Ocean Governance and Conflict in the East and South China Sea

Ocean Governance and Conflict in the East and South China Sea

Negotiating Natural Resources, Institutions and Power

Christian Schultheiss

Routledge
Taylor & Francis Group
LONDON AND NEW YORK

First published in 2024 by Amsterdam University Press Ltd.

Published 2025 by Routledge
4 Park Square, Milton Park, Abingdon, Oxon OX14 4RN
605 Third Avenue, New York, NY 10158

Routledge is an imprint of the Taylor & Francis Group, an informa business

ISBN: 9789463728997 (hbk)
ISBN: 9781041183693 (pbk)
ISBN: 9781003700791 (ebk)
NUR 697

Cover photo: Improvisation (Sea Battle) by Wassily Kandinsky. Courtesy National Gallery of Art, Washington

Cover design: Coördesign, Leiden

DOI: 10.5117/9789463728997

Ocean Governance and Conflict in the East and South China Sea

Negotiating Natural Resources, Institutions and Power

Christian Schultheiss

Routledge
Taylor & Francis Group
LONDON AND NEW YORK

First published in 2024 by Amsterdam University Press Ltd.

Published 2025 by Routledge
4 Park Square, Milton Park, Abingdon, Oxon OX14 4RN
605 Third Avenue, New York, NY 10158

Routledge is an imprint of the Taylor & Francis Group, an informa business

ISBN: 9789463728997 (hbk)
ISBN: 9781041183693 (pbk)
ISBN: 9781003700791 (ebk)
NUR 697

Cover photo: Improvisation (Sea Battle) by Wassily Kandinsky. Courtesy National Gallery of Art, Washington

Cover design: Coördesign, Leiden

DOI: 10.5117/9789463728997

For Product Safety Concerns and Information please contact our EU representative:
GPSR@taylorandfrancis.com
Taylor & Francis Verlag GmbH, Kaufingerstraße 24, 80331 München, Germany

For Selma

Table of Contents

List of Maps

List of Tables

Acknowledgements

This work would not have been possible without the support of many colleagues, universities, and research institutes. I have benefited from the collegial environments of Cambridge's Department of Politics and International Studies, and Centre for Geopolitics and Lauterpacht Centre for International Law, as well as the Max Planck Institute for Comparative Public Law and International Law in Heidelberg. As this book has evolved over several years, I have benefited from discussions with many colleagues. I am very greatly indebted to Kun-Chin Lin and Marc Weller for their detailed criticism and numerous suggestions with respect to the direction the content of this book has taken. I wish to give thanks to the members of the Asian Center of the University of the Philippines, the National Institute for South China Sea Studies, Renmin University, and Keio University for hosting me during field research. Special thanks go to Yuichi Hosoya and his team for their research support in Tokyo. I would like to posthumously acknowledge Aileen Baviera for her invaluable research support in Manila. I owe her many thanks. Many officials and experts from China, Japan, the Philippines, Malaysia, Vietnam, and Taiwan generously offered their time and experience, and I am most grateful for their inspiring interviews. I thank Amrita Narlikar, Stein Tønnesson, John Nilsson-Wright, Peter Dutton, and the anonymous reviewers for Amsterdam University Press for the insightful and constructive comments and suggestions regarding earlier versions of this manuscript. The book also benefited from very helpful suggestions from Carolyn Moser and the entire ENSURE team at the Max Planck Institute. I thank Rocío Bargon Sánchez and Jule Sommer for editorial support. For supporting my research and making this book possible, I wish to thank the Friedrich-Ebert-Stiftung, the University of Cambridge, and the Max Planck Institute for Comparative Public Law and International Law. Finally, I am appreciative of the support of the production team at Amsterdam University Press who guided me throughout the process.

I Introduction – Three Decades of Negotiations in the East and South China Sea Disputes

Abstract

This book explains why claimant states in the East and South China Sea disputes reach agreements on oil and gas, fisheries, crisis communication, and conflict behaviour in some cases, but not in others. Negotiations about cooperative institutions governing marine natural resources are almost as old as the disputes themselves. This is the first comprehensive and theoretically informed investigation that analyses how East and Southeast Asia's middle powers negotiate with China about dispute settlement and ocean governance in Asia's maritime disputes. To this end, this book analyses the bargaining processes of the past three decades and how the law of the sea and the UN Convention on the Law of the Sea (UNCLOS) affects negotiations. To cooperate, state actors need to be confident that a cooperative institution does not expand an opponent's bargaining power in disputes.

Keywords: East and South China Sea, law of the sea, UNCLOS, dispute settlement, natural resource institutions, ocean governance, cooperation, bargaining

This book in a nutshell

Why have claimant states in the East and South China Sea disputes reached agreements for oil and gas, fisheries, crisis communication, and conflict behaviour in some cases, but not in others? Why, for example, did Japan and China agree on a fisheries agreement that covers most disputed areas, but an arrangement on a small bloc for joint gas development reached after

Schultheiss, Christian: *Ocean Governance and Conflict in the East and South China Sea. Negotiating Natural Resources, Institutions and Power.*
Taylor & Francis Group, 2024
DOI: 10.5117/9789463728997_CH01

twenty-three years of consultations ran aground? Why did all negotiations between China and the Philippines on joint oil and gas projects end in an impasse except for one arrangement concluded over the period 2004- 2005? Why did China and Vietnam agree on a sea boundary and joint natural resource governance in the Gulf of Tonkin while several attempts to extend this cooperation into small parts of the South China Sea ended in an impasse? Why did South Korea's forceful response to rampant Chinese fishing activities not escalate in the Yellow Sea while much less severe incidents escalated in the South China Sea? Why is it so difficult to design incident prevention and crisis communication arrangements, even if the disputing states know from experience that frighteningly mundane incidents can escalate beyond measure? What has prevented members of the Association of Southeast Asian Nations (ASEAN) from developing a strong internal consensus around a code of conduct?

These questions represent central knowledge gaps in our understanding of the East and South China Sea disputes. When negotiating options to resolve disputes, the disputing states have almost exclusively considered institutions for marine natural resources and conflict behaviour. The efforts to reach cooperative arrangements in a step-by-step process are anything but recent; they go back at least three decades and, in some cases, up to six decades. Yet China, Japan, South Korea, Taiwan, the Philippines, Vietnam, Malaysia, and Brunei have hardly ever negotiated the settlement of territorial disputes and have considered sea boundary delimitation in only a few cases in the East and South China Sea. The question of when and why claimant states reach and implement agreements on marine natural resources and rules for conduct, and when and why negotiations end in an impasse is therefore central to the East and South China Sea disputes, and by extension, to international security in the Indo-Pacific. This book is the first study to ask and answer this question. It offers, for the first time, a comprehensive and theoretically informed analysis of the claimant states' efforts to design institutions governing marine natural resources and conflict behaviour.

This book argues that the claimant states have recognized that the specific types of agreements under consideration prevent further clashes, help overcome escalatory risks, and allow coordinated action on natural resources without touching directly upon territorial and sea boundary settlements. Yet, while the disputing actors have treated the respective institutions as enablers for limited and voluntary cooperation, they have also realized and know from experience that these institutions help an opponent to expand its power in these disputes and consolidate unilateral advancements with institutional means. To cooperate, the disputing parties have needed not only to reconcile security-related or economic interests, align with geopolitical objectives, or agree on a division of gains from joint action. The agreements have not been prevented by disagreements regarding these questions. To reach and implement agreements, the parties need to be confident that a cooperative institution does not expand a rival's power in disputes.

This book has the following objectives: First, it seeks to explain when and why negotiations on agreements for the common governance of marine natural resources and conflict behaviour result in agreements in some cases but end in impasses in other cases. Island and maritime disputes in the East and South China Sea are central drivers for escalation, instability, destruction of the marine environment, and great power competition in the Indo-Pacific. Yet the claimant states – China, Japan, South Korea, Taiwan, Philippines, Vietnam, and other members of ASEAN – have hardly ever negotiated the settlement of territorial (island) disputes. Instead, claimants have negotiated about institutions for the common governance of marine natural resources and conflict behaviour. This book, therefore, focuses on the interactions about the types of agreement that the disputing states have considered in the past decades – fisheries agreements, agreements for the joint development or exploration of offshore oil and gas, agreements for maritime law enforcement cooperation, codes of conduct, and arrangements for incident prevention and crisis communication.

Second, claimant states in the East and South China Sea interact 'in the shadow' of the law of the sea. In contrast to, for instance, territorial disputes, claims to maritime zones are subject to a relatively well-codified legal regime – the law of the sea and the United Nations Convention of the Law of the Sea (UNCLOS).[1] Beyond questions of compliance or non-compliance with UNCLOS, the existence of a relatively well-codified legal regime impacts relations in several ways. UNCLOS clarifies the maritime rights that states can claim at sea. Claimant states, therefore, negotiate based on existing (or non-existing) legal entitlements to maritime zones. UNCLOS also contains a comprehensive dispute settlement system that has allowed the Philippines to initiate arbitral proceedings. While the issue of the existence or absence of legal entitlements has a distinct effect on resource-sharing negotiations, this book illustrates that this effect results from a broader, underlying factor. Moreover, some of the types of agreements the claimants consider, such as agreements for the joint development of hydrocarbon resources and fisheries agreements, have emerged in international law through subsequent state

1 United Nations Convention on the Law of the Sea (adopted 10 December 1982, entered into force 16 November 1994) 1833 UNTS 396.

practice. UNCLOS adopts these as 'provisional arrangements of a practical nature.'[2] The law of the sea hence offers cooperative governance options in lieu of and in addition to comprehensive sea boundary delimitation. Some negotiators characterize these options as pragmatic step-by-step approaches to the resolution of disputes. To better understand the relationship between natural resource cooperation and conflict,[3] this book examines how these types of arrangements contribute to reducing conflict risks. This book shows that, when comparing all the agreements negotiated in the East and South China Sea, the most effective instruments in preventing an escalation of Asia's maritime disputes have been the fisheries agreements in the East China Sea – even if these agreements have been subject to profound challenges. These arrangements not only prevent conflict over fisheries, but also help avoid escalation in disputes subject to rivalry and great power confrontation. This then raises the question of why claimants have not reached more agreements for marine natural resources and why states in the South China Sea have not emulated the fisheries agreements of the East China Sea.

Third, to understand the observable barriers in the negotiations and the variation between agreement and impasse it is necessary to recognize that two different aspects of institutions are closely interwoven. While institutions make cooperative behaviour durable, they can also help one actor make an opponent do what the opponent would not otherwise do. On the one hand, institutions restrain behaviour, overcome collective action problems, and allow durable, coordinated, and joint action in response to problems actors face.[4] Disputing states in the East and South China Sea have sought cooperative institutions in response to the problems they face, namely escalatory risks, costs to bilateral and regional relations, and access to natural resources. Some surprisingly resilient institutions allow durable

2 UNCLOS, articles 74(3) and 83(3).

3 For a recent review of the literature, see Nina von Uexkull and Halvard Buhaug, 'Security Implications of Climate Change: A Decade of Scientific Progress', *Journal of Peace Research* 58, no. 1 (January 2021): 3–17; also see Nils Petter Gleditsch, 'Whither the Weather? Climate Change and Conflict', *Journal of Peace Research* 49 (2012): 3–9; Nils Petter Gleditsch, 'Armed Conflict and the Environment: A Critique of the Literature', *Journal of Peace Research* 35, no. 3 (1998): 381–400. Many studies focus on river agreements. Also see Jaroslav Tir and Douglas M. Stinnett, 'Weathering Climate Change: Can Institutions Mitigate International Water Conflict?', *Journal of Peace Research* 49, no. 1 (January 2012): 211–25; and Paul R. Hensel et al., 'Bones of Contention: Comparing Territorial, Maritime, and River Issues', *Journal of Conflict Resolution* 52, no. 1 (2008): 117–43.

4 Elinor Ostrom, *Governing the Commons, The Evolution of Institutions for Collective Action* (CUP, 1990); Thráinn Eggertsson, *Economic Behavior and Institutions*, Cambridge Surveys of Economic Literature (CUP, 1990); Barbara Koremenos et al., 'The Rational Design of International Institutions', *International Organization* 55, no. 4 (2001): 761–99.

and coordinated action even in the face of repeated incidents. On the other hand, institutions can also serve as 'weapons of coercion'[5] from which actors gain 'strategic advantages'[6] that consolidate predatory behaviour[7] and bring about vulnerabilities.[8] This raises the question of how institutions can be 'weaponized'. This book argues that the underlying theoretical condition for the possibility of institutions being weaponized is that some institutions increase or decrease actors' power in their interactions.[9] Yet the possibility that actors gain power advantages does not make institutions undesirable. In the East and South China Sea, claimants continue to consult on institutions. It is therefore important to understand when actors agree on institutions even if these can be weaponized. This raises several questions: first, how institutions alter power between actors and, second, how this condition affects negotiation processes about institutions. This book identifies characteristics by virtue of which the institutions under consideration in the East and South China Sea can affect the disputing states' power.

Furthermore, this book describes how rival claimants have implemented agreements to address these concerns. Various actors have sought to reach the benefit of cooperative institutions without the peril of exposing a claim to vulnerability. But when actors have realized that an opponent could use an institution as a 'weapon of coercion', actors have then not reached an effective agreement or let agreements expire. The cost of cooperation between rival actors in the East and South China Sea is not so much the possibility that actors renege on terms or the costs associated with creating an institution but that actors gain power advantages. Sticking points in negotiations have revolved around neutralizing potential perils. Negotiations have been more likely to reach an agreement if negotiators are confident that an implemented agreement will not expose a claim to perils; otherwise, they have resulted in impasses. To cooperate, actors need then not only to

5 Terry M. Moe, 'Political Institutions: The Neglected Side of the Story', *Journal of Law, Economics, and Organization* 6 (1990): 213–53, 213. For a recent adoption of the 'institutions as weapons' metaphor, see Henry Farrell and Abraham L. Newman, 'Weaponized Interdependence: How Global Economic Networks Shape State Coercion', *International Security* 44, no. 1 (July 2019): 42–79.

6 Gregory K. Dow, 'The Function of Authority in Transaction Cost Economics', *Journal of Economic Behavior & Organization* 8, no. 1 (March 1987): 13–38, 20.

7 R. Harrison Wagner, *War and the State: The Theory of International Politics* (University of Michigan, 2007), chapter 5, 184–7.

8 Barbara F. Walter, *Committing to Peace: The Successful Settlement of Civil Wars* (Princeton UP, 2002).

9 Terry M. Moe, 'Power and Political Institutions', *Perspectives on Politics* 3, no. 2 (2005): 215–33.

agree on a division of gains from joint action and on measures to improve compliance, but they need to rule out the expansion of an opponent's power.

Fourth, this book discusses alternative explanations for the observable variation, namely the influence of domestic politics and nationalism, as well as the impact of some characteristics of multilateral negotiations. It considers the question of whether disputed islands are located within the geographic scope of agreements and power asymmetries. While these variables and perspectives offer important insights into disputes and negotiations, they do not explain the observable variation. Moreover, this book goes beyond a focus on China. Undoubtedly, China's claims and behaviour underlie most changes to the status quo. Yet this book shows that interactions and negotiations in cases excluding China have often been no less difficult than negotiations including China. This book attempts not to read history 'backwards' nor to look at the interactions of the past decades through the lenses of current levels of great power confrontations. In this vein, this book corrects the literature on the East and South China Sea that often focuses on China and great power struggles but neglects the perspectives of East and Southeast Asian middle powers.

Fifth, this is the first theoretically informed study that analyses how East and Southeast Asia's middle powers have negotiated with China (and with each other) about institutions in a context where China's outward expansion challenges the existing law of the sea and where geopolitics, lifelines of global trade, and the need to protect the marine environment intersect. The literature discusses many aspects of the East and South China Sea disputes, the historical and legal contexts of the claims and the role of the law of the sea, the issues at stake, and a characterization of China's tactics as well as the relationship between China's rise and great power competition. The literature also refers to single cooperative agreements as role models for moving forward. Numerous authors conclude their papers with a call for practical cooperation, confidence building, and measures for conflict management. However, there is no comprehensive analysis of the disputing countries' attempts to reach agreements for the maritime domain. An explanation for the observable variation between agreements and impasses is missing.

The research puzzle

At first glance, one may be tempted to construe the puzzle in the following way: As sensitive territorial disputes and claims to large maritime zones are interconnected in complex ways in the East and South China Sea, as control over strategic waterways and rich natural resources, reputation, and the reordering of East Asia are at stake, and as China intransigently pursues partly invalid claims, it is surprising that claimants have reached cooperative agreements at all. At second glance, however, it may appear possible to construe the puzzle in the opposite way. A body of literature refers to the parties' efforts to devise cooperative arrangements on 'low-hanging fruits',[10] as 'a creative approach',[11] and as 'all the more attractive when considering alternatives'.[12] Emphasizing the claimants' decades-long efforts to initiate a 'step-by-step'[13] process of 'face-saving' compromises, looking at myriad policy proposals, and describing single agreements as 'role models' for that process, the question is why the disputing actors have not reached more arrangements. Both views, however, are simplistic and disregard the observable variation of agreements and impasses.

In the South China Sea, China, the Philippines, Vietnam, Malaysia, Brunei, and other ASEAN members have negotiated in bilateral, trilateral, and multilateral formats about institutions for fisheries, hydrocarbon resources and seismic research, crisis communication, and codes of conduct for three decades. In the East China Sea, China, Japan, South Korea, and Taiwan[14] have negotiated bilateral institutions for fisheries, the joint development of oil and gas, and incident prevention over several decades. In both China Seas, claimant states have hardly ever negotiated the settlement of territorial disputes. The parties have adopted an incremental approach whereby the negotiated options are agreements about single issues such as natural resources and measures to prevent incidents and reduce tensions. None of the agreements at the negotiation table would settle the territorial and maritime disputes comprehensively. The parties have entered into ten arrangements between the 1990s and the early 2020s and continue consultations about further arrangements at the time of writing.[15] Eight of these ten

10 See subsection below: 'Ocean governance as a step-by-step approach to conflict resolution'.

11 M. Taylor Fravel, 'Explaining Stability in the Senkaku (Diaoyu) Islands Dispute', in *Getting the Triangle Straight: Managing China–Japan–US Relations*, edited by G. Curtis et al. (Brookings Institution Press, 2010), 144–164, 160.

12 Robert Beckman et al., 'Moving Forward on Joint Development in the South China Sea', in *Beyond Territorial Disputes in the South China Sea: Legal Frameworks for the Joint Development of Hydrocarbon Resources*, edited by Robert Beckman et al. (Edward Elgar, 2013), 312–31, 330.

13 Hasjim Djalal, 'The South China Sea: The Long Road towards Peace and Cooperation', in *Freedom of Seas, Passage Rights and the 1982 Law of the Sea Convention*, edited by Tommy T. B Koh et al. (Brill, 2009), 25–50.

14 On Taiwan's status question, see the respective case studies.

15 See the tables in the appendix.

arrangements have been fully implemented, a ninth was implemented but expired, and a tenth has been partly implemented. In another ten cases, negotiations have stalled or ended in an impasse. All parties have suggested agreements that go beyond existing agreements. China itself has entered into seven arrangements, of which five are currently implemented, a sixth was implemented but expired and a seventh is partly implemented. This number excludes ineffective arrangements such as the Declaration on Conduct of 2002. Some bilateral negotiations between claimant states excluding China – for example, between the Philippines and Taiwan, or Brunei and Malaysia – were no less difficult than negotiations including China. While access to marine natural resources has been subject to confrontations, claimants have agreed on the shared governance of these in some cases. While territorial disputes are always sensitive, six agreements have a geographic scope covering disputed territories. It is because of the escalation risks that stem from the combination of territorial and maritime disputes with potential for great power confrontations that the parties have sought ways to manage their disputes.

Moreover, the fact that China has claimed maritime rights beyond the limits of UNCLOS in the South China Sea offers a possible and intuitive explanation for the absence of more negotiation processes on resource sharing in the South China Sea.[16] However, in most cases where China and other claimants have negotiated, China has had valid maritime claims. Thus, this fact alone cannot generally explain the variation between agreements and impasses. To make matters more complex, the Philippines and China have engaged in detailed exchanges and come to an agreement despite the absence of valid Chinese claims.[17] While China's insistence on invalidated maritime claims in the South China Sea is a central driver in these disputes, this factor alone cannot explain the cases and only adds to the puzzle.

The argument

Claimant states of the East and South China Sea have chosen to consult on a code of conduct, agreements for fisheries regulations, joint development of oil and gas, and other practical measures because the parties have seen little room for compromise on territorial issues and sea boundary delimitation. The parties have sought a code of conduct to define the basic rules for

16 See Chapter II 3.1.
17 See Chapter III 1.

reducing escalatory behaviour and enabling practical cooperation in the South China Sea. In both China Seas, several parties have considered the joint development of hydrocarbon resources as a means to replace highly escalatory, unilateral exploration activities with an agreed legal framework for joint exploration or exploitation. As states do not have reliable information about the potential for recoverable resources without exploratory activities, states require such activities to establish the economic value of an area. As parties have tended to regard fishing incidents as competitions in demonstrating superior jurisdiction and superior claims, fishing activities in disputed areas have repeatedly resulted in clashes with coast guards and law enforcement agencies. The parties have negotiated fisheries agreements to dissociate fishing activities from the escalatory logic of clashing claims. Claimant states have sought to devise crisis communication and incident prevention mechanisms to acquire the capability to de-escalate incidents before action–reaction cycles render incidents unmanageable. Under international law, agreements for practical cooperation are without prejudice to claims.[18] Such agreements affect neither boundary delimitation nor territorial settlements; nor, under these agreements, will states acquiesce in another state's claim. In principle, states could define common rules for specific geographic areas in various ways without an agreement prejudicing a state's claim to that particular geographic area *de jure*.

Several obstacles have resulted in impasses or delays in the claimant states' exchanges and what they have in common is the idea that institutions can ameliorate the options of one disputing actor to make an opponent do what it would not otherwise do. Claimant states have considered that the terms of agreements for voluntary and practical cooperation, even if yielding economic and security benefits, could compromise a claim, expose a claimant to vulnerabilities, or expand a rival's power in the disputes. The claimant states treated the agreements and rules under consideration as incremental steps towards cooperation *and* as a 'trap' or a 'slice of the salami'.[19] The disputing states have realized that some agreements could

18 UNCLOS, articles 74(3) and 83(3); Rainer Lagoni, 'Interim Measures Pending Maritime Delimitation Agreements', *The American Journal of International Law* 78, no. 2 (1984): 345–68; Robert Beckman et al. (eds.), *Beyond Territorial Disputes in the South China Sea Legal Frameworks for the Joint Development of Hydrocarbon Resources*, (Edward Elgar, 2013); Christian Schultheiss, 'Overcoming Violence in Maritime Conflicts with Provisional Arrangements: A Legal Tool for Conflict Resolution', in *International Law and Peace Settlements*, edited by Mark Weller et al. (CUP, 2021), 525–44; The Minquiers and Ecrehos Case [Judgment of 17 November 1953] ICJ 47, 58–9.

19 Quotes are from the case studies.

justify and increase an opponent's coast guard or navy patrols in disputed zones. The parties have expected that agreements might 'consolidate' a rival's unilateral advancements and 'cement' a rival's use of unilateral tactics. Various actors were concerned that an opponent's proposed terms would restrict the means the parties rely on to advance or defend their claims. A few actors have seen the possibility that cooperative agreements would allow an opponent to manipulate risk in favour of the opponent's strategy. Some agreements have broken down and others were challenged when the disputing states sensed that the agreement exposed their position to vulnerabilities. Negotiations frequently ended in an impasse when negotiators from all claimant states considered that an agreement could 'recognize', 'validate', or 'legitimise' a rival claim to a particular geographic area such that an opponent could leverage an agreement as 'precedent' in its favour.

Although the agreements under consideration do not prejudice territorial and maritime claims *de jure*, precedent or validation without legal force matters nevertheless. Why precedent without legal force matters is one of the questions that requires a theoretical explanation.[20] This negotiation behaviour can be observed across twenty cases, which represent: (i) various subject matters (agreements for fisheries, oil and gas, crisis communication, and code of conduct); (ii) two regions (the East and South China Sea); (iii) bilateral, trilateral, and multilateral negotiations; (iv) different combinations of states including and excluding China; and (v) cases where China is entitled to claim maritime zones and where China lacks legally valid entitlements.

While the literature recognizes that power has a role to play in the theory of institutions, two questions are central to better understanding the implications of the idea that some institutions allow a state to expand its power and to use it as a weapon of coercion. First, by which characteristics could a cooperative agreement of limited scope increase one actor's power? Second, how do disputing actors negotiate about and implement agreements that prescribe common rules on dispute interactions when, at the same time, these agreements could also affect opponents' power in subsequent interactions? This book identifies several characteristics and discusses three in detail that are particularly relevant to the East and South China Sea: (i) focal points as a source of power in interactions; (ii) restrictions on conflict behaviour, on coalition formation, and access; and (iii) the management and the manipulation of risk.

20 See Chapter II 2.

While it is intuitive to assume that relatively smaller states are particularly risk averse[21] and particularly cautious about giving China opportunities to leverage agreements in disputed seas, China has also rejected several proposed agreements because of similar concerns. This problem has been the rule, not the exception. Nonetheless, this behaviour has not made cooperative institutions less desirable in the eyes of claimant states, nor has it reduced the relevance of these institutions. Claimant states have persistently negotiated about institutions for fisheries, oil and gas, conflict management, and incident prevention. The problem that an opponent can leverage cooperative agreements and that some agreements expose a state to vulnerability has also applied to cases where an agreement was reached. Even when disputing parties have assumed an opponent's bad faith, they have still entered into agreements once they were confident that the opponent could not use institutions as a weapon of coercion. Some implemented agreements have proven resilient against challenges and even against widespread violations of the agreement. An explanation of the East and South China Sea disputes and the actors' interactions that analyses natural resource institutions and rules for conflict behaviour solely in a manipulative perspective cannot explain why the actors have agreed on some institutions and why they have adhered to them despite their shortcomings. At the same time, an explanation that neglects the ways in which institutions are sources of power in interactions cannot explain the course of negotiations and the obstacles the parties encountered within them.

What is at stake in the East and South China Sea disputes?

Territorial disputes – especially when strategic, economic, or ideational interests, or rivalries or questions of reputation are at stake[22] – and a rapidly

21 Brantly Womack, *Asymmetry and International Relationships* (CUP, 2016), 44–45.

22 John A. Vasquez and Valeriano Brandon, 'Territory as Source of Conflict and Road to Peace', in *The SAGE Handbook of Conflict Resolution*, edited by Jacob Bercovitch et al. (SAGE, 2009), 193–209; David B. Carter, 'The Strategy of Territorial Conflict', *American Journal of Political Science* 54, no. 4 (2010): 969–87; Paul R. Hensel et al., 'Bones of Contention: Comparing Territorial, Maritime, and River Issues', *Journal of Conflict Resolution* 52, no. 1 (2008): 117–43; Karen A. Rasler and William R. Thompson, 'Contested Territory, Strategic Rivalries, and Conflict Escalation', *International Studies Quarterly* 50, no. 1 (2006): 145–68; Barbara F. Walter, 'Explaining the Intractability of Territorial Conflict', *International Studies Review* 5, no. 4 (2003): 137–53; Paul D. Senese and John A. Vasquez, 'Assessing the Steps to War', *British Journal of Political Science* 35, no. 4 (2005): 607–33; Beth A. Simmons, 'Rules over Real Estate Trade, Territorial Conflict, and International Borders as Institution', *Journal of Conflict Resolution* 49, no. 6 (2005): 823–48;

changing balance of power[23] are primary causes of interstate conflict and war. In the East and South China Seas, all these factors have been present. The literature identifies many interests of the claimant- and non-claimant states and suggests varying descriptions and explanations for China's behaviour in the disputes.

The East and South China Seas are undoubtedly vital areas for world trade. Trade and access to markets via sea routes are also pillars of China's rapid development. Estimates suggest that a third of world trade, and between 60 per cent and 80 per cent of China's, Korea's, and Japan's energy supplies pass through the South China Sea's chokepoints annually, resulting in a total of $5.3 trillion in trade flows.[24] Analyses of trade economics, however, question this figure, and present data according to which half of Japan's energy imports circumvent the South China Sea, and argue that China is the most vulnerable country with respect to the openness of Southeast Asia's sea routes.[25] While incidents may disrupt trade, risks to trade routes should be assessed realistically.[26]

The East China Sea and the South China Sea have both been referred to as new 'Persian Gulfs' in a UN Economic Commission report of 1969 as

Jean-Marc F. Blanchard, 'Linking Border Disputes and War: An Institutional-Statist Theory', *Geopolitics* 10, no. 4 (2005): 688–711; Áslaug Ásgeirsdóttir and Martin Steinwand, 'Dispute Settlement Mechanisms and Maritime Boundary Settlements', *The Review of International Organizations* 10, no. 2 (June 2015): 119–43; Stephen C. Nemeth et al., 'Ruling the Sea: Managing Maritime Conflicts through UNCLOS and Exclusive Economic Zones', *International Interactions* 40, no. 5 (2014): 711–36.

23 R. Harrison Wagner, 'Peace, War, and the Balance of Power', *American Political Science Review* 88, no. 3 (1994): 593–607; James D. Fearon, 'Rationalist Explanations for War', *International Organization* 49, no. 3 (June 1995): 379–414; Robert Powell, 'Stability and the Distribution of Power', *World Politics* 48, no. 2 (1996): 239–67; Robert Powell, 'War as a Commitment Problem', *International Organization* 60, no. 1 (2006): 169–203; Matthew O. Jackson and Massimo Morelli, 'The Reasons for Wars: An Updated Survey', in *The Handbook on the Political Economy of War*, edited by Christopher J. Coyne and Rachel L. Mathers (Edward Elgar, 2011), 34–57. In the literature, war needs to be explained. Restraint is not an anomaly as Chin-Hao Huang claims in *Power and Restraint in China's Rise* (Columbia UP, 2022), 13.

24 Robert D. Kaplan, *Asia's Cauldron: The South China Sea and the End of a Stable Pacific* (Random House, 2014); Sarah Raine and Christian Le Mière, *Regional Disorder: The South China Sea Disputes*, IISS Adelphi Series (Routledge, 2013); Nong Hong, *UNCLOS and Ocean Dispute Settlement: Law and Politics in the South China Sea* (Routledge, 2012).

25 James Laurenceson, 'Economics and Freedom of Navigation in East Asia', *Australian Journal of International Affairs* (2017), 1–13; CSIS, 'How Much Trade Transits the South China Sea?', *ChinaPower Project* (blog), 2 August 2017, https://chinapower.csis.org/much-trade-transits-south-china-sea/ (last accessed 23 March 2022).

26 Laurenceson, 'Economics and Freedom of Navigation in East Asia'.

well as in several recent works of scholarship,[27] suggesting the existence of 'abundant' hydrocarbon resources.[28] Chinese estimates and estimates of industry sources or of US institutions, however, diverge considerably for both seas. The reports from US institutions are much more pessimistic.[29] Proven and probable reserves of oil and gas are mainly in undisputed areas. The estimates for disputed areas are based on geological information about undiscovered resources.[30] Given these estimates, the hydrocarbon resources at, for instance, the Spratly Islands, would not be relevant to China's energy security; in the same way, the Reed Bank would be important only for Philippine energy supply.[31] China's unilateral hydrocarbon resource exploitation is still confined to areas on its side of UNCLOS-based median lines. China is not able to develop oil in disputed areas of the East or South China Seas beyond that.[32] Chinese and Vietnamese concession blocs overlap widely, but oil and gas are exploited mainly in undisputed areas. The operations of the China National Offshore Oil Company (CNOOC) in the East China Sea (on China's side of a geographic median line) contribute only 1 per cent to its daily production.[33] This 1 per cent of CNOOC's total production represents a minuscule fraction of China's total consumption. Furthermore, fisheries are undoubtedly an important marine natural resource in both China Seas. The growing demand for fisheries in domestic consumption across China and Southeast Asia, as well as changing eating habits, have made fishing a profitable, growing, and most-disputed industry.[34] Land reclamation and

27 UN Economic Commission for Asia and the Far East, *Report of the Sixth Session of the Committee for Coordination of Joint Prospecting for Mineral Resources in Asian Offshore Areas* (CCOP), E/CN.11/L.239, 26 June 1969, 5.

28 Zhao Huanting et al., *Geomorphology and Environment of the South China Coast and the South China Sea Islands* (Science Press, 1999) (in Chinese), quoted in Keyuan Zou, 'Joint Development in the South China Sea: A New Approach', *The International Journal of Marine and Coastal Law* 21, no. 1 (2006): 83–109.

29 US Energy Information Administration, 'South China Sea', 7 February 2013; US Energy Information Administration, 'East China Sea', September 2014.

30 Bill Hayton, *The South China Sea: The Struggle for Power in Asia* (Yale UP, 2014), chapter 5, 147–50.

31 See Chapter III 1.

32 International Crisis Group, 'Stirring up the South China Sea (IV): Oil in Troubled Waters', *Asia Report No. 275*, 26 January 2016, https://www.crisisgroup.org/asia/north-east-asia/china/stirring-south-china-sea-iv-oil-troubled-waters (last accessed 23 March 2022); see Chapter IV 1.

33 CNOOC Limited, http://www.cnooctd.com/col/col7311/index.html (last accessed 23 March 2024).

34 Hongzhou Zhang, 'Chinese Fishermen in Disputed Waters: Not Quite a "People's War"', *Marine Policy* 68 (June 2016): 65–73; Hongzhou Zhang and Sam Bateman, 'Fishing Militia, the Securitization of Fishery and the South China Sea Dispute', *Contemporary Southeast Asia*,

antagonistic fishing practices in disputed areas have resulted in depleted fisheries and environmental destruction.[35]

Beyond economic interests, strategic interests clearly are at stake. The strategic value of disputed islands and land reclamation requires a nuanced assessment. China benefits from building outposts at disputed features for surveillance and for a greater reach and frequency of coast guard, navy, submarine, and air force operations.[36] At the same time, these outposts are non-moving targets and extremely vulnerable to attack. The US Navy considers 'taking down small islands' a 'core competency'.[37] While the additional military capabilities China derives from the outposts are vulnerable in a wartime scenario, the installations extend Chinese maritime law enforcement capabilities in Southeast Asia into peacetime scenarios.[38] China could not otherwise maintain a regular coast guard presence in disputed areas given the distance between the mainland and the claimed waters. Some voices also attribute a military value to the islands in China–US wartime scenarios.[39] The apparent consensus, however, insists that the

2017, 288–314; Erica Gies, 'The Consequences of China's Booming Demand for Seafood', *Hakai Magazine*, 28 June 2018, https://www.hakaimagazine.com/news/the-consequences-of-chinas-booming-demand-for-seafood/ (last accessed 23 March 2022).

35 John W. McManus, 'Offshore Coral Reef Damage, Overfishing, and Paths to Peace in the South China Sea', *The International Journal of Marine and Coastal Law* 32, no. 2 (2017), 199–237; Thang Dang Nguyen, 'Fisheries Co-Operation in the South China Sea and the (Ir)relevance of the Sovereignty Question', *Asian Journal of International Law* 2, no. 1 (2012): 59–88.

36 On the military–strategic value of the island features, see Sarah Kirchberger and Patrick O'Keeffe, 'Military-Strategic Aspects of the South China Sea Issue', in *Traversing the Challenges. Political, Economic and Environmental Dimensions of Maritime and Regional Security*, edited by Benedikt Seemann and Sebastian Bersick (Konrad Adenauer Stiftung, 2017), 27–40. For publicly available imagery of the island-building programs of all claimant states since 2013, see the Asia Maritime Transparency Initiative and Center for Strategic and International Studies, https://amti.csis.org/island-tracker/ (last accessed 23 March 2024).

37 'U.S. Could Take Down Islands in SCS If it Needed To, Says Pentagon Official', Newsweek, 1 June 2018, https://www.newsweek.com/us-could-take-down-man-made-islands-south-china-sea-if-it-needed-says-pentagon-952451 (last accessed 23 March 2024). The official reassured the audience that this statement is no more 'than a simple statement of historical fact'.

38 David Axe, 'Sunk: How China's Man-Made Islands Are Falling Apart and Sinking Into the Ocean', *The National Interest*, 12 March 2020, https://nationalinterest.org/blog/buzz/sunk-how-chinas-man-made-islands-are-falling-apart-and-sinking-ocean-132047 (last accessed 23 March 2022); Christian Becker, 'Die militärstrategische Bedeutung des südchinesischen Meeres', *SWP Aktuell 82*, September 2015.

39 Alessio Patalano, 'When Strategy Is "Hybrid" and Not "Grey": Reviewing Chinese Military and Constabulary Coercion at Sea', *The Pacific Review* 31, no. 6 (2 November 2018): 811–39; Michael O'Hanlon and Gregory Poling, 'Rocks, Reefs, and Nuclear War', *AMTI Update*, 14 January 2020, https://amti.csis.org/rocks-reefs-and-nuclear-war/ (last accessed 23 March 2022).

islands are a strategic liability for China in wartime, not an asset.[40] It is not the artificial islands but China's technological defence advancements that raise the question of how the US could make combat in the Western Pacific viable.[41] Arguably, the artificial islands do not improve China's sea lane security substantively. Sea lane security is a global problem, not a regional one. Control over the China Seas does not give China control over the sea lanes from its mainland to its major markets in Europe, North America, or the Middle East.

The International Crisis Group questioned whether a coherent picture of China's objectives and behaviour can be identified at all, as a range of different Chinese actors pursue different objectives.[42] The tense nature of the disputes, though, remains an observable fact. Activities in disputed maritime zones such as fishing, seismic research, marine scientific research, even tourist cruises, coast guard patrols, navy patrols, and overflights have caused many incidents in the last decades. There is some quantitative and qualitative evidence that China's activities in the East and South China Sea are reactions to perceived challenges from other claimant states.[43] Although this observation fits to some extent with descriptions of China's security posture as that of a vulnerable nation,[44] it is doubtful whether the 'defence' of partially invalid legal claims could be considered 'defensive'. The idea of the 'Chinese cult of the defence' and the tendency of Chinese decision-makers to rationalize the uses of violent means as defensive ends may be applicable.[45] Fravel and Hayer, writing independently, find that China's behaviour in

40 Olli Pekka Suorsa, 'The Conventional Wisdom Still Stands: America Can Deal with China's Artificial Island Bases', *War on the Rocks*, 6 February 2020, https://warontherocks.com/2020/02/the-conventional-wisdom-still-stands-america-can-deal-with-chinas-artificial-island-bases/ (last accessed 23 March 2022).

41 Michael Beckley, 'The Emerging Military Balance in East Asia: How China's Neighbors Can Check Chinese Naval Expansion', *International Security* 42, no. 2 (November 2017): 78–119. Beckley has referred to the neglect among US analysts for the military potential of East and Southeast Asia states as 'bilateral bias'.

42 International Crisis Group, 'Stirring up the South China Sea (I)', *Asia Report No. 223*, 23 April 2012, https://www.crisisgroup.org/asia/south-east-asia/south-china-sea/stirring-south-china-sea-i. See chapter II 3.

43 Ketian Zhang, 'Cautious Bully: Reputation, Resolve, and Beijing's Use of Coercion in the South China Sea', *International Security* 44, no. 1 (July 2019): 117–59; Christopher D. Yung and Patrick McNulty, 'An Empirical Analysis of Claimant Tactics in the South China Sea', in *Strategic Forum* (National Defense UP, 2015), 1–13; Greg Austin, *China's Ocean Frontier: International Law, Military Force, and National Development* (Allen & Unwin, 1998), 300 and 326.

44 Andrew J. Nathan and Andrew Scobell, *China's Search for Security* (Columbia UP, 2015).

45 Andrew Scobell, *China's Use of Military Force: Beyond the Great Wall and the Long March* (CUP, 2003), chapter 2, 15–39.

island disputes differs from behaviour in land border disputes; China has shown a greater willingness to compromise on the latter.[46] This greater willingness to compromise in land border disputes can be attributed to the domestic security benefits China derives from border settlements – a benefit absent in the case of offshore island disputes.[47] Regarding the ideational value attached to historic claims, historic studies suggest that the historic element of claims is more imagined than historic.[48]

Tensions have gone up and down periodically, but the number and presence of Chinese patrols and vessels has increased continuously.[49] China's policy has been characterized as one instance of 'assertiveness'.[50] Doubts have been raised, however, as to whether assertiveness is an analytically useful concept at all.[51] Relatively mundane – but for the claimant states

46 M. Taylor Fravel, *Strong Borders, Secure Nation. Cooperation and Conflict in China's Territorial Disputes* (Princeton UP, 2008); Eric Hyer, *The Pragmatic Dragon: China's Grand Strategy and Boundary Settlements* (UBC Press, 2015).
47 M. Taylor Fravel, 'Regime Insecurity and International Cooperation: Explaining China's Compromises in Territorial Disputes', *International Security* 30, no. 2 (2005): 46–83.
48 Ulises Granados, 'As China Meets the Southern Sea Frontier: Ocean Identity in the Making, 1902–1937', *Pacific Affairs* 78, no. 3 (2005): 443–61; Bill Hayton, 'When Good Lawyers Write Bad History: Unreliable Evidence and the South China Sea Territorial Dispute', *Ocean Development & International Law* 48, no. 1 (2 January 2017): 17–34; William Choong, *The Ties That Divide. History, Honour and Territory in Sino-Japanese Relations*, IISS Adelphi Series (Routledge, 2014); Stein Tønnesson, 'Why Are the Disputes in the South China Sea So Intractable? A Historical Approach', *Asian Journal of Social Science* 30, no. 3 (2002): 570–601.
49 Andrew S. Erickson and Joshua Hickey, 'Surging Second Sea Force: China's Maritime Law-Enforcement Forces, Capabilities, and Future in the Gray Zone and Beyond', *Naval War College Review* 72, no. 2 (2019): 1–25; Japan Ministry of Defense, 'China's Activities in East China Sea, Pacific Ocean, and Sea of Japan', March 2024, https://www.mod.go.jp/en/d_act/sec_env/pdf/ch_d-act_a.pdf (last accessed 24 April 2024); Lyle J. Morris, 'Blunt Defenders of Sovereignty: The Rise of Coast Guards in East and Southeast Asia', *Naval War College Review* 70, no. 2 (2017): 75-112.
50 Aaron L. Friedberg, 'The Sources of Chinese Conduct: Explaining Beijing's Assertiveness', *The Washington Quarterly* 37, no. 4 (2014): 133–50; Michael Yahuda, 'China's New Assertiveness in the South China Sea', *Journal of Contemporary China* 22, no. 81 (2013): 446–59; Michael D. Swaine and M. Taylor Fravel, 'China's Assertive Behavior: Part Two: The Maritime Periphery', *China Leadership Monitor* 35 (2011): 1–29; You Ji, 'The PLA and Diplomacy: Unraveling Myths about the Military Role in Foreign Policy Making', *Journal of Contemporary China* 23, no. 86 (4 March 2014): 236–54.
51 Alastair Iain Johnston, 'How New and Assertive Is China's New Assertiveness?', *International Security* 37, no. 4 (2013): 7–48; Dingding Chen et al., 'Debating China's Assertiveness', *International Security* 38, no. 3 (2014): 176–83; Steve Chan, *China's Troubled Waters: Maritime Disputes in Theoretical Perspective* (CUP, 2016). Chan analyses the disputes in broader theoretical perspectives. Also see Andy Yee, 'Maritime Territorial Disputes in East Asia: A Comparative Analysis of the South China Sea and the East China Sea', *Journal of Current Chinese Affairs* 40, no. 2 (2011): 165–93.

serious – incidents escalated to month-long international crises despite crisis management efforts of the involved parties.[52] The entanglement of territorial disputes with maritime disputes and great power competition[53] results in a situation where structural bureaucratic obstacles[54] and questions of linkage limit effective crisis management.[55] Officials and scholars have acknowledged that 'frighteningly mundane'[56] incidents have escalated and that such incidents have the potential to escalate even to the point of a US–China military confrontation.[57]

While the East and South China Sea disputes are closely linked to China's regional and geopolitical aspirations, various scholars have also pointed to the contradictions between China's conflict behaviour and its regional objectives. Undoubtedly, China's navy and capability to exert control over maritime areas have expanded rapidly over the last two decades.[58] China's sea power ambition has affected the regional balance of power in East and Southeast

52 Ja Ian Chong and Todd H. Hall, 'One Thing Leads to Another: Making Sense of East Asia's Repeated Tensions', *Asian Security* 13, no. 1 (2 January 2017): 20–40; Michael Green et al., *Countering Coercion in Maritime Asia The Theory and Practice of Gray Zone Deterrence* (Center for Strategic and International Studies, 2017); Yingxian Long, 'China's Decision to Deploy HYSY-981 in the South China Sea: Bureaucratic Politics with Chinese Characteristics', *Asian Security* 12, no. 3 (September 2016): 148–65.

53 Peter Dutton, 'Three Disputes and Three Objectives. China and the South China Sea', *Naval War College Review* 64, no. 4 (2011): 42–67; Patrick M. Cronin and Robert Kaplan, 'Cooperation from Strength US Strategy and the South China Sea', in *Cooperation from Strength. The United States, China and the South China Sea*, edited by Patrick M. Cronin (Center for a New American Century, 2012), 3–30.

54 Sanaa Yasmin Hafeez, 'The Senkaku/Diaoyu Islands Crises of 2004, 2010, and 2012: A Study of Japanese-Chinese Crisis Management', *Asia-Pacific Review* 22, no. 1 (2 January 2015): 73–99.

55 Wiegand found evidence for linkage in the time period before 2005, but not after 2005. Krista E. Wiegand, 'China's Strategy in the Senkaku/Diaoyu Islands Dispute: Issue Linkage and Coercive Diplomacy', *Asian Security* 5, no. 2 (5 June 2009): 170–93; Krista Eileen Wiegand, *Enduring Territorial Disputes: Strategies of Bargaining, Coercive Diplomacy, and Settlement* (University of Georgia Press, 2011).

56 Graham T. Allison, *Destined for War: Can America and China Escape Thucydides's Trap?* (Mariner Books, 2017), 167.

57 Charles L. Glaser, 'A U.S.-China Grand Bargain? The Hard Choice between Military Competition and Accommodation', *International Security* 39, no. 4 (April 2015): 49–90; Avery Goldstein, 'First Things First: The Pressing Danger of Crisis Instability in U.S.-China Relations', *International Security* 37, no. 4 (April 2013): 49–89; Lyle Goldstein, *Meeting China Halfway: How to Defuse the Emerging US–China Rivalry* (Georgetown UP, 2015); also see Kenneth Lieberthal and Wang Jisi, *Addressing U.S.–China Strategic Distrust* (Brookings Monograph Series 4, 2012), https://www.brookings.edu/wp-content/uploads/2016/06/0330_china_lieberthal.pdf (last accessed 23 September 2023).

58 Peter Dutton and Ryan D Martinson, eds., *Beyond the Wall: Chinese Far Seas Operations* (Naval War College Press, 2015); Andrew S. Erickson et al., 'Surging Second Sea Force: China's

Asia. China's objectives in the maritime disputes include an intention to realize its maritime claims and replace the US as the dominant power in East and Southeast Asia.[59] Given the maritime geography of East Asia, the concept of the first island chain, that is, the chain of islands separating the East Asian continent from the Pacific, and the capability to break out of it are focuses for China's sea power strategists not least for sea route security.[60] Several descriptions of China's dispute behaviour describe attempts to gradually reverse the status quo by using grey-zone strategies creatively while seeking to remain below the level of war[61] and by delaying a resolution.[62] China's behaviour in the maritime disputes has been one important factor in the US's reassessment of China's global intentions.[63] US national security and defence strategy documents have come to regard China's maritime claims

Maritime Law-Enforcement Forces, Capabilities, and Future in the Gray Zone and Beyond', *Naval War College Review* 72, no. 2 (2019): 1–25.

59 Aaron L. Friedberg, 'The Sources of Chinese Conduct: Explaining Beijing's Assertiveness', *The Washington Quarterly* 37, no. 4 (2014): 133–50; Aaron L. Friedberg, *A Contest for Supremacy: China, America, and the Struggle for Mastery in Asia* (Norton, 2012), 142–81; Toshi Yoshihara and James R. Holmes, *Red Star over the Pacific: China's Rise and the Challenge to U.S. Maritime Strategy* (Naval Institute Press, 2013); Tetsuo Kotani, 'China and Russia in the Western Pacific: Implications for Japan and the United States', *Maritime Awareness Project*, 18 April 2019, https://map.nbr.org/wp-content/uploads/2020/09/Analysis-Kotani-China-and-Russia-in-the-Western-Pacific-Implications-for-Japan-and-the-United-States-041819.pdf (last accessed 23 September 2023).

60 Leszek Buszynski, 'The South China Sea: Oil, Maritime Claims, and US–China Strategic Rivalry', *The Washington Quarterly* 35, no. 2 (2012): 139–56; Andrew S. Erickson and Joel Wuthnow, 'Barriers, Springboards and Benchmarks: China Conceptualizes the Pacific "Island Chains"', *The China Quarterly* 225 (2016): 1–22; Toshi Yoshihara, 'China's Vision of Its Seascape: The First Island Chain and Chinese Seapower', *Asian Politics & Policy* 4, no. 3 (2012): 293–314.

61 Michael Green et al., *Countering Coercion in Maritime Asia*; Patrick M. Cronin and Robert Kaplan, 'Cooperation from Strength US Strategy and the South China Sea', in *Cooperation from Strength The United States, China and the South China Sea*, edited by Patrick M. Cronin (Center for a New American Century, 2012), 3–30; Daniel Russel, Assistant Secretary of State, Bureau of East Asian and Pacific Affairs, US Department of State *Testimony Before the House Committee on Foreign Affairs Subcommittee on Asia and the Pacific*, 5 February 2014, https://docs.house.gov/meetings/FA/FA05/20140205/101715/HHRG-113-FA05-Wstate-RusselD-20140205.pdf (last accessed 23 March 2022).

62 M. Taylor Fravel, 'China's Strategy in the South China Sea', *Contemporary Southeast Asia* 33, no. 3 (2011): 292–319.

63 Michael Green, 'Trump and Asia: Continuity, Change, and Disruption', *ASAN Open Forum*, 18 April 2019, http://www.theasanforum.org/trump-and-asia-continuity-change-and-disruption/?utm_source=CSIS+All&utm_campaign=7f60856cac-EMAIL_CAMPAIGN_2019_04_26_06_46&utm_medium=email&utm_term=0_f326fc46b6-7f60856cac-160737973 (last accessed 23 June 2023); Phuong Nguyen, 'Deciphering the Shift in America's South China Sea Policy', *Contemporary Southeast Asia* 38, no. 3 (31 December 2016): 389–421.

and behaviour in maritime disputes as evidence for China's 'revisionist' designs.[64] Critiques of the US and the Freedom of Navigation Operations argue that these operations failed to deter China's advancements in the East and South China Sea.[65] In this view, China's activities in the East and South China Sea are evidence of China's objectives to replace the US in the Asia–Pacific.

Several Chinese scholars maintain that China's claims and activities in the East and South China Sea are a liability for China's regional and global objectives.[66] China's activities in the China Seas hamper China's sea power transformation and give the US an easy opening to contain China and forge regional alliances. It is China's conflict behaviour that turns Southeast Asian states and Japan into 'enemies' and US allies.[67] Whether or not China acts with 'strategic confusion',[68] China has not yet prioritized between the objective to manage its territorial and maritime disputes – thereby reducing Chinese exposure to US coalition building – and the objective to maximise its claims, made possible by the perceived decline of the US.[69] In this view, China's pursuit of excessive claims, such as the nine-dash line, is

64 The United States of America, 'Summary of the National Defense Strategy Sharping the American Military's Competitive Edge', 2018; US Department of Defense, 'Indo-Pacific Strategy Report. Preparedness, Partnerships, and Promoting a Networked Region', 1 June 2019.

65 Zack Cooper and Gregory Poling, 'America's Freedom of Navigation Operations Are Lost at Sea', *Foreign Policy*, 8 January 2019, https://foreignpolicy.com/2019/01/08/americas-freedom-of-navigation-operations-are-lost-at-sea/; Brahma Chellaney, 'Who Lost the South China Sea?', *The Strategist*, 15 June 2018, https://www.aspistrategist.org.au/who-lost-the-south-china-sea/ (last accessed 23 March 2022). On US Freedom of Navigation Operations more generally, see Rachel Odell, 'How Strategic Norm-Shaping Undergirds America's Command of the Commons', *MIT Political Science Department Research Paper* 23 (2019), https://doi.org/10.2139/ssrn.3451412.

66 Zongyou Wei, 'China's Maritime Trap', *The Washington Quarterly* 40, no. 1 (2 January 2017): 167–84, https://doi.org/10.1080/0163660X.2017.1302745; Wenjuan Nie, 'Xi Jinping's Foreign Policy Dilemma: One Belt, One Road or the South China Sea?', *Contemporary Southeast Asia: A Journal of International and Strategic Affairs* 38, no. 3 (2016): 422–44; Zhengyu Wu, 'Rimland Powers, Maritime Transformation, and Policy Implications for China', in *Beyond the Wall: Chinese Far Seas Operations*, edited by Peter Dutton and Ryan D. Martinson (Naval War College Press, 2015), 13–22; Feng Zhang, 'Assessing China's South China Sea Policy, 2009–2015', *East Asian Policy* 8, no. 3 (July 2016): 100–9; Xiaobo Liu, 'How China Can Resolve the FONOP Deadlock in the South China Sea', *CSIS AMTI Update*, 1 March 2019, https://amti.csis.org/how-china-can-resolve-fonop-deadlock/ (last accessed 23 March 2022).

67 Hailong Ju, *China's Maritime Power and Strategy: History, National Security and Geopolitics* (Hackensack, World Scientific, 2015), 213. 'If such images [of China's tough activities] become popular in public opinion, then the U.S. ... will be able to effortlessly... destroy the strategic environment of China... there is also the risk of losing Southeast Asia and making Japan a mortal enemy.'

68 Wenjuan Nie, 'China's Domestic Strategic Debate and Confusion over the South China Sea Issue', *The Pacific Review* 31, no. 2 (4 March 2018): 188–204.

69 Ibid.

a liability for the objective of replacing the US in East and Southeast Asia.[70] China's behaviour has raised the demand for a US presence among East and Southeast Asian smaller and middle powers and has incentivised collaboration between the US, Japan, Australia, and some ASEAN members.[71] This has resulted in a rapprochement between the US and Vietnam,[72] restored access for US forces to Philippine military facilities,[73] and a strengthened the US–Japan alliance.[74] Japan and ASEAN states also improved coast guard cooperation in response to China's activities.[75] On the one hand, China has risen and so have the maritime activities of the state, its agencies, and nationals.[76] Chinese actors have extended their reach over the surrounding seas and their uses. China pursues many strategic, geopolitical, and economic interests and many of these are rooted in China's rapid development. On the other hand, China's attempts to enforce its claims are producing geopolitical blowback in attempts to build countervailing coalitions.[77]

70 Further Chinese scholars make this point. Alexandre Sheldon-Duplaix, 'Beyond the China Seas: Will China Become a Global "Sea Power"?', *China Perspectives* 2016, no. 3 (1 September 2016): 43–52.

71 Robert S. Ross, 'The Problem with the Pivot: Obama's New Asia Policy Is Unnecessary and Counterproductive', *Foreign Affairs* 91 (December 2012): 70–78; Sarah Raine and Christian Le Mière, *Regional Disorder: The South China Sea Disputes*, IISS Adelphi Series (Routledge, 2013), 173; Cheng-Chwee Kuik, 'Explaining the Contradiction in China's South China Sea Policy: Structural Drivers and Domestic Imperatives', *China: An International Journal* 15, no. 1 (2017): 163–86.

72 Nguyen, 'Deciphering the Shift in America's South China Sea Policy'.

73 The depth of the Philippines–US alliance was affected, among other factors, by China's presence on features in Philippine waters (Mischief Reef in 1995 and Scarborough Shoal in 2012). Philippine President Duterte had decided to cancel the Visiting Forces Agreement in 2020, but then cancelled the cancellation in the wake of tensions. It will be important to observe the future course of this decision. Renato Cruz De Castro, 'The 21st Century Philippine-US Enhanced Defense Cooperation Agreement (EDCA): The Philippines' Policy in Facilitating the Obama Administration's Strategic Pivot to Asia', *The Korean Journal of Defense Analysis* 26, no. 4 (2014): 427–46; Leszek Buszynski, 'ASEAN, the Declaration on Conduct, and the South China Sea', *Contemporary Southeast Asia* (2003), 343–62. For a description of the fluctuation of the US 'pivot', 'rebalancing', and Asia's maritime disputes, see Michael Green, *By More Than Providence: Grand Strategy and American Power in the Asia Pacific Since 1783* (Columbia UP, 2017), chapter 15, 518–40.

74 Yuichi Hosoya, 'FOIP 2.0: The Evolution of Japan's Free and Open Indo-Pacific Strategy', *Asia-Pacific Review* 26, no. 1 (2 January 2019): 18–28.

75 Ian Storey, 'Japan's Maritime Security Interests in Southeast Asia and the South China Sea Dispute', *Political Science* 65, no. 2 (December 2013): 135–56.

76 On the multiplicity of China's domestic actors in the maritime disputes see Chapter II 3.

77 US Department of State, 'A Free and Open Indo-Pacific Advancing a Shared Vision', 4 November 2019; US Department of Defense, 'Indo-Pacific Strategy Report. Preparedness, Partnerships, and Promoting a Networked Region', 1 June 2019.

Moreover, even as China's reputation among Southeast Asian audiences deteriorates,[78] Southeast Asian states attempt to evade a choice between the US as a security provider and China as an indispensable economic partner by combining engagement and 'soft balancing'.[79] Singapore's Prime Minister Lee Hsien Loong stated that Southeast Asian states 'fervently hope not to be forced to choose between the United States and China'.[80] While China cannot replace the US as a security provider, not least due to its claims and behaviour in disputes, Southeast Asian states 'cannot afford to alienate China and other Asian countries will try their best not to let any single dispute dominate their overall relationships with Beijing'.[81] Southeast Asian states have adopted diverging approaches to limit the effect of the disputes on their overall relationships with China.[82] The objective of Southeast Asian states to not be caught in the middle of a US–China confrontation also applies to the South China Sea disputes and appears to limit, to some extent, the receptiveness of some Southeast Asian states to direct military support of the US. Fravel and Glaser suggested that a US Navy presence could counter China's interference in Malaysia's or Vietnam's resource activities in their respective Exclusive Economic Zones (EEZ).[83] Malaysia, however, did not welcome US Navy support in its EEZ even as the US Navy came to help Malaysia against Chinese vessels harassing the *West Capella*, a drill ship hired by Malaysia's state-owned Petronas. While this incident was regarded as the

78 Sharon Seah et al., *The State of Southeast Asia: 2023* (Singapore: ISEAS-Yusof Ishak Institute, 2023), https://www.iseas.edu.sg/wp-content/uploads/2025/07/The-State-of-SEA-2023-Final-Digital-V4-09-Feb-2023.pdf.

79 Evelyn Goh, *Meeting the China Challenge: The U.S. in Southeast Asian Regional Security Strategies* (East-West Center Washington, 2005); Cheng-Chwee Kuik, 'How Do Weaker States Hedge? Unpacking ASEAN States' Alignment Behavior towards China', *Journal of Contemporary China* 25, no. 100 (3 July 2016): 500–14; Van Jackson, 'Power, Trust, and Network Complexity: Three Logics of Hedging in Asian Security', *International Relations of the Asia-Pacific* 14, no. 3 (2014): 331–56.

80 Hsien Loong Lee, 'The Endangered Asian Century', *Foreign Affairs* 99, no. 4 (August 2020): 51–64, 59.

81 Ibid., 61.

82 Sarah Raine and Christian Le Mière, *Regional Disorder The South China Sea Disputes*, IISS Adelphi Series (Routledge, 2013), chapter 3, 110–128; Ian Storey, 'Malaysia and the South China Sea Dispute: Policy Continuity amid Domestic Political Change', *ISEAS Perspective* 2020, no. 18, 20 March 2020, 1–10, https://www.iseas.edu.sg/wp-content/uploads/2020/02/ISEAS_Perspective_2020_18.pdf.

83 M. Taylor Fravel and Charles L. Glaser, 'How Much Risk Should the United States Run in the South China Sea?', *International Security* 47, no. 2 (2022): 88–134, 130.

US's failure to reassure,[84] it may be better interpreted as illustrating the limits of Malaysia's receptiveness to US military support. The unresolved and unmanaged maritime disputes challenge the cohesion of ASEAN, 'ASEAN centrality', and the 'ASEAN way' of informality, consensus, and process orientation.[85]

In sum, the change in the regional balance of power, sea routes for trade in goods and energy, sea power competition, access to resources, some strategic value of islands, the future regional order, and a recalibration of China's relations with its neighbours[86] are at stake in the East and South China Sea. These are important factors for the territorial and maritime disputes and help explain why the claimant states have not even begun negotiation processes on the settlement of sovereignty disputes. These factors, however, do not explain when and why the disputing parties have reached agreements on natural resource cooperation and measures for conflict management, or when and why exchanges have ended in an impasse.

Ocean governance as a step-by-step approach to conflict resolution

Claimant states, officials, and scholars have been very well aware of the fact that ineffective management of disputes is a great impediment to the regions' stability and development, and a potential source for conflict escalation. Existing institutions such as UNCLOS and regional organizations have neither settled disputes nor resulted in effective regional governance of the disputed seas. The idea that institutional processes could socialize China[87] did not noticeably affect China's conduct in maritime disputes. Attempts, however, to create institutions that reconcile single interests, incentivise cooperation and prevent conflict are virtually as old as the

84 Euan Graham, 'US Naval Standoff with China Fails to Reassure Regional Allies', *Foreign Policy*, 4 May 2020, https://foreignpolicy.com/2020/05/04/malaysia-south-china-sea-us-navy-drillship-standoff/ (last accessed 23 June 2023).

85 Dylan M. H. Loh, 'The Disturbance and Endurance of Norms in ASEAN: Peaceful but Stressful', *Australian Journal of International Affairs* 72, no. 5 (3 September 2018): 385–402; Shaun Narine, 'ASEAN and the ARF: The Limits of the "ASEAN Way"', *Asian Survey* 37, no. 10 (1997): 961–78; Samuel Sharpe, 'An ASEAN Way to Security Cooperation in Southeast Asia?', *The Pacific Review* 16, no. 2 (1 March 2003): 231–50.

86 Brantly Womack, *Asymmetry and International Relationships* (CUP, 2016); see Chapter II 2.2.

87 Alastair I. Johnston, *Social States: China in International Institutions, 1980–2000* (Princeton UP, 2008).

disputes themselves. The literature proposes virtually all possible instruments of ocean governance for overcoming the disputes.

The South China Sea can be regarded as a common pool of fisheries resources 'because of the combination of highly migratory species and a high degree of larval connectivity'.[88] It is 'near the world centre of marine biodiversity' by harbouring 22 per cent of fish species in only 8.6 per cent of the ocean's surface.[89] The member states of ASEAN called for a code of conduct for the South China Sea for the first time in 1992. The idea of a code of conduct is twofold. It could provide the basic political commitments to enable pragmatic governance of single and common issue areas and it could provide rules for managing conflict behaviour. In this vein, ASEAN members and China declared in 2002 to undertake cooperative measures on environmental protection, marine science, search and rescue, the security of shipping lanes, and other issue areas without prejudice to claims.[90] Proposals about institutions for shared maritime governance include agreements for fisheries, oil and gas, proposals for a marine protected areas network, large marine ecosystems, and the preservation of the marine environment, as well as proposals on maritime security, marine scientific research, and peace parks.[91] Djalal and several others authors make the case that

88 John W. McManus, 'Offshore Coral Reef Damage, Overfishing, and Paths to Peace in the South China Sea', *The International Journal of Marine and Coastal Law* 32, no. 2 (2017): 199–237, 234.

89 Daniel Pauly and Cui Liang, 'The Fisheries of the South China Sea: Major Trends since 1950', *Marine Policy* 121, no. 103584 (November 2020): 1–7; Kent E. Carpenter and Victor G. Springer, 'The Center of the Center of Marine Shore Fish Biodiversity: The Philippine Islands', *Environmental Biology of Fishes* 72, no. 4 (April 2005): 467–480.

90 The 2002 Declaration on the Conduct of Parties in the South China Sea, article 6, adopted at the 8th ASEAN Summit in Phnom Penh, 4 November 2002, accessible at https://asean.org/declaration-on-the-conduct-of-parties-in-the-south-china-sea-2/ (last accessed 23 June 2023).

91 Robert C. Beckman et al., eds., *Beyond Territorial Disputes in the South China Sea Legal Frameworks for the Joint Development of Hydrocarbon Resources*, NUS Centre for International Law (Edward Elgar, 2013); Thang Dang Nguyen, 'Fisheries Co-Operation in the South China Sea and the (Ir)relevance of the Sovereignty Question', *Asian Journal of International Law* 2, no. 1 (2012): 59–88; Hai Dang Vu, *Marine Protected Areas Network in the South China Sea: Charting a Course for Future Cooperation* (Brill, 2014); John W. McManus et al., 'Toward Establishing a Spratly Islands International Marine Peace Park: Ecological Importance and Supportive Collaborative Activities with an Emphasis on the Role of Taiwan', *Ocean Development & International Law* 41, no. 3 (2010): 270–80; Nong Hong, *UNCLOS and Ocean Dispute Settlement: Law and Politics in the South China Sea* (Routledge, 2012); Shicun Wu and Nong Hong, eds., *Recent Developments in the South China Sea Dispute: The Prospect of a Joint Development Regime* (Routledge, 2014); Gregory B. Poling et al., *Defusing the South China Sea Disputes A Regional Blueprint* (Center for Strategic and International Studies, 2018), https://www.csis.org/analysis/defusing-south-china-sea-disputes (last accessed 23 June 2023); James Borton, 'Science Diplomacy and Dispute Management in the

cooperation on functional issue areas should 'start with what is possible and follow a step by step approach'.[92] The international legal discussion on the joint development of hydrocarbon resources in the South China Sea began in the early 1980s.[93] Chinese scholars joined the discussion on the joint development of oil and gas in the early 1990s.[94] In practice, bilateral and multilateral negotiations involved state actors, national oil companies, fisheries associations, and further non-state actors. Officials and scholars from all claimant states developed, through regional elite networks and track II (expert-level) diplomacy, a long list of policy proposals.[95] Thirteen different ASEAN-related bodies work on topics related to maritime security.[96] Numerous bilateral and multilateral diplomatic fora such as the ASEAN Regional Forum (ARF), the South China Sea Initiative, or the Council for Security Cooperation in the Asia Pacific (CSCAP) regularly discuss measures for enhancing confidence building and cooperation.[97] Claimant states nevertheless could not agree on a greater role for existing

South China Sea', in *Enterprises, Localities, People, and Policy in the South China Sea: Beneath the Surface*, edited by Jonathan Spangler, Dean Karalekas, and Moises Lopes de Souza (Springer, 2018), 195–216. More publications make the case for issue-specific cooperation and conflict management. I can cite only a selection.

92 Hasjim Djalal, 'The South China Sea: The Long Road towards Peace and Cooperation', in *Freedom of Seas, Passage Rights and the 1982 Law of the Sea Convention*, edited by Tommy T. B. Koh, Myron H Nordquist, and John Norton Moore (Brill, 2009), 25–50, 47.

93 Rainer Lagoni, 'Interim Measures Pending Maritime Delimitation Agreements', *The American Journal of International Law* 78, no. 2 (1984): 345–68.

94 Keyuan Zou, 'Joint Development in the South China Sea: A New Approach', *The International Journal of Marine and Coastal Law* 21, no. 1 (2006): 83–109. The concept of joint development of hydrocarbon resources in international law is usually traced back to the North Sea Continental Shelf Case, although some agreements existed before. Masahiro Miyoshi, *The Joint Development of Offshore Oil and Gas in Relation to Maritime Boundary Delimitation*, Maritime Briefing v. 2, no. 5 (International Boundaries Research Unit, University of Durham, 1999).

95 Sam G. Bateman and Ralf Emmers, eds., *Security and International Politics in the South China Sea: Towards a Cooperative Management Regime* (Routledge, 2009); Kun-Chin Lin and Andrés Villar Gertner, *Maritime Security in the Asia-Pacific: China and the Emerging Order in the East and South China Seas*, Research Paper (Royal Institute of International Affairs, 2015); Ramses Amer and Keyuan Zou, *Conflict Management and Dispute Settlement in East Asia* (Ashgate, 2011); Mark John Valencia et al., *Sharing the Resources of the South China Sea* (Martinus Nijhoff Publishers, 1997).

96 'ASEAN Regional Forum Work Plan For Maritime Security 2018–2020', 5, http://aseanregionalforum.asean.org/wp-content/uploads/2019/01/ARF-Maritime-Security-Work-Plan-2018-2020.pdf (last accessed 23 March 2024); also see Christian Bueger, 'What Is Maritime Security?', *Marine Policy*, 53 (2015): 159–64.

97 Hasjim Djalal, 'Indonesia and the South China Sea Initiative', *Ocean Development & International Law* 32, no. 2 (2001): 97–103; Sheldon W. Simon, 'Evaluating Track II Approaches to Security Diplomacy in the Asia-Pacific: The CSCAP Experience', *The Pacific Review* 15, no. 2

regional organisations for fisheries and marine environmental protection. These organisations exclude the South China Sea entirely or in substantial part. The Western and Central Pacific Fisheries Commission (WCPFC), for instance, 'notionally extends to the east Asian seaboard, [but] it is understood that the Convention Area does not include the South China Sea.'[98] Regional initiatives such as the Partnerships in Environmental Management for the Seas of East Asia (PEMSEA) or the United Nations Environment Programme (UNEP) project on the South China Sea proposed regional approaches to marine environmental protection but focused only on undisputed coastal areas.[99]

In the East China Sea, China and Japan have established, with interruptions, various joint fisheries agreements since the mid-1950s, Japan and Korea since the mid-1960s. All three states negotiated fisheries agreements anew in the late 1990s after they ratified UNCLOS. Attempts to negotiate agreements for the joint development of hydrocarbon resources started in the 1970s between Japan, Korea, and Taiwan.[100] The earliest Sino-Japanese exchanges date back to the 1980s. Negotiations about rules for marine scientific research and conflict management followed the rise of tensions in the 2000s. Scholars refer to these efforts as maritime regime building[101] and as 'alternate means', a 'functional' and 'creative approach'.[102]

Institutions of ocean governance could subject incident-prone activities such as fishing, seismic research, and others to common rules that, given their transboundary nature, require a common approach. Such institutions could thereby make single steps towards overcoming environmentally destructive and escalatory behaviour.[103] Under article 123 of UNCLOS, littoral states of a 'semi-enclosed sea' should cooperate on the management of living

(2002): 167–200; Mikael Weissmann, 'The South China Sea Conflict and Sino-ASEAN Relations: A Study in Conflict Prevention and Peace Building', *Asian Perspective* (2010), 35–69.

98 The Western and Central Pacific Fisheries Commission, 'Frequently Asked Questions and Brochures', https://www.wcpfc.int/doc/commission-faqs (last accessed 23 March 2024).

99 Sulan Chen, 'Environmental Cooperation in the South China Sea: Factors, Actors and Mechanisms', *Ocean & Coastal Management* 85 (2013): 131–40.

100 Hurng-Yu Chen, 'The Prospects for Joint Development in the South China Sea', *Issues and Studies* 27, no. 12 (1991): 112–25.

101 Mark J. Valencia, ed., *Maritime Regime Building Lessons Learned and Their Relevance for Northeast Asia* (Martinus Nijhoff, 2001).

102 M. Taylor Fravel, 'Explaining Stability in the Senkaku (Diaoyu) Islands Dispute', *Getting the Triangle Straight: Managing China–Japan–US Relations, Washington, DC: The Brookings Institution* 159 (2010): 144–64, 160.

103 John W. McManus, 'Offshore Coral Reef Damage, Overfishing, and Paths to Peace in the South China Sea', *The International Journal of Marine and Coastal Law* 32, no. 2 (2017): 199–237.

resources, marine science, and the preservation of the marine environment.[104] The proposed instruments could transform the disputed maritime domain from a sea of conflict into a sea of cooperation where maritime commons are governed regionally. Some of the cited works present their proposals as being tailored to the interests, as well as socioeconomic and ecological conditions in the East and South China Sea. Claimant states have negotiated in at least twenty cases about concrete agreements for the governance of marine natural resources, incident prevention, and codes of conduct. This book analyses these cases.

Negotiation and escalation at low levels of violence

The East and South China Sea disputes are coined by the simultaneity of, on the one hand, incidents, crises, coercion, and changes in the territorial status quo and, on the other hand, periods of negotiation. While negotiation attempts are several decades old, China has continuously improved its capabilities to unilaterally enforce claims with coercive means. This raises two questions: Firstly, whether China pursues negotiations with a genuine interest in agreements or whether negotiations are merely a façade to delay reactions; and secondly, and more generally, how negotiations about agreements for natural resources and conflict management interact with escalation at low levels of violence.

To begin with the first question, a few turning points should be summarized. China occupied the Paracel Islands after fighting South Vietnam in 1974. In the 'race' to the Spratly Islands in the 1970s and 1980s, China was a latecomer and found itself in the position to claim features already occupied by Southeast Asian states.[105] China took control of several of the Spratly Islands, for instance Johnson Reef, only in 1988 after fighting Vietnam.[106] Further changes to the territorial status quo occurred in 1995 when China erected installations on Mischief Reef and in 2012 when China took control of Philippine-administered Scarborough Shoal. While several claimants built

104 For the legal debate on the extent of the duty to cooperate in semi-enclosed seas, see Erik Franckx and Marco Benatar, 'The "Duty" to Co-Operate for States Bordering Enclosed or Semi-Enclosed Seas', in *Chinese (Taiwan) Yearbook of International Law and Affairs, Volume 31 (2013)* (Brill Nijhoff, 2016), 66–81.
105 Stein Tønnesson, 'Why Are the Disputes in the South China Sea So Intractable? A Historical Approach', *Asian Journal of Social Science* 30, no. 3 (2002): 570–601; Austin, *China's Ocean Frontier.*
106 Sarah Raine and Christian Le Mière discuss various sources regarding battle casualties. *Regional Disorder: The South China Sea Disputes*, IISS Adelphi Series (Routledge, 2013), 42.

smaller structures on features in the 1990s, China's large-scale island-building program started in 2013.[107] China's tactics were variably described as 'grey zone coercion',[108] 'hybrid warfare',[109] action 'little different from that of other countries',[110] or as attempts to build a reputation for resolve.[111] Legally, China's behaviour raises the question under which conditions coercive maritime law enforcement activities amount to the prohibited threat or use of force.[112] While parts of the literature suggest China's assertiveness began at various points in the 2000s, China's intent to extend its jurisdiction in the South China Sea originated in the 1970s. Revelations of scientific and oceanographic surveys, UNCLOS negotiations, and the temptation of 'territorialising' maritime spaces, as well as domestic legislation, have contributed to the emergence of a bureaucratically entrenched policy within China.[113] In the East China Sea, China has increasingly challenged Japan's control of the Senkaku/Diaoyu Islands and greatly expanded its navy, coast guard, and air patrols in and over the East China Sea and through several straits.[114] Several

107 Armed Forces of the Philippines, *Chronological Development of Artificial Structures on Features*, available in The Republic of Philippines, 'The Memorial of the Philippines Volume IV', (30 March 2014) (Annex 96) https://files.pca-cpa.org/pcadocs/The%20Philippines%27%20Memorial%20-%20Volume%20IV%20%28Annexes%2061-102%29.pdf (last accessed 24 April 2024). On the use of documents from the Philippine diplomatic record, see Chapter II 4.

108 Michael Green et al., *Countering Coercion in Maritime Asia: The Theory and Practice of Gray Zone Deterrence* (Center for Strategic and International Studies, 2017); Lyle J. Morris, 'Organizing for the Gray Zone: Assessing the Rights Protection Capabilities of the New China Coast Guard', in *China's Maritime Gray Zone Operations*, edited by Ryan D Martinson and Andrew S. Erickson (Naval Institute Press, 2019), 1–15 (preprint).

109 Alessio Patalano, 'When Strategy Is "Hybrid" and Not "Grey": Reviewing Chinese Military and Constabulary Coercion at Sea', *The Pacific Review* 31, no. 6 (2 November 2018): 811–39; Chiyuki Aoi et al., 'Introduction "Hybrid Warfare in Asia: Its Meaning and Shape"', *The Pacific Review* 31, no. 6 (2 November 2018): 693–713. For a critique of the term 'hybrid threat', see Michael Rühle, 'Deterring Hybrid Threats: The Need for a More Rational Debate', *NATO Defense College Policy Brief*, no. 15 (July 2019).

110 Austin, *China's Ocean Frontier*, 301.

111 Ketian Zhang, 'Cautious Bully: Reputation, Resolve, and Beijing's Use of Coercion in the South China Sea', *International Security* 44, no. 1 (July 2019): 117–59.

112 Steven Haines, 'War at Sea: Nineteenth Century Laws for Twenty-First Century Wars?' *International Review of the Red Cross* 98, no. 902 (August 2016): 419–47; Wolff Heintschel von Heinegg, 'The Difficulties of Conflict Classification at Sea: Distinguishing Incidents at Sea from Hostilities', *International Review of the Red Cross* 98, no. 902 (August 2016): 449–64.

113 Andrew Chubb, 'PRC Assertiveness in the South China Sea: Measuring Continuity and Change, 1970–2015', *International Security* 45, no. 3 (January 2021): 79–121. On 'territorializing' maritime spaces', see Bernard H. Oxman, 'The Territorial Temptation: A Siren Song at Sea', *American Journal of International Law* 100 (2006): 830–51.

114 Japan Ministry of Defense, 'China's Maritime Expansion', April 2017 (on file with the author); Japan Ministry of Defense, 'China's Activities in East China Sea, Pacific Ocean, and Sea of

crises related to seismic or drilling activities and fisheries have involved clashes between coast guards and navy vessels in the East China Sea.[115]

In the time between 1990 and 2019, China also entered into eight agreements for natural resource cooperation and conflict behaviour with Japan, South Korea, the Philippines, and Vietnam, *not* counting the ineffective 2002 Declaration on Conduct or any other document in its context.[116] Six agreements have been implemented (three fisheries agreements, one boundary plus joint development agreement, the non-binding Code for Unplanned Encounters (CUES), and a previous notice arrangement for marine scientific research).[117] A seventh agreement for joint oil and gas exploration was partly implemented until the Philippines let it expire in 2008. China and Japan agreed on the establishment of a crisis communication mechanism in 2019, which is only partially implemented at the time of writing.[118] While most of China's agreements were reached before 2010, China adopted CUES in 2014 and the crisis communication mechanism with Japan in 2019. In addition to these agreements, multilateral (code of conduct) and bilateral negotiation processes are ongoing at the time of writing. In some of these cases, an agreement was reached after long and difficult negotiations, providing ample pretexts to sabotage negotiations if this had been the intention. Moreover, the joint fisheries agreements in the East China Sea contain unilateral termination clauses; China or Japan could easily terminate these agreements. Fishing incidents in the East China Sea between 2010 and 2018 would have provided ample excuses to terminate the agreements.[119] Neither party did that. China, Korea, and Japan prefer interacting based on these specific agreements. While it could be argued that China delayed negotiations on a code of conduct in some periods, the existing agreements are direct evidence that China negotiated with a genuine interest in the cases where it reached and implemented agreements. As China and the Southeast and East

Japan', March 2024, https://www.mod.go.jp/en/d_act/sec_env/pdf/ch_d-act_a.pdf (last accessed 24 April 2024).

115 Reinhard Drifte, 'The Japan-China Confrontation over the Senkaku/Diaoyu Islands: Between "Shelving" and "Dispute Escalation"', *The Asia-Pacific Journal* 12, no. 30 (2014): 1–26.

116 For an overview of cases, see tables in the appendix. I wrote 'Declaration on Conduc' with capital letters to denote the agreed document, but 'code of conduct' with small letters since no code was agreed upon.

117 Akira Takada, 'Marine Scientific Research in the Exclusive Economic Zone and Japan-China Agreement for Prior Notification (1995–2001)', *Japanese Annual of International Law* (2001), 134–50.

118 I regard this MoU as a case of impasse as implementation has remained controversial after a ten-year negotiation period.

119 Chapter IV 1.4 and 2.2.

Asian claimant states have implemented several agreements and are still negotiating others, the question is not so much whether China really wants agreements. Rather, the question is how negotiations about agreements for natural resources and conflict behaviour relate to coercive activities at low levels of violence. The literature on negotiation and escalation,[120] as well as the literature on bargaining while fighting[121], identifies several ways in which negotiation and escalation interact.[122] In this perspective, escalation and bargaining are part of the same structure where conflicting and common interests are mixed.[123]

First, a straightforward way in which negotiation relates to escalation is that negotiations are a response to instances of escalation. When parties realize that escalatory behaviour does not achieve the desired objectives but entails costs and risks, parties may decide to explore negotiated options.[124] Additionally, parties to a dispute may realize that single issues of a wider dispute entail escalatory risks that are disproportionate to the attention parties have devoted to the issue. And then this might trigger a search for some common rules for this single issue. Instances of escalation serve as a reminder to involved parties that the absence of effective tools to prevent escalatory action–reaction cycles increases a region's instability. The case studies will illustrate that, while incidents interrupted exchanges and attempts to negotiate specific agreements for resource sharing and conflict management, they also responded to instances of escalation.

120 I. William Zartman et al., eds., *Escalation and Negotiation in International Conflicts* (CUP, 2005). Zartman and Faure define escalation as 'a specific increase in conflict, a tactical step that marks a qualitative difference in conflict relations'. Guy Olivier Faure and I. William Zartman, 'The Dynamics of Escalation and Negotiation', in ibid., 3–20, 4. The authors suggest conceptual specifications along various dimensions, e.g., escalation of means, ends, space, or risk. They distinguish between, on the one hand, 'transitive escalation' as purposeful and deliberate actions and, on the other hand, 'intransitive escalation' as the 'inherent tendency of escalation to proceed on its own', ibid., 8.

121 R. Harrison Wagner, 'Bargaining and War', *American Journal of Political Science* (2000), 469–84; Robert Powell, 'Bargaining and Learning While Fighting', *American Journal of Political Science* 48, no. 2 (2004): 344–61; Matthew O. Jackson and Massimo Morelli, 'The Reasons for Wars: An Updated Survey', *The Handbook on the Political Economy of War* 34 (2011): 34–57.

122 Note that negotiation and bargaining analysis often focuses on the interplay of bargaining and uses of force at higher levels of violence (war). Applying these insights to disputes at lower levels of violence would require a detailed analysis. Here I can only raise some general points. For a discussion of China's maritime disputes in the context of the bargaining literature, see Steve Chan, *China's Troubled Waters: Maritime Disputes in Theoretical Perspective* (CUP, 2016).

123 Thomas C. Schelling, *The Strategy of Conflict*, 2nd ed. (Harvard UP, 1980).

124 I. William Zartman, 'Structures of Escalation and Negotiation', in *Escalation and Negotiation in International Conflict* (CUP, 2005), 165–84.

Secondly, one actor may use escalation to hurt and to impose costs on a rival that does not acquiesce in demands and thereby try to coerce this rival into an agreement or compel concessions.[125] In this vein, worsening one actor's outside option or best alternative to a negotiated agreement (BATNA)[126] can be part of a bargaining strategy. One strategic use of escalation may occur in cases where actors can only achieve an objective with an opponent's consent but not without it. In this vein, China's coercive interferences in the continental shelf activities of Southeast Asian states have the effect of worsening Southeast Asian states' alternatives to joint oil or gas development. While the use of coercion at sea appears not to be primarily directed at compelling Southeast Asian states' consent to joint development, the coercion has the effect of worsening Southeast Asian prospects of unilaterally exploiting hydrocarbon resources. China has not been able to exploit oil and gas resources in disputed areas beyond UNCLOS-based claims.[127] China was only able to conduct seismic research. What China can do, however, is to thwart Philippine, Vietnamese, or Malaysian attempts to exploit oil and gas by physically interfering in their continental shelves.[128] China has offered joint development as a negotiated option, but either the Philippines or Vietnam rejected China's plans for joint development in several cases. China's interferences ensure that the Philippines, Malaysia, or Vietnam would need joint development agreements to begin novel hydrocarbon projects in areas claimed by China.[129]

A third way that escalation and bargaining processes interact is that a party may use coercive means to reveal an opponent's resolve and capability to resist concessions. In the literature that understands war as a bargaining

125 Thomas C. Schelling, *Arms and Influence*, New ed. (Yale UP, 1966), 69–91; Thomas C. Schelling, *The Strategy of Conflict*, 2nd ed. (Harvard UP, 1980), 195–199.

126 John Odell, 'Negotiation and Bargaining', in *Handbook of International Relations*, 2nd ed., edited by Thomas Risse, Walter Carlsnaes, and Beth Simmons (SAGE, 2011), 379–99. On concepts related to a BATNA, see Sally Blount White and Margaret A. Neale, 'Reservation Prices, Resistance Points, and BATNAs: Determining the Parameters of Acceptable Negotiated Outcomes', *Negotiation Journal* 7 (1991): 379–88.

127 International Crisis Group, 'Stirring up the South China Sea (IV): Oil in Troubled Waters', *Asia Report No. 275*, 26 January 2016, https://www.crisisgroup.org/asia/north-east-asia/china/stirring-south-china-sea-iv-oil-troubled-waters (last accessed 23 June 2023).

128 CSIS, 'China Risks Flare-Up Over Malaysian, Vietnamese Gas Resources', *AMTI Update*, 16 July 2019, https://amti.csis.org/china-risks-flare-up-over-malaysian-vietnamese-gas-resources/; Bill Hayton, 'South China Sea: Vietnam "Scraps New Oil Project"', *BBC*, 23 August 2018, http://www.bbc.com/news/world-asia-43507448 (last accessed 23 March 2022).

129 Note that this analysis does not apply directly to negotiations on fisheries or a code of conduct.

process,[130] fighting is 'considered part of the bargaining process that leads to a negotiated settlement and not as an alternative to it.'[131] Fighting plays a role in screening between strong or weak opponents.[132] Periods of fighting serve to reveal the actors' resolve and reservation points. Fighting brings about a (new) understanding of the true balance of power between two or more opponents on an issue. While the escalation of crises in the East and South China Sea remained at low levels of violence, various accounts of the conflict behaviour during several crises – crises at Scarborough Shoal in April 2012, at the Senkaku/Diaoyu Islands in 2010 and 2012, or the oil rig standoff in 2014 – pointed out that the revelation of claimants' various costs of holding out and levels of resolve was a crucial factor for the outcomes of these crises.[133] The escalation during the Scarborough Shoal standoff revealed, for instance, the lack of Philippine resolve and US backing for the Philippines.[134] This was one factor contributing to China ultimately taking control of the shoal.

A fourth relation between escalation and negotiation is based on the idea that an actor can derive strategic advantages from a negotiated agreement for ameliorating its position and unilateral advancements in a dispute. When escalation and bargaining are part of the same structure of conflict interaction, not only does escalation affect bargaining processes, agreed outcomes of negotiations can also affect, prepare, consolidate, or support escalatory behaviour in some cases. Actors in a dispute seek, for instance, a rival's consent to agreements that retrospectively consolidate gains made through unilateral escalatory action. When actors can gain strategic advantages from a cooperative agreement, the agreement can represent an incremental step towards cooperation and a tool for the continuation of conflict by other means. This fourth relationship raises the question through which characteristics an institution could increase one actor's power, and under which conditions a second actor would nevertheless consent to this institution.

130 Dan Reiter, 'Exploring the Bargaining Model of War', *Perspectives on Politics* 1, no. 1 (2003): 27–43.

131 R. Harrison Wagner, 'Bargaining and War', *American Journal of Political Science* (2000), 469–84, 469.

132 James D. Fearon, 'Fighting Rather than Bargaining', in *Annual Meetings of the American Political Science Association* (2013), 1–46.

133 Zhang, 'Cautious Bully: Reputation, Resolve, and Beijing's Use of Coercion in the South China Sea'; Michael Green et al., *Countering Coercion in Maritime Asia: The Theory and Practice of Gray Zone Deterrence* (Center for Strategic and International Studies, 2017), chapter 3, cases 2, 3, and 7.

134 Chapter III 1.5.

How this book is organized

The next chapter (Chapter II) begins by conceptualizing the types of agreements the disputing parties in the East and South China Sea negotiate about. This includes fisheries and joint development arrangements – UNCLOS refers to these as 'provisional arrangements of a practical nature' – as well as codes of conduct and incident prevention and communication mechanisms. This conceptualization discusses characteristics of incremental approaches to conflict resolution and analyses how the availability of gradual options in an ongoing dispute is likely to affect calculations of disputing parties. Subchapter 2 two addresses the question of how institutions could be sources of power. It identifies how the agreements and institutions under considerations in the East and South China Sea could impact disputing actors' power in subsequent dispute interactions and how this factor is likely to affect negotiations. Subchapter 3 discusses the impact of alternative variables on the negotiation processes, namely nationalism and domestic politics, the existence (or absence) of legal entitlements and international arbitration, and characteristics of multilateral negotiations.

Chapters III, IV, and V present the case studies. Chapter III offers an analysis of the negotiations about joint development and fisheries agreements in the South China Sea. It begins with an overview of the legal claims in the South China Sea. It then examines the past three decades of interactions between Chinese and Philippine negotiators on a variety of arrangements for oil and gas and for fishing activities (subchapter 1). This is followed by a presentation of the exchanges between Chinese and Vietnamese actors (subchapter 2). Two case studies in chapter III exclude China, namely the negotiations between the Philippines and Taiwan on an arrangement for law enforcement and fishing activities (subchapter 3) and between Brunei and Malaysia on boundary delimitation and resource sharing (subchapter 4). Chapter IV begins with an overview of the legal claims in the East China Sea. It then discusses the two and a half decades-long negotiations between various Chinese and Japanese negotiators about different models for oil and gas sharing in several parts of the East China Sea (subchapter 1). This is followed by an examination of the negotiations leading to a set of four partly overlapping fisheries agreements, namely the fisheries agreements between China and Japan (subchapter 1), South Korea and Japan, South Korea and China (subchapter 2), and Japan and Taiwan (subchapter 3). This chapter concludes with a comparison of the role of fishing incidents and fisheries agreements in the East and South China Sea (subchapter 4). Chapter V deals with the negotiations about codes of conduct and incident prevention and communication mechanisms. It begins with an analysis of the past thirty years of negotiations on a code of conduct for the South China Sea (subchapter 1). It then examines the exchanges between China and Japan on a communication arrangement. This is followed by an analysis of the Code for Unplanned Encounters at Sea (subchapter 2). Tables with an overview of the cases are provided in the appendix. This book presents synthetic discussions and theoretical implications of the cases in several subchapters, especially in subchapters II 3, III 1.4 and 2.4, IV 4, V 1.4, and V 2.4 and in the conclusions.

II Natural Resource Institutions, Conflict Management, and the Perils of Cooperation

Abstract
This chapter shows how natural resource institutions, such as joint development and fisheries agreements, and rules for conflict behaviour, such as codes of conduct, contribute to the management of conflicts. Bargaining processes about these institutions differ from bargaining processes about territorial settlements. While disputing actors derive multiple benefits from such institutions, the problem that they can result in vulnerabilities is a major barrier to agreement. This chapter shows that power is central to explaining how cooperative institutions can be weaponized. It identifies how the institutions under consideration in the East and South China Sea impact disputing actors' bargaining power in subsequent interactions. It presents and discusses three alternative explanations for the variation between agreement and impasse.

Keywords: Conflict management, conflict resolution, territorial dispute settlement, natural resource institutions, bargaining, power, negotiation

Claimant states in the East and South China Sea have largely focused on establishing institutions governing marine natural resources and conflict behaviour, rather than on territorial (island) settlements. They have attempted to manage the disputes and improve cooperation within them, but, with few exceptions, not to settle boundaries. An analysis of the East and South China Sea disputes reveals gaps in the literature on the multifaceted relationship between conflict management, natural resource institutions, and territorial and boundary disputes. Access to natural resources is one of several interests that countries pursue in the East and South China Sea

Schultheiss, Christian: *Ocean Governance and Conflict in the East and South China Sea. Negotiating Natural Resources, Institutions and Power.*
Taylor & Francis Group, 2024
DOI: 10.5117/9789463728997_CH02

disputes.[1] The relevance of natural resources beyond their economic value stems from the fact that natural resource activities are an immediate trigger for incidents and escalation, as the case studies will illustrate. 'Frighteningly mundane'[2] fishing incidents, for instance, have caused major crises in the East and South China Sea. While marine natural resources are common pool resources that require transboundary governance,[3] disputes over islands and sea boundaries are a barrier to transboundary governance. Moreover, natural resource cooperation can be a central component of (land) territorial settlements, but the latter has been regarded as a precondition for transboundary cooperation.[4] In the case of marine natural resources, though, sea boundary delimitation and territorial (island) settlements are much less a precondition for natural resource cooperation. Fisheries agreements and agreements for the joint development of hydrocarbon resources allow natural resource cooperation in lieu of sea boundary delimitation. The UN Convention on the Law of the Sea (UNCLOS) refers to these as 'provisional arrangements of a practical nature' (Articles 74(3) and 83(3)). These types of arrangements originated in international legal practice. It is therefore perhaps unsurprising that few studies outside international law or maritime affairs explicitly examine these arrangements and their contribution to the management of disputes.[5] Studies on natural resource institutions have focused to some extent on the question of how a natural resource institution – for example, a river arrangement – prevents conflict over this natural resource.[6] But here the crucial question is how natural

1 See the subsection of the Introduction, 'What is at stake in the East and South China Sea.'

2 Graham T. Allison, *Destined for War: Can America and China Escape Thucydides's Trap?* (Mariner Books, 2017), 167.

3 Elinor Ostrom, 'The Challenge of Common-Pool Resources', *Environment: Science and Policy for Sustainable Development* 50, no. 4 (July 2008): 8–21; Thomas Dietz et al., 'The Struggle to Govern the Commons', *Science* 302, no. 5652 (2003): 1907–12; V. K. Aggarwal and C. Dupont, 'Goods, Games, and Institutions', *International Political Science Review* 20, no. 4 (1999): 393–409; Elinor Ostrom, *Governing the Commons: The Evolution of Institutions for Collective Action* (CUP, 1990).

4 Paul K. Huth, *Standing Your Ground Territorial Disputes and International Conflict* (University of Michigan, 1998), chapter 7, 192; Thomas Diez, 'The Paradoxes of Europe's Borders', *Comparative European Politics*, 4 (2006): 235–52, 238.

5 An exception is Song Xue, 'Why Joint Development Agreements Fail', *Contemporary Southeast Asia* 41, no. 3 (2019): 418–46.

6 Nina von Uexkull and Halvard Buhaug, 'Security Implications of Climate Change: A Decade of Scientific Progress', *Journal of Peace Research* 58, no. 1 (January 2021): 3–17, 6; Jaroslav Tir and Douglas M Stinnett, 'Weathering Climate Change: Can Institutions Mitigate International Water Conflict?', *Journal of Peace Research* 49, no. 1 (January 2012): 211–25; Jaroslav Tir and Douglas Stinnett, 'The Institutionalization of River Treaties', *International Negotiation* 14, no. 2 (2009):

resource agreements that are established within a dispute contribute to managing broader disputes while not settling them.

Moreover, disputing actors have negotiated agreements for incident prevention, codes of conduct, and crisis communication in the East and South China Sea. These are crucial tools for disputing parties to manage conflict behaviour, but they are also distinct from natural resource agreements. This then results in the following three questions: How do natural resource institutions, such as joint development and joint fisheries agreements, and rules for conflict behaviour, such as codes of conduct, contribute to the management of conflicts (subchapter 1)? How do bargaining processes about such arrangements differ from bargaining processes about territorial or boundary settlements (subchapter 1)? And which barriers prevent claimants from reaching agreements even if claimants derive multiple benefits from them? Subchapter 2 shows how agreements can result in vulnerabilities that negatively affect states' bargaining power, which is a major barrier to agreements. Subchapter 3 presents and discusses three alternative explanations for the variation between agreements and impasses.

1 Conflict Management and Natural Resource Institutions

Conflicting actors will often not negotiate about a comprehensive resolution to a conflict, but they will instead negotiate about provisional rules, principles and procedural issues, cooperation frameworks, joint projects, confidence building, incident prevention, and further rules for the management of conflict behaviour. In intractable disputes, comprehensive settlements of the basic conflict issues may not be on the negotiation table at all, and many dispute resolution options will be exhausted. Disputing actors may then focus on gradual or step-by-step processes that do not settle a conflict comprehensively. To conceptualize such approaches, the literature proposes concepts such as conflict management, partial settlements, conflict transformation, cooperation on issue areas other than the conflict issue, and confidence building.[7] Several studies ask whether

229–51; also see Paul R. Hensel et al., 'Bones of Contention: Comparing Territorial, Maritime, and River Issues', *Journal of Conflict Resolution* 52, no. 1 (2008): 117–43.

7 I. William Zartman, 'Conflict Resolution and Negotiation', in *The SAGE Handbook of Conflict Resolution*, edited by Jacob Bercovitch, Viktor Aleksandrovich Kremeniuk, and I. William Zartman (SAGE, 2009), 322–39; John W. Burton and Frank Dukes, *Conflict. Practices in Management, Settlement, and Resolution*, vol. 4 (Macmillan, 1990); Johannes Botes, 'Conflict Transformation: A Debate over Semantics or a Crucial Shift in the Theory and Practice of Peace and Conflict

step-by-step approaches contribute to conflict resolution incrementally or prolong conflicts by reducing the parties' incentives to seek a comprehensive resolution. Metaphorically speaking, the question is whether incremental approaches are steps on a ladder to an eventual dispute resolution, or whether incremental approaches prevent progress.[8]

The literature is divided on this question. Roger Fisher recommends the 'fractionation' of disputes as 'almost invariably the best tactic' to bring about long-term change in a conflict by separating conflicts into components and dealing with the components one by one.[9] Where 'islands of agreements'[10] – cooperative agreements among conflicting actors on issue areas without a necessarily direct and close connection with a conflict – offer a long-term perspective or where conflict management helps end escalatory processes,[11] these approaches can lead to conflict resolution. Conflict management as the attempt to reduce 'violence without touching the basic conflict issue' can be distinguished from conflict resolution as the attempt to resolve the underlying core issues.[12] 'Gradualism' is often characterized as a logical, practical, and cautious sequencing strategy that is widely used by practising mediators at various levels.[13] Yet several studies caution that gradualism is susceptible to manipulation[14] and that 'incrementalism'[15] can result in prolonged conflict or addresses only minor issues.[16] Mattes, however, finds that 'piecemeal approaches' defined as 'partial settlements pave the way for comprehensive dispute resolution'.[17]

Studies?', *International Journal of Peace Studies* (2003), 1–27; Ramses Amer and Keyuan Zou, *Conflict Management and Dispute Settlement in East Asia* (Ashgate, 2011); Ho-Won Jeong, *Conflict Management and Resolution: An Introduction* (Routledge, 2010).

8 I thank Stein Tønnesson for suggesting this metaphor.

9 Roger Fisher, 'Fractionating Conflict', *Daedalus* 93, no. 3 (1964): 920–41, 934, 939.

10 Gabriella Blum, *Islands of Agreement: Managing Enduring Armed Rivalries* (Harvard UP, 2007).

11 Guy Olivier Faure and I. William Zartman, 'The Dynamics of Escalation and Negotiation', in *Escalation and Negotiation in International Conflicts*, edited by I. William Zartman, Guy Olivier Faure, and the International Institute for Applied Systems Analysis (CUP, 2005), 3–20, 11.

12 I. William Zartman, 'Conflict Resolution and Negotiation', 331.

13 Joshua N. Weiss, 'Trajectories Toward Peace: Mediator Sequencing Strategies in Intractable Communal Conflicts', *Negotiation Journal* 19, no. 2 (2003): 109–15.

14 Ibid., 111.

15 Sumantra Bose, *Contested Lands: Israel-Palestine, Kashmir, Bosnia, Cyprus, and Sri Lanka* (Harvard UP, 2007), 4.

16 T. Clifton Morgan, 'Issue Linkages in International Crisis Bargaining', *American Journal of Political Science*, 1990, 311–33.

17 Michaela Mattes, '"Chipping Away at the Issues" Piecemeal Dispute Resolution and Territorial Conflict,' *Journal of Conflict Resolution* 62, no. 1 (2018): 94–118 treats a partial territorial

Confidence building is an incremental approach whereby actors seek to build trust in each other, but also in the arrangements under consideration and their consequences. The literature uses the broad term 'confidence building' in different ways. Bilateral cooperation on issue areas other than the disputed issue, such as trade in the context of a territorial dispute, can amount to confidence building.[18] Others reserve the term for informal approaches.[19] A narrow concept of confidence building includes informal exchanges, workshops between officials, and track II diplomacy.[20] In contrast to the studies that ask whether incremental approaches contribute to a comprehensive settlement of disputes, this book focuses on the question of whether disputing actors can agree on concrete agreements in the first place and whether these agreements, if implemented, make a difference in an ongoing dispute.

The idea of 'fractionating' applies to disputing states' approaches in the East and South China Sea. These disputes involve different sets of conflicted issues, namely disputes over territorial sovereignty,[21] over the existence of maritime rights (entitlements) and sea boundary delimitation, and disputes regarding access to marine natural resources. The disputes also concern issues regarding the jurisdiction of maritime law enforcement agencies, the scope of navigational rights, and the prohibition of coercive conflict behaviour. On the one hand, these different issue areas are closely related. States can claim maritime rights based on sovereignty over territory or features. In turn, states then have rights to fisheries, oil, and gas based on valid maritime rights. On the other hand, disputing actors have tried to dissociate single issue areas from a dispute by agreeing on common rules for a specific issue. This includes the possibility that actors accumulate issue areas subject to common rules one by one.

Agreements for the joint development of hydrocarbon resources in areas of overlapping claims are one type of agreement that allows such an approach. The use of joint development agreements has emerged in international law

settlement as an independent variable and finds that partial territorial settlements contribute to comprehensive territorial settlements.

18 Krista E. Wiegand and Emilia Justynia Powell, 'Unexpected Companions: Bilateral Cooperation Between States Involved in Territorial Disputes', *Conflict Management and Peace Science* 28, no. 3 (July 2011): 209–29.

19 Blum, *Islands of Agreement: Managing Enduring Armed Rivalries*.

20 Mikael Weissmann, 'The South China Sea Conflict and Sino-ASEAN Relations: A Study in Conflict Prevention and Peace Building', *Asian Perspective*, (2010), 35–69.

21 Lake congruously regards sovereignty as a bundle of rights. David A. Lake, *Hierarchy in International Relations*, (Cornell UP, 2009), 3.

through subsequent state practice.[22] UNCLOS absorbed such practice and adopted the term 'provisional arrangements of a practical nature' to refer to agreements for hydrocarbons, fisheries, and further issues in areas of overlapping claims. Such agreements can have a provisional or interim character in the sense of identically worded Articles 74(3) and 83(3) of UNCLOS, but they can also be durable.

> Pending agreement as provided for in paragraph 1, the States concerned, in a spirit of understanding and cooperation, shall make every effort to enter into provisional arrangements of a practical nature and, during this transitional period, not to jeopardize or hamper the reaching of the final agreement. Such arrangements shall be without prejudice to the final delimitation.[23]

Joint development agreements establish rules for joint exploration or joint exploitation of oil and gas in disputed areas.[24] Such agreements dissociate this issue from a maritime dispute by providing a legal framework within which state or non-state actors (e.g., energy companies) can operate. International law distinguishes between joint development in lieu of sea boundary delimitation and joint development straddling a boundary. Cooperation only extends to the activities specified in the agreement and does not resolve overlapping claims. Where parties agree on several agreements for various issue areas, parties accumulate settled issues. Joint fishery agreements allow disputing actors to establish common rules for fisheries in disputed areas. Such an agreement defines joint fishery zones geographically and defines the rules applicable to fishing activities of private actors (fishermen) and law enforcement activities of state actors (e.g., coast guards) of two or more

22 Miyoshi defines a joint development arrangement as '[a]n inter-governmental arrangement of a provisional nature, designed for functional purposes of joint exploration and/or exploitation of hydrocarbon resources of the seabed beyond the territorial sea'. Masahiro Miyoshi, *The Joint Development of Offshore Oil and Gas in Relation to Maritime Boundary Delimitation* 2, no. 5, Maritime Briefing (University of Durham, 1999), 3; Vasco Becker-Weinberg, *Joint Development of Hydrocarbon Deposits in the Law of the Sea* (Springer, 2014).

23 For a legal analysis of articles 74(3) and 83(3) and their relevance for maritime disputes, see British Institute of International and Comparative Law, ed., *Report on the Obligations of States under Articles 74(3) and 83(3) of UNCLOS in Respect of Undelimited Maritime Areas* (British Institute of International and Comparative Law, 2016); Christian Schultheiss, 'Overcoming Violence in Maritime Conflicts with Provisional Arrangements: A Legal Tool for Conflict Resolution', in *International Law and Peace Settlements*, edited by Mark Retter, Andrea Varga, and Marc Weller (CUP, 2021), 525–44.

24 Rainer Lagoni, 'Interim Measures Pending Maritime Delimitation Agreements', *The American Journal of International Law* 78, no. 2 (1984): 345–68.

states in a disputed area. The agreement separates the issue of fisheries from sea boundary delimitations and from territorial disputes (where islands or features are disputed), and thus reduces the range of disputed issues. It does not settle only the issue of fisheries for their own sake. Where fishing activities repeatedly trigger incidents and escalation, agreements on this issue can also reduce the potential for escalation in the wider conflict.

To what extent an agreement on a single issue can contribute to reducing escalation risks depends, among other things, on the escalatory potential of the specific issue. This book does not assume that disputing actors negotiate such agreements primarily with the intent to produce momentum towards resolution of the broader conflict. The negotiators I interviewed, though, were generally aware that settling one issue helps manage the broader conflict by reducing the number of issue areas prone to escalation. Hence, a joint fishery agreement is an alternative to sea boundary delimitation for the limited purpose of fisheries, but it can also contribute to the resolution of a broader dispute by reducing escalation risks. This latter point is then another reason why incremental approaches may have a positive impact on comprehensive settlements. In principle, several agreements could allow disputing actors to define rules for various issues. If claimant states agreed on a combination of different arrangements in the East and South China Sea, this would result in the institutions for the shared governance of the maritime domain that various scholars suggest.[25]

The types of agreements in incremental approaches can be categorized in a number of ways. The first type of agreements for issue-specific and limited cooperation separates specific issues from a wider dispute – e.g., agreements on resource sharing (fisheries, oil and gas, rivers), joint projects or joint regulations, or cooperation on specific goods. The link between a cooperative arrangement and a dispute can be close and direct as in a joint fishery arrangement in a maritime dispute. Second, agreements for conflict behaviour (conflict management) – e.g., codes of conduct, crisis communication and hotline arrangements, restrictions on conflict behaviour, and measures for stabilization – provide rules for conflict behaviour and seek to reduce violence.[26] Such agreements can prohibit certain types of behaviour actors adopt to pursue their interests, but they can also make certain procedures mandatory or recommendatory to prevent escalation. Agreements of this category could be subdivided into agreements on behaviour (e.g., prohibition of the use of force, restrictions on the use of certain types of coercive

25 See subsection of the Introduction, 'Ocean governance as a step-by-step approach to conflict'.
26 I William Zartman, 'Conflict Resolution and Negotiation', 331.

behaviour), agreements on assets (e.g., arms limitation and disarmament arrangements, prohibitions of certain types of weapons), and prescriptive arrangements (e.g., prescriptions about de-escalating steps). In both China Seas, various actors suggest restrictions on the use of violent means and coercive law enforcement practices as well as prohibiting the occupation of islands or certain military operations. Actors have negotiated prescriptions for the use of communication protocols during incidents and crises.[27] Third, procedural agreements prepare negotiations on specific issues of a dispute or a wider settlement (e.g., 'talks about talks', access to negotiations, agreements on sequencing and principles). Fourth, partial settlements as understood by Mattes[28] refer to a partial settlement within one issue area – e.g., a partial territorial settlement in the context of a territorial dispute. Fifth, confidence building measures can be formal or informal measures or one-time measures (e.g., joint exercises) that aim at building trust between parties or trust in the types of agreements under consideration. Agreements that fit broadly into these five categories can be further characterized as written arrangements except for some informal confidence-building measures. This includes treaties, agreements, notes verbales, and exchanges of letters or memoranda of understanding. They are concluded between disputing parties; they also define rules for non-state and private actors (e.g., fishermen). Some agreements define an institutional mechanism (e.g., a joint committee) that allows actors to address incidents (e.g., a fishing incident) that may arise after an agreement and that are within its scope. Some agreements define practical measures. Whether or not an agreement is effective is a question that can be asked in relation to any specific agreement.

Agreements belonging to these categories are also institutions. Institutions are defined as '*explicit arrangements, negotiated among international actors, that prescribe, proscribe, and/or authorize behaviour.* Explicit arrangements are public, at least among the parties themselves. According to our definition, they are also the fruits of agreement.'[29] This definition theorizes institutions 'as arrangements that make cooperation more feasible and durable, at least in some circumstances.'[30] Institutions are treated 'as rational, negotiated responses to the problems international actors face.'[31] In the East and South China Sea, claimant states negotiate about institutions

27 Chapter V.

28 Michaela Mattes, 'Chipping Away at the Issues'.

29 Barbara Koremenos et al., 'The Rational Design of International Institutions', *International Organization* 55, no. 4 (2001): 761–99, 762 (emphasis in the original).

30 Ibid., 764.

31 Ibid., 766.

for fisheries, oil and gas, marine scientific research, conflict behaviour, and other issue areas that prescribe, allow, or prohibit behaviour in response to the problems that the parties face in the disputed maritime domain.[32]

The disputing states of the East and South China Sea have not sought settlements of territorial disputes. Only one territorial settlement has taken place over the last sixty years while more than a hundred islets, reefs and sandbanks are disputed – in 1957 China handed White Dragon Tail Island (*bailongwei dao*) in the Gulf of Tonkin to North Vietnam.[33] While some maritime boundaries are delimited in the southern part of the South China Sea,[34] China entered into only one maritime boundary agreement, namely with Vietnam in the Gulf of Tonkin. China, Japan, and South Korea have consulted on boundary delimitations without result, as their respective positions are too far apart. Claimant states have negotiated various arrangements for natural resources and conflict management and have been able to implement some. The focus of this book is therefore on agreements for issue-specific and limited cooperation and on agreements for conflict behaviour. China and Vietnam as well as Brunei and Malaysia have reached a partial boundary settlement in a package with an agreement for issue-specific cooperation. This book will discuss the specific nature of the package in the respective case studies. Some important procedural agreements in the context of the negotiations on a code of conduct (Chapter V) and Sino-Vietnamese negotiations (chapter III) will be discussed, but not further theorized. Nor will this book attempt to theorize confidence-building measures. While thirteen different ASEAN-related bodies talk about various maritime security issues, it is sometimes difficult to identify concrete proposals in these talks. Where talks can be characterized as confidence building, they are not part of this book.

1.1 Cooperative Response and Continuation of Conflict by Other Means?

The argument for why claimant states have reverted to agreements regarding natural resources, crisis communication, and conduct in the East and South

32 While many international institutions may be the result of an incremental process, the empirical focus of this book is on agreements that actors negotiate in the context of territorial and sea boundary disputes.

33 M. Taylor Fravel, 'Regime Insecurity and International Cooperation: Explaining China's Compromises in Territorial Disputes', *International Security* 30, no. 2 (2005): 46–83, 63.

34 Tara Davenport, 'Southeast Asian Approaches to Maritime Boundaries', *Asian Journal of International Law* 4, no. 02 (2014): 309–57; Bich Tran, 'The Significance of the Vietnam-Indonesia Exclusive Economic Zone Demarcation', *Fulcrum* (blog), 20 January 2023, https://fulcrum.sg/the-significance-of-the-vietnam-indonesia-exclusive-economic-zone-demarcation/.

China Sea appears intuitively logical. Parties have various incentives to limit escalatory dynamics and to contribute to a positive long-term perspective for the disputes in a situation where parties have not begun consultations on territorial settlements.

Take agreements for the joint development of hydrocarbon resources in disputed maritime zones as one example. Such agreements reconcile disputing positions *partly* by allowing joint action on specified issues. They provide a legal framework within which state or non-state actors can explore for oil and gas, or, in case of findings, exploit oil and gas in an area of overlapping claims.[35] A joint development agreement is without prejudice to claims.[36] Unilateral attempts by China, the Philippines, and Vietnam to explore for oil have led to the most intense incidents and crises in both China Seas.[37] The states cannot exploit resources in the most disputed areas at the time of writing. Arrangements for natural resource sharing help unlock common economic interests. Joint development agreements provide the disputing states with the option to separate joint exploration or exploitation activities from disputes on a provisional basis. By entering into such agreements, states get access to resources they cannot otherwise exploit. States neutralize one trigger for escalation, derive economic and security benefits, ameliorate overall relations, and might enter into a reinforcing, reciprocity-based pattern of cooperation.[38] The objective of Southeast Asian countries to protect their overall relationships with China and not allow single disputes to define the relationship[39] requires the management of territorial and maritime disputes. Glaser refers to resource sharing as an 'ideal solution' for China and its neighbours.[40] Some Chinese analysts regard resource sharing as a way out of the double challenge of pursuing China's claims in the disputes and of preventing the US from forming a countervailing coalition with China's opponents.[41]

35 Robert C. Beckman et al., *Beyond Territorial Disputes in the South China Sea: Legal Frameworks for the Joint Development of Hydrocarbon Resources* (Edward Elgar, 2013).

36 Becker-Weinberg, *Joint Development of Hydrocarbon Deposits in the Law of the Sea*.

37 Chapters III and IV.

38 Robert M. Axelrod, *The Evolution of Cooperation* (Basic Books, 1984).

39 Hsien Loong Lee, 'The Endangered Asian Century', *Foreign Affairs* 99, no. 4 (August 2020): 51–64, 59.

40 Charles L. Glaser, 'A U.S.-China Grand Bargain? The Hard Choice between Military Competition and Accommodation', *International Security* 39, no. 4 (April 2015): 49–90, 80.

41 Interviews with scholars on maritime security of a leading think tank on maritime affairs affiliated with China's Ministry of Foreign Affairs, China, 11 April 2017 and 18 April 2017 (interview 20 and 22).

This argument about the benefits of natural resource agreements and conflict management does not explain, though, why disputing actors should be able to reach such agreements when, at the same time, territorial settlements are outside the bargaining range. Bargaining concepts suggest an intuitive argument for why agreements on natural resources can be inside the bargaining range while comprehensive settlements of sovereignty or boundaries are outside. Scholars argue that issue indivisibilities prevent agreement on territorial disputes.[42] A single island or island group, due to its strategic or ideational properties, may be indivisible. Negotiators cannot compromise if a disputed good cannot be divided, this is, if it is indivisible. The natural resources and fisheries around a disputed island, however, are highly divisible; they can be shared. A fisheries agreement divides indivisibles by regulating fishing activities around an island without having a bearing on the status of the island. A long time horizon or a long 'shadow of the future', was found to prevent an agreement when states were cautious about the long-term consequences of an agreement.[43] In contrast, states can change and define the duration of provisional arrangements. The duration of the resource-sharing agreements discussed in this book is between three and fifty years. Some agreements contain unilateral termination clauses giving state actors further options regarding the long-term consequences of an agreement. Moreover, questions of resolve,[44] reputation,[45] and domestic audiences[46] affect bargaining processes about territorial conflict. Assuming that bargaining processes about issue-specific and limited cooperation within disputes are relatively less affected by these factors, negotiators should face fewer obstacles in their negotiations. This assumption has some plausibility, as claimant states have entered into arrangements on natural resources and conflict management, while not a single island dispute has

42 Stacie E. Goddard, 'Uncommon Ground: Indivisible Territory and the Politics of Legitimacy', *International Organization* 60, no. 1 (2006): 35–68; James D. Fearon, 'Rationalist Explanations for War', *International Organization* 49, no. 3 (June 1995): 379–414.

43 James D. Fearon, 'Bargaining, Enforcement, and International Cooperation', *International Organization* 52, no. 2 (1998): 269–305. Once agreement is reached, a long shadow of the future is conducive to reciprocity-based cooperation, Axelrod, *The Evolution of Cooperation*.

44 Robert Powell, 'Bargaining Theory and International Conflict', *Annual Review of Political Science* 5, no. 1 (2002): 1–30; Andrew H. Kydd, 'Rationalist Approaches to Conflict Prevention and Resolution', *Annual Review of Political Science* 13 (2010): 101–21.

45 Barbara F. Walter, 'Explaining the Intractability of Territorial Conflict', *International Studies Review* 5, no. 4 (2003): 137–53.

46 James D. Fearon, 'Domestic Political Audiences and the Escalation of International Disputes', *American Political Science Review* 88, no. 03 (1994): 577–92.

been settled in the past three decades and, in cases involving China, only one maritime boundary.

This intuitive, cooperative logic arguably underlays the initiation of various regional and bilateral diplomatic processes that have tried to adopt agreements for various issue areas. The agreements that claimants have reached and implemented exemplify this logic to some extent. However, this cooperative logic fails to explain the variation between agreements and impasses or the observable obstacles in the negotiation processes even in cases of agreement. There is more to the agreements for natural resource cooperation and conflict management than cooperative logic. Perhaps it is fair to say that the literature on cooperative models for the East and South China Sea does not pay enough attention to the potential of, at least, some cooperative institutions to extend a disputing actor's power.

Where struggling actors bargain about step-by-step approaches to dispute resolution, it is common knowledge that disputes do not end with successful bargains and that competing interests remain unaligned, as commitments made in incremental approaches are limited. The availability of agreements for natural resource cooperation and conflict management as negotiated options is then likely to affect parties' calculations in several ways. For some actors, it may be particularly attractive to reach arrangements on specific issues of interest while upholding core claims. For instance, China's alternative to a territorial or boundary settlement in the East and South China Sea is not just the continuation of the disputes, but the possibility of maintaining claims while reaching arrangements on specific issues of interest to China. By establishing a cooperative relationship on single issues, China may be able to realize some interests while continuing to build up a position unilaterally and without giving up claims. In short, actors can get what they want with another actor's consent but without having to commit to a profound change of claims. Joint development and joint fisheries agreements are then an attractive alternative option to a negotiated territorial or boundary settlement as they only commit disputing actors to the purpose specified in the arrangement. Moreover, it is also possible that the limited nature of commitments affects an actor's calculation of the viability of compellence strategies. While one actor may be pessimistic about the ability to compel another actor to recognize its territorial claims, it may be more optimistic about the chances of making another actor accept resource-sharing agreements.[47]

47 On joint development and escalation as a bargaining strategy, see the subsection of the Introduction, 'Negotiation and escalation at low levels of violence'.

Furthermore, conflicts are bargaining situations where actors manoeuvre for advantages and jockey for positions.[48] Agreements, not only unilateral changes of the status quo, are one possible medium through which actors could improve their bargaining position. In situations where conflicting interests and common interests are mixed, one party may gain possibilities to advance conflicting interests by acting on common interests. The agreements in incremental approaches to conflicts do not give rise to the expectation that no further demands will be made. The availability of institutions that separate specific issue areas from a wider dispute and define rules for conflict behaviour gives rival parties options to shape the course of ongoing disputes. Claimant states may then regard cooperative institutions as tools for the continuation of conflict behaviour by other means. In the East and South China Sea, claimant states have disagreed on specific terms of the institutions under consideration. Negotiators would not enter into agreements if specific terms of an agreement were to 'consolidate' or 'cement' a rival's unilateral advancements, 'validate' or 'recognize' a rival's claim, or amount to a 'slippery slope', a 'slice of the salami', or even a trap.[49] What these problems have in common is that they display actors' concerns that one actor could leverage institutions for natural resource cooperation and conflict management to gain power advantages. This raises two questions: How or by virtue of which characteristics can seemingly benign institutions for natural resources, joint exploration, crisis communication, incident prevention or codes of conduct be weaponized and result in power advantages? How do actors negotiate about the creation of institutions and their implementation when these alter an actor's power in subsequent interactions?

2 Power – How Institutions Can Be Weaponized

This subchapter begins with a short definition of the concept of power and then discusses the literature on how institutions affect actors' power. Dahl defines power as a relational concept: 'A has power over B to the extent that he can get B to do something that B would not otherwise do.'[50] Baldwin distils four points about power from the literature in Dahl's tradition: first, power should be regarded as a causal concept; second, power should be regarded

48 Thomas C. Schelling, *The Strategy of Conflict* (Harvard UP, 1980), 5.

49 These quotes are from the case studies.

50 Robert A. Dahl, 'The Concept of Power', *Behavioral Science* 2, no. 3 (1957): 201–215, 202–203. Dahl further distinguishes between the source, the means, the amount, and the scope of power.

as a relational concept and not as a property; third, power has various dimensions; and fourth, there are various bases or sources of power and there is no permanent hierarchy among the sources of power.[51] Within this concept of power, the power relation between two or more actors can change in the course of interactions depending on actors' choices and moves.[52] Institutional choices in strategic interactions can be one possible source that alters downstream power.[53] This condition is a central element of the interactions between the parties in the East and South China Sea.

Institutions are responses to situations where collective action problems and transaction costs prevent cooperative behaviour.[54] Various scholars have argued that the question of how institutions impact the downstream power of actors needs to be integrated into the theory of institutions. According to Moe, the theory of institutions recognizes the relevance of power but reduces its role to choices among multiple equilibria and the division of gains from joint action.[55] 'Power is typically just an add-on to the underlying cooperationist theory, playing a peripheral role that leaves the fundamentals of voluntarism and mutual benefit unchanged. Predation and other downsides of power are acknowledged, but the focus tends to be on cooperative solutions.'[56] He criticises scholarship that neglects the question of how institutions alter power and only treats institutions primarily as solutions to collective action problems. The ways institutions alter power plays an important role in addition to their cooperative functions:

> Political institutions serve two very different purposes. On the one hand, they help mitigate collective-action problems, particularly the

51 David A. Baldwin, *Power and International Relations: A Conceptual Approach* (Princeton UP, 2016), 49–59.

52 Schelling, *The Strategy of Conflict*, 22, see 22–80; James D. Fearon, 'Bargaining over Objects That Influence Future Bargaining Power', Conference Paper, *Annual Meeting of the American Political Science Association*, (1996), 1–25. For Schelling, greater bargaining power is a greater ability to define the outcomes of bargaining processes and does not necessarily stem from an actor's greater material resources or greater skill.

53 Baldwin, *Power and International Relations: A Conceptual Approach*; David A. Baldwin, 'Power and International Relations', in *Handbook of International Relations*, edited by Walter Carlsnaes, Thomas Risse, and Beth Simmons (SAGE, 2012), 273–297, 291.

54 Elinor Ostrom, *Governing the Commons: The Evolution of Institutions for Collective Action* (CUP, 1990); Thráinn Eggertsson, *Economic Behavior and Institutions*, Cambridge Surveys of Economic Literature (CUP, 1990); Robert O. Keohane, 'The Demand for International Regimes', *International Organization* 36, no. 2 (1982): 325–55.

55 Terry M. Moe, 'Power and Political Institutions', *Perspectives on Politics* 3, no. 2 (2005): 215–33, 225.

56 Ibid., 229.

> commitment and enforcement problems…, and allow the various actors in politics to cooperate.… On the other hand, political institutions are also weapons of coercion and redistribution. They are the structural means by which political winners pursue their own interests, often at the expense of political losers.[57]

Similar points are made in the literature. The transaction cost theory of institutions sees institutionalized authority 'primarily as a *remedy* for opportunism', while it might also be a 'device which might be *abused* in an opportunistic fashion. Little attention is given to the prospect that agents holding positions of authority might… gain strategic advantages.'[58] International trade institutions, for instance, 'consolidate' asymmetric positions of bargaining power by 'entrenching opportunity structures'.[59] Institutions then need to reflect a balance between informal and formal rules, whereas informal rules serve the big actors and formal rules protect the weak against the abuse of an institution by the powerful.[60] Note that these arguments about power in institutions do *not* argue that various actors are unlikely to be constrained by rules, or that institutions are ineffective or mere epiphenomena of extrinsic power games.[61] On the contrary, institutions are not only likely to impact and constrain interactions between actors, but institutions could also become weapons of coercion and allocate strategic advantages. According to these arguments, institutions impact interactions in addition to and beyond responses to collective action problems. Institutions not only constrain but also extend state power, as states wield influence through institutions. If institutions play a role in distributing power, negotiations leading to their creation are likely to reflect that. Actors

57 Terry M. Moe, 'Political Institutions: The Neglected Side of the Story', *Journal of Law, Economics, & Organization* 6 (1990): 213–53, 213.

58 Gregory K. Dow, 'The Function of Authority in Transaction Cost Economics', *Journal of Economic Behavior & Organization* 8, no. 1 (March 1987): 13–38, 20 (emphasis in the original).

59 Rorden Wilkinson, 'Building Asymmetry Concluding the Doha Development Agenda', in *The WTO after Hong Kong: Progress in, and Prospects for, the Doha Development Agenda*, edited by Donna Lee and Rorden Wilkinson (Routledge, 2007), 248–61; Rorden Wilkinson, 'Power, Performance and the WTO' (International Studies Association Venture Workshop on International Organisation Performance, 25 March 2008). China has also tried to consolidate its trading practices institutionally by perpetuating asymmetric bargaining positions. Michael Sampson, 'The Evolution of China's Regional Trade Agreements: Power Dynamics and the Future of the Asia-Pacific', *The Pacific Review* (2019): 1–31.

60 Randall W. Stone, *Controlling Institutions: International Organizations and the Global Economy* (CUP, 2011).

61 But see John J. Mearsheimer, 'The False Promise of International Institutions', *International Security* 19, no. 3 (1994): 5–49.

then need not only to agree on how to organize joint action and distribute gains from joint action. They also need to settle on the question of how power is distributed and how to bring about safeguards and checks against the potential strategic advantages that an actor can gain as a result of an institution.

The literature identifies several mechanisms that demonstrate how institutions affect actors' power in ways that are pertinent to the case studies. First, institutions alter power between state actors and bureaucracies by distributing public authority and the right to use force.[62] In line with that, the case studies about the fisheries agreements in the East China Sea will illustrate that one core aspect of the practical implementation of these agreements is the spatial and functional allocation of enforcement authority. During the negotiations and implementation of the fisheries agreements, the question of which state's coast guard or maritime law enforcement agency would be allowed to exercise jurisdiction against which fishermen and under which conditions was very contentious. The case studies illustrate severe challenges to the agreements. Japan has experienced that China will use the law enforcement authority, gained under the joint fisheries agreement, to improve the China Coast Guard's effective control of disputed areas and to advance China's claims to the Senkaku/Diaoyu islands.

Another mechanism that demonstrates how institutions affect actors' power is inspired by network theory. In the context of the idea of 'weaponized interdependence', Farrell and Newman argue that institutional networks 'designed to… reduce transaction costs can be deployed for coercive ends'.[63] Control over networks that channel information allows actors in the United States to generate leverage by using information advantages. Such institutions do not need to be intentionally designed as tools of statecraft to become weaponizable.[64] In the South China Sea, the experience that 'power with'[65],

62 Terry M. Moe, 'Political Institutions: The Neglected Side of the Story', 250; Terry M. Moe, 'Power and Political Institutions', 226–228. Lake defined authority as one form of power, namely rightful rule including the right to enforce. David A. Lake, *Hierarchy in International Relations*, (Cornell UP, 2009), 17–21.

63 Henry Farrell and Abraham L. Newman, 'Weaponized Interdependence: How Global Economic Networks Shape State Coercion', *International Security* 44, no. 1 (July 2019): 42–79, 46–47.

64 Ibid. 54.

65 For the distinction between 'power with' and 'power over', see Anne-Marie Slaughter, *The Chessboard and the Web Strategies of Connection in a Networked World.* (Yale UP, 2017), 163; cited in ibid., 49. See Bruce K. Berger, 'Power Over, Power With, and Power to Relations: Critical Reflections on Public Relations, the Dominant Coalition, and Activism', *Journal of Public Relations Research* 17, no. 1 (January 2005): 5–28.

in cooperative institutions, can translate into information advantages and 'power over' was a central aspect in Sino-Philippine relations. The case studies will illustrate the Philippine experience with an agreement for joint seismic research. An issue was to what extent China gained asymmetric information advantages by manipulating joint seismic activities – an advantage China could not have gained were it not for the arrangement.

Cooley and Spruyt demonstrate another mechanism, namely how initial contract choices that split use and control rights over an asset in incomplete contracts can affect downstream bargaining power via hold-up strategies. 'With incomplete contracts... bargaining leverage may change over time and in unforeseen directions.'[66] Their example is of an energy company that sank investments into a foreign country but continues to require cooperation from that country's government with control rights over an asset. The energy company is likely to have lost bargaining power and the government to have gained leverage because the company is vulnerable to hold-up by the government.[67] There are at least two responses to the problem of incomplete contracts: flexibility procedures and intensive negotiations over the implementation of an agreement. Actors rely on flexibility procedures in the design of an institution in response to the possibility of unforeseen developments and to address distributional issues.[68] Unforeseen developments may include not only opportunistic behaviour in the sense of non-compliance but also opportunities to leverage elements of an institution. In the East and South China Sea, actors have included unilateral termination clauses and clauses of limited duration to increase the flexibility of their agreements. As several case studies will illustrate, negotiations over the implementation of an agreement were often no less contentious than the negotiations over the agreements themselves. While these were distinct phases in some cases, it is fair to say that actors did not reach an agreement unless they also agreed on their implementation. Before identifying further characteristics of how the institutions examined in this book could become sources of leverage, the problem of how actors bargain about objects that are themselves sources of power will be discussed.

66 Alexander Cooley and Hendrik Spruyt, *Contracting States Sovereign Transfers in International Relations* (Princeton UP, 2009), 11.

67 Ibid., 9, citing Oliver E. Williamson, *The Economic Institutions of Capitalism: Firms, Markets, Relational Contracting* (Collier Macmillan, 1987), 52–56. Investment protection agreements can then be regarded as strengthening the bargaining power of the side with use rights against the side with control rights.

68 Barbara Koremenos et al., 'The Rational Design of International Institutions', 773.

Bargaining over power in strategic interactions and commitment problems

Fearon formalizes a bargaining problem 'in which the objects bargained over are themselves determinants of future bargaining power'.[69] Bargaining power increases where an agreement at one point in time affects 'the terms of deals struck in the future'.[70] The model is illustrated with an actor conceding strategically relevant territory. The formal model demonstrates under which conditions one actor makes a series of small concessions to the demands of a second actor whereby each concession decreases the conceding side's bargaining power, and under which condition the actor resists these concessions. One outcome of the game is the dismantling of the conceding actor's position ('appeasement' and 'salami-tactic').[71] Although Fearon acknowledges that the problem of how actors agree on a division of power 'is clearly central to much of the bargaining that takes place between states in international relations',[72] he only mentions potential examples (oligopolistic price wars, electoral reform) where this might be the case without identifying specific cases.

Note that in this model, actors' power changes as a result of them implementing an agreement. An increase in power is not the result of one side reneging on terms or of one side not committing to terms. Nevertheless, there is a commitment problem at work, namely the difficulty that one side cannot commit to not use an increase in power that it might gain from an agreement to make further demands. Commitment problems prevent the reaching of agreements when an agreement is not self-enforcing. Actors in civil wars, for instance, expect that vulnerabilities result from the risky process of implementing conflict settlement agreements and that guarantees of a third party are necessary to protect civil war actors against vulnerabilities.[73] When one civil war group lays down arms, it gives up its major bargaining asset – the ability to fight – which incentivised other groups to negotiate with it in the first place. This is then another mechanism by which actors acquire advantages because an actor complied with an agreement. Refraining from a power advantage may not be self-enforcing.

69 James D. Fearon, 'Bargaining over Objects That Influence Future Bargaining Power', Conference Paper, *Annual Meeting of the American Political Science Association*, (1996), 1–25, 16.

70 Ibid., 1.

71 Ibid., 17.

72 Ibid., 16.

73 Barbara F. Walter, *Committing to Peace: The Successful Settlement of Civil Wars* (Princeton UP, 2002), chapter 2, 21.

Two types of commitment problems can then be distinguished depending on the question of what exactly it is that is not self-enforcing. Whether the implementation of the terms of an agreement is self-enforcing or not is a problem of committing to compliance with an agreement. Whether an actor's use of the increase in bargaining power as a result of an implemented agreement is self-enforcing or not is a problem of committing to the non-exploitation of an advantage gained as a result of an implemented agreement. Wagner presents the problem of bargaining over power as this second type of commitment problem.[74] The barriers that prevent the resolution of conflict are the 'inability to craft an agreement that everyone is sufficiently confident will not place them at a disadvantage in the future'.[75] From this perspective, agreement on at least some institutions also reflects a bargain about an allocation of power, not only an allocation of gains from joint action. Negotiators are then likely to resist an institution unless its implementation safeguards against opportunities of leverage. This consideration is likely to be part of an actor's minimum demand. But then again, even an actor assuming a rival's bad faith might enter into a cooperative agreement once the actor is confident that a rival could not gain a power advantage from an institution under plausible circumstances.

2.1 Three Mechanisms: Precedent without Legal Force, Restrictions on Conflict Behaviour, and the Manipulation of Risk

The following discussion describes three characteristics that underlie the idea that an institution for natural resources and conflict management established at one point in time could alter a rival claimants' power at a later point in time. The mechanisms are (i) the establishment of focal points, (ii) restrictions on conflict behaviour, coalition formation, and access, as well as (iii) manipulation of the level of risk. Claimant states were less likely to reach an agreement unless they were confident that a rival could not leverage an agreement to its advantage via one or several of the mechanisms.

2.2 Precedent without Legal Force and Focal Points

Negotiators in the East and South China Sea did not come to an agreement in many cases when they expected an agreement to 'validate' a rival's claim

74 R. Harrison Wagner, *War and the State: The Theory of International Politics* (University of Michigan, 2007), 184–87; R. Harrison Wagner, 'Peace, War, and the Balance of Power', *American Political Science Review* 88, no. 3 (1994): 593–607.

75 R. Harrison Wagner, *War and the State*, 237.

and to result in a 'precedent' in favour of a rival claim.[76] 'Without prejudice clauses notwithstanding, the use of unilateral maritime claims as the limits of a joint area to an extent validates such claims, giving them practical impact and thereby a degree of endorsement and legitimacy which they may not, in fact warrant.'[77] Under international law, though, joint development, joint fisheries, or other practical arrangements do not prejudice a claim. Such agreements do not represent a precedent for a claim and do not validate a claim *de jure*.[78] In short, precedent without legal force or validation without legal force matters in the East and South China Sea. The idea that agreements bring about focal points for future interactions could offer a theoretical explanation for the parties' concern that agreements validate a rival claim despite the *de jure* exclusion of this effect.

Schelling suggests that legal rules, moral or cultural properties, precedent, fairness, and prominent numerical properties of goods (e.g., equal divisions) can affect outcomes of bargaining processes by being focal points.[79] The reason why prominent points influence bargaining outcomes is that focal points affect the expectations of actors regarding what a likely outcome of a bargaining process could be from which no actor would retreat.[80] Focal points may not only have suggestive force for outcomes, but also for preference formation. Some negotiators define initial bargaining positions to make them credible; focal points can serve this function.[81]

76 These are quotes from the case studies. While there are differences between 'A is a precedent for B' and 'A validates B', negotiators and officials have used such terms in a broad and almost interchangeable way during interviews. Precedent narrowly construed refers to a legal practice where judges are bound by previous court decisions. International law does not know such a narrow concept of precedent (Article 59 of the Statute of the International Court of Justice).

77 Clive Schofield, 'Defining Areas for Joint Development in Disputed Waters', in *Recent Developments in the South China Sea Dispute. The Prospect of a Joint Development Regime*, edited by Shicun Wu and Nong Hong, (Routledge, 2014), 78–98, 78.

78 UNCLOS Article 74(3) and 83(3); Rainer Lagoni, 'Interim Measures Pending Maritime Delimitation Agreements', *The American Journal of International Law* 78, no. 2 (1984): 345–68; Vasco Becker-Weinberg, *Joint Development of Hydrocarbon Deposits in the Law of the Sea* (Springer, 2014); Christian Schultheiss, 'Overcoming Violence in Maritime Conflicts with Provisional Arrangements: A Legal Tool for Conflict Resolution', in *International Law and Peace Settlements*, edited by Mark Retter, Andrea Varga, and Marc Weller (CUP, 2021), 525–544.

79 Schelling, *The Strategy of Conflict*, 60, 67, 73, 113.

80 Ibid., 70.

81 Alvin E. Roth, 'Toward a Focal Point Theory of Bargaining,' *Game-Theoretic Models of Bargaining* 259 (1985): 265–67, 259. Although the conspicuousness of particular claims is to some extent context dependent, scholars analyse 'how labels can influence decisions in games' in order to formalize the impact of focal points. Robert Sugden, 'A Theory of Focal Points', *The Economic Journal* (1995): 533–50, 534; Judith Mehta et al., 'Focal Points in Pure Coordination Games: An Experimental Investigation,' *Theory and Decision* 36, no. 2 (1994): 163–85.

Empirical research shows that international legal doctrines, institutions, and third-party decisions shape bargaining processes by serving as focal points. If one state's claim and negotiation position in a territorial dispute is clearly favoured by legal doctrines on territorial sovereignty, a territorial settlement is likely to reflect the state's stronger legal claim. A clear legal advantage translates into bargaining power via focal points.[82] Moreover, international institutions are effective in solving treaty ambiguities by constructing focal points for state interactions.[83] Adjudication 'under anarchy' is effective because it gives particular claims prominence and establishes focal points for state interactions.[84] Furthermore, even if judicial decisions do not have a precedent character as a matter of international legal doctrine,[85] precedent and contestations over what is precedent are arguably 'ubiquitous' in international legal practice.[86] Precedent does not exert an influence in international relations as a matter of legal doctrine, but it does so empirically in state practice.[87] Focal point theory could explain why precedent is politically powerful despite the non-existence of precedent authority in international law. Avoiding setting a precedent can then be a powerful motivation. The US State Department, for instance, has justified the US Freedom of Navigation Operations with the objective to 'avoid setting the precedent that the international community has accepted these unlawful

82 Paul K. Huth et al., 'Bringing Law to the Table: Legal Claims, Focal Points, and the Settlement of Territorial Disputes Since 1945,' *American Journal of Political Science* 57, no. 1 (2013): 90–103; Paul K. Huth et al., 'Does International Law Promote the Peaceful Settlement of International Disputes? Evidence from the Study of Territorial Conflicts since 1945', *American Political Science Review* 105, no. 2 (2011): 415–36; Paul Huth et al., 'Law and the Use of Force in World Politics: The Varied Effects of Law on the Exercise of Military Power in Territorial Disputes,' *International Studies Quarterly* 56, no. 1 (2012): 17–31.

83 Barry Weingast and Geoffrey Garrett, 'Ideas, Interests, and Institutions: Constructing the EC's Internal Market,' in *Ideas and Foreign Policy*, edited by Robert O. Keohane and R. Goldstein (Cornell UP, 1993), 173–206.

84 Tom Ginsburg and Richard H. McAdams, 'Adjudicating in Anarchy: An Expressive Theory of International Dispute Resolution,' *William & Mary Law Review* 45 (2003): 1229–339; Richard H. McAdams and Janice Nadler, 'Testing the Focal Point Theory of Legal Compliance: The Effect of Third-Party Expression in an Experimental Hawk/Dove Game,' *Journal of Empirical Legal Studies* 2, no. 1 (2005): 87–123; Richard H. McAdams, 'A Focal Point Theory of Expressive Law,' *Virginia Law Review* (2000), 1649–729.

85 Article 59 of the Statute of the International Court of Justice: 'The decision of the Court has no binding force except between the parties and in respect of that particular case.'

86 Harlan Grant Cohen, 'Theorizing Precedent in International Law,' in *Interpretation in International Law* edited by Andrea Bianchi, Daniel Peat, and Matthew Windsor (OUP, 2015), 268–89, 269.

87 Krzysztof J. Pelc, 'The Politics of Precedent in International Law: A Social Network Application', *American Political Science Review* 108, no. 3 (August 2014): 547–64.

[maritime] claims'.[88] Another prominent example is the former US Trade Representative who referred to the WTO Appellate Body's alleged practice of treating its decisions as binding precedent as an invalid 'manufacture of precedent authority'.[89]

In sum, a focal point can favour or disfavour an actor in a dispute. A focal point increases an actor's bargaining power if it lends support to the actor's claim; it decreases an actor's bargaining power if it reflects a rival's claim. Negotiators are then likely to be concerned about the possibility that an agreement establishes certain terms, a geographic area, a principle, or a method as a focal point for subsequent bargaining processes. In this way, actors may sometimes expect that a cooperative agreement will build a meaningful layer of validity in favour of a rival's claim.

This leads to the following explanation for claimant states' behaviour in the East and South China Sea. When one party in a dispute anticipates that an agreement or its provisions result in a focal point that reflects a rival's claim, then this party is less likely to accept the agreement because it would support a rival's bargaining power. The incentive to not accept an arrangement that entrains a focal point in support of a rival's claim is particularly pronounced in cases where a rival lacks a legally valid claim.[90] These concerns have led to situations where cooperative arrangements need to reflect original claims even if these arrangements are specifically designed to separate disputes from practical cooperation. The case studies in chapters III, IV, and V will illustrate how negotiators have tried to 'square this circle' in practice.

2.3 Restrictions on Conflict Behaviour, Coalition Formation, and Access

Institutions aimed at managing conflict attempt to reduce 'violence without touching the basic conflict issue'.[91] They require that conflicting

88 US Department of State, 'Military Operational Issues', Archive, https://2001-2009.state.gov/t/pm/iso/c21539.htm (last accessed 23 June 2023); see US Department of Defense, 'Annual Freedom of Navigation Report', 31 December 2018.

89 Office of the United States Trade Representative, 'Report on the Appellate Body of the World Trade Organization', February 2020, https://ustr.gov/sites/default/files/Report_on_the_Appellate_Body_of_the_World_Trade_Organization.pdf (last accessed 23 June 2023). 'The Appellate Body's manufacture of precedent authority has profound implications for the WTO system and WTO Members' (55). Under the heading of 'The Dispute Settlement Understanding Does Not Permit a Panel to Treat a Prior Appellate Body Interpretation as Law or Controlling "Precedent"', the report notes 'The DSU explicitly notes that the dispute settlement system operates without prejudice to this interpretative authority' (56).

90 Chapter II 3.2.

91 I William Zartman, 'Conflict Resolution and Negotiation', 331.

parties reach an agreement on mechanisms to restrain claim-ameliorative behaviour or resorting to violence. This involves, for instance, that parties define restrictions on specific capabilities, coalition formation, or various types of activities that conflicting actors rely on to advance or defend their claims. A difficulty in the negotiations about such restrictions is how one actor can get an opponent's consent to restrict the activities that the opponent relies on to advance or defend a claim. Wide-ranging restrictions on conflict behaviour could amount to a freeze of the status quo.

Various actors in maritime disputes propose many possible restrictions. Specific restrictions on violent and coercive activities could include military operations and exercises, the use of islands as military outposts, or various types of maritime law enforcement operations. A code of conduct, for instance, that were to prohibit all activities an actor could use to enforce its claims – coercive law enforcement activities, an extension of jurisdictional powers, occupations of unoccupied islands, land reclamation, etc. – would come close to freezing the status quo (to the extent actors were to comply with the code). From a legal perspective, some proposals of members of the Association of Southeast Asian Nations (ASEAN) can be regarded as attempts to extend the prohibition of the threat or use of force to activities at lower levels of violence.[92] For China, for instance, to accept limits on coercive activities below the level of the use of force would amount to limiting or offsetting the tactical and strategic advantages China has in this regard.[93] It is possible to say that, through such restrictions, ASEAN members try to distribute power away from China. Other limitations that could offset an actor's power are limits for capabilities – e.g., limits to the construction of outposts and their militarization or limits to the number of ships and level of armaments.

Restrictions on the formation of coalitions matter in several ways. Membership rules limit states' choices about eligible partners for coalitions or alliances. Lascurette illustrates that great powers define membership rules of international orders to exclude threats; they establish an 'order of

92 For the difficulty of distinguishing between maritime law enforcement and the use of force, see Steven Haines, 'War at Sea: Nineteenth-Century Laws for Twenty-First Century Wars?', *International Review of the Red Cross* 98, no. 902 (August 2016): 419–47; Wolff Heintschel von Heinegg, 'The Difficulties of Conflict Classification at Sea: Distinguishing Incidents at Sea from Hostilities', *International Review of the Red Cross* 98, no. 902 (August 2016): 449–64.

93 On China's maritime law enforcement agencies, see Andrew S. Erickson et al., 'Surging Second Sea Force: China's Maritime Law- Enforcement Forces, Capabilities, and Future in the Gray Zone and Beyond', *Naval War College Review* 72, no. 2 (2019): 1–25.

exclusion'.[94] Selection criteria for membership include sovereignty and regime type. In the context of disputes, a state has various incentives to define membership rules. A state may seek to restrict opponents from joining a counterbalancing coalition. Geography is a further and straightforward membership criterion with which an actor can seek to exclude perceived threats from a region – a rule, for instance, that says that only states from a certain region are allowed to build a coalition or to pursue certain types of military activities in this region. In the context of the code of conduct, China has aimed at establishing restrictions on coalition formation between Southeast Asian and non-regional states (e.g., the US) as well as on military activities from non-regional states. Such restrictions would greatly diminish the bargaining power of ASEAN members, namely their option to join or deepen partnerships with the US.

Moreover, where a state's access to a disputed region benefits from local partnerships, restrictions on coalition building create access barriers to a distant power. A great power can then try to define what may be called 'access rules' – rules that govern which actors have a right to access a region. The law of the sea specifies access rules for warships, commercial ships, and aircraft in the context of navigational freedoms.[95] Access rules underpin actors' options to enter a certain geographic area in that they seek to project power. Restricting access is restricting an actor's reach. China put forward proposals that have sought to enlist ASEAN members in the effort to establish restricted access rules for non-regional navies to the South China Sea. This proposal could also be read as an institutional element of an order of exclusion.

Negotiations about such restrictions are negotiations about rival claimants gaining and giving up options to wield power. Each state has an incentive to seek limitations to the activities, capabilities, and coalition options in which a rival claimant has an advantage or that a claimant adopted in the past to advance their claims. An agreement between disputing actors on limiting specific activities, capabilities, and coalition options is therefore unlikely unless disputing actors do not or no longer rely on the specific activities. According to this logic, the primary obstacle to reaching an agreement does not have to be a commitment problem. It is not because limiting one side's resort to violent means is not self-enforcing that two

94 Kyle M. Lascurettes, *Orders of Exclusion: Great Powers and the Strategic Sources of Foundational Rules in International Relations* (OUP, 2020), 37–41.

95 Myron H. Nordquist et al., eds., *Freedom of Seas, Passage Rights and the 1982 Law of the Sea Convention* (Martinus Nijhoff, 2009).

sides do not reach an agreement, but that an actor does not want to forgo such options in the first place. Moreover, actors' preferences regarding restrictions may change over time. An actor that rejected restrictions on, for instance, occupations of islands may promote these very same restrictions once it has occupied the islands it wanted to occupy but also wants to deny the same option to rival claimants. A state may seek restrictions on maritime law enforcement in cases where its nationals are objects of another state's maritime law enforcement. The same state may reject restrictions on maritime law enforcement once its maritime law enforcement agencies are the enforcers against another state's nationals. While this analysis is particularly relevant for chapter V, it also applies to cases about fisheries agreements and maritime law enforcement.

2.4 The Management and Manipulation of Risk

The objective of institutionalized crisis communication and incident prevention measures is to avoid escalation in cases where misperception, misinformation, human or technical error, or bureaucratic (intragovernmental) obstacles to direct communication hinder effective responses to incidents.[96] Crisis communication arrangements involve narrow commitments that apply to situations before or after an incident arises. One assumption that is partially instrumental for the possibility of crisis management is that rules about specified communication procedures could prevent action–reaction cycles towards conflict in cases where actors have an interest in preventing armed conflict as the outcome of an escalatory process. In this vein, an objective is to reduce escalatory risks. It has been argued, however, that risk can also have a protective function, as the risk of escalation can also restrain an actor in its choices. 'It may seem to the advantage of one side to avoid agreement on limits, in order to enhance the other's fear of war.'[97] Townshend and Medcalf advance a related argument: China could use 'tactical stability' brought about by crisis communication measures for

96 Sanaa Yasmin Hafeez, 'The Senkaku/Diaoyu Islands Crises of 2004, 2010, and 2012: A Study of Japanese-Chinese Crisis Management', *Asia-Pacific Review* 22, no. 1 (2 January 2015): 73–99; David A. Welch, 'Crisis Management Mechanisms Pathologies and Pitfalls', *CIGI Papers*, 40 (September 2014): 1–19; Forrest E. Morgan, et al., *Dangerous Thresholds: Managing Escalation in the 21st Century* (Rand Corporation, 2008).

97 Schelling, *The Strategy of Conflict*, 53.

the purpose of 'strengthen[ing] its strategic position' by 'ensur[ing] that its efforts to establish a new status quo do not provoke conflict'.[98]

Under which conditions could an actor exploit an institution for the management of risk as an institution for the manipulation of risk? If a certain activity (e.g., a navy or coast guard operation) is associated with a certain level of risk and more of this activity leads to more risk, an actor might expect that an agreement reducing this risk is likely to give another actor the option to intensify its activities. Maintaining a certain level of risk, for instance, the risk of accidental escalation may therefore induce an actor to act with self-restraint. Maintaining the risk of escalation serves as protection against an increase in an opponent's actions. In short, risk has a protective function. Once risk is off the table, actors expect certain activities of a rival to occur with higher frequency. If actors expect a certain agreement to reduce the protective function of risk, actors are less likely to conclude such an arrangement.

Which effect the risk reduction resulting from institutionalized crisis communication will have on future interactions is part of actors' assessment. The commitment problem here is that a state cannot commit to not misuse a communication procedure to gain strategic advantages. The case studies in chapter V will illustrate that some ministries of some claimant states are indeed concerned with this problem, but that many other state bureaucracies are not.

2.5 Power Asymmetries and Institutions that Alter Power

Although an indication of the exact balance of power between two states is a difficult undertaking and dependent on many variables,[99] most observers would concur that power is distributed unevenly between China and Southeast Asian states and, to a lesser degree, between China and Japan in their maritime disputes.[100] According to Womack, an asymmetrical relationship is coined by the fact that 'B [the smaller power] cannot challenge A [the big power] but A cannot dominate B' and by 'a mix of convergent and different interests'.[101] In this account, conflict in asymmetric relationships

98 Ashley Townshend and Rory Medcalf, *Shifting Waters: China's New Passive Assertiveness in Asian Maritime Security* (Lowy Institute for International Policy, Report 2016), 18–9.

99 Baldwin, *Power and International Relations: A Conceptual Approach*, 59–90.

100 Womack regards the Sino-Japanese relationship as a relationship of 'countervailing asymmetries' in which each side has advantages over the other in some dimensions but disadvantages in others. Brantly Womack, *Asymmetry and International Relationships* (CUP, 2016), 46.

101 Womack, *Asymmetry and International Relationships*, 55. For another account of asymmetric relations in a different geographic region, see Anthony Payne, 'Rethinking United

is an instance of calibrating or recalibrating the relatively smaller power's deference to the larger power and the smaller power's autonomy from the larger power.[102] Former Singaporean diplomat Kausikan argues in a similar vein that China's activities in the South China Sea try to instil 'correct thinking' and 'deference to its interests to be internalized in Southeast Asian states as a mode of thought'.[103] The building of maritime order in the East and South China Sea can then be regarded as one instance of the calibration of asymmetric relations whereas the autonomy of relatively smaller powers involves a reallocation of legal rights and political commitments.[104] Single agreements and institutions are, though, not only a manifestation of recalibrated relations. Institutions are also instruments of and vehicles for recalibration. The question then arises as to which attitude a relatively less powerful state and a relatively more powerful state are likely to have in negotiations about institutions for marine natural resources or conflict management that might increase or decrease the parties' power in subsequent interactions.

A relatively less powerful state that negotiates with a relatively more powerful state might be particularly concerned about the possibility that an institution could give the relatively more powerful state opportunities to leverage the institution against the smaller state. 'Proportionally, the weaker side is more exposed in an asymmetric relationship, and thus it needs guarantees not only that the current interaction is beneficial but that the overall development of the relationship will not endanger its vital interests.'[105] An underlying assumption would be that relatively less powerful states are particularly risk-averse when dealing with more powerful ones. A relatively less powerful state would, however, also benefit particularly from interactions based on formal rules that restrict a more powerful state during disputes. It can be assumed that these two incentives are present at the same time. Moreover, whether an agreement would increase a smaller state's autonomy from or its deference to a great power depends on the exact

States – Caribbean Relations: Towards a New Mode of Trans-Territorial Governance', *Review of International Studies* 26, no. 1 (January 2000): 69–82.

102 Womack, *Asymmetry and International Relationships*, 2016, 93.

103 Bilahari Kausikan, 'Dealing with an Ambiguous World Lecture III: ASEAN & US-China Competition in Southeast Asia', (March 2016), https://lkyspp.nus.edu.sg/docs/default-source/ips/ips-nathan-lectures_lecture-iii_asean-us-china-competition-in-southeast-asia_300316.pdf (last accessed 23 August 2023).

104 Evelyn Goh, *The Struggle for Order: Hegemony, Hierarchy, and Transition in Post-Cold War East Asia* (OUP, 2013).

105 Brantly Womack, 'The Spratlys: From Dangerous Ground to Apple of Discord', *Contemporary Southeast Asia* 33, no. 3 (2011): 370–87, 384.

terms of the agreement. For these reasons, I do not expect that a general statement can be made based on given power asymmetries whether East and Southeast Asia's relatively smaller states are likely or unlikely to enter into agreements with China. Smaller powers, though, have reason to be risk averse in negotiations and to be particularly concerned about excluding that an agreement weakens their bargaining position in subsequent interactions.

A relatively more powerful state may not be willing to accept restrictions limiting its options for future interactions, especially if the state assumes that its power advantage may further increase. At the same time, however, a relatively more powerful state may attempt to consolidate its advancements institutionally and 'lock in'[106] its dominant position for which it needs the smaller states' consent. The relatively more powerful state must also consider how to prioritize disputes with neighbours and competition with other great powers.[107] In the case of China, this includes the question of to what extent China's dispute behaviour encourages the building of a US-led countervailing coalition.[108] It can be assumed that these incentives are present at the same time. Again, whether an agreement would increase a smaller state's deference to a great power or restrain the great power depends on the exact terms. For these reasons, I do not expect that a general statement can be made about whether China is likely or unlikely to enter into agreements solely based on considerations about power asymmetries.

3 Alternative Explanations: Legal Entitlements, Domestic Politics, and Fragmented Coalitions in Negotiations

3.1 The Nine-Dash Line and Negotiations with(out) Legal Entitlements

The tribunal in the South China Sea Arbitration ruled on 12 July 2016 that China is not entitled to claim maritime zones beyond the limits that the

106 G. John Ikenberry, 'State Power and the Institutional Bargain: America's Ambivalent Economic and Security Multilateralism', in *US Hegemony and International Organizations*, edited by Rosemary Foot, Michael Mastanduno, and S. Neil MacFarlane (OUP, 2003), 49–70, 50.

107 Womack, *Asymmetry and International Relationships*, 2016, 47.

108 Wenjuan Nie, 'China's Domestic Strategic Debate and Confusion over the South China Sea Issue', *The Pacific Review* 31, no. 2 (4 March 2018): 188–204; US Department of Defense, 'Indo-Pacific Strategy Report. Preparedness, Partnerships, and Promoting a Networked Region', 1 June 2019; US Department of State, 'A Free and Open Indo-Pacific Advancing a Shared Vision', 4 November 2019.

law of the sea provides for.[109] Subsequent to this award, China is entitled to claim the normal maritime zones, e.g., an Exclusive Economic Zone (EEZ) and continental shelf generated from its mainland as well as the territorial seas of certain features in the Spratly Islands and Scarborough Shoal.[110] The award effectively invalidated the nine-dash line as a claim to maritime zones beyond the normal zones. The tribunal thereby confirmed the Philippine position on the lack of a valid Chinese claim to the Philippine EEZ and continental shelf in the eastern South China Sea.[111] Applying the award to the South China Sea,[112] China's EEZ and continental shelf claims do not overlap with the EEZ claims of Brunei, Indonesia, or Malaysia. China's EEZ and continental shelf claims overlap only with Vietnam's and the Philippines' EEZs in northern parts of the South China Sea,[113] but not in central parts. China accepts neither the tribunal's jurisdiction nor the award and has continued to assert rights within the nine-dash line.

The lack of China's entitlements to maritime zones could be an explanation for the failure to reach agreements in the South China Sea. By refusing to align its claims with UNCLOS, China blocks a starting point for compromise. The expectation is that Southeast Asian claimant states are less likely to enter into or merely negotiate agreements for geographic areas to which China is not legally entitled. This is likely to be the case even if an agreement may come with some economic or security gains and is without prejudice to claims. This argument assumes that the willingness of actors to reach agreements increases or decreases with the existence or absence of legally valid claims. Behavioural economics and the negotiation literature offer some insights into this expectation. Behavioural economics provides some

109 The South China Sea Arbitration (The Republic of Philippines v. The People's Republic of China) Award on Jurisdiction and Admissibility (29 October 2015); The South China Sea Arbitration (The Republic of Philippines v. The People's Republic of China) Merits Award (12 July 2016), https://pca-cpa.org/en/cases/7/ (accessed 13 April 2024).

110 Christian Schultheiss, '"One of the First Matters to Be Addressed but Distinct" or "Distinct but Inseparable"? The Distinction Between Maritime Entitlement and Sea Boundary Delimitation in the Philippines v. China Arbitration', *Asian Journal of International Law* 11, no. 1 (January 2021): 24–35; Lucy Reed and Kenneth Wong, 'Marine Entitlements in the South China Sea: The Arbitration Between the Philippines and China', *American Journal of International Law* 110, no. 4 (2016): 746–60; Kate Parlett, 'Jurisdiction of the Arbitral Tribunal in Philippines v. China under UNCLOS and in the Absence of China', *American Journal of International Law* 110 (2016): 266–72.

111 The Philippines initiated this case in 2013. Undersecretary Severino argued already in 1997 that China does not have a legally valid claim to some maritime zones. See chapter III 1.

112 Strictly speaking, the award is only legally binding between China and the Philippines (Art. 296(2) of UNCLOS).

113 The extent of the overlap between China and the Philippines in the northern South China Sea also depends on the claims and status of Taiwan.

evidence that actors with valid claims (entitlements) to a certain good regard bargains that reflect existing entitlements as fair.[114] While behavioural economics provides evidence for a self-serving bias[115] – the tendency of players to defend the normative views that support their claims – concepts of fairness can also exclude self-serving invocations of fairness. The role of fairness considerations in negotiation behaviour could then contribute to an understanding of negotiations with legal entitlements. To begin with, fairness considerations can have an impact on the parties' minimum demands.[116] Fairness considerations modify the definition of a party's best alternative to a negotiated agreement (BATNA) and result in subjective resistance points that set a party's minimum demand above or below a BATNA.[117] As a potential result, 'fairness considerations can lead negotiators to opt for joint outcomes that leave both parties worse off than they would have been had fairness considerations been ignored.'[118] In some cases, a party is likely to prefer an impasse even if an unfair agreement offered a party tangible gains. The existence or absence of legal entitlements can then affect a party's resistance points and determine a party's definition of the fair minimum demand.

A part of the observable behaviour in the South China Sea can indeed be attributed to the lack of legal status of parts of China's claims. The fact that China sticks to an invalidated claim blocks cooperation in many ways. The lack of Chinese entitlements to parts of the South China Sea can explain why there were not more negotiation attempts about resource sharing. Indonesia, for instance, rejected negotiating with China about maritime

114 Simon Gächter and Arno Riedl, 'Moral Property Rights in Bargaining with Infeasible Claims', *Management Science* 51, no. 2 (2005): 249–63; Simon Gächter and Arno Riedl, 'Dividing Justly in Bargaining Problems with Claims', *Social Choice and Welfare* 27, no. 3 (2006): 571–94.

115 Ibid.

116 Cecilia Albin, 'The Role of Fairness in Negotiation', *Negotiation Journal* 9, no. 3 (1993): 223–44. Albin distinguishes between structural, process, procedural, and outcome fairness. Franck associates fairness with legitimacy and distributive justice. Thomas M. Franck, *Fairness in International Law and Institutions* (OUP, 1995), 26–7; also see Amrita Narlikar, 'Fairness in International Trade Negotiations: Developing Countries in the GATT and WTO', *World Economy* 29, no. 8 (2006): 1005–29.

117 White and Neale distinguish between reservation value, BATNA, and resistance point. A reservation value is a BATNA plus or minus transaction costs. Sally Blount White and Margaret Ann Neale, 'Reservation Prices, Resistance Points, and BATNAs: Determining the Parameters of Acceptable Negotiated Outcomes', *Negotiation Journal* 7 (1991): 379–88.

118 Max H. Bazerman and Margaret Ann Neale, 'The Role of Fairness Considerations and Relationships in a Judgment Perspective of Negotiation', in *Barriers to Conflict Resolution*, edited by Keneth Arrow et al. (Norton, 1995), 86–106, 89, quoted in Amrita Narlikar, ed., *Deadlocks in Multilateral Negotiations: Causes and Solutions* (CUP, 2010), 10.

rights, because China lacks entitlements.[119] The fact that China sticks to an invalidated claim could also explain why there are fewer agreements in the South China Sea than in the East China Sea where China's EEZ claim is within its maximum entitlement.[120]

When looking at a larger sample, however, the lack of China's entitlements cannot explain three things. First, the Philippines (and a reluctant Vietnam) entered into an arrangement for joint seismic research with China in 2004 and 2005 covering an area to which China has no EEZ or continental shelf entitlements.[121] After the South China Sea Arbitration, China and the Philippines resumed negotiations under the Bilateral Consultation Mechanism. This resulted in a memorandum of understanding in 2018 on further negotiations about the joint exploration of areas to which China lacks valid claims. Manila resumed exchanges with Beijing *after* the tribunal's ruling confirmed the Philippine view that China lacks a valid claim to these areas. Even if Manila is under no obligation to negotiate joint development and fisheries agreements in areas to which China is not entitled,[122] Manila has done so until 2022. Second, negotiations about geographic areas to which China has a valid entitlement (e.g., Sino-Japanese and Sino-Vietnamese negotiations in parts of the East or South China Sea) prove as difficult as negotiations regarding areas to which China has no legal entitlement (for example, Sino-Philippine negotiations). The common underlying problem in negotiations where China has a valid claim, where China lacks a valid claim, and even in cases excluding China was the parties' expectation that an agreement would extend an opponent's bargaining power. Third, the explanation that the lack of China's entitlements makes agreements with Southeast Asian states less likely only applies to resource-sharing arrangements, not to codes of conduct or incident prevention arrangements. ASEAN members negotiate the code of conduct because China is trying to advance (invalid) claims. The concern of all negotiators that the respective opponents could leverage substantial provisions of a code of conduct,

119 Permanent Mission of the Republic of Indonesia, 'Communication of the Republic of Indonesia to the United Nations No. 148/POL-703/VI/20', 12 June 2020, https://www.un.org/Depts/los/clcs_new/submissions_files/mys_12_12_2019/2020_06_12_IDN_NV_UN_002_ENG.pdf (last accessed 23 March 2022).

120 See chapter IV.

121 See chapter III 1.1. Beyond its claims from the mainland, China can only legally claim the twelve-nautical-mile territorial sea around the high tide features of the Spratly Islands and Scarborough Shoal ('rocks' in the meaning of Article 121 (3) of UNCLOS).

122 Christian Schultheiss, 'Joint Development of Hydrocarbon Resources in the South China Sea After the Philippines Versus China Arbitration?', *Ocean Development & International Law* 51, no. 3 (3 August 2020): 241–62.

though, is also a key barrier to code of conduct negotiations. In sum, the lack of China's entitlements to some maritime zones then plays the role of reinforcing Southeast Asian states' concern not to accept resource-sharing arrangements that would ameliorate China's position. Southeast Asian states' reluctance to create a layer of validity in favour of China's claims is particularly strong and pronounced in cases where China lacks legal entitlements to maritime areas. But this reluctance is not unique to cases where China lacks valid legal claims.

3.2 The Role of Domestic Politics and Nationalism in Negotiations

The idea of two-level games captures the interactions between international diplomacy and domestic politics.[123] Negotiators need, for instance, to not only reach an agreement on an international level, but also to find support for agreements among domestic constituencies. Potentially relevant factors for the interactions between domestic and international levels are competition between various domestic actors, leadership struggles, regime type, the impact of nationalist sentiments, and the use of international institutions for domestic agendas.

Various domestic actors are involved in the decision-making processes of the claimant states of the East and South China Sea. Changes concerning the number of and coordination among various bureaucratic actors has taken place in several countries, especially within China. The International Crisis Group identifies eleven ministerial-level government agencies, including five different maritime law enforcement agencies, the Communist Party of China (CPC) bodies, the People's Liberation Army (PLA) Navy, provincial governments, and commercial groups that try to advance their respective, particularistic bureaucratic interests and compete for national influence.[124] While China's various bureaucratic actors have had an entrenched consensus about the need to assert China's claims,[125] the report raises doubts about whether China's various agencies are pursuing a single aggregate interest. Moreover, initial attempts to centralize China's policymaking on maritime

123 Robert D. Putnam, 'Diplomacy and Domestic Politics: The Logic of Two-Level Games', *International Organization* 42, no. 3 (1988): 427–60; Peter B. Evans et al., *Double-Edged Diplomacy: International Bargaining and Domestic Politics* (University of California, 1993).

124 International Crisis Group, 'Stirring up the South China Sea (I)', *Asia Report*, no. 223, 23 April 2012, 8.

125 Andrew Chubb, 'PRC Assertiveness in the South China Sea: Measuring Continuity and Change, 1970–2015', *International Security* 45, no. 3 (January 2021): 79–121.

disputes failed.[126] This changed, to some extent, under the leadership of General Secretary Xi Jinping with the consolidation of maritime law enforcement agencies into China's Coast Guard in 2013[127] and with the centralization of foreign policymaking processes.[128] Several case studies (e.g., Sino-Philippine and Sino-Japanese negotiations and negotiations about the Code for Unplanned Encounters at Sea) will indeed reveal domestic, bureaucratic competition and competing assessments about the utility and danger of the respective agreements. For example, different Japanese government agencies have held competing assessments about the utility and danger of crisis communication arrangements. An important point in these case studies is not only that different domestic actors within states have diverging assessments, but that different domestic actors across China, the Philippines, Japan, or Taiwan attributed similar costs and benefits to potential agreements and reject agreements because of similar assessments. The case studies will also demonstrate that similar barriers have prevented agreements before and after China's consolidation of foreign policy decision-making processes. The sample of cases does not suggest that China's perspective and negotiation behaviour on resource-sharing and conflict-management arrangements changed significantly as a result of China's administrative reforms or that the variation in the negotiation outcomes could be attributed to these domestic, institutional changes. An exception to that is China's acceptance of the Code for Unplanned Encounters at Sea (CUES) in 2014 which was previously rejected by the PLA Navy.[129]

Leadership struggle is another potential domestic factor relevant to outcomes of dispute behaviour. While Chinese leadership has had to deal with elite power struggles, leadership transitions are not associated with times of heightened maritime coercion and crises.[130] Leadership transitions occurred in China in 1997, 2002, and 2012, but this book does not find that instances of impasse (or agreement) cluster around these three periods.

126 International Crisis Group, 'Stirring up the South China Sea (I)', *Asia Report N°223*, 23 April 2012, 18. On foreign-policy making in China, see e.g. Linda Jakobson and Ryan Manuel, 'How Are Foreign Policy Decisions Made in China? Foreign Policy Decisions Made in China', *Asia & the Pacific Policy Studies* 3, no. 1 (January 2016): 101–10.

127 Erickson, et al. 'Surging Second Sea Force: China's Maritime Law- Enforcement Forces'.

128 Ji You, 'The PLA and Diplomacy: Unraveling Myths about the Military Role in Foreign Policy Making', *Journal of Contemporary China* 23, no. 86 (4 March 2014): 236–54; Jing Sun, 'Growing Diplomacy, Retreating Diplomats – How the Chinese Foreign Ministry Has Been Marginalized in Foreign Policymaking', *Journal of Contemporary China* 26, no. 105 (4 May 2017): 419–33.

129 Chapter V 2.

130 Ketian Zhang, 'Cautious Bully: Reputation, Resolve, and Beijing's Use of Coercion in the South China Sea', *International Security* 44, no. 1 (July 2019): 117–59, 155.

Similarly, domestic resistance conceptualized as weak leadership, lack of internal consensus, or nationalist resistance could not explain failures to implement joint development agreements.[131] Moreover, the case studies do not allow an inference about the impact of regime type on claimant states' attitudes towards the types of agreements under negotiation.[132] Authoritarian China or Vietnam have entered into arrangements with both their democratic and authoritarian neighbours. Democratic Japan and South Korea have not entered into more arrangements than China or Vietnam. Coalition building occurred across regime types as illustrated by both the attempts of the heterogeneous members of ASEAN to build a common approach and the emerging Vietnam–US partnership.[133]

While commentaries refer regularly to the influence of nationalist sentiments on dispute behaviour, several studies could find no evidence connecting China's assertiveness in foreign policy to rising nationalism.[134] Evidence for a causal link between Chinese nationalism and foreign policy is not conclusive.[135] Evidence is also lacking that nationalist public opinion exerts a decisive influence on China's behaviour in maritime crises[136] or prevents China from de-escalation.[137] At times, China has used popular, nationalist sentiments instrumentally as a tool.[138] Moreover, Zhang argues that 'the need to establish resolve precedes concerns about domestic legitimacy'.[139] A further attempt to find a potential impact of nationalism could be

131 Song Xue, 'Why Joint Development Agreements Fail', *Contemporary Southeast Asia* 41, no. 3 (2019): 418–46, 420.

132 See, for instance, William J. Dixon, 'Democracy and the Peaceful Settlement of International Conflict', *American Political Science Review* 88, no. 1 (1994): 14–32.

133 Phuong Nguyen, 'Deciphering the Shift in America's South China Sea Policy', *Contemporary Southeast Asia* 38, no. 3 (31 December 2016): 389–421.

134 Alastair Iain Johnston, 'Is Chinese Nationalism Rising? Evidence from Beijing', *International Security* 41, no. 3 (2017): 7–43.

135 Xiaolin Duan, 'Unanswered Questions: Why We May Be Wrong about Chinese Nationalism and Its Foreign Policy Implications', *Journal of Contemporary China* 26, no. 108 (2 November 2017): 886–900.

136 Andrew Chubb, 'Assessing Public Opinion's Influence on Foreign Policy: The Case of China's Assertive Maritime Behavior', *Asian Security* (7 March 2018), 1–21; Andrew Chubb, *Chinese nationalism and the 'gray zone': case analyses of public opinion and PRC Maritime Policy* (Naval War College, 2021).

137 Kai Quek and Alastair Iain Johnston, 'Can China Back Down? Crisis de-Escalation in the Shadow of Popular Opposition', *International Security* 42, no. 3 (2018): 7–36.

138 Jessica Chen Weiss, *Powerful Patriots: Nationalist Protest in China's Foreign Relations* (OUP, 2014).

139 Zhang, 'Cautious Bully: Reputation, Resolve, and Beijing's Use of Coercion in the South China Sea', 128.

conceptualized with the notion of framing[140] and the observation that media reports of several claimant states framed access to natural resources in a nationalist way. While media outlets in, for example, China, Malaysia, and the Philippines portray access to natural resources in a nationalist way in the context of resource-sharing arrangements,[141] this does not prevent their governments from signing and implementing arrangements. Some, but not all, attempts to challenge one specific Sino-Philippine-Vietnamese arrangement on seismic surveys have framed this issue in nationalist terms.[142] These critiques, though, began only three years after the conclusion of the arrangement. Moreover, Philippine officials had already resisted the arrangement because of other reasons before it was even publicly known. Although some scholars referred to nationalist media attacks against the Sino-Japanese Principled Consensus, these attacks came after the public learned about the already faltering Sino-Japanese Consensus.[143] Even in cases where access to resources was portrayed in a nationalist way, this alone does not explain why negotiations ended in an impasse or why agreements were not implemented. At most, it might be argued that nationalist sentiments reinforced underlying obstacles.

Another approach to the influence of domestic politics assumes that different domestic actors use international agreements to empower particular bureaucratic agendas that are blocked by domestic resistance. International institutions are then attractive options to overcome domestic resistance against specific agendas.[144] The constellation among Chinese domestic

140 See, for instance, John Odell and Susan Sell, 'Reframing the Issue: The WTO Coalition on Intellectual Property and Public Health 2001' (Developing Countries and the Trade Negotiation Process UNCTAD, Geneva, 2003); Daniel Kahneman and Amos Tversky, 'Rational Choice and the Framing of Decisions', *Journal of Business* 59, no. 4 (1986): 251–78, 257.

141 Robert C. Beckman et al., 'Factors conducive to joint development in Asia – lessons learned for the South China Sea', in *Beyond Territorial Disputes in the South China Sea: Legal Frameworks for the Joint Development of Hydrocarbon Resources*, edited by Robert C. Beckman et el. (Edward Elgar, 2013), 291–311; Aileen Baviera, 'The Influence of Domestic Politics on Philippine Foreign Policy: The Case of Philippines-China Relations since 2004', *RSIS Working Paper*, 2012, 1–36.

142 Baviera, 'The Influence of Domestic Politics on Philippine Foreign Policy'.

143 Chapter IV 1.2.

144 Lieberthal explains China's acceptance of the terms for WTO accession in 2001 with the central government's need to lock in an economic reform agenda and to provide leverage against provincial governments that resisted reform of China's state-owned enterprises. Kenneth Lieberthal, *Governing China: From Revolution through Reform*, 2nd ed (Norton, 2004), 271. Simmons explains the use of third-party dispute settlement procedures with the need to overcome domestic resistance against territorial settlements. Beth A. Simmons, 'Capacity, Commitment, and Compliance: International Institutions and Territorial Disputes', *Journal of Conflict Resolution* 46, no. 6 (December 2002): 829–56.

actors responsible for fisheries policies in the East and South China Sea changed as a result of joint fisheries agreements. China's fisheries policy was, to some extent, affected as the constellation among domestic actors changed.[145] However, unlike China's accession to the WTO, the empirical evidence does not suggest that a domestic reform agenda was a motivation for signing fisheries agreements.

3.3 ASEAN as a Fragmented Coalition in Multilateral Negotiations

While the majority of cases on marine natural resources in the East and South China Sea are bilateral, the negotiations on a code of conduct between China and ASEAN members and on CUES were multilateral. An important element of multilateral negotiations is the issue of coalition formation and fragmentation.[146] Tactics in multilateral negotiations include building and holding coalitions together and splitting rival coalitions. Coalitions with heterogeneous preferences are expected to achieve less than coalitions with homogenous preferences.[147] ASEAN members have heterogeneous preferences with regard to their general strategies towards China[148] and concerning specific terms for a code of conduct. In addition, one crucial factor that also contributes to the existence of heterogeneous preferences is the existence of boundary delimitations and territorial disputes among ASEAN members. Malaysia, for instance, protested the 'excessive nature' of the Philippine claim to the 'Kalayaan Island Group'.[149] The Philippines upheld its territorial claim to North Borneo in Malaysia and protested Malaysia's submission for an extended continental shelf.[150] Malaysia and Brunei came close to conflict over a sea boundary dispute in 2003.[151] Even if Southeast

145 Chapter IV 4.

146 Amrita Narlikar and John Odell, 'The Strict Distributive Strategy for a Bargaining Coalition: The Like Minded Group in the World Trade Organization', in *Negotiating Trade: Developing Countries in the WTO and NAFTA*, edited by John Odell (CUP, 2006), 115–44; also see Amrita Narlikar, ed., *Deadlocks in Multilateral Negotiations: Causes and Solutions* (CUP, 2010).

147 John Odell, 'Negotiation and Bargaining', in *Handbook of International Relations*, edited by Thomas Risse, Walter Carlsnaes, and Beth Simmons (SAGE, 2011), 379–99, 386.

148 Sarah Raine and Christian Le Mière, *Regional Disorder The South China Sea Disputes*, IISS Adelphi Series (Routledge, 2013), chapter 3,110–28.

149 Permanent Mission of Malaysia to the United Nations, 'Note Verbale to the United Nations', 27 August 2020, https://www.un.org/Depts/los/clcs_new/submissions_files/mys_12_12_2019/2020_08_27_MYS_NV_UN_003.pdf (last accessed 23 March 2022).

150 Permanent Mission of the Republic of the Philippines, 'Note Verbale No. 000192-2020', 6 March 2020, https://www.un.org/Depts/los/clcs_new/submissions_files/submission_mys_12_12_2019.html (last accessed 23 March 2022).

151 Chapter III 4.

Asian states settled some sea boundary disputes in the southern part of the South China Sea,[152] these disputes imply that some ASEAN members are not only partners facing a common threat but also opponents in their own disputes.

ASEAN members therefore require a genuine effort to develop a common position regarding the code of conduct. ASEAN members have engaged in procedural negotiations and coalition building.[153] However, these efforts have resulted in several delays without producing a substantial consensus among ASEAN members. Not much is required for China to split ASEAN members in code of conduct negotiations. Although ASEAN members have adopted different negotiation procedures in the code of conduct negotiations, this has not overcome their internal fragmentation problem. From 1996 to 1999, ASEAN negotiated first an informal ASEAN draft code of conduct and only then started negotiating with China. The ASEAN draft code was a consensus between different positions. When China rejected important provisions of the draft, the ASEAN consensus faltered, and ASEAN members were left without a common negotiating position. The case studies will illustrate that if a loose coalition does not have a fallback negotiation position, it might find itself *without* a negotiation position. In the subsequent negotiation approach, ASEAN states tried to get China's consent to a negotiation procedure that would formalize internal ASEAN coordination. As China rejected this, ASEAN members continued to coordinate informally. After these experiences, claimants shifted to a third negotiation procedure based on a Single Draft Negotiating Text. According to this procedure, each party interacts directly with every other party. As a matter of formal negotiation procedures, ASEAN members do not negotiate with China as a bloc.

While the fragmented nature of ASEAN members on the South China Sea disputes is a distinct feature of code of conduct negotiations, the disagreements that have thwarted agreement on a code of conduct fit into a pattern of disagreements that have also blocked bilateral agreements. Disagreements on essential substantive provisions that blocked an effective code occurred between ASEAN members and China as well as between ASEAN members. Disagreements have revolved around the question of which conflict behaviours should be prohibited and the geographic scope and legal status of a code. Disagreements about the geographic scope have also blocked bilateral joint development agreements. Competing views on restrictions for conflict behaviour

152 Tara Davenport, 'Southeast Asian Approaches to Maritime Boundaries', *Asian Journal of International Law* 4, no. 02 (2014): 309–57.
153 Chapter V.

have also delayed crisis communication agreements. Similar disagreements also hindered a Philippine attempt in 2012 to achieve a consensus among ASEAN members on a code of conduct that would have established – with hindsight – an ASEAN draft code in line with the arbitral tribunal's ruling of 2016. Such an ASEAN draft code would have been a strategic asset for post-arbitration diplomacy. This is a lost opportunity to be explained.

4 Methodology

Inductive research design and cross validation

This book adopts an inductive research design in order to generate a theory that builds on the literature on conflict resolution, institutions, and negotiation, and to integrate concepts from international law. Six initial case studies were conducted.[154] The initial sample comprised three agreements about the common utilization of natural resources (the Sino-Japanese Principled Consensus, the China–Japan fisheries agreement, and the expired Sino-Philippine-Vietnamese Joint Marine Seismic Undertaking), one agreement on sea boundary delimitation that includes an arrangement for the joint development of hydrocarbon resources in the Gulf of Tonkin, one fisheries agreement in the Gulf of Tonkin, and one arrangement for conflict management (the negotiation process leading to the Declaration on the Conduct of Parties). I inductively derived an explanation for the observed patterns from the initial case studies. About one half of the cases on resource-sharing agreements were set aside to cross validate the results of the inductive examination. Four more cases on conflict management were also set aside in order to cross validate the results and to use another issue area for an out-of-sample test.

Case studies

The empirical analysis consists of twenty case studies.[155] Cases are defined in the following way. Negotiators reached an agreement if negotiators accepted a document and implemented it, and the agreement was effective within

154 On theory development based on case studies see, Alexander L. George et al., *Case Studies and Theory Development in the Social Sciences* (MIT Press, 2005).

155 'Case connotes a spatially delimited phenomenon (a unit) observed at a single point in time or over some period of time. It comprises the type of phenomenon that an inference attempts to explain.' John Gerring, *Case Study Research: Principles and Practices* (CUP, 2006), 19.

the limits of its scope. Negotiations resulted in an impasse if negotiators did not agree on a document despite a negotiation process, if negotiators reached a document that was not implemented, or if arrangements reached were not effective within the limits of their scope. A negotiation process is defined as genuine negotiations at the level of officials or working groups, including the exchange of draft documents throughout the course of at least one year. Consultations that do not discuss specific proposals are excluded. To develop the case studies, five questions were asked: What was the parties' motivation for negotiating the agreements? What is the evidence for the actual negotiations, and which proposals did the negotiators exchange? Which barriers prevented an agreement? How did the claimant states circumvent or solve the obstacles if they reached an agreement despite barriers? What were the consequences of the implementation of an agreement or of an impasse? This book does not aim to present an innovative account of the effectiveness of agreements. The question arises, though, which difference the agreements make and how. As noted, claimants did not negotiate about a settlement of territorial disputes. The effectiveness of agreements needs therefore to be assessed against their (limited) scope. To assess the effectiveness of agreements, this book presents both the consequences of implemented agreements and the course of events following an impasse. This book assumes, for example, that a fisheries agreement is effective when it prevents fishing incidents, or should they occur nevertheless, when it prevents their escalation. While this book reviews several incidents, it does not seek to explain the variation of escalation below the level of war.

Case selection and comparison

This book identifies twenty cases of agreement and impasse with the following selection criteria. It examines cases where state actors or non-state actors negotiated about common rules for marine natural resources (living and non-living resources) in disputed areas and about rules for the management of conflict behaviour. This includes cases of the joint development of hydrocarbon resources but excludes cooperation in the energy sector or in oil and gas services. The geographic scope extends to the South China Sea, including the Gulf of Tonkin, and the East China Sea, including the Yellow Sea. The analysis covers bilateral, trilateral, and multilateral cases. This book includes the attempts of ASEAN members and China to reach a code of conduct even if not all ASEAN members have claims in the South China Sea (e.g., Cambodia, Laos, Myanmar, Singapore, and Thailand). However, the joint development agreements outside the East and South China Sea (e.g., in the Gulf of Thailand or Timor Sea) are excluded. While two agreements on marine scientific research between, on the one hand, China and Japan, and, on the other hand, China, the Philippines, and Vietnam could provide further cases, this book does not discuss them separately. These agreements would add another policy area to the case studies.[156]

This book does not define on-and-off negotiations between China and the Philippines on oil and gas exploration or between China and ASEAN members on the code of conduct as one long case. The definition of agreement and impasse suggest the following count. China and the Philippines reached an agreement for joint seismic research in 2004; Vietnam joined the agreement in 2005. The agreement was partly implemented and then expired in 2008. This period defines the first case. China and the Philippines resumed negotiations and exchanged proposals in 2011 (second case). Both resumed negotiations in 2017 after the decision of the South China Sea Arbitration (third case). About three-quarters of the cases include China. This is because China is involved in many maritime disputes with all its maritime neighbours. Most cases of impasse include China, but China also entered into the highest number of agreements. About one quarter of the cases exclude China, and a comparison of China's participation is possible. Two cases involve Taiwan. Even if Taiwan is not recognized by a large majority of states,[157] Taiwan has deep and comprehensive relations with neighbouring states in various policy areas. The relevance of Taiwan's status is discussed in the case studies. Indonesia considers itself a 'non-claimant state' in the South China Sea. Indonesia has also explicitly rejected entering into negotiations on marine natural resources with China, as China and Indonesia do not have overlapping entitlements under international law.[158]

156 Akira Takada, 'Marine Scientific Research in the Exclusive Economic Zone and Japan-China Agreement for Prior Notification (1995–2001)', *Japanese Annual of International Law*, 2001, 134–50; Mark J. Valencia and Yoshihisa Amae, 'Regime Building in the East China Sea', *Ocean Development & International Law*, 34 (2003), 189–208; Henry S. Bensurto, 'Cooperation in the South China Sea: Views on the Philippines–Vietnam Cooperation on Maritime and Ocean Concerns', *East Sea Studies*, 2011, 1–12 (URL no longer available); Vietnam Academy of Science and Technology – Institute of Oceanography, 'Philippines–Vietnam Joint Oceanographic and Marine Scientific Research Expedition in the South China Sea (JOMSRE-SCS), 1996–2007', 24 October 2012, http://www.vnio.org.vn/Home/tabid/107/ctl/Details/mid/579/ItemID/798/language/en-US/Default.aspx (last accessed 29 April 2023).

157 177 states do not recognize Taiwan; seventeen states recognize Taiwan as of 2019. The book uses the word 'Taiwan' without intending any implications regarding Taiwan's status.

158 Permanent Mission of the Republic of Indonesia. 'Communication of the Republic of Indonesia to the United Nations No. 148/POL-703/VI/20', 12 June 2020, https://www.un.org/Depts/los/clcs_new/submissions_files/mys_12_12_2019/2020_06_12_IDN_NV_UN_002_ENG.pdf (last accessed 24 April 2024); 'Note Verbale to the United Nations No. 480/POL-703/VII/10', 8 July 2010.

Therefore, no bilateral case study is devoted to Indonesia even if the country has reached boundary agreements in the southern part of the South China Sea.[159] Indonesia has played an important role in code of conduct negotiations as will be shown in the respective chapter.

Applying these criteria yields a set of twenty cases. This book might have discounted the number of genuine negotiations that resulted in an impasse because some negotiations were not made public or substantive data are not available. Counting the number of negotiation rounds or meetings would have resulted in a much higher number of cases. But this would have led to the methodological difficulty that some announced negotiation rounds did not occur (for instance, between ASEAN and China in the context of the code of conduct) and that precise data are not available for each negotiation round. While the case studies principally cover the period between 1992 and 2022, this book briefly refers to earlier agreements. Namely the joint development agreement between South Korea and Japan of 1974 and six historic fisheries agreements that have been replaced by more recent agreements in the East China Sea and the Gulf of Tonkin. The twenty cases allow comparison in several dimensions and across several fields.[160] Comparison is possible in the five dimensions of issue area, region, number of involved parties, combination of parties, and legal character of claims. Cases cover: (i) four different issue areas (fisheries, oil and gas, crisis management, and rules for conduct), (ii) two regions, (iii) bilateral, trilateral, and multilateral negotiations, (iv) different combinations of states including and excluding China, and (v) cases where China's claims are within the limits of the law of the sea and where China's claims go beyond limits of the law of the sea.

Data

As regards data on the negotiation processes, I analysed official documents such as the agreements themselves, various forms of communications

159 Tara Davenport, 'Southeast Asian Approaches to Maritime Boundaries', *Asian Journal of International Law* 4, no. 02 (2014): 309–57; Bich Tran, 'The Significance of the Vietnam-Indonesia Exclusive Economic Zone Demarcation', *Fulcrum* (blog), 20 January 2023, https://fulcrum.sg/the-significance-of-the-vietnam-indonesia-exclusive-economic-zone-demarcation/ (last accessed 20 February 2023).

160 On the comparative method, Giovanni Sartori, 'Concept Misformation in Comparative Politics', *American Political Science Review* 64, no. 4 (1970): 1033–53; David Collier, 'The Comparative Method: Two Decades of Change', in *Comparative Political Dynamics: Global Research Perspectives*, edited by Dankwart Rustow and Kenneth Paul Erickson (HarperCollins Publishers, 1991), 7-31; Charles C. Ragin, *The Comparative Method: Moving beyond Qualitative and Quantitative Strategies* (University of California Press, 2014).

to the United Nations, declarations, official position papers, minutes of parliamentary sessions, public statements, press conferences, and other officially released information on the actors' negotiation positions. Forty-six semi-structured expert interviews were conducted with ministers, generals, admirals, senior officials, and experts from leading government affiliated think tanks. Due to practical limitations, I had to restrict field research to the Philippines, China, Taiwan, Vietnam, and Japan. For three reasons, some of the case studies are shorter than others. First, the length of the underlying negotiation periods varies. Second, data were not available to the same extent for all cases. Third, it was not possible to do field research in all claimant states due to practical limitations. For the admittedly shorter treatment of the positions of Brunei, Malaysia, Indonesia, and South Korea, I had to rely on the literature. Where possible, I identified the officials that participated in the negotiation processes and interviewed them. To encourage a frank and open interview environment, the interviews were conducted anonymously. Given the sensitivity of the disputes, almost all officials of the claimant states requested to remain unnamed.

In the context of the South China Sea Arbitration, the Philippines decided to publish a collection of forty volumes of supporting documents. These volumes contain close to 1,000 documents and, among other documentation, a part of the Philippines' diplomatic record on exchanges with China for the period of 1992 to 2015.[161] This collection includes formerly classified documents – the highest classification is 'secret' – such as memoranda from the Department of Foreign Affairs or the Secretary of Foreign Affairs to the Philippine President. It also comprises minutes about high-level Sino-Philippine negotiations, reports of the Philippine Armed Forces and Coast Guard, internal assessments, and others. The collection contains the record of negotiations and consultations about agreements and incidents between Chinese and Philippine officials and members of government. The collection of documents also contains China's draft code of conduct and further documents on China–ASEAN exchanges. A researcher would

161 Available for download at the website of the Permanent Court of Arbitration (PCA) http://www.pcacases.com/web/view/7 (last accessed 24 April 2024). The PCA made the documents available for download in the section 'Written submission' in late 2016. The updated PCA website no longer indicates at which date the collection of documents went online. I cite the documents of the collection in this way – e.g., *Letter* from the Virgilio A. Hernandez, Major General, Armed Forces of the Philippines, to the Secretary of Foreign Affairs, Department of Foreign Affairs of Republic of the Philippines (10 March 2014) (Annex 99), Vol IV, https://files.pca-cpa.org/pcadocs/The%20Philippines%27%20Memorial%20-%20Volume%20IV%20%28Annexes%2061-102%29.pdf (last accessed 24 April 2024).

normally not be able to access such documents in a timely manner. Usually, a researcher would only be able to make use of such documents after (and if at all) they were declassified. This is the first study to utilize these documents.

The collection of documents is a selection of the diplomatic record prepared by the legal team of the Philippines for the specific purpose of winning the arbitration. The reader cannot expect the documents to be unbiased. The international legal requirements of arbitral proceedings specifically necessitate that the Philippines demonstrates the existence of a dispute and that bilateral means to address the disputes have been exhausted. Nevertheless, the documents are an invaluable source of data for research on Sino-Philippine exchanges and incidents and on China–ASEAN code of conduct negotiations. I decided, therefore, to use the documents and to adopt several methodological safeguards against the potential bias. The first methodological safeguard is that the collection of documents provides data on cases involving the Philippines only. The collection is silent about cases not involving the Philippines. This allows assessing whether the data contained in the documents reflect a broader pattern or are specific to the arbitral proceedings. Second, I researched data about all cases, including the cases involving the Philippines, independently of the Philippines' record, so as to be able to assess whether data in the documents are biased in relation to the proceedings. Third, I conducted field research in the Philippines before analysing the documents. A part of the documents became available only after field research in the Philippines was completed. This book, therefore, does not look at Philippine interview sources through the lens of the documents. The case studies explored in this book do not rely on these documents for contextual information which was research independently. The 1,000 documents presented in the collection are one and only one source of data for the cases involving China and the Philippines.

III Institutions for Marine Natural Resources in the South China Sea

Abstract
This chapter analyses disputing states' negotiations about agreements for the joint development of hydrocarbon resources and for fisheries in the South China Sea. It explains why, after three decades of exchanges, claimants have reached agreements in some cases but not in others. It shows that actors from different claimant states believe, and, in some cases, have experienced that a natural resource institution results in vulnerabilities and strengthens a rival bargaining position. This chapter illustrates how a combination of agreements on boundary delimitations and natural resources offers safeguards against such vulnerabilities.

Keywords: South China Sea disputes, joint development of oil, fisheries agreements, crises, boundary delimitation, negotiation

This chapter analyses disputing states' negotiations about agreements for the joint development of hydrocarbon resources and for fisheries in the South China Sea. It explains why, after three decades of exchanges, claimants have reached agreements in some cases but not in others. It shows that actors from different claimant states have believed and, in some cases, experienced that a natural resource institution results in vulnerabilities and strengthens a rival bargaining position. This chapter illustrates how a combination of agreements on boundary delimitations and natural resources has offered safeguards against such vulnerabilities.

This chapter first examines the past three decades of exchanges between China and the Philippines about the common exploration of oil and gas and fisheries. While these exchanges have produced the only arrangement on natural resource cooperation in waters around some of the Spratly Islands

Schultheiss, Christian: *Ocean Governance and Conflict in the East and South China Sea. Negotiating Natural Resources, Institutions and Power.*
Taylor & Francis Group, 2024
DOI: 10.5117/9789463728997_CH03

between China and a Southeast Asian country, these exchanges have ultimately ended in an impasse (subchapter 1). This chapter then turns to two agreements – one boundary delimitation and one fisheries agreement that China and Vietnam concluded simultaneously for the Gulf of Tonkin (subchapter 2). Thirdly, it presents two case studies that exclude China. To some extent, this allows to assess whether the identified effects are specific to the involvement of China in the case studies. Subchapter 3 examines how Taiwan got the Philippines to agree to a fisheries law enforcement agreement. Subchapter 4 illustrates why a combined boundary and joint development arrangement between Brunei and Malaysia has enabled natural resource cooperation in contested areas.

Moreover, additional puzzles within the single case studies should be highlighted. First, despite the Philippines advocating for a common approach by members of the Association of Southeast Asian Nations (ASEAN) to disputes, Manila was the first country to strike a bilateral arrangement on seismic research with China in the early 2000s. While the Philippine president heralded this arrangement as a 'historic breakthrough', Manila let the agreement expire soon after. This was Manila's second U-turn on the South China Sea within a few years. Moreover, after the South China Sea Arbitration contradicted China's claims beyond the normal limits under the UN Convention on the Law of the Sea (UNCLOS), the Philippines, to the surprise of many observers, resumed negotiations on joint developments with China. The question arises: what explains Manila's zigzag course on common oil and gas activities (subchapter 1)? Second, five years after the battle at the Spratly Islands, in 1993, China and Vietnam began negotiations on sea boundary delimitations, joint development of oil and gas, and fisheries cooperation in the Gulf of Tonkin. While these agreements provided the basis for various joint activities in the Gulf of Tonkin, attempts to extend this cooperation model into small, adjacent areas of the South China Sea have stalled, and the question is why (subchapter 2). Third, the agreement between the Philippines and Taiwan on law enforcement and fisheries appears unsurprising at first glance, as both have a cooperative relationship. However, Manila rejected all Taiwanese proposals about fisheries cooperation, even though escalating fishing incidents called for such cooperation. The question then becomes why Manila was reluctant to cooperate and how Taipei has nevertheless succeeded in getting Manila's consent to the agreement (subchapter 3). Finally, a shorter case study illustrates that some incidents between Brunei and Malaysia, two members of ASEAN, escalated even when they sought restrictions on conflict behaviour vis-à-vis China. While barriers similar to those in Sino-Philippine negotiations initially blocked agreement on joint development in lieu of boundary delimitations, the combination of boundary delimitations and joint development of oil and gas offered a way out (subchapter 4).

Who Claims What: Territorial and Maritime Claims in the South China Sea

This section provides an overview of the claims to features and maritime zones in the South China Sea. Map 1 illustrates these claims. The South China Sea encompasses nearly 3.5 million square kilometres and hundreds of features. The Spratly Islands[1] consist of more than a hundred mostly submerged reefs, shoals, and rocks.[2] They cover an area of between 240,000 square kilometres and 410,000 square kilometres.[3] China, the Philippines, Vietnam, Malaysia, Brunei, and Taiwan claim some or all of the Spratly Islands. Of these, fifty-one features are currently occupied. China and Vietnam claim the Paracel Islands, a second group of islands. China and the Philippines claim Scarborough Shoal.[4] Taiwan claims the 'South China

1 For satellite images and a geographic description of the Spratly Islands, see Clive Schofield et al., *An Appraisal of the Geographical Characteristics and Status of Certain Insular Features in the South China Sea* (March 2015), (Annex 513), Supplemental Written Submission of the Philippines Vol IX, https://files.pca-cpa.org/pcadocs/The%20Philippines%27%20Supplemental%20Written%20Submission%20-%20Volume%20IX%20%28Annexes%20500-521%29.pdf (last accessed 24 April 2024). In the context of the South China Sea Arbitration, a collection of about 1,000 documents were published in forty volumes as annexes to the Memorial of the Philippines (written submission). These volumes are accessible at https://pca-cpa.org/en/cases/7/ (last accessed 24 April 2024). Chapter II 4 discusses how this book uses these documents. The following references will provide the title of the document, its date (if available), the number of the annex and the volume of the memorial. When many annexes are cited, only the number is indicated.

2 Charles S. Hutchison and V. R. Vijayan, 'What Are the Spratly Islands?' *Journal of Asian Earth Sciences* 39, no. 5 (2010): 371–85; David J. Hancox and John R. V. Prescott, *A Geographical Description of the Spratly Islands and an Account of Hydrographic Surveys amongst Those Islands*, Maritime Briefing (University of Durham, 1995). A collection of maps, charts and figures of the South China Sea and the Spratly Islands is available in Vol II of the Memorial of the Philippines, https://files.pca-cpa.org/pcadocs/Memorial%20of%20the%20Philippines%20Volume%20II.pdf (last accessed 24 April 2024).

3 Robert Beckman, 'The UN Convention on the Law of the Sea and the Maritime Disputes in the South China Sea', *The American Journal of International Law*, (2013): 142–63, 143.

4 Various interactive maps of the Asia Maritime Transparency Initiative (CSIS) illustrate claims to features https://amti.csis.org/maps/ (last accessed 24 April 2024).

Map 1 Claims in the South China Sea[5]

Sea Islands and their relevant waters in accordance with international law and the law of the sea' but does not further specify this position.[6]

5 Map prepared by Andi Arsana and Clive Schofield, in Lori Fisler Damrosch and Bernard H. Oxman, 'Agora: The South China Sea: Editors' Introduction', *The American Journal of International Law* 107, no. 1 (2013): 95–7. Reproduced with permission. The map was prepared before the arbitral award. Some features have a territorial sea (visualised by a small circle) that the award considers a low-tide elevation. These would not receive a territorial sea.

6 Ministry of Foreign Affairs, Republic of China (Taiwan), 'South China Sea', https://en.mofa.gov.tw/theme.aspx?n=1462&s=40&sms=294 (last accessed 23 June 2023).

China's nine-dash line can be interpreted as a claim to territorial sovereignty and maritime zones.[7] The country claims all features inside the nine-dash line: it claims the Spratly Islands and occupies seven.[8] And it controls all the Paracel Islands, where it has twenty outposts. China also controls Scarborough Shoal since 2012. Vietnam claims all the Paracel Islands, but controls none. It claims all the Spratly Islands and occupies twenty-seven with forty-nine outposts. The Philippines claims many of the Spratly Islands as the 'Kalayaan Island Group' and controls seven features. Manila also claims Scarborough Shoal, which was administered by the Philippines until 2012. Taiwan claims all Spratly and Paracel islands, but occupies only one, Itu Aba. Malaysia controls five features of the Spratly Islands and claims eleven. Brunei claims Louisa Reef.[9]

The claimant states occupy and control effectively only a minority of features they claim. To provide evidence for the legally critical standard of effective control over features, the claimant states rely to a large extent on historical maps, the concept of discovery, and on economic activities of private actors for the period before the twentieth century.[10] The level of claimant states' effective control over the Spratly Islands was necessarily limited in the past, as nautical administrations considered the waters around

7 'Statement of the Government of the People's Republic of China on China's Territorial Sovereignty and Maritime Rights and Interests in the South China Sea', *Chinese Journal of International Law* 15, no. 4 (December 2016): 903–4; Zhiguo Gao and Bing Bing Jia, 'The Nine-Dash Line in the South China Sea: History, Status, and Implications,' *American Journal of International Law* 107, no. 1 (2013): 98–124.

8 Cuarteron Reef, Fiery Cross Reef, Gaven Reef (North), Hughes Reef, Johnson Reef, Mischief Reef, and Subi Reef.

9 Sources differ in the number of features occupied by claimants, depending on the classification of features. List of Occupied Spratly Features: Geographic Coordinates, Claimants and Occupants (Annex 97), Vol IV, https://files.pca-cpa.org/pcadocs/The%20Philippines%27%20 Memorial%20-%20Volume%20IV%20%28Annexes%2061-102%29.pdf . The Asia Maritime Transparency Initiative (CSIS) provides photographic material of the development of outposts since 2013 https://amti.csis.org/island-tracker/ (last accessed 24 April 2024).

10 Greg Austin, *China's Ocean Frontier: International Law, Military Force, and National Development* (Allen & Unwin, 1998); Monique Chemillier-Gendreau, *Sovereignty over the Paracel and Spratly Islands* (Kluwer Law, 2000); Shicun Wu, *Solving Disputes for Regional Cooperation and Development in the South China Sea: A Chinese Perspective* (Elsevier, 2013); Ulises Granados, 'Chinese Ocean Policies Towards the South China Sea in a Transitional Period, 1946–1952', *China Review*, (2006), 153–81; Antonio Carpio, 'Historical Truths and Lies. Scarborough Shoal in Ancient Maps. A Cartographic Exhibit Based on the 6 June 2014 Lecture of Supreme Court Senior Associate Justice Antonio T. Carpio' (Institute for Maritime and Ocean Affairs, 2014), http://www.imoa.ph/historical-truths-lies-series/; Institute for Maritime and Ocean Affairs, 'Spratlys and "Pulo" in Ancient Maps' (The Exhibit Catalogue, 2014), http://www.imoa.ph/?s=spratlys+and+pulo (last accessed 23 June 2023).

these islands 'dangerous ground' – an area that is best to be avoided.[11] Austin argues that China has a superior claim to sovereignty over the Paracel Islands and a strong claim to sovereignty over the Spratly Islands because of inspections undertaken by the Republic of China in the Spratly Islands between 1946 and the early 1950s.[12] Chen et al., however, have illustrated that authorities of Republican China and the Qing Dynasty had limited geographic knowledge of the South China Sea or confused the Paracel with the Spratly Islands.[13] Several scholars maintain that evidence for claims to the Paracel and Spratly Islands by all claimants are inconclusive and that no claimant has a clearly superior legal claim.[14] Besides many other issues, it remains an entirely open question whether inspection or even occupation of a few features can give rise to a title of sovereignty over an entire group of islands spread out over approximately 410,000 square kilometres – as is the case with the Spratly Islands. It seems hard to rule out the possibility that one state has a superior claim to one feature and a second state has a superior claim to a different feature. In this case, each claimant state would need to provide evidence of effective control for each claimed feature *individually*. Then, the best evidence claimant states may have for having exercised effective control over features may be the acts of occupying these features in the second half of the twentieth century.

The territorial and maritime disputes over exclusive rights to maritime zones of the South China Sea are closely interwoven via the 'regime of islands' (Article 121 of UNCLOS). States are only entitled to claim maritime zones based on the possession of land under the doctrine of '*la terre domine la mer*'

11 Stein Tønnesson, 'Why Are the Disputes in the South China Sea So Intractable? A Historical Approach', *Asian Journal of Social Science* 30, no. 3 (2002): 570–601; Brantly Womack, 'The Spratlys: From Dangerous Ground to Apple of Discord', *Contemporary Southeast Asia* 33, no. 3 (2011): 370–87.

12 Austin, *China's Ocean Frontier*, chapters 4 and 5.

13 Hsin-Chih Chen, 'La Réponse Chinoise à l'occupation Française Des Îles Spratly En 1933', *Guerres Mondiales et Conflits Contemporains* (2001), 5–24; Ulises Granados, 'The South China Sea and Its Coral Reefs during the Ming and Qing Dynasties: Levels of Geographical Knowledge and Political Control', *East Asian History* 32/33 (2006): 109–28; Bill Hayton, 'When Good Lawyers Write Bad History: Unreliable Evidence and the South China Sea Territorial Dispute', *Ocean Development & International Law* 48, no. 1 (2 January 2017): 17–34.

14 Mark John Valencia et al., *Sharing the Resources of the South China Sea* (Martinus Nijhoff, 1997), chapter 3, 17–76; Stein Tønnesson, 'Why Are the Disputes in the South China Sea So Intractable? A Historical Approach'; Ulises Granados, 'Ocean Frontier Expansion and the Kalayaan Islands Group Claim: Philippines' Postwar Pragmatism in the South China Sea', *International Relations of the Asia-Pacific* 9, no. 2 (2008): 267–94; J. Ashley Roach, 'Malaysia and Brunei: An Analysis of Their Claims in the South China Sea' (CNA Occasional Paper, 2014).

('the land dominates the sea').[15] Depending on the status of a feature as an 'island' (Article 121 (2) of UNCLOS) or a 'rock' (Article 121 (3)), states can claim an Exclusive Economic Zone (EEZ) and continental shelf or only a territorial sea. If a feature is only a 'low-tide elevation', it does not generate maritime entitlements by itself.[16] China has not expressly specified the scope and status of the maritime zones within the nine-dash line.[17] It stated on 12 July 2016 that it claims 'inter alia' internal waters, a territorial sea, a contiguous zone, an EEZ, a continental shelf, and historic rights.[18] The country also has the position that these claims are in accordance with UNCLOS.[19] This statement does not specify whether all waters within the nine-dash line are covered by the claimed zones, or which claimed zone applies to which part of the nine-dash line. An arbitral tribunal constituted under Annex VII of UNCLOS ruled that China is not entitled to maritime areas beyond the zones that the law of the sea and UNCLOS provide for:[20] 'historic rights' have been extinguished.[21] All the features in the Spratly Islands are 'rocks' or 'low-tide elevations' and cannot generate entitlements to an EEZ or continental shelf.[22]

15 *North Sea Continental Shelf Cases (Federal Republic of Germany/Denmark; Federal Republic of Germany/Netherlands)*, (1969) ICJ Reports 3, para 96.
16 The South China Sea Arbitration (The Republic of Philippines v. The People's Republic of China) Award (12 July 2016), part VI; Robert C. Beckman and Clive H. Schofield, 'Defining EEZ Claims from Islands: A Potential South China Sea Change', *The International Journal of Marine and Coastal Law* 29, no. 2 (2014): 193–243; Roberto Lavalle, 'Not Quite a Sure Thing: The Maritime Areas of Rocks and Low-Tide Elevations under the UN Law of the Sea Convention', *The International Journal of Marine and Coastal Law* 19, no. 1 (2004): 43–69; Barbara Kwiatkowska and Alfred H. A. Soons, 'Entitlement to Maritime Areas of Rocks Which Cannot Sustain Human Habitation or Economic Life of Their Own', *Netherlands Yearbook of International Law* 21 (1990): 139–81.
17 Robert Beckman, 'The UN Convention on the Law of the Sea and the Maritime Disputes in the South China Sea,' *The American Journal of International Law*, 2013, 142–63.
18 'Statement of the Government of the People's Republic of China on China's Territorial Sovereignty and Maritime Rights and Interests in the South China Sea', 12 July 2016, http://english.www.gov.cn/archive/publications/2016/07/12/content_281475391807773.htm#:~:text=China%20is%20the%20first%20to,in%20the%20South%20China%20Sea. (accessed 23 August 2023).
19 Ibid.
20 The South China Sea Arbitration, Award, 2016. Lucy Reed and Kenneth Wong. 'Marine Entitlements in the South China Sea: The Arbitration Between the Philippines and China'. *American Journal of International Law* 110, no. 4 (2016): 746–60; Christian Schultheiss, '"One of the First Matters to Be Addressed but Distinct" or "Distinct but Inseparable"? The Distinction Between Maritime Entitlement and Sea Boundary Delimitation in the Philippines v. China Arbitration', *Asian Journal of International Law* 11, no. 1 (January 2021): 24–35.
21 The South China Sea Arbitration, Award, 2016, part V, paras 257–272.
22 Ibid. Part VI, paras. 643–648. Scarborough Shoal, Cuarteron Reef, Johnson Reef, Fiery Cross Reef, Gaven Reef (North), and McKennan Reef are rocks and occupied or controlled by China. The tribunal considered Mischief Reef (occupied by China) and Second Thomas Shoal low-tide elevations.

The Spratly Islands can neither generate entitlements collectively as a unit nor be enclosed with archipelagic or straight baselines.[23] In combination, the ruling invalidated China's claim to maritime zones beyond the normal zones. Malaysia, the Philippines, and Vietnam have largely aligned their claims to continental shelves and EEZs with UNCLOS over the last decade.[24] This is the case even some of Vietnam's straight baselines appear excessive.[25] While the Philippines' baseline law of 2009 has implemented UNCLOS,[26] the status of the waters within the 'Kalayaan Island Group' and beyond the 200-nautical-mile limits remains unclear.[27] In contravention of the tribunal's ruling, China continues to assert maritime rights within the nine-dash line.[28] These overlap with the claims of the Philippines, Vietnam, Brunei, Malaysia, and Indonesia. Indonesia has characterized itself as a non-claimant state, as it does not claim features in the South China Sea. However, Indonesia has also rejected the validity of the nine-dash line as a claim to maritime zones, especially as a claim to zones claimed by Indonesia.[29]

After initially receiving cautious reactions from the Philippines in 2016 ('the Philippines [will] study… the award'),[30] the Philippines stated that the South China Sea Arbitration 'conclusively settled the issue of historic rights

23 Ibid., paras. 573–576.

24 Peter Dutton, 'Three Disputes and Three Objectives. China and the South China Sea,' *Naval War College Review* Vol. 64, No. 4 (2011): 42–67.

25 Ashley Roach and Robert W. Smith, 'Straight Baselines: The Need for a Universally Applied Norm', *Ocean Development & International Law* 31, no. 1–2 (2000): 47–80.

26 The Philippines' Republic Act No. 9522, Presidential Decree No. 1596, 1978, available at https://www.lawphil.net/statutes/repacts/ra2009/ra_9522_2009.html; see Rodolfo C. Severino, 'The Philippines' National Territory', *Southeast Asian Affairs*, 2012, 257–62; United States Department of State Bureau of Oceans and International Environmental and Scientific Affairs, 'Limits in the Seas No. 142 Philippines: Archipelagic and Other Maritime Claims and Boundaries', 15 September 2014, https://www.state.gov/wp-content/uploads/2019/10/LIS-142.pdf (last accessed 23 June 2023).

27 Malaysia has protested the 'excessive maritime claims arising from Kalayaan Island Group'. Permanent Mission of Malaysia to the United Nations, 'Note Verbale to the United Nations', 27 August 2020, https://www.un.org/Depts/los/clcs_new/submissions_files/mys_12_12_2019/2020_08_27_MYS_NV_UN_003.pdf (last accessed 23 June 2023).

28 Government of the People's Republic of China, 'Position Paper of the Government of the People's Republic of China on the Matter of Jurisdiction in the South China Sea Arbitration Initiated by the Republic of the Philippines', December 2014, https://www.fmprc.gov.cn/mfa_eng/wjdt_665385/2649_665393/201412/t20141207_679387.html (last accessed 23 06 2023); Chinese Society of International Law, 'The South China Sea Arbitration Awards: A Critical Study', *Chinese Journal of International Law* 17, no. 2 (14 May 2018): 207–748.

29 Permanent Mission of the Republic of Indonesia, 'Note Verbale to the United Nations No. 480/POL-703/VII/10', 8 July 2010.

30 Statement of the Secretary of Foreign Affairs of the Philippines, 12 July 2016, (on file with the author).

and entitlements in the South China Sea' on 6 March 2020, three years after the award.[31] In response to Malaysia's submission for an extended continental shelf in December 2019, Malaysia, Indonesia, Vietnam, and the Philippines sent notes verbales to the UN supporting various elements of the South China Sea Arbitration.[32] The Chairman's statement of the 37^{t}h ASEAN Summit made one cautious step towards adopting a general element of the award by stating that 'the 1982 UNCLOS is the basis for determining maritime entitlements, sovereign rights, jurisdiction and legitimate interests over maritime zones'.[33] The US, Australia, France, Germany, and the UK, as well as Japan and New Zealand have also sent notes verbales supporting various substantive parts of the arbitral award.[34] Some maritime boundaries are delimited in the southern part of the South China Sea.[35]

1 China and the Philippines

1.1 The Joint Marine Seismic Undertaking: From 'Breakthrough for Peace' to Liability

The context

China and the Philippines claim many of the Spratly Islands, Scarborough Shoal, and the waters around these features. China's nine-dash line overlaps

31 Permanent Mission of the Philippines to the United Nations, 'Notes Verbales 000191-2020', 6 March 2020, https://www.un.org/Depts/los/clcs_new/submissions_files/submission_mys_12_12_2019.html (last accessed 23 June 2023).

32 The submission is accessible at the website of the Commission on the Limits of the Continental Shelf (CLCS) https://www.un.org/Depts/los/clcs_new/submissions_files/submission_mys_12_12_2019.html (last accessed 23 June 2023).

33 'Chairman's Statement of the 37th ASEAN Summit: Cohesive and Responsive', 12 November 2020, https://asean.org/wp-content/uploads/43-Chairmans-Statement-of-37th-ASEAN-Summit-FINAL.pdf (last accessed 23/06/2023).

34 The notes verbales are accessible at the website of the Commission on the Limits of the Continental Shelf (CLCS) https://www.un.org/Depts/los/clcs_new/submissions_files/submission_mys_12_12_2019.html (last accessed 23 June 2023).

35 Tara Davenport, 'Southeast Asian Approaches to Maritime Boundaries', *Asian Journal of International Law* 4, no. 02 (2014): 309–57; Bich Tran, 'The Significance of the Vietnam-Indonesia Exclusive Economic Zone Demarcation', *Fulcrum* (blog), 20 January 2023, https://fulcrum.sg/the-significance-of-the-vietnam-indonesia-exclusive-economic-zone-demarcation/; Joint Statement by the Honourable Prime Minister of Malaysia and His Excellency President of the Republic of Indonesia, 8 June 2023, https://demaribus.files.wordpress.com/2023/06/joint-statement-8-june-2023.pdf (last accessed 14/06/2023).

widely with the Philippines' EEZ and continental shelf (Map 2). Estimates of the prospects for substantial hydrocarbon resources in the Spratly area are pessimistic, but it may have deposits of undiscovered resources.[36] Prospects for gas fields in the Reed Bank are more promising. Chinese sources suggest more optimistic estimates.[37] Joint development and joint exploration of the offshore oil and gas resources in disputed areas has been on the Sino-Philippine agenda for more than twenty-five years. China and the Philippines reached an agreement for seismic surveys in 2004. Vietnam joined the agreement in 2005. The Philippines, though, let the agreement expire in 2008. New negotiations were held in 2011 but were without result. After the South China Sea arbitration in 2016, negotiations resumed and resulted in a memorandum of understanding in 2018. No agreement, though, materialized by mid-2023. Why did the Philippines agree to an exploration agreement in the first place? Why did the Philippines then allow it to expire? And how has this affected subsequent exchanges on offshore oil and gas resources?

About 30 per cent of the Philippine national energy consumption is provided by the offshore Malampaya gas field, located in Service Sector 38 in an undisputed area close to the north-western cost of Palawan.[38] Former members of the Philippine government and energy experts expected the gas field to be depleted within ten years in 2016.[39] Accordingly, the Philippines needs alternatives. The prospects for new gas discoveries based on sedimentary data suggests undertaking more seismic and exploratory research in areas located within the Philippine EEZ and close to Palawan, but also within the nine-dash line. Prospects for resources are especially good in the Reed Bank, an area between the northern part of the Spratly Islands and the main Philippine archipelago. The Philippines' technological

36 US Energy Information Administration, 'South China Sea', 7 February 2013, updated in March 2024 https://www.eia.gov/beta/international/regions-topics.php?RegionTopicID=SCS (last accessed 24 April 2024).

37 Keyuan Zou, 'Joint Development in the South China Sea: A New Approach', *The International Journal of Marine and Coastal Law* 21, no. 1 (2006): 83–109, quoting Zhao Huanting et al., *Geomorphology and Environment of the South China Coast and the South China Sea Islands* (Beijing, Science Press, 1999) (in Chinese).

38 Shell Philippines, 'Malampaya Gas Production', 2015, https://www.shell.com.ph/media/media-releases/2015-media-releases/malampaya-begins-gas-production.html (last accessed 23 March 2024).

39 Interviews with two ministers of the administration of President Arroyo, held in Manila on 2 and 6 December 2016 (Interview 7 and 8). Also see, 'Philippines needs to discover new gas field', 09 March 2015, https://www.philstar.com/business/2015/03/09/1431428/philippines-needs-discover-new-gas-field-experts (last accessed 24 April 2024).

capability for exploration and exploitation is too limited, and Manila needs foreign partners. The Philippines has relied on foreign energy companies for oil exploration in the Reed Bank since 1976. Both China and Vietnam have protested Philippine activities.[40] The Philippines has tried repeatedly to conduct seismic research in the Reed Bank, but China has protested and interfered physically in these attempts on several occasions.[41]

Under circumstances of legal uncertainty, foreign companies are unwilling to invest in Philippine concession blocs or service contracts in disputed areas. Moreover, the Philippines needs a foreign partner for technology. As China has resisted unilateral exploration attempts that escalated in some instances, the continuous existence of the disputes represents a de facto moratorium on hydrocarbon-related activity in the area. Given this inefficient and costly situation, economic and security incentives exist for the Philippines to partner with Chinese companies under some cooperative framework. Such cooperation would be without prejudice to claims. A Philippine senior official dealing with security puts it this way: 'The obstacles to joint development are not primarily security questions. If a security question at all, then it is the Philippines' minor technological capabilities in offshore drilling. The difference in technological capabilities is an incentive, not an obstacle, to do joint development. It is an incentive because technology is needed, Philippines cannot do it alone.'[42] If energy security amounted to a priority, then it should have incentivised cooperation rather than prevented it. Although these conditions have applied for a number of years, the Philippine Department of Foreign Affairs did not follow up on Chinese proposals on joint development before or after the Joint Marine Seismic Undertaking (JMSU).

The Joint Marine Seismic Undertaking

The Philippines and China consulted on joint development many times over a period of twenty-five years. In 2004, both sides reached the only agreement that was ever (partially) implemented. The Philippines let it expire in 2008. Both states signed 'An Agreement for Joint Marine Seismic Undertaking in Certain Areas in the South China Sea By and between the

40 Leszek Buszynski and Iskandar Sazlan, 'Maritime Claims and Energy Cooperation in the South China Sea', *Contemporary Southeast Asia* 29, no. 1 (2007): 143–71, 161.

41 Senate of the Philippines, 'Statement on the Reed Bank Incident', Press Release, 08 March 2011, https://www.senate.gov.ph/press_release/2011/0308_angara2.asp (last accessed 23 June 2023).

42 Interview with a senior official of the Philippine National Security Council, Manila, 01 December 2016 (Interview 6); Interviews 7 and 8.

China National Offshore Corporation and Philippine National Oil Company' on 1 September 2004.[43] This is the first bilateral agreement between China and any other claimant state applying for a part of the South China Sea's most disputed areas – the Spratly Islands. Vietnam protested the agreement because it covers an area where Vietnam's claims feature, too. Half a year later, Vietnam reluctantly joined the agreement on 14 March 2005 after negotiations with the Philippine Department of Foreign Affairs.[44] As Vietnam joined, the bilateral agreement was replaced by the trilateral 'A Tripartite Agreement for Joint Marine Seismic Undertaking in the Agreement Area in the South China Sea' (JMSU).[45] Map 2 shows the geographic location of the JMSU.

Manila did not consult ASEAN members before the 2004 agreement, and they were surprised by the Philippine decision to enter into a bilateral agreement with China. The Philippines called for a concerted ASEAN approach and a regional code of conduct after China built installations on the low-tide feature Mischief Reef, which is located on the Philippine continental shelf, in 1995.[46] Then, the Philippines was the first to reach a bilateral agreement with China. At the same time, the agreement was concluded two years after the 2002 Declaration on Conduct called for bilateral or multilateral 'cooperative activities' (paragraph 6 of the Declaration).[47] Former Philippine President Arroyo regarded the JMSU as the first agreement implementing the 2002 Declaration on Conduct.[48] The Philippines let the agreement expire in accordance with the agreement in 2008 after several allegations discredited the agreement. A few joint seismic surveys were undertaken under the agreement. This situation leads to two questions: Why did the Philippines accept the agreement in the first place? Why did the Philippines allow it to expire?

The Philippine top leadership was determined in 2004 and 2005 to sidestep reluctant officials from the Department of Foreign Affairs (DFA) and to enter

43 Available at https://www.spratlys.org/documents/agreement_bilateral_marine_seismic_undertaking.pdf (last accessed 24 April 2024).

44 Interviews with a former minister of the administration of President Arroyo, held in Manila on 2 December 2016 (Interview 7).

45 A copy of the agreement is available at https://maritimeindex.org/wp-content/uploads/2021/12/VN-China-Philippines-tripartite-agreement-adopted-from-nghiencuubiendong.pdf (last accessed 24 April 2024).

46 Chapter V 1.

47 ASEAN Member States and People's Republic of China, 'Declaration on the Conduct of Parties in the South China Sea', 4 November 2002.

48 Radio Free Asia, 'China, Philippines, Vietnam Sign Joint South China Sea Oil Search Accord', *Radio Free Asia*, 14 March 2005, https://www.rfa.org/english/news/business/china_vietnam_spratlys-20050314.html. (last accessed 23 June 2023).

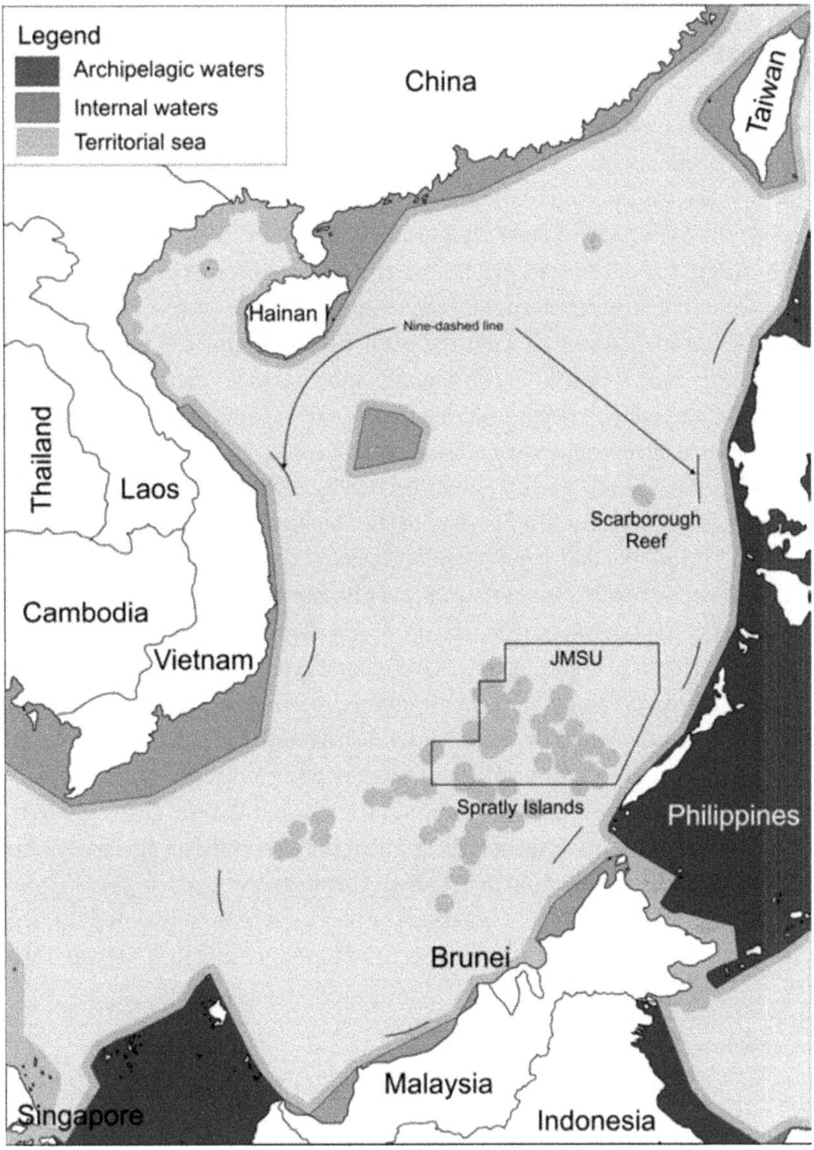

Map 2 The Joint Marine Seismic Undertaking (JMSU)[49]

into the agreement. Former President Arroyo overruled the officials' concerns with a strong portion of political will. The 2004 and 2005 agreements were

49 Map prepared by Andi Arsana and Clive Schofield, in Ben Milligan, 'Legal and Policy Options for the Provisional Joint Management of Maritime Spaces Subject to Overlapping Jurisdictional Claims' (PhD Thesis, University of Wollongong, 2012). Reproduced with permission.

negotiated solely by the president of the Philippine National Oil Company (PNOC) Eduardo Mañalac. Mañalac negotiated the agreement directly with representatives of China National Offshore Oil Company (CNOOC), sidestepping the responsible Philippine officials from the DFA and Department of Energy.[50] I am not aware at which point the Secretary of Foreign Affairs was able to voice the opinion of the DFA's officials about the agreement. But the Philippine Secretary of Foreign Affairs Delia Albert resigned from office on 18 August 2004, two weeks before the agreement was concluded. The new secretary, Alberto Romulo, considered to pursue a pro-China foreign policy, entered office on 23 August 2004. Mañalac signed the agreement on 1 September 2004.[51] Only after the 2004 agreement was reached, the Philippine DFA was charged with negotiating Vietnam's participation and with replacing the bilateral agreement with a trilateral one in 2005. Mañalac could not have negotiated such an agreement on his own terms. He had the support of President Arroyo and the Speaker of the House of Representatives Jose de Venecia.[52] Mañalac had strong connections to the Chinese energy industry and de Venecia to the Communist Party of China.[53] De Venecia was a long-time supporter of joint development, and proposed already in 1988 a motion in the Philippine House of Representatives in favour of a joint development model.[54] President Arroyo and de Venecia attended the ceremonial signature of the JMSU which was signed by the presidents of PNOC (Mañalac), CNOOC (Fu Chengyu), and the Vietnam Oil and Gas Corporation (Tran Ngoc Canh).[55] The Philippine top leadership wanted progress in bilateral relations with China despite the concerns of the DFA, and they believed an agreement for joint seismic research would bring about this progress.

The text of the agreement expresses the parties' intention to downplay the involvement of states in the agreement and to reduce any link between the

50 Interview 7.

51 Aileen Baviera, 'The Influence of Domestic Politics on Philippine Foreign Policy: The Case of Philippines-China Relations since 2004', *RSIS Working Paper* 241 (2012): 1–36.

52 Interview 7.

53 Mañalac has had a professional background in the energy industry in mainland China and contributed to the discovery of China's largest offshore oil field in 2000. He received China's Friendship Award. Baviera, 'The Influence of Domestic Politics', 14–17.

54 Hurng-Yu Chen, 'The Prospects for Joint Development in the South China Sea', *Issues and Studies* 27, no. 12, (1991): 112–25, 115.

55 For photographic evidence of the ceremony, Embassy of the People's Republic of China in the Philippines, 'Oil Companies of China, the Philippines and Vietnam signed Agreement on South China Sea Cooperation', 15 March 2005, http://ph.china-embassy.gov.cn/eng/zt/nhwt/200503/t20050315_1334600.htm#:~:text=On%2014%20March%202005%2C%20representatives,South%20China%20Sea%20in%20Manila (last accessed 23 June 2023).

agreement and the competing claims. The signatories of the agreement are the national oil companies, not the states, giving the agreement ostensibly a corporate rather than international legal character. The substantive activity the JMSU provides for is joint 'Seismic Work' (article 4) in an area of 142,886 square kilometres (article 2). This geographic area encompasses the Reed Bank as well as a part of the Spratly Islands. The scope of the agreement is limited to joint seismic research. The preamble establishes that the national oil companies act 'under the authorization' of their respective governments, that they have the 'exclusive right' to sign the agreement, and that the 'Parties' respective governments have expressed their commitment to pursue peaceful efforts to transform the South China Sea into an area of peace.' Paragraph 6 of article 11 requires the respective governments' approval for the agreement to enter into force. At the signing ceremony of the agreement, former President Arroyo, the Philippines House Speaker Jose De Venecia, Secretary of Energy Vicente Perez, Under Secretary of Foreign Affairs Sonia Brady of the Philippines, Chinese Ambassador Wu Hongbo, and Vietnamese Ambassador Dinh Tich were present.[56]

UNCLOS does not require a specific form or content for provisional arrangements.[57] The JMSU can be understood as an international provisional agreement whereby national companies are authorized by their respective governments. In addition to downplaying states' role in the agreement, an additional safeguard in the preamble excludes prejudice: The 'Parties recognize that the signing of this Agreement shall not undermine the basic position held by the Government of each Party on the South China Sea issue.' The text of the agreement was to be kept confidential (article 10), implying that the exact agreement area was not revealed at the time (see Map 2). The parties did not conceal the fact that the agreement was signed or its content, as will be discussed.

The downfall of the JMSU

On the day the trilateral JMSU was signed, 14 March 2005, international media quoted former Philippine President Arroyo. She hailed the agreement as a 'breakthrough for peace and stability', a 'historic event' and for being the

56 Embassy of the People's Republic of China in the Philippines, 'Oil Companies of China, the Philippines and Vietnam signed Agreement on South China Sea Cooperation', 15 Mach 2005.
57 British Institute of International and Comparative Law, ed., *Report on the Obligations of States under Articles 74(3) and 83(3) of UNCLOS in Respect of Undelimited Maritime Areas* (British Institute of International and Comparative Law, 2016), para 50.

first agreement implementing the 2002 Declaration on Conduct.[58] The assessment of, on the one hand, Arroyo and her advisors, and, on the other hand, the Philippine bureaucracy was diametrically opposed. The latter considered the arrangement inconsistent with the Philippine approach to the 2002 Declaration on Conduct.[59] Three years later, from 2008 onwards, the JMSU was attacked for being 'unconstitutional',[60] a 'sell-out'[61] of the Philippines, the result of a 'tale of secrecy',[62] and for having given 'legitimacy'[63] to China's claims. In response to these charges, the Philippines let the JMSU expire in 2008. This illustrates the utility of the option of terminating an agreement unilaterally as a safeguard against unforeseen developments. Territorial or boundary agreements do not normally have unilateral termination clauses.

I will discuss the four critiques of secrecy, unconstitutionality, selling-out, and legitimation of China's claim in turn. Although the negotiations leading to the agreement and its text remained secret in 2005, the fact that an agreement was signed between the national oil companies of China, the Philippines, and Vietnam in the presence of President Arroyo was made public on the day of signature.[64] One day after the signature of the agreement, China's Embassy in Manila published a 'Joint Statement issued by the three companies: CNOOC/ PETROVIETNAM/ PNOC' on 'the Signing of a Tripartite Agreement for Joint Marine Seismic Undertaking in The Agreement Area in the South China Sea'. It said that the agreement was for 'joint marine seismic' research in the South China Sea in an area of '143,000 square km', and that it 'will not undermine the basic positions held by their respective Governments on the South China Sea issue'.[65]

58 Radio Free Asia, 'China, Philippines, Vietnam Sign Joint South China Sea Oil Search Accord'.
59 Baviera, 'The Influence of Domestic Politics', 15.
60 Neri Javier Colmenares, 'Spratlys Deal Unconstitutional: Joint Marine Seismic Undertaking Void', *GMA News*, 17 March 2008, https://www.gmanetwork.com/news/topstories/specialreports/85173/spratlys-deal-unconstitutional-joint-marine-seismic-undertaking-void/story/ (last accessed 23 June 2023).
61 Mark Valencia, quoted in Barry Wain, 'Manila's Bungle in The South China Sea', *Far Eastern Economic Review*, February 2008, http://realpolitikasia.blogspot.com/2016/08/manilas-bungle-in-south-china-sea-barry.html; Philippine Center for Investigative Journalism, 'The Spratlys deal: Selling out Philippine sovereignty?' PCIJ Blog, 17 March 2008, https://old.pcij.org/blog/2008/03/17/the-spratlys-deal-selling-philippine-sovereignty (last accessed 23 June 2023).
62 Ernst Bower, 'The JMSU: A Tale of Bilateralism and Secrecy in the South China Sea', *CSIS Analysis*, July 2010, https://www.csis.org/analysis/jmsu-tale-bilateralism-and-secrecy-south-china-sea (last accessed 23 June 2023).
63 Barry Wain, 'Manila's Bungle in The South China Sea'.
64 Radio Free Asia, 'China, Philippines, Vietnam Sign Joint South China Sea Oil Search Accord'.
65 Embassy of the People's Republic of China in Manila, 'Oil Companies of China, the Philippines and Vietnam signed Agreement on South China Sea Cooperation', 15 March 2005.

The Embassy's press release also shows President Arroyo shaking hands with CNOOC representatives. To any Philippine or international observer with an interest in the South China Sea, it must have been clear already on 14 March 2005, at the latest on 15 March 2005, that the three countries had come to a provisional arrangement on oil or gas for disputed areas of the South China Sea. The agreement came under attack for 'secrecy' only three years *after* its signature was *made public*.

The charge of unconstitutionality had been pending with the Philippine Supreme Court since 2008. Various domestic Philippine actors repeatedly called for a decision.[66] Some lawyers criticised only the lack of Senate approval for the arrangement as unconstitutional and did not regard the agreement as unconstitutional per se.[67] They failed to note and to explain why the Senate did not act in 2005. Any Philippine senator with an interest in the South China Sea disputes must have noted from reading the news that PNOC concluded an oil deal with China. The Philippine Senate appears not to have been concerned with giving its approval in 2005. Other lawyers deemed the whole agreement unconstitutional. They argued with reference to article XII, section 2 of the Philippine constitution that joint development requires a 60 per cent Philippine ownership of natural resources.[68] The JMSU, though, did not contain a clause about the ownership or exploitation of natural resources. Justice Antonio Carpio, a former judge of the Supreme Court, has advocated against joint development agreements for political and legal reasons, but did not comment on the constitutionality of the agreement.[69] Fifteen years later, in 2023, the Supreme Court declared the JMSU unconstitutional because the JMSU 'illegally compromised the control and supervision of the State over [the] information' that was generated by the joint exploration activities.[70]

66 Colmenares, 'Spratlys deal unconstitutional: Joint Marine Seismic Undertaking void'; Edu Punay, 'SC Asked to Rule on Legality of JMSU', *Philstar*, May 2014, https://www.philstar.com/headlines/2014/05/30/1329017/sc-asked-rule-legality-jmsu (last accessed 23 June 2023).

67 PCIJ, 'The Spratlys Deal Selling Out Philippine Sovereignty?'.

68 Manuel Laserna, 'West Philippine Sea: Unconstitutional and Much-Abused Concept of "joint Development"', *Attylaserna*, July 2017, https://attylaserna.blogspot.com/2017/07/west-philippine-sea-unconstitutional.html. (last accessed 23 June 2023).

69 Interview with Supreme Court Justice Antonio Carpio, Manila, 29 November 2016 (Interview 5). Also see Antonio Carpio, 'The Rule of Law in the West Philippine Sea Dispute', *Speech Delivered before the Philippine Bar Association*, 29 August 2013, https://www.imoa.ph/speech-the-rule-of-law-in-the-west-philippine-sea-dispute/ (last accessed 23 March 2022).

70 Supreme Court of the Philippines, *Bayan Muna Party-List vs President Macapal-Arroyo*, G.R. No. 182734, 10 January 2023. The Supreme Court also noted the absence of Presidential authorisation for the agreement. https://sc.judiciary.gov.

The third critique linked the agreement's origin to the concurrent decision to accept Chinese loans for infrastructure, especially a national broadband network. The JMSU was attacked in the context of several corruption and electoral scandals in 2008. Critics of Arroyo's conciliatory approach towards maritime disputes with China and the JMSU involved the agreement in the scandals. The critique of the pro-China approach and the JMSU became part of the anti-Arroyo campaign in the following Presidential campaign of Aquino. Baviera has noted on this point that 'suspicion of a sell-out of Philippine territorial integrity in exchange for sweetened business deals... might have been avoided if the regular institutional channels for decision-making on such a critical issue as territorial claims had been honoured'.[71]

The fourth critique was that the JMSU legitimised China's claim. For the JMSU to represent a 'sell-out' of Philippine sovereignty, it needed to affect the Philippine position in the disputes. The text of the agreement itself reflects the negotiators' attempt to reduce the possibility of making a connection between the agreement and the states' claims. Corporations rather than governments are signatories, and prejudice to claims is explicitly excluded. The legal analysis of the agreement and of the question of prejudice implies that the JMSU did not affect claims *de jure*. Nevertheless, President Aquino's spokesperson Lacierda led the charge in 2011, arguing that 'China started claiming the Reed Bank... only after the JMSU was signed' and that 'the JMSU provided them [China] an opening for that [claiming the Reed Bank]'.[72]

In which way was the JMSU to be detrimental to the Philippines, and did it 'create' China's claim? The geographic scope of the agreement covered parts of China's nine-dash line (Map 2). Both China and Vietnam claimed sovereignty over the part of the Spratly Islands covered by the agreement before the agreement was signed. China has had an ambiguous claim to waters around the islands before the JMSU, too. Although China claimed the nine-dash line before 2009, the claim was published in an official international document only in 2009.[73] Maňalac, who negotiated the

ph/182734-bayan-muna-party-list-representative-satur-c-ocampo-and-teodoro-a-casino-anakpawis-representative-crispin-b-beltran-gabriela-womens-party-representatives-liza-l-maza-and-luzviminda-c-i/ (accessed 23 August 2023).

71 Baviera, 'The Influence of Domestic Politics', 17 has details on the telecommunication deal and corruption allegations.

72 'JMSU Gave China the Opening to Claim Reed Bank, Says Lacierda', *Gmanetwork*, July 2011, https://www.gmanetwork.com/news/topstories/nation/225527/jmsu-gave-china-the-opening-to-claim-reed-bank-says-lacierda/story/ (last accessed 24 April 2024).

73 'Note Verbale Of the People's Republic of China' (CML/17/2009, 7 May 2009), http://www.un.org/depts/los/clcs_new/submissions_files/mysvnm33_09/chn_2009re_mys_vnm_e.pdf (last accessed 24 April 2024).

JMSU, admitted that the JMSU gave too much to China but insisted that it was in the Philippines' interest. 'The real question, however, is what's our national interest? If there's no joint development, nobody will come to help us develop it. We don't have the money to explore it ourselves. ... Who else will come if China claims it?'[74] The accusation that the JMSU compromised Philippine sovereignty in return for investments essentially claimed that the JMSU resulted in a Philippine vulnerability that China could leverage to its advantage. An agreement of limited scope that started as a 'breakthrough' and a 'historic event' became derided as the agreement that produced China's claim to Philippine waters. The reason why the agreement was detrimental to the Philippines in the view of Philippine officials and observers was that it gave prominence to China's claim and hence established a practical precedent for future interactions. This practical precedent, however, is not a legal precedent, which is excluded in the agreement. China achieved with the JMSU 'the recognition that China has some kind of interest or right in the area. There is a lack of reciprocity because the area is entirely within the Philippines' area. Because of this experience, there is a negative political reaction.'[75] An official from the Philippine DFA held a similar view on the JMSU: 'But what if there is a questionable claim in the first place? Then there is the recognition that this area is disputed. It was not clear that the Reed Bank is disputed. So, why are we legitimising the nine-dash line even before China submitted it formally to the UN?'[76]

1.2 Resource Sharing after the JMSU: Philippine Law vs Joint Jurisdiction

Chinese officials offered a revival of the JMSU on two occasions in 2011 and 2012 despite the Philippine experience and although the JMSU was challenged before the Philippine Supreme Court.[77] In March 2011 and after

74 Quoted in: International Crisis Group, 'Stirring up the South China Sea (IV)', 19.

75 Interview with a professor of international law at the University of the Philippines, Manila, 22 November 2016 (Interview 4).

76 Interview with a senior official of the Philippine Foreign Service Institute, Manila, 07 December 2016 (Interview 10).

77 *Memorandum* from Assistant Secretary, Asian and Pacific Affairs, Department of Foreign Affairs of the Republic of the Philippines, to Secretary of Foreign Affairs of the Republic of the Philippines (7 February 2011) (Annex 68), Vol IV; *Memorandum* from the Embassy of the Republic of the Philippines in Beijing to the Secretary of Foreign Affairs of the Republic of the Philippines, No. ZPE-064-2011-S (21 June 2011) (Annex 72), Vol IV, https://files.pca-cpa.org/pcadocs/The%20Philippines%27%20Memorial%20-%20Volume%20IV%20%28Annexes%2061-102%29.pdf (last accessed 24 April 2024).

repeated incidents related to seismic research and fisheries, Ning Fukui, the Director-General of the Ocean and Boundary Affairs Department of China's Ministry of Foreign Affairs, repeated China's proposals and offered his Philippine counterpart Henry Bensurto the establishment of a working group on maritime issues, joint development, and fisheries. According to Bensurto's confidential memorandum, he recommended that China's proposal for a working group be accepted. Bensurto suggested that his own idea for an 'initiative of Zone of Peace, Freedom, Friendship, and Cooperation (ZoPFFaC)' be introduced into this working group, too.[78]

Bensurto proposed the approach of distinguishing between 'areas under dispute' and 'areas not in dispute' and to examine the legal basis for claims to maritime zones.[79] In 1997, Undersecretary Severino had already advocated a similar approach for Scarborough Shoal.[80] Bensurto's proposal became then the official Philippine position. This memorandum contains all the pieces that, set together, explain the Philippine position not to accept any of China's proposals on joint development or a (however minimal) understanding for fisheries.[81] Bensurto's approach would narrow down the disputes by two steps. First, it distinguished between territorial disputes over islands (Spratly and Paracel Islands) and claims to maritime zones. Second, it applied article 121 of UNCLOS (Regime of Islands) to the disputed islands. In the Philippine view, the Spratly Islands do not qualify as islands, but as rocks – generating merely a 12-nautical-mile territorial sea – or as low-tide elevations that cannot be claimed as territory. The eastern low-tide elevations of the Spratly Islands would then be located on the continental shelf of the Philippines. Accordingly, Bensurto maintained that 'the waters (and continental shelves) beyond the disputed islands (except those adjacent to the islands) are and ought to be not in dispute'.[82] 'Not in dispute' means that these waters are part of the Philippine EEZ because the Philippines is the

78 *Memorandum* from Secretary General, Commission on Maritime and Ocean Affairs Secretariat, Department of Foreign Affairs of the Republic of the Philippines to the Secretary of Foreign Affairs of the Republic of the Philippines (28 March 2011) (Annex 71), Vol IV.

79 Ibid.

80 Department of Foreign Affairs of the Republic of the Philippines, Press Release No. 69: RP, PRC To Convene Working Group for Talks on South China Sea (28 May 1997) (Annex 26), Vol III https://files.pca-cpa.org/pcadocs/The%20Philippines%27%20Memorial%20-%20Volume%20III%20%28Annexes%201-60%29.pdf (last accessed 24 April 2024).

81 Chapter III 1.5.

82 *Memorandum* from Secretary General, Commission on Maritime and Ocean Affairs Secretariat, Department of Foreign Affairs of the Republic of the Philippines to the Secretary of Foreign Affairs of the Republic of the Philippines (28 March 2011) (Annex 71), Vol IV.

only country that could possibly claim them from its mainland. The South China Sea Arbitration followed this argumentation in its decision in 2016.

The Philippine unwillingness to agree to provisional rules follows from a specification of its claim and the refusal to accept any proposal that could be interpreted as being detrimental to the Philippine claim. The Philippines was willing to accept joint development in what it defines as 'areas under dispute.' As China disagreed with the Philippine definition of which areas are 'under dispute', no agreement was possible. The political implication of this legal interpretation manifests itself in Bensurto's conversation with his counterpart Ning. Ning warned that 'if [Philippine unilateral exploration at the Reed Bank] happens, China will have reason to do *exploration* as well *on areas it deems as its own*. Joint development is the best and most practical way to approach the issue.'[83] Bensurto stuck to his interpretation of the law of the sea and replied: The Reed Bank is 'part of the continental shelf of Palawan. PH, in the context of friendly relations with China, is open to Chinese investment in the Reed Bank under *PH laws*.'[84] Ning also urged Bensurto not to file a protest note against China's publication of the nine-dash line in 2009, as this publication 'was *not* directed *against* the Philippines but was something that it had to do in *reaction* to the submission by Vietnam and Malaysia for extended continental shelf'.[85] This request was unacceptable for a similar reason. Bensurto argued that the Philippines had 'no choice but to express its position on the nine-dash line claim of China. To do otherwise, could be *misinterpreted* as *acquiescence*.'[86]

The Philippine officials in 2012 followed this strict interpretation of the Philippines' claim in response to all Chinese offers on joint development agreements. Special Assistant Bensurto and Assistant Secretary Asuque reported in a secret memorandum to the Secretary of Foreign Affairs on a meeting with Deng Zhonghua, Director of the Department of Boundary and Ocean Affairs of China, and Yang Li, the Deputy Director. Bensurto and Asuque explained the Philippine position on joint development agreements in the Reed Bank:

> The abovesigned [Bensurto and Asuque] indicated that joint development would only be proper in an area that is legitimately disputed. Reed Bank is *not a disputed area*. Therefore, the Philippines would *not* be *amenable* to a

83 Ibid., emphasis in the original.
84 Ibid., emphasis in the original.
85 Ibid., emphasis in the original.
86 Ibid., emphasis in the original.

> *joint development* in the Reed Bank area. The Philippines is, however, *open* to *Chinese investment* in the area *under Philippine law.* China's counter-proposal on Reed Bank: Deng indicated that the Philippine proposal would not be acceptable to China because it involves the surrender of China's sovereignty over the Reed Bank.[87]

According to the Philippine view, China had no valid legal claim to the Reed Bank; hence it is 'not a disputed area.' As joint development is predicated on the existence of two equally valid overlapping claims – 'an area under dispute', according to the Philippines – joint development is not an option and Chinese investments have to comply with Philippine law. In China's perspective, accepting the Philippine proposal amounted to recognizing the Philippines' jurisdiction over the Reed Bank; this would have been tantamount to China dropping its claim to the Reed Bank.

The proposals that followed make sense if both sides believe that a joint development agreement under the terms proposed by the respective counterpart would recognize the respective opponent's claim and establish a practically meaningful precedent. Deng understood the Philippine rejection of an agreement for areas Manila considered 'not in dispute'. Deng proposed a non-governmental arrangement to sidestep the question of Philippine jurisdiction:

> Deng instead proposed the following *modality* for consideration by the Philippines: *To let the two private companies of the two countries to negotiate and come to terms among themselves and make separate reports to their governments. Under this scheme, either of the two governments should not take any unilateral action to the detriment of the other.*[88]

To what extent this proposal differs from the JMSU is unclear as the latter had an international legal character. In reply, Bensurto and Asuque reiterated their position of having exclusive jurisdiction over this area and that they did not accept the validity of any rules other than Philippine jurisdiction. In their view, the Philippines had the right to demand that Chinese companies act under Philippine license. They also understood the consequences of demanding Chinese participation under Philippine

87 *Memorandum* from Gilberto G.B. Asuque & Henry B. Bensurto, Jr., Department of Foreign Affairs of the Republic of the Philippines, to the Secretary of Foreign Affairs of the Republic of the Philippines (23 March 2012) (Annex 76), Vol IV, emphasis in the original.
88 Ibid., emphasis in the original.

law, namely that this implied some Chinese recognition of the Philippine claim. Bensurto suggested options for how China could re-structure their state-owned companies such as to sidestep the concern about recognizing the Philippine claim:

> *OPTION #1.* For China to de-link Reed Bank from the Spratlys as they exactly are under international law. Accordingly, participation by China as investor in the Reed Bank under PH law would not compromise China's political position for claim of sovereignty in the land features of 'Nansha.'[89]

'De-linking' the Reed Bank from the Spratly Islands, however, would imply that China accepts that it has no legal claim to the Reed Bank.

> *OPTION#2.* Separate the legal personality of the Chinese National Offshore Oil Company (CNOOC) from the political legal personality of the Chinese National Government. In such a case, an investment by CNOOC either as 100% equity owner or as an investor partner with another company under license from the PH government would not compromise the political sovereign position of China's political government because of the distinct personality of the CNOOC from that of the government. As an additional measure, the Chinese government can also issue a Note Verbale to the Philippine Government to the effect that CNOOC's investment in the Reed Bank should not be interpreted as surrender of China's claim.[90]

This second proposal aimed at circumventing the problem that joint development would be perceived as entailing a de facto recognition of claims. The idea that a suitable company structure could circumvent this problem, however, was overly optimistic.

> *OPTION #3.* China and CNOOC can create a Third Company which will do the investing in Reed Bank under PH law. The distinct and separate personality of such Third Company would not compromise the political position of the political government.[91]

Philippine top-level officials believed that entering into a joint development agreement would result in a pre-decision about the status of an area and

89 Ibid., emphasis in the original.
90 Ibid.
91 Ibid.

would validate China's claim. Their Chinese counterparts believed that the institutional arrangements proposed by the Philippines would entail a pre-decision that an area is *not* disputed, hence invalidating China's own claim. Both were aware of these concerns and tried to alleviate them with the quoted proposals. China could not accept proposals to participate under Philippine law because accepting them would imply they acquiesced in the Philippines' exclusive jurisdiction in the area. The Philippines was unable to accept China's proposals on various formulas for resource sharing because accepting them would imply an acknowledgment that China had a legally valid claim. Philippine lawyers have defended this position consistently. For them, joint development is not possible in a 'completely arbitrary area without overlapping legitimate claims'.[92] To some extent, Chinese and Philippine officials appeared to understand their respective counterparts' reluctance because both prepared proposals to overcome their reluctance. Philippine officials recommended a procedure to diffuse China's concern about recognizing the Philippine claim if China were to act under Philippine law. Bensurto argued that 'the ZPFFC concept will not have negative implications on Philippine sovereignty and future energy contracts in the area, while satisfying China's quest to pursue cooperation in the SCS'.[93] Chinese officials recommended modalities such as to diffuse the Philippine concern that allowing Chinese activities under common rules would imply a validation of China's claims. But both sides did not have a realistic assessment of the proposals' feasibility.

Records of similar exchanges dominated by similar problems are available. Vice-Foreign Minister Zhang Zhijun suggested to de-link the question of jurisdiction from the practical activities undertaken in disputed areas: 'On the government level, we can say all this cooperation is conducted according to each other's law but when it comes to specifics, it is actions of businesses.'[94] The rationale behind this proposal appears to be to circumvent the issue of joint jurisdiction by only non-state actors (referred to as 'businesses') engaging in activities. The problem of this offer is that Zhang proposed that China's jurisdiction should exist alongside Philippine jurisdiction ('each other's law'). This formula for jurisdiction was not acceptable to the Philippines in the context of fisheries because then Manila would accept

92 Interview with Supreme Court Justice Antonio Carpio, Manila, 29 November 2016 (interview 5).

93 *Memorandum* from Acting Assistant Secretary of the Department of Foreign Affairs of the Republic of the Philippines to the Secretary of Foreign Affairs (10 March 2011) (Annex 70), Vol IV.

94 *Record of Discussion: 17th Philippines-China Foreign Ministry Consultations* (14 January 2012) (Annex 204), Vol VI.

that China's regulations apply to Chinese nationals. In an interesting role reversal, Philippine embassy officials in Beijing assumed that 'China may also be hesitant to start bilateral talks on issues besides sovereignty, as it does not trust us not to slip in the sovereignty issues at the talks'.[95] It appears the authors of this memorandum were unfamiliar with the negotiations at the higher level six months earlier. There, it was the Philippines that feared China could leverage a joint development agreement harming the Philippines.

The exchanges illustrate that the Philippines did not oppose resource sharing with China per se even if Philippine officials regarded Chinese claims as invalid. The exchanges also illustrate that the question of how both would divide energy resources in an eventual arrangement did not feature prominently. Bensurto's proposals foresaw that Chinese energy corporations would participate in Philippine energy projects under the condition of China's acceptance that such projects take place under Philippine law. China rejected this as a surrender of their claims. Philippine officials rejected the joint development proposals of Chinese officials. They maintained that Manila would validate China's claim if the Philippines accepted joint development under Sino-Philippine jurisdiction. Both sides were chiefly worried that resource sharing on the opponent's terms would improve the opponent's bargaining position. The failure to find an agreement structure that reconciled these two basic positions on resource sharing was the major obstacle preventing any practical arrangement on hydrocarbon resources. As the following will illustrate, the arbitral award did not reconcile the competing positions regarding oil and gas arrangements.

1.3 Joint Development after the South China Sea Arbitration?

On 12 July 2016, the South China Sea Arbitration ruled that China was not entitled to claim maritime zones beyond the normal zones. Rights based on historic practices ('historic rights') had been extinguished in the EEZ.[96] None of the features of the Spratly Islands represented an island in the meaning of article 121 of UNCLOS, and China could not claim the Spratly Islands as a group of islands.[97] The award effectively invalidated a good part of China's claims to the Philippine EEZ and continental shelf. Surprisingly,

95 *Memorandum* from the Embassy of the Republic of the Philippines in Beijing to the Secretary of Foreign Affairs of the Republic of the Philippines, No. ZPE-110-2012-S (26 July 2012) (Annex 84), Vol IV.

96 The South China Sea Arbitration, Award, 12 June 2016, para 247.

97 Ibid., part VI.

the Philippines responded very cautiously to the award ('the Philippines [will] study the award') and did not even demand that China implemented the arbitral tribunal's ruling in 2016.[98] Only in 2020 did the Philippines state that the South China Sea Arbitration 'conclusively settled the issue of historic rights and entitlements in the South China Sea'.[99] One reason for Manila's initial reluctance was arguably that the Philippines did not prepare a plan for how the legal victory could be implemented in concert with international support for the ruling.[100] Right after the award, there was no ASEAN statement, no joint statement of Southeast Asian claimant states, and no joint statement of the Philippines with other partners to support the award. Moreover, the new Philippine administration of Duterte was preoccupied with the internal transition process, and the award caught the transiting Philippine administration by surprise. Two further reasons for the reluctant reaction may be found in Duterte's priority of establishing closer relations with China and in a hedging strategy that sought to minimise risks of confrontation in the post-arbitration context.[101]

Different expectations about the impact of the arbitral award on Sino-Philippine interactions about joint development appear possible at first glance. First, as the arbitral tribunal confirmed the Philippines' view that China is not entitled to claim maritime rights beyond the normal zones, the Philippines under Duterte might have continued the Aquino administration's position to accept joint projects only under the premise of Philippine jurisdiction. Pursuant to the South China Sea Arbitration, the Philippines is under no obligations to negotiate joint development (or joint fisheries) agreements with China.[102] In contrast to this expectation, the new administration under President Duterte had an ambiguous stance on whether Manila would insist on resource sharing under Philippine law or accept joint development under Sino-Philippine jurisdiction. The second possible expectation could have been that the tribunal's decision facilitated an understanding on joint resource projects. The award created the expectation in Manila that China

98 Statement of the Department of Foreign Affairs of the Philippines, 12 July 2016.

99 Permanent Mission of the Philippines to the United Nations, 'Notes Verbales 000191-2020', 6 March 2020.

100 Interviews 4, 5, and 7.

101 Lowell Bautista, 'The South China Sea Arbitral Award: Evolving Post-Arbitration Strategies, Implications and Challenges', *Asian Politics & Policy* 10, no. 2 (2018): 178–89; see the articles in this special volume of *Asian Politics & Policy*.

102 Christian Schultheiss, 'Joint Development of Hydrocarbon Resources in the South China Sea After the Philippines Versus China Arbitration?', *Ocean Development & International Law* 51, no. 3 (3 August 2020): 241–62. Even if the Philippines is under no obligation to negotiate with China, joint development or exploration would still not prejudice the Philippines' claim *de jure*.

had to offer something, and Duterte tried to maximise concessions from China in post-arbitration negotiations. Moreover, the tribunal's decision brought about strong third-party confirmation of the Philippine claim. This line of reasoning suggests that both Manila's leverage and bargaining range on practical cooperative arrangements increased because of the legal protection the award lent to the Philippine claims. However, despite some reports that a Sino-Philippine arrangement is imminent, no agreement has materialized.

The Philippines has resumed negotiations with China on joint exploration in geographical areas to which China is not entitled according to the ruling.[103] Some media reports citing Philippine sources suggest that the focus of the negotiations is on a company-level arrangement under Philippine jurisdiction.[104] Other media reports, citing Chinese sources, suggest that China has insisted on arrangements under joint jurisdiction.[105] Notwithstanding this central jurisdictional issue, Duterte encouraged talks on joint exploration with China, arguing that joint exploration is better than 'armed conflict'.[106] This position, however, produced a substantial backlash in the Philippines. Critics of joint development agreements opposed Duterte's plans with arguments that were also used against the JMSU in the late 2000s, namely that such agreements would validate China's claims. In a congressional hearing of 30 May 2018, Philippine Foreign Secretary Cayetano defended joint development, quoting security and economic gains.[107] Philippine lawyers criticised political accommodation and argued that '[g]iven that we have the arbitration ruling on our side, it's really hard

103 Jay Batongbacal, 'Philippine-China Joint Development Talks still at an Impasse despite Green Light', AMTI 13 April 2018, https://amti.csis.org/philippine-china-joint-development-impasse/; Patricia Lourdes Viray, 'What Cayetano Missed in Justifying South China Sea Joint Development', *Philstar*, May 2018, https://www.philstar.com/headlines/2018/05/31/1820359/what-cayetano-missed-justifying-south-china-sea-joint-development (last accessed 23 June 2023).

104 'Duterte to Allow PH Oil Exploration with Chinese, Malaysian Firms: DOE', *ABS-CBN*, 27 September 2017, http://news.abs-cbn.com/business/09/27/17/duterte-to-allow-ph-oil-exploration-with-chinese-malaysian-firms-doe (last accessed 23 June 2023).

105 Willard Cheng, 'China, PH Discussing Joint Dev't in West PH Sea: Envoy', *ABS-CBN*, September 2017, https://news.abs-cbn.com/news/09/27/17/china-ph-discussing-joint-devt-in-west-ph-sea-envoy (last accessed 23 June 2023).

106 Gabriel Pabico Lalu, 'Duterte Told: Joint Exploration with China in West PH Sea Unconstitutional', *Inquirer*, 11 September 2019, https://newsinfo.inquirer.net/1163359/duterte-told-joint-exploration-with-china-in-west-ph-sea-unconstitutional (last accessed 23 June 2023).

107 Viray, 'What Cayetano missed in justifying South China Sea joint development', referring to Jay Batongbacal and Aileen Baviera, 'When Will Conditions Be Ripe? Prospects for Joint Development in the South China Sea', paper presented at *13th Asia-Pacific Roundtable Kuala Lumpur*, 1999.

to think of a way to proceed with this joint development without somehow giving up the arbitration ruling'.[108] Former Supreme Court Justice Carpio argued that joint development would weaken the Philippine position even if legal prejudice was excluded.[109] These concerns assumed that a joint development agreement would strengthen China's bargaining position and imperil the leverage Manila gained from the South China Sea Arbitration. 'The accommodation of joint exploration and development in the West Philippine Sea—under the premise that its status is still "disputed" rather than "settled"—is a step backward from the tribunal award's vindication of the Philippines' exclusive economic zone and continental shelf.'[110]

Despite these concerns, China and Philippines signed a memorandum of understanding that established two working groups for government- and company-level negotiations on oil and gas cooperation on 22 November 2018.[111] The MoU provides for further specific exchanges on oil and gas and does not establish a resource-sharing arrangement. Despite further Sino-Philippine negotiations in 2019 and suggestions that a Sino-Philippine company-level arrangement is under way,[112] negotiations have remained at an impasse. In June 2022, the Philippine Foreign Secretary announced the termination of oil and gas negotiations with China.[113] Negotiations in the shadow of the South China Sea Arbitration did not result in China or the Philippines altering their irreconcilable preferences regarding the exact terms of a resource-sharing agreement – a company-level arrangement under Philippine jurisdiction or a joint development arrangement under Sino-Philippine jurisdiction. This impasse also blocked agreement during the Aquino-period consultations. The JMSU of 2005 did not overcome this impasse either, even if the negotiators tried to give it an ostensibly ambiguous character between a company-level

108 Ibid.

109 Interview 5.

110 Viray, 'What Cayetano missed in justifying South China Sea joint development'.

111 Pia Ranada, 'Document: Oil, Gas Development Deal between Philippines, China', *Rappler*, 26 November 2018, https://www.rappler.com/nation/memorandum-understanding-philippines-china-oil-gas-development-deal; Senate Opposition leader Senator Antonio Trillanes IV published a draft arrangement, 'Framework Agreement on Joint Maritime Oil and Gas Exploration between China and the Philippines', https://www.philstar.com/headlines/2018/11/20/1870227/china-claims-draft-oil-exploration-deal-have-no-bearing-sovereignty (last accessed 23 June 2023).

112 Renato Cruz De Castro, 'A Philippine-China Deal on Joint Development in the Making?', *AMTI Update*, 3 November 2020, https://amti.csis.org/a-philippine-china-deal-on-joint-development-in-the-making/ (last accessed 23 June 2023).

113 Department of Energy of the Philippines, 'DOE Statement on the Announcement of the Termination of Joint Oil and Gas Negotiations with China', 25 June 2022, https://www.doe.gov.ph/press-releases/doe-statement-announcement-termination-joint-oil-and-gas-negotiations-china (last accessed 23 March 2024).

arrangement and a joint development arrangement under international law. This impasse is not caused by either side opposing resource-sharing per se, or by the problem of agreeing on a division of oil and gas gains. Rather, the impasse results from the problem of agreeing on joint action without strengthening an opponent's bargaining position.

1.4 The Politics of Sino-Philippine Joint Development Reconsidered

Presidents Arroyo and Duterte pursued a South China Sea policy that centred on ameliorating the bilateral relationship with China through cooperation on specific issues prone to escalation – oil and gas exploration activities and fisheries. Arroyo leaned heavily on Philippine individuals with strong business and party connections to China who believed that cooperation with China was the best option for the Philippines. Duterte's policy after the South China Sea Arbitration followed a similar assessment. In their view, lacking realistic alternatives, the Philippines' best option was to define practical measures with China.

The decision of Arroyo and her advisors to enter into the JMSU in 2004 by sidestepping the Department of Foreign Affairs and Department of Energy reflected badly on the Presidency of Arroyo, the JMSU itself, and the approach of seeking practical cooperative agreements with China. Some members of the Aquino administration considered that the JMSU had not only validated and strengthened China's claims, but that the JMSU hardened China's claim to the Reed Bank and empowered its intransigence. The Philippine officials' concern centred on the problem that China's bargaining power had improved from joint exploration in geographic areas close to the Philippines. A particular institution for resource sharing that the Philippine leadership and international media heralded as a 'historic breakthrough' became a Philippine vulnerability and practical precedent supporting China's claims. This experience with the JMSU has informed the consultations between Bensurto and his Chinese counterparts in subsequent years. After the JMSU, the Philippines has insisted on provisional arrangements that imply China's recognition of a superior Philippine claim. All Philippine proposals on joint oil and gas projects have been based on the exclusive jurisdiction of the Philippines. China has insisted, however, on resource sharing based on joint Sino-Philippine jurisdiction. Thus, negotiations have ended in an impasse.

Philippine officials remain concerned about the possibility that the specific geographic area of the JMSU has created a layer of validity for China's claims even after the JMSU expired. The diplomatic record of the Philippines shows that two years after the Philippines let the JMSU expire, Bensurto, Secretary General of CMOAS (Commission on Maritime and Ocean Affairs of the Philippine Department of Foreign Affairs), was still suspicious of Chinese inquiries that could establish a link between the geographic scope of the JMSU and China's claims. According to a confidential memorandum, Chinese Embassy's Deputy Chief of Mission in Manila, Bai Tian, requested clarification on Service Contract 55. Bensurto noted about this request (but did not reply to Tian):

> Based on a map obtained by CMOAS from the Department of Energy, part of the area covered by SC 55 is located within the JMSU area; this is probably why information on SC 55 was specifically requested. China, however, did not make any reference to JMSU during the meeting.[114]

The question arises whether China was able to leverage the JMSU as much as Philippine officials have feared it did. The agreement was only partly implemented and allowed to expire in 2008. The three implementing national oil companies from China, Vietnam, and the Philippines undertook only a few seismic surveys under the agreement. Some projected joint surveys in 2007 had to be postponed to 2008 due to bad weather conditions.[115] The survey data were not generally promising about findings. Only the survey results for the Reed Bank suggested that more seismic research is worthwhile in the Reed Bank. However, these images – CNOOC was responsible for the survey devices – were of bad quality. At an operational level, an advantage China had gained and a disadvantage the Philippines had incurred comes from allegations that CNOOC did not share all data on the Reed Bank or deliberately manipulated them such as to hand over data of bad quality. This led to the suspicion among former Philippine members of government and senior officials that China found prospective gas sites but did not share the data with the Philippines.[116] In other words, Chinese actors

114 *Memorandum* from Rafael E. Seguis, Undersecretary for Special and Ocean Concerns, Department of Foreign Affairs, Republic of the Philippines, to the Secretary of Foreign Affairs of the Republic of the
Philippines (30 July 2010) (Annex 63), Vol IV. Apparently, the office of the Philippine Secretary General of Ocean Affairs did not have a detailed map of the JMSU (see Map 2). A map of the Department of Energy of the Philippines is available in Rino E. Abad, 'Philippine Offshore Oil and Gas Interests in the West Philippine Sea', *4th Roundtable Discussion Philippine Offshore Oil and Gas industry: Prospects for Competition/ Cooperation*, 28 February 2016, https://slideplayer.com/slide/10115380/ (last accessed 25 June 2023).

115 Interview 7.

116 Interviews 4 and 7.

have gained an information advantage from the data CNOOC acquired in implementation of a cooperative arrangement – information Chinese actors could not have acquired unilaterally at all or only at great cost, since any Chinese unilateral seismic research activity in the Reed Bank would have encountered Philippine resistance.

According to a former minister of the Arroyo administration, the information that CNOOC has gained under the JMSU contributed to the hardening of China's claim to the Reed Bank.[117] CNOOC established the commercial potential of some sites, and China would no longer retreat from the claim to the Reed Bank. In line with that, Aquino's spokesperson Lacierda maintained that China started interfering in Philippine seismic research at the Reed Bank only after the JMSU.[118] The Reed Bank has become an area of enhanced Chinese interest after the JMSU and Chinese law enforcement vessels resisted Philippine seismic surveys in the Reed Bank.[119] The Philippine Supreme Court adopted this view in its justification for the unconstitutionality of the JMSU in 2023, even if these interferences also fit a broader pattern of increased Chinese law enforcement activities in the South China Sea.[120] The Supreme Court, citing another case and former Justice Carpio, noted that 'the State cannot allow foreign corporations, except as contractual agents… to explore our natural resources because information derived from such exploration may have national security implications.'[121] Thus, 'PNOC bargained away the State's supposed full control of all the information acquired from the survey.'[122] By making this point, the Supreme Court also defined constitutional constraints for the potential participation of the Philippines in resource-sharing arrangements.

The point that China could improve its bargaining position by obtaining strategically relevant data under a practical cooperative arrangement also played a role in deliberations about joint oceanographic research. While the benevolent objective of joint marine scientific research is to reduce the

117 Interview 7.

118 'JMSU Gave China the Opening to Claim Reed Bank, Says Lacierda', 6 July 2011.

119 Armed Forces of the Philippines, Special Report: The Jackson Atoll and Reed Bank Incident in West Philippine Sea (2011) (Annex 67), Vol IV.

120 Andrew Chubb, 'PRC Assertiveness in the South China Sea: Measuring Continuity and Change, 1970–2015', *International Security* 45, no. 3 (January 2021): 79–121; Christopher D. Yung and Patrick McNulty, 'An Empirical Analysis of Claimant Tactics in the South China Sea', in *Strategic Forum* (National Defense UP, 2015), 1–13.

121 Supreme Court of the Philippines, *Bayan Muna Party-List vs President Macapal-Arroyo*, No. G.R. No. 182734 (10 January 2023), 28–29.

122 Ibid., 30.

lack of data on the marine environment of the South China Sea'[123] and to prevent the escalation of unilateral research activities, the dual use nature of oceanographic knowledge directly connects oceanographic research to the disputes. Knowledge of the topography of the sea, of layers of salinity in the sea, and of underwater currents is essential for submarine operations. Several ASEAN members have believed that joint marine scientific research would allow China to gather strategically relevant data without reciprocation from China.[124] This incentive not to contribute to China gaining strategically relevant data was a barrier to the implementation of the trilateral Sino-Philippine-Vietnamese Joint Oceanographic and Marine Scientific Research Expedition in the South China Sea (JOMSRE) in 2007.[125] China insisted on marine scientific research projects in the most contested central parts of the South China Sea – conducting research in the area from Scarborough Shoal through the Spratly Islands to Vietnam.[126] China, the Philippines, and Vietnam could then not agree on a geographic scope for the joint research activities.

The policy discussion within the Philippines about joint development and exploration is split into two camps. Advocates of joint development such as Arroyo and Duterte have emphasized its economic, political and security benefits – access to resources and the prevention of escalation. Advocates against their use, especially officials from the DFA and lawyers, have argued that if such agreements apply to areas to which China is not entitled, then such agreements compromise the Philippines' negotiating position. The latter cite concepts such as acknowledgment, recognition, validation, precedent, and areas in dispute vs. areas not in dispute. They accept that joint development is without legal prejudice but insist that joint

123 Angel Alcala, 'Environmental Protection in the Spratlys, South China Sea, under the UNCLOS: JOMSRE-SCS III & IV' (2019), https://aseanregionalforum.asean.org/wp-content/uploads/2019/10/Annex-S-Dr.-Alcala-environmental-protection-in-the-Spratlys-SCS.pdf. (last accessed 23 March 2024).

124 Sophie Boisseau du Rocher, 'Scientific Cooperation in the South China Sea. Another Lever for China', *Australian Strategic Policy Institute*, October 2015, https://www.aspi.org.au/report/scientific-cooperation-south-china-sea-another-lever-china (last accessed 23 June 2023).

125 The Philippines-Vietnam Joint Oceanographic and Marine Scientific Research Expedition in the South China Sea was originally a bilateral Philippine-Vietnamese project pursuant to an agreement of December 1995. Four expeditions took place. Vietnam Academy of Science and Technology – Institute of Oceanography, 'Philippines-Vietnam Joint Oceanographic and Marine Scientific Research Expedition in the South China Sea (JOMSRE-SCS), 1996–2007', 24 October 2012, http://www.vnio.org.vn/Home/tabid/107/ctl/Details/mid/579/ItemID/798/language/en-US/Default.aspx (last accessed 23 March 2024).

126 Interview 7.

development agreements weaken the Philippine bargaining position exceeding the legal force of such concepts. Precedent without legal force matters, as parties have feared and in one case experienced that it contributes to the validation and hardening of an opponent's claims. Additionally, China may have also gained an information advantage from the JMSU. The irreconcilable disagreement between Chinese and Philippine negotiators did not turn around the question of how proceeds from oil or gas exploitation should be divided or around a general unwillingness to compromise on energy resources. Philippine officials, including Bensurto, did not reject China's participation in the exploitation of hydrocarbon resources in the Reed Bank per se. They have insisted that such projects must be conducted exclusively under Philippine jurisdiction. The unsurmountable disagreement has been rooted in the inability to define an agreement on natural resources that does not alter the opponents' bargaining power.

1.5 Fisheries in Sino-Philippine Relations: Incidents, Impasse, Scarborough Shoal, and Arbitration

The context

The exchanges on oil and gas arrangements raise the question of how fisheries and fishing incidents have affected Sino-Philippine relations. The presence of Chinese fishermen in waters around the Spratly Islands and Scarborough Shoal has greatly increased over the last decades. There are several structural, economic reasons for the outward movement of Chinese fishing activities.[127] Historically, the majority of Chinese fishing activities occurred in China's coastal waters. Technological change and the change of corporate structures within China made larger ships for distant fishing available. China has become the biggest exporter of fishery products and achieved a high self-sufficiency rate for fishery products.[128] Overfishing appears inevitable if a country with the population of China exports fishery products and supplies its own market.[129] Island building and dredging are likely to decrease larval flow and to exacerbate the

127 Hongzhou Zhang, 'Chinese Fishermen in Disputed Waters: Not Quite a "People's War"', *Marine Policy* 68 (June 2016): 65–73; Daniel Pauly and Cui Liang. 'The Fisheries of the South China Sea: Major Trends since 1950'. *Marine Policy* 121, no. 103584 (November 2020): 1–7.
128 Zhang, 'Chinese Fishermen in Disputed Waters', 69.
129 John W. McManus, 'Offshore Coral Reef Damage, Overfishing, and Paths to Peace in the South China Sea', *The International Journal of Marine and Coastal Law* 32, no. 2 (2017): 199–237; Erica Gies, 'The Consequences of China's Booming Demand for Seafood', *Hakai Magazine*,

'destructive free-for-all race to resources'.[130] The pollution of China's coastal waters reduces their biological productivity further. China has the world's biggest fishing fleet; the availability of fishing fuel subsidies and the huge domestic market makes fishing a profitable business.[131] China's fishing industry ventured further into the sea. In contrast, Philippine fishing practices consist to some degree of small-boat fishing. The reduction of the number of Chinese fishing vessels in the Gulf of Tonkin by 6,000 following the Sino-Vietnamese fisheries agreement has resulted in a relocation of fishing activities, with some fishermen fishing further south in the South China Sea.[132] China's annual fishing moratorium has not applied to areas south of 12 degrees north, and fishing practices in these waters have further increased.

Only approximations regarding the number of Chinese fishing vessels operating around the Spratly Islands are possible. According to Chinese sources, the number of Chinese vessels operating in these waters multiplied from only thirteen in 1985 to 700 in 2013.[133] The number tends to be highest around the features China occupies. Based on data from Visible Infrared Imaging Radiometer Suite (VIIRS) and satellite images, Poling quotes a number of about 300 Chinese vessels fishing around Subi and Mischief Reefs at peak level in August 2018.[134]

Fishing incidents between the Philippine Coast Guard and Navy and Chinese fishermen result from the increased presence of Chinese fishermen in areas claimed by the Philippines. Incidents have become a heavy burden

28 June 2018, https://www.hakaimagazine.com/news/the-consequences-of-chinas-booming-demand-for-seafood/ (last accessed 23 June 2023).

130 Eric Wolanski et al., 'Island Building and Overfishing in the Spratly Islands Archipelago Are Predicted to Decrease Larval Flow and Impact the Whole System', *Estuarine, Coastal and Shelf Science* 233 (February 2020): 106545.

131 Roland Blomeyer et al, *The Role of China in World Fisheries* (European Parliament Study IP/B/PECH/IC/2011-107, 2012), https://www.europarl.europa.eu/meetdocs/2009_2014/documents/pech/dv/chi/china.pdf.

132 See chapter III 2.

133 Hongzhou Zhang and Sam Bateman, 'Fishing Militia, the Securitization of Fishery and the South China Sea Dispute', *Contemporary Southeast Asia*, 2017, 288–314, 292, quoting numbers from the Guangdong Economics Association. Observers regard parts of China's fishing fleet as a maritime militia. Andrew S. Erickson and Conor M. Kennedy, 'Tanmen Militia: China's "Maritime Rights Protection" Vanguard', *The National Interest*, 6 May 2015, https://nationalinterest.org/feature/tanmen-militia-china%E2%80%99s-maritime-rights-protection-vanguard-12816 (last accessed 23 June 2023).

134 Gregory Poling, 'Illuminating the South China Sea's Dark Fishing Fleets', *CSIS AMTI*, 9 January 2019, https://ocean.csis.org/spotlights/illuminating-the-south-china-seas-dark-fishing-fleets/ (last accessed 23 June 2023).

on Sino-Philippine relations in the last three decades. Reports from the Philippine Coast Guard and Navy present photographic evidence of Chinese fishermen engaging in unlawful fishing practices including dynamite or cyanide fishing and harvesting endangered species such as giant clams.[135] These practices have destroyed coral reefs.[136] Chinese fishing operations directly around disputed rocks, shoals, and reefs proved particularly contentious. Fishing incidents initiated escalatory action–reaction cycles when they turned into a contest about which side has superior jurisdiction over an area or sovereignty over a feature.[137] Both sides appear to have acted in the belief that superior law enforcement could be used to support claims to contested zones.

The prevention of incidents and escalation has provided an incentive for exploring some form of fisheries cooperation. A joint fisheries agreement could sidestep claims to territory and maritime rights and replace the clash of competing jurisdictions with common provisional rules without prejudice to claims. China and the Philippines started talks on a fisheries agreement in 1995 and subsequently set up a working group. China's main interest was to get access to fishing grounds Beijing considers historic fishing grounds without interference from the Philippines. The Philippines' main objective was to reduce Chinese fishing activities and to defend its claim to exclusive rights. No formal agreement on fisheries was reached. In contrast, China entered into fisheries agreements with Japan and South Korea in the East China Sea and with Vietnam in the Gulf of Tonkin between 1997 and 2004. These agreements are far from perfect but have ensured that crises like the crisis at Scarborough Shoal in 2012 did not occur within their areas of application. The Philippines signed an agreement on fisheries law enforcement cooperation with Taiwan in 2015. The question is then: what

135 Reports of the Philippine Coast Guard and Navy include photographic evidence of unlawful fishing activities, harvesting of endangered species and incidents involving Chinese vessels between 1992 and 2014. These reports are available as annexes 16, 23, 25, 40, 42, 43, 44, 46, 47, 49, 50, 51, 54, 55, 56, 58, 59 and 75 of the Memorial of the Philippines, Vol III and Vol IV, available at https://pca-cpa.org/en/cases/7 (last accessed 24 April 2024).

136 John W. McManus, 'Offshore Coral Reef Damage, Overfishing, and Paths to Peace in the South China Sea', *The International Journal of Marine and Coastal Law* 32, no. 2 (2017): 199–237; Victor Robert Lee, 'Satellite Imagery Shows Ecocide in the South China Sea', *The Diplomat*, 15 January 2016, https://thediplomat.com/2016/01/satellite-images-show-ecocide-in-the-south-china-sea (last accessed 24 April 2024).

137 Reports of the Philippine Coast Guard, Navy and Department of Foreign Affairs detail fishing incidents involving Chinese vessels. See Annexes 16, 23, 25, 40, 42, 43, 44, 46, 47, 49, 50, 51, 54, 55, 56, 58, 59, 75, Vol III and Vol IV.

prevented the Philippines and China from reaching at least some provisional rules on fisheries?

Fishing incidents

The fisheries relationship between the Philippines and China in the South China Sea is troublesome. A pattern of repeated fishing incidents has occurred at least since March 1992.[138] The Philippines Navy and Coast Guard apprehended and detained Chinese fishermen found to be fishing in disputed areas. Chinese fishing activities near Thitu Islands, Mischief Reef, Scarborough Shoal, and other features claimed by the Philippines were particularly sensitive to the Philippines. China has reacted to the detentions by demanding the immediate release of their fishermen, and several diplomatic exchanges followed the detentions. China detained Filipino fishermen on a few occasions – for instance, at Mischief Reef in February 1995[139] – and fired warning shots at Filipino fishermen in 2011.[140] In many instances, Chinese officials explained China's position that Chinese fishing activities are 'traditional and normal fishing activities within the Chinese territorial waters.'[141] The detention of Chinese fishermen amounts, according to China, to a 'violation and an infringement of legitimate rights and interests of the Chinese fishermen'. According to the Philippine officials, detentions are 'necessary' and a 'defensive [action] aimed at protecting our territory'[142] as Chinese fishing occurs in Philippine waters. Neither country has changed these positions, and many more fishing incidents have bedevilled the bilateral relationship between 1995 and 2019. The Philippine law enforcement agencies established photographic evidence of the use of dynamite and cyanide fishing, the damage this made to coral reefs, and the repeated harvest of giant claims.[143] The Philippines tried to demonstrate the existence of its laws and factual jurisdiction.

138 *Memorandum* for the Assistant Secretary, Office of Asian and Pacific Affairs, Department of Foreign Affairs, Republic of the Philippines (23 March 1992) (Annex 16), Vol III.
139 *Memorandum* from the Undersecretary of Foreign Affairs of the Republic of the Philippines to the
Ambassador of the People's Republic of China in Manila (6 February 1995) (Annex 17), Vol III.
140 Armed Forces of the Philippines, *Special Report: The Jackson Atoll and Reed Bank Incident in West Philippine Sea* (2011) (Annex 67), Vol IV.
141 *Memorandum* from Erlinda F. Basilio, Acting Assistant Secretary, Office of Asian and Pacific Affairs, Department of Foreign Affairs, Republic of the Philippines, to the Secretary of Foreign Affairs of the Republic of the Philippines (29 March 1995) (Annex 19), Vol III.
142 Ibid.
143 Annexes 16, 23, 25, 40, 42, 43, 44, 46, 47, 49, 50, 51, 54, 55, 56, 58, 59, 75.

Throughout the next two decades, Chinese officials demanded that the Philippines stop detaining its fishermen and refrain from increasing their physical presence on features. The Philippines demanded that Chinese fishermen operate outside the Philippines-claimed EEZ, and that China does not increase its physical presence on features. The potential for escalation was inherent in this situation because Chinese officials suspected that the Philippines would take advantage of detentions 'to stress that "these waters" are within the 200 EEZ of the Philippines'.[144] China was especially wary about the Philippines' intention to file criminal charges against Chinese fishermen, as the Philippines prosecuted them in the 1990s. According to Chinese officials, if China acquiesced in the Philippines subjecting Chinese nationals to Philippine criminal law for fishing in waters claimed by China, this would be tantamount to acquiescing in the Philippines' claims.[145]

Moreover, the Philippine diplomatic record illustrates that it was predominantly the Philippine Coast Guard that enforced Philippine laws against Chinese fishermen. Chinese maritime law enforcement agencies were less present in the 1990s and early 2000s. This pattern began to change with China's decision to regularly protect its fishing fleet with coast guard patrols in 2010.[146] At Scarborough Shoal in April 2012, a relatively mundane fishing incident triggered a dangerous crisis and displayed the parties' inability to manage escalatory action–reaction cycles. After that crisis, China's maritime law enforcement agencies and the China Coast Guard, created in 2013,[147] provided an umbrella for Chinese fishing activities. Lately, it has been the Chinese Coast Guard that has interrupted Philippine fishermen.

144 *Memorandum* from Lauro L. Baja, Jr., Assistant Secretary, Office of Asian and Pacific Affairs, Department of Foreign Affairs, Republic of the Philippines, to the Secretary of Foreign Affairs of the Republic of the Philippines (7 April 1995) (Annex 20), Vol III.

145 *Memorandum* from the Ambassador of the Republic of the Philippines in Beijing to the Undersecretary of Foreign Affairs of the Republic of the Philippines (10 April 1995) (Annex 21), Vol III.

146 Thang Nguyen Dang, 'Fisheries Co-Operation in the South China Sea and the (Ir)Relevance of the Sovereignty Question', *Asian Journal of International Law* 2, no. 01 (2012): 59–88, 65.

147 China's maritime law enforcement agencies have undergone several reforms. In 2013, the China Coast Guard (CCG) was created. The CCG underwent further reforms subsequently. Andrew S. Erickson et al., 'Surging Second Sea Force: China's Maritime Law- Enforcement Forces, Capabilities, and Future in the Gray Zone and Beyond', *Naval War College Review* 72, no. 2 (2019): 1–25; Ryan D Martinson, 'Early Warning Brief: Introducing the "New, New" China Coast Guard', *Jamestown China Brief*, 25 January 2021, https://jamestown.org/program/early-warning-brief-introducing-the-new-new-china-coast-guard/?mc_cid=od3ae43feb&mc_eid=6f43e1d88e (last accessed 23 June 2023).

Proposals, negotiations, and impasse

Diplomats from Beijing and Manila acknowledge that regular fishing incidents are escalatory. Officials from both sides have suggested looking for some provisional rules as a logical undertaking. The Philippine diplomatic correspondence suggests that Manila has sought a modus vivendi since the early 1990s. Besides achieving a modus vivendi on fisheries, the Philippines also proposed a code of conduct in the early 1990s with a view to defining UNCLOS-based rules for the South China Sea at a time when UNCLOS had not yet entered into force.[148] Chinese officials followed up on the idea of a modus vivendi for fisheries in 1995 and suggested several options for a fisheries agreement.

The first documentary evidence for bilateral exchanges between Philippine and Chinese officials on a fisheries arrangement is from 29 March 1995. The former acting Assistant Secretary of the Philippine Department of Foreign Affairs Erlinda Basilio met the Chinese Deputy Chief of Mission Peng Zengjiu in Manila to discuss the release of sixty-two Chinese fishermen that the Philippines detained while fishing off Palawan. Basilio suggested in this conversation that 'China and the Philippines can undertake joint projects to prevent such [illegal fishing methods]' and that 'perhaps both sides could delineate an area where both can fish'.[149] Twelve days after Basilio's and Peng's conversation in Manila, Philippine Ambassador Romualdo Ong met Assistant Minister Wang Yingfan at the Chinese Ministry of Foreign Affairs in Beijing. According to Ambassador Ong 's memorandum, Wang proposed that:

> China's and RP's Foreign Ministries and fishing authorities get together and work closely to reach agreement on "arrangements" to avoid similar situations in the future. (AMPHIL COMMENT: To my recollection, this is the first time Chinese side has responded to RP's proposal of a "modus vivendi." I recommend this matter be taken up seriously and quickly).[150]

148 Chapter V.

149 *Memorandum* from Erlinda F. Basilio, Acting Assistant Secretary, Office of Asian and Pacific Affairs, Department of Foreign Affairs, Republic of the Philippines, to the Secretary of Foreign Affairs of the Republic of the Philippines (29 March 1995) (Annex 19), Vol III.

150 *Memorandum* from the Ambassador of the Republic of the Philippines in Beijing to the Undersecretary of Foreign Affairs of the Republic of the Philippines (10 April 1995) (Annex 21), Vol III.

Wang proposed talks in line with China's 'shelving of the disputes over sovereignty'.[151] In April 1995, officials from both the Philippines and China proposed different models of fisheries cooperation. The objective was to prevent fishing activities in disputed areas from resulting in regular incidents and damaging the bilateral relationship. Three and a half months later, China's Vice-Premier and Foreign Minister Qian Qichen reiterated China's offer in a conversation with the Philippines' Secretary of Foreign Affairs Siazon. According to a secret memorandum from Siazon to President Ramos of 31 July 1995, Qian Qichen noted 'that while the South China Sea is a traditional Chinese fishing ground, fishing vessels of many countries operate in the area. An agreement between the Philippines and China would help avoid conflicts that fisheries disputes have caused in other regions.'[152] In reply, Siazon stated 'that while we could examine the possible merits of the Chinese proposal, the proposal should be discussed with other claimant countries as well'.[153]

Siazon's reply to Qian reflects the Philippines' preference for building a common ASEAN position before entering into talks with China about specific agreements. After China built installations on Mischief Reef in 1995, the Philippines tried to bring about a common ASEAN approach to prevent ASEAN countries from being split by China in many bilateral agreements. However, this Philippine preference for a multilateral approach cannot answer the question of why both did not establish a minimum of rules for fisheries in the 1990s. Most of the fishing incidents between China and the Philippines occurred in areas only claimed by China and the Philippines and amount to a bilateral dispute. Only China and the Philippines claim Scarborough Shoal, even if the Philippine Coast Guard recorded Vietnamese fishermen at the Shoal. There is no reason to assume the Philippines considered Malaysia's or Vietnam's participation in a fisheries arrangement for waters only claimed by the Philippines and China. Moreover, despite Siazon's preference for a multilateral ASEAN approach, the Philippines was the first to break ranks with ASEAN and come to a bilateral agreement with China on hydrocarbon resources nine years later in 2004 (the JMSU).

According to diplomatic correspondence from the Philippine record, China proposed a fisheries agreement that 'cover[s] principles, content, rights

151 Ibid.

152 *Memorandum* from the Secretary of Foreign Affairs of the Republic of the Philippines to the President of the Republic of the Philippines (31 July 1995) (Annex 23), Vol III.

153 Ibid.

and obligations, procedures for settling disputes and wind sheltering for fishermen' in August 1995.[154] Vice-Minister Wang proposed as an alternative a non-enforcement arrangement with a smaller scope, committing both sides to 'refrain from unilaterally exercising compulsory jurisdiction over the fishermen of the other side that are fishing on the disputed area.'[155] Wang suggested that multilateral cooperation was conceivable for areas that were claimed by more than two parties, but bilateral cooperation was the basis for areas that were claimed by only two. Wang also offered another option for fisheries cooperation in case a governmental agreement was not in reach: 'Apart from governmental agreement, we can explore in a non-governmental way. Actually, China and other countries have fishing association [sic] which in nature is non-governmental.'[156] Vice-Minister Wang presumably referred to the fisheries agreements that China concluded with Japan in the 1950s and 1960s. Before Japan recognized the People's Republic of China, the fisheries relations between China and Japan were governed by fishing associations.[157]

By 1995, China's proposals included a substantive fisheries agreement, a non-enforcement agreement and non-governmental agreements. China had experience with these types of fisheries agreements in the Gulf of Tonkin and East China Sea. Chinese and Philippine diplomats set up a bilateral working group to discuss a fisheries arrangement that met for the first time in the Philippines in September 1996.[158] Chinese Vice Foreign Minister Tang Jiaxuan repeated China's proposals on fisheries cooperation on 27 May 1997.[159] The working group reported progress in 1998.[160] In 2001, however, Chinese and Philippine diplomats focused their efforts on an agreement of minimal scope: setting up a 'direct line of communication between the fisheries department

154 Government of the Republic of the Philippines and Government of the People's Republic of China, *Agreed Minutes on the First Philippines-China Bilateral Consultations on the South China Sea Issue* (10 August 1995) (Annex 180), Vol VI, https://files.pca-cpa.org/pcadocs/The%20Philippines%27%20Memorial%20-%20Volume%20VI%20%28Annexes%20158-221%29.pdf (last accessed 24 April 2024).

155 Government of the Republic of the Philippines, Transcript of Proceedings Republic of the Philippines-People's Republic of China Bilateral Talks (10 August 1995) (Annex 181), Vol VI.

156 Ibid.

157 Chapter IV 1.3.

158 Department of Foreign Affairs of the Republic of the Philippines, *Press Release No. 69: RP, PRC To Convene Working Group for Talks on South China Sea* (28 May 1997) (Annex 26), Vol III.

159 *Memorandum* from Rodolfo C. Severino, Undersecretary, Department of Foreign Affairs of the Republic of the Philippines, to the President of the Republic of the Philippines (27 May 1997) (Annex 25), Vol III.

160 Department of Foreign Affairs of the Republic of the Philippines, *Record of Proceedings: 10th Philippines-China Foreign Ministry Consultations* (30 July 1998) (Annex 184), Vol VI.

of both countries' for managing incidents.[161] Administratively, the proposal would have necessitated close coordination between the Philippine Bureau of Fisheries, the fisheries law enforcement unit, and the Philippine Coast Guard.[162] The direct line would have placed the Bureau of Fisheries in an important position for the management of incidents. Moreover, an agreement on a direct communication mechanism would have involved a minimal commitment. Such an arrangement neither establishes joint regulation for fisheries nor commits both parties to refrain from enforcing their rules against fishermen of the other side (a non-enforcement agreement). The arrangement would only say who must call whom *after* an incident arose. Such an agreement only serves to minimise the risk of incidents, not to prevent them. Although Chinese and Philippine negotiators agreed 'in principle' on setting up such a direct line,[163] there is no evidence that the line was ever implemented. The available diplomatic correspondence on how Chinese and Philippine authorities dealt with incidents suggests that no direct communication line between law enforcement agencies or fisheries administrations was ever established.

Under former President Arroyo, the Department of Agriculture of the Philippines and the Ministry of Agriculture of China continued exchanges and signed a memorandum of understanding on fisheries cooperation on 1 September 2004.[164] Already two months later, on 31 October 2004, however, an incident occurred close to Scarborough Shoal and involved Chinese fishing vessels that were found harvesting giant clams. In 2004, the Philippine Coast Guard identified a total of forty-eight foreign (Chinese, Vietnamese, and Taiwanese) fishing boats at Scarborough Shoal, down from a total of seventy-two foreign fishing boats in 2003.[165] China's Vice-Minister protested the apprehension of four Chinese fishing vessels by the Philippine Navy and

161 *Memorandum* from Josue L. Villa, Embassy of the Republic of the Philippines in Beijing, to the Secretary of Foreign Affairs of the Republic of the Philippines (21 May 2001) (Annex 48), Vol III.

162 Interview with a Division Chief of the Philippine Bureau on Fisheries and Aquatic Resources, Manila, 09 December 2016 (Interview 11).

163 Government of the Republic of the Philippines and Government of the People's Republic of China, *Joint Statement: 3rd Philippines-China Experts' Group Meeting on Confidence-Building Measures*, Manila, 3–4 April 2001 (4 April 2001) (Annex 506), Vol IX Supplemental Written Submission.

164 Memorandum of Understanding between the Department of Agriculture of the Republic of the Philippines and the Ministry of Agriculture of the People's Republic of China on Fisheries Cooperation, signed in Beijing on 1 September 2004.

165 *Report* from Lt. Commander Angeles, Philippine Navy, to Flag Officer in Command, Philippine Navy, No. N2E-F-1104-012 (18 November 2004) (Annex 55), Vol III.

the alleged shooting at Chinese fishing vessels inside Scarborough Shoal on 30 December 2005.[166] The memorandum of understanding did not lead to the implementation of an understanding on fisheries. After nine years of consultations and working-group-level negotiations on various models for fisheries cooperation – substantive agreement, non-enforcement agreement, and hotline – no agreement was reached.

This leads to the question of why China and the Philippines did not emulate the approach of Japan, South Korea, and China that agreed on various joint fisheries zones, sidestepping sovereignty disputes. The Philippines approached negotiations with China with two seemingly inconsistent conceptions. Undersecretary Severino argued in 1997 that China could not claim Scarborough Shoal as a territory because it is too small.[167]Accordingly, China would neither have a valid claim to the waters around the shoal nor to fisheries.[168] This appears to confirm the expectation that claimant states are disinclined to consider cooperative arrangements for maritime zones to which a rival claimant is not entitled. While offering an intuitive explanation for the lack of agreement, the expectation is at odds with the observation that Philippine officials were not against a fisheries agreement per se in the 1990s and 2000s. Even if they considered that the Philippines had exclusive rights in waters off the Philippine archipelago and around Scarborough Shoal, Philippine officials initiated and conducted consultations on fisheries agreements over a period of nine years. This mirrors the Sino-Philippine exchanges on joint oil and gas exploration, where the Philippines entered into an arrangement and explored company-level options even if the Philippines maintained that China was not entitled to claim continental shelf rights off the Philippine archipelago.

The Sino-Philippine exchanges also mirrored the talks on joint development in the following way. Philippine officials rejected Chinese joint development models because they judged that these gave China an easy

166 *Memorandum* from the Secretary of Foreign Affairs of the Republic of the Philippines to the President of the Republic of the Philippines (11 January 2006) (Annex 58), Vol III.

167 Department of Foreign Affairs of the Republic of the Philippines, *Press Release No. 69: RP, PRC To Convene Working Group for Talks on South China Sea* (28 May 1997) (Annex 26), Vol III.

168 The Philippines made the same argument in the arbitral proceedings in 2013. The tribunal, however, ruled that Scarborough Shoal is a 'rock.' China can therefore claim sovereignty over the shoal and a territorial sea in its vicinity. The tribunal did not rule on the merits of sovereignty claims. The tribunal also found the existence of 'traditional fishing rights' of both Chinese and Philippine fishermen in the Shoal's territorial seas. The South China Sea Arbitration, 12 June 2016, paras 792–804. The South China Sea Arbitration 2016, paras 643–648.

opening to claim areas in which China had no rights.[169] The terms of a fisheries agreement that would have been acceptable to the Philippines are the terms that would not have legitimised China's presence and fishing activities in Philippine-claimed waters. This would have been a fisheries arrangement that provided for restrictions on Chinese fishing activities and the jurisdiction of the Philippine law enforcement agencies. Such an arrangement, however, would have amounted to the surrender of China's claims in China's perspective. Philippine officials rejected the Chinese proposals on joint fisheries agreements because such an agreement would have created a de facto layer of validity in favour of China's claim and thus a Philippine vulnerability. This was the case even though a fisheries agreement would have been without legal prejudice to Manila's position. Theoretically, this problem can be construed as the problem of how validation without legal force weakens an actor's position. The need to find an agreement that does not strengthen an opponent's bargaining position was a barrier to agreement. Thus, the Philippines decided against the approach of Japan, Korea, and China to jointly define a common framework for fishing activities that includes limits to maritime law enforcement and fishing activities. For the Philippines, the cost of non-agreement is that Chinese fishing activities have expanded and continued unilaterally, without any bilaterally agreed limits, and without China and the Philippines having an agreed mechanism to diffuse fishing incidents.

The escalation of fishing incidents at Scarborough Shoal in 2012

Philippine officials have consistently rejected suggestions from Chinese diplomats during bilateral exchanges that the Philippine Coast Guard refrain from enforcing Philippine laws against Chinese fishermen.[170] Philippine officials have generally regarded law enforcement as crucial to upholding claims to exclusive rights. After twenty years of regular incidents and deadlocked diplomatic efforts to jointly manage fisheries, a crisis at Scarborough Shoal started on 10 April 2012. This incident caused an international crisis lasting three months and involving cat and mouse games between maritime law enforcement and navy vessels.

169 *Memorandum* from Secretary General, Commission on Maritime and Ocean Affairs Secretariat, Department of Foreign Affairs of the Republic of the Philippines to the Secretary of Foreign Affairs of the Republic of the Philippines (28 March 2011) (Annex 71), Vol VI.
170 For this Philippine position, see the following documents from the Philippines' Memorial: Annexes 16, 23, 25, 40, 42, 43, 44, 46, 47, 49, 50, 51, 54, 55, 56, 58, 59, 75, Vol III and Vol IV.

During the bilateral Foreign Minister Consultations in January 2012, Vice Foreign Minister Zhang Zhijun still described the disputes in the typical way:

> I believe that we should have a clear understanding of the damage these disputes might cause if they are not managed well. We are also aware that no country will make compromise on territorial sovereignty… First is what Chinese leadership has repeatedly stressed that is we need to shelve disputes and seek joint development and cooperation. The premise of such cooperation is that it shall not damage the claims of sovereignty of each country.[171]

Assistant Minister Liu Zhenmin proposed establishing a hotline for law enforcement incidents during these consultations.[172] Three months later, a fishing incident at Scarborough Shoal escalated and brought China and the Philippines into near-armed conflict. The incident began when Chinese fishing vessels and maritime law enforcement vessels resisted the Philippine attempt to detain Chinese fishermen who operated inside Scarborough Shoal.[173] The Philippines replaced a navy vessel at some stage with a Philippine Coast Guard ship as it considered this to be less escalatory. Both sides withdrew some vessels at some point from the shoal. China may have withdrawn two ships from the shoal on April 23 in an early attempt to de-escalate the situation.[174] Manila denounced this as not true. Chinese ships appear to have been withdrawn over the horizon only. Sino-Philippine miscommunication due to the existence of various simultaneous channels of communication, unclear inter-agency processes within the Philippines and China,[175] as well as the expectation that backing down amounted to

171 *Record of Discussion: 17th Philippines-China Foreign Ministry Consultations* (14 January 2012) (Annex 204), Vol VI, 30.

172 Ibid.

173 *Memorandum* from Col. Nathaniel Y. Casem, Philippine Navy, to Chief of Staff, Armed Forces of the Philippines, No. N2E-0412-008 (11 April 2012) (Annex 77), Vol IV; Special Report on Scarborough Shoal (19 April 2012) (Annex 77), Vol IV; *Report* from Relly B. Garcia, et al., FRPLEU/QRT Officers, Bureau of Fisheries and Aquatic Resources, Republic of the Philippines, to Director, Bureau of Fisheries and Aquatic Resources, Republic of the Philippines (2 May 2012) (Annex 80), Vol IV; *Memorandum* from the Embassy of the Republic of the Philippines in Beijing to the Secretary of Foreign Affairs of the Republic of the Philippines, No. ZPE-080-2012-S (24 May 2012) (Annex 81), Vol IV.

174 Michael Green et al., *Countering Coercion in Maritime Asia The Theory and Practice of Gray Zone Deterrence* (Center for Strategic & International Studies, 2017),108.

175 Inter-departmental processes within China were presumably also fragmented but there is not a lot of data on inter-departmental processes during the Scarborough Shoal crisis. See in general, Andrew S. Erickson and Adam P. Liff, 'Installing a Safety on the "Loaded Gun"? China's

acquiescence in the opponent's claims thwarted de-escalation and crisis management.[176] In addition to these factors, the chain of events suggests that two problems prevented the chance that an early mutual withdrawal understanding could have solved the crisis. First, vessels sailed on some occasions in the direction of the shoal, presumably as reinforcement or replacement. Chinese and Philippine vessels were stationed nearby the shoal but out of sight. Each side could have read these vessel activities as reneging on a withdrawal understanding. Second, as the Philippines did not consider China's claim to have withdrawn vessels true, Manila did not reciprocate. As a result, confidence in further mutual withdrawal commitments diminished.

The crisis escalated after early withdrawal efforts failed. Chinese maritime law enforcement vessels reverted to pressure tactics by steering collision courses.[177] China imposed banana import restrictions and reduced travel to the Philippines.[178] Philippine Foreign Secretary del Rosario called for 'maximum benefits' from the Mutual Defense Treaty with the US.[179] This call came just two days after the Philippines and the US staged an unrelated and pre-scheduled war game exercising the occupation of a small island on 25 April 2012.[180] Thereafter, Chinese diplomats accused the Philippines of calling for a US military intervention.[181] Three simultaneous high-level diplomatic channels tried to defuse the tensions,[182] but the three channels appear to have been unaware of each other. The existence of concurrent but uncoordinated channels resulted in the squandering of trust. One channel

Institutional Reforms, National Security Commission and Sino–Japanese Crisis (in) Stability', *Journal of Contemporary China* 25, no. 98 (2016): 197–215.

176 *Memorandum* from the Embassy of the Republic of the Philippines in Beijing to the Secretary of Foreign Affairs of the Republic of the Philippines, No. ZPE-080-2012-S (24 May 2012) (Annex 81); *Memorandum* from the Embassy of the Republic of the Philippines in Beijing to the Secretary of Foreign Affairs of the Republic of the Philippines, No. ZPE-110-2012-S (26 July 2012) (Annex 84), Vol IV.

177 Ibid., 109.

178 Green et al., *Countering Coercion in Maritime Asia,* 114.

179 'Chinese military vows to defend sea claim', The Philippine Star, 28 April 2012, https://www.pressreader.com/philippines/the-philippine-star/20120428/281479273420701 (last accessed 20 June 2023).

180 Manuel Mogato, 'Philippines, U.S. stage war games in face of China warning', Reuters, 25/04/2012, https://www.reuters.com/article/us-southchinasea-idUSBRE83O06220120425 (last accessed 20 June 2023).

181 *Memorandum* from the Embassy of the Republic of the Philippines in Beijing to the Secretary of Foreign Affairs of the Republic of the Philippines, No. ZPE-080-2012-S (24 May 2012) (Annex 81), Vol IV.

182 Green et al., *Countering Coercion in Maritime Asia,*116–118.

claimed to have reached an unconfirmed commitment to a mutual ship withdrawal of which the other channels were not aware, but that withdrawal never materialized. A sticking point apart from the question of who would withdraw first was the issue of how the Chinese fishermen inside the shoal should be treated. There are different versions of whether China committed to a mutual withdrawal in consultations with the US in early June and then reneged on this commitment, or whether China only committed to a gradual, sequential withdrawal.[183] The crisis ended with China taking control of previously Philippine-administered Scarborough Shoal by placing coast guard vessels in the shoal and by blocking the entrance into the shoal with concrete blocks in early July 2012.[184] The crisis not only produced a change of the territorial status quo. It also reflected to what extent China's approach to the South China Sea disputes had changed. In 2005, the Philippine Navy still apprehended and allegedly shot at Chinese fishing vessels inside Scarborough Shoal, with China only protesting diplomatically. In 2012, China responded to the Philippine attempt to confiscate catch from Chinese fishermen by taking control of the Shoal.

Scarborough Shoal, the South China Sea Arbitration and land reclamation

The Scarborough Shoal crisis in 2012 started as an attempt of the Philippines to detain Chinese fishermen and to stop illegal fishing practices. The crisis resulted in China taking control of a previously Philippine-administered shoal. The objective of a fisheries agreement would have been to prevent fishing incidents from arising in the first place. The objective of a law enforcement hotline would have been to provide a specified communication procedure to de-escalate incidents. Beijing and Manila consulted without result on various types of fisheries agreements, including non-enforcement and hotline arrangements. As pre-established communication mechanisms did not exist in 2012,[185] Manila and Beijing set up various ad hoc diplomatic channels to diffuse the escalation at Scarborough Shoal. The limitations of the ad hoc channels played a role in thwarting early efforts to reach a ship withdrawal understanding when both parties appear to have been willing

183 Ibid., 119.

184 The arbitral tribunal considered China's blockade of Scarborough Shoal a violation of China's obligation to allow Philippine traditional fishing in and around the shoal. The South China Sea Arbitration, 2016, paras 758–814.

185 Chapter V analyses efforts to negotiate direct communication arrangements.

to de-escalate. In contrast, fisheries agreements in the Gulf of Tonkin and East China Sea illustrate how such agreements prevent the escalation of incidents.[186]

This crisis had important ramifications for the further development of the South China Sea disputes. The change in the territorial status quo tilted the balance within the administration of former President Aquino in favour of launching arbitral proceedings.[187] Six months after China took control of the shoal on 22 January 2013, the Philippines initiated arbitral proceedings against China.[188] The timing of China's land reclamation activities suggests that China's large-scale land reclamation has been, at least partially, a response to the initiation of arbitral proceedings, even if deliberations within the PLA about island building have existed at least since 2009.[189] China initiated its island construction program in 2013.[190] Before that, China's constructions on features were relatively small.[191] The initial Statement of Claim of the Philippines did not ask the tribunal to rule on China's small installations on the features. The Philippines added the submission that China's land reclamation violated the Philippines' rights only two years later, on 21 May 2015.[192] The arbitral tribunal notes that 'since the commencement of the arbitration, China has greatly intensified its programme of building artificial islands and installations.'[193]

After the ruling of the arbitral tribunal in 2016, China and the Philippines launched a bilateral consultation mechanism.[194] Under this mechanism,

186 Chapters III 2 and IV.

187 Interview 7.

188 Notification and Statement of Claim of the Republic of the Philippines (22 January 2013) (Annex 1); *Note Verbale* from the Department of Foreign Affairs of the Republic of the Philippines to the Embassy of the People's Republic of China in Manila, No. 13-0211 (22 January 2013) (Annex 2); China returned the Note Verbale and Statement of Claim to the Philippines. *Note Verbale* from the Embassy of the People's Republic of China in Manila to the Department of Foreign Affairs of the Republic of the Philippines, No. (13) PG-039 (19 February 2013) (Annex 3), Vol III.

189 Russel Hsiao, 'PLA General Advises Building Bases in the South China Sea', *Jamestown China Brief*, 24 June 2009, 1.

190 For publicly available imagery of the island building programs since 2013, see the Asia Maritime Transparency Initiative of the Center for Strategic and International Studies, 'Island tracker', https://amti.csis.org/island-tracker/ (last accessed 23 June 2023).

191 Armed Forces of the Philippines, *Chronological Development of Artificial Structures on Features* (Annex 96), Vol IV.

192 The South China Sea Arbitration, 2016, para 46.

193 Ibid, para 1128. The tribunal found that China's land reclamation aggravated the disputes, para 1181.

194 Rommel Banlaoi, 'The Bilateral Consultative Mechanism on the South China Sea and Philippines-China Relations', *ISEAS Commentary*, 2021, https://www.iseas.edu.sg/

Chinese and Philippine officials from various departments have met several times to discuss fisheries, oil and gas projects, and marine environmental protection.[195] According to a well-placed Chinese official with direct knowledge of the consultations,[196] Beijing and Manila have reached an arrangement not to enforce each side's fisheries laws against the fishing activities of the other side – a non-enforcement arrangement – for some disputed areas. But this verbal understanding,[197] if it existed, was never implemented. Incidents with fishing vessels have continued and intensified, despite Duterte toying with a Sino-Philippine rapprochement. From December 2018 to April 2019, between ninety-five and 275 Chinese fishing and coast guard vessels surrounded Philippines-held Thitu Island,[198] the largest Philippine-occupied feature and second largest Spratly Island. Some media sources referred to an informal Sino-Philippine agreement on a marine sanctuary for protecting the marine environment inside Scarborough Shoal in 2016.[199] Supreme Court Justice Carpio warned against turning the China-controlled and Philippines-claimed Scarborough Shoal into a fisheries sanctuary for Philippine fishermen, as this would impair the tribunal's decision.[200] While China has allowed the return of Philippine fishing boats, but not inside the shoal, Chinese fishermen have continued fishing inside the shoal, including

articles-commentaries/iseas-perspective/2021-51-the-bilateral-consultative-mechanism-on-the-south-china-sea-and-philippines-china-relations-by-rommel-c-banlaoi/ (last accessed 23 June 2023).

195 Department of Foreign Affairs of the Philippines, 'Joint Press Release for the Second Meeting of the Philippines-China Bilateral Consultative Mechanism on the South China Sea', 13 February 2018, https://dfa.gov.ph/dfa-news/dfa-releasesupdate/15562-second-meeting-of-the-philippines-china-bilateral-consultation-mechanism-on-the-south-china-sea (last accessed 23 June 2023).

196 Interview with an official of China's Ministry of Foreign Affairs who contributed to the Sino-Philippine consultations, China, November 2019 (Interview 46).

197 The Duterte administration insists that a verbal understanding was reached. Azer Parrocha, 'Duterte-Xi Verbal Fishing Deal Still Legally Binding: Palace', *Philippine News Agency*, 1 July 2019, https://www.pna.gov.ph/articles/1073792 (last accessed 23 March 2024).

198 Mark J. Valencia, 'Parsing the Present Philippines-China Contretemps', Eurasia Review, 19 April 2019, https://www.eurasiareview.com/19042019-parsing-the-present-philippines-china-contretemps-analysis/; 'Hundreds of Chinese vessels circling Pag-asa Island: military', 29 March 2019, https://news.abs-cbn.com/news/03/29/19/hundreds-of-chinese-vessels-circling-pag-asa-island-military?fbclid=IwAR1t_HVt71bOo2WwHntddR3MH_vmnhXKSw5HnWNM4R-PVNIPUjC7xpBUXpwM (last accessed 23 June 2023).

199 Mike Ives, 'Philippines to Declare Marine Sanctuary in South China Sea', 21 November 2016, New York Times, https://www.nytimes.com/2016/11/22/world/asia/philippines-rodrigo-duterte-scarborough-shoal-china.html (last accessed 23 June 2023).

200 Interview with Philippine Supreme Court Justice Antonio Carpio, Manila, 29/11/2016 (Interview 5).

harvesting endangered giant clams.[201] In short, there is no evidence that an agreement on a marine sanctuary emerged.

Although Duterte has discontinued his predecessor's policy of opposing Chinese fishing activities near disputed features such as Scarborough Shoal, his administration has not entered into a fisheries agreement with China either. Previous Philippine administrations rejected provisional rules for fisheries, considering such arrangements tantamount to a recognition of China's claims. At times, the Philippines under Duterte has given the impression of having acquiesced in Chinese fishing operations in parts of the Philippine EEZ.[202] Where this has been the case, the Philippines' approach to the South China Sea has shifted considerably – from rejecting a fisheries agreement that would have allowed Chinese fishing operations subject to common rules to virtually acquiescing in Chinese fishing operations unconditionally.

In summary, the Philippines and China have continued consultations on fisheries, marine environmental protection, and, as noted above, offshore oil and gas even after the South China Sea Arbitration invalidated parts of China's claims. On the one hand, Manila has decided against emulating the approach of Vietnam, Korea, and Japan regarding fisheries agreements and against the joint development of oil and gas. Essentially, Philippine actors have assessed and, in some instances, experienced that such cooperation results in vulnerabilities that Chinese actors can exploit to advance their claims. On the other hand, China has responded to Philippine attempts to resist China's unilateral fishing activities and seismic research with escalation – escalation China has used to dominate and expand its presence and enforce its claims.

2 China and Vietnam

In contrast to China and the Philippines, China and Vietnam have concluded a boundary delimitation and a separate fisheries agreement. This boundary is the only sea boundary agreement China has concluded – anywhere. It applies to the Gulf of Tonkin but does not extend into the South China Sea.

201 The arbitral award notes regarding the harvesting of sea turtles, a species threatened with extinction, and giant claims that 'China must have known of, and deliberately tolerated and protected the harmful acts.' This is a breach of articles 192 and 194(5) of UNCLOS. The South China Sea arbitration, 2016, para 960.

202 Parrocha, 'Duterte-Xi Verbal Fishing Deal Still Legally Binding: Palace'.

This subchapter explains why the combination of a boundary delimitation and a fisheries agreement has been mutually enabling in this case. It also examines why the attempts to extend this cooperation into the South China Sea have ended in impasses.

The context

The claims of China and Vietnam overlap widely in the South China Sea and overlapped in the Gulf of Tonkin until two agreements were concluded. Chinese and Vietnamese hydrocarbon exploration and exploitation projects have collided repeatedly in the South China Sea since the 1990s. Vietnam has opened many offshore exploration blocks along its coastline[203] and China's concession blocks overlap widely with Vietnamese blocks. China and Vietnam moved ahead unilaterally and invited foreign companies for tenders. The American enterprise Crestone Energy Corporation, for instance, got a Chinese concession in the southern part of the South China Sea in an area in relative proximity to Vietnam in 1992.[204] Vietnam involved foreign energy companies from Europe, Russia, and India, presumably to gain international support.[205] The Indian national oil company ONGC Videsh, for instance, had dropped some exploration projects in areas claimed by Vietnam and China, but resumed them at the insistence of India's Ministry of Foreign Affairs.[206] This situation produced several incidents whereby Chinese naval vessels blocked Vietnamese oil rigs in July 1994. Vietnamese naval vessels interfered with Chinese exploration activities in April 1994. Buszynski and Sazalan comment that 'conflict was narrowly avoided'.[207] This situation remained tense until the early 2000s when China and Vietnam established the Gulf of Tonkin cooperation and when Vietnam joined the Sino-Philippine Joint Marine Seismic Undertaking in 2005.

The Gulf of Tonkin cooperation is based on two agreements, a boundary agreement, and an additional and transitional joint fisheries agreement. While the scope and depth of the cooperation has improved slowly, the two agreements set the basic framework for Sino-Vietnamese interactions in the

203 International Crisis Group, 'Stirring up the South China Sea (IV): Oil in Troubled Waters', *Asia Report*, no. 275, 26 January 2016, 7, https://www.crisisgroup.org/asia/north-east-asia/china/stirring-south-china-sea-iv-oil-troubled-waters (last accessed 23 August 2023).
204 Ibid., 6.
205 Leszek Buszynski and Iskandar Sazlan, 'Maritime Claims and Energy Cooperation in the South China Sea', *Contemporary Southeast Asia* 29, no. 1 (2007): 143–71.
206 International Crisis Group, 'Stirring up the South China Sea (IV): Oil in Troubled Waters', 12.
207 Buszynski and Sazlan, 'Maritime Claims and Energy Cooperation', 158.

Gulf of Tonkin. Attempts to extend the maritime boundary and cooperation model into the South China Sea began in the late 2000s. Boundary negotiations, however, stalled and the talks turned around a small block for common natural resource projects in the 'mouth of the Tonkin Gulf'.

2.1 Boundary Delimitation and Trans-Boundary Cooperation in the Gulf of Tonkin

The Gulf of Tonkin is a gulf of approximately 126,000 square kilometres engulfed by the coastlines of Vietnam, China, and Hainan Island. Sino-Vietnamese attempts to delimit the Gulf of Tonkin date back to the mid-1970s.[208] Vietnam proposed a vertical line that the Sino-French Convention of 1887 utilized for the allocation of Chinese and Vietnamese islands.[209] Vietnam stated in 1982 that the maritime boundary in the Gulf of Tonkin 'is delineated according to the 26 June 1887 Convention of frontier boundary signed between France and the Qing Dynasty of China'.[210] Vietnam also claimed that the Vietnamese side of the line 'constitutes the historic waters and is subjected to the juridical regime of internal waters'.[211] China rejected both positions, and negotiations resumed only in 1993.[212] The resumption of exchanges followed the normalization of diplomatic relations in 1991 and the Sino-Vietnamese battle at Johnson South Reef in 1988.

China and Vietnam came to a general understanding of intent to settle the maritime boundary in the Gulf of Tonkin and to 'apply international law and adapt to international practices, while taking into account the special circumstances of the Gulf in order to reach an equitable solution'.[213]

208 Hong Thao Nguyen, 'Maritime Delimitation and Fishery Cooperation in the Tonkin Gulf', *Ocean Development & International Law* 36, no. 1 (2005): 25–44, 26; Stein Tønnesson, 'The Tonkin Gulf Agreements: A Model of Conflict Resolution?', in *The South China Sea: A Crucible of Regional Cooperation or Conflict-Making Sovereignty Claims?* Edited by C. J. Jenner and Truong Thuy Tran (CUP, 2016), 151–170.

209 The line in the Sino-French Convention was only used to allocate islands. Even though it served some jurisdictional functions, it was not used as a boundary. Benoît De Tréglodé, 'Maritime Boundary Delimitation and Sino-Vietnamese Cooperation in the Gulf of Tonkin (1994–2016)', *China Perspectives*, 2016, 33–41, 35.

210 'Statement of 12 November 1982 by the Government of the Socialist Republic of Viet Nam on the Territorial Sea Baseline of Viet Nam', in United Nations Office for Ocean Affairs and the Law of the Sea, *The Law of the Sea Baselines: National Legislation With Illustrative Maps*, 1989, 384.

211 Ibid.

212 Keyuan Zou, 'The Sino-Vietnamese Agreement on Maritime Boundary Delimitation in the Gulf of Tonkin', *Ocean Development & International Law*, 36 (2005), 13–24.

213 Nguyen Thi Hanh, 'Vinh Bac Bo trong Quan he Viet Nam va Trung Quoc: van de va lich su' (The Gulf of Tonkin's role in Sino-Vietnamese relations: Questions and history), *Nghien Cuu*

China's goal was to delimit a boundary that would result in an equitable result. Vietnam suggested an adjusted median line that gives effect to Bach Long Vi, a Vietnamese island.[214] The leaders of both sides set 1999 as a deadline for the negotiators to arrive at a boundary.[215] It took a total of seventy-seven rounds of negotiation, including talks at the level of heads of government and at the working group and technical group level.[216] The compromise between China's and Vietnam's positions has been to give Vietnam's longer coastline and islands an effect on boundary delimitation, but to limit the effect given to islands.[217] This resulted in a 53.23 per cent share of the gulf for Vietnam and a 46.77 per cent share for China. China and Vietnam signed the 'Agreement on the Delimitation of the Territorial Seas, Exclusive Economic Zones and Continental Shelves in the Beibu Gulf/Bac Bo Gulf between the People's Republic of China and the Socialist Republic of Vietnam' on 25 December 2000.[218] Article 7 of the boundary agreement provides for the joint development of oil and gas deposits in zones straddling the boundary. In 2006 and 2013, Chinese and Vietnamese negotiators agreed on two joint development zones across the boundary to implement this provision.[219] The boundary agreement does not give any side the option of unilateral termination. Crucial conditions for reaching a compromise were the top leadership's determination to settle the Gulf of Tonkin boundary and both sides' acceptance of the law of the sea and UNCLOS as the basic framework for negotiations.

2.2 The Sino-Vietnamese Fisheries Agreement 2004

However, one more issue needed to be solved: China made its consent to the boundary agreement conditional on the conclusion of a fisheries agreement. Access to fisheries was a key issue for both sides. Zou refers to

Lich Su (Historical studies) 4, no. 444 (2013): 69–79, quoted in Benoît De Tréglodé, 'Maritime Boundary Delimitation and Sino-Vietnamese Cooperation in the Gulf of Tonkin (1994–2016)', *China Perspectives*, 2016, 33–41, 36.

214 Nguyen, 'Maritime Delimitation and Fishery Cooperation in the Tonkin Gulf', 28; Zou, 'The Sino-Vietnamese Agreement on Maritime Boundary Delimitation', 15, based on Chinese sources of the negotiation history; de Tréglodé, 'Maritime Boundary Delimitation', 36 based on Vietnamese sources of the negotiation history.

215 Tønnesson, 'The Tonkin Gulf Agreements: A Model of Conflict Resolution?', 152.

216 Zou, 'The Sino-Vietnamese Agreement on Maritime Boundary Delimitation', 13.

217 Tønnesson, 'The Tonkin Gulf Agreements: A Model of Conflict Resolution?', 163.

218 UN Treaty Series 2336, 2005. An unofficial English translation of the agreement is also available in Zou, 'The Sino-Vietnamese Agreement on Maritime Boundary Delimitation'.

219 De Tréglodé, 'Maritime Boundary Delimitation'.

700,000 Chinese fishermen whose living depends on the Gulf.[220] Although Nguyen states that boundary and fisheries negotiations were conducted independently of each other,[221] China linked the acceptance of a boundary agreement to the simultaneous conclusion of a fisheries agreement according to Chinese sources.[222] While a basic fisheries agreement was concluded in 2000,[223] it took another four years to negotiate additional protocols about its implementation.[224] Both the boundary and the fisheries agreement could only be ratified after China and Vietnam compromised on the implementation of the agreements. Both agreements were ratified on 30 June 2004. Map 3 illustrates the agreements.

China and North Vietnam established fisheries cooperation in the late 1950s and early 1960s, but this cooperation stopped in the 1970s as bilateral relations deteriorated.[225] The agreement signed in 2000 is the first Sino-Vietnamese fisheries agreement since the 1970s. Vietnamese negotiators refused to define common fisheries zones in the Gulf of Tonkin until 1998 when negotiations on the boundary proceeded. China insisted on a package trading concession on boundary delimitation against a larger fisheries zone than Vietnam was willing to consider initially. The fisheries zones straddle the boundary. Rich fishing grounds are supposed to be on the Vietnamese side of the boundary.[226]According to de Tréglodé, '[s]ix series of talks were necessary before the Vietnamese side… came to agree with Beijing not only on the shape this zone would take, but also on the cooperation in terms of protection of the marine environment.'[227] China blocked the ratification of the boundary and the fisheries agreements until 2004. An additional protocol and a policy document on management measures specified procedures for how fishermen would obtain fishing permits and how both sides would

220 Zou, 'The Sino-Vietnamese Agreement on Maritime Boundary Delimitation', 16.

221 Nguyen, 'Maritime Delimitation and Fishery Cooperation in the Tonkin Gulf', 30.

222 Interview with a scholar on maritime economy of a leading think tank on maritime affairs affiliated with China's Ministry of Foreign Affairs, China, 19 April 2017 (Interview 24); Zou, 'The Sino-Vietnamese Agreement on Maritime Boundary Delimitation', 16; Keyuan Zou, 'Sino-Vietnamese Fishery Agreement for the Gulf of Tonkin', *International Journal of Marine and Coastal Law*, 17 (2002), 127–48, 132.

223 'Agreement on Fishery Cooperation in the Beibu Gulf/Bac Bo Gulf between the Government of the People's Republic of China and the Government of Socialist Republic of Vietnam.' An unofficial English translation of the agreement is available in Zou, 'Sino-Vietnamese Fishery Agreement for the Gulf of Tonkin'.

224 Nguyen, 'Maritime Delimitation and Fishery Cooperation in the Tonkin Gulf', 30.

225 Zou, 'Sino-Vietnamese Fishery Agreement for the Gulf of Tonkin'.

226 Ibid., 128; Zou, 'The Sino-Vietnamese Agreement on Maritime Boundary Delimitation', 16.

227 De Tréglodé, 'Maritime Boundary Delimitation', 37.

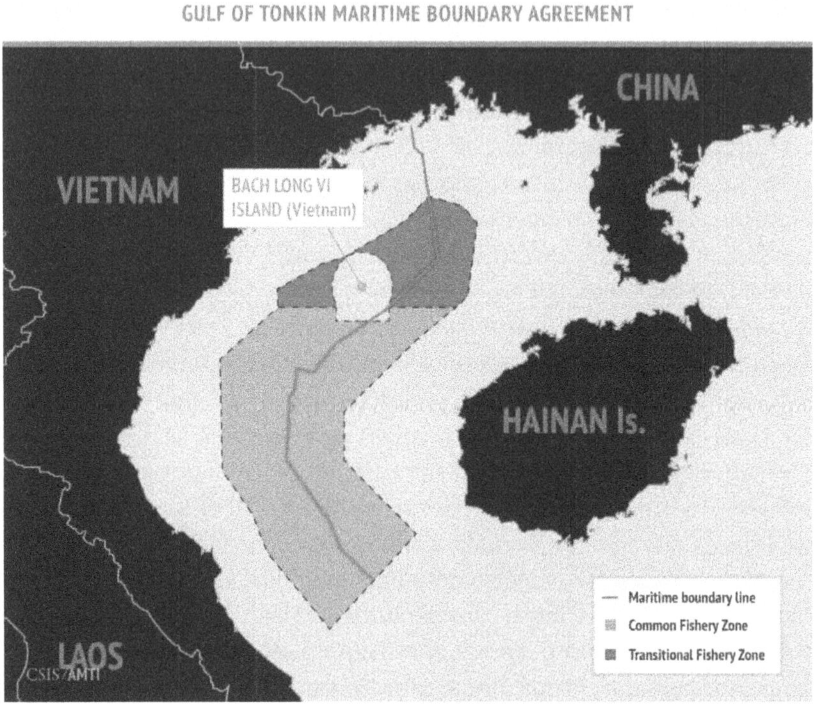

Map 3 Maritime boundary agreement and fisheries agreement in the Gulf of Tonkin[228]

handle fishing incidents if fishermen ventured outside the defined joint zones.[229] China was ready to accept a sea boundary only after relatively specific modalities guaranteed Chinese fishing practices.

The fisheries agreement establishes three subzones. A common fisheries zone is established in a band of a width of 30.5 nautical miles along the boundary line (article 3). A joint commission (article 6) determines annually the number of fishing vessels and the catch level based on joint surveys. Article 12 establishes a buffer zone for small fishing boats transgressing the zone. Each side commits to refrain from detaining or arresting small boats that accidentally enter the other side's waters in this buffer zone. In implementation of the agreement, both sides have agreed that fishing vessels should not be operating within 15 nautical miles of Vietnam's Bac Long Vi Island. Article 11 provides for a transitional arrangement in a fishing zone north of the common fisheries zone where each side has to reduce its fishing

228 The map is drawn from the CSIS Asia Maritime Transparency Initiative, https://amti.csis.org/maritime-disputes/territory_prc_vn/ (last accessed 23 June 2023). Reproduced with permission.
229 Zou, 'The Sino-Vietnamese Agreement on Maritime Boundary Delimitation', 17.

operations within four years. Article 22 limits the validity of the agreement to 15 years and says that the 'extension of cooperation shall be negotiated between the two parties through consultation' (article 22). The agreement expired on 30 June 2019. China has no legal right to an extended duration, but Vietnam agreed to extend the agreement for one year until June 2020.[230]

In the wake of the agreement, China has reduced the number of fishermen in the Gulf by about 6,000 vessels and relocated, compensated, or retrained fishermen for other employment.[231] The decrease in the number of fishermen was an issue between provincial (Hainanese) and central bureaucracies of China. The Hainanese provincial government and the Hainan office of China's Ministry of Foreign Affairs represented the interests of Hainan's fishing industry with a view to mitigate the effects of the agreement on the Hainanese fishing industry.[232]

2.3 Extending the Gulf of Tonkin Cooperation into the South China Sea

China and Vietnam initiated a series of talks at multiple levels to extend the maritime cooperation into the mouth of the Gulf of Tonkin in 2006.[233] Rising tensions in the South China Sea in 2009 revealed the necessity of doing so. This approach has produced a general 'Agreement on basic principles guiding the settlement of sea related issues' in October 2011.[234] Similar to 1993, a general agreement on principles was taken as the basis for negotiations about extending the boundary plus transboundary cooperation framework into an adjacent area. The 'mouth of the Gulf of Tonkin' connects the Gulf of Tonkin with the South China Sea.[235] An additional achievement of the Gulf of Tonkin agreements of 2000 was therefore to provide a framework for further Sino-Vietnamese talks.[236] China's Premier Li Keqiang publicly

230 Interview with a senior official of China's Ministry of Foreign Affairs, China, 2019 (Interview 46).

231 Interview 24; Zhang quotes another source on this point. Hongzhou Zhang, 'Chinese Fishermen in Disputed Waters: Not Quite a "People's War"', *Marine Policy* 68 (June 2016): 65–73.

232 Interview 24.

233 Tønnesson, 'The Tonkin Gulf Agreements: A Model of Conflict Resolution?', 164.

234 Ramses Amer, 'The South China Sea: Achievements and Challenges to Dispute Management', *Asian Survey*, 55 (2015), 618–39, 631.

235 De Tréglodé, 'Maritime Boundary Delimitation', 40.

236 Stein Tønnesson, 'Could China and Vietnam Resolve the Conflicts in the South China Sea', in *Major Law and Policy Issues in the South China Sea: European and American Perspectives*, ed. Yann-Huei Song and Keyuan Zou (Ashgate, 2014), 207–233; also see Ramses Amer and Keyuan Zou, *Conflict Management and Dispute Settlement in East Asia* (Ashgate, 2011).

endorsed the talks and urged substantive progress: 'With the utmost discretion, groups of experts from both countries met seven times between 2010 and 2011, and from 2012 onwards,' but the talks 'became extremely blunt, and the debate has barely progressed at all in the last two years.'[237] The talks were interrupted by an incident on 26 May 2011 whereby a Chinese maritime surveillance vessel cut the exploration cable of a seismic vessel of PetroVietnam, the Binh Minh02.[238] Escalation risks became once more apparent.

The talks initially focused on maritime boundary delimitation, but both sides disagreed on how to draw a median line.[239] The negotiators also disagreed on priorities and sequences. Beijing wanted to focus on joint development talks, while Vietnam preferred to focus on boundary delimitation.[240] Note that both China and Vietnam have valid legal entitlements to an EEZ and continental shelf in this geographic area. Talks on joint development did not result in an agreement. The definition of the geographic area for Sino-Vietnamese cooperation in the South China Sea proved to be a non-circumventable obstacle. As both sides claim the Paracel Islands, a compromise would need to protect against vulnerabilities arising from an arrangement for sovereignty claims.[241] One negotiation round was reportedly coined by Vietnam insisting on a wider area in the eastern direction and China on a longer area in the southern direction.[242] China has preferred a joint development agreement but has rejected any arrangement that could be construed as merely acknowledging the existence of a dispute over the Paracel Islands. According to a former Vietnamese diplomat, 'joint development is Vietnam's leverage, but China doesn't want to discuss the Paracel, so it's deadlocked.'[243] The compromise appeared to be a tiny block for joint exploration activities located directly

237 De Tréglodé, 'Maritime Boundary Delimitation', 41 quoting a Vietnamese source.

238 Ministry of Foreign Affairs of Vietnam, *Press Conference on Chinese maritime surveillance vessel's cutting exploration cable of PetroViet Nam Seismic Vessel* (2011), http://www.mofa.gov.vn/en/tt_baochi/pbnfn/ns110530220030/ (last visited 22 March 2022).

239 International Crisis Group, 'Stirring up the South China Sea (IV): Oil in Troubled Waters', 22.

240 Ibid.

241 Interview with a scholar of a leading think tank on international relations affiliated with Vietnam's Ministry of Foreign Affairs, Nha Trang, 14 November 2016; interview with a security expert of the Vietnamese armed forces, London, 23/09/2016 (Interviews 16 and 17); Chinese sources did not contradict this account.

242 Ibid.

243 A former Vietnamese foreign ministry official, quoted in International Crisis Group, 'Stirring up the South China Sea (IV): Oil in Troubled Waters', 22.

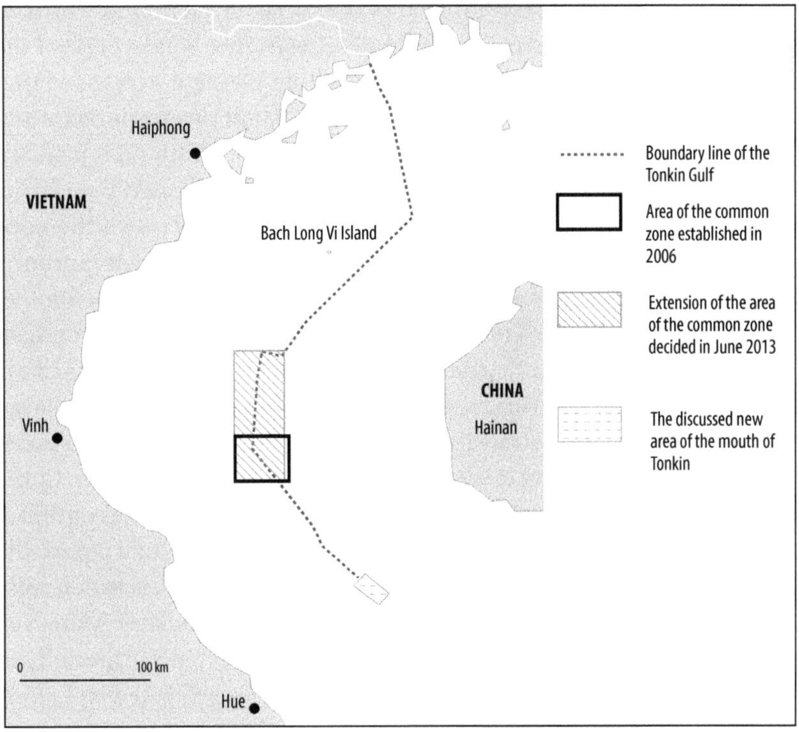

Map 4 Areas for joint surveys in the Gulf of Tonkin[244]

at the mouth of the Gulf of Tonkin rather than a larger area extending further into the South China Sea. Map 4 illustrates the common zones for exploration activities.

Despite the lack of an agreed boundary or provisional rules on hydrocarbon resources in the South China Sea, China moved ahead unilaterally. On 1 May 2014, China moved the oil rig HYSY 981 into an area of overlapping claims 17 nm to the south of Triton Island, part of the Paracel Islands Group occupied by China and claimed by Vietnam, 130 nm to the east of Vietnam's coastline and 180 nm to the south of Hainan.[245] The Sino-Vietnamese relations faced a tense crisis, leading to near-armed conflict. A two-month-long crisis escalated when Vietnam dispatched six coast guard vessels to

244 In Benoît De Tréglodé, 'Maritime Boundary Delimitation and Sino-Vietnamese Cooperation in the Gulf of Tonkin (1994–2016)', *China Perspectives*, 2016, 33–41, 39. Reproduced with permission.
245 Embassy of Vietnam to Germany, 'Viet Nam's International Press Conference', 7 May 2014, http://www.vietnambotschaft.org/viet-nams-international-press-conference-on-7th-may-2014/ (last accessed 23 June 2023).

demand the immediate withdrawal of the oil rig. A Vietnamese official explained that the objective of Vietnamese resistance was to prevent the rig from 'establishing a fixed position'.[246] While Vietnam demanded that China 'immediately end acts of violating Viet Nam's sovereign rights and jurisdiction',[247] China defended the rig's activities.[248] Both sides justified their deployment of up to a total of 200 navy and coast guard vessels, the use of water cannons, and the ramming of rival vessels with the need to protect their sovereign rights. Beijing accused Vietnam of ramming its vessels 171 times in only four days between 3 May and 7 May 2014.[249] Chinese sources refer to a total of sixty Vietnamese vessels that rammed Chinese vessels more than 500 times.[250] Vietnamese sources cite a total of 137 Chinese vessels and overflights of Chinese bomber aircraft. China deployed its ships in three concentric circles around the rig, with the navy vessels being located in the inner circle.[251] The situation deescalated when China withdrew its oil rig. Exploration activities in disputed areas have continued to raise Sino-Vietnamese tensions. In 2018, for instance, China reportedly threatened the Spanish oil company Repsol with market exclusion from China if it remained active in Vietnamese concession blocks.[252] Moreover, fishing incidents have also continued to occur repeatedly, especially in the waters around the Paracel Islands, as China has protected its fishing fleet from enforcement action of other coast guards since 2010.[253] Later, the character of the mission of the China Coast Guard around the Paracel Islands

246 Chris Brummit, 'Vietnam Tries to Stop China Oil Rig Deployment', *USA Today*, May 2014, https://eu.usatoday.com/story/news/world/2014/05/07/vietnam-china-oil-rig/8797007/ (last accessed 23 June 2023).
247 Embassy of Vietnam to Germany, 'International Press Conference on the situation in the East Sea', 5 June 2014, http://www.vietnambotschaft.org/international-press-conference-on-the-situation-in-the-east-sea/ (last accessed 23 June 2023).
248 State Council of the People's Republic of China, 'China urges against Vietnamese interference in territorial water exploration activities in Xisha Islands', 8 May 2014, https://english.www.gov.cn/state_council/state_councilors/2014/08/23/content_281474983036388.htm (last accessed 22 June 2023).
249 'China, Vietnam hold talks on recent anti-China violence', *China Daily*, 17 May 2014, https://www.chinadaily.com.cn/world/2014-05/17/content_17514753.htm (last accessed 23 June 2023).
250 'Beijing urges Vietnam to stop disruptive activities', 17 May 2014, http://www.chinadaily.com.cn/china/2014-05/17/content_17514575.htm (last accessed 23 June 2023).
251 Embassy of Vietnam to Germany, 'International Press Conference on the situation in the East Sea, 5 June 2014.
252 Bill Hayton, 'South China Sea: Vietnam 'scraps new oil project'', *BBC*, 23 March 2018, http://www.bbc.com/news/world-asia-43507448 (last accessed 23 June 2023).
253 Dang Thang Nguyen, 'Fisheries Co-Operation in the South China Sea and the (Ir)Relevance of the Sovereignty Question', *Asian Journal of International Law* 2, no. 01 (2012): 59–88, 65.

has evolved from protecting Chinese fishermen to expelling Vietnamese fishing vessels.[254]

2.4 Gulf of Tonkin Agreements Reconsidered

One major lesson from the Gulf of Tonkin cooperation is that a fisheries agreement and joint development across an established boundary can be politically feasible, even when joint development or a fisheries agreement in lieu of a boundary is not feasible. Vietnam has consented to hold joint seismic surveys with China in blocs across the agreed maritime boundary, and it has accepted a common fisheries zone across the boundary. Joint exploration of hydrocarbon resources and fisheries regulation without a simultaneous boundary agreement was not an acceptable option for Vietnam. As the Sino-Vietnamese boundary agreement established institutional protection against the possibility that a resource-sharing arrangement becomes a layer of validity and hence a vulnerability for future boundary negotiations, China and Vietnam have agreed on joint patrols, the sharing of fisheries, and some level of common regulation. Once both have decided which state has the exclusive sovereign rights on which side of a boundary, it has become feasible to create common fishing zones. In other words, as the basic allocation of jurisdiction and state authority was settled, transboundary cooperation has become an option. In this case, the problem whether a cooperative agreement strengthens one side's bargaining power in subsequent interactions on boundaries does not arise. Thus, the boundary agreement has enabled Vietnam's consent to transboundary cooperation. Vietnam's commitment to transboundary marine economic cooperation has enabled China's consent to the boundary in the Gulf of Tonkin, as the transboundary cooperation has given China access to resources beyond the boundary. As will be shown below, Brunei and Malaysia have also come to a compromise by combining a boundary with a resource-sharing arrangement.[255]

In contrast, the disagreement between Chinese and Vietnamese negotiators on agreements for the South China Sea was motivated by both sides' expectation that an arrangement could validate the opponent's claim and

254 Thanh Trung Nguyen, 'Davids and Goliath: Time for Southeast Asian Fishery Cooperation in the South China Sea', *AMTI*, 20 June 2019, https://amti.csis.org/davids-and-goliath-time-for-southeast-asian-fishery-cooperation-in-the-south-china-sea/; 'South China Sea: Fishing on the front line of Beijing's ambitions', *Financial Times*, 24 January 2019, https://www.ft.com/content/fead89da-1a4e-11e9-9e64-d150b3105d21 (last accessed 23 June 2023).
255 Chapter III 4.

thereby increase its leverage in future interactions. Note that China and Vietnam have negotiated about areas to which both have legally valid maritime entitlements. While the Gulf of Tonkin model could, in principle, offer an option for Sino-Vietnamese cooperation in the north-western South China Sea,[256] this model is unlikely to be emulated in other parts of the South China Sea where maritime boundary delimitation is not an option given China's invalidated claims.

The willingness of both China and Vietnam to enter into a negotiation process based on a clarification of the legal grounds of their claims proved a precondition for reaching a boundary agreement. Once such a boundary is established, parties have the possibility to establish governance mechanisms for transboundary cooperation on fisheries, law enforcement, seismic surveys, and marine scientific research across the boundary. In the Gulf of Tonkin, the boundary does not build a fence separating each parties' activities once and for all. The two agreements design the boundary as an initial distribution of state authority under which various economic activities can take place. Although the boundary agreement has been an initial agreement that enabled rather than prevented transboundary cooperation, the cooperative activities at sea have been limited. The law enforcement cooperation appears to be a confidence-building measure rather than a functional common enforcement effort. Both held seventeen joint patrols in fifteen years.[257] The work of the joint committee is described as 'rigid political rituals, yielding few results'.[258] The limited common activities reflect both sides' concerns about preserving their exclusive sovereign rights. CNOOC and Petro Vietnam have initiated joint exploration activities in 2006 in accordance with the boundary agreement (article 7). Both sides have agreed on a larger area for joint exploration in 2013. Although some exploration activities took place, including seismic research and the drilling of one well, there have not yet been commercially viable findings.[259] Furthermore, despite Chinese attempts to extend the duration of the Gulf of Tonkin fisheries agreement beyond 2020, the agreement expired in June 2020 (after

256 Tønnesson, 'The Tonkin Gulf Agreements: A Model of Conflict Resolution?'.

257 'Vietnam, China begin fishery inspection in Gulf of Tonkin', *Vietnam Plus*, 25 April 2019, https://en.vietnamplus.vn/vietnam-china-begin-fishery-inspection-in-gulf-of-tonkin/151573.vnp (last accessed 23 June 2023).

258 De Tréglodé, 'Maritime Boundary Delimitation', 38, quoting Vietnamese sources.

259 'Petrovietnam and CNOOC signed the 4th Amendment to the Agreement on Joint Exploration in the Gulf of Tonkin', Press Release PetroVietnam, 20 June 2013, http://www.pvcoating.vn/en/shareholders/details/petrovietnam-and-cnooc-signed-the-4th-amendment-to-the-agreement-on-joint-exploration-in-the-gulf-of-tonkin-139/ (last accessed 23 June 2023).

an extension of one year).[260] Officials from both countries' Ministries of Foreign Affairs have resumed negotiations on the delimitation of the sea boundary 'beyond the mouth of the Gulf of Tonkin',[261] in the South China Sea, on 1 December 2021. However, the negotiations have not progressed at the time of writing.

The successful conclusion of a boundary agreement and an additional fisheries agreement for the Gulf of Tonkin has not produced a reciprocity-based dynamic towards further extending this cooperation into the South China Sea. Despite negotiation efforts, the need to prevent escalation and interests in utilizing natural resources, China and Vietnam have not reached any agreements – neither a boundary arrangement, possibly with a resource-sharing arrangement straddling the boundary, nor a joint development agreement in lieu of a boundary. Both have chosen persistent stalemate, fearing the impact of agreement on their claims more than the risk of conflict.

3 The Philippines and Taiwan: Comprehensive Pressure, Minimal Cooperation

The preceding case studies illustrate that not only the Philippines and Vietnam but also China have worried about cooperative agreements resulting in vulnerabilities that a rival could weaponize in subsequent interactions. The question arises whether this is a result of the involvement of China, an effect of power asymmetries, or of a greater level of Vietnamese or Philippine mistrust towards China. The following two case studies on interactions between, on the one hand, the Philippines and Taiwan and, on the other hand, Brunei and Malaysia exclude China. The case studies show that similar barriers have blocked agreement in these two cases.

The Philippines entered into a law enforcement agreement on fisheries with Taiwan in 2015. In contrast, the Philippines did not accept any Chinese proposal on fisheries cooperation. At first glance, there may be various political, geopolitical, and security-related reasons why the Philippines

260 Interview with a senior official of China's Ministry of Foreign Affairs, China, 2019 (Interview 46); Xiaodong Xu, 'China-Vietnamese Fishery Co-Op Needs New Perspectives', *China Daily*, 1 February 2021, https://www.chinadaily.com.cn/a/202102/01/WS601754e3a31024ad0baa655e.html.

261 Vietnam News Agency, 'Vietnam, China Hold Talks on Maritime Issues', *VietnamPlus*, 2 December 2021, https://en.vietnamplus.vn/vietnam-china-hold-talks-on-maritime-issues/216502.vnp (last accessed 23 June 2023).

entered into an agreement with Taiwan on an issue about which it has refused to reach agreement with China. However, this view is misplaced. This chapter shows that the Philippines rejected all Taiwanese proposals until Taiwan applied comprehensive pressure to make the Philippines accept an agreement against Manila's wishes. Why was Manila so reluctant to cooperate with Taipei?

The context

The political situation for the Philippines in the South China Sea was worrisome in 2012. During 2012, China took control of Scarborough Shoal from the Philippines. This has illustrated that Manila needs partners to defend against China's activities. Furthermore, Manila has had an incentive to pre-empt some form of coordination between China and Taiwan on the South China Sea. The government of the Republic of China conceived of the nine-dash line during the 1930s and published it on a map in 1948.[262] Taipei hosts the archives of the Republic of China, containing historical documents necessary to provide legal evidence for the nine-dash line. From Taipei's decisions on sovereignty claims may thus follow some degree of validity, if not legitimacy, for the claims illustrated by the nine-dash line. Taiwan claims all features within the nine-dash line, but its claims to maritime zones are different from mainland China's. Taiwan emphasizes the relevance and application of the law of the sea and UNCLOS.[263] Moreover, the Philippines and Taiwan are both democracies that have faced an increasingly assertive China and have a common ally in the US. Hence, one could have expected that these contextual reasons incentivised some form of provisional cooperation on an aspect of the disputes between Manila and Taipei.

However, the Philippines rejected Taiwan's calls for fisheries cooperation for many years. Manila also rejected negotiations on the agreement it ultimately accepted. Taiwan tried to reach provisional rules for overlapping claims with the Philippines since 1998 when it passed its EEZ

262 Hsin-Chih Chen, 'La Réponse Chinoise à l'occupation Française Des Îles Spratly En 1933', *Guerres Mondiales et Conflits Contemporains*, 2001, 5–24; Bill Hayton, 'When Good Lawyers Write Bad History: Unreliable Evidence and the South China Sea Territorial Dispute', *Ocean Development & International Law* 48, no. 1 (2 January 2017): 17–34.

263 Ministry of Foreign Affairs, Republic of China (Taiwan), 'South China Sea', https://en.mofa.gov.tw/theme.aspx?n=1462&s=40&sms=294; Republic of China (Taiwan), 'Position Paper on ROC South China Sea Policy', 21 March 2016, https://multilingual.mofa.gov.tw/web/web_UTF-8/South/Position%20Paper%20on%20ROC%20South%20China%20Sea%20Policy.pdf (last accessed 23 June 2023).

and Continental Shelf law.[264] Taiwan's and the Philippines' legally valid EEZ claims overlap widely in the Luzon Strait and in parts of the South China Sea and Western Pacific. Taipei claims that Itu Aba is entitled to an EEZ and there is also a dispute about the existence of maritime rights in the Spratly Islands.[265] Lacking a boundary or a fisheries agreement, fishing incidents occurred. Even after two deadly incidents, including in the Balintang Channel, Taiwan still had to force the Philippines to the negotiation table in 2013. This was the case even though the two countries have had legally valid claims, are both democracies, have a common ally, have faced a worsening geopolitical context, and have had leaders that take international legal options seriously.[266] Moreover, China's island construction program that built artificial islands on the Philippines' continental shelf seems not to have contributed to the Philippines willingness to negotiate an agreement with Taiwan either. The Philippines was aware of the large-scale program at least since early 2013.[267] Even the loss of Scarborough Shoal in April 2012 did not contribute to Manila's willingness to consider measures that could avoid incidents with Taiwanese vessels. After two more years of painful negotiations and a comprehensive Taiwanese pressure campaign, both sides reached an agreement on maritime law enforcement cooperation in 2015 – the agreement with the smallest scope of all fisheries agreements in the East and South China Sea. This raises the question of why the Philippines were so reluctant to negotiate this agreement with Taiwan?

264 Keyuan Zou and Yann-Huei Song, 'Maritime Legislation of Mainland China and Taiwan: Developments, Comparison, Implications, and Potential Challenges for the United States', *Ocean Development & International Law* 31, no. 4 (2000): 303–45.

265 Taiwan does not accept the ruling of the South China Sea Arbitration. Ministry of Foreign Affairs of Taiwan, 'ROC position on the South China Sea Arbitration', 12 July 2016, https://www.mofa.gov.tw/en/News_Content.aspx?n=1EADDCFD4C6EC567&s=5B5A9134709EB875 (last accessed 23 June 2023); see Nigel N. T. Li, 'Amicus Curiae Submission by the Chinese (Taiwan) Society of International Law in the South China Sea Arbitration: An Introductory Note', in *Chinese (Taiwan) Yearbook of International Law and Affairs* (2017), 167–227.

266 President Ma Ying-jeou wrote his PhD thesis at Harvard University about joint development agreements and the law of the sea ('Trouble Over Oily Waters: Legal Problems of Seabed Boundaries and Foreign Investments in the East China Sea') in 1980. Yoshiyuki Ogasawara, 'Ma Ying-jeou's Doctoral Thesis and Its Impact on the Japan-Taiwan Fisheries Negotiations', *Journal of Contemporary East Asia Studies* 4, no. 2 (2015): 67–92. President Aquino launched arbitral proceedings against China.

267 Armed Forces of the Philippines, *Ayungin Shoal: Situation Update* (11 May 2013) (Annex 95); Armed Forces of the Philippines, *Chronological Development of Artificial Structures on Features* (Annex 96), Vol IV.

Incidents, sanctions, navy exercises, and an international diplomatic campaign

On 9 May 2013, the Taiwanese fishing vessel Guang Da Xing No. 28 operated in an area of overlapping EEZ claims. The area was in the east of the Balintang Channel, which is in the east of the Luzon Strait. It is approximately 40 nautical miles from the nearest Philippine island and 170 nautical miles from the nearest Taiwanese island. The incident occurred on the Philippine side of a hypothetical median line and outside the Philippine territorial sea. Philippine Coast Guard personnel of the Philippine vessel BFAR MCS-3001 tried to stop and board the Taiwanese fishing vessel. When the fishing crew did not comply, the Philippine Coast Guard fired shots at the vessel and killed Hung Shih-cheng. The Taiwanese inspection found fifty-two bullet holes in the ship.[268] Mainland China protested the shooting of the Taiwanese fishermen.[269] The Philippine Coast Guard reported that a few shots in 'self-defence' were fired at the 'engine section of said vessel in order to stop it'.[270] A subsequent report by the Philippine Department of Justice, undertaken independently of the Philippine Coast Guard and at the insistence of Taiwan, questioned the first Philippine report, particularly the assertion of self-defence.[271] The report recommended that eight crew members be charged with homicide.

This incident was the second deadly incident, as Philippine officers killed a Taiwanese fisherman in 2006.[272] President Ma of Taiwan, an international lawyer and law, adopted the position that the Philippines' forcible law enforcement violated the law of the sea. States must exercise self-restraint in areas of overlapping claims; they cannot endanger life or use excessive violence.[273] Accordingly, Taiwan reacted with a strong protest and four demands: The Philippines should, first, admit responsibility and make an official apology; second, punish the responsible crew members for homicide

268 'Taiwan ultimatum to Philippines over fisherman's death', *BBC*, 12 May 2013, https://www.bbc.com/news/world-asia-22499246 (last accessed 23 June 2023).
269 'China condemns fisherman's death', *China Daily*, 11 May 2013, http://www.chinadaily.com.cn/cndy/2013-05/11/content_16491942.htm (last accessed 23 June 2023).
270 Department of Justice of the Philippines, 'Balintang Channel Incident Report', originally published in the Official Gazette, available at http://newsinfo.inquirer.net/460753/balintang-channel-incident-report (last accessed 23 June 2023).
271 Ibid.
272 'Government slams Manila over death', *Taipei Times*, 11 May 2013, http://www.taipeitimes.com/News/front/archives/2013/05/11/2003561976/2 (last accessed 23 June 2023).
273 Interview with a former senior Taiwanese official, Ministry of Foreign Affairs, Taipei, 05 April 2017 (Interview 12).

and obstruction of justice; third, compensate the victim family; and, fourth, negotiate a fisheries agreement that prevents similar incidents.[274] Taiwan issued an ultimatum on 15 May 2013 and demanded a response within twenty-four hours. The Philippines refused to admit responsibility or to meet any other demand.

On 16 May 2013, Taiwan mounted a campaign and put pressure on the Philippines: Taiwan imposed economic sanctions, froze visa application for Philippine migrant workers (an important source of incomes for Philippine families), recalled its representative in Manila, asked the Philippine representative to leave Taiwan, issued a travel alert on the Philippines, and discouraged Taiwanese to visit the Philippines. Taiwan froze high-level official exchanges, exchanges on trade, civil aviation, and the visa waiver program for businesses.[275] The sanctions imposed costs on both countries.

The same day, Taiwan held joint navy and coast guard drills in the disputed area close to the location of the incident 'to protect Taiwan's fishing rights'.[276] Although Taiwan has a valid EEZ claim to the area, it would not normally cross the parallel of 20 degrees north to protect fishing rights. This time, however, the exercises involved a Taiwanese destroyer, two frigates, helicopters, fighter jets and simulated missile launches. This show of force in disputed waters brought the Philippines to the negotiation table. Manila continued to reject talks on a fisheries agreement, however, and its first apology did not meet Taiwan's expectation.[277] When the talks stalled, Taiwan started an international media campaign lobbying US media to criticise the Philippines and US congressmen, for instance Steve Chabot, to support their position.[278] The US government intervened diplomatically and urged the Philippines to settle as fast as possible.[279] After another three months of intensive negotiations, Manila announced it would prosecute the coast guard members on 7 August 2013, issued an apology on 8 August 2013, and promised talks about fisheries. Taiwan lifted all sanctions. Incidents, however, continued. Two years later, in May 2015, the Philippine Coast

274 Ministry of Foreign Affairs, 'Taiwan Press Announcement No. 202', 08 August 2013, https://www.mofa.gov.tw/en/News_Content.aspx?n=539A9A50A5F8AF9E&sms=37B41539382B84BA&s=C9567323DE86F532 (last accessed 23 June 2023).

275 Interview 12.

276 Lawrence Chung, 'Taiwan's Military Drills in Disputed Waters to Step up Pressure on Manila', *SCMP*, May 2013, https://www.scmp.com/news/china/article/1237123/taiwans-military-drills-disputed-waters-step-pressure-manila (last accessed 23 June 2023).

277 'Talk of the Day – Taiwan, Philippines duel for global support', 2013/05/18, *Focus Taiwan*, https://focustaiwan.tw/politics/201305180026 (last accessed 23 June 2023).

278 Ibid.

279 Interview 12.

Guard apprehended a Taiwanese fishing boat. As a Taiwanese Coast Guard vessel blocked the Philippine vessel, a four-hour standoff followed until the Taiwanese fishing boat was released.[280]

3.1 The Fisheries Law Enforcement Agreement and its Barriers

Despite Taiwanese pressure, it took another two years and three months for both sides to agree on the 'Agreement Concerning the Facilitation of Cooperation on Law Enforcement in Fisheries Matters between The Taipei Economic and Cultural Office in the Philippines and The Manila Economic and Cultural Office in Taiwan' on 5 November 2015.[281] The agreement provides for the law enforcement authorities to 'avoid using violence or unnecessary force' (article 2). Attachment B establishes how this commitment that merely repeats pre-existing international obligations shall be implemented. If one party plans to take law enforcement activities against fishermen of the other party, it has to 'inform the other party, so that this other party can deal with the situation first'. The first party has to '[g]ive the other side one (1) hour to deal with the situation and for the vessel to leave the area immediately' before it can enforce its laws.

The minimum rules necessary for avoiding fishing incidents are an understanding of not enforcing the laws of one party against the fishermen of another party. Even if the parties cannot reach an agreement on not *applying* their laws to the fishing boats of the other party, another way of preventing escalation is not to *enforce* the laws of one party against the fishing boats of another before a certain time has passed. Here, Manila and Taipei have committed to this minimum requirement for the limited time of one hour. The effect on the ground is likely to be the following. If a Philippine Coast Guard vessel intends to enforce Philippine rules against a Taiwanese fishing boat, the Coast Guard has first to inform the Taiwanese counterpart. The Taiwanese Coast Guard is then going to inform the Taiwanese fishing vessel to leave the area. If the vessel does not leave within one hour, the Philippine Coast Guard can enforce Philippine rules. The arrangement also includes a commitment to release detained crews and boats within three days.

280 Paterno Esmaquel II, 'PH confirms standoff with Taiwan off Batanes', *Rappler*, 03 June 2015, https://www.rappler.com/nation/95156-philippines-fisheries-agreement-taiwan (last accessed 23 June 2023).

281 Agreement Concerning the Facilitation of Cooperation on Law Enforcement in Fisheries Matters between The Taipei Economic and Cultural Office in the Philippines and The Manila Economic and Cultural Office in Taiwan, signed 5 November 2015. Entered into force 5 December 2015, accessible at https://law.moj.gov.tw/ENG/LawClass/LawAll.aspx?pcode=Y0110542 (last accessed 23 March 2024).

Barriers to agreement

The Philippines did not try to settle fisheries disputes with Taiwan and thereby reduce the number of maritime disputes. This would have allowed Manila to focus on China's activities in Philippine-claimed areas. To the contrary, Manila rejected Taipei's proposals. Two answers appear plausible as to why Manila opposed even shallow and rudimentary fisheries cooperation with Taiwan. First, it could be that the Philippines tried not to damage its relations with China by signing an agreement with Taiwan that might potentially affect Manila's One China policy. Second, the Philippines needed to rule out that an agreement could establish a practical precedent supporting Taiwan's EEZ claim. As shown above, this problem blocked negotiations between China and the Philippines and China and Vietnam. I will discuss both explanations in turn.

First, as the Philippines does not recognize Taiwan, the status question of Taiwan would clearly thwart boundary negotiations.[282] Even if boundary questions were not part of the negotiations, the status question of Taiwan might have blocked Philippine consent to a law enforcement arrangement. However, if this were the case, the Philippines would be very selective about when Taiwan's status is a barrier to agreements with Taiwan and when Taiwan's status is not a barrier. The Philippines is not hesitant to engage in practical cooperation with Taiwan in many policy areas. The Manila Economic and Cultural Office and the Taipei Economic and Cultural Office have entered into various agreements on trade, investment, visa waiver programs, aviation, migrant workers, technology, education, and science cooperation. Chinese officials have reminded their Philippine counterparts in bilateral foreign minister consultations in 2012 that '[u]pholding the One China principle is the political foundation of our bilateral relations'.[283] They have also urged the Philippines 'not so sign any agreement with sovereignty implications'.[284] China protested the investment treaty between the Philippines and Taiwan, but this fact did not stop the Philippines from signing the investment treaty.[285] I could not find, however,

282 Rodolfo C. Severino, 'The Philippines' National Territory', *Southeast Asian Affairs*, 2012, 257–62.

283 Record of Discussion: 17th Philippines-China Foreign Ministry Consultations (14 January 2012) (Annex 204), Vol VI.

284 Department of Foreign Affairs of the Republic of the Philippines, *Notes on the 18th Philippines-China Foreign Ministry Consultations* (19 October 2012) (Annex 85), Vol IV.

285 'China unhappy as Philippines signs investment deal with Taiwan', *SCMP*, 09 December 2017, http://www.scmp.com/news/china/diplomacy-defence/article/2123556/

that China protested the Philippine-Taiwanese fisheries law enforcement agreement in 2015. China's Foreign Minister Wang Yi visited the Philippines on 10 November, a few days after the agreement was signed.[286] If China protested, the protest was below the level of public attention. China protested the fisheries agreement between Japan and Taiwan.[287] In sum, there is no sufficient evidence that the status question regarding Taiwan prevented fisheries cooperation in a specific way. Lacking a compelling argument why a law enforcement arrangement would affect Taiwan's status more than an investment treaty, the status question alone cannot explain the reluctant Philippine negotiation position on practical cooperation in the field of fisheries.

Second, a former senior Taiwanese official with direct knowledge of the negotiations commented on the negotiations: 'The Philippines was very hesitant. It claims large portions of waters and does not recognize Taiwanese fishing rights. The legal point of the agreement: Manila did not recognize the ROC's EEZ claim. But now it does implicitly.'[288] The institutional set-up of the agreement needed to find a formula for minimising the Philippines' concern that entering into an agreement would recognize Taiwan's fishing rights and thereby strengthen its claim. Taiwan, however, 'wanted an arrangement similar to the agreement with Japan. Manila blocked.'[289] The arrangement between Taiwan and Japan defines common fishing zones and establishes rules for non-enforcement.[290] China also offered the Philippines such arrangements, but the Philippines did not accept any of them.[291] Philippine officials worried that Taiwan's preferred arrangement would have supported the rights of Taiwan by giving them a reflection in common fisheries zones. The scope and structure of the Taiwanese-Philippine agreement demonstrate the negotiators' attempt to evade any de facto validation of any side's claim. The negotiators have achieved this by writing an agreement with remarkably minimal substantive content – the mere affirmation of a pre-existing international legal obligation and a

china-unhappy-philippines-signs-investment-deal-taiwan (last accessed 23 June 2023).

286 Ministry of Foreign Affairs of China, 'Foreign Ministry Spokesperson Hong Lei's Regular Press Conference on November 9, 2015', https://www.fmprc.gov.cn/ce/cedk/eng/fyrth/t1313261.htm (last accessed 23 March 2022).

287 Chapter IV 3.

288 Interview with a former senior Taiwanese official, Ministry of Foreign Affairs, Taipei, 05 April 2017 (Interview 12).

289 Ibid.

290 Chapter IV 3.

291 Chapter III 1.5.

communication procedure. Manila refused common fishing zones that define catch quotas, the number of fishing vessels or conservation measures. The negotiations did not turn around the question of how to distribute economic gains from joint action. The underlying obstacle was the question of how to find a model for a minimum of coordinated action – time-limited non-enforcement – without this coordination creating a de facto layer of validity in favour of Taiwan's claims. A third potential explanation for Manila's reluctance is the fact that Manila did not want to jeopardize its position on fisheries cooperation vis-à-vis China. However, I am not aware of any Chinese official who has argued that Manila must accept a fisheries agreement with China similar to the agreement with Taiwan.

Philippine and Taiwanese negotiators then had the task of finding terms for an agreement that neither side could leverage to its advantage. In the present case, an agreement that neither specifies a geographic scope nor common jurisdiction has satisfied the negotiators. Only attachment B contains an unspecified reference to the geographic area, 'the Exclusive Economic Zone' (singular in the agreement). This is probably meant to designate the area where both parties' EEZs overlap. The agreement does not even refer to 'Exclusive Economic Zones' (plural) and thereby evades merely mentioning the existence of more than one EEZ. The agreement does not contain provisions which could be interpreted as pre-determining the extent of EEZ claims. Not defining the applicable area, however, leaves an important question unanswered – whether the agreement applies to the disputed area that results from Taiwan's EEZ claim from Itu Aba. It is not clear whether the agreement applies to the waters between Itu Aba and Palawan. Itu Aba is the largest of the Spratly Islands and is occupied by Taiwan. The South China Sea Arbitration ruled that Itu Aba is a rock, not an island, and does not generate an EEZ claim.[292] However, Taiwan does not accept the award and the award is only legally binding between China and the Philippines (Art. 296(2) of UNCLOS).

The Philippines was reluctant to enter into fisheries agreements with China and Taiwan. Why was Taiwan able to reach the only formal agreement on fisheries law enforcement between the Philippines and another claimant in the South China Sea? Three differences with China are now apparent. First, Taiwan used sanctions to bring the Philippines to the negotiations table. Taiwan adopted coercive means exclusively for the objective of institutionalizing specific fisheries cooperation. The terms of the agreement, though, seem fair and balanced. China negotiated fisheries agreements

292 The South China Sea Arbitration, paras 473–625.

with the Philippines over nine years, with China making various proposals between 1995 and 2004. But as the Sino-Philippine talks did not result in an agreement, China continued its unilateral activities. The China Coast Guard has regularly protected its fishermen and has provided an umbrella for their fishing activities since 2010.[293] Second, notwithstanding Taiwan's status question, both Taiwan and the Philippines have valid overlapping EEZ claims in several areas. The agreements proposed by China covered areas in which China lacks valid entitlements. Third, Philippine and Taiwanese negotiators have found an agreement design that has satisfied the negotiators' need to exclude any adverse effects of the agreement on their claims. The agreement avoids mentioning the mere existence of rival EEZ claims. Taiwan has insisted on a procedure allowing Taiwanese fishermen to fish in areas of overlapping EEZs. Thus, it has taken more than two years to turn a simple commitment – each side shall give one-hour prior notice before enforcing national laws unilaterally – into an institutionalized procedure that prevents the reoccurrence of violence. Despite its minimal character and ambiguous definition of the geographic scope, the agreement is remarkably effective in preventing incidents. The author is not aware of the occurrence of violent fishing incidents since the agreement was reached. The negotiators have established a suitable procedure based on a minimal commitment.

4 Brunei and Malaysia: From Confrontation to Boundary Delimitation and Resource Sharing

This subchapter further illustrates three points. First, disputes involving China are not the only disputes that have escalated in the South China Sea. Incidents also sparked a confrontation between Brunei and Malaysia, two ASEAN members. Second, barriers similar to those in the preceding cases have blocked the negotiations between these two countries on natural resource agreements. Third, not unlike the Sino-Vietnamese arrangements in the Gulf of Tonkin, the combination of a sea boundary and a natural resource arrangement has enabled resource cooperation between Brunei and Malaysia by offering safeguards against vulnerabilities from such cooperation.

The EEZ and continental shelf claims of Brunei and Malaysia overlapped in the South China Sea (see Map 1) and a maritime boundary dispute arose. This dispute escalated in the early 2000s as efforts to reach a boundary

293 Nguyen, 'Fisheries Co-Operation in the South China Sea', 65; chapter III 1.5.

settlement remained elusive. Brunei and Malaysia have faced a common threat in China's maritime expansion. While this might arguably have incentivised attempts to overcome the bilateral dispute, both countries did not reach a boundary settlement until 2009. Moreover, both countries tried to negotiate a code of conduct with China in the context of ASEAN–China consultations.[294] In the late 1990s, both countries proposed terms for a code with the aim to restricting escalatory behaviour. The 'Declaration on the Conduct of Parties in the South China Sea,' signed by ASEAN members and China in November 2002, called for 'self-restraint in the conduct of activities that would complicate or escalate disputes' (paragraph 5).[295] Shortly after Brunei and Malaysia signed the declaration, however, both countries moved ahead with unilateral exploration activities in disputed areas. The unilateral attempts of Brunei and Malaysia to exploit oil without common rules resulted in severe incidents. In March 2003, a navy vessel from Brunei expelled a Murphy drilling ship commissioned by Malaysia's Petronas. In April 2003, a Malaysian patrol vessel drove away a Total vessel commissioned by Brunei.[296] Smith notes that, '2003 found the two States [Brunei and Malaysia] in near armed conflict over a mutually claimed maritime area, when a Malaysian naval vessel forced an oilfield exploration vessel operated by the French petroleum company TotalFinaElf from the "Block J-K" seabed production area.'[297] The Brunei–Malaysia dispute resulted in a de facto moratorium on hydrocarbon projects in areas of overlapping claims.

In response to these incidents, the opponents began negotiations in 2003 and 2005. Malaysia proposed a joint development agreement like the Malaysia–Thailand agreement in the Gulf of Thailand.[298] Brunei rejected the offer because its British legal advisors warned that a joint development agreement might 'entail conceding territorial rights'.[299] Note that there is

294 See Chapter V.

295 ASEAN Member States and People's Republic of China, 'Declaration on the Conduct of Parties in the South China Sea', 4 November 2002, https://asean.org/declaration-on-the-conduct-of-parties-in-the-south-china-sea-2/ (last accessed 23 March 2022).

296 Leszek Buszynski and Iskandar Sazlan, 'Maritime Claims and Energy Cooperation in the South China Sea', *Contemporary Southeast Asia* 29, no. 1 (2007): 143–71, 163.

297 Jeffrey J. Smith, 'Brunei and Malaysia Resolve Outstanding Maritime Boundary Issues', *LOS Reports* 1 (2010): 1–4, 3.

298 Malaysia and Thailand reached a Memorandum of Understanding (MoU) on the joint development of hydrocarbon resources in the Gulf of Thailand in 1979. For the MoU, see Masahiro Miyoshi, *The Joint Development of Offshore Oil and Gas in Relation to Maritime Boundary Delimitation*, Maritime briefing v. 2, no. 5 (International Boundaries Research Unit, University of Durham, 1999), 13–16.

299 Buszynski and Sazlan, 'Maritime Claims and Energy Cooperation', 164.

agreement among international lawyers that joint development is without prejudice to claims *de jure*. Legal advisors, however, warned against joint development because it could nevertheless weaken Brunei's negotiation positions in subsequent interactions by entailing concessions. Both parties were unable to agree on a joint development agreement because Brunei has believed that the joint area would strengthen Malaysia's claim up to the point of conceding rights. One theoretical mechanism how an agreement could entail concessions exceeding any legal effect – given the without prejudice character – is that an agreement establishes a focal point from which an opponent will not retreat in subsequent interactions. Brunei held this position, although the political context and existing disputes with China arguably should have incentivised compromise between Brunei and Malaysia.

Both countries interacted with the risk of escalation while China's claims and expanded presence in the South China Sea would have required a concerted approach to confronting a common and bigger challenge. Moreover, the dispute between Brunei and Malaysia escalated a few months after ASEAN members and China committed in the 2002 Declaration on Conduct to refrain from escalatory behaviour and, 'in a spirit of cooperation and understanding, to build trust and confidence'.[300] While Bruneian and Malaysian vessels confronted each other in 2003, ASEAN members tried to produce a consensus on a stronger and more effective ASEAN draft code between 2003 and 2006. ASEAN members had to exchange twenty-one drafts before compromise emerged on a common draft.[301] The signal escalating incidents between two ASEAN members sent to China undermined the efforts of committing China to a code of conduct and of producing a consensus among ASEAN members.

In this situation, Brunei and Malaysia had many reasons to try and find a mutually acceptable arrangement. Moreover, another incentive to finalize negotiations came from the continental shelf regime. The rules of the Commission on the Limits of the Continental Shelf (CLCS) require that preliminary submissions of states claiming an extended continental shelf beyond 200 nautical miles had to be made until 2009. The rules also require that the CLCS must refrain from making any recommendation on submissions if the geographic area of the submission is disputed.[302] Thus,

300 'Declaration on the Conduct of Parties in the South China Sea', para 5.

301 Chapter V 1.

302 Rules of Procedure, paragraph 3 of annex I of the Commission for the Limits of the Continental Shelf (CLCS), https://www.un.org/depts/los/clcs_new/commission_rules.htm (last accessed

the rules of the CLCS set 2009 as a deadline for an arrangement between Brunei and Malaysia.

Bilateral negotiations continued after 2005 and Brunei and Malaysia finally settled on a boundary and joint development agreement in March 2009. The boundary agreement delimits a part of the continental shelf boundary of Brunei and Malaysia in the South China Sea. The agreement was reached in the form of an 'Exchange of Letters' after six years and thirty-nine rounds of negotiations.[303] The 'Exchange of Letters' is not published, and not much is known about the negotiation process. Crucially, Malaysia and Brunei agreed on setting up a joint development zone in addition to delimiting the boundary.[304] The joint development zone is part of the boundary agreement. It is unclear whether China protested the agreement, although the agreement has established a maritime boundary within the nine-dash line, as no record of a protest note is publicly available.

The agreement structure with a joint development area in addition to a boundary does not only reflect a quid pro quo. Brunei gave Malaysia joint access to one area within its continental shelf in return for Malaysia accepting the boundary delimitation. The agreement does not reflect a general reluctance against resource sharing, as Brunei and Malaysia ultimately agreed on sharing natural resources. It was not the question of how to distribute gains from joint action on hydrocarbon resources that prevented the reaching of a joint development agreement either. After all, Brunei and Malaysia have agreed on the joint development of the natural resources that are located in a formerly disputed area and on Brunei's side of the newly established boundary. Rather, after the boundary established a safeguard against the possibility that the joint development area could affect subsequent bargaining processes on boundary delimitation, resource sharing has become feasible. Brunei and Malaysia could not agree on sharing the resources through a joint development agreement before the boundary agreement was reached, as Brunei considered this to develop a dynamic towards conceding rights. In this regard, the agreement resembles the Sino-Vietnamese Gulf of Tonkin cooperation, which also combines a boundary agreement with an arrangement for joint exploration and common fisheries zones. However, this model of combining a boundary with a

23 March 2024) and UNCLOS, article 4 of annex II.

303 Jeffrey J. Smith, 'Brunei and Malaysia resolve outstanding maritime boundary issues', *Law of the Sea Reports*, Vol.1 (2010), 1–4.

304 'Petronas: M'sia, Brunei to jointly develop 2 oil-rich areas', *The Star*, 1 May 2010, https://www.thestar.com.my/news/nation/2010/05/01/petronas-msia-brunei-to-jointly-develop-2-oilrich-areas (last accessed 23 March 2024).

resource-sharing agreement is unlikely to serve as a policy model for other cases where the rationale for joint development is to allow practical and provisional cooperation in lieu of boundary delimitation.

Finally, this agreement between Brunei and Malaysia also cleared the way for submissions of several Southeast Asian states for an extended continental shelf. The claimant states' submissions for an extended continental shelf have triggered important incidents in the disputes. Brunei made a submission for an extended continental shelf in 2009.[305] But it was in response to the joint submission for an extended continental shelf of Malaysia and Vietnam that China presented, for the first time, a map of the nine-dash line in a formal communication to the UN.[306] This communication, in turn, has triggered a round of protest notes, assertions of claims, and a series of incidents that have been characteristic of the disputes in the South China Sea.

305 Brunei's preliminary submission for an extended continental shelf is accessible at http://www.un.org/Depts/los/clcs_new/submissions_files/preliminary/brn2009preliminaryinformation.pdf (last accessed 23 March 2024).

306 Malaysia's joint submission with Vietnam and the notes verbales of China, Malaysia, Indonesia, the Philippines, and Vietnam are accessible at http://www.un.org/Depts/los/clcs_new/submissions_files/submission_mysvnm_33_2009.htm (last accessed 23 June 2023).

IV Institutions for Marine Natural Resources in the East China Sea

Abstract

This chapter shows that disputing actors in the East China Sea negotiate about shared marine natural resource governance in contested areas to prevent incidents, enable access to natural resources, and avoid deteriorating relations. In contrast to the South China Sea, China, Japan, and South Korea have reached several bilateral fisheries agreements within a brief negotiation period. This chapter demonstrates how these partly overlapping fisheries agreements have established the most substantial set of common rules for any disputed area of the East or South China Sea, despite severe challenges. It illustrates that claimant states experience that the position of opponents improves in the disputes because of such agreements. It explains why and how negotiators have overcome this barrier in some cases.

Keywords: East China Sea, territorial disputes, sea boundary disputes, UNCLOS, joint development of oil, fisheries agreements, natural resource institutions, crisis management, negotiation

This chapter analyses the efforts of claimant states to negotiate agreements for fisheries and the joint development of hydrocarbon resources in the East China Sea. This chapter first examines the past decades of exchanges between China and Japan about common oil and gas projects and joint fisheries agreements. It then turns to two bilateral joint fisheries agreements that South Korea and Japan, as well as China and South Korea, have concluded. Thirdly, this chapter presents the twenty-two-year-long period of on-and-off exchanges between Japan and Taiwan on a fisheries agreement. It demonstrates that joint fisheries agreements in the East China Sea are the most effective of all institutions in easing tensions in the East and South

Schultheiss, Christian: *Ocean Governance and Conflict in the East and South China Sea. Negotiating Natural Resources, Institutions and Power.*
Taylor & Francis Group, 2024
DOI: 10.5117/9789463728997_CH04

China Sea. It explains why and how negotiators have overcome barriers to agreement in some cases but not in others.

This chapter shows that contending actors have attempted to govern, in a shared way, marine natural resources in disputed areas in order to prevent incidents, access natural resources, and avoid deteriorating bilateral relations. Unlike in the South China Sea, China, Japan, and South Korea have agreed on several bilateral fisheries agreements in a relatively short negotiation period (subchapters 1 and 2). This chapter demonstrates how these partly overlapping fisheries agreements have established the most substantial set of common rules for any disputed area of the East or South China Sea, despite severe challenges. This chapter also answers the questions of why one arrangement about oil and gas agreed to by China and Japan after twenty-three years of negotiations came to a halt (subchapter 1), and why Japan and Taiwan took twenty years longer than Japan and China to reach a fisheries agreement (subchapter 3). This chapter illustrates that claimant states have feared and, in some cases, experienced that an opponent could leverage these institutions to gain a bargaining advantage. This cost of cooperation has been a barrier to agreement in all cases. Unless the negotiators found terms protecting against this cost, negotiations have ended in an impasse.

Moreover, additional puzzles within the single case studies will be highlighted. The East China Sea's energy resources were compared to a 'new Persian Gulf' that energy companies wanted to explore. But as these resources are situated in areas of boundary disputes, the coastal states have discussed various options to jointly utilize oil and gas. Chinese and Japanese energy companies and state actors, though, could not reach an agreement after more than two decades. Then, to the surprise of Japan, China suddenly dropped two of its long-held positions and accepted an arrangement in 2008. Chinese actors, however, let the arrangement run aground soon after. The question arises: what explains Beijing's U-turns (subchapter 1)?

Three aspects of the joint fisheries agreements in the East China Sea add to the puzzles. The Sino-Japanese fisheries agreement covers the southern part of the East China Sea where the disputed Senkaku/Diaoyu Islands are located. The literature and news reports have sometimes overlooked this fact. Incidents related to these islands triggered the most dangerous crises in the Sino-Japanese relationship, including one incident with a fishing vessel. Perhaps somewhat paradoxically, China and Japan have also accorded each other the greatest level of freedom to unilaterally define catch levels and the number of fishing vessels in the southern part of the East China Sea.

The question arises why this is the case and how both countries deal with this situation (subchapter 1). Furthermore, Chinese fishermen have violated in a rampant manner the fisheries agreements of China and South Korea. But even as South Korea has adopted the most forcible response against Chinese fishing vessels of all claimants in the East and South China Sea, this practice did not escalate at the interstate level. China and Korea kept the agreement alive, and the question is how the agreement prevented the escalation of this situation (subchapter 2). In the northern part of the East China Sea, the three Exclusive Economic Zones (EEZ) claimed by China, Japan, and South Korea overlap. Instead of reaching a trilateral agreement, though, the three countries concluded three bilateral agreements that partly overlap. The question then becomes how this unusual arrangement of overlapping bilateral agreements works in practice (subchapter 2). This chapter concludes with a comparison of the role that fisheries, fishing incidents, and the fisheries agreements play in the East and South China Sea (subchapter 4).

Who Claims What: Territorial and Maritime Claims in the East China Sea

This paragraph provides a brief overview of claims. Map 5 illustrates the claims to continental shelves, EEZs, the Senkaku/Diaoyu Islands, and joint development zones. The East China Sea encompasses approximately 1.25 million square kilometres. China and Japan dispute sovereignty over the Senkaku/Diaoyu Islands in the southern part of the East China Sea.[1] The island group of eight features is currently administered by Japan. The East China Sea is approximately 630 nautical miles long in the north–south direction and has a width of approximately between 150 and 360 nautical miles along the east–west axis. During the third UN Conference on the Law of the Sea (1973–1982), members of the Chinese delegation were aware that the EEZ regime of the UN Convention on the Law of the Sea (UNCLOS) would inevitably result in boundary disputes.[2] As the width of the East China Sea

1 Hirose Hajime, 'Japan's Effective Control of the Senkaku Islands', *Review of Island Studies*, June 2013, 1–25; Zhongqi Pan, 'Sino-Japanese Dispute over the Diaoyu/Senkaku Islands: The Pending Controversy from the Chinese Perspective', *Journal of Chinese Political Science* 12, no. 1 (21 June 2007): 71–92; Linus Hagström, 'Quiet Power: Japan's China Policy in Regard to the Pinnacle Islands', *The Pacific Review* 18, no. 2 (June 2005): 159–88; Mark J. Valencia, 'The East China Sea Disputes: History, Status, and Ways Forward', *Asian Perspective* 38, no. 2 (2014): 183–218.

2 Isaac B. Kardon, *China's Law of the Sea: The New Rules of Maritime Order* (Yale UP, 2023), 52.

and Yellow Sea is less than 400 nautical miles (nm), the claims of China, South Korea, and Japan to EEZs and continental shelves overlap.[3] China and Korea[4] base their claims to extended continental shelves on the natural prolongation principle. This would give China a considerable continental shelf extending almost to the territorial seas of Japan's Okinawa and Ryukyu Islands. Japan holds the position that where the distance between two coasts is less than 400 nm, no claim to an extended continental shelf should be accepted. Japan claims a continental shelf of 200 nm and proposes an equidistance line as the boundary. The country did not give up its claim to the areas beyond the median line. Rather, 'Japan decides to temporally limit its exercise of sovereign rights and jurisdiction to the Japanese side of the equidistance line in a period pending delimitation under international law.'[5] Recent decisions by the International Court of Justice (ICJ) and the International Tribunal for the Law of the Sea (ITLOS) applied a 'three stage approach' for boundary delimitation. While an equidistance line was the starting point in several decisions, courts took other, especially geographic, circumstances into consideration and adjusted a median line.[6] Japan uses basepoints at the disputed Senkaku/Diaoyu islands to define a median line, making this median line even less acceptable to China.[7] Taiwan also claims the Senkaku/Diaoyu Islands and its maritime claims overlap with those of Japan.

3 Jonathan I. Charney, 'Central East Asian Maritime Boundaries and the Law of the Sea', *American Journal of International Law* 89, no. 4 (1995): 724–49; Sun Pyo Kim, *Maritime Delimitation and Interim Arrangements in North East Asia* (Martinus Nijhoff, 2004).

4 Republic of Korea, 'Partial Submission to the Commission on the Limits of the Continental Shelf Pursuant to Article 76 Paragraph 8 of the United Nations Convention on the Law of the Sea Executive Summary', December 2012, https://www.un.org/Depts/los/clcs_new/submissions_files/kor65_12/executive_summary.pdf.

5 Ministry of Foreign Affairs of Japan, 'Japan's legal position on the development of natural resources in the East China Sea', 6 August 2015, https://www.mofa.go.jp/a_o/c_m1/page3e_000358.html (last accessed 23 September 2023).

6 Malcolm D. Evans, 'Maritime Boundary Delimitation', in *The Oxford Handbook of the Law of the Sea*, edited by Donald R. Rothwell, Alex G. O. Elferink, Karen Scott, and Tim Stephens (OUP, 2015), 254–81. Evans argues that, while 'equidistance' is the starting point, 'equity' also plays a crucial role in recent case law.

7 Ministry of Foreign Affairs of Japan, 'The Current Status of China's Unilateral Development of Natural Resources in the East China Sea. Map', 5 June 2023, https://www.mofa.go.jp/files/000091724.pdf; Clive H. Schofield and Ian Townsend-Gault, 'Choppy Waters Ahead in "a Sea of Peace Cooperation and Friendship"? Slow Progress towards the Application of Maritime Joint Development to the East China Sea', *Marine Policy* 35, no. 1 (2011): 25–33, 28.

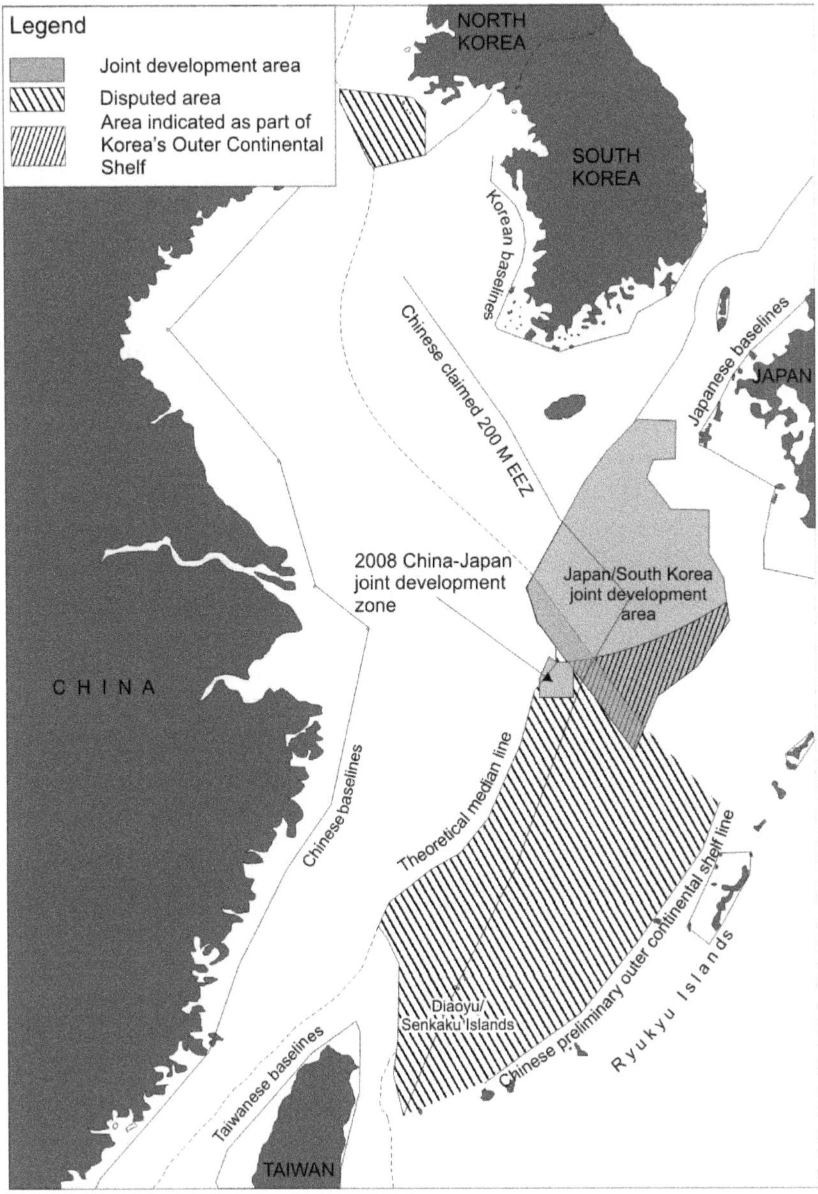

Map 5 Overlapping continental shelf claims and joint development in the East China Sea[8]

8 Map prepared by Andi Arsana and Clive Schofield, in Clive H. Schofield and Ian Townsend-Gault, 'Choppy Waters Ahead in "a Sea of Peace Cooperation and Friendship"? Slow Progress towards the Application of Maritime Joint Development to the East China Sea', *Marine Policy* 35, no. 1 (2011): 25–33. Reproduced with permission.

1 China and Japan

1.1 Energy without Politics? Joint Development Negotiations 1985–2008

China and Japan have the longest coastlines in the East China Sea. Accordingly, the way China and Japan govern their nationals' maritime activities and the changing nature of these activities greatly affects the maritime relations in this sea. The question of the joint development of hydrocarbon resources in the disputed continental shelves of the East China Sea has been on the Sino-Japanese agenda since the 1980s. In June 2008, after a total of twenty-three years of exchanges on joint development of oil and gas resources, China and Japan reached the 'Principled Consensus' (the Consensus).[9] The Consensus is a basic document with three parts: (i) a general commitment to improving maritime cooperation; (ii) a commitment to joint development in a block defined by seven geographic points (map 5) and a commitment to prepare joint development projects in other areas; and (iii) participation of Japanese energy companies in existing operations of Chinese energy companies under China's laws. In the words of China's former Vice-Foreign Minister Wu Dawei, the Consensus marks a 'new historic starting point' for the bilateral relations and the 'settlement of the East China Sea issue indicates' that both 'are capable of solving other sensitive' issues.[10] Expectations could have hardly been higher. Not even two months later, Japan's Foreign Minister Koumura met his counterpart Yang Jiechi in Beijing on 17 August during the Olympic Games. He suggested continuing the process of the Consensus, but 'there was no immediate positive response'.[11] Since then, neither side has made any progress in implementing the Consensus. Japan resumed its resistance against unilateral Chinese gas exploitation in 2009, as it has since 2004 when China announced plans to develop gas fields

9 Ministry of Foreign Affairs of Japan, '2008 China-Japan Principled Consensus on the East China Sea Issue', 18 June 2008 made the text available at a press conference https://www.mofa.go.jp/files/000091726.pdf (last accessed 23 March 2024); also available in the annex to Jianjun Gao, 'A Note on the 2008 Cooperation Consensus Between China and Japan in the East China Sea', *Ocean Development & International Law* 40, no. 3 (August 2009): 291–303.

10 Ministry of Foreign Affairs of China, 'Vice Foreign Minister Wu Dawei Talks About the Principled Consensuses Reached Between China and Japan on the East China Sea Issue', 19 June 2008, https://www.fmprc.gov.cn/eng/wjdt_665385/wshd_665389/200806/t20080623_636938.html (last accessed 23 March 2024).

11 Ministry of Foreign Affairs of Japan, 'Press Conference by Minister for Foreign Affairs Masahiko Koumura', 26 August 2008, https://www.mofa.go.jp/announce/fm_press/2008/8/0826.html (last accessed 23 March 2024).

just a few miles from a geographic equidistance line. Tensions subsequently increased in the East China Sea and Sino-Japanese relations reached a new low point. This leads to three questions: Which obstacles had prevented an agreement for twenty-three years? Why did the opponents reach agreement nevertheless in June 2008? What explains that both reached a 'historic agreement', but China did not want to be reminded of it soon after?

The context: claims and natural resources

The continental shelf claims of China and Japan overlap widely in the East China Sea between mainland China and Japan's Okinawa and Ryukyu Islands. The total distance between Japan's and China's coasts varies roughly between 280 nm and 350 nm. China claims an extended continental shelf with reference to article 76 of UNCLOS. This continental shelf extends between 268 nm and 300 nm from its baseline.[12] Map 5 illustrates the large overlap. China defines this claim by connecting end points with straight lines with reference to Article 76 4 (a) (ii) of UNCLOS. Map 6 shows a profile of China's claim. The point E indicates the end point of China's claim. The point F is a few dozen miles away from Japan's Okinawa. China's continental shelf claim extends almost to Japan's territorial sea. A hypothetical median line as claimed by Japan would be located roughly at a point between 150 nm and 175 nm in this profile (somewhere close to the left of point B). Even if China claimed only a continental shelf of 200 nm (point B), the claim would still overlap with Japan's 200 nm. It would also overlap with the median line Japan proposes. Japan uses the Senkaku/Diaoyu Islands for defining a median line.[13]

Figures assessing the extent of hydrocarbon reserves in the entire East China Sea vary greatly. The Energy Information Agency (EIA) of the US assumes the existence of between sixty and one hundred million barrels of oil and 1 and 2 trillion cubic feet (ft^3) of gas in proven and probable resources.[14]

12 'Preliminary Information Indicative of the Outer Limits of the Continental Shelf Beyond 200 Nautical Miles of the People's Republic of China', 11 May 2009, http://www.un.org/depts/los/clcs_new/commission_preliminary.htm; also see China's partial submission for an extended continental shelf, 14 December 2012, and Japan's protest notes, http://www.un.org/Depts/los/clcs_new/submissions_files/submission_chn_63_2012.htm (last accessed 23 March 2024).

13 Ministry of Foreign Affairs of Japan, 'The Current Status of China's Unilateral Development of Natural Resources in the East China Sea. Map', 5 June 2023, https://www.mofa.go.jp/files/000091724.pdf; Schofield and Townsend-Gault, 'Choppy Waters Ahead in "a Sea of Peace Cooperation and Friendship"?', 27–8.

14 US Energy Information Administration, 'East China Sea', September 2014, https://www.eia.gov/international/analysis/regions-of-interest/East_China_Sea (last accessed 23 March 2024).

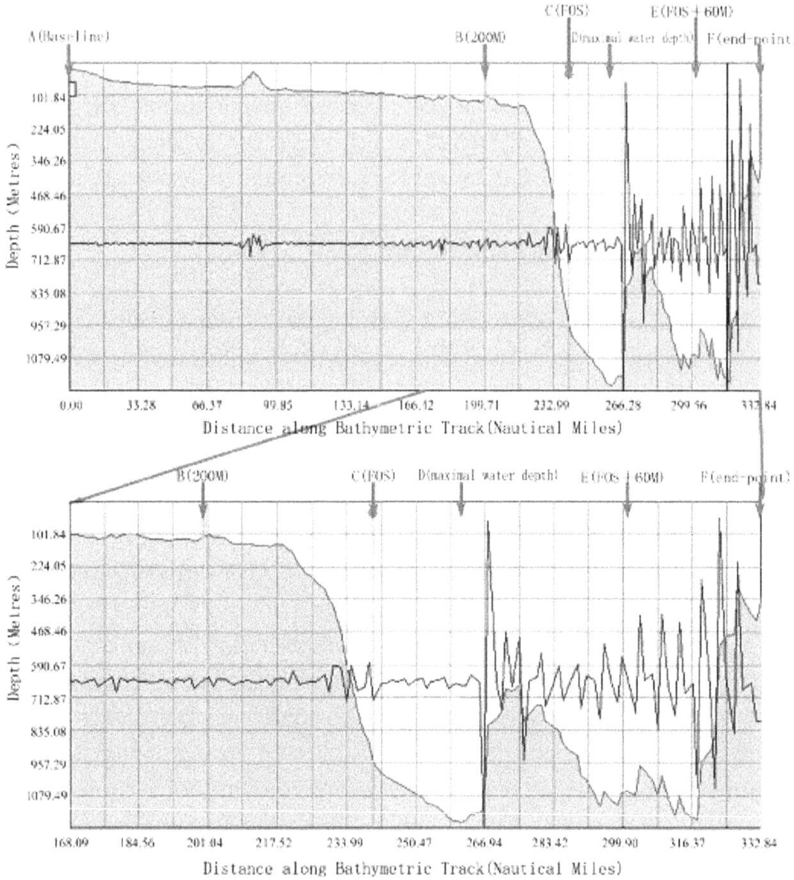

Map 6 Map of one profile of China's continental shelf claim in the East China Sea[15]

The EIA cites Chinese sources for between seventy and 160 billion barrels of oil and 250 trillion ft^3 of gas in undiscovered resources. Chinese estimates of undiscovered oil resources are a thousand times higher than US estimates of proven and probable reserves and 250 times higher for gas resources. Reliable assessments of economically recoverable resources would require exploratory drilling. The uncertainty about the resources dates back to 1969,

15 From 'Preliminary Information Indicative of the Outer Limits of the Continental Shelf Beyond 200 Nautical Miles of the People's Republic of China', by People's Republic of China, © (2009) United Nations, 7. Reprinted with the permission of the United Nations. Accessible with further illustrations, http://www.un.org/depts/los/clcs_new/commission_preliminary.htm (last accessed 23 March 2024).

when a report of the UN Economic Commission for Asia suggested that the 'shallow sea floor between Japan and Taiwan might contain one of the most prolific oil and gas reservoirs in the world, possibly comparing favourably with the Persian Gulf area'.[16] The prospects of findings are high in two areas: the shallow waters around the disputed Senkaku/Diaoyu Islands and, even higher, in the Okinawa Trough where sedimentary deposits have piled up at the rise at the bottom of the Okinawa Trough.[17] Better estimates on commercially viable reserves are lacking, because the disputes thwarted test drilling in either the Okinawa Trough or around the disputed islands. China and Japan must rely on seismic data. The rise of the Okinawa Trough with a depth of between 1,000 meters and 2,500 meters has the highest prospects for substantial reserves. Deep water drilling could reach these deposits but requires higher investments and hence a stable legal framework for exploitation. Model calculations of pipeline construction costs considered the geomorphological conditions of the Okinawa Trough and assessed different end markets for offshore gas extraction.[18] These calculations suggest that the technological requirements of pipeline construction in the Okinawa Trough represent another commercial incentive for resource-sharing agreements.

The China National Offshore Oil Corporation (CNOOC), in joint venture with Sinopec, operated six oil and gas fields in the East China Sea in 2006.[19] According to CNOOC's 2022 figures, its operations in the East China Sea contribute only 3.1 per cent to CNOOC's total reserves and 1.2 per cent to its production.[20] 1.2 per cent of CNOOC's total production represents a miniscule fraction of China's total consumption. Of these six fields, Canxue, Tianwitian, and Chunxiao are located just a few miles west of a median line claimed by Japan.[21] Chunxiao (Shirakaba in Japanese) is located about one mile west

16 UN Economic Commission for Asia and the Far East, *Report of the Sixth Session of the Committee for Coordination of Joint Prospecting for Mineral Resources in Asian Offshore Areas* (CCOP), E/CN.11/L.239, 26 June 1969.

17 Selig Harrison, 'Seabed Petroleum in Northeast Asia: Conflict or Cooperation?', in *Seabed Petroleum in Northeast Asia: Conflict or Cooperation?* (Woodrow Wilson International Center for Scholars, 2005), 3–14.

18 Rongxing Guo, *Territorial Disputes and Seabed Petroleum Exploitation: Some Options for the East China Sea* (The Brookings Institution Center for Northeast Asian Policy Studies, 2010).

19 CNOOC, 'Major Properties', internet archive, https://web.archive.org/web/20060317225747/http://www.cnoocltd.com/Operations/channel/opertions1297.asp (accessed 23 March 2024).

20 CNOOC Limited, 'Key operating areas', http://www.cnoocltd.com/col/col7311/index.html (accessed 23 March 2024).

21 China has a total of sixteen structures in operation. For a map and photographic evidence, see Ministry of Foreign Affairs of Japan, 'The Current Status of China's Unilateral Development of Natural Resources in the East China Sea', 5 June 2023, https://www.mofa.go.jp/a_o/c_m1/page3e_000356.html (last accessed 23 March 2024).

from a median line. Japan argues that the field straddles a median line, and that China is therefore extracting resources that Japan has a right to.

The total oil and gas extraction from the East China Sea is hence minimal in comparison to the potential estimates attributed to it. China became a net oil importer in the early 1990s, and Japan has imported virtually all of its oil. China's unilateral exploration and exploitation activities have caused incidents and negatively affected the bilateral relations since the 2000s.[22] However, their contribution to China's energy security is minimal. If the East China Sea's potential is to play any important role in the provision of energy to Japan or China,[23] both countries need to delimit continental shelf boundaries or agree on the joint development of these resources. Both states therefore have at least three powerful incentives in favour of joint development – the access to energy resources, the prevention of incidents, and the amelioration of the bilateral relationship.[24] Neither party moved on boundary delimitation and the only option pursued by Chinese and Japanese actors became joint development agreements. Exchanges on the joint exploration of hydrocarbon resources started in 1985 and were conducted predominantly by energy companies. Until today, however, no joint development agreement has been reached and neither side has been able to explore, let alone exploit hydrocarbon resources of the most promising areas. Which obstacle has prevented an agreement?

Twenty-three years of negotiations and some escalations

The earliest exchanges on the joint development of hydrocarbon resources in the East China Sea started in 1985 with talks between national energy companies. Susumu Yarita, managing director of Uruma Resources Exploration, reported on the talks between China's CNOOC and Japan's Uruma, Teikoku Oil, Japex, and Japan National Oil Corporation (JNOC).[25] These talks were held secretly and Yarita was the first to provide details about them.

22 Ibid.

23 On China and energy security, see Philip Andrews-Speed et al., *The Strategic Implications of China's Energy Needs* (Routledge, 2014); Erica S. Downs, 'The Chinese Energy Security Debate', *The China Quarterly*, 177 (2004): 21–41; David Zweig and Jianhai Bi, 'China's Global Hunt for Energy', *Foreign Affairs*, 2005, 25–38.

24 Only one interview source, a representative of Sumitomo Corporation, argued that, from a business perspective, joint development with 'difficult business partners' is no longer an attractive option as energy markets are liquid. Interview with a security analyst of Sumitomo Corporation, Tokyo, 28 July 2017 (interview 42).

25 Susumu Yarita, 'Toward Cooperation in the East China Sea', in *Seabed Petroleum in Northeast Asia: Conflict or Cooperation?* (Woodrow Wilson International Center for Scholars, 2005), 23–9.

The governments of both China and Japan appear to have had a favourable view regarding joint development. China's government nominated CNOOC to consult Japanese corporations.[26] The governmental instructions to explore cooperation between corporations signalled that governments prioritized energy interests and practical cooperation over politics. These exchanges lasted until 2001, but several rounds of talks failed to result in a compromise. Based on Yarita, the negotiation history can be reconstructed as follows.

The first attempt, 1985–86: CNOOC proposed and insisted on joint development in the area around the Senkaku/Diaoyu Islands. CNOOC recommended suspending the sovereignty question. Japex and Teikoku Oil suggested joint operations in an area farther to the north of the islands. Both rejected each other's proposal.

The second attempt, 1987–1988: To facilitate compromise, Uruma suggested that neither side raise the question of sovereignty over islands, that Japan does not raise the equidistance line and that China does not raise the issue of the definition of the continental shelf margin. CNOOC proposed an area for joint development located to the east of an equidistance line. Uruma suggested an area straddling an equidistance line. No compromise was reached.

The third attempt, 1988–1992: Japex and JNOC proposed joint operations in a 100,000 square kilometre area straddling a median line that would have had several subzones. Subzones allow the use of multiple formulas for jurisdiction, so that each party could have jurisdictional primacy in particular subzones as might be convenient. The model proposed by Japex and JNOC essentially emulated the Korea–Japan joint development agreement of 1974.[27] CNOOC retracted to its previous proposals. It signalled that a governmental agreement would be necessary for CNOOC to accept any proposal other than the one it proposed.

Fourth attempt, 1992: China's Ministry of Natural Resources unilaterally invited a tender for exploration in areas west of a median line. Japanese companies had previously proposed these areas as part of a joint area for joint operations. Japex and Teikoku participated in the tender and were awarded a few blocks, but they made no substantial findings.

Fifth attempt, 2001: Uruma and CNOOC discussed practical measures to enable joint operations. Despite 'the best efforts of the private sector in

26 Ibid. 24.

27 Republic of Korea and Japan, 'Agreement Concerning Joint Development of the Southern Part of the Continental Shelf Adjacent to the Two Countries' (UN deposit Vol. 1225, No. 1–19778, 30 January 1974).

Japan to find ways to make things move', no compromise was in reach.[28] Uruma suggested an area for joint development across a median line. To accommodate CNOOC's position, Uruma proposed two subzones: a western zone where CNOOC would have a 51 per cent stake and Uruma a 49 per cent stake; an eastern zone with a reversed distribution. Each partner would have a larger share in 'its' subzone reflecting each party's position. CNOOC rejected this because a geographic line would have been necessary to demarcate the subzones. This line would have looked like a median line and would have established a median line as a practically meaningful line. CNOOC proposed then to establish a joint governing body that would act as an international entity such that neither party's domestic laws would apply. As an additional safeguard, it requested that Japan explicitly exclude the application of its laws to the area for joint operations.

This overview demonstrates several points. As could be expected for an area referred to as another 'Persian Gulf', energy companies tried to find a legal framework allowing them to tap into the resources. CNOOC exchanged many proposals on various options with changing Japanese companies over a period of sixteen years. From a purely commercial perspective, none of the proposals stood out dramatically. In principle, the companies could have pursued various – or a mix of – the proposed options at the same time. Their inability to reach a compromise on a geographic area for joint activities was not an economic or commercial problem. The companies of both parties floated proposals covering various geographic areas, with many or few subzones, different formulas for jurisdiction, and a commitment to exclude politically sensitive questions. This gave them many options to bargain about; all these options would have been without prejudice to original claims. Even if these talks were attempts to circumvent political sensitivities by prioritizing business over politics, the political sensitivities attached to the positions proved stronger than energy interests. CNOOC's proposal to establish a joint international entity went far beyond mere business arrangements, illustrating that China's government was closely involved in the search for a practical arrangement.

The disagreements of the company-level talks mirrored the disagreements of subsequent state-level talks. Between 1997 and 2003, officials from the ministries of Foreign Affairs of China and Japan held fourteen rounds of consultations on law of the sea issues.[29] These consultations made no

28 Yarita, 'Toward Cooperation in the East China Sea', 26.

29 Jianjun Gao, 'Joint Development in the East China Sea: Not an Easier Challenge than Delimitation', *The International Journal of Marine and Coastal Law*, 23 (2008), 39–75.

progress on the issue of how to deal with oil and gas on the continental shelf. China's government allowed energy companies to proceed unilaterally with twelve survey operations in 1998 and 1999. Chinese offshore oil companies set up a production platform in the Chunxiao field in August 2003. CNOOC and Sinopec entered into a joint venture with Unocal and Royal Dutch Shell in disputed areas in 2003. Both withdrew from joint projects at the end of 2004, 'citing doubts over the commercial viability of developing energy resources in the disputed area'.[30] Government officials resumed consultations on the East China Sea in June 2004. In these consultations and through protest notes, Japanese officials demanded that China share seismic data with Japan and that it seize all operations: 'Given the straw effect, there is the possibility that some of the reserves on the Japanese side are also being taken out and that was the largest problem.'[31] To the extent that the hydrocarbon deposits extend into the Japanese side of a median line, exploitation of the fields would violate the obligation not to permanently affect the physical unity of the deposit.[32] China's Foreign Minister Li Zhaoxiang suggested to 'shelve this difference and embark on a "joint development" of the field' during consultation in June 2004.[33] Japan's leaders rejected this proposal because China would not share data on the field. When China refused to share data, Japan began its own unilateral seismic operations.

Lacking common rules, China's unilateral seismic operations caused incidents and raised tensions. It is difficult to assess whether China learned from the negotiations with Japan about which Chinese unilateral activities Japan would acquiesce in. Japan resisted Chinese unilateral moves if they crossed a median line, while in the previous negotiations Tokyo had insisted on areas for joint development across a median line. Cat and mouse games involving coast guard and navy vessels followed in November 2004 and January 2005 in response to each other's operations.[34] The number of

30 US Energy Information Administration, 'East China Sea', 25 September 2014, 3.

31 'Joint Press Conference by Minister for Foreign Affairs Masahiko Koumura and Minister of Economy, Trade and Industry Akira Amari (Regarding Cooperation between Japan and China in the East China Sea)', 18 June 2008, https://www.mofa.go.jp/announce/fm_press/2008/6/0618.html (last accessed 13 April 2022).

32 British Institute of International and Comparative Law, ed., *Report on the Obligations of States under Articles 74(3) and 83(3) of UNCLOS in Respect of Undelimited Maritime Areas* (London: British Institute of International and Comparative Law, 2016).

33 Ministry of Foreign Affairs Japan, 'Press Conference 22 June 2004', https://www.mofa.go.jp/announce/press/2004/6/0622.html (last accessed 13 April 2024).

34 Selig Harrison, 'Seabed Petroleum in Northeast Asia: Conflict or Cooperation?', in *Seabed Petroleum in Northeast Asia: Conflict or Cooperation?* (Woodrow Wilson International Center for Scholars, 2005), 3–14, 4.

annual scrambles by Japan's Air Self-Defense Forces against China's aircraft ranged from zero to thirteen until 2004, it jumped to 107 in 2005.[35] Relations deteriorated and both sides had to back up their positions with increased navy operations.[36] The near conflict over unilateral seismic and drilling operations increased the need and the incentive to reach a deal on oil and gas projects. In fact, between the end of 2004 and 2008, both sides held a further eleven rounds of consultations on joint development at the official level. The proposals in these talks mirrored those in the company-level talks. Chinese officials offered and insisted on joint development around the Senkaku/Diaoyu Islands. Japanese officials insisted on an area straddling the median line. In the third round, in 2005, China's position shifted.[37] China offered to carry out joint development in both areas. Japan rejected this. These positions did not change until the twelfth round.

Harrison explains China's negotiation position with the fact that 'the "rise" at the bottom of the trough may well contain the richest petroleum deposits in the East China Sea. This is the underlying explanation for what would otherwise appear to be a completely unreasonable Chinese stance.'[38] However, this is not a good explanation for the otherwise 'completely unreasonable stance'. An area for joint development could, in principle, extend from just west of a median line in the eastern direction to the Okinawa Trough. Such an area would not be spatially wider than the joint development agreement that Japan and Korea agreed on in 1974.[39] It would give both sides access to the possibly richest deposits. Gao discusses Japan's proposal to define a joint development area across the claimed median line. He assumes that Japan proposed this area because Tokyo wanted to include gas fields near the median line in which China was operating. This may be the case but does not explain why China rejected it. In fact, China offered to include Japanese companies in the exploitation of these areas, provided joint projects were under Chinese jurisdiction (part III of the Principled Consensus). Gao also discusses the legal status of the median line. He concludes that an area

35 Japan Ministry of Defence, 'China's Maritime Expansion', April 2017.

36 Ibid.

37 Jianjun Gao, 'Joint Development in the East China Sea: Not an Easier Challenge than Delimitation'; Xinjun Zhang, 'Why the 2008 Sino-Japanese Consensus on the East China Sea Has Stalled: Good Faith and Reciprocity Considerations in Interim Measures Pending a Maritime Boundary Delimitation', *Ocean Development & International Law*, 42 (2011), 53–65; Interviews 25 and 30.

38 Harrison, 'Seabed Petroleum in Northeast Asia: Conflict or Cooperation?', 10.

39 Republic of Korea and Japan, 'Agreement Concerning Joint Development of the Southern Part of the Continental Shelf Adjacent to the Two Countries' (UN deposit 1225, no. 1–19778, January 1974).

for joint development does not have to straddle the median line because a hypothetical median line itself has no legal effect.[40] It is of course true that an area for joint exploration need not straddle a median line, but this still does not explain why China would not accept a geographic area for practical joint projects straddling the median line.

The various uses of legal language (suspension of claim, legal analysis of the median line, precedent) in these explanations contrast with the acknowledgements of Gao, Yarita, and Harrison that any joint development would be without prejudice to claims. They note that both parties had explicitly agreed to separate legal status questions from practical measures. Harrison then argues that, 'the Japanese Foreign Ministry is reluctant to suspend Japanese territorial claims to the Senkakus (Tiao Yu Tai) for the sake of joint exploration and development with China, lest this set a precedent that would jeopardize Japan's position in its dispute with Russia.'[41] A joint development agreement does not suspend territorial claims in a legal sense. The observable need for joint development agreements to incorporate the original claims in this case – the very same original claims the agreement is meant to separate from economic activities – is not a legal problem. It is a problem of preventing one actor from using another actor's consent to a particular geographic scope to its advantage in subsequent interactions.

1.2 From 'New Historic Starting Point' to Conflict – the Principled Consensus

Japanese and Chinese officials and businesses did not reach a compromise because they could not agree on a common geographic area for joint development. Each actor, be it an energy company or an official, rejected joint development models that the rival claimant could have used as acknowledgement or precedent in its favour. Then, in 2008, China suddenly accepted an area for joint development straddling a median line.

On 18 June 2008, China and Japan reached the Principled Consensus. This sudden progress followed the visit of Prime Minister Wen Jiabao in April 2008 and President Hu Jintao in May 2008 to Japan. Although President Hu Jintao's visit on 7 May 2008 ended with a joint declaration about turning the East China Sea into a 'Sea of Peace, Cooperation and

40 Jianjun Gao 'Joint Development in the East China Sea: Not an Easier Challenge than Delimitation', 62–6.

41 Harrison, 'Seabed Petroleum in Northeast Asia: Conflict or Cooperation?', 6.

Friendship',[42] Japan's Foreign Minister Koumnura, speaking on 3 June 2008, did *not* expect that Tokyo and Beijing could reach a compromise.[43] The government of Japan could arguably not believe that China was prepared to drop two of its long-held positions on joint development to reach an agreement. But that is exactly what China did. The text of the Principled Consensus shows that Chinese officials no longer insisted on joint development around the Senkaku/Diaoyu Islands, and that they accepted a joint development area straddling the median line – all Chinese actors had consistently rejected the latter and insisted on the former between 1985 and 2008.

With the Principled Consensus, China's leadership dropped two positions on joint development that it had held for twenty-three years – no joint area can straddle a median line, and joint development in the Senkaku/Diaoyu area must be part of the deal. This enabled the conclusion of the agreement and followed within weeks after Prime Minster Wen and President Hu visited Japan. Indeed, only the top leadership could have decided this change. Chinese and Japanese sources agree on the assessment that China's top leadership had a strong political will to calm down tensions and make progress in the East China Sea. They overruled the Chinese officials who continued to reject joint development under the terms of the Consensus.[44] The course of events provides evidence for this, too. Prime Minister Wen visited Tokyo in April 2008 and President Hu in May 2008. China suddenly accepted Japan's position in mid-June 2008.

The Consensus is a short document containing three parts: First, a general commitment to improve maritime cooperation. The second part establishes a commitment to joint development in a block defined by seven geographic points in the centre of the East China Sea. Map 5 illustrates that the largest part of the area is located to the east of the median line and only a small area extends to the west of a median line. The Consensus also provided for both sides to 'attain joint development in other waters' (part

42 'Joint Statement between the Government of Japan and the Government of the People's Republic of China on Comprehensive Promotion of a "Mutually Beneficial Relationship Based on Common Strategic Interests"', Tokyo, 7 May 2008, https://www.mofa.go.jp/region/asia-paci/china/joint0805.html (last accessed 23 March 2022).

43 'Press Conference by Minister for Foreign Affairs Masahiko Koumura', 3 June 2008, https://www.mofa.go.jp/announce/fm_press/2008/6/0603.html (last accessed 23 March 2024).

44 Interview with a professor of international law at Tsinghua University, Beijing, 24 April 2017 (Interview 25), interview with a professor of international relations of the University of Tokyo, 18 July 2017 (Interview 34), interview with a professor of international security of Hosei University, Tokyo, 20 July 2017 (Interview 36).

II of the Consensus). Third, Japanese energy companies should be given the opportunity to participate in CNOOC's existing operations in the Chunxiao gas field 'in accordance with Chinese laws' (part III of the Consensus). China's acceptance of Japan's position on joint development amounted to a substantial concession. Japan made the concession to participate in the Chunxiao gas field 'in accordance with Chinese laws'.

The best explanation I can give for Hu's and Wen's decision at this stage is the most logical one: the obstacle that prevented access to energy resources and led to escalating incidents was the question of whether a joint development area would extend a few dozen square miles to the east or west of a median line. Chinese officials rejected a joint area straddling the median line, assessing that such an agreement would set a precedent in favour of Japan's claim. Hu and Wen decided to overcome this obstacle. Hu and Wen overruled their officials' assessment that a joint geographic area straddling a median line would weaken China's negotiating position by representing a precedent in favour of Japan. Subsequent events, however, illustrate that this problem could not easily be overruled. The problem re-emerged in the following days and weeks.

On 19 June 2008, the day after the arrangement was publicised, China's Vice-Foreign Minister Wu Dawei hailed it as a 'new historic starting point' and stated that the 'settlement of the East China Sea issue indicates' that both sides can settle other issues.[45] Two Japanese ministers presented the Consensus to the Japanese public. Foreign Minister Koumura presented it as 'cooperation on the premise of not prejudicing positions of both countries'.[46] Economy Minister Akira Amari defended the Consensus as contributing to Japan's 'energy security'.[47] Koumura defended Japanese participation under Chinese laws in Chunxiao (Part III of the document) as 'joint development'. While the Consensus can be called a 'joint development' arrangement, Koumura arguably meant to imply a jurisdictional parity, which was not intended by the language of the document in Part III. Koumura concluded: 'Regarding any statement that was made by the Chinese side to the effect

45 Ministry of Foreign Affairs of China, 'Vice Foreign Minister Wu Dawei Talks About the Principled Consensuses Reached Between China and Japan on the East China Sea Issue', 19 June 2008, https://www.fmprc.gov.cn/eng/wjdt_665385/wshd_665389/200806/t20080623_636938.html (last accessed 12 April 2024).

46 'Joint Press Conference by Minister for Foreign Affairs Masahiko Koumura and Minister of Economy, Trade and Industry Akira Amari (Regarding Cooperation between Japan and China in the East China Sea)', June 18, 2008, https://www.mofa.go.jp/announce/fm_press/2008/6/0618.html (last accessed 12 August 2023).

47 Ibid.

that this is not a joint development, I for my part would say that this is a question of how the definition is drawn.... I think that whether or not you use the term "joint development" it really is just a matter of the definition of a word.[48]

When asked about the role of the median line in the agreement and whether the agreement attributes equal shares to both sides, Koumura replied that: 'it is unquestionable that the median line goes through inside.'[49] Chinese officials did not leave these statements unanswered. The next day, Vice Foreign Minister Wu Dawei defended the agreement as a 'historic change' but stated that 'China does not recognize the so-called "median line" of Japan and there does not exist the issue of drawing the "median line" between China and Japan.'[50] Five days later, Foreign Minister Yang Jiechi gave another press conference on the same agreement. He defended the arrangement as 'mutually beneficial and in line with the fundamental interests of the two countries and the two peoples'.[51] Yang then stated that Japan had agreed to participate in the Chunxiao gas field and 'accept Chinese jurisdiction' and that 'China has never and will not recognize the so-called "median line" as advocated by Japan'. Less than two months later, Japan's Foreign Minister met his counterpart Yang in Beijing on 17 August during the Olympic Games and proposed continuing the joint development process, but 'there was no immediate positive response'.[52]

Leadership struggles, or how the Consensus compromised China's claim

Gao, writing shortly after the Consensus, discussed the geographic definition of the joint development area:

> Had the precedent of the joint development zones between Japan and Korea been followed, the block area between China and Japan would have been located between the median line claimed by Japan and the deepest points line in the Okinawa Trough claimed by China and would

48 Ibid.

49 Ibid.

50 'Vice Foreign Minister Wu Dawei Talks About the Principled Consensuses Reached Between China and Japan on the East China Sea Issue', 19 June 2008.

51 'Chinese Foreign Minister Yang Jiechi Meets the Press on East China Sea Issue', 24 June 2008, http://www.chinaconsulatesf.org/eng/xw/t451127.htm (last accessed 12 April 2022).

52 'Press Conference by Minister for Foreign Affairs Masahiko Koumura', 26 August 2008, https://www.mofa.go.jp/announce/fm_press/2008/8/0826.html (last accessed 12 April 2024).

> not straddle the median line. It should be pointed out that agreeing that the block straddles the median line claimed by Japan does not indicate that China has accepted the claims of Japan on maritime delimitation.[53]

Zhang and Manicom, in separate articles, discuss whether and how the joint development area could represent any Chinese pre-commitment to a later negotiating position on the area, and whether the bloc recognized Japan's claim.[54] Zhang also notes that China's failure to secure concessions from Japan on joint development in the Senkaku/Diaoyu area implied a lack of reciprocity, making it difficult for the Chinese leadership to defend the arrangement. One interviewee perhaps overstated the problem when he argued that 'there are two documents China wants to erase: the award of the South China Sea Arbitration and the Principled Consensus'.[55] Several Japanese interview sources alleged that Xi Jinping factions within China's leadership exploited the agreement in order to attack Hu Jintao and Wen Jiabao for having compromised China's position vis-à-vis Japan. Due to the opacity of leadership interactions in China, little evidence is publicly available on this point. Chinese sources did not comment on this point. Instead, Chinese sources suggest that criticism of the agreement had increased in social media in 2008 without, however, pointing to concrete evidence.[56] This raises the question of why China's censorship did not suppress this criticism, and what impact China's social media had in 2008. Moreover, for some factions to exploit the agreement for a leadership battle requires the possibility to interpret the agreement as resulting in a major concession and in compromising China's claims. Either of these two alleged explanations requires an explanation of why the Consensus should have been detrimental to China and why the Chinese leadership did not see this before accepting the Consensus.

The Consensus would have allowed an ending to the dispute over the Chunxiao field. It would have made it possible to explore an area that

53 Jianjun Gao, 'A Note on the 2008 Cooperation Consensus Between China and Japan in the East China Sea', *Ocean Development & International Law* 40, no. 3 (August 2009): 291–303, 294.

54 Xinjun Zhang, 'Why the 2008 Sino-Japanese Consensus on the East China Sea Has Stalled: Good Faith and Reciprocity Considerations in Interim Measures Pending a Maritime Boundary Delimitation', *Ocean Development & International Law*, 42 (2011): 53–65; James Manicom, 'Sino-Japanese Cooperation in the East China Sea: Limitations and Prospects', *Contemporary Southeast Asia: A Journal of International and Strategic Affairs*, 30 (2008): 455–78.

55 Interview with a Deputy Director-General level official, Ministry of Defence of Japan, Tokyo, 13 July 2017 (Interview 31).

56 Interview 25.

neither side could explore unilaterally without risking armed conflict. It should have initiated a process to unlock the oil and gas potential of the East China Sea. In principle, an agreement is without prejudice to territorial and maritime claims and could cover various geographic areas of the East China Sea. The fact that the joint development area extended by a few dozen square miles to the west of an equidistant line – most of which would have been on the Japanese side – proved too contentious for Chinese actors after the agreement was reached. This fact gave the line too much prominence not to become its dominant political feature. A 'historic' arrangement promising access to the wealth of another 'Persian Gulf' was thwarted by the fact that it extended a few square miles in the wrong direction. If the agreement had legally prejudiced China's claim or had set a legal precedent in favour of Japan's claim, this obstacle to the agreement would be a legal problem. However, the arrangement was without legal prejudice to the claims. The dominant perception among Chinese officials was that the Principled Consensus supported Japan's claim. An agreement that amounts to a potential pre-decision about boundary delimitation would result in a Chinese vulnerability. Given that the Consensus does not affect a claim *de jure*, the idea that an arrangement can establish a focal point in favour of Japan's position from which Japanese negotiators would not retreat in subsequent bargaining processes could provide a theoretical explanation for this behaviour. Even if the political will of China's top leadership was rooted in the promise of access to otherwise unavailable oil and gas and a historic agreement to improve Sino-Japanese relations, and even if this political will was expressed in a legally sound arrangement, it did not overrule this problem.

If this disagreement over whether a geographic area should be extended a few dozen square miles further to the east or west is merely a reflection of a sensitivity, it is a very consequential sensitivity that has blocked two decades of negotiations. In the absence of an agreement, the potential for oil and gas in the East China Sea remains largely unexplored. The East China Sea does not contribute to either China's or Japan's energy security. Disputes escalated further when China sent coast guard vessels into the territorial seas of the Senkaku/Diaoyu Islands for the first time in December 2008.[57] Just six months after China and Japan signed a 'new historic starting point', China saw the need to re-assert its claims. The Sino-Japanese relations in the East China Sea reached their most contentious period in the following

57 Reinhard Drifte, 'The Japan-China Confrontation over the Senkaku/Diaoyu Islands – Between "Shelving" and "Dispute Escalation"', *The Asia-Pacific Journal* 12, no. 30 (2014): 1–26.

years, with two crises related to the Senkaku/Diaoyu islands in 2010 and 2012 and a sharp increase in China's navy and air force presence in the East China Sea.[58]

1.3 The Sino-Japanese Fisheries Agreements in the East China Sea 1950–2000

While China and Japan could not agree on the joint development of oil and gas, they have reached fisheries agreements. This subchapter presents the negotiations leading to the current Sino-Japanese fisheries agreement after briefly introducing earlier agreements. It examines the barriers to agreement and how the negotiators have overcome them. It explains the design of the current agreement and answers why China and Japan have accorded each other greater room to unilaterally regulate fishing activities in the most disputed southern part of the East China Sea. The next subchapter then analyses how China and Japan have dealt with fishing incidents and crises around the Senkaku/Diaoyu Islands.

Prologue: fisheries relations, 1950–1975

The fisheries relationship between China and Japan dates to the 1950s. Fishing technologies and the law of the sea have dramatically changed since then. As the concept of the EEZ did not yet exist in the 1950s – it came into being only with UNCLOS – large parts of the East China Sea were considered high seas. Then, Japanese vessels were larger, numerous and technologically capable of harvesting in biologically productive Chinese coastal areas. Fishing incidents occurred repeatedly between fishing vessels of both countries. China seized 158 Japanese fishing vessels and 1,909 crewmen between 1950 and 1954.[59] To Japanese fishermen operating in Chinese coastal areas, it was unclear which zones China considered to be its territorial sea, its fishing zones, or its military zones. China's law on the territorial sea was promulgated only on 4 September 1958. To avoid disputes, both sides started negotiations on fisheries in 1954. Within Japan's domestic scene, the call for an agreement followed the initiative of the PRC-Japanese Fishing Enterprisers' Association, an association of the fishing industry. In

58 Ibid.; Japan Ministry of Defense, 'China's Maritime Expansion', April 2017; see chapters IV 1.4 and V 2.

59 Zengo Ohira and Terumichi Kuwahara, 'Fishery Problems between Japan and the People's Republic of China', *Japanese Annual of International Law*, 3 (1959), 109–25.

1953, national rallies in Tokyo called for the early conclusion of a fisheries agreement.[60] As Japan and the PRC had no diplomatic relations until 1972, non-governmental groups led the exchanges, and the non-governmental Japan–China Fisheries Council concluded the first Sino-Japanese fisheries agreement in 1955. The first negotiation attempt, however, to define common principles was deadlocked. Japan was mainly interested in preventing the seizure of Japanese fishing vessels; China was interested in restricting these vessels' operations in specific zones. Both sides negotiated based on self-serving principles that could not be reconciled. Japanese negotiators then proposed to discuss practical provisional rules for different subzones that divided a larger area. These subzones reconciled fishing activities and China's military zones.[61] This proposal was followed up in three non-governmental agreements in 1955, 1963, and 1965. After the PRC and Japan established diplomatic relations in 1972, both sides reached a governmental fisheries agreement on 15 August 1975. The agreement followed the previous model in several respects. It regulated Japanese fishing vessels in high seas close to China's coast and reconciled Japanese fishing interests with Chinese security interests around the Korean Peninsula and Taiwan. As few Chinese fishing vessels operated in the high sea areas close to Japan's coastline, these areas were not regulated.

The 1975 agreement's objective to 'preserve fishery resources and utilize them effectively' (article 2) is implemented through the definition of three protection areas, two fisheries suspension areas, and the regulation of ship size, number of ships, and fishing methods.[62] In an additional exchange of letters, China informed Japan about one military warning zone in the Bohai Bay and a fisheries warning zone south of 27 degrees north, an area in proximity of Taiwan. Japan did not endorse these positions, but consented to restrain Japanese fishing vessels, albeit only in the Bohai Bay, 'in consideration of the necessity of preserving fishery resources' and took 'note of the advice' for the waters close to Taiwan.[63] In other words, China and Japan carefully constructed a fisheries agreement that responded to each other's interests and sensitivities. The approach of the 1950s and 1970s established the model for the design of the East China Sea's fisheries agreements. Currently, all fisheries agreements in the East China Sea have

60 Ibid., 112.

61 Ibid.

62 'Fisheries Agreement between the People's Republic of China and Japan 15 August 1975' available in: US Department of State, Limits in the Sea No.70, April 1976, https://www.state.gov/wp-content/uploads/2019/11/LIS-70.pdf., (last accessed 12 June 2023).

63 Ibid.

subzones that combine various allocations of maritime law enforcement authority with different types of fisheries regulation.

UNCLOS, boundary disputes and fisheries negotiations between China and Japan

After four decades of Sino-Japanese fisheries relations in the East China Sea, four changes necessitated a new fisheries agreement. First, UNCLOS established the concept of a 200-nm EEZ. China and Japan ratified UNCLOS in 1996 and claimed an EEZ of 200 nm.[64] As the width of the East China Sea is less than 400 nm, overlapping claims and a boundary dispute resulted. Second, an increase in the size of China's fishing fleet (larger vessels, a greater number of vessels, advancements in fishing technologies, and fuel subsidies)[65] resulted in the situation whereby Chinese fishermen accessed waters in geographic proximity to Japan. As UNCLOS entitled states to claim larger EEZs, the old fisheries agreement of 1975 was no longer suitable. After China and Japan had ratified UNCLOS, what was previously part of the high seas became EEZs of Japan and China. These waters were not covered by the agreement of 1975. Third, fisheries in Chinese coastal waters depleted, giving fishermen an incentive to operate in other areas.[66] Fourth, Japan's fishing industry stagnated and reduced operations in (overfished) areas close to China. In comparison to the 1950s and 60s, when Japanese fishing vessels were operating in western parts of the East China Sea, China's and Japan's fishing roles reversed to some extent in the 1990s.

In the wake of the ratification of UNCLOS, Japan began claiming an EEZ of 200 nm and has insisted that boundary delimitation should be based on a median line.[67] China has claimed an EEZ of 200 nm and

64 China ratified UNCLOS on 7 June 1996; Japan ratified UNCLOS on 20 June 1996. UN Treaty Collection, https://treaties.un.org/pages/ViewDetailsIII.aspx?src=TREATY&mtdsg_no=XXI-6&chapter=21&Temp=mtdsg3&clang=_en#EndDec (last accessed 12 June 2023).

65 Hongzhou Zhang, 'China's Evolving Fishing Industry: Implications for Regional and Global Maritime Security', *RSIS Working Paper* 246/12 (2012), 1-46.

66 Roland Blomeyer et al., *The Role of China in World Fisheries*, IP/B/PECH/IC/2011-107 (European Parliament Study, 2012), https://www.europarl.europa.eu/meetdocs/2009_2014/documents/pech/dv/chi/china.pdf. (last accessed 30 June 2023).

67 Government of Japan, 'Law of the Exclusive Economic Zone and Continental Shelf (Law No. 74 of 1996)' (Law of the Sea Bulletin No 35, 1997). On the role of median lines and equitable principles in maritime boundary delimitation, see Malcolm D Evans, 'Maritime Boundary Delimitation', in *The Oxford Handbook of the Law of the Sea*, edited by Donald R. Rothwell et al. (OUP, 2015), 254–81.

has insisted that a boundary should be based on equitable principles.[68] China suggested taking into consideration the length of the coastline, the existence of economic needs, and fishing practices. Applying these principles would give China a larger EEZ. China's objective was to preserve access to larger fishing grounds in the East China Sea. Japan intended to subject maritime areas that belonged to the high seas in the pre-UNCLOS period to national jurisdiction in accordance with UNCLOS. China also wanted to preserve access to parts of the Japanese EEZ in the Western Pacific (east of Japan) that were part of the high seas in the pre-UNCLOS period.[69] The objectives for China were hence to secure access to larger fishing grounds than UNCLOS attributed to China and to secure some form of access to fishing grounds in Japan's EEZ with Japan's consent. Nevertheless, 'China originally strongly insisted that Japan and the People's Republic of China agree on delimitation of the EEZ before agreeing on a new agreement on fisheries' according to Koreshige Anami, the former director general for Asian Affairs of Japan's Ministry of Foreign Affairs.[70] Although Japan and China have legally valid EEZ claims in the East China Sea, the competing positions on boundaries and applicable legal principles (median line vs. equitable delimitation) were far apart. It soon became clear that compromise on sea boundary delimitation was not in reach. Both sides then began negotiations on a provisional fisheries order and on boundary delimitation in parallel.[71] The parallel negotiations did not progress any more than the boundary talks. China preferred a zone as large as possible and as close as possible to Japan's coast while Japan preferred a zone as small as possible. 'On top of this difference in their basic positions, ... the negotiations concluded at a point that was barely acceptable to both sides.'[72]

68 Sun Pyo Kim, *Maritime Delimitation and Interim Arrangements in North East Asia* (Martinus Nijhoff Publishers, 2004); Jonathan I. Charney, 'Central East Asian Maritime Boundaries and the Law of the Sea', *American Journal of International Law* 89, no. 4 (1995): 724–49.

69 Keyuan Zou, 'Sino-Japanese Joint Fishery Management in the East China Sea', *Marine Policy*, 27 (2003), 125–42, 132.

70 House of Councilors, 142nd Session of the Diet, Minutes of the Standing Committee for Foreign Affairs and Defense, 12th Meeting (April 28, 1998), 1, quoted in Nobukatsu Kanehara and Yutaka Arima, 'New Fishing Order – Japan's New Agreement on Fisheries with the Republic of Korea and with the People's Republic of China', *Japanese Annual of International Law*, 1999, 1–32, 20.

71 China and Vietnam reached a boundary and a separate fisheries agreement after parallel negotiations. Chapter III 2.

72 Kanehara and Arima, 'New Fishing Order – Japan's New Agreement on Fisheries with the Republic of Korea and with the People's Republic of China', 20.

While the basic positions were irreconcilable, the basic interests were not irreconcilable. According to Kanehara, the former Director of the Legal Affairs Division, Ministry of Foreign Affairs of Japan and Arima, the former Assistant Director of the same division, Japan's 'main purpose of negotiating new agreements on fisheries with the People's Republic of China and the Republic of Korea was to establish a fishing order based on [UNCLOS], especially with regard to the recognition of the coastal state's rights to establish the EEZ'.[73] The question was then how to reconcile Japan's objective of establishing a common fishing order that recognized the existence of Japanese sovereign rights and jurisdiction with China's interest in larger fishing areas. In other words, both sides needed to design an agreement that regulated 'in ingenious ways, … fishing activities without a delimitation of the EEZ.'[74]

Squaring the circle: how subzones allowed Chinese and Japanese negotiators to incorporate original claims

The solution to the clash of claims and the parties' inability to agree on one common fisheries zone was to define four different fisheries zones. Map 7 illustrates the fisheries agreements and their subzones. The map also illustrates the joint fishing zones of the Sino-Korean and Korean–Japanese agreements. However, the map does not show the Sino-Japanese fishing zone located in the south of the PMZ that is sometimes called the 'South Water Zone' (SWZ). Even careful studies of this fisheries agreement overlooked this zone that was established by an Exchange of Letters.[75]

Each subzone is subject to a different set of rules about fishing practices and law enforcement. The subzones allocate jurisdiction and clarify how maritime law enforcement agencies of both sides should interact and how one side's maritime law enforcement agency should interact with the fishing vessels of the other side. As the following will illustrate, economic or sustainability issues influenced the design of the fisheries agreement much less than political sensitivities about preventing the agreement from strengthening either side's bargaining position in the disputes. Indeed, it is a distinctive feature of the fisheries agreement that it does not specify any quantitative or qualitative measures for fishing operations at the bilateral level in the

73 Ibid. 2.

74 Ibid. 9.

75 The early English translation of the agreement in Zou, 'Sino-Japanese Joint Fishery Management in the East China Sea', does not contain the Exchange of Letters.

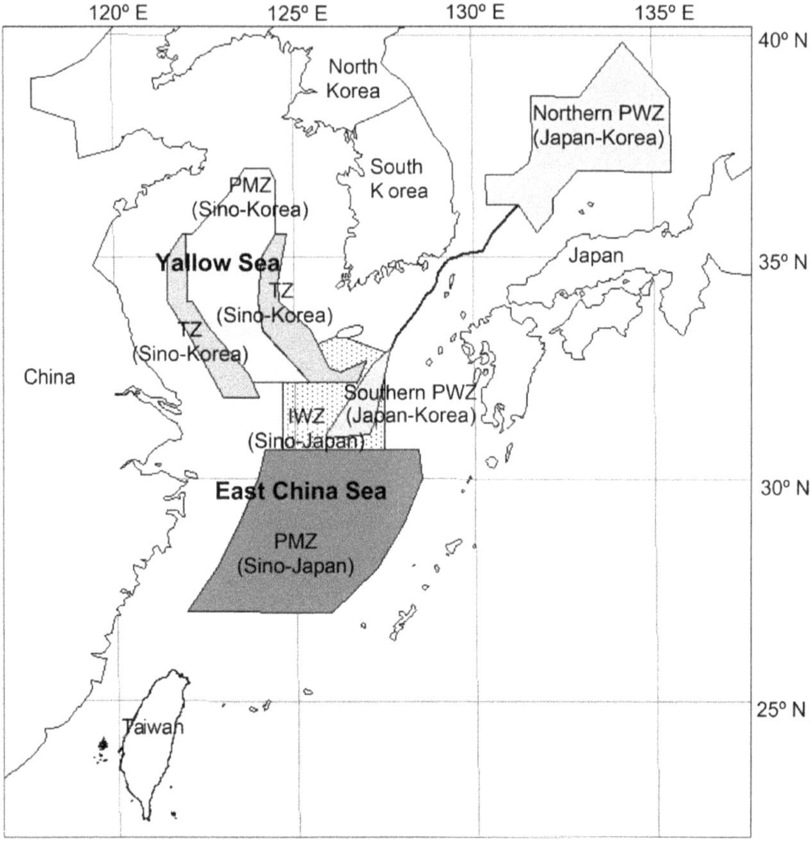

Map 7 Fisheries agreements in the East China Sea[76]

most contentious areas. The negotiations produced the perhaps paradoxical result that the most disputed area, the southern part of the East China Sea where the Senkaku/Diaoyu Islands are located, received the shallowest, most barebone common rules. This implies that China and Japan have accorded each other greater levels of freedom to unilaterally define coast guard presences and fisheries policies in the most intensively disputed areas.

China and Japan reached the 'Agreement on Fisheries' on 11 November 1997.[77] The agreement consists of three documents: one Agreement

76 Ching-Hsiewn Ou and Huan-Sheng Tseng, 'The Fishery Agreements and Management Systems in the East China Sea', *Ocean and Coastal Management* 53, no. 5 (2010): 279–88, 282. Reproduced with permission.

77 Agreement on Fisheries between the People's Republic of China and Japan, signed 11 November 1997, entered into force 1 June 2000. A complete English translation of the agreement, including the Agreed Minute and Exchange of Letters, is available in Sun Pyo Kim, *Maritime*

(detailing obligations in the EEZs and Provisional Measures Zone (PMZ)), one Agreed Minute (on obligations in the zone north of the PMZ), and one Exchange of Letters (on obligations in the zone south of the PMZ). The decreasing depth of joint regulation for each zone corresponds to the decreasing precision with which the three different documents define obligations.

The first zone is each side's EEZ. The agreement requires that each side permits nationals of the other party to fish in its EEZ. Each side must issue permits to fishermen of the other side and may collect a fee (article 2). Each side can determine the number of fishing permits based on estimates about conservation purposes but should do this 'with respect for the result of the consultations in [the] China-Japan Joint Fisheries Committee' (article 3). In other words, Japan should allow Chinese fishing activities in Japan's EEZ subject to Japan's authorization and regulation and vice versa. This provision also gives Chinese fishermen a privileged access to Japan's large EEZ in the Western Pacific east of Japan. The difficulties in the initial allocation of the number of fishing permits for each side's EEZ was an issue before the ratification of the agreement but did not block it. It entered into force in June 2000. Japan's former Foreign Minister Keizo Obuchi commented at the time in the Japanese Diet's Standing Committee for Foreign Affairs and Defense:

> Until now, Chinese fishing boats were not subject to the regulation or enforcement activities of Japan inside Japan's exclusive economic zone. With this new agreement, Chinese fishing boats will, in principle, come under Japan's jurisdiction. Also, Japan's fishing boats, in principle, will fish in China's EEZ with China's permission. As a result of this new agreement, a new fishing order between Japan and China will be established based on UNCLOS.[78]

China and Japan defined the geographic shape of their respective EEZs negatively. The EEZs of China and Japan under the agreement are the waters that China and Japan claim as their EEZ, except for the PMZ, the zone north of the PMZ, the zone south of the PMZ, and China's EEZ in the South

Delimitation and Interim Arrangements in North East Asia (Martinus Nijhoff Publishers, 2004), 338.

78 House of Councilors, 142nd Session of the Diet, *Minutes of the Standing Committee for Foreign Affairs and Defense*, 12th Meeting (April 28, 1998), 1, quoted in Kanehara and Arima, 'New Fishing Order – Japan's New Agreement on Fisheries with the Republic of Korea and with the People's Republic of China', 3.

China Sea. The reason why a fisheries agreement between China and Japan explicitly excludes the South China Sea as an applicable area (Article 6 (b)) is that the agreement gives fishermen of both sides access to both parties' EEZs. China has an EEZ in the South China Sea. The agreement therefore excludes Japanese fishermen from applying for Chinese fishing licences for the South China Sea. The provisions on mutual access to each side's EEZ do not apply to the three separately defined zones: the Provisional Measures Zone (PMZ, defined in article 6), the zone north of the PMZ (defined in the Agreed Minute) and the overlapping EEZs south of 27 degrees north latitude (article 6). Map 7 illustrates the subzones but omits the southern zone which is located south of the PMZ.[79] Several publications were not aware of the Exchange of Letters and do not include a reference to this important zone.

The second zone is the Provisional Measures Zone (PMZ) (article 7). China and Japan agreed to manage this zone jointly through the China–Japan Joint Fisheries Committee that sets quantitative and qualitative conservation measures (article 11). In practice, the committee determines the number of fishing vessels from both sides and the catch limits annually. Both sides exchange lists of fishing vessels authorized to fish in the area and register the name and number of the vessel.[80] The enforcement, however, of the joint rules follows what may be called flag state enforcement. If, for instance, the Japan Coast Guard detects a Chinese fishing vessel in the PMZ that is not registered with the joint committee, Japan is not allowed to arrest the crew. Rather, it will record the presence and notify China. China's maritime law enforcement agencies are then responsible for investigation and enforcement measures and notifying Japan of the result (article 7 (3)). The PMZ combines joint rules with separate law enforcement. Each side's competent coast guard enforces joint rules against its own nationals only. This system makes sure that, although common quantitative and qualitative fishing regulations apply, neither party's law enforcement agency is in the position to subject fishermen of the other party to its jurisdiction when fishing in the PMZ. Both states thereby evade the recognition that the other state has the power to enforce rules against its own nationals. At the same time, this system solves an important problem that has bedevilled the South China Sea disputes. When, for instance, the Philippines detained

79 The Japanese government refers to this zone as 'South Water Zone' (SWZ). Japanese Ministry of Foreign Affairs, 'Outline of the New Japan-China Fisheries Agreement' (on file with the author).
80 Interview with a senior official of Japan's Ministry of Foreign Affairs, Tokyo, 27 July 2017 (Interview 40).

or prosecuted Chinese fishermen in disputed areas, China regarded the Philippines' exercise of jurisdiction against Chinese fishermen as evidence for the Philippines' claim.[81] The combination of joint rules and separated enforcement was politically agreeable, is effective in preventing incidents, and contains some quantitative management measures.

The spatial definition of the PMZ was one intricate question in the negotiations. The difficulties in delimiting a boundary translated into difficulties for defining a provisional zone even if the purpose of the provisional zone is to sidestep delimitation questions. Both sides perceived the spatial shape of the PMZ as pre-determining sea boundary delimitation efforts. Zou notes that the 'PMZ is just designed for fishery management rather than provisional delimitation of the EEZ. On the other hand, since the PMZ has implications for the delimitation of the EEZs, it became the toughest issue in the negotiation.'[82] According to Japanese negotiators, China rejected the use of a provisional median line to demarcate fishing grounds.[83] According to a Chinese source, Chinese negotiators believed that the provisional zone amounts to China's consent to a de facto undisputed status for the areas outside the provisional zone (east and west of it). The spatial scope of a provisional zone therefore amounted to a pre-decision regarding subsequent exchanges on comprehensive boundary delimitation.[84] In other words, the view that the PMZ would pre-commit both parties to a narrower area for boundary delimitation coined the negotiations on the geographic definition of the PMZ even if the entire agreement is without prejudice to claims (article 12, reaffirmed in the Agreed Minute). Each side wanted a PMZ that did not reflect the other's position on boundary delimitation. Japan preferred a small PMZ and suggested that the distance between the PMZ and each side's baseline should be 100 nm; China preferred a large PMZ and proposed that the distance between the PMZ and each side's baseline should be 24 nm. This would leave only a very narrow EEZ to each side.[85] Negotiators had to reconcile both sides' positions on future maritime boundary delimitation and the narrowing down of the disputed area through the PMZ. The compromise defined an area where the distance from the eastern PMZ boundary and Japan's coast, and from the western PMZ boundary and China's coast is

81 Chapter III 1.

82 Zou, 'Sino-Japanese Joint Fishery Management in the East China Sea', 135.

83 Kanehara and Arima, 'New Fishing Order – Japan's New Agreement on Fisheries with the Republic of Korea and with the People's Republic of China', 21.

84 Interview 25.

85 Zou, 'Sino-Japanese Joint Fishery Management in the East China Sea', 135. This negotiation history was confirmed by interviews held in Tokyo with Japanese officials, 27 July 2017.

approximately 52 nm.[86] The distance from Japan's outer PMZ boundary (the western end of the PMZ) and China's outer PMZ boundary (the eastern end of the PMZ) is also less than 200 nm from each side's coastline. Both arrived at this compromise by using an arbitrary distance – 52 nm has no suggestive force in this context – from the coasts rather than a possible maritime boundary (for example a median line) as reference points. The spatial definition of the PMZ follows the logic that even if the PMZ is interpreted as predetermining boundary delimitation (what it does not *de jure*), this would still not support one country's bargaining position.

The Agreed Minute refers to a third zone. It mentions 'a certain area of the East China Sea in the north of the [PMZ]' (Agreed Minute). Japanese sources refer to this zone as 'Median Waters Zone (MWZ)'; Chinese sources call it the 'Intermediate Waters Zone' (IWZ) (Map 7). The Agreed Minute does not specify the size of or the obligations within the zone. The Agreed Minute obliges both parties to 'respect the current fishing operations' and to 'pay due consideration to the traditional fishing of the other country and the resource situation of the other country'. It refers to 'fishing relations with a third country'. This third country is South Korea, which also has claims in northern parts of the East China Sea. China and Japan could not agree in 1997 on more precise rules for the IWZ for two reasons. First, any regulation would have affected Korea's claims, as Korea's claims partly overlap with Japan's and China's claims. Moreover, both China and Japan have had a separate fisheries relationship with Korea. Second, Japan insisted that both sides apply, in principle, the EEZ regime to that area and that Chinese vessels are under some authority of Japan. The same problems that made negotiations of the whole agreement difficult – which side has the power to allocate rights and to enforce them and how to define this power geographically – underlined the IWZ negotiations. China resisted constraints going beyond the status quo and preferred a zone where both can fish without accepting the other's jurisdiction. It took another twenty rounds of consultations until February 2000 to reach agreement on the IWZ.[87] The solution accommodating both positions shrank the size of the IWZ to the zone between 124° 45' east longitude and 127° 30' east longitude.[88] Within the IWZ, fishing vessels of both sides are allowed to operate. Each party's maritime law enforcement agencies enforce rules only against its

86 For the exact coordinates, see article 7 of the agreement.

87 Zou, 'Sino-Japanese Joint Fishery Management in the East China Sea', 134.

88 Kanehara and Arima, 'New Fishing Order – Japan's New Agreement on Fisheries with the Republic of Korea and with the People's Republic of China', 26.

own fishing vessels. Both sides agreed on essentially applying flag state jurisdiction to the parties' fishing vessels in this area. Both sides agreed to exchange information for conservation purposes. Moreover, both sides agreed that Japan has the authority to give fishing permits for areas in the east of the IWZ and China has the authority to issue fishing permits for areas in the west of the IWZ. The IWZ's allocation of authority incorporates both sides' EEZ claims. Neither party could make use of the IWZ in subsequent exchanges to argue that the other recognized its claims.

The fourth zone is the area south of 27 degrees north latitude. It is established through an Exchange of Letters annexed to the agreement. China and Japan only committed to one obligation in this area. Each government expressed in the Exchange of Letters that it 'has the intention not to apply its relevant laws and regulations on fisheries to nationals' of the other party 'on the condition that both... are in cooperative relations in order to ensure that the maintenance of marine living resources is not endangered by over-exploitation'.[89] The Exchange of Letters specifies the obligation concerning 'the area referred to in subparagraph (b) of Article 6'. Article 6 (b) reads, 'the part of the Agreement Zone in the East China Sea below Lat. 27 N. and the part of the Agreement Zone to the west of Long. 125 E. below the East China Sea (excluding the exclusive economic zone of the People's Republic of China in the South China Sea).' Japanese sources sometimes refer to this zone as South Water Zone (SWZ) even if the exchange of letters does not use this term.[90] Map 7 does not indicate any southern zone, presumably because the authors were not aware of the SWZ. The SWZ is located between the PMZ and Taiwan. It covers the southern part of the East China Sea and is within 200 nm of Taiwan. The disputed Senkaku/Diaoyu Islands are also located within it.

The Exchange of Letters provides for the limited obligation of non-enforcement of domestic laws. This commits China's and Japan's maritime law enforcement agencies not to enforce their respective laws against fishermen of the respective other side. It does not commit the parties to accepting the validity of the other party's regulation. The objective of this commitment is to prevent fishing incidents; it is not to regulate fisheries economically or sustainably. In the SWZ, both sides do not recognize the existence of the other side's jurisdiction, but only 'intend not to apply' their own rules.

89 The Exchange of Letters is available in Kim, *Maritime Delimitation and Interim Arrangements in North East Asia*, 338.

90 Japanese Ministry of Foreign Affairs, 'Outline of the New Japan-China Fisheries Agreement' (on file with the author). I will refer to it as SWZ for convenience.

Paradoxically, Japan accepted China's maximum amount of freedom to unilaterally define fisheries regulations and to enforce these regulations with Chinese coast guard agencies in the southern part of the East China Sea – including the waters outside the territorial waters of the Senkaku/Diaoyu Islands. Each party unilaterally decides on fundamental economic questions such as the number of fishing vessels. These economic issues were not even part of the negotiations. The commitment to non-enforcement in the SWZ therefore raises a question. Japan insisted on fisheries regulation for all parts of the East China Sea that reflect, in principle, its UNCLOS-based EEZ claim except for the southern part of the East China Sea. Tokyo's insistence on such regulation in the northern IWZ blocked progress on the whole agreement, but for the southern zone Japan accepted a minimal commitment to 'the intention not to apply its relevant laws'. Why was Japan satisfied with a minimal commitment for the southern part of the East China Sea? Several reasons must be discussed. First, a Japanese outline of the agreement cites the 'complicated pattern'[91] of fishing activities in this area. The complicated pattern probably refers to the difficult trilateral fisheries relationship between Japan, Taiwan, and China. China and Taiwan did not conclude a written fisheries agreement.[92] Both China and Taiwan fish in largely overlapping areas and the cross strait relationship has its own difficulties. Second, the existence of the disputed Senkaku/Diaoyu Islands in this area results in further challenges.[93] Former Foreign Minister Obuchi noted: 'Japan's position is that there is no territorial issue over the Senkaku Islands to be negotiated or to be resolved with China.'[94] Obuchi's argument appears to be that a non-recognized territorial dispute cannot affect the content of an agreement.[95] The former deputy director general of the Treaties Bureau

91 Japanese Ministry of Foreign Affairs, 'Outline of the new Japan-China fisheries Agreement' (on file with the author).

92 China and Taiwan had some exchanges on fisheries in 2009, but these exchanges appear not to have gone beyond an informal understanding. Huan-Sheng Tseng and Ching-Hsiewn Ou, 'Taiwan and China: A Unique Fisheries Relationship', *Marine Policy*, 34 (2010), 1156–62. With the election of President Tsai, official cross strait exchanges discontinued.

93 Zou, 'Sino-Japanese Joint Fishery Management in the East China Sea', 136; Guifang Xue, 'Bilateral Fisheries Agreements for the Cooperative Management of the Shared Resources of the China Seas: A Note', *Ocean Development & International Law*, 36 (2005), 363–74, 369.

94 House of Representatives, 142nd Session, *Minutes of the Standing Committee for Foreign Affairs, 9th* Meeting (April 17, 1998), 2, quoted in: Kanehara, 'New Fishing Order – Japan's New Agreement on Fisheries with the Republic of Korea and with the People's Republic of China', 28.

95 Japan does not recognize the existence of a dispute about the Senkaku /Diaoyu Islands. Hirose Hajime, 'Japan's Effective Control of the Senkaku Islands', *Review of Island Studies*, 2013, 1–25;

of Japan's Ministry of Foreign Affairs Ebihara made a similar statement in Japan's Standing Committee for Foreign Affairs: 'The territorial waters [of the Senkaku Islands] are not an area where the Agreement applies. The status of the territorial waters is unchanged, and this Agreement has no effect on its status.'[96] As Japan does not even recognize the existence of a sovereignty dispute over the Senkaku/Diaoyu Islands, a fisheries agreement cannot contain provisions from which China could infer that a dispute exists. Japan had, in principle, two options to incorporate this position in the agreement. China and Japan could have agreed on a thicker set of rules reflecting EEZ claims combined with a provision explicitly excluding the territorial waters of the disputed islands from these rules. Alternatively, they could agree on minimal rules and leave the geographic scope undefined. The parties chose the second option and agreed only on the 'intention not to enforce' their own rules in an exchange of letters. In this way, no compromise on the geographical scope was necessary and the territorial waters need no mention, however indirect. Regardless of the status of the Senkaku/Diaoyu Islands, or whether these islands are entitled to an EEZ, Japan did not acknowledge the existence of Chinese authority in the wider area around the islands – Japan only committed not to apply its own rules to Chinese nationals. China preferred an arrangement without substantial rules, minimising the reach of Japan's EEZ claims. Both Japan and China evaded the question of how the fisheries agreement could integrate the sovereignty dispute – in Japan's view, a non-existent sovereignty dispute – by combining a shallow commitment with an ambiguously defined area. In sum, even if the fisheries agreement became a focal point in future negotiations, China could not use it for sovereignty or boundary claims. This has, however, resulted in Japan giving China the maximum degree of freedom to unilaterally decide on fishing activities in the southern part of the East China Sea, including in the waters outside the territorial waters of the Senkaku/Diaoyu Islands.

Masahiro Miyoshi, 'Exercising Enforcement Jurisdiction around the Senkaku Islands', *Review of Island Studies*, 2014, 1–18. For an English language publication reviewing the Japanese legal debate on the Senkaku Islands, see Shingo Yamagami, 'Reflections on the Issue of the Senkaku Islands -from the Field of Practice on International Law and Politics', *Japan's Territories Series, Japan Digital Library*, 2016 http://www2.jiia.or.jp/en/digital_library/japan_s_territories.php (last accessed 17 June 2023).

96 House of Representatives, 142nd Session, *Minutes of the Standing Committee for Foreign Affairs, 9th* Meeting (April 17, 1998), 2, quoted in Kanehara, 'New Fishing Order – Japan's New Agreement on Fisheries with the Republic of Korea and with the People's Republic of China', 28.

1.4 The Senkaku/Diaoyu Islands, the Fisheries Agreement, and the Management of Incidents 2010–2017

The fisheries agreement governs the Sino-Japanese fisheries relations in all areas of the East China Sea that China and Japan claim except for the territorial waters around the Senkaku/Diaoyu Islands. It clarifies which country's maritime law enforcement agency has the authority to enforce which rules against which fishermen and in which areas. It also specifies that a country's coast guard does not have the authority to exercise enforcement jurisdiction against the other party's fishermen. With the Joint Committee, the agreement has established a procedure to settle issues. Despite the escalation of incidents and severe challenges to the agreement, neither Tokyo nor Beijing terminated the agreement, which they could have done unilaterally in accordance with article 14 (2).

The only geographic area where the agreement does not apply is also the only area where fishing incidents involving Chinese fishing vessels and the Japan Coast Guard escalated. In September 2010 and after the end of China's annual fishing ban, the Japan Coast Guard warned a total of 430 Chinese fishing vessels to leave the territorial waters of the Senkaku/Diaoyu Islands. One Chinese fishing vessel intentionally collided with two Japan Coast Guard vessels on 7 September 2010. Japan's Coast Guard detained the Chinese crew and its allegedly intoxicated captain that rammed two Japanese vessels.[97] A diplomatic standoff followed. When Japan arrested the fishermen and announced the intention to prosecute them in Japan, China reacted strongly. Beijing regarded Japan's intended prosecution of Chinese fishermen who were apprehended in the territorial waters of the Senkaku/Diaoyu as potential manifestation of Japan's effective control of the islands and therefore as evidence for Japan's claim. According to monthly data from Japan's Ministry of Defence, China did not have a regular coast guard presence in the territorial waters before this incident.[98] China's maritime law enforcement vessels initiated regular patrols within the territorial waters after and in response to this incident and maintained this presence after the incident. The number of Chinese overflights in the East China Sea (outside the airspace of the islands) more than doubled in 2010, too.[99]

97 Ministry of Foreign Affairs of Japan, 'Status of activities by Chinese government vessels and Chinese fishing vessels in waters surrounding the Senkaku Islands', August 26, 2016, https://www.mofa.go.jp/files/000180283.pdf (last accessed 17 March 2024).

98 Japan Ministry of Defence, 'China's Maritime Expansion, Report' ((on file with author), April 2017).

99 Ibid.

Former US Secretary of State Clinton was reportedly prompted to declare that article five of the Japan–US defence treaty applies to the Senkaku/Diaoyu Islands.[100] China suspended a number of bilateral exchanges and allegedly banned the export of rare earth to Japan.[101] In fact, the rare earth price peaked at four times the previous price level during the events in 2010.[102] However, the evidence for China weaponizing rare earth exports in the context of this crisis remains inconclusive, because the observable drop in rare earth exports to Japan can also be explained by policy changes announced before this crisis.[103] Japanese officials and observers agreed with Chinese counterparts that this incident was one of the turning points that produced the tense situation in the East China Sea disputes.[104] It also led to Japan's nationalization of the islands in 2012 which, in turn, triggered the next crisis.[105] Without a minimum of common rules, the Chinese and Japanese governments were unable to prevent the escalation of the disputes triggered by a fishing incident.

Expansion of the China Coast Guard presence and the fisheries agreement

Japan has tried to at least match the China Coast Guard presence around the Senkaku/Diaoyu Islands. As the distance from the bases of the Japan Coast Guard at Ishigaki to the islands is shorter than the distance from Chinese bases, Japan has a geographic advantage. Japan's surveillance provides

100 'Clinton: Senkakus subject to security pact', *The Japan Times*, 25 September 2010, https://www.japantimes.co.jp/news/2010/09/25/national/clinton-senkakus-subject-to-security-pact/ (last accessed 12 March 2024).

101 Keith Bradsher, 'Amid Tension, China Blocks Vital Exports to Japan', *New York Times*, 22 September 2010, https://www.nytimes.com/2010/09/23/business/global/23rare.html (last accessed 12 March 2024).

102 Ian R Coles, 'Strategic Minerals — the New Global Battleground', *Financial Times*, 21 June 2019, https://www.ft.com/content/c553bfc0-890b-11e9-a028-86cea8523dc2. (last accessed 12 March 2024).

103 Michael Green et al. *Countering Coercion in Maritime Asia The Theory and Practice of Gray Zone Deterrence.* (Center for Strategic & International Studies, 2017), 84–94. https://www.csis.org/analysis/countering-coercion-maritime-asia.

104 Interviews 25, 30, 32; Ryoko Nakano, 'The Sino–Japanese Territorial Dispute and Threat Perception in Power Transition', *The Pacific Review*, 29 (2016), 165–86; Drifte, 'The Japan-China Confrontation over the Senkaku/Diaoyu Islands; Yuki Tatsumi, 'Senkaku Islands/East China Sea Disputes – A Japanese Perspective', in *CNA Maritime Asia Project*, 2013, https://www.stimson.org/content/senkaku-islandseast-china-sea-disputes-japanese-perspective (last accessed 12 June 2023).

105 Green et al., *Countering Coercion in Maritime Asia*,128.

the necessary information to anticipate deployments of the China Coast Guards, according to Rear Admiral Awai of the Japan Coast Guard.[106] In early August 2016, however, this was challenged. After the end of China's annual summer fishing ban, several hundred Chinese fishing vessels have been fishing in the southern part of the East China Sea at a time. In August 2016, around 230 Chinese fishing vessels operated in the southern zone of the fisheries agreement in areas around but mainly outside the territorial waters of the Senkaku/Diaoyu Islands. They were accompanied by fifteen China Coast Guard vessels.[107] Japanese media reported on this event ('China's use of an armada of fishing boats — part of its so-called maritime militia', 'potentially significant escalation').[108] These reports failed to note, however, that to the extent that the fishing operations occurred outside the territorial waters of the Senkaku/Diaoyu Islands they complied with the Sino-Japanese fisheries agreement, specifically its Exchange of Letters. When Chinese fishing and Coast Guard vessels entered the territorial waters, the Japanese Coast Guard opposed them. The Sino-Japanese rules for the southern fisheries zone do not mandate a maximum number of fishing vessels. The presence of several hundred Chinese vessels in this area is not unusual, especially after the end of China's summer fishing ban. The real issue in August 2016 was not the large number of Chinese fishing vessels, but the fact that they were escorted by the China Coast Guard.[109]

From Japan's perspective, Chinese fishing activities undertaken in compliance with the fisheries agreement are linked to adversarial political purposes – affecting the sovereignty status of the disputed islands – when China uses fishing activities and the fisheries agreement as pretence to increase the presence of the China Coast Guard. If China were to use fishing activities allowed by the fisheries agreement as a pretext to improve China's de facto authority in the waters around the Senkaku/Diaoyu Islands, this calls into question the whole Sino-Japanese fisheries relationship in the East China Sea. The fisheries agreement essentially serves the purpose of separating fisheries from territorial and maritime boundary disputes. When one party uses fishing practices and provisions of the agreement instrumentally for strengthening its position on territorial issues by expanding its coast guard

106 Tsuguo Awai, *The Silent Guardians of the East China Sea. Unsung heroes of the Japan Coast Guard to stand guard of Senkaku* (Next Publishing Authors Press, 2022), 104.
107 Ibid., 108.
108 Jesse Johnson, 'Chinese Senkaku swarm tactic spells trouble for Japan', Japan Times, 07 August 2016, https://www.japantimes.co.jp/news/2016/08/07/national/politics-diplomacy/senkaku-swarm-tactic-spells-trouble-tokyo/#.W6jVYfkzaij (last accessed 12 April 2024).
109 Interview 40.

presence, this challenges the carefully adjusted fishing order. However, without a fisheries agreement the number of fishing incidents is likely to increase dramatically in the entire East China Sea. Japan appears to have conveyed this message to their Chinese counterparts. In 2017, an even higher number of Chinese fishing vessels operated without incidents in the southern East China Sea.[110]

The political relevance of termination clauses becomes apparent in this context. Article 14 of the agreement allows each party to unilaterally terminate the agreement with a previous notice of six months. This provision gives each side the option to use the continuation of the whole agreement as leverage to request compliance. This provision also serves as a safeguard against the possibility that an interim agreement becomes a permanent institution. Neither state terminated the agreement despite the mentioned challenges.

The fisheries agreement defines a broad mandate for the joint committee (article 11). This allows the joint committee to take up issues flexibly even for zones where the agreement does not mandate substantive cooperation and where the joint committee has no competence. In practice, officials also consult on the 'maintenance of order in fishing activities in the south zone'.[111] Moreover, Japanese officials use the committee to inform Chinese officials about Japan's law enforcement responses to illegal fishing practices such as coral poaching by Chinese fishermen in Japan's EEZ.[112]

Moreover, contrasting the SWZ and the PMZ, another politically important element of this agreement becomes apparent. The practice of jointly setting a maximum number of fishing vessels in the PMZ has an ecologically and politically crucial effect. Both sides get some influence over the maximum number of fishing vessels from *both* parties in the PMZ. In contrast, the agreement does not limit the number of fishing vessels operating in the IWZ or SWZ. After the end of China's summer ban, this number could reach over a thousand vessels that fish at one time in the southern zone. Despite these limitations, China has reduced the number of

110 AMTI, 'Smooth Sailing for East China Sea Fishing', 30 November 2017, https://amti.csis.org/smooth-sailing-east-china-sea/ (last accessed 12 April 2024).

111 Japanese Ministry of Foreign Affairs, 'Outline of the New Japan-China Fisheries Agreement'.

112 Interview 40; Reiji Yoshida, 'Chinese Coral Poachers Encroaching on Japanese Fishermen', *Japan Times*, 6 November 2014, https://www.japantimes.co.jp/news/2014/11/06/national/chinese-coral-poachers-encroaching-japanese-fishermen/; 'Japan sentences Chinese fishing boat captain to prison for poaching coral off Tokyo coast', 27 May 2017, SCMP, https://www.scmp.com/news/asia/east-asia/article/1810107/chinese-fishing-boat-captain-sentenced-prison-poaching-coral (both last accessed 12 April 2024).

fishing vessels in the East China Sea in the wake of the Sino-Japanese and Sino-Korean agreements. Zhang mentions a reduction of 25,000 vessels for the entire East China Sea and Yellow Sea.[113] Although China has reduced the number of vessels in the East China Sea, quantitative restrictions on fishing practices did not represent strong barriers to the agreement. Both parties can unilaterally define quota for the IWZ and SWZ. The scarcity of joint rules for the IWZ and SWZ shows that the principal objective of the agreement is to prevent fishing incidents in these areas rather than to regulate fisheries sustainably. For the EEZs and PMZ, the agreement has the double objective of fisheries governance and provisional dispute settlement. Although one of the objectives of the agreement was the implementation and recognition of UNCLOS as the applicable legal framework, other international agreements pertaining to sustainability or environmental protection did not have any impact on the agreement beyond the general notion of sustainable uses.[114]

The controversial issues in the negotiations as well as the variation and details of the subzones do not correspond to competing positions on fisheries management, sustainable regulation, or monitoring standards. Negotiators instead defined subzones spatially and with varying formulas of jurisdiction to ensure that the institutional arrangement does not strengthen one state's bargaining position over the other. This problem was twofold. First, no agreement was possible without a consensus on the spatial definition of subzones that evade a de facto validation of the parties' claims. This is illustrated in the delay caused by the IWZ and the difficulties of defining the PMZ. The institutional design of the agreement incorporates the expectation that a particular geographic area is a precedent for future negotiations. Negotiators ensured that even if the shape of joint zones amounts to a precedent for future negotiations, this would not be detrimental to the parties. The second controversial point in the negotiations was to determine different allocations of authority to coast guard agencies for different areas. In several instances, Japan has experienced that there is small difference between China's maritime law enforcement agencies advancing China's claims and enforcing fisheries laws in disputed areas. As long as the priority mission of Chinese maritime law enforcement agencies is to safeguard China's claims, any mutually agreed transfer of public authority to the China Coast Guard is a most sensitive issue that requires a prudent approach. China and Japan

113 Hongzhou Zhang, 'Chinese Fishermen in Disputed Waters: Not Quite a "People's War"', *Marine Policy* 68 (June 2016): 65–73, 69.

114 Interview 40.

have squared this circle and upheld the fishery agreement until today. The discussion of the negotiations leading to this agreement illustrates that both parties were prepared to creatively synthesize their opposing claims and institutional design.

2 The Republic of Korea, Japan, and China

The following presents in less detail the exchanges between the Republic of Korea and Japan, and the Republic of Korea and China. It shows how Korea and China have responded to massive violations of the Sino-Korean fisheries agreement. It examines how the bilateral agreements have addressed the overlapping claims of three countries.

2.1 The Republic of Korea and Japan: Fisheries Agreements 1965–1999

The Republic of Korea and Japan had first established a common fisheries regime in the East China Sea and the Sea of Japan (East Sea in Korea) in 1965. In the 1950s and 1960s, fishing incidents, especially around the disputed Dok-do/Takeshima Islands and the Syngman Rhee Line, bedevilled the bilateral relations. Korea and Japan established diplomatic relations in 1965 and this enabled the conclusion of a fisheries agreement. The agreement created an exclusive fisheries zone, a joint regulation zone and a joint survey zone.[115] A new fisheries agreement became necessary after both sides ratified UNCLOS. Similar to the Sino-Japanese relations, the EEZ regime of UNCLOS resulted in overlapping EEZ claims. Korea and Japan reached a fisheries agreement in 1999.[116] Not unlike the Sino-Japanese agreement, Korea and Japan agreed on several subzones with various formulas of jurisdiction that accommodated each side's claims. Map 7 illustrates the subzones (see above). The agreement sets up a northern 'Provisional Waters Zone' (PWZ) and a southern 'Provisional Waters Zone' (PWZ). The agreement allows each side's fishermen access to the other side's EEZ, provided it applied for a licence. Both parties agreed on an ambiguous definition of the southern end of the southern PWZ in the East China Sea to evade the question where the southernmost end of Korea's claim is located. Article 9 (2) reads: 'The provisions

115 'Agreement on Fisheries between the Republic of Korea and Japan of 1965'; available in Kim, *Maritime Delimitation and Interim Arrangements in North East Asia*, 321–38.
116 'Agreement on Fisheries between the Republic of Korea and Japan of 1999'; available in Kim, *Maritime Delimitation and Interim Arrangements in North East Asia*, 321–38.

of Annex I, paragraph 3 shall apply to the area north of the southernmost parallel of the exclusive economic zone of the Republic of Korea.' Japan and Korea have conflicting positions where the southernmost parallel of Koreas' EEZ is located. The fisheries agreement settled this issue by allowing both parties to interpret this formula differently. This works well enough as long as both parties have a consensus for the bigger part of the disputed areas.

Kim has analysed the difficulties in the negotiations and how the disputed island of Dok-do/Takeshima[117] in the Sea of Japan has impacted the design of fishing zones. Kim argues that 'Korea wished to avoid any implication that the joint fishing zone in the East Sea where Dok-do is geographically situated is jointly managed by Korea and Japan' because the Korean government believed that 'the joint fishing zone might affect the territorial issue if it is jointly managed by the joint committee'. Kim then discusses this problem in the following way:

> An important question arises here: if the joint fisheries committee has the competence to prescribe any conservation measures with regard to the zone in the East Sea and thus the zone is to be called a "joint management" zone, then does the competence of the joint committee affect territorial status of Dok-do? It seems unreasonable to suggest that a joint fishing zone affects sovereignty over an island if its fisheries resources are jointly managed.... Interestingly, however, a few Korean scholars have argued that the new fisheries agreement between Korea and Japan affects negatively Korea's territorial sovereignty of Dok-do.[118]

Kim then argues that it is 'absurd to assume that a provisional fisheries agreement affects the issue of territorial sovereignty' and says 'both countries are free from the possible precedence in the Fisheries Agreement'.[119] Despite considering this absurd, he nevertheless argues that 'from close examination of the map, it can be said that the shaping of the joint fishing zone is a precedent where Japan's claim to use Dok-do was denounced whereas Korea's claim is not.'[120] Kim then asks: 'Now a further question can arise: is it Japan's hidden intention, as the Korean public worries, to take some advantage in territorial issues over Dok-do from the fisheries agreement?

117 Lee Chang Wee, 'Legal and Political Aspects of the Dokdo Issue: Interrelationship between International Law and International Relations', *Korean Journal of Defense Analysis*, 2013, 227–42.

118 Kim, *Maritime Delimitation and Interim Arrangements in North East Asia*, 260.

119 Ibid. 258.

120 Ibid. 257.

The answer is unknown to this author. But one thing is very clear. The provisional fisheries agreement cannot affect territorial questions at all as we have discussed fully thus far.'[121]

If it is absurd to assume that a fisheries agreement affects the status of the island, then Japan will not take advantage of it because there are no possible circumstances where Japan could take advantage of it. Alternatively, if Japan has the possibility of taking advantage of the agreement for improving its territorial claims, it is not absurd to assume that the agreement could potentially affect the sovereignty issue. The underlying problem of Kim's discussion is that the questions he raises play, according to Kim, a key role in the negotiations of the agreement. Kim, the lawyer, argues that it is pointless to ask whether the difference between 'joint measures' and 'joint recommendations' can affect the status of Dok-do/Takeshima.[122] Kim, the observer, however, reports the obstacles in the negotiations – whether a fisheries zone could be construed as a precedent of which one party could take advantage. Japan's Foreign Minister Koumura proved no less adept at considering the relevance of different formulas for status questions: 'The territorial issue was not shelved; it was separated. This agreement does not prejudice Japan's legal position concerning Takeshima.'[123] The agreement had to respond to the parties' belief that the agreement amounts to a layer of validity for a rival claim. Otherwise, the parties did not reach agreement. This agreement needed to satisfy the expectation that provisional zones establish a practical precedent in favour of an opponent's claim. The institutional design incorporates both parties' concerns for preventing the creation of this vulnerability. The agreement did this by defining various subzones that reflect original claims. Even if the agreement could be construed as a precedent for territorial issues or boundary delimitation, this would still not improve the bargaining position of one or the other state.

A further factor contributing to the conclusion of the agreement in 1999 was the following. Japan made use of the termination clause of the fisheries agreement of 1965 and unilaterally terminated it with a previous notice of one year. If both parties wanted to preserve joint rules for otherwise disputed areas prone to incidents, they needed to reach a new agreement by 1999.[124] The fisheries agreement of 1999 is largely effective in preventing fishing

121 Ibid. 262.

122 Ibid. 255.

123 Quoted in: Kanehara and Arima, 'New Fishing Order – Japan's New Agreement on Fisheries with the Republic of Korea and with the People's Republic of China', 10.

124 Ibid., 13.

incidents in the East China Sea. The fisheries relations in the Sea of Japan, however, remain contentious. According to the agreement, both parties need to determine annual fishing quota for the Sea of Japan. However, both repeatedly failed to agree on quotas. In consequence, both parties prohibit their own fishermen from fishing in the other party's EEZ.[125]

Korean-Japanese joint development agreement 1974

The Republic of Korea and Japan concluded the 'Agreement concerning joint development of the southern part of the continental shelf adjacent to the two countries' in 1974.[126] This agreement should be briefly mentioned, if only because it 'represented the first application of the idea of joint development of offshore oil where the parties failed to agree on boundary delimitation, as indicated in the ICJ judgment of 1969 [North Sea Continental Shelf Case]'.[127] This agreement illustrates a dynamic similar to the fisheries agreements. Korea and Japan had an unresolved continental shelf dispute in the late 1960s. This dispute intensified after the UN Economic Commission for Asia reported potentially rich deposits in the area.[128] Korea unilaterally announced concession blocks beyond a median line that Japan claimed. Japan resisted Korea's unilateral move and negotiations on a boundary did not progress. While Korea claimed a boundary based on the natural prolongation of the continental shelf, Japan proposed an equidistance line as a boundary. Both sides could not resolve the question of which of the two principles should be applied to delimitation (prolongation of the continental shelf or equidistance) as each side's principle enlarged its share of the continental shelf. Korea rejected Japan's proposal to bring the dispute to the ICJ.[129] In order to overcome the deadlock, both states started negotiations on joint development.[130] These negotiations resulted in the Agreement

125 'Korea, Japan fail to reach fisheries agreement', *The Korea Herald*, 29 June 2016, https://www.koreaherald.com/view.php?ud=20160629000780 (last accessed 12 April 2024).

126 Republic of Korea and Japan, 'Agreement Concerning Joint Development of the Southern Part of the Continental Shelf Adjacent to the Two Countries' (*UN deposit* 1225, no. 1-19778, January 1974).

127 Masahiro Miyoshi, *The Joint Development of Offshore Oil and Gas in Relation to Maritime Boundary Delimitation*, Maritime Briefing (University of Durham, 1999), 2, no. 5, 1.

128 UN Economic Commission for Asia and the Far East, *Report of the Sixth Session of the Committee for Coordination of Joint Prospecting for Mineral Resources in Asian Offshore Areas* (CCOP), E/CN.11/L.239, 26 June 1969.

129 Kim, *Maritime Delimitation and Interim Arrangements in North East Asia*, 282.

130 Japan, Korea, and Taiwan also consulted in a trilateral committee on developing marine resources from 1970 to 1972. When Japan recognized the People's Republic of China, Taiwan

concerning Joint Development in January 1974. The geographic definition of the area for joint development incorporated both countries' positions. It adopted Japan's equidistance line and Korea's prolonged continental shelf line as outer boundaries.[131] The joint area encompasses about 24,101 square miles and was divided into nine subzones. Korea and Japan agreed on a combination of a 'single operator formula' and alternating jurisdiction in the nine subzones.

> This 'operator formula' has made it unnecessary to decide the respective jurisdictions of the two countries.... Thus, Japanese law is applied in a sub-zone where a Japanese concessionaire works as the operator, while in an adjacent sub-zone Korean law is applied.... However, the law shifts from Japanese to Korean law and vice versa as the operator alternates between the concessionaires of the two governments for a sub-zone with the shift of work phase from exploration to exploitation.[132]

This agreement addressed the issues of the geographic definition of a joint area and the allocation of authority by utilizing a model of alternating jurisdiction. Jurisdiction alternates in place and time. Exploration activities will be undertaken under one state's jurisdiction and according to procedures of this side's energy company. The subsequent exploitation phase, however, must be conducted under the other state's jurisdiction and according to the procedures of the company of the other side. From a commercial and legal standpoint, this solution is undesirable as it makes the operations of oil companies complex. Each concessionaire will have to do a complete hand over to a competitor in case of findings. The primary motivation for this institutional design appears to be political rather than economic or legal. The rationale was to establish jurisdictional parity to the point where political incentives take precedence over commercial incentives. No side could use the agreement to construe a precedent or an element of validity in favour of its claim. Thus, the alternating jurisdiction formula has protected claims against this potential vulnerability. It should be noted that Korea and Japan conducted seismic research but did not make economically viable findings.[133]

withdrew from the trilateral committee. Hurng-Yu Chen, 'The Prospects for Joint Development in the South China Sea', *Issues and Studies, Vol. 27, No. 12*, (1991), 112–25.

131 Kim, *Maritime Delimitation and Interim Arrangements in North East Asia*, 282–286.

132 Miyoshi, *The Joint Development of Offshore Oil and Gas in Relation to Maritime Boundary Delimitation*, 12.

133 Kim, *Maritime Delimitation and Interim Arrangements in North East Asia*, 285.

2.2 The Sino-Korean Fisheries Agreement: Effective despite Rampant Violations?

The lack of clarity about sea boundaries and maritime zones has also shaped Sino-Korean relations in the East China Sea and Yellow Sea. The Republic of Korea and China, though, did not follow the Sino-Japanese example of reaching a non-governmental fisheries agreement in the 1960s. Korea and China did not have diplomatic relations at that time. Without diplomatic relations, Korea and China did not negotiate about a fisheries order and had little common rules for the maritime domain. To prevent repeated fishing incidents since the 1950s, the Korean government advised Korean fishermen not to fish in areas beyond the so-called Mao Tse-teung line, a line off the coast of China in the Yellow Sea.[134] Talks at the level of governments only became feasible with the normalization of diplomatic relations in 1992.[135] As both countries have ratified UNCLOS and the Yellow Sea is a narrow sea, their EEZ entitlements overlap widely, as illustrated by Map 7 (see above). Chinese and Korean officials began talks on a fisheries agreement in 1993. Korea insisted on boundary delimitation rather than joint fishing zones in the first four years of negotiations, but these negotiations ended in an impasse. Chinese fishermen continued to fish in areas close to Korea, and Korea faced the challenge of whether and how to enforce its laws unilaterally. Korea's negotiation position changed, and it accepted to negotiate provisional and practical measures for fisheries cooperation. 'From December 1997, various proposals on how to shape a joint fishing zone in the Yellow Sea were exchanged between the two countries. As Korea wished to set up a joint fishing zone of a narrow width whereas China wanted a joint fishing zone of a wide width, it was difficult for the two countries to agree on the shape.'[136] Negotiators resolved this disagreement by defining two joint transitional zones of a wide size that were phased out after four years and another joint zone that would not be phased out. Based on this compromise, China and Korea reached their first formal fisheries agreement in November 1998. The agreement entered into force on 30 June 2001.[137]

The basic design and legal structure of this agreement resembles the Sino-Japanese and the Korean-Japanese agreements in the East China

134 Kim, *Maritime Delimitation and Interim Arrangements in North East Asia*, 269.

135 Ji-Young Lee, *The Geopolitics of South Korea-China Relations: Implications for U.S. Policy in the Indo-Pacific* (RAND Corporation, 2020).

136 Kim, *Maritime Delimitation and Interim Arrangements in North East Asia*, 266.

137 'Agreement on Fisheries between the Republic of Korea and the People's Republic of China', available in Kim, *Maritime Delimitation and Interim Arrangements in North East Asia*, 347–56.

Sea. It establishes subzones with varying allocations of public authority. Each subzone is designed to incorporate the basic positions on maritime boundaries and the preferences on access to fishing grounds. Article 2 allows fishing vessels of both parties to access the other party's EEZ subject to acquiring licences from this state. In the Yellow Sea and the East China Sea, the agreement defines two transitional zones (TZ) close to the respective coasts (article 8) and a provisional measures zone (PMZ) in the centre (article 7). A joint committee (article 13) defines quantitative and conservation measures for the PMZ (article 7.2). Each party shall gradually implement the EEZ rules in the TZ (article 8.2) over a period of four years. After the four-year period, the rules of articles 2–5 should apply in the TZ, which was effectively phased out in 2005. Moreover, article 9 refers to a 'certain area to the north' of the PMZ and 'a certain area' to the south of the PMZ. The memorandum of understanding attached to the agreement specifies that these two areas are distinct. Korea demanded a special prohibition zone in waters close to North Korea, where no foreign fishing vessels are allowed to operate ('a certain area in the north').[138] China insisted on a conservation zone off the mouth of the Yangtze River ('a certain area in the south'). Only local Chinese fishermen are permitted to fish there. The geographic scope of these two zones is not defined precisely. Additionally, both established a zone where the current unilateral fishing pattern is to be maintained in the south of the PMZ.

Managing rampant violations of the Sino-Korean fisheries agreement

The agreement has been subject to severe challenges as Chinese fishermen have continued to fish in the expired TZs and thereby violated the agreement many 10,000 times. The Yellow Sea is an area of particularly dense fishing practices with about 2,000 Chinese vessels operating in the joint fishing zones during fishing season.[139] Chinese fishing operations in the eastern Transitional Zone (TZ) and Korean fishing operations in the western TZ were meant to phase out by 2005 (article 8 of the agreement). Map 7 (see above) illustrates these zones. The two TZs should then have been subject to the EEZ rules as specified in the bilateral agreement. Chinese fishermen, however, did not comply with this provision and have continued fishing in

138 Kim, *Maritime Delimitation and Interim Arrangements in North East Asia*, 271.

139 Ministry of Oceans and Fisheries of the Republic of Korea, 'Press Release', quoted in: 'S. Korea, China to hold joint inspection on illegal fishing in Yellow Sea', *Korean Times*, 5 April 2015, http://www.koreatimes.co.kr/www/news/nation/2015/11/656_176526.html (last accessed 13 April 2024).

the eastern TZ. Chinese fishermen have also tried to take advantage of the absence of coordination between North and South Korean law enforcement agencies by fishing close to North Korean waters. One reason for these fishing activities appears to be the depletion of the Chinese waters in the Yellow Sea.[140] South Korea counted a total of 29,600 Chinese fishing ships operating in its area in the second half of 2014 (adding up repeated entries of fishing vessels).[141] 25,400 vessels entered illegally into Korean waters in the same period in 2013.[142]

South Korean Coast Guard vessels opposed Chinese fishing vessels and violent clashes ensued. One South Korean coast guard officer died in the clashes in 2011. Korea's coast guard acted more resolutely, leaving several Chinese fishermen dead in subsequent years. Further violent clashes between Chinese fishermen and the Korean Coast Guard followed. One Korean Coast Guard vessel sank after a Chinese fishing vessel rammed it; two Korean officers were killed and several injured between 2008 and 2016.[143] In response to this situation, China agreed to conduct joint patrols with Korean law enforcement vessels in 2014 such as to restrain Chinese fishermen. A few joint patrols were conducted in 2015 but did not solve the problem. Chinese fishermen continued their operations in the expired TZ. Not even the joint patrols with the China Coast Guard restricted Chinese fishermen. Both parties did not terminate the agreement article 16 (3) gives both parties the option to unilaterally terminate the agreement with a previous notice of one year – even if Chinese fishermen violated the agreement many 10,000 times, perhaps even several 100,000 times since 2011. Instead, Korea responded by adopting the 'Manual for the Use of Weapons' in 2016 that provides a clear legal basis for the Korea Coast Guard's 'use of force'.[144] As Korea's manual explicitly allows forceful responses, clashes continued in 2017 and 2018. One Chinese vessel was found with 250 bullets from a machine gun. China protested the shooting of Chinese fishermen ('excessive action')

140 Ki Beom Lee, 'The Korea Coast Guard's Use of Force Against Chinese Fishing Vessels: A Note', *Ocean Development & International Law* 49, no. 3 (3 July 2018): 226–35, 227.

141 'S. Korea, China to hold joint inspection on illegal fishing in Yellow Sea'. Zhang also quotes this number based on the same source. Hongzhou Zhang, 'Chinese Fishermen in Disputed Waters: Not Quite a "People's War"', *Marine Policy* 68 (June 2016): 65–73, 65.

142 Hongzhou Zhang and Sam Bateman, 'Fishing Militia, the Securitization of Fishery and the South China Sea Dispute', *Contemporary Southeast Asia*, 2017, 288–314, 293.

143 Lyle J Morris, 'South Korea Cracks Down on Illegal Chinese Fishing, With Violent Results', *The Diplomat*, 03 November 2016, https://thediplomat.com/2016/11/south-korea-cracks-down-on-illegal-chinese-fisherman-with-violent-results/ (last accessed 13 April 2023).

144 Ki Beom Lee, 'The Korea Coast Guard's Use of Force Against Chinese Fishing Vessels: A Note'.

and called for coordination ('strengthen communication with the Chinese side').[145] It is important to note that neither did China respond with violent means nor did Korean sources warn of Chinese reprisals. Lee, a Korean lawyer, expressed concern regarding Korea's 'use of force' on international legal grounds.[146]

China's reaction to the use of machine guns by the Korea Coast Guard against Chinese fishing vessels is striking in comparison to the South China Sea. China did not claim that the Chinese fishermen were operating in Chinese waters. China did not reciprocate with forceful law enforcement operations against Korean fishing vessels. China did not call into question South Korea's jurisdiction in the area east of the PMZ as conveyed on Korea by the Sino-Korean agreement. The agreement offers the basis for joint patrols of China and South Korea.[147] The fisheries agreement was not effective in reducing the number of fishermen to a sustainable level of tension-free fishing activities, but the fisheries agreement prevented that even the shooting of Chinese fishermen would have escalated. Much less severe fishing incidents and much smaller numbers of incidents escalated in the South China Sea far beyond what is observable in the Yellow Sea. China reacted strongly when the Philippines merely detained Chinese fishermen. In 2012, China took control of Philippine-administered Scarborough Shoal when a fishing incident escalated.[148] In the Yellow Sea, however, China did not react to the shooting of Chinese fishermen by interfering with South Korea's Coast Guard. Instead, China issued a protest note and conducted joint patrols.

While Chinese fishermen are not complying with the agreement, Chinese authorities do not provide a protective umbrella for Chinese fishermen against the Korea Coast Guard. In the South China Sea, the China Coast Guard protects fishing vessels. The stark contrast between China's reaction

145 James Griffiths, 'South Korean coast guard fires 250 rounds at Chinese fishing ships', *CNN*, 21 December 2017, https://edition.cnn.com/2017/12/20/asia/south-korea-china-intl/index.html (last accessed 13 April 2024).

146 Ki Beom Lee, 'The Korea Coast Guard's Use of Force Against Chinese Fishing Vessels: A Note'. On the use of force in maritime law enforcement, see Patricia Jimenez Kwast, 'Maritime Law Enforcement and the Use of Force: Reflections on the Categorisation of Forcible Action at Sea in the Light of the Guyana/Suriname Award', *Journal of Conflict and Security Law* 13, no. 1 (2008): 49–91.

147 South Korea and China appear to have continued their efforts to curb illegal Chinese fishing activities in 2023. Seok-Min Oh, 'S. Korea, China to Toughen Crackdown on Illegal Fishing in East Sea', *Yonhap News Agency*, 14 June 2023, https://en.yna.co.kr/view/AEN20230614002300320 (last accessed 20 April 2024).

148 Chapter III 1.5.

to fishing incidents in the South China Sea – escalation, use of forcible means, change of territorial status quo – and China's reaction in the Yellow Sea – protest note and joint patrols – must be explained with the fisheries agreement. Once the question of the basic allocation of state authority is settled, even if this is done in a provisional arrangement only, Chinese and Korean state actors did not regard each other's moves against Chinese fishermen as threatening their claims. Section 4 will further discuss how this situation compares to the South China Sea.

2.3 An Innovative Approach? Three Overlapping Bilateral Fisheries Agreements

One distinctive element of the fisheries relations in the East China Sea is that three bilateral fisheries agreements overlap. South Korea, China, and Japan did not engage in trilateral negotiations regarding fisheries, but instead opted to produce three bilateral agreements that partially overlap. Map 7 illustrates that the Sino-Korean TZ partly overlaps with the Sino-Japanese IWZ and that the Japanese-Korean PWZ partly overlaps with the Sino-Japanese IWZ. The three states have preferred to reach three bilateral agreements over one trilateral agreement. This necessitates a minimum understanding of how the three bilateral agreements relate to each other. China, Japan, and Korea have addressed this situation by including into the Agreed Minutes of the fisheries agreements a paragraph on cooperation with an unnamed third party. The example of the agreement between Japan and Korea reads as the following: 'Governments of both countries have the intention to negotiate specific ways to maintain a good fisheries order in the East China Sea on the basis of fisheries agreements concluded or to be concluded by either Party with a third country.'[149] The third country is China. The Sino-Japanese agreement has a similarly worded provision in its Agreed Minutes implicitly referring to South Korea. In practice, the institutional arrangement results in the following situation. A Chinese fishing vessel fishing in the overlapping area of the Sino-Japanese IWZ and the Japanese-Korean PWZ has to comply with two agreements: The vessel has to comply with the Sino-Japanese agreement and the rules of the IWZ. The fishing vessel also has to comply with the Sino-Korean agreement. According to this agreement, the PWZ of the Japanese-Korean agreement is the EEZ of Korea or China in which

149 'Agreed Minute' of the 'Agreement on Fisheries between the Republic of Korea and Japan of 1999', available in Kim, *Maritime Delimitation and Interim Arrangements in North East Asia*, 327–38.

Chinese fishermen are allowed to fish provided they have a licence from Korea or China (article 2-5 of the Sino-Korean agreement). The rules of the Japanese-Korean PWZ do not apply to Chinese activities, because the Japanese-Korean fishery agreement only applies to Korean and Japanese fishermen. The three bilateral agreements and the overlapping joint fisheries zones do not have an institutional coordinating procedure. Note that in the present case, it is not necessary to have a multilateral agreement for areas claimed by three states. Whether this construct could be a policy option for the parts of the South China Sea where the claims of more than two states overlap would require policy analysis. To my knowledge, this option has not been considered, as talks on fisheries did not progress at the bilateral level in the South China Sea.

3 Japan and Taiwan

Japan and Taiwan started negotiations on a fisheries agreement in 1996 – the same year that Japan started negotiations with China. While Sino-Japanese negotiations resulted in an agreement in 1997 that entered into force in 2000, negotiations between Japan and Taiwan stalled. The latter signed an agreement only in 2013 and continued negotiations until 2018. This raises the question of why it took Japan and Taiwan twenty-two years to negotiate an agreement that is structurally similar to the agreements Japan and China reached within one year and Japan and South Korea within two years. Various contextual conditions might have encouraged an agreement and could have led to the expectation that both countries would reach an agreement faster than Japan and China.

3.1 Agreement between Rivals, Impasse between Partners?

The background

Japan and Taiwan incorporated UNCLOS' provisions on the EEZs into their domestic laws in 1996 and 1998, respectively.[150] As the distance between Taiwan and Japan's Ryukyu Islands is less than 400 nm, overlapping claims

150 Taiwan is not a member of UNCLOS but has adopted a domestic EEZ law. 'Law on the Exclusive Economic Zone and the Continental Shelf of the Republic of China', 21 January 1998, amended 27 January 2021, https://law.moj.gov.tw/ENG/LawClass/LawAll.aspx?pcode=A0000010 (last accessed 13 June 2023).

and a boundary dispute resulted. Taiwan also claims the Senkaku/Diaoyu/Diaoyutai Islands, giving rise to a territorial dispute between Japan and Taiwan.[151] Taiwan unilaterally claimed a temporary enforcement line (TEL) in 2003, which is based on Taipei's claim to the Senkaku/Diaoyutai Islands (see Map 8). The TEL extends 200 nm northward, reaching 29° 18' north latitude, within which Taiwan purports to enforce its regulations.[152] Fishing incidents affected and disturbed the Japanese-Taiwanese relationship no less than the Sino-Japanese relationship. Incidents occurred continuously and sometimes involved confrontations between coast guard vessels.[153] Japan expelled or detained between twenty-three and sixty-one Taiwanese fishermen annually between 2005 and 2013.[154] In one incident, a Taiwanese boat sank after collision with a Japan Coast Guard vessel on 10 June 2008.[155]

Japan, Korea, and China reached agreements in order to overcome similar problems. The existence of sovereignty disputes was also an issue in Sino-Japanese (Senkaku/Diaoyu) and Korean-Japanese (Dok-do/Takeshima) negotiations, but the parties succeeded to accommodate their conflicting positions. Moreover, Japan and Taiwan have a common ally, the US, and both are democracies. The rise of China confronts both Japan and Taiwan with various strategic and geopolitical challenges that are certainly no less important than fisheries. China's increased navy and air force operations in the East China Sea and around the Senkaku/Diaoyu disputes are major security challenges for Japan.[156] China claims sovereignty over and aspires to unify with Taiwan.[157] A common threat should have given Japan and Taiwan strong incentives to settle bilateral fisheries issues, at least through

151 Hui-Yi Katherine Tseng, 'The Taiwan Dilemma in the Diaoyu/Diaoyutai/Senkaku Islands Sovereignty Dispute', *American Journal of Chinese Studies* 21 (2014): 111–26.

152 Yun-Hu Yeh et al., 'Taiwan and Japan: A Complex Fisheries Relationship,' *Marine Policy* 51 (2015): 293–301.

153 Interview with a former senior Taiwanese official, Ministry of Foreign Affairs, Taipei, 05 April 2017 (Interview 12).

154 Taiwan Coast Guard, 'Statistical Yearbook', quoted in Yun-Hu Yeh, 'Taiwan and Japan: A Complex Fisheries Relationship', 298.

155 Yoshiyuki Ogasawara, 'Ma Ying-Jeou's Doctoral Thesis and Its Impact on the Japan-Taiwan Fisheries Negotiations,' *Journal of Contemporary East Asia Studies* 4, no. 2 (2015): 67–92, 76.

156 Japan Ministry of Defense, 'China's Activities in East China Sea, Pacific Ocean, and Sea of Japan', March 2024, https://www.mod.go.jp/en/d_act/sec_env/pdf/ch_d-act_a.pdf (last accessed 24 April 2024); Japan Ministry of Defense, 'China's Maritime Expansion', April 2017 (on file with the author); Yuichi Hosoya, 'Japan's New Security Legislation: What Does This Mean for East Asian Security?', in *Building a Regional Order in East Asia: Community, Competition, Conflict*, (National Committee on American Foreign Policy, 2016), 88–95.

157 Lung-chu Chen, *The U.S.-Taiwan-China Relationship in International Law and Policy* (OUP, 2016); Jing Huang, *Inseparable Separation: The Making of China's Taiwan Policy.* (Hackensack:

a provisional arrangement. Nevertheless, while China and Japan reached a fisheries agreement in 1997, Japan and Taiwan needed to negotiate for seventeen years. After seventeen rounds of consultations, both reached an initial agreement on 10 April 2013. It took another five years of negotiations on specific rules for two subzones. As Japan does not recognize Taiwan as a state, the agreement is formally reached between the Interchange Association of Japan and Taiwan's Association of East Asian Relations. Map 8 illustrates the agreement.

The question is then what prevented an earlier agreement from being reached. In that regard, the status of Taiwan must be discussed. Following the China–Japan joint communique, 1972, Japan recognized the People's Republic of China (PRC) as the sole government of China and stated that it 'fully understands and respects this stand' of the PRC that Taiwan is a 'part of the territory' of the PRC.[158] Taiwan's status, however, is not a barrier to comprehensive relations between Japan and Taiwan. Japan's Ministry of Foreign Affairs regards Taiwan as 'one of the most important economic partners' and characterizes bilateral relations as 'close, friendly'.[159] Their relations cover many issue areas, many aspects of country-to-country relations except for relations that imply formal state recognition. Unless there is a compelling argument why a fisheries agreement should have greater implications for Taiwan's status than the many other issue areas in which Taiwan and Japan have a profound relationship, Taiwan's status could not explain the difficulties in reaching a fisheries agreement.

Moreover, distributional economic issues such as access of foreign fishing vessels to fishing grounds were not an unsolvable barrier in the negotiations. Both countries' choice was not between access of foreign fishing vessels to areas of overlapping claims and denial of this access. The choice was between fishing activities in overlapping areas with common rules and fishing activities without common rules. Given the decreased number of active Japanese fishermen – between 200 and 300 Japanese fishing vessels and around 15,000 Taiwanese operate in the overlapping area in

World Scientific, 2010); Drew Thompson, 'The Rise of Xi Jinping and China's New Era: Implications for the United States and Taiwan', *Issues & Studies* 56, no. 01 (March 2020): 1–25.

158 'Joint Communique of the Government of Japan and the Government of the People's Republic of China', 29 September 1972, https://www.mofa.go.jp/region/asia-paci/china/joint72.html (last accessed 13 April 2024.

159 First and Second China and Mongolia Division, Asian and Oceanian Affairs Bureau, Ministry of Foreign Affairs of Japan, 'Recent Japan-Taiwan Relations and the Taiwan Situation', July 2013, https://www.mofa.go.jp/region/asia-paci/taiwan/pdfs/japan-taiwan_relations.pdf (last accessed 13 April 2024).

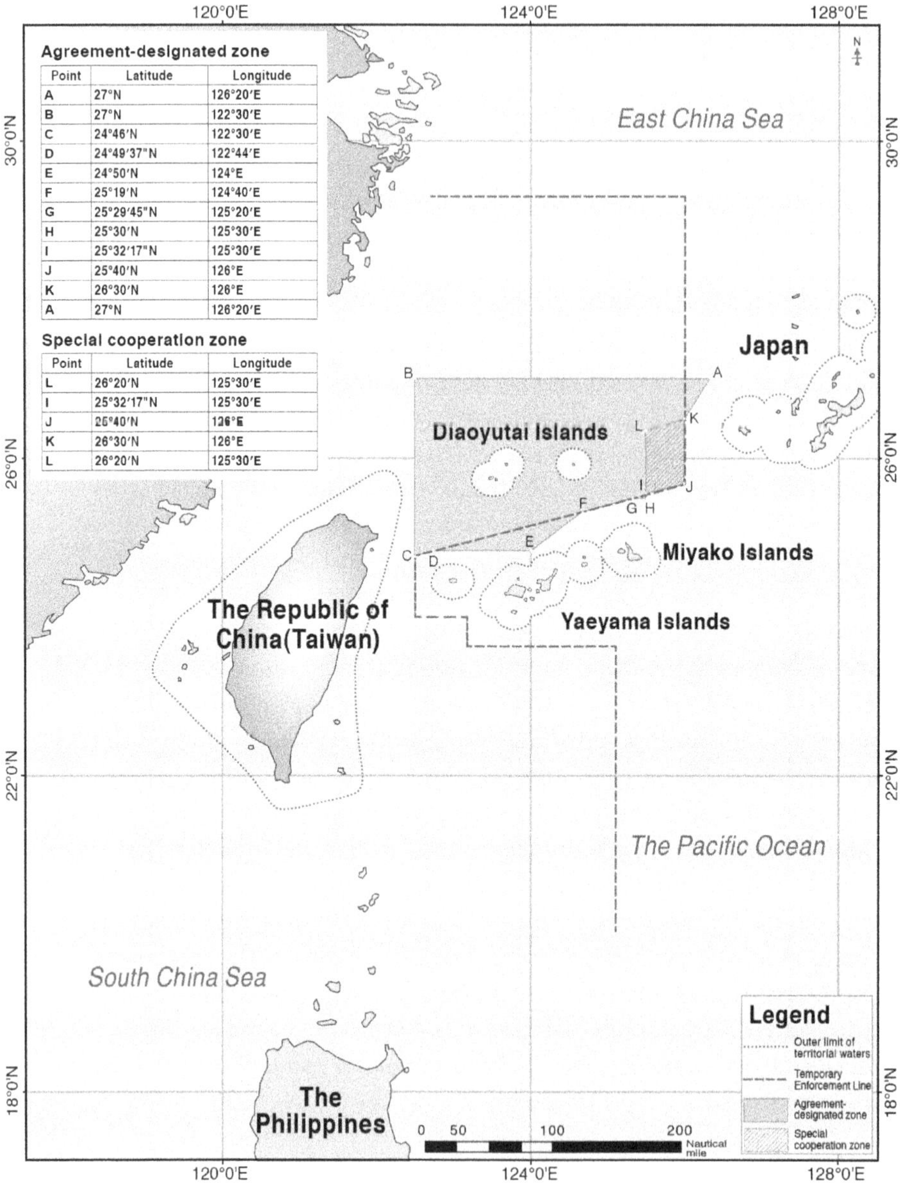

Map 8 Japan–Taiwan Fisheries Agreement[160]

160 In 'The Taiwan-Japan Fisheries Agreement – Embodying the Ideals and Spirit of the East China Sea Peace Initiative', The Ministry of Foreign Affairs of Taiwan, August 2013, Catalogue Card No. MOFA-EN-FO-102-006-I-1. https://chinaus-icas.org/wp-content/uploads/2019/08/Taiwan-Japan-Fisheries-Agreement-Pamphlet.pdf (last accessed 11 January 2024). Reproduced with permission. A copy of the original agreement is on file with the author (in Japanese).

the southern East China Sea[161] – the resistance of Japanese lobby groups representing a few hundred fishermen is hardly a convincing explanation for the long negotiation process. Finally, Taiwan's President in 2008 Ma Ying-jeou had studied resource-sharing agreements in detail.[162] Still, even as Ma got personally involved in the fisheries negotiations,[163] Taiwan and Japan needed five years (2008–2013) to come to an agreement and another five years for some specific regulations.

Negotiations and Impasse (1996–2013)

Despite many common interests, agreement was blocked by the inability of the parties to design an agreement that would have reflected each party's original claims in the negotiations from 1996 until 2009. In the first two rounds of negotiations, in 1996, both sides insisted on their sovereignty and sea boundary claims to no effect. From 1997 on, both started focusing on fisheries issues, similar to the bilateral talks that were under way between Japan, Korea, and China.[164] Between 1998 and 2000, Taiwan proposed a commission to delimit a provisional fisheries boundary based on 'equitable principles' which was rejected by Japan.[165] A provisional fisheries boundary based on equitable principles would have given this fisheries boundary, which would have been disadvantageous to Japan if an EEZ boundary, prominence. Taiwan could have used the line as a starting point for subsequent boundary delimitation. Moreover, even a provisional fisheries line would have needed to take the disputed islands into consideration. After Japan concluded agreements with Korea and China, Taiwanese central government officials insisted on a similar arrangement. From 2000 to 2005, Taiwan signalled that it preferred 'any kind of arrangement to protect

161 Interview with a professor of international relations, Tokyo University of Foreign Studies, Tokyo, 13 July 2017; interview with a senior official of Japan's Ministry of Foreign Affairs, Tokyo, 27 July 2017 (Interviews 32 and 40).

162 Ma Ying-jeou wrote his PhD thesis on 'Trouble Over Oily Waters: Legal Problems of Seabed Boundaries and Foreign Investments in the East China Sea' at Harvard University in 1980. In his thesis, Ma argued that 'the parties will be serious about seeking a settlement of these disputes to clear the way for resource development.' Quoted in: Ogasawara, 'Ma Ying-Jeou's Doctoral Thesis and Its Impact on the Japan-Taiwan Fisheries Negotiations,' 76.

163 Ibid. 67. Ogasawara attributes two political directions to former President Ma: 'the Chinese nationalist who participated in the *baodiao* movement ('Defend the Diaoyu Islands') … and the international law scholar who puts aside sovereignty disputes and advocates joint development.'

164 Shih Hsiu-chuan, 'Taiwan, Japan ink fisheries agreement', *Taipei Times*, 11 April 2013, http://www.taipeitimes.com/News/front/archives/2013/04/11/2003559323/1 (last accessed 13 April 2024).

165 Ibid.

fishermen', but that it did not expect political concessions on boundaries or sovereignty.[166]

Taiwan proposed essentially to define two joint zones: a joint management zone for the waters south of 27 degrees north and some arrangement for the zone between 27 degrees north and 29° 18' north (Taiwan's temporary enforcement line). Japan rejected this proposal, too. At the surface, Taiwan's proposal resembles the Sino-Japanese agreement. It appears puzzling why Japan rejected the two joint zones. But a closer look reveals that the proposals for both joint zones deviate substantively from the Sino-Japanese agreement. First, the zone south of 27 degrees north proposed by Taiwan is problematic. The only area of the Sino-Japanese agreement where Japan preferred a minimal commitment, namely non enforcement of domestic laws, is the area south of 27 degrees north. Taiwan proposed a joint management zone with joint regulation for exactly this area. To accommodate the sovereignty dispute, China and Japan chose a mere non-enforcement commitment minimising the implications of the agreement for sovereignty and boundary issues. An additional, economic explanation why Japan rejected a joint management zone south of 27 degrees north was suggested by a Japanese source. Fishermen from both sides fish the same species, namely tuna, in this area[167] and Japan sought to minimise the impact of the agreement on tuna fishing. Although tuna fishing is of economic and perhaps emotional relevance to Japan, Japanese negotiators accepted in the Sino-Japanese agreement that China unilaterally determines the number of fishing vessels in this area which is at odds with this economic explanation.

Second, regarding the zone between 27 degrees north and 29° 18' north, there is only one possibility how Taiwan can claim this area (or, for that matter, the temporary enforcement line along 29° 18' north), namely, by Taiwan having sovereignty over the Senkaku/Diaoyu Islands. The temporary line is located at a distance of 200 nm from the disputed islands as though Taiwan could claim an EEZ from them. A joint zone defined by a line along 29° 18' north would hence reflect and incorporate Taiwan's sovereignty claim. Given the logic that actors seek to prevent the validation of an opponent's claim through an agreement, any northern terminal line of a joint zone needed to be located way south of this line to be acceptable to Japan. Taiwan's proposal needed to change to accommodate Japan's position. News Agency Reuters suggested an alternative reason why Japan rejected the proposal.

166 Interview with a former senior Taiwanese official, Ministry of Foreign Affairs, Taipei, 5 April 2017 (Interview 12).
167 Interview 40.

Reuters suggested that Taiwan's proposed zone north of 27 degrees north is already subject to the joint Sino-Japanese zone.[168] This, however, is not a good explanation. Japan and Taiwan established a joint zone in 2013 that overlaps with the Sino-Japanese fishery zone: The southern zone of the Sino-Japanese agreement overlaps with the 'designated zone' that the subsequent Taiwan–Japan agreement established south of 27 degrees north. Moreover, China, Korea, and Japan accepted a situation where three bilateral joint zones overlap in the northern East China Sea. If some institutional connection between two overlapping bilateral agreements were necessary, this argument could explain Japan's rejection. Only then would it be necessary to establish a formal and politically sensitive link between a Sino-Japanese and a Taiwanese-Japanese agreement. But no formal link between the different bilateral fisheries agreements is necessary and the agreement Japan and Taiwan ultimately reached overlaps with the Sino-Japanese agreement.[169]

Agreement

Negotiations between Japan and Taiwan resumed only four years later in 2009, after Ma Ying-jeou became President of Taiwan. The sixteenth negotiation round took place in 2009 when both exchanged views on principles about fishing. This, however, did not advance the talks and no further negotiations took place until late 2012. The seventeenth negotiation round began on 30 November 2012 and lasted until 10 April 2013 when both finally signed an agreement. Taiwanese officials were 'surprised by the sudden swift change from the Japanese side under [Prime Minister] Abe' in 2012.[170] What has happened between 2009 and 2013 such that Japan under the leadership of Prime Minister Abe changed its position? Two factors explain why. First, tensions between China and Japan, on the one hand, and Taiwan and Japan, on the other, increased dramatically in the East China Sea from 2010 to 2012 such as to raise the costs for a prolonged impasse between Japan and Taiwan. Second, negotiators of both sides succeeded in designing an agreement and accompanying commitments that incorporates both sides' positions with respect to the sovereignty and boundary disputes. Nevertheless, the agreement in 2013 established only a basic framework. Negotiations on details about its implementation in two subzones continued until March 2018.

168 Shih Hsiu-chuan, 'Taiwan, Japan ink fisheries agreement'.
169 Chapter IV 2.3.
170 Interview 12.

Rising tensions and the East China Sea Peace Initiative

In 2010, a total of 430 Chinese fishing vessels entered the territorial waters of the Senkaku/Diaoyu Islands.[171] One Chinese fishing vessel intentionally collided twice with a Japanese Coast Guard vessel on 7 September 2010.[172] Japan's Coast Guard detained the Chinese crew that rammed Japan's vessel and announced they would prosecute them. This caused a diplomatic standoff that lasted for a month.[173] Japanese sources can only speculate about the question of whether the captain was an intoxicated 'lone wolf' or somehow instigated by Chinese political actors with an interest in sabotaging Sino-Japanese relations.[174] The Japanese reactions revealed limitations in the crisis management capacity of the new government under Prime Minister Naoto Kan.[175] A major issue in Japan appears to have been the question of bureaucratic competence in deciding whether to prosecute or release the Chinese crew.[176] Japan's performance in this crisis set the stage for the next crisis. Tokyo's nationalist governor Ishihara planned to purchase the privately owned Senkaku/Diaoyu Islands in 2011 to bolster Japan's position in the disputes. Japan's national government nationalized then the Senkaku/Diaoyu Islands in September 2012 and communicated to China that it wanted to pre-empt the purchase of these islands by Tokyo's governor Ishihara.[177] China regarded Japan's nationalization of the islands as a change of the territorial status quo and increased maritime patrols and overflights. Japan's Self-Defense Air Force matched these and intercepted Chinese aircraft.[178]

171 Ministry of Foreign Affairs of Japan, 'Status of activities by Chinese government vessels and Chinese fishing vessels in waters surrounding the Senkaku Islands', 26 August, 2016, https://www.mofa.go.jp/files/000180283.pdf (last accessed 17 March 2024).

172 A video of the incident is available at https://www.youtube.com/watch?v=nEDUE60Ri-A and https://www.youtube.com/watch?v=ULHitmtvaFw (last accessed 13 April 2024).

173 'Press Conference by Minister for Foreign Affairs Katsuya Okada', 10 September 2010, https://www.mofa.go.jp/announce/fm_press/2010/9/0910_01.html (last accessed 13 April 2024).

174 Interviews 30 and 31.

175 Sanaa Yasmin Hafeez, 'The Senkaku/Diaoyu Islands Crises of 2004, 2010, and 2012: A Study of Japanese-Chinese Crisis Management', *Asia-Pacific Review* 22, no. 1 (2 January 2015): 73–99.

176 'Press Conference by Minister for Foreign Affairs Seiji Maehara', 28 September 2010 https://www.mofa.go.jp/announce/fm_press/2010/9/0928_01.html (last accessed 13 April 2024).

177 Officials and scholars in Tokyo agree that one motivation for Governor Ishihara to nationalise the islands was to make up for Japan's poor crisis management of the incident in 2010. Interviews held in Tokyo, July 2017.

178 Michael Green et al., *Countering Coercion in Maritime Asia The Theory and Practice of Gray Zone Deterrence* (Center for Strategic & International Studies, 2017), 124–47.

In the wake of the nationalization of the Senkaku/Diaoyu islands, tensions between Taiwan and Japan also rose. Taiwan's Coast Guard started escorting fishermen in disputed areas. When a Taiwanese fishing fleet under escort approached the Senkaku/Diaoyu Islands on 25 September 2012, coast guards of both sides fired water cannons at each other.[179] Chinese officials communicated to Taiwan that they faced a common opponent. Chinese officials from mainland China's Taiwan Affairs Office (under the State Council) publicly asked Taiwan to join hands because 'measures taken by both sides of the strait safeguard the overall interest of the Chinese nation'.[180] President Ma, however, rejected coordination with China on the East China Sea emphasizing Taiwan's own interests.[181] Nevertheless, tensions on Japan's maritime front rose with China and Taiwan simultaneously raising the possibility that Japan might have to cope with two opponents.

Just one month before these tensions arose, President Ma announced the East China Sea Peace Initiative on 6 August 2012. The Peace Initiative called for refraining from antagonistic action, shelving disputes, establishing a code of conduct, and sharing natural resources.[182] Without clear commitments, such calls were without much effect. From October 2012, President Ma repeated his position to not compromise on sovereignty, but to resume talks on a fisheries agreement.[183] Talks resumed on 30 November 2012. Taiwan signalled that it had no intention to cooperate with mainland China. On 24 January 2013, a Taiwanese vessel from the *baodiao* group, an activist group to support territorial claims, approached the Senkaku/Diaoyu Islands. The Japanese Cost Guard shot with water cannons to prevent a landing. Three mainland China maritime law enforcement vessels appeared as though they intended to protect the Taiwanese activists. The approaching Taiwanese Coast Guard then demanded the Chinese vessels leave the territorial waters, as these were the 'territory of the Republic of China', and the Chinese vessels left.[184] Taiwanese vessels must have been instructed to chase away Chinese

179 J.R., 'Taiwan wades in Water-gunfighting', *The Economist*, 26 September 2012, https://www.economist.com/banyan/2012/09/26/water-gunfighting (last accessed 13 April 2024).

180 'Press Conference of the Taiwan Affairs Office of the State Council', 12 September 2012, http://eng.taiwan.cn/Press_conference/201304/t20130424_4122587.htm (last accessed 13 April 2024).

181 Interview 12.

182 Ministry of Foreign Affairs of Taiwan, 'President Ma proposes the East China Sea Peace Initiative, calls on all parties concerned to resolve Diaoyutai dispute peacefully', Press Release, 5 August 2012 https://www.mofa.gov.tw/en/News_Content.aspx?n=539A9A50A5F8AF9E&sms=37B41539382B84BA&s=8791CAB0BB21333B (last accessed 13 April 2022).

183 Ogasawara, 'Ma Ying-Jeou's Doctoral Thesis and Its Impact on the Japan-Taiwan Fisheries Negotiations', 83–4.

184 Ibid., 84.

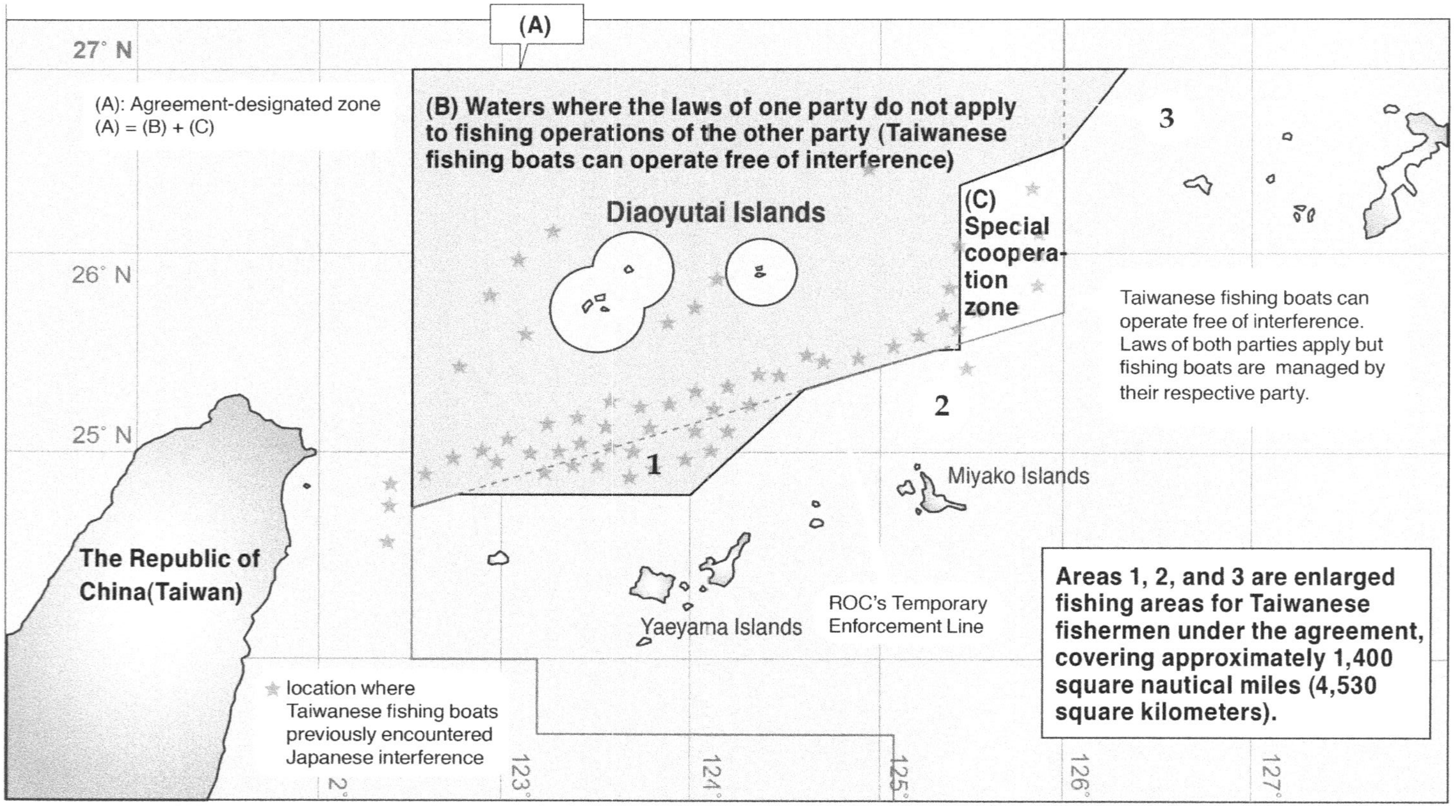

Map 9 Common fishing zones (details)[185]

185 The Ministry of Foreign Affairs of Taiwan, 'The Taiwan-Japan Fisheries Agreement – Embodying the Ideals and Spirit of the East China Sea Peace Initiative', August 2013, Catalogue Card No. MOFA-EN-FO-102-006-I-1. Available at https://chinaus-icas.org/wp-content/uploads/2019/08/Taiwan-Japan-Fisheries-Agreement-Pamphlet.pdf (last accessed 11 April 2024). Reproduced with permission.

vessels. In this way, Taiwan signalled that it would not coordinate its East China Sea policy with the PRC. This signal proved important for Japan's willingness to reconsider a fisheries arrangement with Taiwan.

Design of the fisheries agreement

Japan and Taiwan finally reached a fisheries agreement on 10 April 2013, seventeen years after the first negotiations. China protested the agreement. Notwithstanding whether China's protest was a mild or a strong one,[186] officials in both Taipei and Tokyo expressed the view that China protested only verbally against the agreement without taking any concrete measures against either party.[187] Fishermen of both sides, though, were frustrated with the agreement and how coast guards responded to fishermen.[188] Japan and Taiwan continued negotiations until 2018 to specify rules for some subzones.[189]

The Taiwan–Japan fisheries agreement designates a large zone of 74,000 square kilometres. Map 9 illustrates the subzones of the agreement. The designated area was initially divided into two subzones, the main area (B on map 9) and a special cooperation zone (SCZ) which requires special regulation because of differences in tuna fishing practices. The northern boundary of the joint area is the line along 27 degrees north which also demarcates the boundary between the PMZ and the southern zone (SWZ) of the Sino-Japanese agreement. The joint zone extends *beyond* Taiwan's unilateral Temporary Enforcement Line (TEL) in the east and south. This gives Taiwanese fishermen access to new areas (indicated as 1, 2, and 3 on the map) with an approximate size of 1,400 square nautical miles. In the west, the joint zone extends beyond a Japanese-claimed median line by approximately 1,854 square nautical miles.[190] The spatial definition of the

186 Zhang quotes 'concerns.' Yunbi Zhang, 'Japan-Taiwan fishery agreement raises 'concern'', *China Daily*, 11 April 2013 http://www.chinadaily.com.cn/china/2013-04/11/content_16391602.htm (last accessed 13 April 2024); the BBC quotes 'extreme concerns.' 'China anger at Japan-Taiwan disputed island fishing deal', *BBC*, 10 April 2013 https://www.bbc.com/news/world-asia-china-22092853 (last accessed 13 April 2024).
187 Interview 12 and 40.
188 Ko Shu-Ling, 'Taiwan fisheries pact frustrates both sides', *Japan Times*, 13 June 2013, https://www.japantimes.co.jp/news/2013/06/13/national/politics-diplomacy/taiwan-fisheries-pact-frustrates-both-sides (last accessed 13 April 2024).
189 'Japan-Taiwan talks on fishing near Senkakus end with some progress', *Japan Times*, 18 March 2018, https://www.japantimes.co.jp/news/2018/03/18/national/politics-diplomacy/japan-taiwan-talks-fishing-near-senkakus-end-progress/ (last accessed 13 April 2024).
190 Yun-Hu Yeh, 'Taiwan and Japan: A Complex Fisheries Relationship,' 299.

joint zone neither reflects the Taiwanese TEL nor a Japanese-claimed median line. Areas 1, 2, and the SCZ have witnessed repeated fishing incidents in the past. In area B, each party's laws apply to their nationals only and each party has the authority to enforce its laws against its nationals only – i.e., Taiwan's laws would apply only to Taiwanese fishermen and the Taiwanese Coast Guard would only enforce these laws against Taiwanese fishermen. The agreement does not mandate limits on the number of fishing vessels within this area. Each side has a large amount of discretion in unilaterally determining the number of fishing vessels.

The agreement establishes a Taiwan–Japan Fishery Committee. One of the first tasks of the four committee members was to negotiate the common rules for the special cooperation zone and area 1 that the agreement left unspecified. For the special cooperation zone, the depth of joint regulation needed to go beyond flag state jurisdiction because of the differences in tuna-fishing practices. The SCZ is rich in tuna. Japanese vessels tend to be smaller than Taiwanese vessels and tend to keep a longer safety distance to each other than Taiwanese vessels (four nautical miles against one nautical mile).[191] In order to prevent that too many fishing vessels with different fishing practices cause incidents, the committee needed to find another allocation of jurisdiction reconciling both parties' practices and formal claims. The committee agreed to establish rules for the 'preservation and rational utilization of fishery resources'.[192] This general objective was implemented by subdividing the special cooperation zone into two sectors. The northern sector of the SCZ is governed by Japanese rules. Taiwanese rules apply to the southern sector of the SCZ (zone C on the map is split into two parts). The two sectors have roughly equal size and fishermen of each side are allowed to operate in both sectors as long as they comply with both sides' regulations. This led to a situation whereby Japanese fishermen fish mainly in the northern sector and Taiwanese in the southern sector.[193] Moreover, the southern area, identifiable as an inverted triangle (area 1 on Map 9), was also subdivided into two subzones, a western and an eastern sector.[194] In the eastern sector, Japanese vessels are permitted to fish during daytime under Japanese regulation. Taiwanese vessels are permitted to operate during nighttime under Taiwanese regulation. Only Taiwanese

191 Interview 40.

192 Ibid.

193 Ibid.

194 'Japan–Taiwan talks on fishing near Senkakus end with some progress', *Japan Times*, 18 March 2018, https://www.japantimes.co.jp/news/2018/03/18/national/politics-diplomacy/japan-taiwan-talks-fishing-near-senkakus-end-progress/ (last accessed 13 April 2024).

vessels have operated in the western sector at the time of writing. The rules for the SCZ and the inverted triangle are effective in preventing accidents or competition between fishermen by clarifying which party's rules apply at which time of the day and in which place.[195]

The Fishery Committee has two more important tasks. First, the Committee is also charged with producing some understanding on fishing operations in areas north of 27 degrees north and south of the Yaeyama Islands. As of 2021, however, no common understanding was found. Japan and Taiwan continue to unilaterally enforce their national regulations in these areas. Second, when a fishing incident occurs in or in the proximity of the agreement area and one party enforces its rules against the other party's fishermen, the Committee can pick up the issue and the law enforcement authorities can coordinate their responses.

In sum, the institutional setup of these subzones represents another innovation in the attempts of the disputing parties to reconcile political sensitivities and the need for practical regulation. Both parties established pockets of provisional national jurisdiction in disputed areas. These pockets of provisional national jurisdiction alternate in place and time. Japan agreed to the sole application of Taiwanese rules in the southern sector of the SCZ. This area is in proximity to Japan's Miyako Islands, but far from Taiwan. This pocket of provisional national jurisdiction is surrounded in the south and east by Japan's exclusive jurisdiction and in the north by Japan's provisional exclusive jurisdiction.

3.2 The Japanese–Taiwanese Negotiations Reconsidered

David Lin, Taiwan's former Foreign Minister (2012–2016), led Taiwan's negotiations. He commented that the agreement follows a pragmatic approach that separates sovereignty questions from fishing rights.[196] Both sides, however, were unable to turn this objective into a workable agreement between 1996 and 2013. One could have expected that Japan would have had a strong incentive to prevent its partner Taiwan from moving closer to its rival China on the East China Sea by accepting the Taiwanese proposals on fisheries in the 2000s – especially as only 200–300 Japanese fishermen have been operating in the disputed areas. However, Japan accepted Taiwan's proposals only in 2013 while China and Japan reached a fisheries agreement within one year of negotiations in 1997.

195 Interview 40.

196 Interview held with Ambassdor David Lin, London, 03 March 2017 (Interview 19).

Some analysts have argued that Prime Minister Abe used the opportunity of the fisheries agreement to drive a wedge between China and Taiwan after President Ma signalled not to coordinate with the PRC on the East China Sea disputes.[197] This certainly played a role, but it does not explain why Abe or another prime minister did not act on the same incentive earlier. China continuously increased its presence in the East China Sea since the 1990s. This did not incentivise Japanese negotiators to tilt towards a fisheries agreement with Taiwan. In 2005, when Japan protested in vain against China's unilateral oil exploitation and Sino-Japanese disputes escalated, the same incentive to prevent policy coordination between mainland China and Taiwan could have been present. Japan and Taiwan did not reach an agreement in 2009 either and Japan did not come back to Taiwanese proposals in 2010 and 2012 when Sino-Japanese tensions were highest in the East China Sea.

Japan had to balance between, on the one hand, the geopolitical incentives to reduce tensions with Taiwan and, on the other hand, the expected negative consequences of a joint fisheries agreement in the southern half of the East China Sea. The question then is what these negative consequences would be, especially as the Taiwanese fishing activities occurred with or without an agreement. Recall that the only area where Japan did not insist on specific fisheries regulation with China is the southern half of the East China Sea and that Japan chose a minimal understanding for this area – giving China more freedom to unilaterally define fisheries regulation. Recall that Japan and Japanese oil companies rejected all Chinese proposals on joint development in this area, too. A negative consequence that Japan needed to rule out – and did rule out through an appropriate agreement design – was the possibility that the fisheries agreement would become a vulnerability in future interactions on territorial sovereignty and delimitation. Even if a fisheries agreement did not establish a precedent *de jure*, Japanese negotiators needed to rule out that an agreement could establish a layer of validity in favour of Taiwan's bargaining position. Considering these considerations and the Sino-Japanese negotiations, the proposals Taiwan made could not have been acceptable to Japan.

It took several incidents, collisions, rising tensions, and the possibility of Japan facing another maritime front for Japan under Prime Minister

197 Ogasawara, 'Ma Ying-Jeou's Doctoral Thesis and Its Impact on the Japan-Taiwan Fisheries Negotiations'; Kawashima Shin, 'The Implications of the Japan-Taiwan Fisheries Agreement', Nippon, 5 June 2013, http://www.nippon.com/en/currents/d00081/ (last accessed 13 April 2022).

Abe to change its approach. However, even in this case, the devil is in the details. An initial agreement reflected both parties' formal positions with respect to sovereignty by excluding the territorial waters of the disputed islands. With respect to boundary delimitation, the agreement incorporated both positions by using the 27 degrees north line as a northern boundary of the joint area in combination with a Japanese commitment to continue consultations for further areas. It did not establish either Japan's claimed median line in the west or Taiwan's temporary enforcement line in the east as focal points by having a joint area going beyond these lines. This means that the agreement extends into areas both sides did not commonly operate in. It took another five years for both sides to agree on the implementation of the rules in two subzones. In comparison to the other fisheries agreements in the East and South China Seas, the institutional design is innovative. The agreement has established pockets of provisional national jurisdiction in disputed areas alternating in place and time. A former Taiwanese official and a Japanese official have considered this agreement to be effective in preventing fishing incidents.[198]

4 The Impact of Fisheries Agreements on Incidents and Coast Guard Behaviour in the East and South China Sea

Fisheries agreements in the East China Sea and their design

At the time of writing, most areas of overlapping claims in the East China Sea between China, South Korea, Japan, and Taiwan are covered by joint fisheries agreements. The parties have adopted a subzone approach (table 1): the agreements establish various subzones whereby a different allocation of rights, formula for enforcement powers, and state authority apply to each subzone. This has given states options to accommodate legal positions and various interests, to incorporate original claims, to bring about reciprocity and to protect against potential vulnerabilities. The institutional design with varying allocations of state authority does not respond to diverging positions regarding fisheries management, catch quota, or sustainable fishing practices. Rather, the subzones have created a balance such that no agreement and no subzone can be regarded as ameliorating an opponent's claim. Table 1 provides an overview of the varying scope of fisheries cooperation in different subzones.

198 Interviews 12 and 40.

The fisheries agreements prevent the regular occurrence of fishing incidents. No agreement applies to the territorial waters of the Senkaku/Diaoyu Islands. This area is not governed jointly, and fishing incidents have caused substantial tensions between China and Japan. A geographic area where an existing agreement is not effective is the expired Transitional Zone of the Sino-Korean agreement.[199] Even there, the agreement is the basis for managing regular incidents so that these do not escalate. Incidents did not escalate in areas governed by the agreements. Incidents did not become a contest in the question of which country has a superior claim and superior state authority in the area because the agreements settled this question for the specific issue of fisheries. China and Taiwan do not have a formal fisheries agreement. Some informal exchanges resulted in some preliminary understandings to prevent fishing incidents in 2009.[200] However, this coordination effort was frozen together with other cross strait contacts after the election of President Tsai Ing-Wen.

Table 1 Fisheries agreements and proposals in the East and South China Sea[201]

Scope of cooperation in different subzones	Allocation of law enforcement authority	Fishing activities of a vessel from a disputing state	Examples in the fisheries agreements
Fisheries management (vessel licence system, maximum number of vessels, technical measures)	Cooperative law enforcement, joint commission	Take place under common rules.	Japan–China, Japan–Korea, China–Korea, Japan–Taiwan, China–Vietnam, China's proposal to the Philippines
Each party's rules apply to its nationals only	Flag state jurisdiction	Take place under each party's rules.	Japan–China, Japan–Korea, China–Korea, Japan–Taiwan, China's proposal to the Philippines
One party's rules are not enforced against nationals of a second party	Non-enforcement of domestic rules	Are tolerated.	Japan–China, Japan–Taiwan, China–Vietnam, China's proposal to the Philippines
Rules are not enforced against nationals of a second party for a limited time	Time-limited non-enforcement of domestic rules	Are tolerated for a limited time.	Philippines-Taiwan

199 Chapter IV 2.2.

200 Huan-Sheng Tseng and Ching-Hsiewn Ou, 'Taiwan and China: A Unique Fisheries Relationship', *Marine Policy*, 34 (2010), 1156–62.

201 Source: own compilation.

Scope of cooperation in different subzones	Allocation of law enforcement authority	Fishing activities of a vessel from a disputing state	Examples in the fisheries agreements
Hotline, 'damage control'	None	Are not tolerated. One party's rules are enforced against vessels of a second party.	China's proposal to the Philippines

The politically most contentious issue in all fisheries negotiations in the East China Sea and the South China Sea proved to be the question of how to rule out that an agreement and its provisions on maritime law enforcement would compromise states' claims and bargaining power. If the negotiators found agreeable solutions for this question, they were more likely to reach agreement. While incidents interrupted negotiations in some cases, their inherent escalation risks provided an incentive to negotiate agreements, too. I could not find that the balances of power, alliances or economic interests strongly affected the agreement design. The bilateral agreements between China and South Korea, Korea and Japan, Japan and China, and Japan and Taiwan have a similar design and have had to overcome similar problems. Japan and Taiwan have had the most difficult negotiation process. They reached agreement after seventeen years (implemented after twenty-two years) while China and Japan reached agreement after one year (implemented after three).

The claimant states need safeguards that a rival could not leverage an agreement to their detriment. Japan, Korea, China, and Taiwan negotiated about subzones as though the shape of a subzone pre-committed them to the location of a future maritime boundary. The states negotiated about the area of common rules as though they acquiesced in their rival's entitlement to this area. The states negotiated about the geographic scope as though the outer boundary of a joint zone established the limit of their claim, as though they were estopped from claiming areas beyond it. And the states negotiated the shape of joint zones as though such zones affected sovereignty claims to islands located within the zone. Under international law, prejudice is explicitly excluded in all these respects. Nevertheless, subzones needed to be acceptable under the condition that the subzones amount to a layer of validity in favour of a rival claim and that the defined joint zones affect future interactions. This observable bargaining behaviour was not unique to fisheries. As discussed above, it affected Sino-Japanese exchanges on joint development of oil and gas (the Principled Consensus). The idea that China would use marine scientific operations as a '*fait accompli* so that

China can use them to its advantage in defining a boundary of its own EEZ and its continental shelf' also bedevilled Sino-Japanese exchanges on marine scientific research.[202]

The claimant states have adopted various jurisdictional formulas that allow them to accept some common rules and to allocate public authority while not giving up claims to exclusive territorial and maritime rights. Somewhat paradoxically, Japan has accepted that China has the maximum level of freedom to define fisheries regulation unilaterally in the southern part of the East China Sea, including the areas outside the territorial waters of the Senkaku/Diaoyu islands. Japan has done this to achieve a minimum understanding with China while, at the same time, avoiding any suggestion that more comprehensive cooperation could be construed as Japan's recognition of China's claim to the Senkaku/Diaoyu Islands. The parties to the fisheries agreements need to strike a certain balance. On the one hand, the agreements provide a basic policy framework for incident-prone fisheries and a minimum amount of coordination between otherwise antagonistic behaviour of rival coast guards. They thereby stabilize the overall disputes. On the other hand, the agreements legitimise an opponent's fishing activities and maritime law enforcement operations in disputed areas. The Philippines did not emulate the approach of Korea or Japan because Manila assessed that the second aspects entrain prohibitively detrimental consequences for the Philippine claims in the context of non-existing legal entitlements of China.

The fisheries agreements are remarkable in another aspect. An important aspect of bilateral or regional fisheries governance is usually a procedure to determine some quantitative measures, such as a Total Allowable Catch (TAC).[203] Distributional economic questions such as catch levels and number of fishing vessels, however, have played a minor role in the fisheries agreements of the East China Sea. These issues were less contentious in the negotiations. As noted, in several subzones key aspects of fisheries management are left to unilateral regulation and have not featured in negotiations at all. China preferred in several cases larger common fishing zones and Korea and Japan smaller zones. However, the coastal states did not establish quantitative restrictions inside most

202 Mark J. Valencia and Yoshihisa Amae, 'Regime Building in the East China Sea', *Ocean Development & International Law*, 34 (2003), 189–208, 198 (emphasis in the original); Akira Takada, 'Marine Scientific Research in the Exclusive Economic Zone and Japan-China Agreement for Prior Notification (1995–2001)', *Japanese Annual of International Law*, 2001, 134–50.

203 Richard Caddell and Erik Jaap Molenaar, eds., *Strengthening International Fisheries Law in an Era of Changing Oceans* (Hart Publishing, 2019).

common subzones. The Joint Committees of the agreements have been tasked with defining a maximum number of vessels for only a few subzones. For these, the Joint Committees determine catch quota annually. In most subzones, claimant states set their catch quota and distribute licences unilaterally. Claimant states have been free to set limits on the number of fishing vessels for these subzones. Thus, the key distributional economic issues are either regulated shallowly or it is up to the states to decide them unilaterally. Both the negotiation histories and the content of the agreements demonstrate that the question of how to distribute economic gains from shared fisheries regulation did not represent a key obstacle in the negotiations.

There are clear signs of overfishing in the whole East China Sea – decreasing Catch per Unit Effort (CPUE), smaller fish sizes, and a change in the fish stock – such that stronger ecological measures should be adopted.[204] According to Zhang, China has reduced the total number of fishing boats in the East China Sea by 25,000.[205] Neither the Japanese negotiators Arima and Kanehara nor interview sources nor the literature reported that these reductions in fishing vessels were an issue in the Sino-Japanese fisheries negotiations.[206] Rather, Zou has argued that central Chinese bureaucracies used the fisheries agreement as leverage against local governments to curb domestic illegal and unregistered Chinese fishing vessels.[207] This suggests that China has reduced its fishing fleet unilaterally, but in response to institutionalized fisheries cooperation. The existence of fisheries agreements does not imply that law enforcement agencies cooperate effectively to ensure compliance of fishermen. Although solving illegal fishing often has a positive ecological effect,[208] the clarification of jurisdiction can only be considered a first step towards sustainable governance.

204 Ching-Hsiewn Ou and Huan-Sheng Tseng, 'The Fishery Agreements and Management Systems in the East China Sea', *Ocean and Coastal Management* 53, no. 5 (2010): 279–88.

205 Hongzhou Zhang, 'Chinese Fishermen in Disputed Waters: Not Quite a "People's War"', *Marine Policy* 68 (June 2016): 65–73, 69.

206 Nobukatsu Kanehara and Yutaka Arima, 'New Fishing Order – Japan's New Agreement on Fisheries with the Republic of Korea and with the People's Republic of China', *Japanese Annual of International Law*, 1999, 1–32.

207 Keyuan Zou, 'Sino-Japanese Joint Fishery Management in the East China Sea', *Marine Policy* 27, no. 2 (March 2003): 125–42, 137.

208 Reniel B. Cabral et al., 'Rapid and Lasting Gains from Solving Illegal Fishing', *Nature Ecology & Evolution* 2, no. 4 (2018): 650–58.

Governing fisheries enforcement, stabilizing disputes?

The bilateral fisheries agreements of the East China Sea and Yellow Sea have had several effects on the behaviour of the China Coast Guard and on the constellation between Chinese domestic bureaucratic actors.

The Sino-Korean fisheries agreement has changed the fisheries enforcement game in the Yellow Sea. Even rampant violations of the agreement and forcible action of the Korea Coast Guard against Chinese fishermen did not escalate at the interstate level. In the South China Sea, much less forcible fishing incidents escalated and, at Scarborough Shoal, resulted in a change of the territorial status quo.[209] One role of the China Coast Guard (and China's former maritime law enforcement agencies) is to provide a protective umbrella for Chinese fishing operations in the South China Sea. The China Coast Guard regularly protects Chinese fishing vessels against law enforcement agencies of other claimant states, even in cases where Chinese fishermen use dynamite or harvest endangered species. In the Yellow Sea, the China Coast Guard conducted a few joint patrols with the Korea Coast Guard to enforce the joint fisheries agreement against Chinese fishermen. The China Coast Guard did not protect Chinese vessels and cooperated, even if perhaps only symbolically, in a few instances with the Korea Coast Guard against Chinese fishermen. While Chinese fishermen have violated this agreement close to 100,000 times – this is the highest number of violations against any fisheries agreement in the East and South China Sea – neither party terminated the agreement. China has acquiesced in the forcible law enforcement policy of South Korea. As noted above,[210] the contrast between China's response to fishing incidents in the South China Sea and the Yellow Sea could hardly be higher. As the fisheries agreement has settled the basic allocation of state authority, Chinese and Korean state actors did not regard each other's moves as threatening.

The parties to the East and South China Sea disputes recognize that maritime law enforcement agencies are 'frontline actors' in the maritime disputes.[211] The China Coast Guard is one of China's preferred instruments

209 Chapter III 1.5.

210 Chapter IV 2.2.

211 'ASEAN Regional Forum Ministerial Statement on Enhancing Cooperation among Maritime Law Enforcement Agencies' (23rd ARF Foreign Ministers' Meeting, 26 July 2016), https://aseanregionalforum.asean.org/wp-content/uploads/2019/03/arf-ministerial-statement-on-enhancing-cooperation-among-maritime-law-enforcement-agencies.pdf (last accessed 13 April 2024).

to advance or defend China's claims and has expanded rapidly.[212] It has often been noted that there is a lack of instruments dedicated to managing interactions at sea between coast guards. The Sino-Japanese fisheries agreement, however, illustrates that functional fisheries cooperation provides a framework for two central types of dispute interactions: the interactions between one state's coast guard and a second state's fishing vessels and the interactions between two states' coast guards in the context of fisheries. Japan has also experienced the downside of consenting to the China Coast Guard exercising authority in disputed areas. It is a small step from the China Coast Guard enforcing China's fisheries law near the Senkaku/Diaoyu Islands to the China Coast Guard expanding its presence in the same area. Because safeguarding China's claims is a priority for Chinese maritime law enforcement agencies,[213] accepting the public authority of the China Coast Guard is a most sensitive issue.

The bilateral fisheries agreements in the East China Sea have had a further effect on the constellation among China's domestic bureaucratic actors. Fisheries in the South China Sea are predominantly under the jurisdiction of the provincial governments of Guangdong, Guanxi, and Hainan, while fisheries subject to bilateral agreements are under the jurisdiction of the central government, the Fisheries Management Bureau under the Ministry of Agriculture, and the State Oceanic Administration under the Ministry of Land and Resources.[214] Central Chinese ministries would hence appear to have a greater say in fisheries relations in the East China Sea than in the South China Sea.

An obvious difference between the Yellow Sea and the South China Sea is that there is no sovereignty dispute between China and South Korea in the Yellow Sea, and only EEZ claims overlap. This lowered the bar to reaching a fisheries arrangement in the first place. China and the Philippines did not reach a fisheries agreement and have clashed over fisheries in the belief that

212 Andrew S. Erickson et al., 'Surging Second Sea Force: China's Maritime Law- Enforcement Forces, Capabilities, and Future in the Gray Zone and Beyond', *Naval War College Review* 72, no. 2 (2019): 1–25; Lyle J. Morris, 'Organizing for the Gray Zone: Assessing the Rights Protection Capabilities of the New China Coast Guard', in *China's Maritime Gray Zone Operations*, edited by Ryan D Martinson and Andrew S. Erickson (Naval Institute Press, 2019), 1–15 (preprint); Lyle J. Morris, 'Blunt Defenders of Sovereignty: The Rise of Coast Guards in East and Southeast Asia', *Naval War College Review* 70, no. 2 (2017): 75–112.

213 'Coast Guard Law of the People's Republic of China. Order No. 71 of the President of the People's Republic of China', 22 January 2021, available at https://www.lawinfochina.com/display.aspx?lib=law&id=34610&EncodingName=big5 (last accessed 14 March 2024).

214 Hongzhou Zhang and Sam Bateman, 'Fishing Militia, the Securitization of Fishery and the South China Sea Dispute', *Contemporary Southeast Asia*, 2017, 288–314, 296.

superior law enforcement could be used to support claims to sovereignty and contested maritime zones.[215] Fishing proved very contentious and escalatory in the waters around the Spratly Islands and Scarborough Shoal, and the question arises whether the economic value of fishing could contribute to explaining the more contentious nature of fisheries there. According to available numbers, there are between 700 and 1,000 Chinese fishing vessels in the waters of the Spratly Islands.[216] There are about 2,000 Chinese fishing vessels in the joint zones of the Yellow Sea.[217] Several hundred Chinese fishing vessels are regularly active in waters around the Senkaku/Diaoyu Islands (outside their territorial waters).[218] The mere number of fishing vessels does not suggest that fishing activities around the Spratly Islands are economically more important to China than those in the Yellow Sea or East China Sea.[219] One reason why the presence of between 700 and 1,000 Chinese fishermen in the Spratly Islands is of greater security concerns than the activities of a larger, or at least equal, number of Chinese fishermen in the East China Sea and Yellow Sea is that the Spratly Islands lack any bilateral or multilateral rules for fishing.

The state practice in the East China Sea and Yellow Sea illustrates the gains in terms of improved stability and security that the claimant states derive from institutionalized fisheries cooperation. The exception that demonstrates the rule is that the fishing incidents that escalated and destabilized Sino-Japanese relations occurred in waters that were not covered by the Sino-Japanese agreement – the territorial seas of the Senkaku/Diaoyu Islands. The comparison does not imply, however, that a Sino-Philippine fisheries agreement emulating the East China Sea agreements would prevent Chinese excessive fishing activities. After all, Chinese fishermen have not complied with the Sino-Korean agreement many 10,000 times. Moreover,

215 Chapter III 1.5

216 Zhang and Bateman, 'Fishing Militia, the Securitization of Fishery and the South China Sea Dispute', 292; Gregory Poling refers to 300 vessels around Subi Reef and Mischief Reef, 'Illuminating the South China Sea's Dark Fishing Fleets', *CSIS AMTI*, 9 January 2019, https://ocean.csis.org/spotlights/illuminating-the-south-china-seas-dark-fishing-fleets/ (last accessed 13 April 2024).

217 Ministry of Oceans and Fisheries of the Republic of Korea, Press Release, quoted in: 'S. Korea, China to hold joint inspection on illegal fishing in Yellow Sea', *Korean Times*, 05 April 2015, http://www.koreatimes.co.kr/www/news/nation/2015/11/656_176526.html (last accessed 13 April 2024).

218 Chapter IV 1.4.

219 This does not take into consideration the trade with giant clams or other species, Victor Robert Lee, 'Satellite Imagery Shows Ecocide in the South China Sea', *The Diplomat*, 15 January 2016, https://thediplomat.com/2016/01/satellite-images-show-ecocide-in-the-south-china-sea (last accessed 13 April 2024).

sovereignty issues, hydrocarbon resources and other issue areas would continue to be sources for incidents.

A further difference between the East China Sea and the South China Sea is that the sovereignty disputes in the latter, especially the Spratly Islands, cover a much larger area than sovereignty disputes in the East China Sea and Sea of Japan. The Sino-Japanese, Japanese–Korean and Japanese–Taiwanese fisheries agreements cover areas in which disputed islands are located (Senkaku/Diaoyu, Dok-do/Takeshima), but excluded their territorial seas as the most sensitive areas. Given the larger area the disputed Spratly islands cover, fishing activities in the vicinity of disputed islands are more widespread and contentious in the South China Sea. Unless the claimant states agree on a minimum of common rules for the fisheries of the Spratly Islands, it appears almost inevitable that fisheries will remain a source for incidents. Scholars made various proposals for cooperative fisheries mechanisms.[220] The analysis of the East China Sea offers another noteworthy option. These bilateral fisheries agreements defined bilateral zones that overlap partly with the bilateral zones of other fisheries agreements.[221] In principle, a multiparty dispute does not necessarily require a multilateral arrangement but could also be resolved with overlapping bilateral arrangements. Whether this practice could be applied to the Spratly Islands is doubtful given the large overlaps of multiparty claims, the involvement of multiparty territorial claims and the fact that China has only valid claims to territorial seas and not to an EEZ. The tribunal in the South China Sea Arbitration observed that individually held traditional fishing rights exist in territorial seas around features such as Scarborough Shoal but not in EEZs.[222] This observation of the tribunal, though, has not incentivised fisheries cooperation in the territorial seas.[223]

220 Dang Thang Nguyen, 'Fisheries Co-Operation in the South China Sea and the (Ir)Relevance of the Sovereignty Question', *Asian Journal of International Law* 2, no. 01 (2012): 59–88; John W. McManus, 'Offshore Coral Reef Damage, Overfishing, and Paths to Peace in the South China Sea', *The International Journal of Marine and Coastal Law* 32, no. 2 (2017): 199–237; Gregory B. Poling et al., *Defusing the South China Sea Disputes A Regional Blueprint* (Center for Strategic & International Studies, 2018); James Borton, 'Science Diplomacy and Dispute Management in the South China Sea', in *Enterprises, Localities, People, and Policy in the South China Sea* (Springer, 2018), 195–216.

221 Chapter IV 2.3.

222 The South China Sea Arbitration (The Republic of Philippines v. The People's Republic of China) Award (12 July 2016), (Merits), paras 257–72.

223 Schoenbaum criticised the award for not having provided a basis for negotiation on fisheries between the parties. Thomas J. Schoenbaum, 'The South China Sea Arbitration Decision and a Plan for Peaceful Resolution of the Disputes', *J. Mar. L. & Com.* 47 (2016): 451–77; Stein Tønnesson, 'Fish for Peace in the South China Sea', *AMTI Update*, 11 January 2019, https://amti.csis.org/fish-for-peace-south-china-sea/ (last accessed 13 April 2024).

V Institutions for Conflict Behaviour in the East and South China Sea

Abstract

This chapter examines the efforts of claimants to design institutions for conflict behaviour. Using a code of conduct, communication, and incident prevention mechanisms, disputing actors aim to reduce violence without touching territorial and maritime claims. This chapter illustrates that state actors of all levels of government are aware that such arrangements contribute to reducing escalation risks and to stabilizing disputes. Despite this recognition and top-leadership endorsement, decades-long negotiations have yielded many documents, but few effective ones. The underlying reason for the impasses is the problem of how and under which conditions the arrangements engender vulnerabilities and improve an opponent's bargaining position.

Keywords: South China Sea, East China Sea, ASEAN, conflict management, crisis communication, code of conduct

The present chapter examines the efforts of claimants to design institutions for conflict behaviour and crisis communication. This chapter first analyses the past thirty years of negotiations between China and members of the Association of Southeast Asian Nations (ASEAN) about a code of conduct for the South China Sea. It then presents the past decade of negotiations between China and Japan on a communication and incident prevention mechanism for the East China Sea. Thirdly, it examines the background and implementation of the Code for Unplanned Encounters at Sea, which many Western Pacific countries adopted in 2014. Despite top-leadership endorsement, these decades-long processes have yielded many documents, but few binding and effectively implemented ones.

Schultheiss, Christian: *Ocean Governance and Conflict in the East and South China Sea. Negotiating Natural Resources, Institutions and Power.*
Taylor & Francis Group, 2024
DOI: 10.5117/9789463728997_CH05

This chapter shows that with these arrangements, the disputing actors have sought to reduce violence without touching territorial and maritime claims. They have negotiated restrictions about the types of activities various state actors cannot do and prescriptions about the activities state actors must do to prevent the disputes from getting out of control. This chapter illustrates that state actors of all levels of government were aware that such arrangements contribute to reducing escalation risks and to stabilizing the disputes. Despite this recognition, negotiations have often ended in an impasse. The underlying reason for the impasses has been the problem that an arrangement could result in vulnerabilities that an opponent could use to advance its position in subsequent interactions. This problem found several manifestations in the cases of the code of conduct, and of the communication and incident prevention mechanisms.

Additionally, further puzzles of the cases merit attention that this chapter addresses. In the late 1990s, ASEAN members and China began exchanges on a code of conduct and continued their consultations with interruptions until the time of writing (subchapter 1). China proposed restrictions on coercive coast guard behaviour and on naval activities in 1999 – in the meantime, China has become the one to apply coast guard coercion. Why then did ASEAN members not accept China's restrictions? Moreover, the Philippines, Indonesia, Vietnam, Malaysia, and further ASEAN members proposed different full-draft codes or draft provisions at various stages. Over a period of twenty-five years, ASEAN members missed several opportunities to develop a common ASEAN draft code and a cohesive ASEAN negotiation position. What prevented ASEAN members from building a cohesive coalition?

The case of Sino-Japanese negotiations (subchapter 2.1) reiterates this chapter's question of why it is so difficult to agree on incident prevention mechanisms. After several dangerous incidents between aircraft and navy vessels, Chinese and Japanese security and defence officials attempted to design measures for incident prevention and crisis communication between 2008 and 2021. While both sides reached a memorandum of understanding (MoU) after a ten-year negotiation period, the implementation of core parts of the MoU has remained contentious. This raises the problem of why it is so difficult to reach agreements on direct communication measures, even if such measures have a limited and non-binding scope and top leadership support. This chapter reveals the existence of competing factual assessments among different central-level government bureaucracies. The perspectives of various senior officials differ on the question of whether crisis communication agreements result in Japanese vulnerabilities that Chinese actors could exploit in subsequent encounters.

The case of the non-binding Code for Unplanned Encounters at Sea of 2014 (CUES) (subchapter 2.3) reinforces the question of why incident prevention and communication instruments that claimants are currently contemplating are so contentious. The West Pacific Naval Symposium agreed on applying an earlier version of CUES to encounters of navy vessels in 2003. The People's Liberation Army (PLA) Navy endorsed CUES only eleven years later in 2014, even if, as critics noted, CUES repeats pre-existing legal obligations in a non-binding manner. This step required a policy change within China regarding the desirability of communication mechanisms and a renegotiation of parts of CUES.

1 China and ASEAN Members: The Long March towards a South China Sea Code of Conduct

The idea that a code of conduct could establish the rules necessary to guarantee a peaceful conduct of the rival claimant states in their sovereignty and maritime boundary disputes has been on the agenda in the South China Sea since 1992. Before the UN Convention on the Law of the Sea (UNCLOS) had entered into force in 1994, ASEAN members wanted to define a framework for interactions at sea. They suggested establishing 'a code of international conduct over the South China Sea' for the first time on 22 July 1992.[1] This suggestion reflected their belief 'that any adverse developments in the South China Sea directly affect peace and stability in the region'. In November 2018, China's Prime Minister Li Keqiang said that China aimed at the completion of a code of conduct within three years.[2] As China and ASEAN members did not reach a substantive code by 2023, a thirty-years-long process did not deliver the result envisioned in 1992. China and ASEAN states agreed on many documents between 1995 and 2023 and virtually all of them recognize 'that the maintenance of regional peace and stability served the interests of all parties',[3] that rules on the conduct in the

1 1992 ASEAN Declaration on the South China Sea, Manila, 22 July 1992, accessible at https://cil.nus.edu.sg/wp-content/uploads/2017/07/1992-ASEAN-Declaration-on-the-South-China-Sea.pdf (last accessed 13 April 2024).

2 Catherine Wong, 'South China Sea: Beijing hopes for maritime accord with Asean neighbours in three years', *SCMP*, 13 November 2018, https://www.scmp.com/news/china/diplomacy/article/2172913/south-china-sea-beijing-hopes-maritime-accord-asean-neighbours (last accessed 13 April 2024).

3 Joint Statement of the Meeting of Heads of State/Government of the Member States of ASEAN and the President of the People's Republic of China, Kuala Lumpur, Malaysia, 16 December 1997,

disputes are necessary to prevent escalation, and that such rules do not prejudice final settlements. The reiteration of such objectives reflects the parties' common interest in economic development and the reduction of risks of inadvertent and accidental escalation to war, involving potentially a US–China confrontation.[4]

China's interest in a code of conduct originated historically in the period when the Philippines resumed its military relationship with the US in 1998. The Philippines decided to remove the US naval presence at Subic Bay in 1992 and to re-establish a US presence with the Visiting Forces Agreement in 1998. The incident at Mischief Reef in 1995 and the ensuing construction of Chinese installations on Mischief Reef marked a turning point for the Philippines. According to Buszynski, 'the Chinese became aware of the risks of pushing ASEAN countries militarily closer to the US which would result in greater access to the region's port facilities for the American navy.'[5] He argues that 'most important was the recognition on China's part that a suitably-worded code of conduct could work in its favour in terms of limiting the risk of conflict in the area, which could involve the US in the dispute'.[6] Since 2017, the US has increased its presence in the South China Sea. The US conducted exercises involving different aircraft carrier battle groups and intensified Freedom of Navigation Operations in 2018,[7] reminding China that it is Chinese activities that create a demand for a US military presence. This interest in reducing incentives for various forms of military cooperation between the US and Southeast Asian states appears to be one reason for China's participation in code of conduct negotiations. But this is not the only Chinese interest. Crucially, as the following will illustrate, China proposed provisions that have sought to enlist Southeast Asian states in China's expansion of control in the South China Sea and to restrict their responses to various Chinese activities.

A code of conduct has represented the preferred instrument of ASEAN members for addressing the South China Sea disputes since 1992. The hopes

https://asean.org/joint-statement-of-the-meeting-of-heads-of-state-government-of-the-member-states-of-asean-and-the-president-of-the-peoples-republic-of-china-kuala-lumpur-malaysia-16-december-1997/ (last accessed 13 April 2024).

4 Avery Goldstein, 'First Things First: The Pressing Danger of Crisis Instability in U.S.-China Relations', *International Security* 37, no. 4 (April 2013): 49–89; Graham T. Allison, *Destined for War: Can America and China Escape Thucydides's Trap?* (Mariner Books, 2017).

5 Leszek Buszynski, 'ASEAN, the Declaration on Conduct, and the South China Sea', *Contemporary Southeast Asia*, (2003), 343–62, 352.

6 Ibid, 357.

7 Sam Bateman, 'Favourable Currents for ASEAN–China Relations in the South China Sea', *East Asia Forum*, December 2018, http://www.eastasiaforum.org/2018/12/12/favourable-currents-for-asean-china-relations-in-the-south-china-sea/ (last accessed 13 April 2024).

of Southeast Asian states to come to some understanding with China to the effect that China does not unilaterally enforce its claims have partly rested on a code. While China rammed and sank a Vietnamese fishing vessel near Lincoln Reef in the Paracels in April 2018 and while China blocked Philippine resupply of Philippine-occupied Second Thomas Shoal in the Spratlys multiple times between 2018 and 2023,[8] no party used these incidents as a pretext to cancel the negotiation process on a code of conduct. An effective code would be one that manages the disputes, reduces the risk of escalation, thwarts conflict and contributes to regional stability. The code of conduct negotiations between 1992 and 2018 demonstrate that disagreements between China and ASEAN members and among ASEAN members on essential provisions prevented the conclusion of an effective code. These disagreements centred on the issue that different sets of provisions would distribute power onto a different actor by restricting parties' options to advance or defend claims. The second disagreement was about the problem that a particular geographic scope would build a layer of validity for one or the other party's claim to an area. While a third disagreement turned around the legal status of the code, China and several ASEAN members put forward non-binding documents.

1.1 The First March towards a Code of Conduct: 1992–2002

The 1992 declaration of ASEAN members in Manila was the first call for a code of conduct. Especially the Philippines emphasized the need for some provisional rules governing the sea, as UNCLOS was not yet in force in the early 1990s.[9] UNCLOS entered into force on 16 November 1994 and China ratified UNCLOS on 7 June 1996. Since then, China and the Philippines, China and ASEAN states, and ASEAN states among themselves have negotiated many documents.

The next step towards a code of conduct was undertaken by the Philippines and China in 1995. Fishing disputes between the Philippines and China increased and intensified after 1992.[10] In early 1995, the Philippines'

8 CSIS AMTI, 'Are maritime law enforcement forces destabilizing Asia?', CSIS China Power Project, December 2018 https://csis-ilab.github.io/cpower-viz/csis-china-sea/ (last accessed 13 April 2024).

9 Interview with a ministerial-level official of the administration of President Arroyo, Manila, 02 December 2016 (Interview 7).

10 In the context of the South China Sea Arbitration, a collection of about 1,000 documents were published in forty volumes as annexes to the Memorial of the Philippines (written submission). These volumes are accessible at https://pca-cpa.org/en/cases/7/ (last accessed

law enforcement authorities removed Chinese markers on the Spratly Islands and Mischief Reef as soon as Chinese personnel left the features to remove any visible sign of China's sovereignty claims.[11] As incidents intensified, China built installations on Mischief Reef in 1995. The Philippines did not resist Chinese installations, presumably to prevent further escalation, but protested China's occupation. Undersecretary Severino and Vice-Minister Wang held substantial talks to address these disputes in the context of the first Philippines–China Bilateral Consultations on the South China Sea in August 1995.[12] These talks produced the Sino-Philippine 'Agreed Minutes':

> Pending the resolution of the dispute, the two sides agreed to abide by the following principles for a code of conduct in the area:
> 1. Territorial disputes between the two sides should not affect the normal development of their relations.
> 2. Efforts must be undertaken… to refrain from using force or threat of force to resolve disputes.
> 3. In the spirit of expanding common ground and narrowing differences, a gradual and progressive process of cooperation shall be adopted….
> 4. The two sides agreed to settle their bilateral disputes in accordance with the recognised principles of international law, including the UN Convention of the Law of Sea….[13]

The Agreed Minutes define further objectives such as cooperation on environmental protection, marine scientific research, prevention of piracy,

24 April 2024). Chapter II 4 discusses how this book uses these documents. The following references will provide the title of the document, its date, the number of the annex and the volume of the memorial. When many annexes are cited, only the number is indicated. Annexes 16, 23, 25, 40, 42, 43, 44, 46, 47, 49, 50, 51, 54, 55, 56, 58, 59, 75 in Volume III and IV of the Philippines' Memorial present the diplomatic record and documentary evidence of incidents since 1992.

11 *Memorandum* from the Ambassador of the Republic of the Philippines in Beijing to the Undersecretary of Foreign Affairs of the Republic of the Philippines (10 April 1995) (Annex 21), Vol III, https://files.pca-cpa.org/pcadocs/The%20Philippines%27%20Memorial%20-%20Volume%20III%20%28Annexes%201-60%29.pdf (last accessed 24 April 2024).

12 Department of Foreign Affairs of the Republic of the Philippines, *Transcript of Proceedings: RP-PRC Bilateral Talks* (9 August 1995) (Annex 179), Vol VI, https://files.pca-cpa.org/pcadocs/The%20Philippines%27%20Memorial%20-%20Volume%20III%20%28Annexes%201-60%29.pdf (last accessed 24 April 2024).

13 Government of the Republic of the Philippines and Government of the People's Republic of China, *Agreed Minutes on the First Philippines-China Bilateral Consultations on the South China Sea Issue* (10 August 1995) (Annex 180), Vol VI.

and multilateral cooperation. It specifically provides for consultations on fisheries cooperation in disputed areas and for the Philippines to study the 'Chinese proposal to jointly explore oil and gas resources in the disputed area, including the Reed Bank'.[14] It also provides for dispute settlement 'without prejudice to the freedom of navigation'. The first time China signed on to a document containing the objective of settling disputes based on UNCLOS was in 1995. Some observers point to the significance that China accepted references to UNCLOS in a bilateral memorandum of understanding in 2018.[15] However, the fact that China accepted references to UNCLOS already in 1995 suggests that this does not establish a change in China's policy.

In July 1996 at their 29th meeting, the ASEAN foreign ministers supported the idea of moving forward with a code of conduct 'for which the earlier Philippine-China agreement of 1995 would serve as a model'.[16] Both Vietnam and the Philippines started preparing a draft code of conduct. However, several disagreements among Vietnam and ASEAN members prevented a common position. Firstly, Vietnam and other ASEAN member disagreed about the geographic scope of the draft. Vietnam requested that a code included the Paracel Islands, occupied by China and claimed by Vietnam, and the Spratly Islands.[17] Other ASEAN states, including the Philippines, rejected the inclusion of the Paracel Islands because this island group is subject to a bilateral dispute between China and Vietnam. The reason for this reluctance was that ASEAN members wanted to prevent being drawn into the Sino-Vietnamese bilateral dispute as a result of a code, especially in case this bilateral dispute would escalate.[18] Secondly, the Philippines' draft code resembled a binding treaty. Malaysian and Indonesian officials preferred at this time a non-binding, political document.[19] A third controversial issue was that the Philippines insisted on the prohibition of new occupations of islands.[20] Over the next three years, ASEAN members worked on overcoming differences among ASEAN states, and this resulted in an ASEAN draft agreed on at the ASEAN meeting in Bangkok in 1999. This internal ASEAN process

14 Chapter III 1 presents these negotiations in detail.

15 Jay Batongbacal, 'The Philippines-China MOU on Cooperation in Oil and Gas Development', *AMTI*, 5 December 2018, https://amti.csis.org/philippines-china-mou-cooperation-oil-gas-development/ (last accessed 13 April 2024).

16 Buszynski, 'ASEAN, the Declaration on Conduct, and the South China Sea', 354.

17 Ibid. 354.

18 Interview 7.

19 Buszynski, 'ASEAN, the Declaration on Conduct, and the South China Sea', 355.

20 Ibid.

was presumably encouraged by the first joint China–ASEAN statement on the South China Sea in 1997:

> Recognizing that the maintenance of regional peace and stability served the interests of all parties, they undertook to resolve their differences or disputes through peaceful means, without resorting to the threat or use of force. The parties concerned agreed to resolve their disputes in the South China Sea through friendly consultations and negotiations in accordance with universally recognised international law, including the 1982 UN Convention on the Law of the Sea. While continuing efforts to find solutions, they agreed to explore ways for cooperation in the areas concerned.[21]

In the following, I will first present the ASEAN draft code and China's reactions to it, then China's draft code and ASEAN members' reactions and finally the compromise Declaration on Conduct.

The ASEAN draft code and China's reaction

In comparison to Vietnam's and the Philippines' draft codes, the ASEAN draft was a compromise text.[22] It adopted the definition of the geographic scope of Vietnam's draft ('disputed areas of the Spratlys and the Paracels in the South China Sea'). The Philippines did not suggest the inclusion of Scarborough Shoal, as the Philippines still administered the shoal (until 2012) and considered it an undisputed area. The ASEAN draft adopted the provision from the Philippines' draft to 'refrain from action of inhabiting or erecting structures in presently uninhabited islands... and other features in the Disputed Area' (paragraph 2). Although this provision is just short of a general commitment not to occupy new features – it does not, for instance, explicitly prohibit moving military personnel to an island – it would ban installations. Without installations, the features could not easily sustain a presence. Paragraph seven contained the contentious provision that 'other countries and international organizations are encouraged to subscribe to the principles in this Code of Conduct'. Moreover, the ASEAN draft drew from the Sino-Philippine understanding of 1995 the objective to cooperate in

21 Joint Statement of the Meeting of Heads of State/Government of the Member States of ASEAN and the President of the People's Republic of China Kuala Lumpur, Malaysia, 16 December 1997.
22 The ASEAN draft code is accessible in Carlyle A. Thayer, 'South China Sea: Background to ASEAN-China Code of Conduct,' Thayer Consultancy Background Brief, April 25, 2017.

various maritime issue areas and environmental protection. It added to this list the objective of holding confidence-building measures such as dialogues between military officials and the voluntary exchange of information on planned 'significant measures' in disputed areas.

Philippine Undersecretary Baja consulted China's former Assistant Minister Wang Yi[23] on the ASEAN draft code on October 27, 1999. According to a Philippine memorandum, Wang Yi said that China has a positive attitude towards a code but cannot agree to the ASEAN draft. It was unacceptable because it contained the commitment to 'no new occupation' and this would imply 'some illegal connotation' for recent occupations.[24] In December 1999, China's Minister Counsellor Sun Heping presented in written form a 'Memo of China's position regarding the Latest Draft of the Code of Conduct by the ASEAN' to Philippine Assistant Secretary Wily Gaa. According to this memo, Chinese officials saw 'the following serious problems that China will never agree to':[25]

> a. [T]he draft especially includes the Xisha [Paracel] Islands in the scope of the application, which creates new trouble out of thin air. The Xisha Islands is Chinese inherent territory which is indisputable. This draft seriously breaches the political consensus reached between China and ASEAN and creates a new obstacle… by including the indisputable Xisha Islands.
>
> Accordingly, the Chinese side can't agree to take this draft as a basis for the discussion…. With the Xisha islands included in the draft Code, China won't agree to start any substantive discussion with ASEAN.

China's memo insisted on the exclusion of the Paracel Islands as a precondition for talks and repeated this point several times. Why was the exclusion of the Paracel Islands as an applicable area a precondition to starting talks?

23 Wang Yi became China's Minister of Foreign Affairs in 2013 and State Councillor in 2018.

24 *Memorandum* from Undersecretary of Foreign Affairs to the Republic of the Philippines to the Secretary of Foreign Affairs of the Republic of the Philippines (27 October 1999) (Annex 39), Vol III.

25 *Memorandum* from the Assistant Secretary of Foreign Affairs for Asia and Pacific Affairs of the Republic of the Philippines to the Secretary of Foreign Affairs of the Republic of the Philippines (21 December 1999) (Annex 471), Vol VIII of the Philippines' Supplemental Written Submission, https://files.pca-cpa.org/pcadocs/The%20Philippines%27%20Supplemental%20Written%20Submission%20-%20Volume%20VIII%20%28Annexes%20466-499%29.pdf (last accessed 24 April 2024).

China has had control over the Paracel Islands and deemed this occupation 'indisputable'. From China's perspective, if a code applied to these islands, this would imply China's recognition that the Paracels are disputed and hence acknowledge the existence of Vietnam's claims. As China refuses to consult on the status of the Paracel Islands, China rejects any document that deviates from this position. The memo further notes:

> b. Some wording of the draft like "Without prejudice to existing claims of sovereignty or jurisdiction", "refrain from action of inhabiting or erecting structures in presently uninhabited islands, ... in the disputed areas" ... highlights the most sensitive disputes....
>
> c. The draft encourages other countries and international organizations to subscribe to the principles contained in this Code of Conduct, which runs counter to the common stance that China and ASEAN are consistently opposed to any external interference in and internationalization of the Nansha Issue.[26]

ASEAN's proposal that 'other countries... are encouraged to subscribe' to the code (paragraph 7) would have resulted in the possibility that non-regional states join the code. Had China accepted this, this proposal may have resulted in China's consent to the US or other actors assuming a formal role in the disputes as 'subscribers' to the code. The code would have become what may be called an 'institution of inclusion'. Below, this book will discuss that China has proposed elements of an 'institution of exclusion' in the negotiations since 2018. Another of China's concerns was the use of some legal language that would have resembled a legal document.[27]

China's problem with the commitment to 'refrain from action of inhabiting or erecting structures in presently uninhabited islands' was not so much the commitment to refrain from inhabiting new islands, but the ban on the construction of new structures. China accepted in the Declaration on Conduct to refrain 'from action of inhabiting presently uninhabited islands' (paragraph 5). A ban on building new installations, however, would have affected China's options for future interactions considerably because China's

26 Ibid.

27 Association of Southeast Asian Nations, *Report of the Third Meeting of the Working Group of ASEAN-China Senior Official Consultations on the Code of Conduct in the South China Sea* (11 October 2000) (Annex 498), Vol VIII of the Philippines' Supplemental Written Submission.

structures were relatively small in 1999.[28] China relied on construction upgrades to strengthen its position in the 1990s; its large-scale construction program began in 2013.[29] Furthermore, Wang Yi explained that the commitment 'to no new occupations' would imply 'illegal connotations' for China's recent occupations.[30] This point about 'illegal connotations' reflects an important element of China's position. China was not willing to accept any provision that would have restricted China in changing the status quo of 1999 and that would have thwarted eventual recognition of China's occupations. Chinese officials also suspected that such language could imply some retrospective 'consolidation' of the occupations of ASEAN members which had occupied the majority of Spratly islands in earlier decades.[31] Vice-Minister Wang Yingfan commented to his Philippine counterpart Severino in 1995: '[W]e Chinese think that it is foreign countries that have occupied China's islands and reefs so it is entirely impossible to China to accept the validity of such occupation to accept such status quo [...]. Because maintaining of status quo implies that there is the possibility of accepting and recognizing such occupation.'[32] For China, the bottom line about the code was that any provision that would have frozen the status quo of 1999 was unacceptable. Chinese Vice-Minister Wang Yingfan and former Assistant Minister Wang Yi explained to their Philippine counterparts clearly that Beijing could neither accept the status quo of 1999 nor accept restrictions on China's options to change the status quo. In sum, the ASEAN draft was designed to seek China's cooperation in reducing China's ability to advance or defend its claims. Yet, China wanted to reserve options to do exactly that.

28 See the following reports of the Armed Forces of the Philippines on China's installations before 2013: Armed Forces of the Philippines, *Matrix of Events*: Chigua (Kennan) Reef (2013) (Annex 86), Armed Forces of the Philippines, *Matrix of Events*: Cuarteron (Calderon) Reef (2013) (Annex 87), Armed Forces of the Philippines, *Matrix of Events*: Fiery Cross (Kagitingan) Reef (2013) (Annex 88), Vol IV, https://files.pca-cpa.org/pcadocs/The%20Philippines%27%20Memorial%20-%20Volume%20IV%20%28Annexes%2061-102%29.pdf (last accessed 24 April 2024).

29 Armed Forces of the Philippines, *Chronological Development of Artificial Structures on Features* (Annex 96), Vol IV. For publicly available imagery of the island-building programs since 2013, see the Asia Maritime Transparency Initiative and Center for Strategic and International Studies, https://amti.csis.org/island-tracker/ (last accessed 13 April 2024).

30 *Memorandum* from Undersecretary of Foreign Affairs to the Republic of the Philippines to the Secretary of Foreign Affairs of the Republic of the Philippines (27 October 1999) (Annex 39), Vol III.

31 Interview with an international lawyer of a leading think tank on maritime affairs affiliated with China's Ministry of Foreign Affairs, China, 13 April 2017 (Interview 22).

32 Department of Foreign Affairs of the Republic of the Philippines, *Transcript of Proceedings: RP-PRC Bilateral Talks* (9 August 1995) (Annex 179), Vol VI, 12.

China proposes to restrict coercion: China's draft code

Assistant Minister Wang Yi submitted China's draft code to Philippine Undersecretary Baja on 27 October 1999.[33] Chinese and ASEAN senior officials discussed the draft in March and May 2000 at ASEAN meetings. China's draft defines the geographic scope of a code only as 'disputes relating to the Nansha [Spratly] Islands' (paragraph 4), excluding all other areas and the Paracel Islands. As mentioned above, several ASEAN members also preferred a geographic scope excluding the Paracel Islands in internal ASEAN negotiations in 1996. This was, however, unacceptable to Vietnam who rejected any draft that defines a geographical area without the Paracels. Vietnam's assessment likely was that not mentioning the Paracels while mentioning the Spratlys would have supported China's position that the Paracels' status is 'undisputed'. In paragraph 7, China suggested restricting law enforcement activities:

> The countries concerned shall be encouraged to develop bilateral fishery cooperation, establish channels of consultation and dialogue over issues that may arise in fishing operation....
>
> Refrain from use of threat of force, or taking coercive measures, such as seizure, detention or arrest, against fishing boats or other civilian vessels engaged in normal operations in the disputed areas, nor against nationals of other countries thereon.[34]

This Chinese proposal is significant. China proposed to restrict the very same coercive law enforcement activities that China's maritime law enforcement agencies have adopted themselves a few years later. China's proposal to restrict coercive behaviour, however, did not make it into the Declaration on Conduct in 2002. By not accepting this or a redrafted version of this provision, Southeast Asian countries might have missed an opportunity to establish limits to coercive maritime law enforcement operations at sea. Especially since the late 2000s, China would have been the primary addressee of the second paragraph of this provision. It is China that has repeatedly violated its proposed provision to 'refrain from use of threat of

33 China's draft Code of Conduct is available in: *Memorandum* from Undersecretary of Foreign Affairs to the Republic of the Philippines to the Secretary of Foreign Affairs of the Republic of the Philippines (27 October 1999) (Annex 39), Vol III.

34 Ibid.

force, or taking coercive measures... against fishing boats or other civilian vessels engaged in normal operations in the disputed areas'. China has repeatedly interfered with Southeast Asian seismic research and fishing vessels[35] – these are 'civilian vessels engaged in normal operations in the disputed areas'.

Why did ASEAN members not accept restrictions on coercive coast guard behaviour? The negotiations on fisheries between China and the Philippines suggest the following. China tried to negotiate fisheries agreements with the Philippines between 1995 and 2006. At that time, Philippine maritime law enforcement authorities repeatedly detained Chinese fishermen who were operating inside Philippine waters. As Sino-Philippine negotiations on fisheries stalled,[36] China tried to define restrictions for Philippine law enforcement with the proposed paragraph. China wanted to include this provision in the code during a time when Chinese fishermen were subject to Philippine law enforcement – Chinese fishermen were the enforced and Philippine law enforcement vessels were the enforcer. During the negotiations on fisheries, the Philippines was reluctant to accept rules that would have restricted its enforcement activities against Chinese fishing vessels. This suggests that the Philippines (and perhaps other ASEAN members) did not accept this provision because the Philippines was determined not to accept any limitations on law enforcement against Chinese fishermen in areas Manila regarded as their own.

Moreover, paragraph 9 of China's draft code tried to restrict military exercises in the Spratly Islands:

> Refrain from conducting any military exercises directed against other countries in the Nansha Islands and their adjacent waters, and from carrying out any dangerous and close-in military reconnaissance. Military patrol activities in the area shall be restricted;[37]

Although restricting military exercises in disputed areas could be an effective provision to increase the stability of a dispute, this provision did not make it into the 2002 Declaration. Why did ASEAN states not build on this paragraph or a redrafted version that would have restricted military

35 Chapter III.

36 Chapter III 1.5.

37 *Memorandum* from Undersecretary of Foreign Affairs to the Republic of the Philippines to the Secretary of Foreign Affairs of the Republic of the Philippines (27 October 1999) (Annex 39), Vol III.

activities of their more capable competitor? After all, it was China that used force to occupy islands held by Vietnam at the battle of the Spratlys in 1988 and built installations on Mischief Reef in 1995. 'Military exercises directed against other countries' is a general provision that could be regarded as restricting many types of military activities. If China used 'military patrol activities' to occupy new islands, this provision would have applied to China. At the same time, the specific restrictions of this proposal are directed against reconnaissance that was conducted by the US Navy. ASEAN states presumably saw this provision directed against possible US Navy exercises and as an attempt to restrict US military presence. The Philippines might have regarded this as an attempt to limit its use of the alliance with the US which was reinvigorated in 1998. There is no evidence whether ASEAN members attempted to redraft this proposal in the exchanges between 2000 and 2002 such as to redirect it more specifically to China's military activities. Today, China maintains the largest permanent navy and air force presence on the features China occupies.

The Declaration on the Conduct of Parties in the South China Sea

Two key disagreements about the content of the code blocked the agreement – disagreement on the applicable geographic area and on the question of which types of activities (which conduct) should be restricted. These disagreements reflected the parties' concerns about excluding specific provisions that would reduce their options to advance or defend their claims. When it became clear that China would not accept essential provisions of the ASEAN draft, ASEAN members faced a difficult situation. It took ASEAN members three years to reach consensus on an internal ASEAN draft. But ASEAN had no agreed alternative negotiation position. When China rejected the ASEAN draft, ASEAN had no readily prepared fallback option. Insistence on the ASEAN draft would have prolonged deadlock, but, at the same time, ASEAN did not have an internal consensus on an alternative. ASEAN was left without a workable negotiation position. The Malaysian Foreign Minister Syed Hamid Albar tried therefore to resolve the deadlock by proposing a Declaration on Conduct.[38] The Philippines rejected Syed Hamid Albar's proposal at the beginning, insisting on a more committal and binding document, but accepted the proposal later as the only compromise in reach. China accepted the less committal compromise. The parties made compromise possible by minimising the restrictions on

38 Buszynski, 'ASEAN, the Declaration on Conduct, and the South China Sea', 356.

claimant states' options to advance or defend their claims. This required reducing the substance of the arrangement resulting in the 'Declaration on the Conduct of Parties' adopted on 4 November 2002 (the Declaration).[39]

The disagreement about the geographic scope, whether to include or exclude the Paracel Islands, was resolved by leaving the applicable area undefined and ambiguous. The Declaration only mentions the 'South China Sea' and the 'territorial and jurisdictional disputes' (paragraph 4). The disagreement about the question of which specific dispute activities states should refrain from – restrictions on new occupations as Manila proposed or on military and law enforcement activities as China suggested – was resolved by leaving the restrictions undefined and ambiguous. The parties only 'undertake to exercise self-restraint in the conduct of activities that would complicate or escalate disputes and… refraining from action of inhabiting on the presently uninhabited islands' (paragraph 5).

Paragraph 6 specifies five areas of bilateral or multilateral cooperation: marine environmental protection, marine scientific research, safety of navigation and communication at sea, search and rescue operation, and combating transnational crime. Note that cooperation on fisheries or hydrocarbon resources is not mentioned. China and ASEAN made progress in the field of safety of navigation and communication at sea when they agreed on the Code for Unplanned Encounters at Sea (CUES) in 2014 and when they agreed to apply CUES in 2016.

China was initially reluctant to accept a provision calling for further work towards a code of conduct. The country accepted it after the inclusion of the formula 'on the basis of consensus' (paragraph 10). The Declaration reaffirmed several principles and objectives that were part of the Sino-Philippine framework of 1995 and the ASEAN-China joint statement of 1997 such as the undertaking to cooperate on various maritime issues. The Declaration also contains a commitment to 'freedom of navigation in and overflight above the South China Sea as provided for by the universally recognised principles of international law, including the 1982 UN Convention on the Law of the Sea' (paragraph 3).[40]

39 ASEAN member states and People's Republic of China, 'Declaration on the Conduct of Parties in the South China Sea', 4 November 2002, https://asean.org/declaration-on-the-conduct-of-parties-in-the-south-china-sea-2/ (last accessed 13 August 2023).

40 On the dispute between China and the US about the extent of Freedom of Navigation, see Raul Pete Pedrozo, 'Preserving Navigational Rights and Freedoms: The Right to Conduct Military Activities in China's Exclusive Economic Zone', *Chinese Journal of International Law* 9, no. 1 (2010): 9–29; Haiwen Zhang, 'Is It Safeguarding the Freedom of Navigation or Maritime Hegemony of

This Declaration marked the first multilateral document accepted by China on the South China Sea. Disagreements about substantive provisions of a code of conduct prevented its conclusion. These, in turn, reflect disagreements about the question of which party would have to give up hard power options to advance or defend its claims. Disagreement about the definition of a geographic scope was a prominent obstacle in both the intra-ASEAN negotiations and in the negotiations between China and ASEAN states. This disagreement reflects states' concerns for not creating a layer of validity in favour of an opponent's claim. China proposed restrictions on law enforcement and military activities for the area of the Spratly Islands in 1999. ASEAN members may have benefited from such restrictions for the period between 2009 and 2020, when it was especially China that applied coercive means with maritime law enforcement vessels, the later China Coast Guard, and greatly expanded its military presence. In 1999 and 2000, however, ASEAN members seem to have been more concerned with preventing restrictions on their own law enforcement activities and for allied or supportive US military presences.

For the period until 2002, I could not find that China pursued a deliberate delaying tactic. Rather, delay was the result of disagreements between China and ASEAN members and among ASEAN members. Both ASEAN and China submitted draft codes with more substantial provisions than the 2002 Declaration. In the case of the code, bargaining about a substantial conflict management agreement entailed the problem of securing an opponent's cooperation in giving up options to wield hard power and thereby restricting this party's options to advance its claims. This problem made sure that the first ten-year-long march towards a code resulted in a non-binding, ambiguous, and ineffective Declaration.

1.2 The Second March towards a Code of Conduct: 2003–2016

Bercovitch and Oichi referred to the 2002 Declaration as evidence for a change in the nature of the disputes 'compared with the time [in 1995] when China's aggressive and unilateral behaviours sent an alarm among regional states'.[41] They believed that, with the 2002 Declaration, 'the dragon has been tamed effectively'.[42] With the benefit of hindsight, however, this

the United States?—Comments on Raul (Pete) Pedrozo's Article on Military Activities in the EEZ', *Chinese Journal of International Law* 9, no. 1 (1 March 2010): 31–47.

41 Jacob Bercovitch and Mikio Oichi, *International Conflict in the Asia-Pacific Patterns, Consequences and Management* (Routledge, 2010), chapter 5, 110.

42 Ibid., 110.

judgement appears overly optimistic.[43] Claimant states did not move forward with cooperation agreements as called for in the 2002 Declaration. Lacking clear common rules on conduct and on marine natural resources, tensions rose again following China's first official publication of its nine-dash line in a note verbale of 7 May 2009.[44] China protested Malaysia's and Vietnam's joint submission for an extended continental shelf of 6 May 2009. The joint submission, in turn, was precipitated by the 2009 deadline for partial submissions imposed by the Rules of Procedure (paragraph 3 of annex I) of the Commission for the Limits of the Continental Shelf (CLCS) and UNCLOS (article 4 of annex II).[45]

The course of events and the ASEAN members' negotiation processes demonstrate that ASEAN members did not regard the 2002 Declaration as a sufficiently effective instrument. Beginning in 2003, ASEAN states released annual joint statements reaffirming the Declaration, calling for its implementation and for the adoption of a code of conduct. After two years of consultations among ASEAN states and between ASEAN and China, the parties agreed on a procedure for further steps. The 8th ASEAN–China summit adopted the 'Plan of Action to Implement the Joint Declaration' and provided for a procedure on the 'realisation of the DOC' (Declaration on Conduct) on 29 November 2004.[46] In 'Terms of Reference', ASEAN and China established a joint working group (also referred to as ASEAN-China JWG) 'to study and recommend measures to translate the provisions of the DOC into concrete cooperative activities' that the Senior Officials Meeting (SOM) would then discuss.[47] The first and second meetings of the working

43 Andrew Chubb, 'PRC Assertiveness in the South China Sea: Measuring Continuity and Change, 1970–2015', *International Security* 45, no. 3 (January 2021): 79–121.

44 China's Note Verbale, CML/17/2009, 7 May 2009, http://www.un.org/depts/los/clcs_new/submissions_files/mysvnm33_09/chn_2009re_mys_vnm_e.pdf (last accessed 14 March 2024).

45 The submission was made in accordance with article 76 (8) of UNCLOS. The joint submission together with the protest notes of China, Malaysia, the Philippines, and Vietnam is accessible at http://www.un.org/Depts/los/clcs_new/submissions_files/submission_mysvnm_33_2009.htm (last accessed 14 April 2024).

46 Plan of Action to Implement the Joint Declaration on China-ASEAN Partnership for Peace and Prosperity, Vientiane, 29 November 2004, is accessible at https://cil.nus.edu.sg/wp-content/uploads/2019/02/2004-Plan-of-Action-to-Implement-ASEAN-China-Joint-Declaration-1.pdf (last accessed 14 April 2024).

47 Terms of Reference of the ASEAN–China Joint Working Group on the Implementation of the Declaration on the Conduct of Parties in the South China Sea, Kuala Lumpur, 7 December 2004, accessible at https://cil.nus.edu.sg/databasecil/2004-terms-of-reference-of-the-asean-china-joint-working-group-on-the-implementation-of-the-declaration-on-the-conduct-of-parties-in-the-south-china-sea/ (last accessed 14 April 2024).

group took place in August 2005 and February 2006.[48] After a delay of four years, the JWG resumed its meetings only in April 2010.[49]

Two disagreements resulted in this delay. At the first meeting of the ASEAN–China JWG on 4–5 August 2005, ASEAN member states suggested a procedural guideline, namely that ASEAN members 'consult among themselves before meeting China'.[50] China objected to this procedure and negotiations stalled in the next years. Thuy commented that China preferred consultations 'with "relevant parties" not with ASEAN as a bloc'.[51] This is of course true, but from China's objection follows only that China preferred not to consent to a formal procedure that would establish ASEAN as a single negotiating actor. The absence of a formal two-stage procedure – ASEAN member states produce a common position before negotiating with China – does not by itself preclude ASEAN members from coordinating *informally* and acting *de facto* as a bloc. ASEAN members tried indeed to coordinate their position informally before negotiating with China. The consultations of ASEAN members required twenty-one successive drafts before an internal consensus allowed them to proceed to negotiations with China.[52] This illustrates that the lack of a common position among ASEAN members about the substantial content of the code of conduct was one problem causing delay in ASEAN–China negotiations between 2002 and 2010. In 2012, ASEAN members discussed internally a Philippine draft code of conduct while consulting China through the ASEAN Chair.[53] That illustrates that formal procedural questions did not preclude ASEAN members from trying to produce a common position before meeting China, even if the procedural formula remained contentious between China and ASEAN members.[54]

48 Joint Communiqué of the 38th ASEAN Ministerial Meeting, Vientiane, 26 July 2005, accessible at https://asean.org/joint-communique-of-the-38th-asean-ministerial-meeting-vientiane-26-july-2005/ (last accessed 14 April 2024).

49 Chairman's Statement of the 17th Meeting of the ASEAN Regional Forum, Ha Noi, 23 July 2010, accessible at https://asean.org/43rd-amm-pmc-17th-arf-vietnam-2010-chairmans-statement-17th-asean-regional-forum-ha-noi-23-july-2010/ (last accessed 14 April 2024).

50 Truong Thuy Tran, 'Recent Development In The South China Sea: From Declaration To Code Of Conduct', *East Sea (South China Sea) Studies*, 2011, 1–20, 4.

51 Ibid.

52 Carlyle A. Thayer, 'ASEAN and China Set to Agree on Single Draft South China Sea Code of Conduct', *The Diplomat*, July 2018, https://thediplomat.com/2018/07/asean-and-china-set-to-agree-on-single-draft-south-china-sea-code-of-conduct/ (last accessed 14/04/2022).

53 Carlyle A. Thayer, 'ASEAN'S Code of Conduct in the South China Sea: A Litmus Test for Community-Building?', *The Asia-Pacific Journal* 10, no. 4 (2012): 1–22, 3.

54 Ibid. 2.

Nine years after the 2002 Declaration and after intensive intra-ASEAN consultations, this process resulted in a largely symbolic arrangement. China and ASEAN states agreed on the 'Guidelines for the Implementation of the DOC' in 2011. The guidelines consist of a 'step-by-step approach in line with the provisions of the DOC' on a 'voluntary basis' that should lead to 'the eventual realization of a Code of Conduct'.[55] This wording defined the pace of talks on a code between 2003 and 2012: slow, hardly going beyond the 2002 Declaration, and blocked by disagreements regarding the substantive content similar to the disagreements of the late 1990s and early 2000s.

A code of conduct aligned with the *South China Sea* Arbitration? The Philippines' Draft Code of Conduct 2012

The Philippines tried to accelerate the negotiation process and to build an ASEAN consensus by producing a new draft, the Philippines' Draft Code of Conduct, in January 2012.[56] In terms of substantial provisions, the Philippine draft contained the following proposals:[57] a 'Joint Cooperation Area in the South China Sea' (part III), a 'Joint Permanent Working Committee to implement the Zone of Peace, Freedom, Friendship and Cooperation' (Zone of Peace) (part IV), an application of articles 122 and 123 of UNCLOS on cooperation in semi-enclosed seas to the South China Sea (part V) and provisions on a dispute settlement mechanism (part VI). The essential objective of the Zone of Peace was to distinguish between 'areas in dispute' and 'areas not in dispute' according to the maximum extent of maritime zones as defined in UNCLOS.[58] In the Philippines' perspective, an area to which China is not entitled under the law of the sea should be an 'area not in dispute'.[59] The South China Sea Arbitration vindicated this key distinction four years later in 2016. In other words, the central decision of the South China Sea Arbitration – the judgement that China cannot legally claim rights

55 'Guidelines for the Implementation of the DOC', adopted 19 July 2011, https://www.asean.org/wp-content/uploads/images/archive/documents/20185-DOC.pdf (last accessed 14 April 2024).

56 Thayer, 'ASEAN'S Code of Conduct in the South China Sea: A Litmus Test for Community-Building?', 3.

57 Ibid.

58 The Zone of Peace was proposed by Henry Bensurto, Philippine Secretary-General of the Ocean Affairs Department in the Department of Foreign Affairs and then became the official policy of the Philippines. *Memorandum* from Secretary General, Commission on Maritime and Ocean Affairs Secretariat, Department of Foreign Affairs of the Republic of the Philippines to the Secretary of Foreign Affairs of the Republic of the Philippines (28 March 2011) (Annex 71), Vol IV.

59 Ibid.

beyond the entitlements under UNCLOS – was already the starting point of the Philippine draft code in 2012. No consensus in favour of this draft code emerged among ASEAN members, however. ASEAN members trimmed and replaced the Philippine draft with an ASEAN draft.[60] Disagreements among ASEAN states thwarted that ASEAN's key project of a code of conduct and the award of the South China Sea Arbitration could have reinforced each other early on.

While ASEAN members were curtailing the Philippine draft code and struggling to find an ASEAN compromise, further incidents escalated in 2011 and 2012. In 2011, Chinese fishermen cut the cables of a seismic research vessel commissioned by Vietnam, the Viking II, and, crucially, China took control of Scarborough Shoal in July 2012.[61] Cambodia, however, rejected even general reference to both incidents at the 45th ASEAN Foreign Minister meeting. Cambodia considered both incidents purely bilateral disputes that ASEAN as a grouping should not mention.[62] ASEAN disunity regarding the question of which disputes ASEAN should put on the agenda prevented the adoption of an ASEAN joint communiqué for the first time in ASEAN's history.

To move forward with ASEAN consensus building, Indonesia proposed a so-called Zero Draft code of conduct in September 2012.[63] The Zero Draft draws some of its provisions from the 2002 Declaration. Other provisions existed in a different wording already in the ASEAN draft of 1999 or in China's draft of 1999. The Zero Draft proposed general limitations on military exercises which went beyond China's draft of 1999. It proposed a ban on new occupations and new structures on islands repeating the ASEAN draft of 1999. It proposed a

60 Thayer, 'ASEAN's Code of Conduct in the South China Sea: A Litmus Test for Community-Building?', 4.

61 *Memorandum* from Col. Nathaniel Y. Casem, Philippine Navy, to Chief of Staff, Armed Forces of the Philippines, No. N2E-0412-008 (11 April 2012) (Annex 77); *Memorandum* from the Embassy of the Republic of the Philippines in Beijing to the Secretary of Foreign Affairs of the Republic of the Philippines, No. ZPE-080-2012-S (24 May 2012) (Annex 81), Vol IV. For further details, see chapter III 1.4.

62 The subsequent controversy among ASEAN foreign ministers was partly leaked. Thayer, 'ASEAN's Code of Conduct in the South China Sea: A Litmus Test for Community-Building?'; Termsak Charlermpalanupap, 'Review of the ASEAN-China Declaration of the Conduct of Parties in the South China Sea and Prospects of a Code of Conduct in the South China Sea: An ASEAN Perspective', in *Power, Law, and Maritime Order in the South China Sea*, edited by Truong Thuy Tran and Thuy Trang Le (2015), 37–48, 38.

63 Valencia obtained a copy of the draft. Mark J. Valencia, 'What the "Zero Draft" Code of Conduct for the South China Sea Says (and Doesn't Say)', *Global Asia*, March 2013, https://www.globalasia.org/v8no1/feature/what-the-zero-draft-code-of-conduct-for-the-south-china-sea-says-and-doesnt-say_mark-j-valencia (last accessed 13 April 2024).

new definition for the geographic scope ('Areas of Application'): the code 'shall apply to unresolved maritime boundary areas of the parties concerned'. This definition maintained enough ambiguity to evade the contentious question whether the code should apply to the Paracel Islands but introduced a new difficulty. The formulation would apply to all boundary disputes in the South China Sea: bilateral and multilateral disputes, disputes about 'disputed' and 'undisputed' areas, disputes inside and outside the nine-dash line. Another new proposal focused on creating mechanisms to manage incidents at sea between navies. Outside the framework of ASEAN–China meetings, the West Pacific Naval Symposium established such a mechanism in 2014 (the Code for Unplanned Encounters at Sea, CUES).[64]

While intense diplomacy occurred between 2003 and 2012, the formal start of the next attempt to reach a code of conduct was at the ASEAN–China Senior Officials Meeting in Suzhou, China, in September 2013. The meeting agreed on the procedural point that the code of conduct would be on the agenda of all meetings of senior officials (SOM) and working groups (JWG).[65] It also suggested projects to implement the 2002 Declaration's call for maritime cooperation (paragraph 6 of the 2002 Declaration). China proposed funding through the China–ASEAN Maritime Cooperation Fund to which it allocated about half a billion US dollars.[66] Projects were limited to the holding of workshops on hazard prevention, marine ecosystems, marine ecological monitoring, search and rescue, and a workshop in commemoration of the Declaration.[67] These workshops did not lead to concrete steps.

Considering the negotiations on the code of conduct between 1999 and 2002, the provisions of the Zero Draft had little chance of being acceptable, short of a profound change of policy of several claimants. Familiar disagreements prevented progress on the Zero Draft. According to Tran, 'China can get ASEAN to consent to a new status-quo, including China's occupation of the Scarborough Shoal in 2012 – a situation similar to the DOC negotiation process after the Mischief Reef incidents.'[68] The Philippines saw the application of a code to Scarborough Shoal critically 'as it will legalise China's

64 CUES will be discussed in chapter V 2.

65 Truong Thuy Tran, 'Code of Conduct and the Prevention and Management of Incidents in the South China Sea', in *Power, Law, and Maritime Order in the South China Sea*, edited by Truong Thuy Tran and Thuy Trang Le (Lexington Books, 2015), 317–30, 319.

66 Charlermpalanupap, 'Review of the ASEAN-China Declaration of the Conduct of Parties in the South China Sea', 40.

67 Ibid., 40.

68 Tran, 'Code of Conduct and the Prevention and Management of Incidents in the South China Sea', 323.

occupation' while the inclusion of the Paracels remained a Vietnamese interest.[69] Holmes warned that China would use 'international covenants to cement [its] gains'.[70] These analyses reflect expectations that a code of conduct would contribute to consolidating China's unilateral advancements. Note that Chinese officials used similar arguments in opposing the ASEAN draft code in 1999. As noted above, Wang Yi rejected some provisions of the 1999 ASEAN draft as they implied 'illegal connotations' for China's activities; other Chinese officials suspected the ASEAN draft would 'consolidate' Southeast Asian positions.[71]

1.3 The Third March towards a Code of Conduct after the South China Sea Arbitration: Procedural Novelties and Old Divisions

ASEAN members and China resumed negotiations on a code of conduct with renewed interest after the award of the South China Sea Arbitration on 12 July 2016. Initially, the claimants agreed on three documents: a statement calling for the 'early' rather than 'eventual' realization of a code, guidelines for hotline communication, and a framework for a code of conduct. The documents were agreed on quickly, which suggests that China wanted to make it seem like it was willing to give something after the arbitration. The documents, though, do not contain new commitments other than the guidelines for hotline communication. China and ASEAN members started another attempt to negotiate a code of conduct in August 2018. While China's Premier Li Keqiang publicly expected these negotiations to result in a code in 2021, this did not materialize. The negotiation procedure starting in 2018 underwent a substantive change. In 2018, ASEAN members and China agreed to negotiate based on a Single Draft Negotiation Text. Nevertheless, few proposals for specific provisions appear both substantive and uncontroversial if compared to earlier attempts.

Post-Arbitration Politics

On 12 July 2016, the South China Sea Arbitration ruled that China is not entitled to claim maritime zones beyond the normal zones under UNCLOS

69 Ibid.

70 James Holmes, 'ASEAN Should Reject a Code of Conduct in the South China Sea', *The Diplomat*, September 2013, https://thediplomat.com/2013/09/asean-should-reject-a-code-of-conduct-in-the-south-china-sea/ (last accessed 13 April 2024).

71 Interview with an international lawyer of a leading think tank on maritime affairs affiliated with China's Ministry of Foreign Affairs, China, 12 April 2017 (Interview 21).

and thereby invalidated a good part of China's claim to maritime zones in the South China Sea. As discussed above,[72] the Philippines responded very cautiously to the award ('the Philippines [will] study the award') and did not demand that China implement the arbitral tribunal's ruling in 2016.[73] Only three and half years later, the Philippines asserted that the South China Sea Arbitration 'conclusively settled the issue of historic rights and entitlements in the South China Sea'.[74] Vietnam's initial reaction to the award was also more cautious than could have been expected.[75] There was no ASEAN statement and no joint statement of Southeast Asian claimant states in response to the award in 2016. China declared that the award is 'null and void and has no binding force. China neither accepts nor recognises it'.[76] Given this reaction to the award, the Philippines and Vietnam tried using the award as leverage in bilateral and multilateral interactions rather than pressing for China's compliance. The governments of the Philippines and Vietnam had the expectation that China must make some concessions in negotiations on a code of conduct.[77] According to Chinese sources, China's Ministry of Foreign Affairs believed that the tribunal's award would remain the focal point for interactions if China did not engage in further code of conduct negotiations.[78] As the renewed Sino-Philippine negotiations on joint development cannot reflect a Chinese concession[79] – joint development has been China's preferred instrument

72 Beginning of chapter III and chapter III 1.3.

73 Statement of the Secretary of Foreign Affairs of the Philippines, 12 July 2016.

74 Permanent Mission of the Philippines to the United Nations, 'Notes Verbales 000191-2020', 6 March 2020, https://www.un.org/Depts/los/clcs_new/submissions_files/mys_12_12_2019/2020_03_06_PHL_NV_UN_001.pdf (last accessed 13 June 2023).

75 Remarks of the Spokesperson of the Ministry of Foreign Affairs of Viet Nam, 12 July 2016, http://www.mofa.gov.vn/en/tt_baochi/pbnfn/ns160712211059 (last accessed 13 April 2024).

76 Ministry of Foreign Affairs of the People's Republic of China, 'Statement of the Ministry of Foreign Affairs of the People's Republic of China on the Award of 12 July 2016 of the Arbitral Tribunal in the South China Sea Arbitration Established at the Request of the Republic of the Philippines', July 2016, https://www.fmprc.gov.cn/mfa_eng/wjdt_665385/2649_665393/201607/t20160712_679470.html (last accessed 19 April 2024).

77 Interview with a ministerial-level official of the administration of President Arroyo, Manila, 02 December 2016 (Interview 7); interview with a scholar of a leading think tank on international relations affiliated with Vietnam's Ministry of Foreign Affairs, Nha Trang, 14 October 2016 (Interview 16).

78 Interview with an international lawyer of a leading think tank on maritime affairs affiliated with China's Ministry of Foreign Affairs, China, 13 April 2017 (Interview 22); see Lowell Bautista, 'The South China Sea Arbitral Award: Evolving Post-Arbitration Strategies, Implications and Challenges', *Asian Politics & Policy* 10, no. 2 (2018): 178–89 and this special volume of *Asian Politics & Policy* 10, no.2 for further analyses of post-arbitration politics.

79 Chapter III 1.3.

in the disputes – the negotiations on a code are the area where Southeast Asian claimants expect responsiveness. Moreover, Vietnam used the legal strategy of the Philippines as a model and assembled a legal team to prepare a Vietnamese case against China. Vietnam initially tried to use potential legal proceedings to impose conditions on China.[80] In return for not initiating legal proceedings, Vietnam demanded that China commit to no new occupations of features, no further militarization of features, and no interference in Vietnam's offshore oil and gas projects. China complied only with the first condition but interfered in Vietnam's oil projects and further militarized features.[81] Nevertheless, Vietnam did not initiate arbitral proceedings against China at the time of writing. This illustrates the difficulties Vietnam has had in using the arbitral proceedings to impose some conditionality on China's behaviour.

Three further steps

Thirteen days after the tribunal published its decision, the foreign ministers of ASEAN members and China issued a joint statement 'on the Full and Effective Implementation of the Declaration on the Conduct of Parties in the South China Sea' on 25 July 2016.[82] The statement repeats many provisions of the Declaration and contains one new word. The parties commit to 'the full and effective implementation of the DOC in its entirety and working substantively towards the early adoption of Code of Conduct in the South China Sea based on consensus'. Some officials saw progress in the fact that China accepted language moving from the 'eventual realization' of a code to the 'early adoption' of a code in July 2016.[83] The document contains an indication that the new word 'early' is indeed of political significance, because it needed qualification in paragraph six of the same document: 'The Parties… agree to work, on the basis of consensus towards the eventual attainment of this objective [the adoption of a code].' To the extent that

80 Interview 16.

81 Bill Hayton, 'South China Sea: Vietnam "Scraps New Oil Project"', *BBC*, 23 August 2018, http://www.bbc.com/news/world-asia-43507448; 'China, Vietnam meeting canceled amid South China Sea tensions', *Reuters*, 8 August 2017, https://www.reuters.com/article/us-asean-philippines-china-vietnam-idUSKBN1AO07K (both accessed 19 April 2024).

82 'Joint Statement of the Foreign Ministers of ASEAN Member States and China on the full and effective Implementation of the Declaration on the Conduct of Parties in the South China Sea', 25 July 2016, https://asean.org/wp-content/uploads/2016/07/Joint-Statement-on-the-full-and-effective-implementation-of-the-DOC-FINAL.pdf (last accessed 19 April 2024).

83 Interview with a senior Malaysian official, Ministry of Foreign Affairs, 18 November 2016 (Interview 15).

the word 'early' was a concession by China, this concession needed to be balanced by a repetition of the word 'eventual'.

Another six weeks later, Senior Officials of the disputing states approved 'Guidelines for Hotline Communications Among Senior Officials of Foreign Affairs of ASEAN Member States and China in Response to Maritime Emergencies in the Implementation of the Declaration on the Conduct of Parties in the South China Sea'.[84] The guidelines only provide for China and ASEAN members to designate a director general (or deputy director general) from the respective ministries of foreign affairs as the 'focal point for the MFA's Hotline Communications' (paragraph 4.1). In case of an incident, a party that is called through this mechanism shall ensure 'effective and timely response'. The guidelines are supposed to ensure an effective exchange of information in maritime emergencies that 'require immediate policy level intervention' (paragraph 2). The guidelines do not specify what would amount to 'effective' and 'timely' responses. The guidelines do not mandate a change of behaviour in an incident. Fourteen years after the 2002 Declaration on Conduct, ASEAN and China wanted these guidelines to be understood as an 'Early Harvest Measure' (paragraph 1.2) implementing the 2002 Declaration.

China proposed to establish a law enforcement hotline on fisheries with the Philippines in the late 1990s, early 2000s, and again in 2012,[85] but the Philippines did not follow up on the proposals. The Philippines was reluctant to accept agreements with China (and Taiwan) that had implications for maritime law enforcement activities. Manila believed these to restrict Philippine efforts to rein in Chinese fishing activities in the Philippine Exclusive Economic Zone (EEZ).[86] Two differences allowed Philippine consent in the case of the ASEAN–China guidelines for hotline communication. Foremost, the agreement for hotline communication between ASEAN states and China is a multilateral instrument without a focus on fisheries. Second, this hotline communication is not among frontline actors such as coast guards but among Ministries of Foreign Affairs. Moreover, ASEAN member states under the chairmanship of the Philippines regarded the

84 'Guidelines for Hotline Communications Among Senior Officials of the Ministries of Foreign Affairs of ASEAN Member States and China in Response to Maritime Emergencies in the Implementation of the Declaration on the Conduct of Parties in the South China Sea', 07 September 2016, https://www.fmprc.gov.cn/nanhai/eng/zcfg_1/201704/P020210903716568578083.pdf (last accessed 19 April 2024).

85 *Record of Discussion: 17th Philippines-China Foreign Ministry Consultations* (14 January 2012) (Annex 204), Vol VI.

86 Chapter III 1.5 and III 3.

successful testing of this hotline in 2017 as another step in implementing the 2002 Declaration.[87] Some observers questioned whether China's Ministry of Foreign Affairs had enough authority within China's bureaucratic system to make this hotline an effective instrument.[88] It is not known whether this hotline played a crucial role in defusing tensions in any specific incident, and its effectiveness appears limited.

On 5 August 2017, the foreign ministers of China and ASEAN states adopted the 'Framework for a Code of Conduct' (the Framework).[89] The Framework is one and a half pages long and consists of three parts with bullet points or sentences on (i) preambular provisions, (ii) general provisions (objective, principles, and basic undertakings), and (iii) final clauses.[90] The Framework can be understood as a 'work package' for the negotiations on a code. It does not specify commitments but lists objectives that the code should cover. The objectives of the Framework go beyond the 2002 Declaration in only a few policy areas. The Framework and the 2002 Declaration refer to the promotion of 'maritime cooperation' and 'self-restraint'. The Framework refers to two new elements: 'prevent incidents, manage incidents should they occur' and 'ensure maritime security'. As the Framework does not specify any specific commitments, for instance on how parties should prevent and manage incidents, this question is left entirely to the negotiations on a code. Two novelties stand out. The Framework lists a 'necessary mechanism for monitoring of implementation' and a 'review of the COC'. No previous document aimed at formulating a monitoring mechanism or an in-built review process. An institutionalized procedure for monitoring implementation would be an important step towards incentivising compliance with a code. The Framework, however, does not specify which types of activities it intends to monitor. The preambular provisions note the 'inter-connection and interaction between DOC and COC', but do not specify how both are expected to relate to each other. Storey suggests that in China's view the

87 'Chairman's Statement of the 31st ASEAN Summit', 13 Nov 2017, Manila, Philippines, para 138. https://asean.org/chairmans-statement-of-the-31st-asean-summit/ (last accessed 19 April 2024).

88 Andrew S. Erickson and Adam P. Liff, 'Installing a Safety on the "Loaded Gun"? China's Institutional Reforms, National Security Commission and Sino–Japanese Crisis (in) Stability', *Journal of Contemporary China* 25, no. 98 (2016): 197–215.

89 'Joint Communiqué of the 50th ASEAN Foreign Ministers' Meeting', Manila, Philippines, 5 August 2017, https://asean.org/wp-content/uploads/2021/03/4.pdf (last accessed 19 April 2024).

90 The text of the framework for a COC was made available by Carlyle A. Thayer, 'ASEAN-China: Framework of a COC', *Thayer Consultancy Background Brief*, August 2017.

DOC 'takes precedence over the COC' and that a code is part of the implementation of the 2002 Declaration.[91] He does therefore not expect a code to deviate substantively from the Declaration. Although the experience of the past does not warrant optimism on code of conduct negotiations, the Framework can be understood as a work plan, not as an attempt to specify new obligations. The policy question is hence whether China and ASEAN will find specific and agreeable provisions substantializing what the Framework lays out.

Procedural novelties and old divisions? The Single Draft Code of Conduct Negotiating Text

The next step towards a code followed on 27 June 2018 when senior officials agreed on a 'Single Draft Code of Conduct Negotiating Text' (Single Draft) at the 15th ASEAN–China Senior Officials' Meeting on the 'Implementation of the Declaration on the Conduct of Parties in the South China Sea' in Changsha, China.[92] This meeting specified a procedure for the negotiations. An internal ASEAN report specified that the Single Draft 'will be the basis of COC negotiations [and that it is] a living document. All parties reserved the right to consult their domestic agencies and submit new or revised input.'[93] The Single Draft was an open text serving as a basis for negotiations; ASEAN states and China were free to insert, propose, and withdraw ('revise') proposals on concrete provisions. The second procedural step was that there would be 'at least three readings of the Single Draft' by the ASEAN–China Joint Working Group (JWG).[94] After each 'reading', the Single Draft would move from the working group to a meeting of senior officials. A Chairman's statement of the 21st ASEAN–China summit confirms this negotiation procedure partially: 'We noted the agreement among ASEAN Member States and China on a Single Draft COC Negotiating Text, [and] looked forward to the completion of the first reading of the Single Draft COC Negotiating

91 Ian Storey, 'Assessing the ASEAN China Framework for the Code of Conduct for the South China Sea', *ISEAS Perspective*, 62, 2017, https://www.iseas.edu.sg/wp-content/uploads/2018/02/ISEAS_Perspective_2017_62.pdf (last accessed 19 April 2024).

92 'Joint Communiqué of the 51st ASEAN Foreign Ministers Meeting', Singapore, 2 August 2018, para 74. https://asean.org/asean2020/wp-content/uploads/2021/01/51st-AMM-Joint-Communique-Final.pdf (last accessed 19 April 2024).

93 Quoted in: Carlyle A. Thayer, 'ASEAN and China Set to Agree on Single Draft South China Sea Code of Conduct', *The Diplomat*, July 2018, https://thediplomat.com/2018/07/asean-and-china-set-to-agree-on-single-draft-south-china-sea-code-of-conduct/ (last accessed 19 April 2024).

94 Ibid.

Text by 2019.'[95] The initial indication by Premier Li Keqiang to sign a code of conduct following three readings in 2021 did not materialize.[96] It appears that there is no realistic deadline for the negotiations.

The negotiation procedure based on a Single Draft has important procedural and political implications that break with the past. First, members of ASEAN have abandoned their previous approach of first seeking an ASEAN consensus on a draft code before entering into negotiations with China. With the Single Draft negotiation procedure, ASEAN members do not act as a bloc and, indeed, do not even try to build a coalition behind a common position. Rather, each state can propose and has proposed its preferred provisions. While ASEAN members have attempted to coordinate their positions before negotiating with China, this has not changed the fact that ASEAN did not adopt one or several internal draft codes. Second, a single negotiating text contains various draft provisions for each issue area. Negotiations are not based on entire draft codes from the opposing claimants. It is a negotiating text, not a negotiated text. No party fully commits to the draft provisions it proposes; all parties are free to revise their provisions. This negotiation method was applied at the Third United Nations Conference on the Law of the Sea (1973–1982).[97] It served the purpose of 'pulling states away from their varied starting positions towards a common position'.[98] This negotiating procedure can be useful when intense disagreements of a political nature have prevented agreement in previous attempts – as is the case with the code of conduct. Each state can float proposals in a less committal way than previously, when China and ASEAN each submitted a full draft that engraved the major disagreements. Third, it is noteworthy that China and ASEAN agreed on calling three negotiation rounds 'readings'. This language is used in legislative processes, while the issue of whether a code of conduct should be legally binding is contested.

Possible reasons for this negotiation procedure are the following: Two previous attempts to reach a code – between 1992 and 2002, and between

95 'Chairman's Statement of the 21st ASEAN-China Summit, Singapore', 14 November 2018, https://asean.org/wp-content/uploads/2018/11/ASEANChinaSummitChairmansStatementFinal1.pdf (last accessed 19 April 2024).

96 'South China Sea: Beijing hopes for maritime accord with Asean neighbours in three years', 13 November 2018, *SCMP*.

97 Codification Division Publication, 'Third United Nations Conference on the Law of the Sea 1973–1982', http://legal.un.org/diplomaticconferences/1973_los/ (last accessed 19 April 2024).

98 Barry Buzan, 'Negotiating by Consensus: Developments in Technique at the United Nations Conference on the Law of the Sea', *American Journal of International Law* 75, no. 2 (1981): 324–48, 332.

2003 and 2013 – were unsuccessful. Consensus building among ASEAN members twice caused a delay of several years. As the previous ASEAN draft codes were themselves the result of compromise, the effect of China rejecting essential provisions of the ASEAN draft code was to leave ASEAN without a negotiation position. ASEAN needed to engage in an internal coordination process to adopt a new common negotiating position. ASEAN members saw apparently little benefit in insisting on their position after China rejected it. In other words, the previous ASEAN consensus on a code did not survive first encounters with China. Furthermore, the Single Negotiating Text procedure has its merits. It prevents negotiations from being based on irreconcilable drafts from the beginning. The key question is then whether these procedural novelties can translate into agreement on new substantive provisions, or whether the past disagreements on specific provisions will be replicated in recent negotiations. Thayer made the leaked content of the Single Draft publicly available.[99] In the following, I discuss some draft proposals for the Single Draft in light of previous disagreements.

The Single Draft repeats previous documents by saying that the code is 'not an instrument to settle territorial disputes or maritime delimitation issues'. Malaysia proposed a without prejudice clause excluding that the code would 'affect the Parties' position on legal questions relating to the settlement of disputes, maritime boundaries, or the permissible maritime entitlements of the Parties under international law of the sea and enshrined/reflected in the 1982 UNCLOS'. It is an open question whether China would accept a reference to the concept of maritime entitlement in the code. The South China Sea Arbitration relied on this concept to find jurisdiction and to rule that China is not entitled to waters beyond the normal entitlements.

Regarding the geographic scope of the code, Vietnam suggested that the code 'shall apply to all disputed features and overlapping maritime areas claimed under the 1982 UNCLOS in the South China Sea'. In previous negotiations, Vietnam insisted on the explicit inclusion of the Paracel Islands and China rejected this categorically. The formula 'all disputed features' tries to solve this disagreement with ambiguity. China does not recognize

99 Carlyle A. Thayer, 'A Closer Look at the ASEAN-China Single Draft South China Sea Code of Conduct', *The Diplomat*, August 2018, https://thediplomat.com/2018/08/a-closer-look-at-the-asean-china-single-draft-south-china-sea-code-of-conduct/ (last accessed 19 April 2024). The following quotes of the Single Draft are taken from Thayer. A second source partly confirming the content of the leaked text is the *Straits Times*, 'Tough talks ahead on South China Sea code of conduct as Vietnam seeks to curb China's actions', 31 December 2018, https://www.straitstimes.com/asia/se-asia/tough-talks-ahead-on-south-china-sea-code-of-conduct-as-vietnam-seeks-to-curb-chinas (last accessed 19 April 2024).

the existence of a dispute about the Paracel Islands, but a dispute exists as a matter of fact. 'All disputed features' would hence include the Paracels, but not mention them explicitly. Indonesia proposed the provision that 'the Parties are committed to respect the EEZ, and continental shelf of the coastal states as provided for in the 1982 UNCLOS'. This formula contains some ambiguity, too. In application of the South China Sea Arbitration, the Reed Bank, for instance, is part of the continental shelf of the Philippines. In China's view, China has a valid claim to the Reed Bank. It is not yet clear whether China regards itself as a coastal state of the Reed Bank and, more generally, how China assesses these proposals regarding the geographic scope.

A section on the duty to cooperate repeats provisions deriving from UNCLOS, i.e., the duty to cooperate on environmental protection in semi-enclosed seas.[100] This section also repeats the five areas of cooperation that the 2002 Declaration specified: environmental protection, marine scientific research, safety of navigation, and combatting transnational crime. China has added cooperation in the marine economy and mentioned specifically hydrocarbon resources. China proposed that such cooperation 'shall not be conducted in cooperation with companies from outside the region'. It is very unlikely that ASEAN members will accept this provision. Malaysia, Vietnam, and the Philippines have relied on technology and investments of foreign energy companies, including from the US, Europe, Russia, and India, for exploiting their offshore oil and gas resources and for strategic considerations in the disputes.[101] Malaysia made the counterproposal, asserting that nothing 'shall affect... rights or ability of the Parties to conduct activities with foreign countries... of their own choosing.'

Under the heading of 'Self-restrain/Promotion of trust and confidence', Indonesia proposed measures such as an exchange between military officials, just and humane treatment of persons in distress, the voluntary notification of military exercises, and the exchange of relevant information. These provisions exist already in the 2002 Declaration (paragraph 5). From what is known so far, Indonesia's proposal did not go beyond the 2002 Declaration. China made five proposals under the same heading: 'military

100 UNCLOS, article 123. It will be important to observe which language the parties will finally choose. There is a debate among lawyers whether to interpret article 123 of UNCLOS as mandating or recommending cooperation in semi-enclosed seas. Erik Franckx and Marco Benatar, 'The "Duty" to Co-Operate for States Bordering Enclosed or Semi-Enclosed Seas', in *Chinese (Taiwan) Yearbook of International Law and Affairs, Volume 31 (2013)* (Brill Nijhoff, 2016), 66–81.

101 Leszek Buszynski and Iskandar Sazlan, 'Maritime Claims and Energy Cooperation in the South China Sea', *Contemporary Southeast Asia* 29, no. 1 (2007): 143–71.

activities in the region shall be conducive to enhancing mutual trust'; 'mutual port calls of military vessels and joint patrols on regular basis'; 'joint military exercises among China and ASEAN Member States on a regular basis'.[102] One of China's proposals stands out:

> The Parties shall establish a notification mechanism on military activities, and to notify each other of major military activities if deemed necessary. The Parties shall not hold joint military exercises with countries from outside the region, unless the parties concerned are notified beforehand and express no objection.[103]

This provision would give China a veto over joint military exercises between ASEAN states and, for instance, the US, Japan, European states, or other countries from outside Southeast Asia. ASEAN members are very unlikely to accept this provision. While China's proposed restrictions on military activities in China's 1999 draft code (paragraph 9) would have restricted military activities in general terms, China's proposal of 2018 would restrict joint US–ASEAN exercises, but not China's exercises.

Vietnam proposed a list of specific activities states should refrain from doing: 'construct on any artificial island, militarise features, blockade vessels carrying provisions or personnel for rotation, declare an Air Defense Identification Zone, and conduct simulated attacks at the vessels of other countries.'[104] China conducted these activities in the South or East China Sea – China announced an Air Defense Identification Zone in the East China Sea – in the past. China is unlikely to accept this list of restrictions until the point when China will no longer rely on these activities in the defence or advancement of its claims. Beijing suggested restrictions on law enforcement activities in its 1999 draft code. In 2018, however, as China had the largest law enforcement operations, it was very unlikely to accept these restrictions.

Furthermore, Vietnam proposed that the code of conduct 'be subject to ratification',[105] that it shall be deposited and registered pursuant to the Charter of the United Nations, and that no party may add a reservation when signing the code. These features would turn the code into a legally binding treaty. The Philippines suggested a provision on 'respect of the exercise of

102 Thayer, 'A Closer Look at the ASEAN-China Single Draft South China Sea Code of Conduct'.
103 Ibid.
104 Ibid.
105 Ibid.

traditional fishing rights by fishermen [and] access to features and fishing grounds'.[106] China did not grant Filipino fishermen access to Scarborough Shoal between April 2012 and September 2016 and permitted access to areas around the shoal only occasionally after the arbitral tribunal's decision. The tribunal deemed this practice unlawful and vindicated Philippine traditional fishing rights.[107] Malaysia inserted a formula for the geographic scope of the code. It reads, 'depending on the operative elements/contents of the COC, the geographic scope/scope of application may have to be defined.'[108] This insertion reflects the general problem that challenged negotiations on the code, and on fishery or joint development agreements: the more specific the rules, the more specific states' proposals on the geographic scope need to be. Although a state may be willing to accept stricter rules for some areas, it may not be willing to accept the same rules for other geographic areas. It will be more difficult to find a consensus among claimant states about substantive restrictions for behaviour, e.g., to refrain from certain coercive law enforcement activities, if these commitments are not limited geographically. Agreement between all parties on the geographic scope, though, remains a crucial condition and a most contentious issue.

This overview demonstrates that ASEAN members and China have not yet found specific, substantial, and uncontroversial provisions for a code of conduct as of 2023. The 2002 Declaration and other previous documents already contain several provisions that were also proposed in 2018. These provisions appear uncontroversial but were not effective in preventing the rise of tensions and escalations after 2002. China and ASEAN states also made little progress in cooperative activities in the issue areas the 2002 Declaration mentions. Crucially, earlier draft codes – ASEAN's 1999 draft, China's 1999 draft, the Philippines' 2012 draft, and Indonesia's 2012 zero draft – contained variants of further recently proposed provisions, but one or the other state objected to them in the past. Several new proposals appear to be directed directly against activities claimant states relied on to protect or advance their claims in the past. Short of a profound change of policy, agreement on these provisions is unlikely. Such a change of policy can only be expected when states judge they have achieved what they wanted.

According to one source, Vietnam dropped the proposal to restrict coercive law enforcement, island construction, Air Defense Identification

106 Ibid.

107 The South China Sea Arbitration, 2016 paras. 257–272.

108 Quoted in: Thayer, 'A Closer Look at the ASEAN-China Single Draft South China Sea Code of Conduct'.

Zones, blockades, and the use of force after the Single Draft's first reading in 2019.[109] And China dropped restrictions on military exercises with non-regional states. If these changes were confirmed, they would not only amount to an apparent bilateral Sino-Vietnamese bargain, but also in Vietnam dropping the provisions 'with teeth'. This apparent bilateral bargain would also illustrate that the Single Draft negotiating procedure allows China to make bilateral bargains with single ASEAN members and that ASEAN members did not build a coherent coalition in the current code of conduct negotiations.

In September 2020, China cited the COVID-19 pandemic and the need to resist interference from a 'certain country outside the region' as reasons why China did not consent to the Philippines' efforts to continue the second reading of the Single Draft.[110] The COVID-19 pandemic interrupted the negotiation process but was certainly not a reason for the lack of agreement on a code. China has, however, continued to rhetorically link progress in code of conduct negotiations with 'resist[ing] the interference' from 'outside the region'.[111] China continues to see in the code of conduct a possible instrument for reducing US influence and presence in Southeast Asia.

1.4 Code of Conduct Negotiations Reconsidered

Seven points on the code of conduct result from this analysis. First, several claimants tried to restrict the type of conflict behaviour the respective rival claimant relied on in the past to improve its position unilaterally: occupations, land reclamation, interference with economic activities of another side, forcible coast guard actions, navy operations, military exercises, acts of harassment, etc. The objective to increase stability within a dispute necessitates specific restrictions on conflict behaviour. Such restrictions on conduct, however, require the consent of adversaries to restrict the means they adopted to enforce or defend claims. If rival claimants agree to tie their hands regarding the coercive activities that escalated disputes in the past, this would be an effective management of the disputes. But the more claimants commit to not using their preferred means to defend or advance their claims, the closer they move to a commitment to freezing the status quo.

109 Carlyle A. Thayer, 'ASEAN, China and the South China Sea Code of Conduct' (Presentation to Maritime Security Research Group Workshop, The University of New South Wales, Canberra, 14 October 2019).

110 'Chinese Embassy Spokesperson on Code of Conduct in the South China Sea', 18 September 2020, http://ph.china-embassy.org/eng/sgfyrbt/t1815987.htm (accessed 19 April 2022).

111 Ibid.

This is a high bar for an effective code of conduct. Consequently, an effective code requires greater political commitments than crisis communication, environmental protection, fisheries, or joint development agreements.

Second, core disagreements were not caused by irreconcilable interests or by the question of how to distribute gains from joint action, but by the question of how to distribute power. The rival claimants have bargained about restrictions on the type of behaviour and the options in which respective opponents have had an advantage. One key disagreement that has been preventing a code of conduct is the question of onto which side a code would distribute power. Vietnam and the Philippines proposed substantive provisions requiring China to restrain its activities and to reduce its power advantages in the disputes, e.g., by restricting coercive claimant tactics, island construction, and militarization. Clearly, such restrictions would be effective conflict management, but they would also reduce China's advantages. China had a similar preference: to design an institution that limits Southeast Asian states' use of strategic assets, for instance, cooperation with the US and non-regional actors. Two recent Chinese proposals could be read as Beijing's attempt to define the code of conduct as what may be called an 'institution of exclusion', deriving a term from Lascurettes' 'order of exclusion'.[112] China's proposal to restrict joint military operations with 'countries from outside the region' would restrict ASEAN members' options to form coalitions and to counterbalance militarily. It would also limit non-regional countries' navigational freedoms and access in contravention of the law of the sea. China's proposal to restrict ASEAN members' cooperation with non-regional companies regarding hydrocarbon resources can be regarded as another institution of exclusion. Although ASEAN members' consent to these proposals is very unlikely,[113] China's proposed code aims at enlisting Southeast Asian states in China's efforts to establish an exclusive regional order in terms of naval and strategic issues. Negotiations on a code of conduct are not just a reflection of an underlying and ongoing power game. A code of conduct is itself a tool in the power game.

Third, as noted above, actors expected that various proposals for a geographic scope of a code would 'consolidate' or 'legalize' an opponent's gains or imply 'consent to a new status quo'. In a legal sense, a code does

112 Kyle M. Lascurettes, *Orders of Exclusion: Great Powers and the Strategic Sources of Foundational Rules in International Relations* (OUP, 2020).

113 Philippine Foreign Secretary Locsin rejected this attempt publicly. Aie Balagtas See, 'Philippines Foreign Secretary Challenges "China's Demand" on South China Sea', *Benarnews*, 21 September 2020, https://www.benarnews.org/english/news/philippine/western-powers-09212020142758.html (accessed 19 April 2024).

not legalize an otherwise unlawful status and does not affect the status of claims. Still, the idea that a specific geographic code would establish a layer of validity for a rival position proved a consequential barrier to agreement. Theoretically, this concern could be understood as actors preventing that a code's 'wrong' geographic scope would establish a focal point from which an opponent would not retreat in subsequent interactions. To overcome disagreements, claimant states reduced the code's scope and agreed on non-binding agreements with ambiguous definitions.

Fourth, the fragmented nature of ASEAN delayed negotiations and has implied that ASEAN is less powerful than the sum of its parts. ASEAN members coordinated internally to cope with this difficulty. When China rejected key provisions of a hard-won common ASEAN position in 1999, however, ASEAN members did not pursue the common draft code and were left without a common negotiation position. The effect was that ASEAN would have needed time to coordinate internally to develop a new negotiation position. Not much was required then for China to resist the adoption of a code of conduct. As noted above, previous ASEAN draft codes did not survive first encounters with China. A fragmented coalition without a fallback option risks ending up in a coalition without a negotiation position. Huang observed in 2022 that 'ASEAN committed China to a hard timeline for the completion of the COC agreement, a breakthrough' that he attributed to a strong ASEAN consensus.[114] In retrospect, it is clear that there is no deadline for code of conduct negotiations, nor a breakthrough or strong ASEAN consensus on the substance of a code. The negotiation procedure of the Single Draft Negotiating Text, which was adopted in 2018, differs substantively from previous procedures. In this procedure, ASEAN members have not tried to form an ASEAN coalition before negotiating with China. Vietnam and Malaysia, for example, put forward different provisions regarding the geographic scope during negotiations already involving China. Instead, each ASEAN member and China have proposed their preferred provisions. Each party can respond to each party's proposals. Using the Single Draft negotiation procedure, ASEAN did not enter the negotiations as a bloc.

Fifth, all actors involved needed to balance the potential benefits from cooperation on conflict management against the potential losses in options to advance or defend their claims. On the one hand, disputing countries have an incentive to improve their security by stabilizing a conflict situation through restrictions on conflict behaviour. On the other hand, the disputing

114 Chin-Hao Huang, *Power and Restraint in China's Rise* (Columbia UP, 2022), 73.

parties have an incentive not to accept restrictions on the means with which they advance or defend their claims. Both China and ASEAN states do not want to allow the disputes to dominate the bilateral relations. China is aware that it needs to keep the negotiation processes ongoing to prevent a further deterioration of its relations with several ASEAN states. Despite the many delays, disagreements, and disappointments, ASEAN members and China have continued to negotiate a code. As a settlement of boundary and sovereignty questions is not merely attempted, a code of conduct remains the preferred negotiated option, even if the various declarations and documents did not result in effective institutions for conflict management.

Sixth, since the 2002 Declaration on Conduct various documents called for cooperative practices in functional issue areas such as marine environmental protection, marine scientific research, and combating transnational crime. While more than a dozen ASEAN-related working groups deal with such issues,[115] the pace of consultations between China and ASEAN members on these issue areas has remained slow. Even if hydrocarbon resources are not mentioned in the Declaration, former Philippine President Arroyo still called the Joint Marine Seismic Undertaking (JMSU) the first agreement in the implementation of the Declaration and a 'historic breakthrough'.[116] But as illustrated above, various Philippine officials regarded the JMSU as an institution that expanded China's activities rather than having tamed its behaviour. While the Declaration called for maritime cooperation, it did not lay the basis for it.

Seventh, some preferences regarding the code of conduct have changed over time. China proposed limitations on law enforcement and military activities in 1999 when Chinese fishing boats were subject to Philippine law enforcement. ASEAN members did not accept these limitations at that time. Throughout the 2010s, the situation changed and the preferences regarding restrictions on law enforcement reversed. In 2018, Vietnam proposed restrictions on types of violent law enforcement measures that were conducted by the China Coast Guard. Many coercive law enforcement activities of China would clearly have violated China's draft code of 1999. Still, whether ASEAN members could have used some provisions of China's draft code of 1999 against China's activities is a counterfactual question and an answer can only be speculative.

115 'ASEAN Regional Forum Work Plan For Maritime Security 2018–2020', 5, http://aseanregionalforum.asean.org/wp-content/uploads/2019/01/ARF-Maritime-Security-Work-Plan-2018-2020.pdf (accessed 19 April 2024).
116 Chapter III 1.

2 Institutions for Crisis Management in the East and South China Sea

Officials and analysts from China, Japan, Southeast Asian states, and the US have been aware that the increased presence and use of navy and maritime law enforcement vessels and aircraft in the disputes has resulted in more and more intense incidents and in higher escalation risks.[117] As neither side has wanted conflict, claimant states have sought to improve their capacities to control escalation processes by institutionalizing incident prevention and crisis communication procedures. The objective of such instruments is to prevent escalation in cases where misperception, misinformation, human or technical error, or bureaucratic obstacles to direct communication prevent effective responses to incidents.[118] Where communication procedures apply directly to frontline actors, e.g., navy and coast guard vessels or aircraft, they offer, in principle, the benefit of reducing the likelihood of, first, the occurrence of incidents and, second, the escalation of incidents at source. Communication procedures are narrow instruments. They intend to commit captains, pilots, or, in the case of hotlines, decision makers to communication protocols during encounters or after an incident arises. They do not necessarily mandate a change of the behaviour that can lead to incidents, but they restrict such behaviour. The policy literature and interview sources acknowledge the expected gains of preventing escalation through structured communication.[119] The sources acknowledge the limited

117 Japan Ministry of Defense, 'China's Activities in East China Sea, Pacific Ocean, and Sea of Japan', March 2024, https://www.mod.go.jp/en/d_act/sec_env/pdf/ch_d-act_a.pdf (last accessed 24 April 2024); Alastair Iain Johnston, 'The Evolution of Interstate Security Crisis-Management Theory and Practice in China', *Naval War College Review* 69, no. 1 (2016): 29–72; Andrew S. Erickson and Adam P. Liff, 'Installing a Safety on the "Loaded Gun"? China's Institutional Reforms, National Security Commission and Sino–Japanese Crisis (in) Stability', *Journal of Contemporary China* 25, no. 98 (2016): 197–215; Avery Goldstein, 'First Things First: The Pressing Danger of Crisis Instability in U.S.-China Relations', *International Security* 37, no. 4 (April 2013): 49–89.

118 Sanaa Yasmin Hafeez, 'The Senkaku/Diaoyu Islands Crises of 2004, 2010, and 2012: A Study of Japanese-Chinese Crisis Management', *Asia-Pacific Review* 22, no. 1 (2 January 2015): 73–99; David A. Welch, 'Crisis Management Mechanisms Pathologies and Pitfalls', *CIGI Papers* No. 40 (September 2014): 1–19; Forrest E. Morgan et al., *Dangerous Thresholds: Managing Escalation in the 21st Century* (Rand Corporation, 2008).

119 Takuya Shimodaira, 'Measures to Enhance Maritime Safety —Expansion of Code for Unplanned Encounters at Sea (CUES) Exercise', in *Symposium Maintaining Maritime Order in the Asia-Pacific*, 2017, www.nids.mod.go.jp/english/event/symposium/pdf/2017/e-07.pdf; James Przystup et al., 'Japan-China Maritime Confidence Building and Communications Mechanisms', *Pac Net 67 Pacific Forum CSIS*, August 2013, https://www.cigionline.org/articles/japan-china-maritime-confidence-building-and-communications-mechanisms/; Euan Graham, 'Maritime

nature of the commitments under consideration, including the option of not answering calls made through structured communication procedures. The possibility of crisis management rests then on two conditions: first, the assumption that a set of rules on specified interactions such as communication protocols could prevent that an incident follows an uncontrollable action–reaction cycle towards conflict. Second, the involved actors in an incident have a common interest in preventing armed conflict as an outcome of an escalatory process.

Despite this picture, negotiations on such procedures proved to be controversial, slow, and to require top leadership intervention. Chinese and Japanese officials have negotiated a Maritime Communication Mechanism for the East China Sea since 2008. While they reached a memorandum of understanding in late 2018, its implementation has still been contentious by 2021. Moreover, the members of the West Pacific Naval Symposium, including the navies of China, Japan, South Korea, ASEAN members, and the US, agreed on a non-binding Code for Unplanned Encounters at Sea (CUES) in 2014. As noted in the chapters on the code of conduct, Indonesia's proposal for crisis communication in its Zero Draft Code of Conduct was not adopted in 2013. ASEAN members and China agreed, however, on setting up a hotline between their ministries of foreign affairs in 2016, fourteen years after the 2002 Declaration of Conduct. The question is then why the reaching of agreement on such measures is difficult, even if the involved states recognize the need for improved crisis management capacities and the limited nature of the commitments required.

The next chapter will examine the Sino-Japanese negotiations on a Maritime Communication Mechanism (also known as Air and Sea Communication Mechanism). Key disagreements between China and Japan in the bilateral negotiations were motivated by competing factual assessments within government bureaucracies. Officials have differed on whether the crisis communication agreement would result in vulnerabilities that the opponent could exploit. Some Japanese officials have cautioned whether an arrangement would allow Chinese armed forces to manipulate risk or to restrain Japanese responses to Chinese operations. Note that officials of the Japanese Ministries of Foreign Affairs and Defense as well as the Japanese Self-Defense Forces (JSDF) have disagreed on whether these vulnerabilities would indeed materialize. While the evidence for diverging factual assessments among Japanese agencies is better, some Chinese sources indicate

Hotlines in East Asia', *RSIS Policy Brief*, May 2014, https://www.rsis.edu.sg/rsis-publication/idss/maritime-hotlines-in-east-asia/ (accessed 19 April 2024).

that Chinese officials have held mirror image views. The subsequent chapter on CUES will illustrate that Chinese officials rejected earlier versions of CUES because of the related issues of the geographic scope, restrictions on operations in territorial seas, and implications for China's position on freedom of navigation.

2.1 The Japan–China Air and Sea Communication Mechanism 2008–2020

The context

With an increasing number of Chinese air force and navy operations in the East China Sea, the establishment of an air and sea communication mechanism to improve crisis management capacities became a Sino-Japanese policy objective. In response to China's unilateral hydrocarbon projects in areas of overlapping claims in the centre of the East China Sea, Sino-Japanese tensions rose with increased navy and air force operations in 2005.[120] The number of annual scrambles of Japan's self-defence forces against China's aircraft was between zero and thirteen until 2004; it jumped to 107 in 2005. The number of Japanese annual scrambles scaled back to around forty until 2009. It started moving up continuously and in 2016 Japanese scrambles against Chinese aircraft numbered 851 – on average 2.3 Japanese scrambles against Chinese aircraft per day.[121] Japanese aircraft operate to protect sovereignty when aircraft approach its airspace or the Senkaku/Diaoyu Islands or to be in place in case a Chinese aircraft changes direction. Uncertainty about direction and mission is a characteristic of aircraft operations. Japanese officials do not generally regard the increase in Chinese air operations as an attempt to intimidate Japan.[122] Rather, an increase in the number of China's assets is assumed to have led to an increase in operations. For Japan, however, it is difficult to assess in which cases China's air operations are training or intelligence operations and in which cases the operations want to test Japan's reaction.[123] The ensuing potential for misperception has led to some dangerous and provocative

120 Chapter IV 1.

121 Japanese Ministry of Defence, 'China's Maritime Expansion', April 2017. For comparison, the number of Japanese scrambles during the Cold War peaked at 944 in 1984.

122 Interview with a Deputy Director-General level official, Ministry of Defence of Japan, Tokyo, 13 July 2017 (Interview 31).

123 Interview with a General of the Japanese Self-Defence Forces, Tokyo, 21 July 2017 (Interview 37).

encounters in the air.[124] A Chinese security scholar reports near misses between aircraft.[125] The number of Chinese surface combatant vessels passing annually through Japan's various straits from the East China Sea into the Western Pacific (Soya Straits and Tsugaru Straits, Miyakojima Strait, Nansei Islands) multiplied from one or two in the late 2000s to about twenty in 2017. China also started a routinized monthly presence of coast guard vessels in the territorial waters of the Senkaku/Diaoyu Islands in 2011.[126] From the Japanese perspective, an incident involving a Chinese submarine in Japanese waters further demonstrated the need for crisis communication capacities. While Japan's navy tried to chase and identify the submarine, Japanese diplomats tried to pre-empt escalatory reactions. To the surprise of Japanese defence officials, it became clear that Japan's navy had no direct communication channel to the PLA Navy for such incidents.[127] Interview sources from both sides acknowledged the possibility that incidents involving military assets could escalate quickly and that a shooting war, once started, may not be immediately stoppable.

The possibility to establish direct communication between relevant actors (pilots, captains of involved vessels, and bureaucracies) becomes an urgent matter in this context. Crisis communication capacities at an operational level take on strategic significance. As structural bureaucratic obstacles have limited direct and effective communication during past crises,[128] the case for institutionalized communication procedures has been strong. China reformed its domestic crisis response and inter-agency decision-making structures following several salient incidents.[129] China's and Japan's top leadership acknowledged the need to establish crisis communication procedures already in 2007. A Japan–China Joint Press Statement during the visit of China's Premier Wen Jiabao to Japan in April 2007 noted that 'a communication mechanism between the two defence authorities will be established, and thereby, prevent the occurrence of unforeseen circumstances at sea'.[130] The need for crisis communication has increased

124 Interview 31.

125 Interview with a professor of international security at Peking University, Beijing, 26 April 2017 (Interview 28).

126 Japanese Ministry of Defence, 'China's Maritime Expansion'.

127 Interview 31.

128 Hafeez, 'The Senkaku/Diaoyu Islands Crises of 2004, 2010, and 2012'.

129 Erickson and Liff, 'Installing a Safety on the "Loaded Gun"? China's Institutional Reforms, National Security Commission and Sino–Japanese Crisis (in) Stability'; Johnston, 'The Evolution of Interstate Security Crisis-Management Theory and Practice in China'.

130 Ministry of Foreign Affairs of Japan, 'Japan-China Joint Press Statement', 11 April 2007, https://www.mofa.go.jp/region/asia-paci/china/pv0704/joint.html (last accessed 14 April 2024).

in qualitative and in quantitative terms since 2007. However, both sides could not find terms implementing communication mechanisms by 2020.

Negotiations at the working level started in April 2008 and continued with some interruptions until June 2012. Both sides agreed that they needed to work out terms for three elements: (i) the holding of annual meetings of defence and security experts at working level, (ii) the establishment of hotlines between the defence ministries, and (iii) the adoption of communication procedures between naval vessels and aircraft.[131] Japan and China aimed hence at a more comprehensive agreement than CUES, which is limited to naval communication procedures. Regarding point (i), Japan's SDF and China's PLA had no regular high-level military contact hitherto, and agreement on annual meetings would establish this contact. An open question in the negotiations was about the topic for the annual meetings – whether meetings should focus on increasing military transparency generally (China's position) or also review specific incidents (Japanese position). Regarding point (ii), an important question has been which bureaucracy and what level should be the contact point of a direct communication line.[132] To increase the effectiveness of a hotline, contact points need to have authority in the respective lines of command. While the Japanese Ministry of Defense has such authority, a contact point with operational authority over military operations in China is the PLA.[133] The symmetrical Ministry of Defense or the Ministry of Foreign Affairs lack this authority.[134] I will discuss the negotiations regarding point (iii) in detail below.

Before both sides reached agreement on terms for these three elements, Japan nationalized the Senkaku/Diaoyu Islands in September 2012.[135] Negotiations stopped and resumed only in January 2015. Observers from both sides expected agreement in 2015, but this expectation did not materialize.[136] Interview sources in Beijing and Tokyo expressed their hope for an agreement

131 Shimodaira, 'Measures to Enhance Maritime Safety'.

132 Interview 31.

133 Erickson and Liff, 'Installing a Safety on the "Loaded Gun"? China's Institutional Reforms, National Security Commission and Sino–Japanese Crisis (in) Stability'.

134 Linda Jakobson and Ryan Manuel, 'How Are Foreign Policy Decisions Made in China? Foreign Policy Decisions Made in China', *Asia & the Pacific Policy Studies* 3, no. 1 (January 2016): 101–10.

135 Tokyo's Governor Ishihara Shintaro played a key role in forcing the nationalization of the disputed islands, see Reinhard Drifte, 'The Senkaku/Diaoyu Islands Territorial Disputee Between Japan and China: Between the Materialization of the "China Threat" and Japan "Reversing the Outcome of World War II"?', in *UNISCI Discussion Papers*, no. 32, 2013, 1–55.

136 'Japan, China eye May talks on maritime crisis management mechanism', *The Japan Times*, 14 March 2015, https://www.japantimes.co.jp/news/2015/03/14/national/japan-china-eye-may-talks-on-maritime-crisis-management-mechanism/#.VdMZpxOqqNL (last accessed 19 April 2024).

in mid-2017. Negotiations, however, continued without result. While Japanese news outlets reported a memorandum of understanding on a communication mechanism in June 2018,[137] statements of the Japanese Ministry of Defense clarified that the hotline and essential details of the communication procedures had not been implemented by June 2019.[138] Incidents between Chinese aircraft and Japanese destroyers in August 2019 – Chinese aircraft reportedly used a Japanese destroyer as a mock target during a missile drill[139] – provide further evidence for the lack of any mechanisms. The question is then which obstacles have blocked agreement on an effective instrument over more than ten years.

Diverging assessments about crisis communication among state bureaucracies

A manifest disagreement between China and Japan is about the geographic coverage of the communication procedures for navies and air forces. Japanese officials have insisted on excluding territorial seas from the arrangement; Chinese negotiators have insisted on including the territorial seas.[140] Note that China has not applied the Code for Unplanned Encounters (CUES) in the territorial seas of the South China Sea but has insisted that the territorial seas of the Senkaku/Diaoyu Islands should be included in the Sino-Japanese communication mechanism. Also note that China and Japan agreed on CUES in 2014 such that it cannot be a general unease with communication arrangements that prevents agreement in the present case. The question is then why the inclusion or exclusion of the territorial waters in the crisis communication mechanism is so contentious as to prevent

137 Shinichi Akiyama, 'Japan, China Launch Maritime-Aerial Communication Mechanism', *Mainichi Japan*, 8 June 2018, https://mainichi.jp/english/articles/20180608/p2a/00m/0na/002000c; Michael Kovrig, 'How a Long-Awaited Hotline Could Pave the Way for Calmer China-Japan Relations', *South China Morning Post*, 13 May 2018, https://www.scmp.com/news/china/diplomacy-defence/article/2145811/how-long-awaited-hotline-could-pave-way-calmer-china (last accessed 19 April 2024).

138 Ministry of Defence of Japan, 'Japan-China Defense Ministers' Meeting (Summary)', 1 June 2019, https://www.mod.go.jp/en/d_act/exc/area/docs/2019/20190601_j-china_e.html (last accessed 19 April 2024).

139 'Chinese Aircraft Used Japanese Ships as Targets in East China Sea Drill: Gov't', *Kyodo News*, 19 August 2019, https://english.kyodonews.net/news/2019/08/b9e1c11f12b8-chinese-aircraft-use-japan-ships-as-targets-in-e-china-sea-drill.html (last accessed 19 April 2024).

140 Retired Vice Admiral of Japan's Maritime Self-Defence Forces Hideaki Kaneda, 'Management of Incidents at Sea', paper presented at the 8th South China Sea International Conference, Nha Trang, Vietnam, (13–15 November 2016), (on file with the author). This disagreement was confirmed by several Chinese and Japanese interview sources.

agreement for ten years. There are diverging assessments of this question among Chinese and Japanese officials. An issue about which Japanese officials have diverging views is whether Chinese military actors could exploit an institution for crisis communication in a manipulative way to advance China's objectives.

Different Japanese sources explain Japan's position to exclude the territorial waters from a communication procedure with the following arguments. One defence analyst argued that China could 'use it [the agreement] to justify its presence in the territorial seas'.[141] Japan could not accept the presence of Chinese vessels and aircraft in its (disputed and undisputed) territorial seas. Adopting bilateral measures for the territorial seas would, however, imply to validate a Chinese presence. This would raise the issue of whether the inclusion of the territorial seas could be taken as a first step towards co-management and a 'slice of the salami' in the Senkaku/Diaoyu dispute.[142] In a similar vein, observers argue that Japan regards the inclusion of the territorial seas 'as a ploy to legitimise China's presence in what it claims as sovereign waters'.[143]

Japanese sources also brought forward a more practical assessment of how China could gain advantages from the 'justification' of the presence of Chinese assets in the Senkaku/Diaoyu areas. The inclusion of the airspace above the territorial seas could 'justify' Chinese presence and thereby result in an increased presence of Chinese assets.[144] An increase in the number of Chinese air and navy operations could allow China to 'establish precedent for its behaviour' resulting in even more frequent intrusions.[145] One explanation for Japan's position to exclude the territorial waters could then be that Japanese officials expect the inclusion of the territorial seas to result in an increased Chinese presence in this particular area.[146] While Chinese aircraft entered the territorial airspace of the Senkaku/Diaoyu Islands in only a few

141 Interview with a scholar of a leading think tank on security affiliated with Japan's Ministry of Foreign Affairs, Tokyo, 14 July 2017 (Interview 33).

142 Interview with a senior official of Japan's Ministry of Foreign Affairs, Tokyo, 19 July 2017 (interview 35).

143 Ashley Townshend and Rory Medcalf, *Shifting Waters: China's New Passive Assertiveness in Asian Maritime Security*, Report (Lowy Institute for international Policy, 2016), 11.

144 Interview 35.

145 Marta McLellan Ross, 'The Japan-China Maritime and Air Communication Mechanism: Operational and Strategic Considerations', *Japanese Institute of International Affairs* 30 (2015), 3 https://www2.jiia.or.jp/pdf/fellow_report/150630_Ms_Ross_ECS.pdf (last accessed 19 April 2024).

146 Townshend and Medcaff, *Shifting Waters: China's New Passive Assertiveness* quoting Japanese interview sources.

cases, for instance in December 2012,[147] China's Coast Guard used to enter the territorial waters of the Senkaku/Diaoyu Islands three times per month and has since increased its monthly presence.

The policy literature suggests another argument why communication procedures could result in an increase in Chinese operations. This argument rests on two ideas: the idea that certain levels of risk protect an actor against activities of an opponent that are associated with that risk, and the idea that an opponent could use communication mechanisms to restrain an adversary's response after a certain action is completed. This argument, if correct, would offer another explanation why Japan is reluctant to accept communication capacities. Ross suggests that the crisis communication measures under negotiations could 'constrain Japanese responses to Chinese actions around the Senkaku Islands' while Chinese forces could be 'emboldened to challenge Japan's control … because of their confidence that Japan will rely on the mechanism to diffuse escalation'.[148] Townshend and Medcalf suggest that China is using 'tactical restraint to ensure that its efforts to establish a new status quo do not provoke conflict'.[149] This explanation rests on the expectation that the crisis communication procedures could result in the following Japanese vulnerability. Once risk is off the table, there is a lower barrier to provocative action. To thwart this consequence, Japanese officials are reluctant to agree on procedures.

Japanese defence and security officials were divided on this argument. One senior Japanese defence official argued that crisis communication measures would not restrict Japanese responses to Chinese activities in territorial waters and would not constrain proportionate responses.[150] A Japanese Air Self-Defence Force general maintained that the current number of Chinese aircraft patrols does not depend on the level of risk.[151] Bilateral communication procedures are hence unlikely to affect the number of Chinese air and sea operations. The frequency of the latter is dependent on the exigencies of assets, training, and intelligence operations. A senior defence official and a general-level official further questioned whether the disagreement regarding the geographic scope is

147 'China's Maritime Expansion', Report of Japan's Ministry of Defence, April 2017 (on file with the author).

148 Ross, 'The Japan-China Maritime and Air Communication Mechanism', 3.

149 Townshend and Medcalf, *Shifting Waters: China's New Passive Assertiveness*, 18.

150 Interview 31.

151 Interview with a General of the Japanese Self-Defence Forces, Tokyo, 21 July 2017 (Interview 37).

motivated by operational considerations.[152] According to these sources, the exclusion of the airspace above the territorial waters raises practical considerations, for instance, stemming from the speed with which aircraft operates near the Senkaku/Diaoyu Islands' airspace. The time Chinese aircraft will stay in the islands' airspace in the event of an incursion is likely to be short. If Chinese and Japanese aircraft have established contact, and then one aircraft changes direction and enters the Senkaku/Diaoyu airspace, the question arises as to whether both sides should stop communicating. In this vein, another Japanese source argued that the PLA Navy could accept the exclusion of the territorial sea, but not the PLA Air Force.[153] As noted, the navies of China and Japan adopted the non-binding communication procedures of CUES which are not applied to territorial seas in practice.

Chinese sources argue that the maritime zones and the airspace near the disputed Senkaku/Diaoyu Islands are a hotspot in bilateral relations. Hence, if there is an area where measures for crisis management are most needed, then it is the Senkaku/Diaoyu area.[154] From a Chinese perspective, excluding the hotspot from such measures might look like validating Japan's position that the Senkaku/Diaoyu islands are 'undisputed'.[155] The Chinese argument is that excluding the geographic area for which direct communication is most needed can only have the political motivation of producing evidence against China's claim.

While Ross stated that the air and sea mechanism 'does not apply to a collision within territorial waters or airspace, an incident tantamount to an act of war',[156] the record of existing communication arrangements illustrates that it is up to negotiators to include or exclude a specification of a geographic scope. On the one hand, collisions that occur in disputed territorial seas or airspace are highly escalatory and, accordingly, make crisis communication capacities particularly desirable. On the other hand, the issue of the inclusion or exclusion of the territorial seas has also been a key barrier to agreement. During the Sino-Japanese negotiations, Chinese negotiators have cited the US–China memorandum of understanding regarding the Rules of Behavior for Safety of Air and Maritime Encounters as

152 Interview 37 and Interview 31.

153 Interview 33.

154 Interview 28, with a professor of international security at Peking University, Beijing, 26 April 2017; Interview 31, with a Deputy Director-General level official, Ministry of Defence of Japan, Tokyo, 13 July 2017.

155 Ibid.

156 Ross, 'The Japan-China Maritime and Air Communication Mechanism', 2.

precedent for China's position.[157] This MoU does not exclude some geographic areas specifically. According to Chinese sources, Japanese negotiators have cited their own communication agreements with Russia and the Republic of Korea as precedent; these agreements define a geographic scope where the agreements apply.[158] In the Cold War era, the US and the USSR reached an agreement on the 'Prevention of Incidents On and Over the High Seas' (INCSEA) which defines a geographic scope (the high seas).[159] The US–China MoU regarding the Rules of Behavior for Safety of Air and Maritime Encounters, though, does not specify a geographic area and mentions only encounters 'at sea or in the air'. This MoU is not binding and does not ban specific behaviour.

A further relevant question is the issue of including or excluding coast guards. Although observers from both sides suggested the inclusion of coast guards into the crisis communication mechanism, Chinese and Japanese officials have insisted that they cannot accept formal restrictions on forcible measures of maritime law enforcement agencies. A Japanese official argued that 'the inclusion of law enforcement agencies would establish a "slippery slope" towards joint management of the islands'.[160] Chinese officials stated that China cannot accept restrictions on maritime law enforcement activities because the mission of these is to enforce Chinese laws.[161] Crucially, the inclusion of coast guards would necessitate agreement between China and Japan regarding the application of direct communication mechanisms to the territorial waters of the Senkaku/Diaoyu islands. It is especially in these territorial waters where Japanese and Chinese coast guard vessels confront each other and where Japanese coast guard vessels try to maintain a permanent presence.[162]

157 Interview 28; see the 'Memorandum of Understanding Between the Department of Defense of the United States of America and the Ministry of National Defense of the People's Republic of China Regarding the Rules of Behavior for Safety of Air and Maritime Encounters', 9th and 10th November 2014, https://dod.defense.gov/Portals/1/Documents/pubs/141112_MemorandumOfUnderstandingRegardingRules.pdf (last accessed 19 April 2024).

158 Interview 28.

159 Agreement Between the Government of The United States of America and the Government of The Union of Soviet Socialist Republics on the Prevention of Incidents On and Over the High Seas (INCSEA), 25 May 1972, accessible at https://www.state.gov/t/isn/4791.htm (last accessed 19 April 2024).

160 Townshend and Medcalf, *Shifting Waters: China's New Passive Assertiveness*, 32, quoting Japanese interview sources.

161 Interview with a senior PLA Navy officer, China, 30 October 2019 (interview 45).

162 Japanese Ministry of Defense, 'China's Maritime Expansion. Report'.

2.2 Air and Sea Communication Reconsidered

The analysis of the Sino-Japanese negotiations about crisis communication illustrates the existence of factually diverging assessments among Japanese officials of the Ministries of Foreign Affairs, Defense and the JSDF. These competing assessments are about the question of whether institutions for crisis communication could result in an increase in the frequency of Chinese activities, and whether China could gain advantages from an arrangement to advance claims. Officials from the Ministry of Foreign Affairs have been more concerned about this impact than officials from Defense or the JSDF. A part of the delay appears to be due to competing assessments within the Japanese government about whether a communication agreement would limit Japanese responses to future challenges from China and whether it would incentivise more frequent Chinese operations. Another barrier to agreement was the issue of whether the arrangement would apply to disputed territorial seas and airspace or not. The contentious issues are whether a set of rules that are meant to increase stability in conflict interactions expose a state to threats that emerge because of these rules.

While Chinese and Japanese state actors can readily agree that they need to improve their crisis communication, disagreements about the precise provisions and their institutional design prevent or delay agreement. The diverging positions on the use of incident prevention and direct communication measures for territorial seas demonstrate that claimant states' priority of not exposing their claims to potential vulnerabilities thwarts agreement even if the parties acknowledge the benefits of such measures. The disagreement on the inclusion or exclusion of the disputed territorial seas of the Senkaku/Diaoyu Islands could be understood in the following way. Both sides have tried to prevent the establishment of a layer of validity in favour of the rival claim. The disagreements about the specific provisions turn around the question of how the agreement would affect each party's leverage in future interactions. Unless the agreement includes this concern, there has been no agreement.

In short, the reasons Chinese and Japanese officials and observers bring forward for the delay and contentious nature of the communication agreement revolve around the issue of whether the agreement would result in vulnerabilities that the respective opponent could exploit to make gains. Officials and negotiators are worried about possibilities that institutions for direct communication justify and increase an opponent's air and sea operations, validate a rival claim, restrain responses to a fait accompli, or allow a manipulation of risk. Officials do not agree on the nature of the vulnerability. Especially Japanese officials from different ministries and agencies disagreed in their assessments of which of these vulnerabilities a rival could actually take advantage of. This suggests that a reason for the delay in the negotiations is the existence of factually diverging assessments in the different government agencies. These disagreements, however, are about the question of whether an opponent could use a direct communication agreement to improve their position in a dispute.

2.3 The Code for Unplanned Encounters 2003–2018

Background to the Code for Unplanned Encounters at Sea

An increasing number of incidents, naval standoffs and violent clashes between maritime law enforcement and naval vessels in the East and South China Sea highlights the need for a basic framework for interactions between vessels at sea. Such a basic framework would have various objectives. The Australian Navy proposed a document in 1999 that 'offers means by which navies may safeguard and advance their rights, duties, freedoms and responsibilities, develop… broad-based involvement in establishing international standards in relation to the use of the sea'.[163] The Western Pacific Naval Symposium (WPNS)[164] amended this proposal at the WPNS 2003 and drafted a voluntary code, the Code for Unalerted Encounters at Sea (the 2003 Code).[165] Several navies of the WPNS have adopted the 2003 Code; the US navy has used it since 2011.[166] The 2003 Code defined, among other provisions, measures for casual and unexpected encounters between 'warships, submarines, public vessels or naval aircraft' (paragraph 1.3). The

163 The Editors, 'Code for Unalerted Encounters at Sea', *Australian Journal of Maritime & Ocean Affairs* 4, no. 4 (January 2012): 126–30.
164 The WPNS is a series of multilateral meetings to discuss and improve maritime and naval cooperation among Pacific states and navies. The WPNS has twenty-one member states and four observers. These include the coastal states in the East China Sea (China, Japan, and Republic of Korea) and South China Sea (China, Vietnam, the Philippines, Brunei, Malaysia, Indonesia, and Singapore), the US, Australia, France, Canada, and India. The WPNS holds regular meetings and workshops to discuss naval matters. On the WPNS, see Jie Du and Hao Qui, 'Western Pacific Naval Symposium and Asia-Pacific Multilateral Cooperation on Maritime Security', *China Int'l Stud.* 46 (2014): 57–70; John Mortimer, 'Western Pacific Naval Symposium', *Maritime Studies* 1996, no. 87 (March 1996): 8–9.
165 Anh Duc Ton, 'Code for Unplanned Encounters at Sea and Its Practical Limitations in the East and South China Seas', *Australian Journal of Maritime & Ocean Affairs* 9, no. 4 (2 October 2017): 227–39. The 2003 code is reproduced in The Editors, 'Code for Unalerted Encounters at Sea'.
166 James Kraska, 'Maritime Confidence-Building Measures for Navigation in the South China Sea', *The International Journal of Marine and Coastal Law* 32, no. 2 (2017): 268–97, 284.

geographic scope of the 2003 Code was defined as 'the high seas, territorial waters, contiguous zones, exclusive economic zones (EEZ), and the archipelagic waters of an archipelagic state' (paragraph 1.6). At a meeting of the WPNS held in Malaysia in 2012, China was the only state to object to the adoption of the 2003 Code.[167] China explained its rejection at the subsequent WPNS meeting in 2013. Chinese navy officials argued that any code for encounters at sea cannot apply to territorial seas and cannot be called a Code for 'unalerted' encounters.[168] According to China's national laws, foreign warships need to seek prior authorization from China before entering China's territorial waters.[169] Consequentially, the PLA Navy cannot endorse rules for encounters in China's territorial seas that are 'unalerted'[170] and the PLA Navy rejected the 2003 Code. PLA Navy officials also anticipated that the 2003 Code would have entailed restrictions on its maritime law enforcement activities in claimed territorial seas in the South China Sea.[171] Moreover, Chinese Navy officials expected the word 'code' to entrain legally binding connotations.[172] Note, however, that China has insisted that the communication mechanism with Japan apply to the territorial seas of the Senkaku/Diaoyu Islands.

In consequence, several provisions of the 2003 Code needed to change to accommodate China's concerns regarding innocent passage and maritime law enforcement. China insisted that the new draft no longer included a provision on the geographic scope. The new draft also reiterated the non-binding nature of the arrangement, and it changed its title from 'unalerted' to 'unplanned' encounters at sea. After these changes, the WPNS reached agreement on the *Code for Unplanned Encounters at Sea* (CUES) in Qingdao on 22 April 2014.[173] China and ASEAN members reaffirmed their commit-

167 Anh Duc Ton, 'Code for Unplanned Encounters at Sea and Its Practical Limitations', 229.
168 Ibid.
169 Keyuan Zou, 'Innocent Passage for Warships: The Chinese Doctrine and Practice', *Ocean Development & International Law* 29, no. 3 (1998): 195–223. According to section 3 of UNCLOS all ships enjoy innocent passage in the territorial sea and a prior authorization request is inconsistent with the right to innocent passage. See e.g. Myron H. Nordquist, et al., eds., *Freedom of Seas, Passage Rights and the 1982 Law of the Sea Convention*, Center for Oceans Law and Policy 13 (Martinus Nijhoff Publishers, 2009).
170 Interview with a Senior PLA Navy officer, China, 2019 (Interview 45).
171 Interview 45.
172 Lim Han Wei, 'Code for Unplanned Encounters at Sea and Maritime Stability in the Indo-Pacific', *Journal of the Singapore Armed Forces* 42, no. 2 (2015): 12–24.
173 The Western Pacific Naval Symposium, 'Code for Unplanned Encounters at Sea', 22 April 2014, https://news.usni.org/2014/06/17/document-conduct-unplanned-encounters-sea (last accessed 19 April 2024).

ment to using CUES in September 2016, two years after their navies adopted CUES.[174]

The Code for Unplanned Encounters at Sea

The purpose of CUES is to offer:

> a means by which navies may develop mutually rewarding international cooperation and transparency and provide leadership and broad-based involvement in establishing international standards in relation to the use of the sea. The document is not legally binding; rather, it's a coordinated means of communication to maximise safety at sea (paragraph 1.1.1).

CUES contains 'safety measures and a means to limit mutual interference, to limit uncertainty, and to facilitate communication when naval ships or naval aircraft encounter each other in an unplanned manner' (paragraph 1.1.2). CUES only applies to 'unplanned' encounters when ships meet 'casually or unexpectedly' (paragraph 1.3.2). Moreover, the various national navies 'choose to adopt CUES' and they 'do so on a purely voluntary and non-binding basis' (paragraph 1.4).

The safety procedures include general provisions such as actions to avoid collisions. WPNS navies 'are expected to comply with the 1972 International Regulations of Preventing Collisions at Sea (COLREGs)'.[175] CUES specifies safety measures for formations, convoys, safe distance, and speed. Regarding exercises with submarines, 'surface ships should consider the display of the appropriate signals from the International Code of Signals to indicate the presence of submarine(s) in the area' (paragraph 2.7). Commanding officers also 'need to consider the potential ramifications before engaging in actions which could be misinterpreted'. CUES specifies which actions the 'prudent commander might generally avoid' such as the 'simulation of attacks by aiming guns, missiles, fire control radars', 'the discharge of signal rockets, weapons or other object in the direction of vessels or aircraft encountered', 'the use of laser in such a manner as to cause harm

174 'Joint Statement on the Application of the Code for Unplanned Encounters at Sea in the South China Sea', 7 September 2016, https://asean.org/wp-content/uploads/2016/09/Joint-Statement-on-the-Application-of-CUES-in-the-SCS-Final.pdf (last accessed 19 April 2024).

175 Convention on the International Regulations for Preventing Collisions at Sea, adopted 20 October 1972, entered not force 15 July 1977, https://treaties.un.org/pages/showDetails.aspx?objid=0800000280 0fcf87 (last accessed 19 April 2024).

to personnel' and other activities (paragraph 2.8). It notes that 'interference with command and control systems may constitute a safety hazard' (paragraph 2.9). Some measures are designed to prevent misjudgements due to technical error (e.g., a breakdown, paragraph 2.2). Specified technical details are designed to enable establishing contact in a timely manner (paragraph 3). An annex specifies further signals, including submarine pyrotechnic signals.

All these measures are designed to reduce the risks of accidental incidents that could arise when one vessel encounters another vessel, submarine, or aircraft of another state and needs to assess another state's naval activities before choosing an appropriate response. The possibility to follow specified communication procedures before making decisions and the awareness of the commander of the rules of CUES can be effective in preventing accidental escalation. However, incidents occurred in both the East and South China Sea when a vessel, aircraft, or helicopter intentionally engaged in activities that a 'prudent commander might generally avoid' such as the direction of fire control radars, collisions, the use of lasers, and very close overflights.

CUES does not define a geographic area of application (e.g., high seas, EEZs, or territorial seas) and does not exclude specific areas. As compliance with CUES is purely voluntary, the definition of a geographic area can remain ambiguous. Any adopting state is free to release internal rules on how navy commanders apply CUES and in which maritime zones. Observers noted that the navies do not normally use CUES in territorial seas.[176]

The PLA's shifting attitude towards engagement with foreign navies

CUES illustrates how the stance of China's armed forces towards interstate crisis management with Southeast Asian and US counterparts has changed within a relatively short period of time. The leadership of the PLA resisted entering into crisis management measures with Southeast Asian and US military actors for some time.[177] The PLA Navy objected to CUES in 2012 and 2013 because of CUES' geographic scope and implications for China's position on navigational freedoms and innocent passage. This picture contrasts with China's interactions on crisis communication with Japan which were backed by former Prime Minister Wen Jiabao since 2008.[178] The PLA's resistance

176 Wei, 'Code for Unplanned Encounters at Sea and Maritime Stability in the Indo-Pacific'.

177 Interview 33; Townshend and Medcalf, *Shifting Waters: China's New Passive Assertiveness in Asian Maritime Security*.

178 See chapter V 2.1.

also contrasts with China's Ministry of Foreign Affairs which was more open to maritime law enforcement hotlines.[179] A change of policy within China became visible at a US–China presidential summit in the US in 2013. Townshend and Medcaff quote Chinese officials who argued that 'after Xi made the "political decision [to] pave the way for CBMs [confidence-building measures]" in mid-2013, he issued a "top-down decree" within the PLA urging its leaders to pursue CBM talks with regional militaries'.[180] After Xi Jinping assumed power, the policy of PLA forces changed and negotiations on CUES became possible in 2014. Note, however, that Sino-Japanese exchanges on crisis communication already began in 2007.

Increased research about the utility and risks of crisis management measures within Chinese security and policy institutes preceded China's policy shift chronologically.[181] Chinese experts question whether China's aggressive policy on maritime disputes contradicts China's interests.[182] A major reason for this policy change and the positive attitude towards crisis communication stems arguably from China's assessment that an increased maritime presence and more frequent encounters in the East and South China Sea necessitates measures to reduce escalation risks. Moreover, some Chinese sources argue that embracing measures for crisis management allows China to manage its gradual tactics. Townshend and Medcalf quote Chinese officials to demonstrate how Chinese actors assess crisis communication instruments:

> Because CBMs make it likely that all sides will control and … prevent encounters from escalating … China and Japan can continue to send ships and planes to patrol; Chinese, Filipino, and Vietnamese vessels can all

179 *Memorandum* from Josue L. Villa, Embassy of the Republic of the Philippines in Beijing, to the Secretary of Foreign Affairs of the Republic of the Philippines (21 May 2001) (Annex 48), Vol III; *Record of Discussion: 17th Philippines-China Foreign Ministry Consultations* (14 January 2012) (Annex 204), Vol VI; chapter III 1.5.

180 Townshend and Medcalf, *Shifting Waters: China's New Passive Assertiveness in Asian Maritime Security*, 10; interview with a security analyst of a leading US security think tank, Washington DC, 16 October 2017 (Interview 43).

181 Johnston, 'The Evolution of Interstate Security Crisis-Management Theory and Practice in China'.

182 Hailong Ju, *China's Maritime Power and Strategy: History, National Security and Geopolitics* (World Scientific, 2015); Wenjuan Nie, "Xi Jinping's Foreign Policy Dilemma: One Belt, One Road or the South China Sea?," *Contemporary Southeast Asia: A Journal of International and Strategic Affairs* 38, no. 3 (2016): 422–44; Zongyou Wei, "China's Maritime Trap," *The Washington Quarterly* 40, no. 1 (January 2, 2017): 167–84; Wenjuan Nie, 'China's Domestic Strategic Debate and Confusion over the South China Sea Issue', *The Pacific Review* 31, no. 2 (4 March 2018): 188–204.

be sent to disputed waters; and China can build on disputed islands and keep disrupting US military activities in its EEZs.[183]

According to this argument, Chinese officials have judged that accepting crisis communication does not restrain China's policy but contributes to China's goals at a strategic level. Townshend and Medcalf argue that 'because the risks of military miscalculation are falling that Chinese leaders have grown more confident about taking actions such as island building, expanded military and coastguard patrols.... In fact, China is using CBMs and tactical restraint to ensure that its efforts to establish a new status quo do not provoke conflict.'[184] According to this logic, crisis management reduces the risk of China's coercive behaviour while allowing China to build up a position gradually. The question then becomes whether Southeast Asian claimants have had an incentive to be careful about such arrangements. If a higher level of risk restrains the number of China's activities and thereby protects a country against a higher number of Chinese activities, this country is likely to have an incentive to reject communication procedures and accept risk.

ASEAN members and officials, however, appear not to share this assessment. If the assessment were correct that China could exploit the resulting increase in tactical stability to advance its position gradually, then this assessment should have resonated among the navies of ASEAN members, too. ASEAN states, however, have not been reluctant to accept CUES. To the contrary, some navies of ASEAN members embraced CUES even earlier. Indonesia proposed measures for direct communication procedures already in the Zero Draft Code of Conduct in 2012. It was China that rejected CUES before 2014, not ASEAN navies. While Townshend and Medcalf's argument may be correct about the assessment of Chinese officials and thereby explain the PLA's policy shift towards accepting some incident prevention and communication measures, the navies of ASEAN states or the US do not share this assessment regarding CUES.

Is CUES effective?

The application of CUES is voluntary for 'unexpected' and 'unplanned' encounters. Navies do not have to apply CUES when ships meet in a deliberate or planned encounter. Just nine days after China and Vietnam adopted CUES, one of the South China Sea's major crises began. China

183 Townshend and Medcalf, *Shifting Waters: China's New Passive Assertiveness*, 18.
184 Ibid., 18–19.

moved the oil rig HYSY 981 for drilling operations in an area of overlapping claims south of the Paracel Islands on 1 May 2014. Vietnam resisted China's unilateral move vigorously, and China defended its operation against Vietnam's resistance. Both sides deployed a total of 200 navy and coast guard vessels that frequently rammed each other and justified their activities with the need to protect their sovereign rights.[185] CUES did not play a role in the de-escalation of this crisis. China and Vietnam had further channels of communication available, especially among military officials through party-to-party channels.[186] Neither CUES nor other communication channels, however, could prevent that the operations of a Chinese oil rig in disputed areas escalated to a two and a half-month-long crisis. In another incident, a Chinese destroyer deliberately steered on a collision course within 45 yards of the US destroyer Decatur on 30 September 2018.[187] The US destroyer conducted a freedom of navigation operation within 12 nautical miles of Chinese occupied Gaven Reef. China or the commander of the Chinese destroyer saw this as a threat to China's sovereignty over Gaven Reef and forced the Decatur to change its course by steering on a collision course. This practice shows that China does not apply CUES within areas it claims as territorial seas. Moreover, further incidents occurred after the adoption of CUES that excluded Chinese actors. In December 2018, a South Korean destroyer directed its fire control radar at a Japanese P-1 patrol aircraft.[188] CUES seems not to have played a role in diffusing this incident, even if both Korea and Japan adopted CUES.

Navies do not have to follow CUES when they choose to use escalatory or coercive means for whatever purpose. CUES does not limit the use of intentional escalatory behaviour. Moreover, CUES does not apply to

185 Embassy of Vietnam to Germany, 'International Press Conference on the situation in the East Sea', 5 June 2014, http://www.vietnambotschaft.org/international-press-conference-on-the-situation-in-the-east-sea/ (last accessed 19 April 2024); see chapter III 2.

186 Interview with an international lawyer of a leading think tank on maritime affairs affiliated with China's Ministry of Foreign Affairs, China, 13 April 2017 (Interview 22).

187 Barbara Starr et al., 'Chinese Warship in "unsafe" Encounter with US Destroyer, amid Rising US-China Tensions', *CNN*, 2 October 2018, https://edition.cnn.com/2018/10/01/politics/china-us-warship-unsafe-encounter/index.html; 'Photos Show Confrontation Between USS Decatur and a Chinese Navy Warship in South China Sea', *GCaptain*, 2 October 2018, https://gcaptain.com/photos-show-confrontation-between-uss-decatur-and-chinese-navy-warship-in-disputed-south-china-sea/ (last accessed 19 April 2024).

188 Ministry of Defense of Japan, 'Regarding the incident of an ROK naval vessel directing its fire-control radar at an MSDF patrol aircraft', December 2018, https://www.mod.go.jp/en/d_act/radar/index.html (last accessed 19 April 2024).

coast guard vessels, although these are frontline actors in Asia's maritime disputes. CUES does not contain a strict commitment to refrain from activities that a 'prudent commander might generally avoid'. It applies to commanders of vessels in circumstances each navy is free to define. The practice of not applying CUES to incidents in territorial seas greatly limits its effectiveness for the East and South China Sea disputes, as incidents in territorial seas are most contentious. It does not follow, though, that CUES is altogether an ineffective instrument. According to former US Rear Admiral McDevitt, CUES is often used between the US Navy and the PLA Navy during encounters in the high seas.[189] The Japanese and Chinese navies have also applied CUES during encounters.[190] CUES is not designed to apply to cases where states adopt coercive means as a matter of policy. Coercion is not accidental in these cases, but a deliberate means to an end. CUES does not respond to typical incidents between claimant states in the East and South China Sea.

2.4 Institutions for Crisis Management Reconsidered

Most claimant states in the East and South China Seas have experienced that relatively common maritime activities can trigger incidents. They have also learned that once an incident escalates into a crisis, the combination of obstacles to intragovernmental and intergovernmental communication, and the fear of losing by deescalating prevented the diffusion of crises. This experience explains the efforts of claimant states to institutionalize incident prevention and crisis communication procedures. What it does not explain is the question of why the claimant states cannot agree on instruments that respond to typical incidents, even after more than a decade of exchanges. The analysis reveals that China has insisted on including the territorial seas in the scope of an arrangement with Japan but has demanded excluding the territorial seas in the case of CUES. While Chinese officials began negotiating with Japan about communication procedures already in 2008, the PLA Navy was ready to discuss CUES only in 2014. Moreover, China's position towards crisis communication shifted again in 2023, when China made progress on crisis communication mechanisms with the US conditional on progress in the bilateral relationship. Despite the intuitive logic of crisis communication, different officials and countries have had diverging assessments about

189 Comment of former Rear Admiral Michael McDevitt during the 8th South China Sea International Conference, Nha Trang, Vietnam, 14–15 November 2016.
190 Shimodaira, 'Measures to Enhance Maritime Safety'.

whether such institutions result in vulnerabilities and who benefits from them in which scenarios.

For communication procedures to be effective, actors involved in an incident need to be able to influence escalatory action–reaction cycles. This does not imply, however, that one side gets greater control over deliberate escalation of another side or that one side could use communication procedures in a manipulative way. It is questionable whether communication procedures would allow this, given their limited scope and the fact that any actor has the option to not use the procedure if it is deemed disadvantageous. None of the agreements for crisis communication discussed in the East and South China Sea include an enforcement mechanism. Whenever the various actors specified in an agreement – Japanese or Chinese captains or pilots, a commander of a navy vessel (CUES), or a senior official of a foreign ministry (China–ASEAN Guidelines for Hotline Communication) – find the use of an agreed communication procedure inconvenient for political, operational, or other reasons, these actors have had the option to not communicate. As noted, various actors ignored communication procedures in incidents that had a bearing on the claims of Vietnam, China, South Korea, and Japan.

CUES did not produce new legal obligations as COLREGs and UNCLOS already contain legally binding rules on the prevention of collisions and on signals and communication for all vessels, including navy vessels, submarines, and fishing vessels. One objective of CUES was to use existing international legal rules on encounters between vessels and to facilitate China's increasing compliance with these rules.[191] The approach of reaching non-binding instruments on military communication mechanisms was criticised as potentially eroding existing rules by adding non-binding rules to binding rules on the prevention of collisions.[192] However, the absence of legal requirements beyond COLREGs does not in itself preclude effectiveness. As mentioned in chapter III, the agreement between the Philippines and Taiwan about maritime law enforcement has established a procedure for the prevention of incidents based on a minimal commitment. Another benefit of CUES is that it allows the participating navies to engage in a direct dialogue with the PLA Navy regarding the prevention of incidents.

Despite the limitations of CUES, Southeast Asian states value direct communication mechanisms. At least three diplomatic initiatives to

191 James Kraska, 'Maritime Confidence-Building Measures for Navigation in the South China Sea', *The International Journal of Marine and Coastal Law* 32, no. 2 (2017): 268–97, 280–2.

192 Pete Pedrozo, 'The US-China Incidents at Sea Agreement: A Recipe for Disaster', *Journal of National Security Law & Policy* 6 (2012): 207–26.

produce further instruments have been suggested at the time of writing. First, ASEAN members and ASEAN Regional Forum (ARF) participants have continued to work towards the adoption of guidelines for a broader set of maritime interactions, including between maritime law enforcement vessels.[193] Singaporean Foreign Minister Balakrishnan suggested that CUES should be expanded to coast guards.[194] As illustrated above, however, CUES does not respond to the dynamics that underlie typical incidents in the East and South China Sea. While guidelines are needed for interactions between coast guard vessels, CUES may not offer the best model. The majority of incidents in the South China Sea involve coast guard vessels rather than navy vessels. The ARF recognized that maritime law enforcement vessels are 'front-line actors' and that guidelines are necessary to manage incidents at sea.[195] The EU, Australia and Vietnam co-sponsored an initiative to draft such guidelines at the ARF between 2017 und 2022. Officials of the PLA Navy, however, regard the use of forcible measures in maritime law enforcement as a necessary option for enforcing claims.[196] The protection of maritime claims, sea boundaries, installations, reefs, and islands is a stated priority of the China Coast Guard.[197] As restrictions on coast guard behaviour would limit China's options in an area where China has advantages over its competitors, Chinese officials have rejected developing guidelines for coast guards, including at the ARF. Moreover, the idea of developing incident prevention instruments for coast guards and the thorny issue of defining geographic coverage are closely related. Maritime law enforcement vessels usually operate inside areas of national jurisdiction (EEZs and territorial seas) and an arrangement needs to define whether it applies to disputed territorial seas. This is likely to be an additional barrier to an arrangement for maritime law enforcement vessels. Second, Singapore has proposed a set of guidelines to avoid unintended incidents between aircraft. ASEAN

193 '2019 ASEAN Defence Ministers' Meeting Guidelines for Maritime Interaction', adopted 11 July 2019, para 33, https://cil.nus.edu.sg/wp-content/uploads/2019/11/2019-ADMM-Guidelines-Maritime-Interaction.pdf (last accessed 19 April 2024).

194 Sam Bateman, 'CUES and Coast Guards', *East Asia Forum*, 7 October 2016, https://www.eastasiaforum.org/2016/10/07/cues-and-coast-guards/ (last accessed 19 April 2024).

195 'ASEAN Regional Forum Ministerial Statement on Enhancing Cooperation among Maritime Law Enforcement Agencies', 26 July 2016, https://aseanregionalforum.asean.org/wp-content/uploads/2019/03/arf-ministerial-statement-on-enhancing-cooperation-among-maritime-law-enforcement-agencies.pdf (last accessed 19 April 2024).

196 Interview with a senior PLA Navy officer, (interview 45).

197 'Coast Guard Law of the People's Republic of China. Order No. 71 of the President of the People's Republic of China', 22 January 2021, available at https://www.lawinfochina.com/display.aspx?lib=law&id=34610&EncodingName=big5 (last accessed 14 April 2024).

defence ministers endorsed the 'Guidelines on Air Military Encounters' at the ASEAN Defence Ministers meeting (ADMM) held on 19 October 2018.[198] The ADMM-Plus countries, China and the US, though, could not immediately be convinced to adopt the non-binding guidelines. Third, ASEAN members developed an ASEAN Direct Communications Infrastructure (ADI) between 2014 and 2017. The ADI has the objective of establishing 'permanent, rapid, reliable and confidential means for communication between ASEAN Defence Ministers and arrive at mutual decisions in handling crisis or emergency situations'.[199] While the ADI was first established between ASEAN members, ASEAN invited ADMM-Plus countries (the US, China, India, Russia, Japan, South Korea, Australia, and New Zealand) to join the ADI.

Despite the limited nature of commitments, state actors gain further benefits from exchanges on crisis communication, namely learning processes and domestic bureaucratic adjustments. In response to the experiences gained during crises and concurrently with negotiations about crisis communications, China scrutinized its fragmented interdepartmental procedures and reorganized its information flows and decision-making processes.[200] The attempts to build international institutions for crisis communication were accompanied by additional, albeit limited, improvements in China's domestic crisis management capacities. The Philippines also responded to its fractured crisis management capacities with domestic institutional adjustments, most notably the creation of the National Coast Watch Centre.[201]

Finally, it is insightful to briefly compare CUES with the 'Agreement Between the Government of The United States of America and the Government of The Union of Soviet Socialist Republics on the Prevention of Incidents On and Over the High Seas (INCSEA)', which was the first incident prevention

198 'Guidelines for Air Military Encounters Adopted by the 12th ADMM', 19 October 2018, https://admm.asean.org/dmdocuments/2018_Oct_12th%20ADMM_Singapore,%2019%20October%202018_[Final]%20Guidelines%20for%20Air%20Military%20Encounters.pdf (last accessed 19 April 2024).

199 'Concept Paper on the Expansion of the ASEAN Direct Communications Infrastructure in the ASEAN Defence Ministers' Meeting (ADMM) Process To the Plus Countries', July 2019, https://admm.asean.org/dmdocuments/2019_July_13th%20ADMM_Bangkok,%2011%20July%202019_3.%20(Final)%20The%20Expansion%20of%20the%20ADI%20to%20the%20ADMM-Plus%20Countries.pdf (last accessed 19 April 2024).

200 Erickson and Liff, 'Installing a Safety on the "Loaded Gun"? China's Institutional Reforms, National Security Commission and Sino–Japanese Crisis (In)Stability'.

201 'Briefer: National Coast Watch Center', Official Gazette of the Philippines, 28 April 2015, https://www.officialgazette.gov.ph/2015/04/28/briefer-national-coast-watch-center/ (last accessed 19 April 2024). The crisis at Scarborough Shoal in 2012 was a wake-up call and accelerated the establishment of the centre. Its mandate includes improvements in maritime domain awareness and inter-agency coordination, including during crises.

agreement.[202] The purpose of INCSEA was to prevent incidents at sea in the Cold War context. In contrast to CUES, INCSEA is a binding agreement that commits each side to keep their ships at a sufficient distance to prevent collisions and to not simulate attacks. Potentially escalatory activities that INCSEA prohibits, CUES merely recommends avoiding ('a prudent commander might generally avoid'). In contrast to CUES, INCSEA has a clearly defined geographic area of application – the high seas outside territorial seas.[203] CUES does not prohibit acts of harassment; INCSEA prohibits such acts. China and ASEAN members negotiated about prohibiting acts of harassment in the context of the code of conduct. As noted in the analysis of code of conduct negotiations, China and some Southeast Asian claimants relied on forcible enforcement activities to protect their claims in the last decades and objected to proposals restricting forcible enforcement actions at various stages. CUES' mere commitment to communication procedures and non-committal recommendations cannot replace the rules for conflict behaviour that a code of conduct has sought.

202 Agreement Between the Government of The United States of America and the Government of The Union of Soviet Socialist Republics on the Prevention of Incidents On and Over the High Seas (INCSEA), 25 May 1972, accessible at https://www.state.gov/t/isn/4791.htm (last accessed 19 April 2024).
203 The EEZ regime did not yet exist at the time of the conclusion of INCSEA.

VI Conclusions

Abstract
This chapter illustrates how the disputing claimant states govern marine natural resources in a shared way even under conditions of territorial and boundary disputes and great power competition. It demonstrates that cooperative institutions and conflict are not confined domains of action but part of the same structure of interactions. The notion that cooperative agreements isolate areas of shared interest and encapsulate cooperation from a broader conflict is simplistic. This chapter identifies the commitments that are lacking to move forward with ocean governance in the East and South China Sea. It explores some implications of these findings for great power confrontation and cooperation beyond Asia's maritime disputes.

Keywords: East and South China Sea, dispute settlement, great power confrontation, ASEAN, maritime cooperation, ocean governance, institutions, UNCLOS

This book has analysed the interactions and negotiations that took place between various state bureaucracies and non-state actors in the South China Sea and East China Sea. Different actors have sought to devise practical institutions governing marine natural resources and providing rules for behaviour in disputed areas over several decades. These attempts are almost as old as the disputes themselves. The conflicting parties concluded several agreements since the late 1990s; the parties continue to negotiate about further arrangements or the implementation of existing documents at the time of writing. Previous agreements date back to the 1950s and 1960s. All parties have sought to prevent the maritime disputes from dominating their overall and economic relations by reducing the disputes' escalation risks and the security and economic costs with practical institutions. As the disputing parties have not even attempted

Schultheiss, Christian: *Ocean Governance and Conflict in the East and South China Sea. Negotiating Natural Resources, Institutions and Power.*
Taylor & Francis Group, 2024
DOI: 10.5117/9789463728997_CH06

territorial settlements, and in cases including China have not delimited maritime boundaries except one, the parties have tried to dissociate the governance of specific maritime issue areas from the disputes in an incremental process. This decades-long practice has emerged not in spite of, but in response to irreconcilable claims.

Institutions as cooperative response and as tools that extend power

The book has illustrated how the shared governance of the maritime domain is possible even under conditions of territorial and sea boundary disputes and great power competition. Cooperative institutions and conflict, though, are not confined domains of action in the East and South China Sea, but part of the same structure of interactions. Highly conflicted escalatory behaviour and cooperative action occurred in the case of fisheries, offshore oil and gas, or seismic research, sometimes side by side. For the latter to materialize, numerous actors sought to design various agreements. This book illustrates that negotiators made great efforts to find mutually agreeable terms and to implement some arrangements in the face of regular incidents. But the idea that cooperative agreements isolate issue areas of common interest and encapsulate cooperation from the overall conflict is simplistic. Coordinated action for the purpose of natural resource governance and conflict management does not simply remove a particular type of behaviour or issue area from the disputes. Various actors treated the institutions for the East and South China Sea disputes as both cooperative responses and as tools that help one state make an opponent do what it would not otherwise do. As actors regarded coordinated actions as potential vulnerabilities, their major concern in the negotiations was to minimise risks and protect against the perils of cooperation.

Especially, but not exclusively, claimant states interacting with China have feared that the price for cooperative institutions on natural resources and conflict management is the extension and consolidation of China's influence rather than the taming of their ambitions. Various parties sought to replace fishing incidents with bilateral institutions that make fisheries cooperation durable. But they have expected, and in some instances experienced, a rival claimant use the public authority gained from a fisheries agreement to expand its coast guard presence in disputed areas. Disputing parties tried to dissociate escalation-prone access to hydrocarbon resources from the disputes with joint development arrangements. But they suspected and, in some instances, experienced that consent to joint development implied consent to an opponent's access to maritime zones beyond legal claims and validation of these claims. Members of the Philippine government also assessed that the information the China National Offshore Oil Corporation (CNOOC) gained through joint research activities resulted in a practically relevant Chinese information advantage and led to the hardening of the claim. With the project of a code of conduct, members of the Association of Southeast Asian Nations (ASEAN) and China sought to define the basic rules for a reduction in escalatory activities and to initiate a path towards regional cooperation. Yet, China regarded ASEAN members' draft codes as attempts to restrict China's options to defend and advance their claims and thereby consolidate ASEAN members' territorial possessions. In turn, China's draft codes would have limited the coalition choices of ASEAN members and turned the code into an institution that excludes non-regional states from various activities and navigational rights in the South China Sea.

Various parties attempted to design institutions for incident prevention and crisis communication in a move to prevent the recurrence of escalatory action–reaction cycles. Such cycles began in several instances with 'frighteningly mundane'[1] incidents that the parties were incapable or unwilling to stop due to various obstacles, including fractured crisis management processes between fragmented domestic bureaucracies. Yet, a few actors assessed (others did not) that a rival claimant can manipulate crisis responses through institutions for crisis communication. In short, the parties have regarded institutions for resource sharing and conflict management as much as incremental steps towards conflict resolution as potential sources of leverage that a rival claimant can exploit to its advantage in subsequent interactions.

The central problem in these negotiation processes has not been the parties' inability to agree on a division of economic gains from coordinated action – e.g., which fisheries quota or shares in oil and gas each party would receive. Neither was the most contentious issue the question of how to facilitate compliance with the agreements. The parties treated institutions as weapons of coercion that parties could use to derive strategic advantages, and as objects that are themselves determinants of future power. This problem was not an add-on but a core problem in the negotiations. The parties cherished institutions as remedies against their respective strategic

1 Graham T. Allison, *Destined for War: Can America and China Escape Thucydides's Trap?* (Mariner Books, 2017), 167.

disadvantages and the shortcomings of their approaches to these disputes. Negotiators resisted agreements if they believed an opponent would gain opportunities to weaponize an institution. From the perspective of the negotiators, this is the cost of cooperation. Theoretically, the central problems bedevilling negotiations were questions of which actor would gain power advantages from an (implemented) institution. Once the parties resolved this problem, they could also agree on a division of economic gains. Even an actor that assumed an opponent's bad faith accepted an institution once the actor was confident that a rival claimant could not use the institution as a tool to gain strategic advantages under plausible circumstances. This behaviour does not reduce the relevance of institutions or render cooperation less desirable in the eyes of claimant states. Thus, claimant states have been persistent in negotiating institutions for oil and gas, fisheries, conduct, maritime security, crisis management, and incident prevention at the time of writing. As the actors have sought to prevent escalation and to protect their overall relationships from disputes, cooperative institutions remain in demand.

The multiple roles of institutions for resource sharing and conflict management in the disputes

These points find multiple manifestations in the disputes. First, despite the slow motion of long-standing negotiation processes, despite disappointingly ineffective documents in the context of the code of conduct, and despite China's attempts to advance its claims, parties have continued to negotiate various agreements at the time of writing. China and Japan have sought to implement the crisis communication arrangements they have been contemplating for over a decade. ASEAN members and China have continued the code of conduct negotiations. China and the Philippines established the Bilateral Consultation Mechanism on maritime communication mechanisms, and more than a dozen ASEAN-related bodies deal with various issues regarding maritime security. Moreover, South Korea did not terminate its fisheries agreement with China although Chinese fishermen violated the agreement several 10,000 times. Japanese actors regarded some activities that are compliant with the letter of the Sino-Japanese fisheries agreement as a pretext to improve the China Coast Guard's control of waters in the direct vicinity of the Senkaku/Diaoyu Islands. And yet, Japan did not terminate the fisheries agreement. The fisheries agreements of the East China Sea and Yellow Sea illustrate how close cooperation and the expansion of a state actor's rule are interwoven. On the one hand, of all documents in the East and South China Sea, these fisheries agreements are comparatively the most effective in preventing incidents and, should they occur nevertheless, their escalation.[2] On the other hand, any de facto transfer of public authority via a fisheries agreement to the China Coast Guard is a most sensitive issue that requires a prudent approach as long as safeguarding China's claims is a priority mission of the China Coast Guard. As noted in chapter IV, it is a small step from the China Coast Guard enforcing China's fisheries law in the vicinity of the Senkaku/Diaoyu Islands to the China Coast Guard expanding its presence in the same area. Despite their many shortcomings and barriers, the disputing parties still regard agreements for ocean governance and conflict management as valuable options. This is the case because these have been the only negotiated options in the disputes. Thus, an explanation of the East and South China Sea disputes that analyses the negotiations about institutions solely from a manipulative perspective cannot explain why parties agreed on some institutions and why they have adhered to them. An explanation, however, that neglects in which ways institutions could be sources of vulnerabilities and rival power cannot explain the course of negotiations and the obstacles the parties encountered within them.

Second, different parties displayed similar concerns about the possibility that an opponent could leverage resource-sharing agreements to its advantage. Actors from China, Japan, South Korea, the Philippines, Vietnam, Malaysia, Brunei, and Taiwan rejected draft agreements in bilateral or multilateral contexts because they suspected that the draft agreement could result in a layer of validity and a precedent in favour of an opponent's claim. Practical arrangements for natural resources and conflict management are, however, without prejudice to claims *de jure*; they do not represent precedents, do not recognize claims, and do not affect the status of claims under international law. A theoretical explanation for why states act on precedent without legal force is that agreements or some of their provisions, especially regarding the geographic scope, can establish focal points in subsequent interactions from which an opponent would not retreat. This concern explains why the Sino-Japanese Principled Consensus on joint oil and gas projects ran aground. China's former top leadership, reportedly driven by Wen Jiabao, overruled reluctant Chinese officials, and pushed for the conclusion of the Principled Consensus with Japan – the first and only agreed document on joint development after twenty-three years of

2 Chapter IV 1.4, 2.2, and 4.

consultations. China's former Vice-Foreign Minister Wu Dawei hailed the understanding as a 'new historic starting point' in Sino-Japanese relations.[3] A few days later, however, the dominant element of the Consensus became the fact that China had accepted a joint exploration zone that straddled a Japan-claimed median line by a few dozen square miles and had thereby set a precedent in favour of Japan's claimed median line. China's claim was compromised. In the case of the trilateral Sino-Philippine-Vietnamese Joint Marine Seismic Undertaking (JMSU), it was the Philippine actors that first accepted an arrangement which applied to an area to which China had virtually no maritime entitlement. Then, three years later, Manila allowed it to expire. To reach the JMSU, former Philippine President Arroyo sidestepped the Philippine bureaucracy that opposed such an arrangement and entrusted a Philippine businessman with strong connections to China's energy companies with the negotiation of the arrangement. President Arroyo hailed the JMSU as a 'breakthrough for peace and stability'.[4] Three years later, Philippine opposition figures and lawyers challenged the JMSU on multiple grounds, among them that the JMSU gave China the opening to start claiming the Reed Bank. The Principled Consensus and the JMSU came into being as the top leaderships of China and the Philippines overruled officials who cautioned against the arrangements. Both cases started as 'historic breakthroughs'. Both arrangements run aground as the parties feared the arrangements would improve the respective opponent's bargaining position in subsequent interactions.

The case of the JMSU and the Principled Consensus cannot be dismissed as exemplifying mere sensitivities. The concern not to ameliorate the status of an opponent's claim to a certain maritime zone or territorial sovereignty delayed or thwarted negotiations on fisheries, oil and gas, crisis communication, and on the code of conduct. The concern was the rule and not the exception. It resonated among all parties in cases where China has had or has not had valid entitlements and in cases excluding China. This concern has been particularly pronounced in cases involving disputed territorial claims (e.g., Senkaku/Diaoyu, Dok-do/Takeshima, Paracel, and Spratly Islands) and, among Southeast Asian states, in cases where China's claims

3 Ministry of Foreign Affairs of China, 'Vice Foreign Minister Wu Dawei Talks About the Principled Consensuses Reached Between China and Japan on the East China Sea Issue', 19 June 2008, https://www.fmprc.gov.cn/eng/wjdt_665385/wshd_665389/200806/t20080623_636938.html (last accessed 23 March 2023).

4 'China, Philippines, Vietnam Sign Joint South China Sea Oil Search Accord', *Radio Free Asia*, 14 March 2005, https://www.rfa.org/english/news/business/china_vietnam_spratlys-20050314.html (last accessed 23 March 2024).

to rights inside the nine-dash line exceed the entitlements under the UN Convention on the Law of the Sea (UNCLOS). Southeast Asian states have a particular incentive not to create a layer of validity for Chinese claims that are legally invalid. This also explains why a limited number of attempts to negotiate resource-sharing arrangements occurred in the South China Sea.

The parties of the East China Sea's fisheries agreements circumvented this problem by engaging in complex 'claims arithmetic'. They excluded that the geographic design of an agreement and its subzones could be construed as a de facto precedent in favour of an opponent's claim. To mention an example, Japan rejected geographic scopes for joint fisheries zones that could be construed as reflecting China's claims to the Senkaku/Diaoyu Islands. Japanese negotiators deemed such a geographic scope as an acknowledgement that the islands are disputed. The question of how the parties should distribute economic gains from coordinated action played a smaller role. In few subzones, the fisheries agreements provide for some amount of qualitative and quantitative fisheries regulation. In other subzones, the agreements do not provide for quantitative regulation at all – they do not define quota, not even a maximum number of vessels, and substantive questions of fisheries regulation remain almost entirely within national jurisdiction. The 'claims arithmetic' resulted in the perhaps paradoxical situation whereby China and Japan accorded each other the maximum freedom to define fisheries regulation unilaterally in the most disputed southern part of the East China Sea, including in the vicinity but outside the territorial waters of the Senkaku/Diaoyu Islands. The fisheries agreements in the East China Sea, Yellow Sea, and the Gulf of Tonkin established the basic institutional structure with which their parties can manage even severe incidents. Rampant violations of the Sino-Korean agreement, Korea's forceful response against Chinese fishermen, and incidents in the southern East China Sea would have escalated the disputes dramatically had it not been for the fisheries agreements.[5] Incidents escalated in the parts of the East China Sea where no fisheries agreement applied, namely the territorial waters of the Senkaku/Diaoyu islands. Given China's invalidated claims in the South China Sea, however, Southeast Asian states are unlikely to emulate the agreements of Japan or South Korea regarding these as consequential validations of China's claims.

Several cases illustrate that the disputing actors are not against resource sharing per se. Opponents had fewer difficulties sharing natural resources once they agreed on maritime boundary delimitation. China and Vietnam

5 Chapter IV 2.2 and 4.

agreed on boundary delimitation and joint development of straddling oil and gas resources in the Gulf of Tonkin. In addition, they agreed on a transitional fisheries agreement, also straddling the boundary. At the time of writing, China and Vietnam renewed negotiations on extending the boundary arrangement of the Gulf of Tonkin into adjacent parts of the South China Sea. In the South China Sea, Brunei rejected Malaysian proposals for joint development fearing these would entail conceding Brunei's rights. Instead, Brunei and Malaysia reached a boundary delimitation agreement that includes provisions for the joint development of a block on Brunei's side of the boundary. The cases represent not only package agreements. They illustrate that the parties were willing to share resources once a delimited boundary offered protection against the possibility that an opponent could leverage a joint development or fisheries agreement for its claim. Philippine officials and members of the government did not reject per se involving Chinese energy companies in the exploration or exploitation of areas to which China lacks valid claims. In negotiations in 2011 and 2018–2019, senior Philippine officials made detailed proposals about the participation of Chinese energy companies provided China accepted Philippine jurisdiction. As China, the Philippines, and Japan experienced, politically there is a big difference between joint development under international law and the participation of one side's energy company in an energy project under another state's jurisdiction. While both are pragmatic forms of resource sharing, this difference contributed to the making and breaking of the JMSU and the Principled Consensus.

The interactions in the East and South China Sea illustrate one relevance of international law for negotiations. State actors and non-state actors delegated by the state have negotiated in the shadow of the law of the sea. The law of the sea allocates entitlements to maritime zones; actors negotiate with legal entitlements. The question of the existence or absence of legal entitlements is crucial to the observable negotiation processes even if this factor alone can only explain a part of the variation. Further research could examine how the existence of legal claims affects actors' negotiating behaviour and preference formation in other geographic contexts or the context of different legal regimes.

Third, the disputing parties displayed similar, but not identical concerns about the possibility that an opponent derives strategic advantages from a code of conduct or incident prevention arrangement. Negotiations on the code of conduct illustrate the problem of how states bargain about agreements that restrict claim-ameliorative behaviour, coercive tactics, and coalition options. China and ASEAN members proposed provisions that would have restricted the types of activities that the respective opponent had adopted in the past to advance or defend its claims. Each party envisioned a code that would have restricted and thereby offset the rival's operational and political advantages. At varying points in time, ASEAN members sought to restrict the use of coercive coast guard activities, disruptions of maritime economic activities, occupations and militarization of islands or constructions on islands. The ASEAN members' draft of 1999 encouraged non-regional states, e.g., the United States, to join the code. China rejected what may be called ASEAN's 'institution of inclusion'. The latter would have resulted in China's consent to non-regional states playing a role in the disputes. In the 1990s, China still sought restrictions on coast guard interference with fishing activities. At that time, China did not yet have a regular maritime law enforcement presence in most parts of the South China Sea. In 2018, China proposed that ASEAN members consent to a system of previous notice and 'no objection' from China for non-regional military operations in the South China Sea. China also proposed the exclusion of non-regional energy companies from oil and gas projects. China sought ASEAN's consent to limit the coalition choices of ASEAN members and to limit the navigational freedoms of all states in line with China's geopolitical objectives.

Officials from Malaysia, the Philippines and Vietnam (and possibly other ASEAN members) opposed China's proposals. These Chinese proposals designed the code as an 'institution of exclusion' or, as the proposal may be called, as one element of an 'order of exclusion'.[6] These proposals represent some evidence for China's geopolitical objectives for Southeast Asia, but also reveal that China is not in a position to bring about ASEAN members' acceptance. Moreover, to address the contentious issue of specifying a geographic scope for the code of conduct, the parties reverted to ambiguous formulas. The inability to define a precise geographic scope adds to the difficulty of defining precise restrictions for conflict behaviour. Crucially, as ASEAN members have had diverging preferences regarding a code of conduct and as ASEAN consensus documents tended to represent the lowest common denominator, the bargaining power of ASEAN is less than the sum of ASEAN members.

This book's analysis does not suggest that the occurrence of bilateral or multilateral negotiations is predominantly a function of China's or ASEAN members' preferences. It cannot uphold the idea of 'smoking-gun evidence' for a strong ASEAN consensus and a multilateralization of China–ASEAN

6 Kyle M. Lascurettes, *Orders of Exclusion: Great Powers and the Strategic Sources of Foundational Rules in International Relations* (OUP, 2020).

exchanges in 2016.[7] Not only have the code of conduct negotiations been multilateral for more than twenty-five years, but bilateral exchanges between China and Vietnam or the Philippines also continue regarding geographic areas not claimed by other claimants. Importantly, ASEAN members still propose diverging provisions for key aspects of a code of conduct – its geographic scope and legal status as well as restrictions for conflict behaviour – after more than two decades. Not much is required for China to split ASEAN, as a unified and effective ASEAN coalition remains elusive. Current negotiations are therefore unlikely to yield provisions with more 'teeth' than previous declarations.

Regarding crisis communication arrangements, various bureaucracies had competing assessments of whether China can exploit tools for crisis management in a manipulative way, for instance, by increasing their operations or by restraining rival responses to operations. Some Japanese officials and security experts suspected this possibility. Some Chinese sources rationalized China's consent to crisis communication with the assessment that China derives advantages from a reduction in the risk of accidental escalation. Other Japanese officials and members of the armed services, however, rejected this assessment on factual grounds. They were sceptical about whether crisis communication mechanisms offer such manipulative or abusive opportunities. The assessment that crisis communication mechanisms could be manipulated appears not to have resonated among Southeast Asian states in their dealings with China. The existence of factually diverging assessments among Japan's relevant bureaucracies regarding whether China could leverage crisis communication measures to its advantage in Senkaku/Diaoyu Islands operations was one reason why negotiations stalled for so long. Another possible explanation is the issue of whether to exclude or include territorial waters. Japanese actors have regarded the inclusion of the territorial waters as establishing one layer of validation for China's claim to the Senkaku/Diaoyu Islands, while Chinese actors suspected that excluding the waters would have strengthened Japan's claim.

Fourth, this book does not establish evidence for the following expectations of international relations. This book does not find that the reaching of one or several agreements makes the reaching of further agreements more likely due to reciprocity or greater trust.[8] In some cases, claimant states tried to reach a second or third agreement by either focusing on other issue areas or by extending cooperation geographically. But the attempts to

7 Chin-Hao Huang, *Power and Restraint in China's Rise* (Columbia UP, 2022), 67.

8 Robert M. Axelrod, *The Evolution of Cooperation* (Basic Books, 1984).

reach a second or third agreement were subject to the same conditions as the reaching of a first agreement. China and Japan entered into a fisheries agreement, an arrangement for marine scientific research,[9] and adopted the Code for Unplanned Encounters at Sea (CUES), but negotiations on more substantive crisis management and joint development stalled. China and Vietnam came to a maritime boundary agreement including provisions for joint development and to a fisheries agreement. They undertook some joint patrols in the Gulf of Tonkin and adopted CUES but attempts to extend the cooperation into the South China Sea ended in an impasse.

Furthermore, bilateral negotiations between claimant states with some common geopolitical interests, and shared democratic values, with a common ally and excluding China, did not reach more agreements or have less trouble reaching an agreement than bilateral cases involving China. South Korea, Japan, Taiwan, and the Philippines face the question of how to respond to a risen China; they are democracies and have the US as a common ally. Their bilateral negotiations were nevertheless no less difficult than the negotiations of these countries with China. Japan and Taiwan reached a fisheries agreement after an on-and-off negotiation period of seventeen years; China and Japan reached an agreement after only one year. The Philippines accepted a fisheries law enforcement agreement with Taiwan only after Taiwan pursued a campaign to pressure the Philippines into a minimal, shallow but effective arrangement. Moreover, this book did not find evidence for big bargains or linkages (for example concessions on the South China Sea traded against concessions in another policy area). Furthermore, the existing cooperative arrangements and documents did not noticeably affect alignment choices. No indication could be found that Japanese actors, for instance, worried that fisheries, joint development, or incident prevention arrangements with China would drive a wedge between the US and Japan. Likewise, considerations for US-Philippine relations seem not to have affected Manila's position regarding joint development. Finally, this book did not find that China's power advantage generally translated into favourable terms for the country. East and Southeast Asian states rejected various Chinese proposals that would have been favourable to China. In the case of the JMSU, China provided infrastructure loans as side payments. This was not the case regarding other agreements. The question of whether the terms of the JMSU favoured China, but disfavoured the Philippines is a question of whether the JMSU strengthened China's bargaining power

9 Akira Takada, 'Marine Scientific Research in the Exclusive Economic Zone and Japan-China Agreement for Prior Notification (1995–2001)', *Japanese Annual of International Law*, 2001, 134–50.

but weakened the Philippines' power. Philippine officials and observers believe that the JMSU did that.

Fifth, the question arises whether and to what extent the proposals and draft agreements China put forward during the negotiations of the past three decades reflect an attempt to renegotiate or reinterpret the law of the sea, at least, regarding East and Southeast Asia. China's maritime claims in the South China Sea and the limits to navigational freedoms favoured by China would substantively affect two balances that are fundamental to the law of the sea: first, is the fact that no state is entitled to claim maritime rights in excess of the rights defined in the law of the sea. All coastal states are entitled to claim the same maritime rights. Second, is the balance between the rights of coastal states and the rights of user states. While China seeks to restrict navigational rights in waters claimed by China, the People's Liberations Army (PLA) Navy makes use of navigational freedoms outside the South China Sea. Restrictions on navigational freedoms in the East and South China Sea, if established, would constitute a reinterpretation of UNCLOS and a reorientation towards the primacy of the coastal state. China, however, has not achieved a change in the legal rules but is reducing their importance.[10] Moreover, some of China's draft provisions for a code of conduct would have had the effect of enlisting ASEAN members in this effort. If Southeast Asian claimants were to concede maritime zones beyond the normal limits, this would set apart a law of the sea for the South China Sea and a law of the sea for the rest of the world's ocean. In the context of climate change and international financial institutions, China relied on hold-up strategies to extract concessions in the renegotiation of multilateral institutions.[11] From this perspective, China's coercive activities can also be regarded as holding up East and Southeast Asian countries for concessions that would result in a reorientation of the law of the sea and the primacy of the coastal state. However, this reorientation would not be the result of a comprehensive alternative vision for the law of the sea – China's draft agreements do not reflect that – but of particularistic claims and interests.

Sixth, a few years ago experts were still delving into specificities of joint development arrangements and tried to move forward with identifying geographic areas for joint development.[12] In 2020, US Assistant Secretary

10 Isaac B. Kardon, *China's Law of the Sea: The New Rules of Maritime Order* (Yale UP, 2023), 257.

11 Scott L. Kastner, Margaret M. Pearson, and Chad Rector, *China's Strategic Multilateralism: Investing in Global Governance* (CUP, 2019).

12 Robert C. Beckman et al., *Beyond Territorial Disputes in the South China Sea Legal Frameworks for the Joint Development of Hydrocarbon Resources,* NUS Centre for International Law (Edward Elgar, 2013); Clive Schofield, 'Defining Areas for Joint Development in Disputed Waters', in *Recent*

Stilwell described Beijing's attempts of 'push[ing] other states to accept "joint development"' as 'gangster tactics'.[13] Stilwell's comment arguably reflects the blunt confrontational rhetoric of the Trump administration and the general deterioration of US–China relations. Yet, the South China Sea Arbitration represents a turning point for the South China Sea by bringing about a major clarification of the validity of claims. In the application of the award to the South China Sea,[14] the Philippines, Vietnam, Brunei, Malaysia, and Indonesia are not under an obligation to negotiate joint development with China in most parts of the South China Sea as there are no overlapping entitlements.[15] Whether or not China's coercive activities are intentionally directed at making Southeast Asian states accept resource-sharing arrangements, frequent interferences in Philippine activities keep the idea of giving China access to some maritime zones via some type of resource-sharing arrangements on the agenda in the Philippines. Crucially, China could gain some sort of residual acknowledgement of China's interests beyond the normal entitlements with the consent of Southeast Asian states but not without their consent. It is perhaps not an overstatement to conclude that Southeast Asian claimant states are to some extent gatekeepers of the recognition of China's interests beyond UNCLOS' normal rights. This is a bargaining asset Southeast Asian claimants are unlikely to give up lightly.

Outlook for the South China Sea – coalition building and conditions for regional ocean governance

This book cites many works that propose agreements, models, ways forward, or blueprints for shared ocean governance in the South and East China Sea. It offers, for the first time, an analysis and explanation for the actual and

Developments in the South China Sea Dispute. The Prospect of a Joint Development Regime, edited by Shicun Wu and Nong Hong (Routledge, 2014), 78–98.

13 David R. Stilwell, 'The South China Sea, Southeast Asia's Patrimony, and Everybody's Own Backyard Remarks of David R. Stilwell Assistant Secretary Bureau of East Asian and Pacific Affairs at the CSIS', 14 July 2020, https://2017-2021.state.gov/the-south-china-sea-southeast-asias-patrimony-and-everybodys-own-backyard/index.html (last accessed 19 April 2024).

14 Christian Schultheiss, '"One of the First Matters to Be Addressed but Distinct" or "Distinct but Inseparable"? The Distinction Between Maritime Entitlement and Sea Boundary Delimitation in the Philippines v. China Arbitration', *Asian Journal of International Law* 11, no. 1 (January 2021): 24–35.

15 Christian Schultheiss, 'Joint Development of Hydrocarbon Resources in the South China Sea After the Philippines Versus China Arbitration?', *Ocean Development & International Law* 51, no. 3 (3 August 2020): 241–62.

substantial interactions and negotiations that took place between various state and non-state actors about such options in the past three decades. By doing so, the author hopes to have provided a sober and realistic assessment of the promises and costs such options involve. China currently shows no sign of willingness to align its claims with the South China Sea Arbitration and to effectively drop a part of the claims to maritime rights. Southeast Asian claimants are unlikely to give in and develop resources jointly on China's terms. This book's analysis does not imply, though, that cooperation in the maritime domain and conflict management cannot play a role in overcoming the disputes. As noted, China and Southeast Asian claimants have continued negotiations on maritime cooperation in different constellations while not even consulting on territorial settlements. The question is, therefore, which scenarios and political commitments could enable pragmatic cooperation between China and Southeast Asian claimant states.

This book's analysis revealed one profound shortcoming in the bilateral and multilateral negotiations: China has never committed to altering its posture in the South China Sea if Southeast Asian claimant states were to accept common natural resource institutions or other forms of maritime cooperation. China did not indicate whether and in which ways Chinese actors would reduce pressure on Southeast Asia claimants if these were to cooperate with China. Apart from this, China has never indicated to what extent Chinese actors could accept unilateral activities of Southeast Asian states in areas outside potential joint projects. Generally, China has never indicated to what extent their claims would be satisfied if Southeast Asian claimant states consented to various forms of shared ocean governance. Without China committing to a predictable perspective that maritime cooperation will satisfy China's claims and will alter China's posture, a basis for maritime cooperation is lacking. China cannot defy the idea that self-restraint, especially regarding territorial and maritime claims, and leadership in regional governance and institutions, go hand in hand.[16] Due to the absence of Chinese commitments to these effects, Southeast Asian claimants have good reason to fear that Chinese actors can and will use cooperative arrangements as tools to advance their claims in the disputes.

Moreover, ASEAN members and especially Southeast Asian claimants have made separate steps towards incorporating the tribunal's ruling in

16 G. John Ikenberry, 'State Power and the Institutional Bargain: America's Ambivalent Economic and Security Multilateralism', in *US Hegemony and International Organizations*, edited by Rosemary Foot, Michael Mastanduno, and S. Neil MacFarlane (OUP, 2003), 49–70.

their bargaining position.[17] Southeast Asian claimants have not developed a coherent coalition around the terms based on which they would be prepared to cooperate with China. Even when it comes to code of conduct negotiations, ASEAN members are a fragmented coalition. ASEAN members and especially Southeast Asian claimants need to invest in coalition building. Besides settling their territorial and sea boundary disputes, Southeast Asian claimant states could do this by developing bilateral or regional arrangements on marine natural resources and maritime law enforcement cooperation without China's participation. Such arrangements could establish the basic terms and conditions of Southeast Asian claimants for maritime cooperation in the South China Sea in line with the tribunal's award. CUES is the precedent whereby a whole group of countries adopted a multilateral code that China did not want to join. China reconsidered their position only a decade later after having observed and studied the utility, costs, and benefits of CUES. To get China to participate in some arrangements, it may be necessary to develop the arrangements to which China objects without China's participation.

While the South China Sea Arbitration has clarified which maritime zones China and the Philippines can claim, it leaves important issues undecided. Crucially, the tribunal did not rule on territorial claims and did not have jurisdiction to do so. This includes the territorial seas around the Spratly Islands that qualify as rocks. Around these features, China, the Philippines, Vietnam, Malaysia, Brunei, and Taiwan can claim territorial seas. Fishing, seismic research, or maritime law enforcement activities in disputed territorial seas were among the most escalatory activities. It, therefore, appears desirable that the claimant states would agree that they have valid claims to these areas and that they cooperate in these waters.[18] The territorial seas, however, have been the most sensitive waters that claimants were least likely to cooperate in as they deem provisional cooperation prejudicial to their sovereignty claims.

The claimants have hardly, if at all, discussed the settlement of their territorial claims in the past decades. The fact that territorial settlements are not being considered has been one factor motivating talks on natural resources and conflict management in the first place. The former Prime

17 See their notes verbales at the website of the Commission on the Limits of the Continental Shelf (CLCS) https://www.un.org/Depts/los/clcs_new/submissions_files/submission_mys_12_12_2019.html (last accessed 23 June 2024).

18 Stein Tønnesson, 'Fish for Peace in the South China Sea', *AMTI Update*, 11 January 2019, https://amti.csis.org/fish-for-peace-south-china-sea/ (last accessed 19 April 2024).

Minster of Malaysia, Mahathir Mohamad, may have been the first Southeast Asian leader to hint at what a territorial settlement of the Spratly Islands could look like: 'So, we want to retain, of course, about four or five islands that we have occupied. The rest – whoever thinks it is theirs, they can occupy.'[19] This proposal has merit. As the Spratly Islands spread out over about 410,000 square kilometres, it appears virtually impossible to rule out the possibility that one state has a superior claim to one feature and a second state has a superior claim to a different feature. Therefore, claimant states will need to provide evidence of effective control for claimed features *individually*. To prove a title to sovereignty over all Spratly Islands, it is not enough to show that a state has effectively controlled one or several features, when a second state can show that it is has effectively controlled other features. The current occupational status of features in the Spratly Islands may then be the best evidence most claimants have for effective control of these features and, in turn, for their sovereignty claims. This view also reflects the idea that pursuing a claim to an uninhabitable feature a state does not control is more a liability than an asset. There is, however, nothing in China's, Vietnam's, or the Philippines' current positions that suggests that they would merely consider such a proposal.

Moreover, an issue area that is conspicuous by its absence from the negotiations and considerations of the claimant states is climate change. Ocean warming is already having a negative effect on marine environments, coral reefs, and the abundance of fisheries. Especially in tropical waters such as parts of the South China Sea, ocean warming and acidification is expected to further decrease the productivity of fisheries and to increase competition for scarce marine living resources.[20] Incidents related to fishing activities have played a key role by triggering several crises. The negative effects of ocean warming on fisheries may therefore exacerbate the disputes in the South China Sea by intensifying fishing incidents. While claimants negotiated about the institutions, agreements, and governance tools necessary to regulate fisheries, protect marine environments, and synthesize marine sciences, regional, climate-adaptative

19 Quoted in: Bhavan Jaipragas, 'Forget the Warships: Malaysian PM Mahathir's Peace Formula for South China Sea', *South China Morning Post*, 19 June 2018, https://www.scmp.com/week-asia/geopolitics/article/2151403/forget-warships-malaysian-pm-mahathirs-peace-formula-south (last accessed 19 April 2024).

20 N.L. Bindoff et al. 'Changing Ocean, Marine Ecosystems, and Dependent Communities'. In *IPCC Special Report on the Ocean and Cryosphere in a Changing Climate*, edited by H. O. Pörtner et al. (CUP, 2019), 447–587. https://www.ipcc.ch/srocc/chapter/chapter-5/ (last accessed 19 April 2024).

institutions are yet to emerge. How the fisheries agreements in the East China Sea and Yellow Sea will respond to impacts of ocean warming remains to be seen. Climate change represents one additional factor claimants need to take into consideration when designing institutions for the maritime domain.

Beyond the East and South China Sea

Many scholars acknowledge that heightened great power confrontation impedes the governance of regional and global commons. The maritime disputes and interactions between East and Southeast Asian countries offer some insights into how the simultaneity of confrontational disputes and the need for cooperation affect interactions. For East and Southeast Asian countries, neither confrontation nor cooperation at all costs are strategies for dealing with China in maritime disputes. While unqualified cooperation in the maritime domain may serve as an opponent's springboard to expand their reach, confrontation without agreed limits is the springboard to escalation. Instead, East and Southeast Asian states and non-state actors have focused on the incremental process of devising policy options that manage incidents, de-escalate violence, and transform interactions while hedging against risks from confrontational and cooperative behaviour alike. An era in which great and middle powers recognize the need to simultaneously maintain cooperation on global commons, preparedness for intensified economic competition, and a defensive posture in rivalry should not be surprised to find that, at least in some cases, coordinated, collective action and confrontation are not only concomitant but closely intertwined. The simple dichotomy between traditional security as a force for interstate confrontation and economic interdependence as a driver for cooperation is naïve from several perspectives. Not only can economic interdependence result in security risks,[21] but so does the realm of traditional security not preclude coordinated action. Cooperation, however, does not always yield a confined domain of action. One underlying structural reason for this is that cooperative agreements result in vulnerabilities and alter the power of actors in some cases. A question that warrants further research is then to identify further characteristics by which cooperative institutions alter power between actors and how actors protect against this such as to make

21 Margaret M. Pearson et al., 'China's Party-State Capitalism and International Backlash: From Interdependence to Insecurity', *International Security* 47, no. 2 (2022): 135–76.

coordinated action more likely. While studies address this question in the case of settlements of strategically relevant territory and while it is intuitive that agreements for arms control or non-proliferation of nuclear weapons are about power, the answer to this question is less obvious in the case of institutions for fisheries, codes of conduct, incident prevention, crisis communication, or resource exploitation. This question may therefore be asked for other institutions governing regional or global commons, for instance, international economic institutions, institutions for the management of rivers and freshwater resources, the regulation of global communication, and cyber infrastructure or adaptation to climate change.

Appendix: Overview of Cases

Table 2 Cases in the South China Sea[1]

Case[2]	Claimant states	Negotiation period	Outcome	Scope	Implementation	Are disputed features located within the respective area?	Validity of China's claims to respective maritime zones[3]
1	China–Philippines–Vietnam	2004–2005	Joint Marine Seismic Undertaking (JMSU)	Joint seismic research	Partly implemented expiration in 2008	Yes	Invalid EEZ/CS, valid territorial sea claim around rocks
2	China–Philippines	2011–2012	Impasse	Joint development	No	Yes	Invalid EEZ/CS, valid territorial sea claim around rocks
3	China–Philippines	2017–2022	Memorandum of Understanding	Procedural, further negotiations on seismic research	Not implemented	Yes	Invalid EEZ/CS, valid territorial sea claim around rocks
4	China–Philippines	1995–2004	Memorandum of Understanding	Fisheries cooperation	Not implemented	Yes	Invalid EEZ/CS, valid territorial sea claim around rocks
5	China–Vietnam	1993–2004	Agreement	Sea boundary delimitation, joint development, and patrols	Implemented Some joint exploration activities and patrols	No	Valid EEZ/CS claim

1 Source: own compilation.
2 The book's case studies follow the same order.
3 Pursuant to South China Sea Arbitration, 2016.

Case[2]	Claimant states	Negotiation period	Outcome	Scope	Implementation	Are disputed features located within the respective area?	Validity of China's claims to respective maritime zones[3]
6	China–Vietnam	1993–2004	Agreement	Fisheries, joint committee	Implemented	No	Valid EEZ/CS claim
7	China–Vietnam	2010–2013	Impasse	Boundary, then joint development	No	No	Valid EEZ/CS claim
8	Philippines–Taiwan	2013–2015	Agreement	Fisheries law enforcement	1-hour previous notice before enforcement	Yes	Not applicable
9	Brunei–Malaysia	2003–2009	Agreement	Boundary and joint development	Implemented	No	Not applicable

Table 3 Cases in the East China Sea[4]

Case	Claimant states	Negotiation period	Outcome	Scope	Implementation	Are disputed features located within the respective area?	Validity of China's claims to respective maritime zones
10	China–Japan	1985–2008	Principled Consensus	Joint development, participation of Japanese companies in Chinese projects	Not implemented	No	Valid EEZ/CS claim
11	China–Japan	1996–2000	Agreement	Fisheries, joint committee	Implemented, effective in managing incidents within scope of agreement	Yes	Valid EEZ/CS claim

4 Source: own compilation.

Case	Claimant states	Negotiation period	Outcome	Scope	Implementation	Are disputed features located within the respective area?	Validity of China's claims to respective maritime zones
12	ROK–Japan	1974	Agreement	Joint exploration, joint exploitation of oil and gas	Implemented, no commercially viable findings	No	Not applicable
13	ROK–Japan	1997–1999	Agreement	Fisheries, joint committee	Implemented, some disagreements on annual quota allocation	Yes	Not applicable
14	China–ROK	1993–2001	Agreement	Fisheries, joint committee	Implemented, often violated, effective in preventing interstate crisis	No	Yes
15	Japan–Taiwan	1996–2018	Agreement	Fisheries, joint committee	Implemented	Yes	Not applicable

Table 4 Cases on conflict management in the East and South China Sea[5]

Case	Claimant states	Negotiation period	Outcome	Scope	Implementation	Are disputed features located within the respective area?	Validity of China's claims to maritime zones
16	China–ASEAN members	1996–2002	Declaration on Conduct	Conflict management foundation for practical cooperation	Not implemented	Yes	Invalid beyond normal zones, valid territorial sea claim around rocks

5 Source: own compilation.

17	China–ASEAN members	2003–2016	Various non-binding documents	Conflict management foundation for practical cooperation procedural issues	Not implemented	Yes	Invalid beyond normal zones, valid territorial sea claim around rocks
18	China–ASEAN members	2016–ongoing	Various non-binding documents	Conflict management foundation for practical cooperation procedural issues	Not implemented	Yes	Invalid beyond normal zones, valid territorial sea claim around rocks
19	All claimants, some non-claimant states	2003–2014	Code for Unplanned Encounters at Sea	Communication and navigation procedures, de-escalatory behaviour recommended	Voluntary implementation	Claimants do not generally apply CUES during incidents in territorial seas	Invalid beyond normal zones, valid territorial sea claim around rocks Not applicable outside SCS/ECS
20	China–Japan	2008–ongoing	Memorandum of Understanding	Crisis communication, confidence-building	Partly, implementation ongoing	Yes	Yes

Bibliography

Cited Documents

'2019 ASEAN Defence Ministers' Meeting Guidelines for Maritime Interaction', 11 July 2019. https://cil.nus.edu.sg/wp-content/uploads/2019/11/2019-ADMM-Guidelines-Maritime-Interaction.pdf (last accessed 24 April 2024).

'A Tripartite Agreement for Joint Marine Scientific Research in Certain Areas in the South China Sea By and Among China National Offshore Oil Corporation Vietnam Oil and Gas Corporation Philippine National Oil Company', 14 March 2005. https://maritimeindex.org/wp-content/uploads/2021/12/VN-China-Philippines-tripartite-agreement-adopted-from-nghiencuubiendong.pdf (last accessed 24 April 2024).

'Agreement Between the Government of The United States of America and the Government of The Union of Soviet Socialist Republics on the Prevention of Incidents On and Over the High Seas', 25 May 1972. https://www.state.gov/t/isn/4791.htm (last accessed 24 April 2024).

'Agreement Concerning the Facilitation of Cooperation on Law Enforcement in Fisheries Matters between The Taipei Economic and Cultural Office in the Philippines and The Manila Economic and Cultural Office in Taiwan', 5 November 2015. https://law.moj.gov.tw/ENG/LawClass/LawAll.aspx?pcode=Y0110542 (last accessed 24 April 2024).

'Agreement on Fisheries between the People's Republic of China and Japan', 11 November 1997. An English translation is available in Sun Pyo Kim, *Maritime Delimitation and Interim Arrangements in North East Asia* (Martinus Nijhoff Publishers, 2004), 338–347.

'Agreement on Fisheries between the Republic of Korea and Japan', 1965. An English translation is available in Sun Pyo Kim, *Maritime Delimitation and Interim Arrangements in North East Asia* (Martinus Nijhoff Publishers, 2004), 321–327.

'Agreement on Fisheries between the Republic of Korea and Japan', 1999. An English translation is available in Sun Pyo Kim, *Maritime Delimitation and Interim Arrangements in North East Asia* (Martinus Nijhoff Publishers, 2004), 327–338.

'Agreement on Fisheries between the Republic of Korea and the People's Republic of China', 2000. An English translation is available in Sun Pyo Kim, *Maritime Delimitation and Interim Arrangements in North East Asia* (Martinus Nijhoff Publishers, 2004), 347–356.

'Agreement on Fishery Cooperation in the Beibu Gulf/Bac Bo Gulf between the Government of the People's Republic of China and the Government of Socialist Republic of Vietnam', 25 December 2000. An English translation is available in Keyuan Zou, 'Sino-Vietnamese Fishery Agreement for the Gulf of Tonkin', *International Journal of Marine and Coastal Law* 17/1 (2002): 127–148.

'Agreement on the Delimitation of the Territorial Seas, Exclusive Economic Zones and Continental Shelves in the Beibu Gulf/Bac Bo Gulf between the People's Republic of China and the Socialist Republic of Vietnam'. UN Treaty Series 2336, 2005, 25 December 2000.

'An Agreement for Joint Marine Seismic Undertaking in Certain Areas in the South China Sea By and Between the China National Offshore Corporation And Philippine National Oil Company', 1 September 2004. https://www.spratlys.org/documents/agreement_bilateral_marine_seismic_undertaking.pdf (last accessed 24 April 2024).

'ASEAN Declaration on the South China Sea, Manila', 22 July 1992. https://cil.nus.edu.sg/wp-content/uploads/2017/07/1992-ASEAN-Declaration-on-the-South-China-Sea.pdf (last accessed 24 April 2024).

ASEAN Member States and People's Republic of China. 'Declaration on the Conduct of Parties in the South China Sea', 4 November 2002. https://asean.org/declaration-on-the-conduct-of-parties-in-the-south-china-sea-2/ (last accessed 24 April 2024).

ASEAN Member States and People's Republic of China. 'Guidelines for the Implementation of the DOC', 19 July 2011. https://www.asean.org/wp-content/uploads/images/archive/documents/20185-DOC.pdf (last accessed 24 April 2024).

'ASEAN Regional Forum Ministerial Statement on Enhancing Cooperation among Maritime Law Enforcement Agencies'. 23rd ARF Foreign Ministers' Meeting, 26 July 2016. https://aseanregionalforum.asean.org/wp-content/uploads/2019/03/arf-ministerial-statement-on-enhancing-cooperation-among-maritime-law-enforcement-agencies.pdf (last accessed 24 April 2024).

'ASEAN Regional Forum Work Plan For Maritime Security 2018–2020', http://aseanregionalforum.asean.org/wp-content/uploads/2019/01/ARF-Maritime-Security-Work-Plan-2018-2020.pdf (last accessed 24 April 2024).

'Briefer: National Coast Watch Center'. Official Gazette of the Philippines, 28 April 2015. https://www.officialgazette.gov.ph/2015/04/28/briefer-national-coast-watch-center/ (last accessed 24 April 2024).

Brunei Darussalam. 'Preliminary submission for an extended continental shelf', 2009, http://www.un.org/Depts/los/clcs_new/submissions_files/preliminary/brn2009preliminaryinformation.pdf (last accessed 24 April 2024).

'Chairman's Statement of the 37th ASEAN Summit: Cohesive and Responsive', 12 November 2020, https://asean.org/wp-content/uploads/43-Chairmans-Statement-of-37th-ASEAN-Summit-FINAL.pdf (last accessed 24 April 2024).

'Chairman's Statement of the 31st ASEAN Summit', 13 Nov 2017, Manila, Philippines, para 138. https://asean.org/chairmans-statement-of-the-31st-asean-summit/ (last accessed 24 April 2024).

'Chairman's Statement of the 21st ASEAN-China Summit, Singapore', 14 November 2018, https://asean.org/wp-content/uploads/2018/11/ASEANChinaSummitChairmansStatementFinal1.pdf (last accessed 24 April 2024).

'Chairman's Statement of the 17th Meeting of the ASEAN Regional Forum', Ha Noi, 23 July 2010, accessible at https://asean.org/43rd-amm-pmc-17th-arf-vietnam-2010-chairmans-statement-17th-asean-regional-forum-ha-noi-23-july-2010/ (last accessed 24 April 2024).

'Chinese Embassy Spokesperson on Code of Conduct in the South China Sea', 18 September 2020, http://ph.china-embassy.org/eng/sgfyrbt/t1815987.htm (accessed 19 April 2022).

'Chinese Foreign Minister Yang Jiechi Meets the Press on East China Sea Issue', 24 June 2008, http://www.chinaconsulatesf.org/eng/xw/t451127.htm (last accessed 12 April 2022).

Chinese (Taiwan) Society of International Law. 'Amicus Curiae On the Issue of the Feature of Taiping Island (Itu Aba) Pursuant to Article 121 (1) and (3) of the 1982 United Nations Convention of the Law of the Sea', 23 March 2016. Available in Nigel N.T. Li, 'Amicus Curiae Submission by the Chinese (Taiwan) Society of International Law in the South China Sea Arbitration: An Introductory Note'. *Chinese (Taiwan) Yearbook of International Law and Affairs*, 33, (2017), 167–227.

CNOOC. 'Key operating areas', http://www.cnoocltd.com/col/col7311/index.html (last accessed 23 March 2024).

CNOOC. 'Major Properties', internet archive, https://web.archive.org/web/20060317225747/http://www.cnoocltd.com/Operations/channel/opertions1297.asp (accessed 23 March 2024).

'Coast Guard Law of the People's Republic of China. Order No. 71 of the President of the People's Republic of China', 22 January 2021. https://www.lawinfochina.com/display.aspx?lib=law&id=34610&EncodingName=big5 (last accessed 24 April 2024).

Codification Division Publication. 'Third United Nations Conference on the Law of the Sea 1973–1982'. Accessed 20 May 2019. http://legal.un.org/diplomaticconferences/1973_los/ (last accessed 24 April 2024).

Commission for the Limits of the Continental Shelf (CLCS). 'Rules of Procedure', https://www.un.org/depts/los/clcs_new/commission_rules.htm (last accessed 23 March 2024)

'Concept Paper on the Expansion of the ASEAN Direct Communications Infrastructure in the ASEAN Defense Ministers' Meeting (ADMM) Process To the Plus Countries', July 2019. https://admm.asean.org/dmdocuments/2019_July_13th%20ADMM_Bangkok,%2011%20July%202019_3.%20(Final)%20The%20Expansion%20of%20the%20ADI%20to%20the%20ADMM-Plus%20Countries.pdf (last accessed 24 April 2024).

'Convention on the International Regulations for Preventing Collisions at Sea', adopted 20 October 1972, entered not force 15 July 1977, https://treaties.un.org/pages/showDetails.aspx?objid=08000002800fcf87 (last accessed 24 April 2024).

Department of Energy of the Philippines. 'DOE Statement on the Announcement of the Termination of Joint Oil and Gas Negotiations with China', 25 June 2022, https://www.doe.gov.ph/press-releases/doe-statement-announcement-termination-joint-oil-and-gas-negotiations-china (last accessed 24 April 2024).

Department of Foreign Affairs of the Philippines. 'Joint Press Release for the Second Meeting of the Philippines-China Bilateral Consultative Mechanism on the South China Sea', 13 February 2018. https://dfa.gov.ph/dfa-news/dfa-releasesupdate/15562-second-meeting-of-the-philippines-china-bilateral-consultation-mechanism-on-the-south-china-sea (last accessed 24 April 2024).

Department of Justice of the Philippines. 'Balintang Channel Incident Report'. http://newsinfo.inquirer.net/460753/balintang-channel-incident-report (last accessed 24 April 2024).

Embassy of the People's Republic of China in the Philippines. 'Oil Companies of China, the Philippines and Vietnam signed Agreement on South China Sea Cooperation', 15 March 2005, http://ph.china-embassy.gov.cn/eng/zt/nhwt/200503/t20050315_1334600.htm#:~:text=On%2014%20March%20 2005%2C%20representatives,South%20China%20Sea%20in%20Manila (last accessed 24 April 2024).

Embassy of Vietnam to Germany. 'Viet Nam's International Press Conference', 7 May 2014, http://www.vietnambotschaft.org/viet-nams-international-press-conference-on-7th-may-2014/ (last accessed 24 April 2024).

Embassy of Vietnam to Germany. 'International Press Conference on the Situation in the East Sea', 5 June 2014. http://www.vietnambotschaft.org/international-press-conference-on-the-situation-in-the-east-sea/ (last accessed 24 April 2024).

First and Second China and Mongolia Division Asian and Oceanian Affairs Bureau, Ministry of Foreign Affairs of Japan. 'Recent Japan-Taiwan Relations and the Taiwan Situation', July 2013. https://www.mofa.go.jp/region/asia-paci/taiwan/pdfs/japan-taiwan_relations.pdf (last accessed 24 April 2024).

'Fisheries Agreement between the People's Republic of China and Japan 15 August 1975'. U.S. Department of State, Limits in the Sea No.70, 6 April 1976. https://www.state.gov/wp-content/uploads/2019/11/LIS-70.pdf (last accessed 24 April 2024).

'Framework Agreement on Joint Maritime Oil and Gas Exploration between China and the Philippines (Chinese Draft)', 22 November 2018. Available at https://www.philstar.com/headlines/2018/11/20/1870227/china-claims-draft-oil-exploration-deal-have-no-bearing-sovereignty (last accessed 24 April 2024).

Government of Japan. 'Japan's Submission to the Commission on the Limits of the Continental Shelf', 2008. https://www.un.org/Depts/los/clcs_new/submissions_files/jpn08/jpn_execsummary.pdf (last accessed 24 April 2024).

Government of Japan. 'Law of the Exclusive Economic Zone and Continental Shelf (Law No. 74 of 1996)'. Law of the Sea Bulletin No 35, 1997.

Government of the People's Republic of China. 'Position Paper of the Government of the People's Republic of China on the Matter of Jurisdiction in the South China Sea Arbitration Initiated by the Republic of the Philippines', 7 December 2014. https://www.fmprc.gov.cn/mfa_eng/wjdt_665385/2649_665393/201412/t20141207_679387.html (last accessed 24 April 2024).

Government of the People's Republic of China. 'Declaration under Article 298', 25 August 2006. https://treaties.un.org/Pages/ViewDetailsIII.aspx?src=TREATY&mtdsg_no=XXI-6&chapter=21&Temp=mtdsg3&clang=_en#EndDec (last accessed 24 April 2024).

'Guidelines for Air Military Encounters Adopted by the 12th ADMM', 19 October 2018. https://admm.asean.org/dmdocuments/2018_Oct_12th%20ADMM_Singapore,%2019%20October%202018_[Final]%20Guidelines%20for%20Air%20Military%20Encounters.pdf (last accessed 24 April 2024).

'Guidelines for Hotline Communications Among Senior Officials of the Ministries of Foreign Affairs of ASEAN Member States and China in Response to Maritime Emergencies in the Implementation of the Declaration on the Conduct of Parties in the South China Sea', 7 September 2016. https://cil.nus.edu.sg/wp-content/uploads/2019/10/2016-ASEAN-China-Guidlines-for-Hotline-Communications.pdf (last accessed 24 April 2024).

'Guidelines for the Implementation of the DOC', 19 July 2011. https://www.asean.org/wp-content/uploads/images/archive/documents/20185-DOC.pdf (last accessed 24 April 2024).

International Court of Justice. 'The Minquiers and Ecrehos Case. Judgement'. I.C.J. Reports 1953, p. 47, 17 November 1953.

Japan Coast Guard. 'Annual Report 2016'. https://www.kaiho.mlit.go.jp/e/anuual_report_of_jcg.html (last accessed 24 April 2024).

Japan Ministry of Defense. 'China's Activities in East China Sea, Pacific Ocean, and Sea of Japan', March 2024. https://www.mod.go.jp/en/d_act/sec_env/pdf/ch_d-act_a.pdf (last accessed 24 April 2024).

Japan Ministry of Defense. 'Japan-China Defense Ministers' Meeting (Summary)', 1 June 2019. https://www.mod.go.jp/en/d_act/exc/area/docs/2019/20190601_j-china_e.html (last accessed 24 April 2024).

Japan Ministry of Defense. 'Regarding the incident of an ROK naval vessel directing its fire-control radar at an MSDF patrol aircraft', December 2018, https://www.mod.go.jp/en/d_act/radar/index.html (last accessed 24 April 2024).

Japan Ministry of Defense. 'China's Maritime Expansion Report', April 2017. (on file with the author).

'Joint Communiqué of the 51st ASEAN Foreign Ministers Meeting Singapore', 2 August 2018. https://asean.org/speechandstatement/joint-communique-of-the-51st-asean-foreign-ministers-meeting/ (last accessed 24 April 2024).

'Joint Communiqué of the 50th ASEAN Foreign Ministers' Meeting', Manila, Philippines, 5 August 2017. https://asean.org/wp-content/uploads/2021/03/4.pdf (last accessed 24 April 2024).

'Joint Communiqué of the 38th ASEAN Ministerial Meeting', Vientiane, 26 July 2005. https://asean.org/joint-communique-of-the-38th-asean-ministerial-meeting-vientiane-26-july-2005/ (last accessed 24 April 2024).

'Joint Communiqué of the Government of Japan and the Government of the People's Republic of China', 29 September 1972. https://www.mofa.go.jp/region/asia-paci/china/joint72.html (last accessed 24 April 2024).

'Joint Press Conference by Minister for Foreign Affairs Masahiko Koumura and Minister of Economy, Trade and Industry Akira Amari (Regarding Cooperation between Japan and China in the East China Sea)', 18 June 2008. https://www.mofa.go.jp/announce/fm_press/2008/6/0618.html (last accessed 12 August 2023).

'Joint Statement between the Government of Japan and the Government of the People's Republic of China on Comprehensive Promotion of a "Mutually Beneficial Relationship Based on Common Strategic Interests"', Tokyo, 7 May 2008. https://www.mofa.go.jp/region/asia-paci/china/joint0805.html (last accessed 23 March 2022).

'Joint Statement between the People's Republic of China and Brunei Darussalam', 5 April 2013. https://www.fmprc.gov.cn/mfa_eng/wjdt_665385/2649_665393/201304/t20130409_679342.html (last accessed 24 April 2024).

'Joint Statement of the Foreign Ministers of ASEAN Member States and China on the Full and Effective Implementation of the Declaration on the Conduct of Parties in the South China Sea', 25 July 2016. https://asean.org/wp-content/uploads/2016/07/Joint-Statement-on-the-full-and-effective-implementation-of-the-DOC-FINAL.pdf (last accessed 24 April 2024).

'Joint Statement of the Meeting of Heads of State/Government of the Member States of ASEAN and the President of the People's Republic of China Kuala Lumpur', 16 December 1997. https://asean.org/joint-statement-of-the-meeting-of-heads-of-state-government-of-the-member-states-of-asean-and-the-president-of-the-peoples-republic-of-china-kuala-lumpur-malaysia-16-december-1997/ (last accessed 24 April 2024).

'Joint Statement on the Application of the Code for Unplanned Encounters at Sea in the South China Sea', 7 September 2016. https://asean.org/wp-content/

uploads/2016/09/Joint-Statement-on-the-Application-of-CUES-in-the-SCS-Final.pdf (last accessed 24 April 2024).

'Joint Statement by the Honourable Prime Minister of Malaysia and His Excellency President of the Republic of Indonesia', 8 June 2023. https://demaribus.files.wordpress.com/2023/06/joint-statement-8-june-2023.pdf (last accessed 24 April 2024).

'Law on the Exclusive Economic Zone and the Continental Shelf of the Republic of China', 21 January 1998. https://law.moj.gov.tw/ENG/LawClass/LawAll.aspx?pcode=A0000010 (last accessed 24 April 2024).

'Malaysia and Vietnam Joint Submission for an Extended Continental Shelf', 6 May 2009. http://www.un.org/Depts/los/clcs_new/submissions_files/submission_mysvnm_33_2009.htm (last accessed 24 April 2024).

Malaysia. 'Submission for an Extended Continental Shelf', Commission on the Limits of the Continental Shelf (CLCS), 12 December 2019 https://www.un.org/Depts/los/clcs_new/submissions_files/submission_mys_12_12_2019.html (last accessed 24 April 2024).

'Memorandum of Understanding Between the Department of Defense of the United States of America and the Ministry of National Defense of the People's Republic of China Regarding the Rules of Behavior for Safety of Air and Maritime Encounters', 9 November 2014. https://dod.defense.gov/Portals/1/Documents/pubs/141112_MemorandumOfUnderstandingRegardingRules.pdf (last accessed 24 April 2024).

'Memorandum of Understanding on Cooperation on Oil and Gas Development between the Government of People's Republic of China and the Government of the Republic of the Philippines', 20 November 2018. https://www.mfa.gov.cn/eng/wjdt_665385/2649_665393/201811/t20181127_679548.html (last accessed 24 April 2024).

'Memorandum of Understanding between the Department of Agriculture of the Republic of the Philippines and the Ministry of Agriculture of the People's Republic of China on Fisheries Cooperation', signed in Beijing on 1 September 2004.

Minquiers and Ecrehos (France/United Kingdom), (1953) ICJ Reports 47.

Ministry of Foreign Affairs of China. 'Statement of the Ministry of Foreign Affairs of the People's Republic of China on the Award of 12 July 2016 of the Arbitral Tribunal in the South China Sea Arbitration Established at the Request of the Republic of the Philippines', 12 July 2016. https://www.fmprc.gov.cn/mfa_eng/wjdt_665385/2649_665393/201607/t20160712_679470.html (last accessed 24 April 2024).

Ministry of Foreign Affairs of China. 'Foreign Ministry Spokesperson Hong Lei's Regular Press Conference on November 9, 2015'. https://www.fmprc.gov.cn/ce/cedk/eng/fyrth/t1313261.htm (last accessed 23 March 2022).

Ministry of Foreign Affairs of China. 'Vice Foreign Minister Wu Dawei Talks About the Principled Consensuses Reached Between China and Japan on the East China Sea Issue', 19 June 2008. https://www.fmprc.gov.cn/eng/wjdt_665385/wshd_665389/200806/t20080623_636938.html (last accessed 24 April 2024).

Ministry of Foreign Affairs of Japan. 'The Current Status of China's Unilateral Development of Natural Resources in the East China Sea. Map', 5 June 2023. https://www.mofa.go.jp/files/000091724.pdf (last accessed 24 April 2024).

Ministry of Foreign Affairs of Japan. 'Status of activities by Chinese government vessels and Chinese fishing vessels in waters surrounding the Senkaku Islands', 26 August 2016. https://www.mofa.go.jp/files/000180283.pdf (last accessed 24 April 2024).

Ministry of Foreign Affairs of Japan. 'Japan's legal position on the development of natural resources in the East China Sea', 6 August 2015, https://www.mofa.go.jp/a_o/c_m1/page3e_000358.html (last accessed 24 April 2024).

Ministry of Foreign Affairs of Japan. 'Press Conference by Minister for Foreign Affairs Masahiko Koumura', 26 August 2008. https://www.mofa.go.jp/announce/fm_press/2008/8/0826.html (last accessed 24 April 2024).

Ministry of Foreign Affairs of Japan. 'China-Japan Principled Consensus on the East China Sea Issue', 18 June 2008. https://www.mofa.go.jp/files/000091726.pdf (last accessed 24 April 2024).

Ministry of Foreign Affairs of Japan. 'Japan-China Joint Press Statement', 11 April 2007. https://www.mofa.go.jp/region/asia-paci/china/pv0704/joint.html (last accessed 24 April 2024).

Ministry of Foreign Affairs of Japan. 'Press Conference 22 June 2004'. https://www.mofa.go.jp/announce/press/2004/6/0622.html (last accessed 24 April 2024).

Ministry of Foreign Affairs of Japan. 'Outline of the New Japan-China Fisheries Agreement', (on file with the author).

Ministry of Foreign Affairs of Taiwan. 'South China Sea', https://en.mofa.gov.tw/theme.aspx?n=1462&s=40&sms=294 (last accessed 24 April 2024).

Ministry of Foreign Affairs of Taiwan. 'ROC position on the South China Sea Arbitration', 12 July 2016. https://www.mofa.gov.tw/en/News_Content.aspx?n=1EADDCFD4C6EC567&s=5B5A9134709EB875 (last accessed 24 April 2024).

Ministry of Foreign Affairs of Taiwan. 'Taiwan Press Announcement No. 202', 08 August 2013. https://www.mofa.gov.tw/en/News_Content.aspx?n=539A9A50A5F8AF9E&sms=37B41539382B84BA&s=C9567323DE86F532 (last accessed 23 June 2023).

Ministry of Foreign Affairs of Taiwan. 'The Taiwan-Japan Fisheries Agreement – Embodying the Ideals and Spirit of the East China Sea Peace Initiative', August 2013, Catalogue Card No. MOFA-EN-FO-102-006-I-1. https://chinaus-icas.

org/wp-content/uploads/2019/08/Taiwan-Japan-Fisheries-Agreement-Pamphlet.pdf (last accessed 24 April 2024).

Ministry of Foreign Affairs of Taiwan. 'President Ma proposes the East China Sea Peace Initiative, calls on all parties concerned to resolve Diaoyutai dispute peacefully', Press Release, 5 August 2012. https://www.mofa.gov.tw/en/News_Content.aspx?n=539A9A50A5F8AF9E&sms=37B41539382B84BA&s=8791CAB0BB21333B (last accessed 13 April 2022).

Ministry of Foreign Affairs of Vietnam. 'Statement of the MOFA Spokesperson on the Violations of Viet Nam's EEZ and Continental Shelf by the Chinese Survey Ship, Haiyang Dizhi 8, and Its Escort Vessels', 26 July 2019. http://www.vietnamembassy.at/en/news/statement-spokesperson-vietnamese-ministry-foreign-affairs-le-thi-thu-hang-regarding-chinese (last accessed 24 April 2024).

Ministry of Foreign Affairs of Vietnam. 'Press Conference on Chinese Maritime Surveillance Vessel's Cutting Exploration Cable of PetroViet Nam Seismic Vessel', 29 May 2011. http://www.mofa.gov.vn/en/tt_baochi/pbnfn/ns110530220030/ (last accessed 13 April 2022).

North Sea Continental Shelf Cases (*Federal Republic of Germany/Denmark; Federal Republic of Germany/Netherlands*), (1969) ICJ Reports 3.

Office of the United States Trade Representative. 'Report on the Appellate Body of the World Trade Organization', February 2020. https://ustr.gov/sites/default/files/Report_on_the_Appellate_Body_of_the_World_Trade_Organization.pdf (last accessed 24 April 2024).

People's Republic of China. 'Partial Submission for an Extended Continental Shelf', 14 December 2012. http://www.un.org/Depts/los/clcs_new/submissions_files/submission_chn_63_2012.htm (last accessed 24 April 2024).

People's Republic of China. 'Preliminary Information Indicative of the Outer Limits of the Continental Shelf Beyond 200 Nautical Miles', 11 May 2009. http://www.un.org/depts/los/clcs_new/commission_preliminary.htm (last accessed 24 April 2024).

Permanent Mission of Malaysia to the United Nations. 'Note Verbale to the United Nations', 27 August 2020. https://www.un.org/Depts/los/clcs_new/submissions_files/mys_12_12_2019/2020_08_27_MYS_NV_UN_003.pdf (last accessed 24 April 2024).

Permanent Mission of the People's Republic of China to the United Nations. 'Note Verbale'. CML/17/2009, 7 May 2009. http://www.un.org/depts/los/clcs_new/submissions_files/mysvnm33_09/chn_2009re_mys_vnm_e.pdf (last accessed 24 April 2024).

Permanent Mission of the Republic of Indonesia. 'Communication of the Republic of Indonesia to the United Nations No. 148/POL-703/VI/20', 12 June 2020. https://www.un.org/Depts/los/clcs_new/submissions_files/

mys_12_12_2019/2020_06_12_IDN_NV_UN_002_ENG.pdf (last accessed 24 April 2024).

Permanent Mission of the Republic of Indonesia. 'Note Verbale to the United Nations No. 480/POL-703/VII/10', 8 July 2010. https://www.un.org/depts/los/clcs_new/submissions_files/mysvnm33_09/idn_2010re_mys_vnm_e.pdf (last accessed 24 April 2024).

Permanent Mission of the Republic of the Philippines. 'Note Verbale No. 000192-2020', 6 March 2020. https://www.un.org/Depts/los/clcs_new/submissions_files/submission_mys_12_12_2019.html (last accessed 24 April 2024).

Permanent Mission of the Republic of the Philippines. 'Notes Verbales 000191-2020', 6 March 2020. https://www.un.org/Depts/los/clcs_new/submissions_files/submission_mys_12_12_2019.html (last accessed 24 April 2024).

Permanent Mission of the Republic of the Philippines. 'Note Verbale No. 000228', 5 April 2011. https://www.un.org/depts/los/clcs_new/submissions_files/vnm37_09/phl_re_chn_2011.pdf (last accessed 24 April 2024).

PetroVietnam. 'Petrovietnam and CNOOC signed the 4th Amendment to the Agreement on Joint Exploration in the Gulf of Tonkin', Press Release, 20 June 2013. http://www.pvcoating.vn/en/shareholders/details/petrovietnam-and-cnooc-signed-the-4th-amendment-to-the-agreement-on-joint-exploration-in-the-gulf-of-tonkin-139/ (last accessed 24 April 2024).

'Philippines' Memorial – Volume II', 30 March 2014. https://files.pca-cpa.org/pcadocs/Memorial%20of%20the%20Philippines%20Volume%20II.pdf (last accessed 24 April 2024).

'Philippines' Memorial – Volume III (Annexes 1-60)', 30 March 2014. https://files.pca-cpa.org/pcadocs/The%20Philippines%27%20Memorial%20-%20Volume%20III%20%28Annexes%201-60%29.pdf (last accessed 24 April 2024).

'Philippines' Memorial – Volume IV (Annexes 61-102)', 30 March 2014. https://files.pca-cpa.org/pcadocs/The%20Philippines%27%20Memorial%20-%20Volume%20IV%20%28Annexes%2061-102%29.pdf (last accessed 24 April 2024).

'Philippines' Memorial – Volume V (Annexes 103-157)', 30 March 2014. https://files.pca-cpa.org/pcadocs/The%20Philippines%27%20Memorial%20-%20Volume%20V%20%28Annexes%20103-157%29.pdf (last accessed 24 April 2024).

'Philippines' Memorial – Volume VI (Annexes 158-221)', 30 March 2014. https://files.pca-cpa.org/pcadocs/The%20Philippines%27%20Memorial%20-%20Volume%20III%20%28Annexes%201-60%29.pdf (last accessed 24 April 2024).

'Philippines' Memorial – Volume VII (Annexes 222-255)', 30 March 2014. https://files.pca-cpa.org/pcadocs/The%20Philippines%27%20Memorial%20-%20Volume%20VII%20%28Annexes%20222-255%29.pdf (last accessed 24 April 2024).

'Philippines' Memorial – Volume VIII (Annexes 256-275)', 30 March 2014. https://files.pca-cpa.org/pcadocs/The%20Philippines%27%20Memorial%20

-%20Volume%20VIII%20%28Annexes%20256-275%29.pdf (last accessed 24 April 2024).
'Philippines' Memorial – Volume IX (Annexes 276-306)', 30 March 2014. https://files.pca-cpa.org/pcadocs/The%20Philippines%27%20Memorial%20-%20Volume%20IX%20%28Annexes%20276-306%29.pdf (last accessed 24 April 2024).
'Philippines' Memorial – Volume X (Annexes 307-343)', 30 March 2014. https://files.pca-cpa.org/pcadocs/The%20Philippines%27%20Memorial%20-%20Volume%20X%20%28Annexes%20307-343%29.pdf (last accessed 24 April 2024).
'Philippines' Supplemental Written Submission — Volume III (Annexes 344-385)', 16 March 2015. https://files.pca-cpa.org/pcadocs/The%20Philippines%27%20Supplemental%20Written%20Submission%20-%20Volume%20III%20%28Annexes%20344-385%29.pdf (last accessed 24 April 2024).
'Philippines' Supplemental Written Submission — Volume IV (Annexes 386-442)', 16 March 2015. https://files.pca-cpa.org/pcadocs/The%20Philippines%27%20Supplemental%20Written%20Submission%20-%20Volume%20IV%20%28Annexes%20386-442%29.pdf (last accessed 24 April 2024).
'Philippines' Supplemental Written Submission — Volume V (Annexes 443-465)', 16 March 2015. https://files.pca-cpa.org/pcadocs/The%20Philippines%27%20Supplemental%20Written%20Submission%20-%20Volume%20V%20%28Annexes%20443-465%29.pdf (last accessed 24 April 2024).
'Philippines' Supplemental Written Submission — Volume VIII (Annexes 466-499)', 16 March 2015. https://files.pca-cpa.org/pcadocs/The%20Philippines%27%20Supplemental%20Written%20Submission%20-%20Volume%20VIII%20%28Annexes%20466-499%29.pdf (last accessed 24 April 2024).
'Philippines' Supplemental Written Submission — Volume IX (Annexes 500-521)', 16 March 2015. https://files.pca-cpa.org/pcadocs/The%20Philippines%27%20Supplemental%20Written%20Submission%20-%20Volume%20IX%20%28Annexes%20500-521%29.pdf (last accessed 24 April 2024).
'Philippines' Supplemental Documents – Volume I (Annexes 607-667)', 19 November 2015. https://files.pca-cpa.org/pcadocs/The%20Philippines%27%20Supplemental%20Documents%20-%20Volume%20I%20%28Annexes%20607-667%29.pdf (last accessed 24 April 2024).
'Philippines' Supplemental Documents – Volume II (Annexes 608-709)', 19 November 2015. https://files.pca-cpa.org/pcadocs/The%20Philippines%27%20Supplemental%20Documents%20-%20Volume%20II%20%28Annexes%20608-709%29.pdf (last accessed 24 April 2024).
'Philippines' Supplemental Documents – Volume V (Annexes 807-819)', 19 November 2015. https://files.pca-cpa.org/pcadocs/The%20Philippines%27%20Supplemental%20Documents%20-%20Volume%20V%20%28Annexes%20807-819%29.pdf (last accessed 24 April 2024).

Philippines' Republic Act No. 9522, Presidential Decree No. 1596, 1978. https://www.lawphil.net/statutes/repacts/ra2009/ra_9522_2009.html (last accessed 24 April 2024).

'Plan of Action to Implement the Joint Declaration on China-ASEAN Partnership for Peace and Prosperity', Vientiane, 29 November 2004. https://cil.nus.edu.sg/wp-content/uploads/2019/02/2004-Plan-of-Action-to-Implement-ASEAN-China-Joint-Declaration-1.pdf (last accessed 24 April 2024).

'Press Conference by Minister for Foreign Affairs Seiji Maehara', 28 September 2010. https://www.mofa.go.jp/announce/fm_press/2010/9/0928_01.html (last accessed 24 April 2024).

'Press Conference by Minister for Foreign Affairs Katsuya Okada', 10 September 2010. https://www.mofa.go.jp/announce/fm_press/2010/9/0910_01.html (last accessed 24 April 2024).

'Press Conference by Minister for Foreign Affairs Masahiko Koumura', 26 August 2008. https://www.mofa.go.jp/announce/fm_press/2008/8/0826.html (last accessed 24 April 2024).

'Press Conference by Minister for Foreign Affairs Masahiko Koumura', 3 June 2008. https://www.mofa.go.jp/announce/fm_press/2008/6/0603.html (last accessed 24 April 2024).

'Press Conference of the Taiwan Affairs Office of the State Council', 12 September 2012. http://eng.taiwan.cn/Press_conference/201304/t20130424_4122587.htm (last accessed 24 April 2024).

'Remarks of the Spokesperson of the Ministry of Foreign Affairs of Viet Nam', 12 July 2016. http://www.mofa.gov.vn/en/tt_baochi/pbnfn/ns160712211059 (last accessed 24 April 2024).

Republic of China (Taiwan). 'Position Paper on ROC South China Sea Policy', 21 March 2016. https://multilingual.mofa.gov.tw/web/web_UTF-8/South/Position%20Paper%20on%20ROC%20South%20China%20Sea%20Policy.pdf (last accessed 24 April 2024).

Republic of Korea. 'Partial Submission To the Commission on the Limits of the Continental Shelf Pursuant to Article 76 Paragraph 8 of the United Nations Convention on the Law of the Sea Executive Summary', December 2012. https://www.un.org/Depts/los/clcs_new/submissions_files/kor65_12/executive_summary.pdf (last accessed 24 April 2024).

Republic of Korea and Japan. 'Agreement Concerning Joint Development of the Southern Part of the Continental Shelf Adjacent to the Two Countries'. UN deposit Vol. 1225/1-19778, 30 January 1974.

Republic of the Philippines. 'Notification and Statement of Claim', Memorial of the Philippines Volume III (Annex 1), 22 January 2013. https://files.pca-cpa.org/

pcadocs/The%20Philippines%27%20Memorial%20-%20Volume%20III%20%28Annexes%201-60%29.pdf (last accessed 24 April 2024).

Senate Armed Services Committee. 'Advance Policy Questions for Admiral Philip Davidson, USN Expected Nominee for Commander, U.S. Pacific Command', 20 August 2019. https://www.armed-services.senate.gov/imo/media/doc/Davidson_APQs_04-17-18.pdf (last accessed 24 April 2024).

Senate of the Philippines. 'Statement on the Reed Bank Incident', Press Release, 08 March 2011. https://www.senate.gov.ph/press_release/2011/0308_angara2.asp (last accessed 24 April 2024).

Shell Philippines. 'Malampaya Gas Production', 2015. https://www.shell.com.ph/media/media-releases/2015-media-releases/malampaya-begins-gas-production.html (last accessed 24 April 2024).

South China Sea Arbitration (*The Republic of Philippines v. The People's Republic of China*) Award (12 July 2016).

South China Sea Arbitration (*The Republic of Philippines v. The People's Republic of China*) Award on Jurisdiction and Admissibility (29 October 2015).

State Council Information Office of the People's Republic of China. 'China Adheres to the Position of Settling Through Negotiation the Relevant Disputes Between China and the Philippines in the South China Sea. White Paper', 13 July 2016. http://english.www.gov.cn/state_council/ministries/2016/07/13/content_281475392503075.htm (last accessed 24 April 2024).

State Council Information Office of the People's Republic of China. 'China's National Defense in the New Era', 2019. https://english.www.gov.cn/archive/whitepaper/201907/24/content_WS5d3941ddc6d08408f502283d.html (last accessed 24 April 2024).

State Council of the People's Republic of China. 'China urges against Vietnamese interference in territorial water exploration activities in Xisha Islands', 8 May 2014. https://english.www.gov.cn/state_council/state_councilors/2014/08/23/content_281474983036388.htm (last accessed 24 April 2024).

'Statement of the Government of the People's Republic of China on China's Territorial Sovereignty and Maritime Rights and Interests in the South China Sea'. *Chinese Journal of International Law* 15/4 (1 December 2016): 903–4. https://doi.org/10.1093/chinesejil/jmw045.

'Statement of the Secretary of Foreign Affairs of the Philippines', 12 July 2016. (on file with the author).

'Statement of 12 November 1982 by the Government of the Socialist Republic of Viet Nam on the Territorial Sea Baseline of Viet Nam', in United Nations Office for Ocean Affairs and the Law of the Sea, ed., *The Law of the Sea Baselines: National Legislation With Illustrative Maps*, (1989), 384-87.

Supreme Court of the Philippines. *Bayan Muna Party-List vs President Macapal-Arroyo*, No. G.R. No. 182734 (10 January 2023). https://sc.judiciary.gov.ph/182734-bayan-muna-party-list-representative-satur-c-ocampo-and-teodoro-a-casino-anakpawis-representative-crispin-b-beltran-gabriela-womens-party-representatives-liza-l-maza-and-luzviminda-c-i/ (last accessed 24 April 2024).

'Terms of Reference of the ASEAN-China Joint Working Group on the Implementation of the Declaration on the Conduct of Parties in the South China Sea, Kuala Lumpur', 7 December 2004. https://cil.nus.edu.sg/databasecil/2004-terms-of-reference-of-the-asean-china-joint-working-group-on-the-implementation-of-the-declaration-on-the-conduct-of-parties-in-the-south-china-sea/ (last accessed 24 April 2024).

United States of America. 'Summary of the National Defense Strategy Sharping the American Military's Competitive Edge', 2018. https://dod.defense.gov/Portals/1/Documents/pubs/2018-National-Defense-Strategy-Summary.pdf (last accessed 24 April 2024).

UN Economic Commission for Asia and the Far East. 'Report of the Sixth Session of the Committee for Coordination of Joint Prospecting for Mineral Resources in Asian Offshore Areas (CCOP), E/CN.11/L.239', 26 June 1969.

United Nations Convention on the Law of the Sea, adopted 10 December 1982, entered into force 16 November 1994, 1833 UNTS 396, https://legal.un.org/avl/ha/uncls/uncls.html (last accessed 24 April 2024).

US Department of Defense. 'Annual Freedom of Navigation Report', 31 December 2018. https://policy.defense.gov/OUSDP-Offices/FON/ (last accessed 24 April 2024).

US Department of Defense. 'Indo-Pacific Strategy Report. Preparedness, Partnerships, and Promoting a Networked Region', 1 June 2019. https://media.defense.gov/2019/Jul/01/2002152311/-1/-1/1/DEPARTMENT-OF-DEFENSE-INDO-PACIFIC-STRATEGY-REPORT-2019.PDF (last accessed 24 April 2024).

US Department of State. 'A Free and Open Indo-Pacific Advancing a Shared Vision', 4 November 2019. https://www.state.gov/wp-content/uploads/2019/11/Free-and-Open-Indo-Pacific-4Nov2019.pdf (last accessed 24 April 2024).

US Department of State. 'Military Operational Issues', 2009. Archive. https://2001-2009.state.gov/t/pm/iso/c21539.htm (last accessed 24 April 2024).

US Energy Information Administration. 'East China Sea', September 2014. https://www.eia.gov/beta/international/regions-topics.php?RegionTopicID=ECS (last accessed 24 April 2024).

US Energy Information Administration. 'South China Sea', updated 21 March 2024. https://www.eia.gov/beta/international/regions-topics.php?RegionTopicID=SCS (last accessed 24 April 2024).

Western and Central Pacific Fisheries Commission. 'Frequently Asked Questions and Brochures', 2010. https://www.wcpfc.int/doc/commission-faqs (last accessed 24 April 2024).

Western Pacific Naval Symposium. 'Code for Unplanned Encounters at Sea', 22 April 2014. https://news.usni.org/2014/06/17/document-conduct-unplanned-encounters-sea (last accessed 24 April 2024).

Cited Literature

Abad, Rino E., 'Philippine Offshore Oil and Gas Interests in the West Philippine Sea', *4th Roundtable Discussion Philippine Offshore Oil and Gas industry: Prospects for Competition and Cooperation*, 28 February 2016, https://slideplayer.com/slide/10115380/ (last accessed 25 March 2024).

Alcala, Angel, 'Environmental Protection in the Spratlys, South China Sea, under the UNCLOS: JOMSRE-SCS III & IV' (2019), https://aseanregionalforum.asean.org/wp-content/uploads/2019/10/Annex-S-Dr.-Alcala-environmental-protection-in-the-Spratlys-SCS.pdf.

Aggarwal, V. K., and C. Dupont, 'Goods, Games, and Institutions', *International Political Science Review* 20/4 (1999), 393–409.

Akiyama, Shinichi, 'Japan, China Launch Maritime-Aerial Communication Mechanism', *Mainichi Daily News* (8 June 2018), https://mainichi.jp/english/articles/20180608/p2a/00m/0na/002000c (last accessed 24 April 2024).

Albin, Cecilia, 'The Role of Fairness in Negotiation', *Negotiation Journal*, 9/3 (1993), 223–44.

Allison, Graham T, *Destined for War: Can America and China Escape Thucydides's Trap?* (Mariner, 2017).

Amer, Ramses, 'The South China Sea: Achievements and Challenges to Dispute Management', *Asian Survey*, 55/3 (2015), 618–39. https://doi.org/10.1525/as.2015.55.3.618.

Amer, Ramses, and Keyuan Zou, *Conflict Management and Dispute Settlement in East Asia* (Ashgate, 2011).

Andrews-Speed, Philip, Xuanli Liao, and Roland Dannreuther, *The Strategic Implications of China's Energy Needs* (Routledge, 2014).

Aoi, Chiyuki, Madoka Futamura, and Alessio Patalano, 'Introduction "Hybrid Warfare in Asia: Its Meaning and Shape"', *The Pacific Review*, 31/6 (November 2018), 693–713. https://doi.org/10.1080/09512748.2018.1513548.

Ásgeirsdóttir, Áslaug, and Martin Steinwand, 'Dispute Settlement Mechanisms and Maritime Boundary Settlements', *The Review of International Organizations*, 10/2 (June 2015), 119–43. https://doi.org/10.1007/s11558-015-9217-9.

Asia Maritime Transparency Initiative of the Center for Strategic and International Studies, 'Island-tracker', https://amti.csis.org/island-tracker/ (last accessed 23 March 2024).

Asia Maritime Transparency Initiative of the Center for Strategic and International Studies, 'Smooth Sailing for East China Sea Fishing', 30 November 2017, https://amti.csis.org/smooth-sailing-east-china-sea/ (last accessed 12 April 2024).

Asia Maritime Transparency Initiative of the Center for Strategic and International Studies, 'China Risks Flare-Up Over Malaysian, Vietnamese Gas Resources', *AMTI Update* (July 2019), https://amti.csis.org/china-risks-flare-up-over-malaysian-vietnamese-gas-resources/ (last accessed 12 April 2024).

Austin, Greg, *China's Ocean Frontier: International Law, Military Force, and National Development* (Allen & Unwin, 1998).

Awai, Tsuguo, *The Silent Guardians of the East China Sea. Unsung Heroes of the Japan Coast Guard to Stand Guard of Senkaku* (NextPublishing, 2022).

Axe, David, 'Sunk: How China's Man-Made Islands Are Falling Apart and Sinking Into the Ocean', *The National Interest* (12 March 2020), https://nationalinterest.org/blog/buzz/sunk-how-chinas-man-made-islands-are-falling-apart-and-sinking-ocean-132047 (last accessed 12 April 2024).

Axelrod, Robert, and William Donald Hamilton, 'The Evolution of Cooperation', *Science,* 211/4489 (1981), 1390–6.

Axelrod, Robert M., *The Evolution of Cooperation* (Basic Books, 1984).

Baldwin, David A., 'Power and International Relations', in Walter Carlsnaes, Thomas Risse, and Beth Simmons, eds., *Handbook of International Relations* (SAGE, 2012), 273–97.

Baldwin, David A. *Power and International Relations: A Conceptual Approach* (Princeton UP, 2016).

Banlaoi, Rommel, 'The Bilateral Consultative Mechanism on the South China Sea and Philippines-China Relations', *ISEAS Commentary* (2021), https://www.iseas.edu.sg/articles-commentaries/iseas-perspective/2021-51-the-bilateral-consultative-mechanism-on-the-south-china-sea-and-philippines-china-relations-by-rommel-c-banlaoi/ (last accessed 24 April 2024).

Bateman, Sam. 'CUES and Coast Guards', *East Asia Forum* (October 2016), https://www.eastasiaforum.org/2016/10/07/cues-and-coast-guards/ (last accessed 24 April 2024).

Bateman, Sam. 'Favourable Currents for ASEAN–China Relations in the South China Sea'. *East Asia Forum*, (December 2018), http://www.eastasiaforum.org/2018/12/12/favourable-currents-for-asean-china-relations-in-the-south-china-sea/ (last accessed 24 April 2024).

Bateman, Sam. 'Hydrographic Surveying in the EEZ: Differences and Overlaps with Marine Scientific Research', *Marine Policy*, 29/2 (March 2005), 163–74. https://doi.org/10.1016/j.marpol.2004.08.011.

Bateman, Sam. 'Prospective Guidelines for Navigation and Overflight in the Exclusive Economic Zone', *Maritime Studies*, 144 (2005), 17–28.

Bateman, Sam and Ralf Emmers, eds., *Security and International Politics in the South China Sea: Towards a Cooperative Management Regime*, vol. 9 of Routledge Security in Asia Pacific Series (Routledge, 2009).

Batongbacal, Jay, 'Philippine-China Joint Development Talks Still at an Impasse despite Green Light', *AMTI* (23 April 2018), https://amti.csis.org/philippine-china-joint-development-impasse/ (last accessed 24 April 2024).

Batongbacal, Jay, 'The Philippines-China MOU on Cooperation in Oil and Gas Development', *AMTI* (5 December 2018), https://amti.csis.org/philippines-china-mou-cooperation-oil-gas-development/ (last accessed 24 April 2024).

Batongbacal, Jay, and Aileen Baviera, 'When Will Conditions Be Ripe? Prospects for Joint Development in the South China Sea', *13th Asia-Pacific Roundtable Kuala Lumpur* (1999).

Bautista, Lowell, 'The South China Sea Arbitral Award: Evolving Post-Arbitration Strategies, Implications and Challenges', *Asian Politics & Policy*, 10/2 (2018), 178–89.

Baviera, Aileen, 'The Influence of Domestic Politics on Philippine Foreign Policy: The Case of Philippines-China Relations since 2004', *RSIS Working Paper* (2012), 1–36.

Bazerman, Max H., and Margaret Ann Neale, 'The Role of Fairness Considerations and Relationships in a Judgment Perspective of Negotiation', in Keneth Arrow et al., eds., *Barriers to Conflict Resolution* (Norton, 1995), 86–106.

Becker, Christian, 'Die Militärstrategische Bedeutung Des Südchinesischen Meeres', *SWP-Aktuell*, 82 (21 September 2015), https://www.swp-berlin.org/publikation/die-militaerstrategische-bedeutung-des-suedchinesischen-meeres/ (last accessed 24 April 2024).

Becker-Weinberg, Vasco, *Joint Development of Hydrocarbon Deposits in the Law of the Sea*, vol. 30 of Hamburg Studies on Maritime Affairs (Springer, 2014).

Beckley, Michael, 'The Emerging Military Balance in East Asia: How China's Neighbors Can Check Chinese Naval Expansion', *International Security*, 42/2 (November 2017), 78–119. https://doi.org/10.1162/ISEC_a_00294.

Beckman, Robert C., 'The UN Convention on the Law of the Sea and the Maritime Disputes in the South China Sea', *The American Journal of International Law*, 107/1 (January 2013), 142–63.

Beckman, Robert C., and Clive H. Schofield, 'Defining EEZ Claims from Islands: A Potential South China Sea Change', *The International Journal of Marine and Coastal Law*, 29/2 (2014), 193–243.

Beckman, Robert C., and Zhen Sun, 'The Cooperative Mechanism for the Straits of Malacca and Singapore', in Robert C. Beckman et al., eds., *Governance of Arctic Shipping* (Brill 2017).

Beckman, Robert C. et al., eds., *Beyond Territorial Disputes in the South China Sea Legal Frameworks for the Joint Development of Hydrocarbon Resources*, NUS Centre for International Law (Edward Elgar, 2013).

Beckman, Robert C. et al., 'Moving Forward on Joint Development in the South China Sea', in Robert C. Beckman et al, eds., *Beyond Territorial Disputes in the South China Sea: Legal Frameworks for the Joint Development of Hydrocarbon Resources* (Edward Elgar, 2013), 312–331.

'Beijing Urges Vietnam to Stop Disruptive Activities', *China Daily* (17 May 2014), http://www.chinadaily.com.cn/china/2014-05/17/content_17514575.htm (last accessed 24 April 2024).

Bercovitch, Jacob, and Mikio Oichi, *International Conflict in the Asia-Pacific Patterns, Consequences and Management* (Routledge, 2010).

Bercovitch, Jacob, Victor Kremenyuk, and I. William Zartman, 'Introduction: The Nature of Conflict and Conflict Resolution', in Bercovitch, Jacob, Viktor Aleksandrovich Kremeniuk, and I. William Zartman, eds., *The SAGE Handbook of Conflict Resolution* (SAGE, 2009).

Berger, Bruce K, 'Power Over, Power With, and Power to Relations: Critical Reflections on Public Relations, the Dominant Coalition, and Activism', *Journal of Public Relations Research*, 17/1 (January 2005): 5–28. https://doi.org/10.1207/s1532754xjprr1701_3.

Bernard, Vincent. 'War and Security at Sea: Warning Shots', *International Rc view of the Red Cross*, 98/902 (August 2016): 383–92. https://doi.org/10.1017/S1816383117000443.

Biddle, Stephen, and Ivan Oelrich, 'Future Warfare in the Western Pacific: Chinese Anti-Access/Area Denial, U.S. AirSea Battle, and Command of the Commons in East Asia', *International Security*, 41/1 (July 2016), 7–48. https://doi.org/10.1162/ISEC_a_00249.

Bindoff, N.L. et al. 'Changing Ocean, Marine Ecosystems, and Dependent Communities', in H. O. Pörtner et al., eds., *IPCC Special Report on the Ocean and Cryosphere in a Changing Climate* (CUP, 2019), 447–587. https://www.ipcc.ch/srocc/chapter/chapter-5/ (last accessed 24 April 2024).

Blanchard, Jean-Marc F., 'Linking Border Disputes and War: An Institutional-Statist Theory', *Geopolitics*, 10/4 (2005), 688–711.

Blomeyer, Roland et al., *The Role of China in World Fisheries*. IP/B/PECH/IC/2011-107. (European Parliament Study, 2012), https://www.europarl.europa.eu/meetdocs/2009_2014/documents/pech/dv/chi/china.pdf (last accessed 24 April 2024).

Blum, Gabriella, *Islands of Agreement: Managing Enduring Armed Rivalries* (Harvard UP, 2007).

Borton, James, 'Science Diplomacy and Dispute Management in the South China Sea', in Jonathan Spangler, Dean Karalekas, and Moises Lopes de Souza, eds.,

Enterprises, Localities, People, and Policy in the South China Sea (Springer, 2018), 195–216.

Bose, Sumantra, *Contested Lands: Israel-Palestine, Kashmir, Bosnia, Cyprus, and Sri Lanka* (Harvard UP, 2007).

Botes, Johannes, 'Conflict Transformation: A Debate over Semantics or a Crucial Shift in the Theory and Practice of Peace and Conflict Studies?' *International Journal of Peace Studies*, 8/2 (2003), 1–27.

Bower, Ernst, 'The JMSU: A Tale of Bilateralism and Secrecy in the South China Sea', *CSIS Analysis* (27 July 2010), https://www.csis.org/analysis/jmsu-tale-bilateralism-and-secrecy-south-china-sea (last accessed 24 April 2024).

Brands, Hal, and Jake Sullivan, 'China Has Two Paths to Global Domination', *Foreign Policy* (May 2020), https://foreignpolicy.com/2020/05/22/china-superpower-two-paths-global-domination-cold-war/ (last accessed 24 April 2024).

British Institute of International and Comparative Law, ed., *Report on the Obligations of States under Articles 74(3) and 83(3) of UNCLOS in Respect of Undelimited Maritime Areas* (British Institute of International and Comparative Law, 2016).

Brummit, Chris, 'Vietnam Tries to Stop China Oil Rig Deployment', *USA Today* (7 May 2014), https://eu.usatoday.com/story/news/world/2014/05/07/vietnam-china-oil-rig/8797007/ (last accessed 24 April 2024).

Bueger, Christian, 'What Is Maritime Security?', *Marine Policy*, 53 (2015), 159–64.

Bukh, Alexander, *These Islands Are Ours: The Social Construction of Territorial Disputes in Northeast Asia*, Studies in Asian Security (Stanford UP, 2020).

Burton, John W., and Frank Dukes, *Conflict Practices in Management, Settlement, and Resolution* (Macmillan, 1990).

Buszynski, Leszek, 'ASEAN, the Declaration on Conduct, and the South China Sea', *Contemporary Southeast Asia*, 25/3 (December 2003), 343–62.

Buszynski, Leszek, 'The South China Sea: Oil, Maritime Claims, and US–China Strategic Rivalry', *The Washington Quarterly*, 35/2 (2012), 139–56.

Buszynski, Leszek, and Christopher B Roberts, eds., *The South China Sea Maritime Dispute: Political, Legal, and Regional Perspectives*, Routledge Security in Asia Pacific Series (Routledge, 2014).

Buszynski, Leszek, and Iskandar Sazlan, 'Maritime Claims and Energy Cooperation in the South China Sea', *Contemporary Southeast Asia*, 29/1 (2007), 143–71.

Buzan, Barry, 'Negotiating by Consensus: Developments in Technique at the United Nations Conference on the Law of the Sea', *American Journal of International Law*, 75/2 (1981), 324–48.

Cabral, Reniel B. et al., 'Rapid and Lasting Gains from Solving Illegal Fishing', *Nature Ecology & Evolution*, 2/4 (2018), 650–58.

Caddell, Richard, and Erik Jaap Molenaar, eds., *Strengthening International Fisheries Law in an Era of Changing Oceans* (Hart, 2019).

Calder, Kent E., and Min Ye, *The Making of Northeast Asia* Studies in Asian Security (Stanford UP, 2010).

Carlsnaes, Walter, Thomas Risse, and Beth A Simmons, *Handbook of International Relations* (SAGE Publications, 2013).

Carpenter, Kent E., and Victor G. Springer, 'The Center of the Center of Marine Shore Fish Biodiversity: The Philippine Islands', *Environmental Biology of Fishes*, 72/4 (April 2005), 467–80. https://doi.org/10.1007/s10641-004-3154-4.

Carpio, Antonio. 'Historical Truths and Lies. Scarborough Shoal in Ancient Maps. A Cartographic Exhibit Based on the 6 June 2014. Lecture of Supreme Court Senior Associate Justice Antonio T. Carpio' (Institute for Maritime and Ocean Affairs, 2014). http://www.imoa.ph/historical-truths-lies-series/ (last accessed 24 April 2024).

Carpio, Antonio, 'The Rule of Law in the West Philippine Sea Dispute', *Speech Delivered before the Philippine Bar Association* (August 2013). https://www.imoa.ph/speech-the-rule-of-law-in-the-west-philippine-sea-dispute/ (last accessed 24 April 2024).

Carter, David B., 'The Strategy of Territorial Conflict', *American Journal of Political Science*, 54/4 (2010), 969–987.

Chachavalpongpun, Pavin, ed., *Entering Uncharted Waters? ASEAN and the South China Sea* (ISEAS, 2014).

Chan, Steve, *China's Troubled Waters: Maritime Disputes in Theoretical Perspective* (CUP, 2016).

Charlermpalanupap, Termsak, 'Review of the ASEAN-China Declaration of the Conduct of Parties in the South China Sea and Prospects of a Code of Conduct in the South China Sea: An ASEAN Perspective', in Truong Thuy Tran and Thuy Trang Le, eds., *Power, Law, and Maritime Order in the South China Sea* (Lexington, 2015), 37–48.

Charney, Jonathan I., 'Central East Asian Maritime Boundaries and the Law of the Sea', *American Journal of International Law*, 89/4 (1995), 724–49.

Chellaney, Brahma, 'Who Lost the South China Sea?' *The Strategist* (15 June 2018). https://www.aspistrategist.org.au/who-lost-the-south-china-sea/ (last accessed 24 April 2024).

Chemillier-Gendreau, Monique, *Sovereignty over the Paracel and Spratly Islands* (Kluwer Law, 2000).

Chen, Dingding, and Jianwei Wang, 'Lying Low No More? China's New Thinking on the Tao Guang Yang Hui Strategy', *China: An International Journal*, 09/02 (September 2011), 195–216. https://doi.org/10.1142/S0219747211000136.

Chen, Dingding, Xiaoyu Pu, and Alastair Iain Johnston, 'Debating China's Assertiveness', *International Security*, 38/3 (2014), 176–183.

Chen, Hsin-Chih, 'La Réponse Chinoise à l'occupation Française Des Îles Spratly En 1933', *Guerres Mondiales et Conflits Contemporains*, (2001), 5–24.

Chen, Hurng-Yu, 'The Prospects for Joint Development in the South China Sea', *Issues and Studies*, 27/12 (1991), 112–25.

Chen, Lung-chu, *The U.S.–Taiwan–China Relationship in International Law and Policy* (OUP, 2016).

Chen, Sulan, 'Environmental Cooperation in the South China Sea: Factors, Actors and Mechanisms', *Ocean & Coastal Management*, 85 (2013), 131–140. https://doi.org/doi.org/10.1016/j.ocecoaman.2013.02.004.

Cheng, Willard, 'China, PH Discussing Joint Dev't in West PH Sea: Envoy', *ABS-CBN* (27 September 2017), https://news.abs-cbn.com/news/09/27/17/china-ph-discussing-joint-devt-in-west-ph-sea-envoy (last accessed 24 April 2024).

'China Anger at Japan-Taiwan Disputed Island Fishing Deal', *BBC News* (10 April 2013), https://www.bbc.com/news/world-asia-china-22092853 (last accessed 21 April 2024).

'China Condemns Fisherman's Death, *China Daily* (11 May 2013), http://www.chinadaily.com.cn/cndy/2013-05/11/content_16491942.htm (last accessed 18 April 2024).

'China, Philippines, Vietnam Sign Joint South China Sea Oil Search Accord', *Radio Free Asia* (14 March 2005), https://www.rfa.org/english/news/business/china_vietnam_spratlys-20050314.html (last accessed 24 April 2024).

'China Unhappy as Philippines Signs Investment Deal with Taiwan', *South China Morning Post* (8 December 2017), https://www.scmp.com/news/china/diplomacy-defence/article/2123556/china-unhappy-philippines-signs-investment-deal-taiwan (last accessed 18 April 2024).

'China, Vietnam Hold Talks on Recent Anti-China Violence', *China Daily* (17 May 2014), https://www.chinadaily.com.cn/world/2014-05/17/content_17514753.htm (last accessed 18 April 2024)

'China, Vietnam Meeting Canceled amid South China Sea Tensions', *Reuters* (8 August 2017) https://www.reuters.com/article/us-asean-philippines-china-vietnam-idUSKBN1AO07K/ (last accessed 22 April 2024).

'Chinese Aircraft Use Japan Ships as Targets in E. China Sea Drill', *Kyodo News* (19 August 2019), https://english.kyodonews.net/news/2019/08/b9e1c11f12b8-chinese-aircraft-use-japan-ships-as-targets-in-e-china-sea-drill.html (last accessed 24 April 2024).

'Chinese Aircraft Used Japanese Ships as Targets in East China Sea Drill: Gov't', *Japan Today* (19 August 2019). https://japantoday.com/category/national/chinese-aircraft-use-japan-ships-as-targets-in-e.-china-sea-drill (last accessed 24 April 2024).

'Chinese Military Vows to Defend Sea Claim', *The Philippine Star* (28 April 2012), https://www.pressreader.com/philippines/the-philippine-star/20120428/281479273420701 last accessed 24 April 2024).

Chinese Society of International Law, 'The South China Sea Arbitration Awards: A Critical Study', *Chinese Journal of International Law*, 17/2 (May 2018), 207–748.

Chong, Ja Ian, and Todd H. Hall, 'One Thing Leads to Another: Making Sense of East Asia's Repeated Tensions', *Asian Security*, 13/1 (January 2017), 20–40. https://doi.org/10.1080/14799855.2017.1284795.

Choong, William, *The Ties That Divide: History, Honour and Territory in Sino-Japanese Relations*, IISS Adelphi Series (Routledge, 2014).

Chubb, Andrew, 'Assessing Public Opinion's Influence on Foreign Policy: The Case of China's Assertive Maritime Behavior', *Asian Security*, 15/2 (7 March 2018), 159-179.

Chubb, Andrew, 'PRC Assertiveness in the South China Sea: Measuring Continuity and Change, 1970–2015', *International Security*, 45/3 (January 2021), 79–121. https://doi.org/10.1162/isec_a_00400.

Chubb, Andrew, *Chinese nationalism and the 'gray zone': case analyses of public opinion and PRC Maritime Policy* (Naval War College, 2021).

Chung, Lawrence, 'Taiwan's Military Drills in Disputed Waters to Step up Pressure on Manila', *South China Morning Post* (14 May 2013), https://www.scmp.com/news/china/article/1237123/taiwans-military-drills-disputed-waters-step-pressure-manila (last accessed 18 April 2024).

Cohen, Harlan Grant, 'Theorizing Precedent in International Law', in Andrea Bianchi et al., eds., *Interpretation in International Law* (OUP, 2015), 268–89. https://doi.org/10.1093/acprof:oso/9780198725749.003.0013.

Colaresi, Michael, and William R. Thompson, 'Strategic Rivalries, Protracted Conflict, and Crisis Escalation', *Journal of Peace Research*, 39/3 (2002), 263–87.

Coles, Ian R., 'Strategic Minerals – the New Global Battleground', *Financial Times* (June 2019), https://www.ft.com/content/c553bfc0-890b-11e9-a028-86cea8523dc2 (last accessed 24 April 2024).

Collier, David, 'The Comparative Method: Two Decades of Change', in Dankwart A. Rustow and Kenneth Paul Erickson, eds., *Comparative Political Dynamics: Global Research Perspectives* (HarperCollins, 1991), 7-31.

Collier, John Greenwood, and Vaughan Lowe, *The Settlement of Disputes in International Law: Institutions and Procedures* (OUP, 2000).

Colmenares, Neri Javier, 'Spratlys Deal Unconstitutional: Joint Marine Seismic Undertaking Void', *GMA News* (17 March 2008), https://www.gmanetwork.com/news/topstories/specialreports/85173/spratlys-deal-unconstitutional-joint-marine-seismic-undertaking-void/story/ (last accessed 24 April 2024).

Cooley, Alexander, and Hendrik Spruyt, *Contracting States Sovereign Transfers in International Relations* (Princeton UP, 2009).

Cooper, Zack, and Gregory Poling, 'America's Freedom of Navigation Operations Are Lost at Sea', *Foreign Policy* (January 2019), https://foreignpolicy.com/2019/01/08/americas-freedom-of-navigation-operations-are-lost-at-sea/ (last accessed 24 April 2024).

Cronin, Patrick M. and Robert Kaplan, 'Cooperation from Strength: US Strategy and the South China Sea', in Patrick M. Cronin, ed., *Cooperation from Strength The United States, China and the South China Sea* (Center for a New American Century, 2012), 3–30.

Center for Strategic and International Studies, 'Are Maritime Law Enforcement Forces Destabilizing Asia?' *ChinaPower Project* (blog), 2019. https://chinapower.csis.org/maritime-forces-destabilizing-asia/ (last accessed 24 April 2024).

Center for Strategic and International Studies, 'How Much Trade Transits the South China Sea?' *ChinaPower Project* blog (August 2017), https://chinapower.csis.org/much-trade-transits-south-china-sea/ (last accessed 24 April 2024).

Dahl, Robert A., 'The Concept of Power', *Behavioral Science*, 2/3 (1957), 201–15.

Damrosch, Lori Fisler, and Bernard H. Oxman, 'Agora: The South China Sea: Editors' Introduction', *The American Journal of International Law*, 107/1 (2013), 95–7.

Davenport, Tara, 'Southeast Asian Approaches to Maritime Boundaries', *Asian Journal of International Law*, 4/02 (2014), 309–57. https://doi.org/10.1017/S2044251313000313.

De Castro, Renato Cruz, 'A Philippine-China Deal on Joint Development in the Making?' *AMTI Update* (November 2020), https://amti.csis.org/a-philippine-china-deal-on-joint-development-in-the-making/ (last accessed 24 April 2024).

De Castro, Renato Cruz, 'The 21st Century Philippine-US Enhanced Defense Cooperation Agreement (EDCA), The Philippines' Policy in Facilitating the Obama Administration's Strategic Pivot to Asia', *The Korean Journal of Defense Analysis*, 26/4 (2014), 427–446.

De Tréglodé, Benoît, 'Maritime Boundary Delimitation and Sino-Vietnamese Cooperation in the Gulf of Tonkin (1994–2016)', *China Perspectives* (2016), 33–41.

Diehl, Paul F., and Thorin M. Wright, 'A Conditional Defense of the Dyadic Approach', *International Studies Quarterly*, 60/2 (2016), 363–8.

Dietz, Thomas, Elinor Ostrom, and Paul C. Stern, 'The Struggle to Govern the Commons', *Science*, 302/5652 (2003), 1907–12.

Diez, Thomas, 'The Paradoxes of Europe's Borders', *Comparative European Politics*, 4/2–3 (2006), 235–52.

Dixon, William J., 'Democracy and the Peaceful Settlement of International Conflict', *American Political Science Review*, 88/1 (1994), 14–32.

Djalal, Hasjim, 'Indonesia and the South China Sea Initiative', *Ocean Development & International Law*, 32/2 (2001), 97–103.

Djalal, Hasjim, 'The South China Sea: The Long Road towards Peace and Cooperation', in Tommy T. B Koh, Myron H Nordquist, and John Norton Moore, eds., *Freedom of Seas, Passage Rights and the 1982 Law of the Sea Convention* (Brill, 2009), 25–50.

Dow, Gregory K., 'The Function of Authority in Transaction Cost Economics', *Journal of Economic Behavior & Organization*, 8/1 (March 1987), 13–38. https://doi.org/10.1016/0167-2681(87)90019-9.

Downs, Erica S., 'The Chinese Energy Security Debate', *The China Quarterly*, 177 (2004), 21–41. https://doi.org/10.1017/S0305741004000037.

Downs, George W., and Michael A. Jones, 'Reputation, Compliance, and International Law', *The Journal of Legal Studies*, 31/S1 (2002), 95–114.

Drifte, Reinhard, 'The Japan-China Confrontation over the Senkaku/Diaoyu Islands – Between "Shelving" and "Dispute Escalation"', *The Asia-Pacific Journal*, 12/30 (2014), 1–26.

Drifte, Reinhard, 'The Senkaku/Diaoyu Islands Territorial Dispute Between Japan and China: Between the Materialization of the "China Threat" and Japan "Reversing the Outcome of World War II"?', *UNISCI Discussion Papers*, 32 (2013), 1–55.

Du, Jie, and Hao Qui, 'Western Pacific Naval Symposium and Asia-Pacific Multilateral Cooperation on Maritime Security', *China International Studies*, 46 (2014), 57–70.

Duan, Xiaolin, 'Unanswered Questions: Why We May Be Wrong about Chinese Nationalism and Its Foreign Policy Implications', *Journal of Contemporary China*, 26/108 (November 2017), 886–900. https://doi.org/10.1080/10670564.2017.1337312.

Dupuy, Florian, and Pierre-Marie Dupuy, 'A Legal Analysis of China's Historic Rights Claim in the South China Sea', *American Journal of International Law*, 107/1 (2013), 124–41.

'Duterte to Allow PH Oil Exploration with Chinese, Malaysian Firms: DOE', *ABS-CBN* (27 September 2017), http://news.abs-cbn.com/business/09/27/17/duterte-to-allow-ph-oil-exploration-with-chinese-malaysian-firms-doe (last accessed 14 August 2019).

Dutton, Peter, 'Three Disputes and Three Objectives. China and the South China Sea', *Naval War College Review*, 64/4 (2011), 42–67.

Dutton, Peter, and Ryan D Martinson, eds., *Beyond the Wall: Chinese Far Seas Operations* (Naval War College, 2015).

'Editor's Note: Code for Unalerted Encounters at Sea', *Australian Journal of Maritime & Ocean Affairs*, 4/4 (January 2012), 126–30. https://doi.org/10.1080/18366503.2012.10815721.

Eggertsson, Thráinn, *Economic Behavior and Institutions*, Cambridge Surveys of Economic Literature (CUP, 1990).

Elemia, Camille, '2 Senators Ask Duterte to Release Details of Draft Deals with China', *Rappler* (20 November 2018), https://www.rappler.com/nation/217038-trillanes-pangilinan-duterte-release-draft-ph-china-oil-deals-details (last accessed 24 April 2024).

Erickson, Andrew S., and Adam P. Liff, 'Installing a Safety on the "Loaded Gun"? China's Institutional Reforms, National Security Commission and Sino–Japanese Crisis (in) Stability', *Journal of Contemporary China*, 25/98 (2016), 197–215.

Erickson, Andrew S., and Conor M. Kennedy, 'Tanmen Militia: China's "Maritime Rights Protection" Vanguard', *The National Interest* (May 2015), https://nationalinterest.org/feature/tanmen-militia-china%E2%80%99s-maritime-rights-protection-vanguard-12816 (last accessed 24 April 2024).

Erickson, Andrew S., and Joel Wuthnow, 'Barriers, Springboards and Benchmarks: China Conceptualizes the Pacific "Island Chains"', *The China Quarterly*, 225 (2016), 1–22.

Erickson, Andrew S., Joshua Hickey, and Henry Holst, 'Surging Second Sea Force: China's Maritime Law- Enforcement Forces, Capabilities, and Future in the Gray Zone and Beyond', *Naval War College Review*, 72/2 (2019), 1–25.

Esmaquel II, Paterno Esmaquel, 'PH Confirms Standoff with Taiwan off Batanes', *Rappler* (2015) https://www.rappler.com/nation/95156-philippines-fisheries-agreement-taiwan/ (last accessed 18 April 2024).

Evans, Malcolm D., 'Maritime Boundary Delimitation', in Donald R. Rothwell et al., eds., *The Oxford Handbook of the Law of the Sea* (OUP, 2015), 254–81.

Evans, Paul M., 'Building Security: The Council for Security Cooperation in the Asia Pacific (CSCAP)', *The Pacific Review*, 7/2 (January 1994), 125–39. https://doi.org/10.1080/09512749408719081.

Evans, Peter B, Harold Karan Jacobson, and Robert D Putnam, *Double-Edged Diplomacy: International Bargaining and Domestic Politics* (University of California, 1993).

Farrell, Henry, and Abraham L. Newman, 'Weaponized Interdependence: How Global Economic Networks Shape State Coercion', *International Security*, 44/1 (July 2019), 42–79. https://doi.org/10.1162/isec_a_00351.

Faure, Guy Olivier, and I. William Zartman, 'The Dynamics of Escalation and Negotiation', in I. William Zartman, Guy Olivier Faure, and the International Institute for Applied Systems Analysis, eds., *Escalation and Negotiation in International Conflicts* (CUP, 2005), 3–20.

Fearon, James D., 'Bargaining, Enforcement, and International Cooperation', *International Organization*, 52/02 (1998), 269–305.

Fearon, James D., 'Bargaining over Objects That Influence Future Bargaining Power', *Annual Meetings of the American Political Science Association* (1996), 1–25.

Fearon, James D., 'Domestic Political Audiences and the Escalation of International Disputes', *American Political Science Review*, 88/03 (1994), 577–92.

Fearon, James D., 'Fighting Rather than Bargaining', *Annual Meetings of the American Political Science Association* (2007).

Fearon, James D., 'Rationalist Explanations for War', *International Organization*, 49/03 (June 1995), 379–414.

Fisher, Roger, 'Fractionating Conflict', *Daedalus*, 93/3 (1964), 920–41.

Foot, Rosemary, S. Neil MacFarlane, and Michael Mastanduno, eds., *U.S. Hegemony and International Organizations the United States and Multilateral Institutions* (OUP, 2003).

Franck, Thomas M., *Fairness in International Law and Institutions* (OUP, 1995).

Franckx, Erik, and Marco Benatar, 'The "Duty" to Co-Operate for States Bordering Enclosed or Semi-Enclosed Seas', *Chinese (Taiwan) Yearbook of International Law and Affairs*, 31 (2013), 66–81.

Fravel, M. Taylor, 'China's Strategy in the South China Sea', *Contemporary Southeast Asia*, 33/3 (2011), 292–319. https://doi.org/10.1355/cs33-3b.

Fravel, M. Taylor. 'Explaining Stability in the Senkaku (Diaoyu) Islands Dispute'. In *Getting the Triangle Straight: Managing China–Japan–US Relations*, G. Curtis, R. Kokubun, and J. Wang eds. (Brookings Institution Press, 2010), 144–164.

Fravel, M. Taylor, 'Regime Insecurity and International Cooperation: Explaining China's Compromises in Territorial Disputes', *International Security*, 30/2 (2005), 46–83.

Fravel, M. Taylor, *Strong Borders, Secure Nation. Cooperation and Conflict in China's Territorial Disputes* (Princeton UP, 2008).

Fravel, M. Taylor, and Charles L. Glaser, 'How Much Risk Should the United States Run in the South China Sea?' *International Security* 47/2 (2022), 88–134.

Friedberg, Aaron L., *A Contest for Supremacy: China, America, and the Struggle for Mastery in Asia* (Norton, 2012).

Friedberg, Aaron L., 'The Sources of Chinese Conduct: Explaining Beijing's Assertiveness', *The Washington Quarterly*, 37/4 (2014), 133–50.

Gächter, Simon, and Arno Riedl, 'Dividing Justly in Bargaining Problems with Claims', *Social Choice and Welfare*, 27/3 (2006), 571–94.

Gächter, Simon, and Arno Riedl, 'Moral Property Rights in Bargaining with Infeasible Claims', *Management Science*, 51/2 (2005), 249–63.

Gao, Jianjun, 'A Note on the 2008 Cooperation Consensus Between China and Japan in the East China Sea', *Ocean Development & International Law*, 40/3 (August 2009), 291–303. https://doi.org/10.1080/00908320903077100.

Gao, Jianjun, 'Joint Development in the East China Sea: Not an Easier Challenge than Delimitation', *The International Journal of Marine and Coastal Law*, 23/1 (2008), 39–75.

Gao, Zhiguo, and Bing Bing Jia, 'The Nine-Dash Line in the South China Sea: History, Status, and Implications', *American Journal of International Law*, 107/1 (2013), 98–124.

George, Alexander L. et al., *Case Studies and Theory Development in the Social Sciences* (MIT, 2005).

Gerring, John, *Case Study Research: Principles and Practices* (CUP, 2006).

Gies, Erica, 'The Consequences of China's Booming Demand for Seafood', *Hakai Magazine* (June 2018), https://www.hakaimagazine.com/news/the-consequences-of-chinas-booming-demand-for-seafood/ (last accessed 24 April 2024).

Ginsburg, Tom, and Richard H. McAdams, 'Adjudicating in Anarchy: An Expressive Theory of International Dispute Resolution', *William & Mary Law Review*, 45 (2003), 1229–339.

Gioia, Dennis A., Kevin G. Corley, and Aimee L. Hamilton, 'Seeking Qualitative Rigor in Inductive Research: Notes on the Gioia Methodology', *Organizational Research Methods*, 16/1 (2013), 15–31.

Glaser, Charles L., 'A U.S.-China Grand Bargain? The Hard Choice between Military Competition and Accommodation', *International Security*, 39/4 (April 2015), 49–90. https://doi.org/10.1162/ISEC_a_00199.

Gleditsch, Nils Petter, 'Whither the Weather? Climate Change and Conflict', *Journal of Peace Research*, 49 (2012), 3–9.

Gleditsch, Nils Petter, 'Armed Conflict and the Environment: A Critique of the Literature'. *Journal of Peace Research* 35, no. 3 (1998), 381–400.

Goddard, Stacie E, 'Uncommon Ground: Indivisible Territory and the Politics of Legitimacy', *International Organization*, 60/1 (2006), 35–68.

Goh, Evelyn, *Meeting the China Challenge: The U.S. in Southeast Asian Regional Security Strategies*, Policy Studies 16 (East-West Center, 2005).

Goh, Evelyn, *The Struggle for Order: Hegemony, Hierarchy, and Transition in Post-Cold War East Asia* (OUP, 2013).

Goldstein, Avery, 'First Things First: The Pressing Danger of Crisis Instability in U.S.-China Relations', *International Security*, 37/4 (April 2013), 49–89. https://doi.org/10.1162/ISEC_a_00114.

Goldstein, Avery, *Rising to the Challenge: China's Grand Strategy and International Security* (Stanford UP, 2005).

Goldstein, Lyle, *Meeting China Halfway: How to Defuse the Emerging US-China Rivalry* (Georgetown UP, 2015).

'Government Slams Manila over Death', *Taipei Times* (11 May 2013), https://www.taipeitimes.com/News/front/archives/2013/05/11/2003561976 (last accessed 18 April 2024).

Graham, Euan, 'Maritime Hotlines in East Asia', *RSIS Policy Brief* (May 2014), https://www.rsis.edu.sg/rsis-publication/idss/maritime-hotlines-in-east-asia/ (last accessed 24 April 2024).

Graham, Euan, 'US Naval Standoff with China Fails to Reassure Regional Allies', *Foreign Policy* (May 2020), https://foreignpolicy.com/2020/05/04/malaysia-south-china-sea-us-navy-drillship-standoff/ (last accessed 24 April 2024).

Granados, Ulises, 'As China Meets the Southern Sea Frontier: Ocean Identity in the Making, 1902–1937', *Pacific Affairs*, 78/3 (2005), 443–61.

Granados, Ulises, 'Chinese Ocean Policies Towards the South China Sea in a Transitional Period, 1946—1952', *China Review* (2006), 153–81.

Granados, Ulises, 'Ocean Frontier Expansion and the Kalayaan Islands Group Claim: Philippines' Postwar Pragmatism in the South China Sea', *International Relations of the Asia-Pacific*, 9/2 (2008), 267–94.

Granados, Ulises, 'The South China Sea and Its Coral Reefs during the Ming and Qing Dynasties: Levels of Geographical Knowledge and Political Control', *East Asian History*, 32/33 (2006), 109–28.

Green, Michael, *By More Than Providence: Grand Strategy and American Power in the Asia Pacific Since 1783* (Columbia UP, 2017).

Green, Michael, 'Trump and Asia: Continuity, Change, and Disruption', *ASAN Open Forum* (April 2019), http://www.theasanforum.org/trump-and-asia-continuity-change-and-disruption/?utm_source=CSIS+All&utm_campaign=7f60856cac-EMAIL_CAMPAIGN_2019_04_26_06_46&utm_medium=email&utm_term=0_f326fc46b6-7f60856cac-160737973 (last accessed 24 April 2024).

Green, Michael et al., *Countering Coercion in Maritime Asia: The Theory and Practice of Gray Zone Deterrence* (Center for Strategic & International Studies, 2017). https://www.csis.org/analysis/countering-coercion-maritime-asia (last accessed 24 April 2024).

Guo, Rongxing, *Territorial Disputes and Seabed Petroleum Exploitation: Some Options for the East China Sea* (The Brookings Institution Center for Northeast Asian Policy Studies, 2010).

Hafeez, Sanaa Yasmin, 'The Senkaku/Diaoyu Islands Crises of 2004, 2010, and 2012: A Study of Japanese-Chinese Crisis Management', *Asia-Pacific Review*, 22/1 (January 2015), 73–99. https://doi.org/10.1080/13439006.2015.1038885.

Hagström, Linus, 'Quiet Power: Japan's China Policy in Regard to the Pinnacle Islands', *The Pacific Review*, 18/2 (June 2005), 159–88. https://doi.org/10.1080/09512740500162923.

Haines, Steven, 'War at Sea: Nineteenth-Century Laws for Twenty-First Century Wars?' *International Review of the Red Cross* 98/902 (August 2016), 419–47. https://doi.org/10.1017/S1816383117000418.

Hajime, Hirose, 'Japan's Effective Control of the Senkaku Islands', *Review of Island Studies* (June 2013), 1–25.

Hamzah, B. A. et al., 'The Maritime Boundaries of Malaysia and Indonesia in the Malacca Strait: An Appraisal', *Australian Journal of Maritime & Ocean Affairs*, 6/4 (October 2014), 207–26. https://doi.org/10.1080/18366503.2014.956856.

Hancox, David J., and John R. V. Prescott, *A Geographical Description of the Spratly Islands and an Account of Hydrographic Surveys amongst Those Islands*, Maritime Briefing (University of Durham, 1995).

Harrison, Selig, 'Seabed Petroleum in Northeast Asia: Conflict or Cooperation?', in Selig S. Harrison, ed., *Seabed Petroleum in Northeast Asia: Conflict or Cooperation?* (Woodrow Wilson International Center for Scholars, 2005), 3–14.

Hayton, Bill, 'South China Sea: Vietnam "Scraps New Oil Project"', *BBC* (August 2018), http://www.bbc.com/news/world-asia-43507448 (last accessed 24 April 2024).

Hayton, Bill, 'The Modern Creation of China's "Historic Rights" Claim in the South China Sea', *Asian Affairs*, 49/3 (July 2018), 370–82. https://doi.org/10.1080/03068374.2018.1487689.

Hayton, Bill. *The South China Sea: The Struggle for Power in Asia* (Yale UP, 2014).

Hayton, Bill. 'When Good Lawyers Write Bad History: Unreliable Evidence and the South China Sea Territorial Dispute', *Ocean Development & International Law*, 48/1 (January 2017), 17–34. https://doi.org/10.1080/00908320.2017.1265362.

Heinegg, Wolff Heintschel von, 'The Difficulties of Conflict Classification at Sea: Distinguishing Incidents at Sea from Hostilities', *International Review of the Red Cross*, 98/902 (August 2016), 449–64. https://doi.org/10.1017/S1816383117000327.

Hensel, Paul. R. et al., 'Bones of Contention: Comparing Territorial, Maritime, and River Issues', *Journal of Conflict Resolution*, 52/1 (2008), 117–143. https://doi.org/10.1177/0022002707310425.

Heydarian, Richard Javad, 'Mare Liberum: Aquino, Duterte, and The Philippines' Evolving Lawfare Strategy in the South China Sea', *Asian Politics & Policy*, 10/2 (April 2018), 283–99. https://doi.org/10.1111/aspp.12392.

Ho, Joshua H., 'Enhancing Safety, Security, and Environmental Protection of the Straits of Malacca and Singapore: The Cooperative Mechanism', *Ocean Development & International Law*, 40/2 (May 2009), 233–47. https://doi.org/10.1080/00908320902864854.

Holmes, James, 'ASEAN Should Reject a Code of Conduct in the South China Sea', *The Diplomat* (September 2013), https://thediplomat.com/2013/09/asean-should-reject-a-code-of-conduct-in-the-south-china-sea/ (last accessed 24 April 2024).

Hong, Nong, *UNCLOS and Ocean Dispute Settlement: Law and Politics in the South China Sea* (Routledge, 2012).

Hosoya, Yuichi, 'FOIP 2.0: The Evolution of Japan's Free and Open Indo-Pacific Strategy', *Asia-Pacific Review*, 26/1 (January 2019), 18–28. https://doi.org/10.1080/13439006.2019.1622868.

Hosoya, Yuichi, 'Japan's New Security Legislation: What Does This Mean for East Asian Security?', in National Committee on American Foreign Policy, ed., *Building a Regional Order in East Asia: Community, Competition, Conflict* (National Committee on American Foreign Policy, 2016), 88–95.

Hsiao, Russel, 'PLA General Advises Building Bases in the South China Sea', *Jamestown China Brief* (24 June 2009).

Huang, Chin-Hao, *Power and Restraint in China's Rise* (Columbia UP, 2022).

Huang, Jing, *Inseparable Separation: The Making of China's Taiwan Policy* (Hackensack, World Scientific, 2010).

Huang, Kristin, '"Prepare for War", Xi Jinping Tells Military Region That Monitors South China Sea, Taiwan', *South China Morning Post* (26 October 2018), https://www.scmp.com/news/china/military/article/2170452/prepare-war-xi-jinping-tells-military-region-monitors-south (last accessed 24 April 2024).

Hutchison, Charles S., and V. R. Vijayan, 'What Are the Spratly Islands?' *Journal of Asian Earth Sciences* 39/5 (2010), 371–85.

Huth, Paul, Sarah Croco, and Benjamin Appel, 'Law and the Use of Force in World Politics: The Varied Effects of Law on the Exercise of Military Power in Territorial Disputes', *International Studies Quarterly*, 56/1 (2012), 17–31. https://doi.org/10.1111/j.1468-2478.2011.00695.x.

Huth, Paul K., *Standing Your Ground Territorial Disputes and International Conflict* (University of Michigan, 1998).

Huth, Paul K., Sarah E. Croco, and Benjamin J. Appel, 'Bringing Law to the Table: Legal Claims, Focal Points, and the Settlement of Territorial Disputes Since 1945', *American Journal of Political Science*, 57/1 (2013), 90–103. https://doi.org/10.1111/j.1540-5907.2012.00607.x.

Huth, Paul K., Sarah E. Croco, and Benjamin J. Appel, 'Does International Law Promote the Peaceful Settlement of International Disputes? Evidence from the Study of Territorial Conflicts since 1945', *American Political Science Review*, 105/2 (2011), 415–36.

Hyer, Eric, *The Pragmatic Dragon: China's Grand Strategy and Boundary Settlements* (UBC, 2015).

Ikenberry, G. John, *After Victory: Institutions, Strategic Restraint, and the Rebuilding of Order after Major Wars*, Princeton Studies in International History and Politics 117 (Princeton UP, 2001).

Ikenberry, G. John, 'State Power and the Institutional Bargain: America's Ambivalent Economic and Security Multilateralism', in Rosemary Foot, Michael Mastanduno, and S. Neil MacFarlane, eds., *US Hegemony and International Organizations* (OUP, 2003), 49–70.

Institute for Maritime and Ocean Affairs, 'Spratlys and "Pulo" in Ancient Maps' (The Exhibit Catalogue, 2014), https://www.imoa.ph/spratlys-pulo-ancient-maps/ (last accessed 24 April 2024).

International Crisis Group, 'Stirring up the South China Sea (I)', *Asia Report*, 223 (April 2012).

International Crisis Group, 'Stirring up the South China Sea (IV): Oil in Troubled Waters', *Asia Report*, 275 (January 2016), https://www.crisisgroup.org/asia/north-east-asia/china/stirring-south-china-sea-iv-oil-troubled-waters (last accessed 24 April 2024).

Ives, Mike, 'Philippines to Declare Marine Sanctuary in South China Sea', *The New York Times* (21 November 2016), https://www.nytimes.com/2016/11/22/world/asia/philippines-rodrigo-duterte-scarborough-shoal-china.html (last accessed 15 April 2024).

Jackson, Matthew O., and Massimo Morelli, 'The Reasons for Wars: An Updated Survey', *The Handbook on the Political Economy of War*, 34 (2011), 34–57.

Jackson, Van, 'Power, Trust, and Network Complexity: Three Logics of Hedging in Asian Security', *International Relations of the Asia-Pacific*, 14/3 (2014), 331–56.

Jaipragas, Bhavan, 'Forget the Warships: Mahathir's Peace Formula for South China Sea', *South China Morning Post* (19 June 2018), https://www.scmp.com/week-asia/geopolitics/article/2151403/forget-warships-malaysian-pm-mahathirs-peace-formula-south (last accessed 24 April 2024).

Jakobson, Linda, and Ryan Manuel, 'How Are Foreign Policy Decisions Made in China? Foreign Policy Decisions Made in China', *Asia & the Pacific Policy Studies*, 3/1 (January 2016), 101–10.

'Japan, China Eye May Talks on Maritime Crisis Management Mechanism', *The Japan Times* (14 March 2015), https://www.japantimes.co.jp/news/2015/03/14/national/japan-china-eye-may-talks-on-maritime-crisis-management-mechanism/ (last accessed 24 April 2024).

'Japan-Taiwan Talks on Fishing near Senkakus End with Some Progress', *The Japan Times* (18 March 2018), https://www.japantimes.co.jp/news/2018/03/18/national/politics-diplomacy/japan-taiwan-talks-fishing-near-senkakus-end-progress/ (last accessed 21 April 2024).

Jayakumar, Shunmugam, Tommy Koh, and Robert C. Beckman, eds., *The South China Sea Disputes and Law of the Sea*, NUS Centre for International Law (Elgar, 2014).

Jenner, C. J. and Truong Thuy Tran, eds., *The South China Sea: A Crucible of Regional Cooperation or Conflict-Making Sovereignty Claims?* (CUP, 2016).

Jennings, Robert Yewdall, *The Acquisition of Territory in International Law* (Manchester UP, 1963).

Jeong, Ho-Won, *Conflict Management and Resolution: An Introduction* (Routledge, 2010).

Ji, You, 'The PLA and Diplomacy: Unraveling Myths about the Military Role in Foreign Policy Making', *Journal of Contemporary China*, 23/86 (4 March 2014), 236–54. https://doi.org/10.1080/10670564.2013.832526.

'JMSU Gave China the Opening to Claim Reed Bank, Says Lacierda', *Gmanetwork* (6 July 2011), https://www.gmanetwork.com/news/topstories/nation/225527/jmsu-gave-china-the-opening-to-claim-reed-bank-says-lacierda/story/ (last accessed 24 April 2024).

Johnston, Alastair Iain, 'China in a World of Orders: Rethinking Compliance and Challenge in Beijing's International Relations', *International Security*, 44/2 (October 2019), 9–60.

Johnston, Alastair Iain, 'How New and Assertive Is China's New Assertiveness?' *International Security*, 37/4 (2013), 7–48.

Johnston, Alastair Iain, 'Is Chinese Nationalism Rising? Evidence from Beijing', *International Security*, 41/3 (2017), 7–43.

Johnston, Alastair Iain, *Social States: China in International Institutions, 1980–2000*, Princeton Studies in International History and Politics (Princeton UP, 2008).

Johnston, Alastair Iain, 'The Evolution of Interstate Security Crisis-Management Theory and Practice in China', *Naval War College Review*, 69/1 (2016), 29–72.

Ju, Hailong, *China's Maritime Power and Strategy: History, National Security and Geopolitics* (World Scientific, 2015).

Kahneman, Daniel, and Amos Tversky, 'Rational Choice and the Framing of Decisions', *Journal of Business*, 59/4 (1986), 251–78.

Kaneda, Hideaki, 'Management of Incidents at Sea' (Nha Trang, Vietnam, 2016).

Kanehara, Nobukatsu, and Yutaka Arima, 'New Fishing Order – Japan's New Agreement on Fisheries with the Republic of Korea and with the People's Republic of China', *Japanese Annual of International Law* (1999), 1–32.

Kaplan, Robert D., *Asia's Cauldron: The South China Sea and the End of a Stable Pacific* (Random House, 2014).

Kardon, Isaac B., *China's Law of the Sea: The New Rules of Maritime Order* (Yale UP, 2023).

Kastner, Scott L., Margaret M. Pearson, and Chad Rector, *China's Strategic Multilateralism: Investing in Global Governance* (CUP, 2019).

Kausikan, Bilahari, 'Dealing with an Ambiguous World Lecture III: ASEAN & US-China Competition in Southeast Asia' (presented at the IPS-Nathan Lectures, March 2016), https://lkyspp.nus.edu.sg/docs/default-source/ips/ips-nathan-lectures_lecture-iii_asean-us-china-competition-in-southeast-asia_300316.pdf (last accessed 24 April 2024).

Keohane, Robert O., 'The Demand for International Regimes', *International Organization*, 36/2 (1982), 325–55.

Kim, Sun Pyo, *Maritime Delimitation and Interim Arrangements in North East Asia* (Martinus Nijhoff, 2004).

Kirchberger, Sarah, and Patrick O'Keeffe, 'Military-Strategic Aspects of the South China Sea Issue', in Benedikt Seemann and Sebastian Bersick, eds., *Traversing the Challenges. Political, Economic and Environmental Dimensions of Maritime and Regional Security* (Konrad Adenauer Stiftung, 2017), 27–40.

Klein, Natalie, *Maritime Security and the Law of the Sea* (OUP, 2015).

Ko, Shu-ling, 'Taiwan Fisheries Pact Frustrates Both Sides', *The Japan Times* (13 June 2013), https://www.japantimes.co.jp/news/2013/06/13/national/politics-diplomacy/taiwan-fisheries-pact-frustrates-both-sides/ (last accessed 21 April 2024).

Koh, Tommy T. B., 'A Constitution for the Oceans. Remarks by Tommy T.B. Koh, of Singapore, President of the Third United Nations Conference on the Law of the Sea' (December 1982), https://www.un.org/depts/los/convention_agreements/texts/koh_english.pdf (last accessed 24 April 2024).

Koremenos, Barbara, Charles Lipson, and Duncan Snidal, 'The Rational Design of International Institutions', *International Organization*, 55/4 (2001), 761–99. https://doi.org/10.1162/002081801317193592.

Kotani, Tetsuo, 'China and Russia in the Western Pacific: Implications for Japan and the United States', *Maritime Awareness Project* (April 2019), https://map.nbr.org/wp-content/uploads/2020/09/Analysis-Kotani-China-and-Russia-in-the-Western-Pacific-Implications-for-Japan-and-the-United-States-041819.pdf (last accessed 24 April 2024).

Kotani, Tetsuo, 'Issues in the South China Sea Explain the Disturbance around the Senkaku Islands', *Japan Policy Forum* (2017), https://www.japanpolicyforum.jp/pdf/2017/no36/DJweb_36_dip_03.pdf (last accessed 24 April 2024).

Kovrig, Michael, 'How a Long-Awaited Hotline Could Pave the Way for Calmer China-Japan Relations', *South China Morning Post* (13 May 2018), https://www.scmp.com/news/china/diplomacy-defence/article/2145811/how-long-awaited-hotline-could-pave-way-calmer-china (last accessed 24 April 2024).

Kraska, James, 'Maritime Confidence-Building Measures for Navigation in the South China Sea', *The International Journal of Marine and Coastal Law*, 32/2 (2017), 268–97.

Kuik, Cheng-Chwee, 'Explaining the Contradiction in China's South China Sea Policy: Structural Drivers and Domestic Imperatives', *China: An International Journal*, 15/1 (2017), 163–86.

Kuik, Cheng-Chwee, 'How Do Weaker States Hedge? Unpacking ASEAN States' Alignment Behavior towards China', *Journal of Contemporary China*, 25/100 (July 2016), 500–14. https://doi.org/10.1080/10670564.2015.1132714.

Kuok, Lynn. 'Tides of Change: Taiwan's Evolving Position in the South China Sea | Brookings Institution', *Brookings* (7 May 2015), https://www.brookings.edu/research/tides-of-change-taiwans-evolving-position-in-the-south-china-sea/ (last accessed 24 April 2024).

Kwast, Patricia Jimenez, 'Maritime Law Enforcement and the Use of Force: Reflections on the Categorisation of Forcible Action at Sea in the Light of the Guyana/Suriname Award', *Journal of Conflict and Security Law*, 13/1 (2008), 49–91.

Kwiatkowska, Barbara, and Alfred HA Soons, 'Entitlement to Maritime Areas of Rocks Which Cannot Sustain Human Habitation or Economic Life of Their Own', *Netherlands Yearbook of International Law*, 21 (1990), 139–81.

Kydd, Andrew H., 'Rationalist Approaches to Conflict Prevention and Resolution', *Annual Review of Political Science*, 13 (2010), 101–21.

Lagoni, Rainer, 'Interim Measures Pending Maritime Delimitation Agreements', *The American Journal of International Law*, 78/2 (1984), 345–68. https://doi.org/10.2307/2202280.

Lagoni, Rainer, 'Oil and Gas Deposits Across National Frontiers', *The American Journal of International Law*, 73/2 (1979), 215–43. https://doi.org/10.2307/2201608.

Lai, Hongyi, and Su-Jeong Kang, 'Domestic Bureaucratic Politics and Chinese Foreign Policy', *Journal of Contemporary China*, 23/86 (2014), 294–313.

Lake, David A., *Hierarchy in International Relations* (Cornell UP, 2009).

Laksmana, Evan, and Waffaa Kharisma, 'Safeguarding The Shared Maritime Domain Between Indonesia, Vietnam, and Malaysia' CSIS Event Report (CSIS Indonesia, 2020).

Lalu, Gabriel Pabico, 'Duterte Told: Joint Exploration with China in West PH Sea Unconstitutional', *Inquirer* (11 September 2019), https://newsinfo.inquirer.net/1163359/duterte-told-joint-exploration-with-china-in-west-ph-sea-unconstitutional (last accessed 24 April 2024).

Laserna, Manuel, 'West Philippine Sea: Unconstitutional and Much-Abused Concept of "joint Development "', *Attylaserna* (2017), https://attylaserna.blogspot.com/2017/07/west-philippine-sea-unconstitutional.html (last accessed 24 April 2024).

Lascurettes, Kyle M., *Orders of Exclusion: Great Powers and the Strategic Sources of Foundational Rules in International Relations* (OUP, 2020).

Laurenceson, James, 'Economics and Freedom of Navigation in East Asia', *Australian Journal of International Affairs* (2017), 1–13.

Lavalle, Roberto, 'Not Quite a Sure Thing: The Maritime Areas of Rocks and Low-Tide Elevations under the UN Law of the Sea Convention', *The International Journal of Marine and Coastal Law*, 19/1 (2004), 43–69.

Lee, Chang Wee, 'Legal and Political Aspects of the Dokdo Issue: Interrelationship between International Law and International Relations', *Korean Journal of Defense Analysis*, (2013), 227–42.

Lee, Hsien Loong, 'The Endangered Asian Century', *Foreign Affairs*, 99/4 (August 2020), 51–64.

Lee, Ji-Young, *The Geopolitics of South Korea-China Relations: Implications for U.S. Policy in the Indo-Pacific* (RAND Corporation, 2020). https://doi.org/10.7249/PEA524-1.

Lee, Ki Beom, 'The Korea Coast Guard's Use of Force Against Chinese Fishing Vessels: A Note', *Ocean Development & International Law*, 49/3 (July 2018), 226–35. https://doi.org/10.1080/00908320.2018.1443416.

Lee, Peter, 'China Not Leaving the "South China Sea"', *The Asia-Pacific Journal Japan Focus Volume*, 14/6 (2016). https://apjjf.org/2016/06/lee (last accessed 24 April 2024).

Lee, Victor Robert, 'Satellite Imagery Shows Ecocide in the South China Sea', *The Diplomat* (January 2016), https://thediplomat.com/2016/01/satellite-images-show-ecocide-in-the-south-china-sea (last accessed 24 April 2024).

Li, Jinming, and Dexia Li, 'The Dotted Line on the Chinese Map of the South China Sea: A Note', *Ocean Development & International Law*, 34/3–4 (2003), 287–95. https://doi.org/10.1080/00908320390221821.

Li, Nigel N.T, 'Amicus Curiae Submission by the Chinese (Taiwan) Society of International Law in the South China Sea Arbitration: An Introductory Note', *Chinese (Taiwan) Yearbook of International Law and Affairs, 33*, (2015), 167–227.

Lieberthal, Kenneth, *Governing China: From Revolution through Reform* (2nd ed., Norton, 2004).

Lieberthal, Kenneth, and Wang Jisi. *Addressing U.S.-China Strategic Distrust* (Brookings Monograph Series 4, 2012).

Lin, Kun-Chin, and Andrés Villar Gertner, *Maritime Security in the Asia-Pacific. China and the Emerging Order in the East and South China Seas*, Research Paper (Royal Institute of International Affairs, 2015).

Lipscy, Phillip Y., *Renegotiating the World Order: Institutional Change in International Relations* (CUP, 2017).

Liu, Xiaobo, 'How China Can Resolve the FONOP Deadlock in the South China Sea', *CSIS AMTI Update* (March 2019), https://amti.csis.org/how-china-can-resolve-fonop-deadlock/ (last accessed 24 April 2024).

Loh, Dylan M. H., 'The Disturbance and Endurance of Norms in ASEAN: Peaceful but Stressful', *Australian Journal of International Affairs*, 72/5 (September 2018), 385–402. https://doi.org/10.1080/10357718.2018.1488939.

Long, Yingxian, 'China's Decision to Deploy HYSY-981 in the South China Sea: Bureaucratic Politics with Chinese Characteristics', *Asian Security*, 12/3 (September 2016), 148–65. https://doi.org/10.1080/14799855.2016.1227322.

Manicom, James, 'Sino-Japanese Cooperation in the East China Sea: Limitations and Prospects', *Contemporary Southeast Asia: A Journal of International and Strategic Affairs* 30/3 (2008), 455–478.

Martin, Lisa L., and Beth A Simmons, 'International Organizations and Institutions', in Walter Carlsnaes, Thomas Risse, and Beth A Simmons, eds., *Handbook of International Relations* (2012), 327–51.

Martinson, Ryan D., 'Early Warning Brief: Introducing the "New, New" China Coast Guard', *Jamestown China Brief* (January 2021), https://jamestown.org/wp-content/uploads/2021/02/Read-the-2.4.21-Issue-in-PDF.pdf (last accessed 24 April 2024).

Mattes, Michaela, '"Chipping Away at the Issues" Piecemeal Dispute Resolution and Territorial Conflict', *Journal of Conflict Resolution*, 62/1 (2018), 94–118.

McAdams, Richard H., 'A Focal Point Theory of Expressive Law', *Virginia Law Review*, (2000), 1649–729.

McAdams, Richard H., and Janice Nadler, 'Testing the Focal Point Theory of Legal Compliance: The Effect of Third-Party Expression in an Experimental Hawk/Dove Game', *Journal of Empirical Legal Studies*, 2/1 (2005), 87–123.

McLaughlin, Rob. 'Authorizations for Maritime Law Enforcement Operations', *International Review of the Red Cross*, 98/902 (August 2016), 465–90. https://doi.org/10.1017/S1816383117000340.

McManus, John W., 'Offshore Coral Reef Damage, Overfishing, and Paths to Peace in the South China Sea', *The International Journal of Marine and Coastal Law*, 32/2 (2017), 199–237.

McManus, John W., Kwang-Tsao Shao, and Szu-Yin Lin, 'Toward Establishing a Spratly Islands International Marine Peace Park: Ecological Importance and Supportive Collaborative Activities with an Emphasis on the Role of Taiwan', *Ocean Development & International Law*, 41/3 (2010), 270–80. https://doi.org/10.1080/00908320.2010.499303.

Mearsheimer, John J., 'The False Promise of International Institutions', *International Security*, 19/3 (1994), 5–49. https://doi.org/10.2307/2539078.

Mehta, Judith, Chris Starmer, and Robert Sugden, 'Focal Points in Pure Coordination Games: An Experimental Investigation', *Theory and Decision*, 36/2 (1994), 163–85.

Merrills, J. G., *International Dispute Settlement* (5th ed., CUP, 2011).

Milligan, Ben, 'Legal and Policy Options for the Provisional Joint Management of Maritime Spaces Subject to Overlapping Jurisdictional Claims', PhD thesis, University of Wollongong, 2012.

Mitchell, Ronald B., and Patricia M. Keilbach, 'Situation Structure and Institutional Design: Reciprocity, Coercion, and Exchange', *International Organization*, 55/4 (2001), 891–917. https://doi.org/10.1162/002081801317193637.

Miyoshi, Masahiro, 'Exercising Enforcement Juridiction around the Senkaku Islands', *Review of Island Studies* (October 2014), 1–18.

Miyoshi, Masahiro, *The Joint Development of Offshore Oil and Gas in Relation to Maritime Boundary Delimitation*, Maritime Briefing, v. 2/5 (University of Durham, 1999).

Moe, Terry M., 'Political Institutions: The Neglected Side of the Story', *Journal of Law, Economics, & Organization*, 6 (1990), 213–53.

Moe, Terry M., 'Power and Political Institutions', *Perspectives on Politics*, 3/2 (2005), 215–33.

Mogato, Manuel, 'Philippines, U.S. Stage War Games in Face of China Warning', *Reuters* (25 April 2012), https://www.reuters.com/article/us-southchinasea-idUSBRE83O06220120425 (last accessed 24 April 2024).

Morgan, Forrest E. et al., *Dangerous Thresholds: Managing Escalation in the 21st Century* (Rand Corporation, 2008).

Morgan, T. Clifton, 'Issue Linkages in International Crisis Bargaining', *American Journal of Political Science* (1990), 311–33.

Morris, Lyle J., 'Blunt Defenders of Sovereignty: The Rise of Coast Guards in East and Southeast Asia', *Naval War College Review*, 70/2 (2017), 75–112.

Morris, Lyle J., 'Organizing for the Gray Zone: Assessing the Rights Protection Capabilities of the New China Coast Guard', in Ryan D Martinson and Andrew S. Erickson, eds., *China's Maritime Gray Zone Operations* (Naval Institute, 2019), 1–15 (preprint).

Morris, Lyle J., 'South Korea Cracks Down on Illegal Chinese Fishing, With Violent Results', *The Diplomat* (November 2016), https://thediplomat.com/2016/11/south-korea-cracks-down-on-illegal-chinese-fisherman-with-violent-results/ (last accessed 24 April 2024).

Mortimer, John, 'Western Pacific Naval Symposium', *Maritime Studies*, 1996/87 (March 1996), 8–9. https://doi.org/10.1080/07266472.1996.10878449.

Nakano, Ryoko, 'The Sino–Japanese Territorial Dispute and Threat Perception in Power Transition', *The Pacific Review*, 29/2 (2016), 165–86.

Narine, Shaun, 'ASEAN and the ARF: The Limits of the "ASEAN Way"', *Asian Survey*, 37/10 (1997), 961–78. https://doi.org/10.2307/2645616.

Narlikar, Amrita, ed., *Deadlocks in Multilateral Negotiations: Causes and Solutions* (CUP, 2010).

Narlikar, Amrita, 'Fairness in International Trade Negotiations: Developing Countries in the GATT and WTO', *World Economy*, 29/8 (2006), 1005–29.

Narlikar, Amrita, and John Odell, 'The Strict Distributive Strategy for a Bargaining Coalition: The Like Minded Group in the World Trade Organization', in John Odell, ed., *Negotiating Trade: Developing Countries in the WTO and NAFTA* (CUP, 2006), 115–44.

Nathan, Andrew J., and Andrew Scobell, *China's Search for Security* (Columbia UP, 2015).

Nemeth, Stephen C. et al., 'Ruling the Sea: Managing Maritime Conflicts through UNCLOS and Exclusive Economic Zones', *International Interactions*, 40/5 (2014), 711–36.

Nguyen, Dang Thang, 'Fisheries Co-Operation in the South China Sea and the (Ir) Relevance of the Sovereignty Question', *Asian Journal of International Law*, 2/01 (2012), 59–88. https://doi.org/10.1017/S2044251311000099.

Nguyen, Hong Thao, 'Maritime Delimitation and Fishery Cooperation in the Tonkin Gulf', *Ocean Development & International Law*, 36/1 (2005), 25–44.

Nguyen Minh Quang, 'Saving the China-ASEAN South China Sea Code of Conduct', *The Diplomat* (29 June 2019), https://thediplomat.com/2019/06/saving-the-china-asean-south-china-sea-code-of-conduct/ (last accessed 24 April 2024).

Nguyen, Phuong, 'Deciphering the Shift in America's South China Sea Policy', *Contemporary Southeast Asia*, 38/3 (December 2016), 389–421. https://doi.org/10.1355/cs38-3b.

Nguyen, Thanh Trung, 'Davids and Goliath: Time for Southeast Asian Fishery Cooperation in the South China Sea', *AMTI* (24 June 2019), https://amti.csis.org/davids-and-goliath-time-for-southeast-asian-fishery-cooperation-in-the-south-china-sea/ (last accessed 24 April 2024).

Nie, Wenjuan, 'China's Domestic Strategic Debate and Confusion over the South China Sea Issue', *The Pacific Review*, 31/2 (March 2018), 188–204. https://doi.org/10.1080/09512748.2017.1370608.

Nie, Wenjuan. 'Xi Jinping's Foreign Policy Dilemma: One Belt, One Road or the South China Sea?' *Contemporary Southeast Asia* (2016), 422–44.

Nordquist, Myron H., John Norton Moore, and Tommy T. B Koh, eds., *Freedom of Seas, Passage Rights and the 1982 Law of the Sea Convention*, Center for Oceans Law and Policy, 13 (Martinus Nijhoff, 2009).

Odell, John, 'Negotiation and Bargaining', in Thomas Risse, Walter Carlsnaes, and Beth Simmons, eds., *Handbook of International Relations* (SAGE, 2011), 379–99.

Odell, John, and Susan Sell, 'Reframing the Issue: The WTO Coalition on Intellectual Property and Public Health 2001' (Geneva, 2003).

Odell, Rachel, 'How Strategic Norm-Shaping Undergirds America's Command of the Commons', *MIT Political Science Department Research Paper*, 23 (2019). https://doi.org/10.2139/ssrn.3451412

Odgaard, Liselotte, *Maritime Security between China and Southeast Asia: Conflict and Cooperation in the Making of Regional Order* (Routledge, 2017).

Ogasawara, Yoshiyuki, 'Ma Ying-Jeou's Doctoral Thesis and Its Impact on the Japan-Taiwan Fisheries Negotiations', *Journal of Contemporary East Asia Studies*, 4/2 (2015), 67–92.

O'Hanlon, Michael, and Gregory Poling, 'Rocks, Reefs, and Nuclear War', *AMTI Update* (January 2020), https://amti.csis.org/rocks-reefs-and-nuclear-war/ (last accessed 24 April 2024).

Oh, Seok-Min, 'S. Korea, China to Toughen Crackdown on Illegal Fishing in East Sea', *Yonhap News Agency* (14 June 2023), https://en.yna.co.kr/view/AEN20230614002300320 (last accessed 24 April 2024).

Ohira, Zengo, and Terumichi Kuwahara, 'Fishery Problems between Japan and the People's Republic of China', *Japanese Annual of International Law*, 3 (1959), 109–25.

Olson, Mancur, *Power and Prosperity: Outgrowing Communist and Capitalist Dictatorships* (Basic Books, 2000).

Ordaniel, Jeffrey, 'The Philippines and Joint Development in the South China Sea', *PacNet*, 75 (October 2017), https://pacforum.org/wp-content/uploads/2019/02/171016_PacNet_75.pdf (last accessed 24 April 2024).

Ostrom, Elinor, *Governing the Commons: The Evolution of Institutions for Collective Action* (CUP, 1990).

Ostrom, Elinor, 'The Challenge of Common-Pool Resources', *Environment: Science and Policy for Sustainable Development*, 50/4 (July 2008), 8–21. https://doi.org/10.3200/ENVT.50.4.8-21.

Ou, Ching-Hsiewn, and Huan-Sheng Tseng, 'The Fishery Agreements and Management Systems in the East China Sea', *Ocean and Coastal Management*, 53/5 (2010), 279–88. https://doi.org/10.1016/j.ocecoaman.2010.04.004.

Oxman, Bernard H., 'The Territorial Temptation: A Siren Song at Sea', *American Journal of International Law*, 100 (2006), 830–51.

Pan, Zhongqi, 'Sino-Japanese Dispute over the Diaoyu/Senkaku Islands: The Pending Controversy from the Chinese Perspective', *Journal of Chinese Political Science*, 12/1 (June 2007), 71–92. https://doi.org/10.1007/s11366-007-9002-6.

Parlett, Kate, 'Jurisdiction of the Arbitral Tribunal in Philippines v. China under UNCLOS and in the Absence of China', *American Journal of International Law*, 110 (2016), 266–272. https://doi.org/10.1017/S2398772300009144.

Parrocha, Azer, 'Malacañang Maintains Duterte Not Surrendering PH Sovereignty', *Republic of the Philippines News Agency* (July 2019), https://www.pna.gov.ph/articles/1073915 (last accessed 24 April 2024).

Parrocha, Azer, 'Duterte-Xi Verbal Fishing Deal Still Legally Binding: Palace', *Philippine News Agency* (1 July 2019), https://www.pna.gov.ph/articles/1073792 (last accessed 15 April 2024).

Patalano, Alessio, 'When Strategy Is "Hybrid" and Not "Grey": Reviewing Chinese Military and Constabulary Coercion at Sea', *The Pacific Review*, 31/6 (November 2018), 811–39. https://doi.org/10.1080/09512748.2018.1513546.

Pauly, Daniel, and Cui Liang, 'The Fisheries of the South China Sea: Major Trends since 1950', *Marine Policy*, 121/103584 (November 2020), 1–7. https://doi.org/10.1016/j.marpol.2019.103584.

Payne, Anthony, 'Rethinking United States–Caribbean Relations: Towards a New Mode of Trans-Territorial Governance', *Review of International Studies*, 26/1 (January 2000), 69–82. https://doi.org/10.1017/S0260210500000693.

Pearson, Margaret M., Meg Rithmire, and Kellee S. Tsai, 'China's Party-State Capitalism and International Backlash: From Interdependence to Insecurity', *International Security* 47/2 (October 2022), 135–176. https://doi.org/10.1162/isec_a_00447.

Pedrozo, Raul Pete, 'The US-China Incidents at Sea Agreement: A Recipe for Disaster', *Journal of National Security Law & Policy*, 6 (2012), 207–26.

Pedrozo, Raul Pete, 'Preserving Navigational Rights and Freedoms: The Right to Conduct Military Activities in China's Exclusive Economic Zone', *Chinese Journal of International Law*, 9/1 (2010), 9–29.

Pejsova, Eva, ed., *Sense and Sensibility: Addressing the South China Sea Disputes*, ISS Reports, 28 (EU Institute for Security Studies, 2016).

Pelc, Krzysztof J., 'The Politics of Precedent in International Law: A Social Network Application', *American Political Science Review*, 108/3 (August 2014), 547–64. https://doi.org/10.1017/S0003055414000276.

Pemmaraju, Sreenivasa Rao, 'The South China Sea Arbitration (The Philippines v. China), Assessment of the Award on Jurisdiction and Admissibility', *Chinese Journal of International Law*, 15/2 (2016), 265–307.

'Petronas: M'sia, Brunei to Jointly Develop 2 Oil-Rich Areas', *The Star* (01 May 2010), https://www.thestar.com.my/news/nation/2010/05/01/petronas-msia-brunei-to-jointly-develop-2-oilrich-areas (last accessed 18 April 2024).

Philippine Center for Investigative Journalism, 'The Spratlys Deal: Selling out Philippine Sovereignty?', *PCIJ Blog* (17 March 2008), https://old.pcij.org/blog/2008/03/17/the-spratlys-deal-selling-philippine-sovereignty (last accessed 24 April 2024).

'PHL Stops Oil and Gas Drilling in Reed Bank, Cites Dispute with China', *Gmanetwork*, (3 March 2015), https://www.gmanetwork.com/news/money/companies/445665/phl-stops-oil-and-gas-drilling-in-reed-bank-cites-dispute-with-china/story/(last accessed 24 April 2024).

'Photos Show Confrontation Between USS Decatur and a Chinese Navy Warship in South China Sea', *gCaptain* (2 October 2018), https://gcaptain.com/photos-show-confrontation-between-uss-decatur-and-chinese-navy-warship-in-disputed-south-china-sea/ (last accessed 24 April 2024).

Poling, Gregory B., Michael J. Green, Christopher K. Johnson, Murray Hiebert, Matthew P. Funaiole, Bonnie S. Glaser, and Amy Searight, *Defusing the South China Sea Disputes A Regional Blueprint* (Center for Strategic & International Studies, 2018). https://www.csis.org/analysis/defusing-south-china-sea-disputes (last accessed 24 April 2024).

Poling, Gregory, 'China's Hidden Navy', *Foreign Policy* (June 2019), https://foreignpolicy.com/2019/06/25/chinas-secret-navy-spratlys-southchinasea-chinesenavy-maritimemilitia/ (last accessed 24 April 2024).

Poling, Gregory, 'Illuminating the South China Sea's Dark Fishing Fleets', *CSIS AMTI* (January 2019), https://ocean.csis.org/spotlights/illuminating-the-south-china-seas-dark-fishing-fleets/ (last accessed 24 April 2024).

Powell, Robert, 'Bargaining and Learning While Fighting', *American Journal of Political Science*, 48/2 (2004), 344–61.

Powell, Robert, 'Bargaining Theory and International Conflict', *Annual Review of Political Science* 5/1 (2002), 1–30.

Powell, Robert, 'Stability and the Distribution of Power', *World Politics*, 48/2 (1996), 239–67.

Powell, Robert, 'War as a Commitment Problem', *International Organization*, 60/1 (2006), 169–203.

Przystup, James, John Bradford, and James Manicom, 'Japan-China Maritime Confidence Building and Communications Mechanisms', *Pac Net 67 Pacific Forum CSIS* (August 2013).

Punay, Edu, 'SC Asked to Rule on Legality of JMSU', *Philstar* (30 May 2014), https://www.philstar.com/headlines/2014/05/30/1329017/sc-asked-rule-legality-jmsu (last accessed 24 April 2024).

Putnam, Robert D., 'Diplomacy and Domestic Politics: The Logic of Two-Level Games', *International Organization*, 42/3 (1988), 427–60.

Qu, Xiaobo, and Qiang Meng, 'The Economic Importance of the Straits of Malacca and Singapore: An Extreme-Scenario Analysis', *Transportation Research Part E: Logistics and Transportation Review*, 48/1 (January 2012), 258–65. https://doi.org/10.1016/j.tre.2011.08.005.

Quek, Kai, and Alastair Iain Johnston, 'Can China Back down? Crisis de-Escalation in the Shadow of Popular Opposition', *International Security*, 42/3 (2018), 7–36.

Ragin, Charles C., *The Comparative Method: Moving beyond Qualitative and Quantitative Strategies* (University of California, 2014).

Raine, Sarah, and Christian Le Mière, *Regional Disorder: The South China Sea Disputes*, IISS Adelphi Series (Routledge, 2013).

Ranada, Pia, 'Document: Oil, Gas Development Deal between Philippines, China', *Rappler* (26 November 2018), https://www.rappler.com/nation/memorandum-understanding-philippines-china-oil-gas-development-deal (last accessed 24 April 2024).

Ranada, Pia, 'Philippines, China Form Groups to Implement Oil, Gas Exploration Deal', *Rappler* (30 August 2019), https://www.rappler.com/nation/238821-philippines-china-form-groups-implement-oil-gas-exploration-deal (last accessed 24 April 2024).

Rasler, Karen A., and William R. Thompson, 'Contested Territory, Strategic Rivalries, and Conflict Escalation', *International Studies Quarterly*, 50/1 (2006), 145–68.

Reed, Lucy, and Kenneth Wong, 'Marine Entitlements in the South China Sea: The Arbitration Between the Philippines and China', *American Journal of International Law*, 110/4 (2016), 746–60. https://doi.org/10.1017/S0002930000763202.

Reilly, James, 'A Wave to Worry About? Public Opinion, Foreign Policy and China's Anti-Japan Protests', *Journal of Contemporary China*, 23/86 (March 2014), 197–215. https://doi.org/10.1080/10670564.2013.832519.

Reiter, Dan, 'Exploring the Bargaining Model of War', *Perspectives on Politics*, 1/01 (2003), 27–43.

Ren, Xiaofeng, and Xizhong Cheng, 'A Chinese Perspective', *Marine Policy*, 29/2 (March 2005), 139–46. https://doi.org/10.1016/j.marpol.2004.08.007.

Roach, J. Ashley, 'Marine Scientific Research and the New Law of the Sea', *Ocean Development & International Law*, 27/1–2 (January 1996), 59–72. https://doi.org/10.1080/00908329609546075.

Roach, J. Ashley, 'Malaysia and Brunei: An Analysis of Their Claims in the South China Sea' (A CNA Occasional Paper, 2014).

Roach, J. Ashley, and Robert W. Smith, 'Straight Baselines: The Need for a Universally Applied Norm', *Ocean Development & International Law*, 31/1–2 (2000), 47–80.

Roberts, Christopher, 'The South China Sea: Beijing's Challenge to ASEAN and UNCLOS and the Necessity of a New Multi-Tiered Approach', *RSIS Working Paper*, 307 (2017), 1–33.

Rocher, Sophie Boisseau du, 'Scientific Cooperation in the South China Sea. Another Lever for China', *Australian Strategic Policy Institute*, (October 2015), https://www.aspi.org.au/report/scientific-cooperation-south-china-sea-another-lever-china (last accessed 24 April 2024).

Ross, Marta McLellan, 'The Japan-China Maritime and Air Communication Mechanism: Operational and Strategic Considerations', *Japanese Institute of International Affairs*, 30 (2015). https://www2.jiia.or.jp/pdf/fellow_report/150630_Ms_Ross_ECS.pdf (last accessed 24 April 2024).

Ross, Robert S., 'The Problem with the Pivot: Obama's New Asia Policy Is Unnecessary and Counterproductive', *Foreign Affairs*, 91 (December 2012), 70–8.

Roth, Alvin E., 'Toward a Focal Point Theory of Bargaining', *Game-Theoretic Models of Bargaining*, 259 (1985), 265–67.

Rühle, Michael, 'Deterring Hybrid Threats: The Need for a More Rational Debate', *NATO Defense College Policy Brief*, 15 (July 2019).

Russel, Daniel, 'Assistant Secretary of State Bureau of East Asian and Pacific Affairs at the US Department of State, Testimony to United States House Committee on Foreign Affairs, Subcommittee on Asia and the Pacific', (February 2014),

https://docs.house.gov/meetings/FA/FA05/20140205/101715/HHRG-113-FA05-Wstate-RusselD-20140205.pdf (last accessed 24 April 2024).
'S. Korea, China to Hold Joint Inspection on Illegal Fishing in Yellow Sea', *The Korea Times* (5 April 2015), http://www.koreatimes.co.kr/www/news/nation/2015/11/656_176526.html (last accessed 21 April 2024).
Sampson, Michael, 'The Evolution of China's Regional Trade Agreements: Power Dynamics and the Future of the Asia-Pacific', *The Pacific Review* (September 2019), 1–31. https://doi.org/10.1080/09512748.2019.1660397.
Sartori, Giovanni, 'Concept Misformation in Comparative Politics', *American Political Science Review*, 64/4 (1970), 1033–53.
Schelling, Thomas C., *Arms and Influence* (Yale UP, 1966).
Schelling, Thomas C., *The Strategy of Conflict* (2nd ed., Harvard UP, 1980).
Schoenbaum, Thomas J., 'The South China Sea Arbitration Decision and a Plan for Peaceful Resolution of the Disputes', *Journal of Maritime Law and Commerce*, 47 (2016), 451–77.
Schofield, Clive, 'Defining Areas for Joint Development in Disputed Waters', in Shicun Wu and Nong Hong, eds., *Recent Developments in the South China Sea Dispute: The Prospect of a Joint Development Regime* (Routledge, 2014), 78–98.
Schofield, Clive H., and Ian Townsend-Gault, 'Choppy Waters Ahead in "a Sea of Peace Cooperation and Friendship"? Slow Progress towards the Application of Maritime Joint Development to the East China Sea', *Marine Policy*, 35/1 (2011), 25–33.
Schultheiss, Christian, 'Challenges for Joint Development in the SCS', in Eva Pejsova, ed., *Sense and Sensibility – Addressing the South China Sea Disputes*, EUISS 28 (2016) 35–44. https://www.iss.europa.eu/content/sense-and-sensibility-%E2%80%93-addressing-south-china-sea-disputes (last accessed 24 April 2024).
Schultheiss, Christian, 'Joint Development of Hydrocarbon Resources in the South China Sea After the Philippines Versus China Arbitration?', *Ocean Development & International Law*, 51/3 (August 2020), 241–262. https://doi.org/10.1080/00908320.2020.1781381.
Schultheiss, Christian, '"One of the First Matters to Be Addressed but Distinct" or "Distinct but Inseparable"? The Distinction Between Maritime Entitlement and Sea Boundary Delimitation in the Philippines v. China Arbitration', *Asian Journal of International Law*, 11/1 (January 2021), 24–35. https://doi.org/10.1017/S2044251320000235.
Schultheiss, Christian, 'Overcoming Violence in Maritime Conflicts with Provisional Arrangements: A Legal Tool for Conflict Resolution', in Mark Retter, Andrea Varga, and Marc Weller, eds., *International Law and Peace Settlements* (CUP, 2021), 525–44.

Scobell, Andrew, *China's Use of Military Force: Beyond the Great Wall and the Long March* (CUP, 2003).

Scott, David, 'Conflict Irresolution in the South China Sea', *Asian Survey*, 52/6 (December 2012), 1019–42. https://doi.org/10.1525/as.2012.52.6.1019.

Seah, Sharon et al., *The State of Southeast Asia: 2023* (ISEAS-Yusof Ishak Institute, 2023), https://www.iseas.edu.sg/wp-content/uploads/2025/07/The-State-of-SEA-2023-Final-Digital-V4-09-Feb-2023.pdf (last accessed 24 April 2024).

See, Aie Balagtas, 'Philippines Foreign Secretary Challenges "China's Demand" on South China Sea', *Benarnews* (21 September 2020), https://www.benarnews.org/english/news/philippine/western-powers-09212020142758.html (last accessed 24 April 2024).

Senese, Paul D., and John A. Vasquez, 'Assessing the Steps to War', *British Journal of Political Science*, 35/04 (2005), 607–33.

Severino, Rodolfo C., 'The Philippines' National Territory', *Southeast Asian Affairs*, 2012, 257–62.

Sharpe, Samuel, 'An ASEAN Way to Security Cooperation in Southeast Asia?', *The Pacific Review*, 16/2 (March 2003), 231–50. https://doi.org/10.1080/0951274032000069624.

Sheldon-Duplaix, Alexandre, 'Beyond the China Seas: Will China Become a Global "Sea Power"?' *China Perspectives*, 2016/3 (September 2016), 43–52. https://doi.org/10.4000/chinaperspectives.7041.

Shimodaira, Takuya, 'Measures to Enhance Maritime Safety – Expansion of Code for Unplanned Encounters at Sea (CUES) Exercise', in NIDS, ed., *Symposium Maintaining Maritime Order in the Asia-Pacific* (2017), 113-31 https://www.nids.mod.go.jp/english/publication/symposium/e2017.html (last accessed 24 April 2024).

Simmons, Beth A., 'Capacity, Commitment, and Compliance: International Institutions and Territorial Disputes', *Journal of Conflict Resolution*, 46/6 (December 2002), 829–56. https://doi.org/10.1177/002200202237931.

Simmons, Beth A., 'Rules over Real Estate Trade, Territorial Conflict, and International Borders as Institution', *Journal of Conflict Resolution*, 49/6 (2005), 823–48.

Simon, Sheldon W., 'Evaluating Track II Approaches to Security Diplomacy in the Asia-Pacific: The CSCAP Experience', *The Pacific Review*, 15/2 (2002), 167–200.

Simon, Sheldon W., 'Safety and Security in the Malacca Straits: The Limits of Collaboration', *Asian Security*, 7/1 (February 2011), 27–43. https://doi.org/10.1080/14799855.2011.548208.

Slaughter, Anne-Marie, *The Chessboard and the Web: Strategies of Connection in a Networked World.* (Yale UP, 2017).

Smith, Jeffrey J., 'Brunei and Malaysia Resolve Outstanding Maritime Boundary Issues', *LOS Reports*, 1 (2010), 1–4.

Starr, Barbara, et al., 'Chinese Warship in "unsafe" Encounter with US Destroyer, amid Rising US-China Tensions', *CNN* (2 October 2018), https://edition.cnn.com/2018/10/01/politics/china-us-warship-unsafe-encounter/index.html (last accessed 24 April 2024).

Stashwick, Steven, 'China's South China Sea Militarization Has Peaked', *Foreign Policy* (August 2019), https://foreignpolicy.com/2019/08/19/chinas-south-china-sea-militarization-has-peaked/ (last accessed 24 April 2024).

Stilwell, David R., 'The South China Sea, Southeast Asia's Patrimony, and Everybody's Own Backyard. Remarks of David R. Stilwell Assistant Secretary Bureau of East Asian and Pacific Affairs at the CSIS' (July 2020), https://2017-2021.state.gov/the-south-china-sea-southeast-asias-patrimony-and-everybodys-own-backyard/ (last accessed 24 April 2024).

Stone, Randall W., *Controlling Institutions: International Organizations and the Global Economy* (CUP, 2011).

Storey, Ian, 'Assessing the ASEAN China Framework for the Code of Conduct for the South China Sea', *ISEAS Perspective*, 62 (2017), https://www.iseas.edu.sg/articles-commentaries/iseas-perspective/201762-assessing-the-aseanchina-framework-for-the-code-of-conduct-for-the-south-china-sea/ (last accessed 24 April 2024).

Storey, Ian, 'Japan's Maritime Security Interests in Southeast Asia and the South China Sea Dispute', *Political Science*, 65/2 (December 2013), 135–56. https://doi.org/10.1177/0032318713508482.

Storey, Ian, 'Malaysia and the South China Sea Dispute: Policy Continuity amid Domestic Political Change', *ISEAS Perspective*, 18 (2020), https://www.iseas.edu.sg/wp-content/uploads/2020/02/ISEAS_Perspective_2020_18.pdf (last accessed 24 April 2024).

Storey, Ian, 'Sino-Philippine and Sino-US Tensions Persist in the South China Sea', *ISEAS Commentary* (February 2019), https://sealionplus.iseas.edu.sg/nodes/view/23915 (last accessed 24 April 2024).

Sugden, Robert, 'A Theory of Focal Points', *The Economic Journal* (1995), 533–50.

Sun, Jing, 'Growing Diplomacy, Retreating Diplomats – How the Chinese Foreign Ministry Has Been Marginalized in Foreign Policymaking', *Journal of Contemporary China*, 26/105 (May 2017), 419–33. https://doi.org/10.1080/10670564.2016.1245895.

Suorsa, Olli Pekka, 'The Conventional Wisdom Still Stands: America Can Deal with China's Artificial Island Bases', *War on the Rocks* (February 2020), https://warontherocks.com/2020/02/the-conventional-wisdom-still-stands-america-can-deal-with-chinas-artificial-island-bases/ (last accessed 24 April 2024).

Swaine, Michael D., and M. Taylor Fravel. 'China's Assertive Behavior–Part Two: The Maritime Periphery', *China Leadership Monitor* 35 (2011), 1–29.

Takada, Akira, 'Marine Scientific Research in the Exclusive Economic Zone and Japan-China Agreement for Prior Notification (1995–2001)', *Japanese Annual of International Law* (2001), 134–50.

'Taiwan Ultimatum to Philippines over Fisherman's Death', *BBC News* (12 May 2013), https://www.bbc.com/news/world-asia-22499246 (last accessed 18 April 2024).

'Talk of the Day – Taiwan, Philippines Duel for Global Support', *Focus Taiwan* (18 May 2013), https://focustaiwan.tw/politics/201305180026 (last accessed 18 April 2024).

Talmon, Stefan, and Bing Bing Jia, *The South China Sea Arbitration: A Chinese Perspective* (Bloomsbury, 2014).

Tamacruz, Sofia, 'PH, China Eye Marine Research, Protection in South China Sea', *Rappler* (29 October 2019), https://www.rappler.com/nation/philippines-china-eye-marine-research-protection-south-china-sea (last accessed 24 April 2024).

Tatsumi, Yuki, 'Senkaku Islands/East China Sea Disputes – A Japanese Perspective', *CNA Maritime Asia Project Policy Paper* (2013), https://www.stimson.org/content/senkaku-islandseast-china-sea-disputes-japanese-perspective (last accessed 24 April 2024).

Taylor, Brendan, 'The South China Sea Is Not a Flashpoint', *The Washington Quarterly*, 37/1 (January 2014), 99–111. https://doi.org/10.1080/0163660X.2014.893176.

Thayer, Carlyle A., 'A Closer Look at the ASEAN-China Single Draft South China Sea Code of Conduct', *The Diplomat* (August 2018), https://thediplomat.com/2018/08/a-closer-look-at-the-asean-china-single-draft-south-china-sea-code-of-conduct/ (last accessed 24 April 2024).

Thayer, Carlyle A., 'ASEAN and China Set to Agree on Single Draft South China Sea Code of Conduct', *The Diplomat* (July 2018), https://thediplomat.com/2018/07/asean-and-china-set-to-agree-on-single-draft-south-china-sea-code-of-conduct/ (last accessed 24 April 2024).

Thayer, Carlyle A., 'ASEAN, China and the South China Sea Code of Conduct', Presentation to Maritime Security Research Group Workshop (The University of New South Wales Canberra, October 2019).

Thayer, Carlyle A., 'ASEAN-China: Framework of a COC', *Thayer Consultancy Background Brief* (August 2017), https://www.scribd.com/document/355938565/Thayer-ASEAN-China-Framework-of-a-COC-August-6-2017 (last accessed 24 April 2024).

Thayer, Carlyle A., 'ASEAN'S Code of Conduct in the South China Sea: A Litmus Test for Community-Building?' *The Asia-Pacific Journal*, 10/4 (2012), 1–22.

Thayer, Carlyle A., 'South China Sea: Background to ASEAN-China Code of Conduct', *Thayer Consultancy Background Brief* (April 2017), https://www.scribd.com/document/346497873/Thayer-ASEAN-China-South-China-Sea-Code-of-Conduct-Background (last accessed 24 April 2024).

Thompson, Drew, 'The Rise of Xi Jinping and China's New Era: Implications for the United States and Taiwan', *Issues & Studies*, 56/01 (March 2020), 1–25. https://doi.org/10.1142/S1013251120400044.

Till, Geoffrey, *Seapower: A Guide for the Twenty-First Century* (Routledge, 2018).

Tir, Jaroslav, and Douglas Stinnett, 'The Institutionalization of River Treaties', *International Negotiation*, 14/2 (2009), 229–51. https://doi.org/10.1163/157180609X432815.

Tir, Jaroslav, and Douglas M Stinnett, 'Weathering Climate Change: Can Institutions Mitigate International Water Conflict?' *Journal of Peace Research*, 49/1 (January 2012), 211–25. https://doi.org/10.1177/0022343311427066.

Ton, Anh Duc, 'Code for Unplanned Encounters at Sea and Its Practical Limitations in the East and South China Seas', *Australian Journal of Maritime & Ocean Affairs*, 9/4 (October 2017), 227–39. https://doi.org/10.1080/18366503.2017.1326075.

Tønnesson, Stein, 'Could China and Vietnam Resolve the Conflicts in the South China Sea', in Yann-Huei Song and Keyuan Zou, eds., *Major Law and Policy Issues In the South China Sea: European and American Perspectives* (Ashgate, 2014), 207–33.

Tønnesson, Stein, *Explaining the East Asian Peace: A Research Story* (Nordic Institute of Asian Studies Press, 2017).

Tønnesson, Stein, 'Fish for Peace in the South China Sea', *AMTI Update* (January 2019), https://amti.csis.org/fish-for-peace-south-china-sea/ (last accessed 24 April 2024).

Tønnesson, Stein, 'The Tonkin Gulf Agreements: A Model of Conflict Resolution?' in C. J. Jenner and Tran Truong Thuy, eds., *The South China Sea: A Crucible of Regional Cooperation or Conflict-Making Sovereignty Claims?* (CUP, 2016), 151–70.

Tønnesson, Stein, 'Why Are the Disputes in the South China Sea So Intractable? A Historical Approach', *Asian Journal of Social Science*, 30/3 (2002), 570–601.

'Tough Talks Ahead on South China Sea Code of Conduct as Vietnam Seeks to Curb China's Actions', *The Straits Times* (31 December 2018), https://www.straitstimes.com/asia/se-asia/tough-talks-ahead-on-south-china-sea-code-of-conduct-as-vietnam-seeks-to-curb-chinas (last accessed 22 April 2024).

Townshend, Ashley, and Rory Medcalf, *Shifting Waters: China's New Passive Assertiveness in Asian Maritime Security*, Report (Lowy Institute for international Policy, 2016).

Tran, Bich, 'The Significance of the Vietnam-Indonesia Exclusive Economic Zone Demarcation', *Fulcrum* (January 2023), https://fulcrum.sg/the-significance-of-the-vietnam-indonesia-exclusive-economic-zone-demarcation/ (last accessed 24 April 2024).

Tran, Truong Thuy, 'Code of Conduct and the Prevention and Management of Incidents in the South China Sea', in Tran Truong Thuy and Le Thuy Trang, eds., *Power, Law, and Maritime Order in the South China Sea* (Lexington Books, 2015), 317–30.

Tran, Truong Thuy, 'Recent Development In The South China Sea: From Declaration To Code Of Conduct', *East Sea (South China Sea) Studies* (2011), 1–20.

Tran, Truong Thuy, and Le Thuy Trang, eds., *Power, Law, and Maritime Order in the South China Sea* (Lexington Books, 2015).

Tseng, Huan-Sheng, and Ching-Hsiewn Ou, 'Taiwan and China: A Unique Fisheries Relationship', *Marine Policy*, 34/6 (November 2010), 1156–62. https://doi.org/10.1016/j.marpol.2010.03.015.

Tseng, Hui-Yi Katherine, 'The Taiwan Dilemma in the Diaoyu/Diaoyutai/Senkaku Islands Sovereignty Dispute', *American Journal of Chinese Studies*, 21 (2014), 111–26.

Uexkull, Nina von, and Halvard Buhaug, 'Security Implications of Climate Change: A Decade of Scientific Progress', *Journal of Peace* Researc,h 58/1 (January 2021), 3–17. https://doi.org/10.1177/0022343320984210.

United States Department of State Bureau of Oceans and International Environmental and Scientific Affairs, 'Limits in the Seas No. 142 Philippines: Archipelagic and Other Maritime Claims and Boundaries' (September 2014), https://www.state.gov/wp-content/uploads/2019/10/LIS-142.pdf (last accessed 24 April 2024).

'U.S. Could Take Down Islands in SCS If It Needed To, Says Pentagon Official', *Newsweek* (1 June 2018), https://www.newsweek.com/us-could-take-down-man-made-islands-south-china-sea-if-it-needed-says-pentagon-952451 (last accessed 24 April 2024).

Valencia, Mark J., 'Parsing the Present Philippines-China Contretemps', *Eurasia Review* (April 2019), https://www.eurasiareview.com/19042019-parsing-the-present-philippines-china-contretemps-analysis/ (last accessed 24 April 2024).

Valencia, Mark J., 'The "Blueprints for Management of the South China Sea": A Critique', *IPP Review* (November 2018).

Valencia, Mark J., 'The East China Sea Disputes: History, Status, and Ways Forward', *Asian Perspective*, 38/2 (2014), 183–218.

Valencia, Mark J., 'What the "Zero Draft" Code of Conduct for the South China Sea Says (and Doesn't Say)', *Global Asia* (March 2013), https://www.globalasia.org/v8no1/feature/what-the-zero-draft-code-of-conduct-for-the-south-china-sea-says-and-doesnt-say_mark-j-valencia (last accessed 24 April 2024).

Valencia, Mark J., ed., *Maritime Regime Building: Lessons Learned and Their Relevance for Northeast Asia* (Martinus Nijhoff, 2001).

Valencia, Mark J., and Yoshihisa Amae, 'Regime Building in the East China Sea', *Ocean Development & International Law*, 34/2 (April 2003), 189–208. https://doi.org/10.1080/00908320390209636.

Valencia, Mark John, Jon M. Van Dyke, and Noel A. Ludwig, *Sharing the Resources of the South China Sea* (Martinus Nijhoff, 1997).

Van Dyke, Jon M., and Robert A. Brooks, 'Uninhabited Islands: Their Impact on the Ownership of the Oceans' Resources', *Ocean Development & International Law*, 12/3–4 (1983), 265–300.

Vasquez, John A. and Valeriano Brandon. 'Territory as Source of Conflict and Road to Peace', in Jacob Bercovitch, Viktor Aleksandrovich Kremeniuk, and I William Zartman, eds., *The SAGE Handbook of Conflict Resolution*, (SAGE, 2009), 193–209.

Vicedo, Christian. 'Balikatan 2019 and Philippine Policy on the South China Sea', *PacNet*, 25 (April 2019), https://pacforum.org/publications/pacnet-25-balikatan-2019-and-philippine-policy-on-the-south-china-sea/ (last accessed 24 April 2024).

Vietnam Academy of Science and Technology – Institute of Oceanography, 'Philippines–Vietnam Joint Oceanographic and Marine Scientific Research Expedition in the South China Sea (JOMSRE-SCS), 1996–2007' (October 2012), http://www.vnio.org.vn/Home/tabid/107/ctl/Details/mid/579/ItemID/798/language/en-US/Default.aspx (last accessed 24 April 2024).

'Vietnam, China Hold Talks on Maritime Issues', *VietnamPlus* (2 December 2021), https://en.vietnamplus.vn/vietnam-china-hold-talks-on-maritime-issues/216502.vnp (last accessed 24 April 2024).

'Vietnam, China Begin Fishery Inspection in Gulf of Tonkin', *VietnamPlus* (24 April 2019), https://en.vietnamplus.vn/vietnam-china-begin-fishery-inspection-in-gulf-of-tonkin/151573.vnp (last accessed 15 April 2024).

Viray, Patricia Lourdes, 'China Claims Draft Oil Exploration Deal to Have No Bearing on Sovereignty', *Philstar* (20 November 2018), https://www.philstar.com/headlines/2018/11/20/1870227/china-claims-draft-oil-exploration-deal-have-no-bearing-sovereignty (last accessed 24 April 2024).

Viray, Patricia Lourdes, 'What Cayetano Missed in Justifying South China Sea Joint Development', *Philstar* (31 May 2018), https://www.philstar.com/headlines/2018/05/31/1820359/what-cayetano-missed-justifying-south-china-sea-joint-development (last accessed 24 April 2024).

Vu, Hai Dang, *Marine Protected Areas Network in the South China Sea: Charting a Course for Future Cooperation* (Brill Nijhoff, 2014).

Wagner, R. Harrison, 'Bargaining and War', *American Journal of Political Science* (2000), 469–84.

Wagner, R. Harrison, 'Peace, War, and the Balance of Power', *American Political Science Review*, 88/3 (1994), 593–607.

Wagner, R. Harrison, *War and the State: The Theory of International Politics* (University of Michigan, 2007).

Wain, Barry, 'Manila's Bungle in The South China Sea', *Far Eastern Economic Review* (February 2008), http://realpolitikasia.blogspot.com/2016/08/manilas-bungle-in-south-china-sea-barry.html (last accessed 24 April 2024).

Walter, Barbara F., 'Bargaining Failures and Civil War', *Annual Review of Political Science*, 12 (2009), 243–61.

Walter, Barbara F., *Committing to Peace: The Successful Settlement of Civil Wars* (Princeton UP, 2002).

Walter, Barbara F., 'Explaining the Intractability of Territorial Conflict', *International Studies Review*, 5/4 (2003), 137–53.

Wang, Kuan-Hsiung, 'The ROC's Maritime Claims and Practices with Special Reference to the South China Sea', *Ocean Development & International Law*, 41/3 (2010), 237–52. https://doi.org/10.1080/00908320.2010.499282.

Wei, Lim Han, 'Code for Unplanned Encounters at Sea and Maritime Stability in the Indo-Pacific', *Journal of the Singapore Armed Forces*, 42/2 (2015), 12–24.

Wei, Zongyou, 'China's Maritime Trap', *The Washington Quarterly*, 40/1 (January 2017), 167–84. https://doi.org/10.1080/0163660X.2017.1302745.

Weingast, Barry, and Geoffrey Garrett, 'Ideas, Interests, and Institutions: Constructing the EC's Internal Market', in Robert O. Keohane and R. Goldstein, eds., *Ideas and Foreign Policy* (Cornell UP, 1993), 173–206.

Weiss, Jessica Chen, *Powerful Patriots: Nationalist Protest in China's Foreign Relations* (OUP, 2014).

Weiss, Joshua N., 'Trajectories Toward Peace: Mediator Sequencing Strategies in Intractable Communal Conflicts', *Negotiation Journal*, 19/2 (2003), 109–15. https://doi.org/10.1111/j.1571-9979.2003.tb00770.x.

Weissmann, Mikael, 'The South China Sea Conflict and Sino-ASEAN Relations: A Study in Conflict Prevention and Peace Building', *Asian Perspective* (2010), 35–69.

Welch, David A., 'Crisis Decision Making Reconsidered', *Journal of Conflict Resolution*, 33/3 (1989), 430–45.

Welch, David A., 'Crisis Management Mechanisms Pathologies and Pitfalls', *CIGI Papers*, 40 (September 2014), 1–19.

White, Sally Blount, and Margaret A. Neale, 'Reservation Prices, Resistance Points, and BATNAs: Determining the Parameters of Acceptable Negotiated Outcomes', *Negotiation Journal*, 7 (1991), 379–88.

Wiegand, Krista E., 'China's Strategy in the Senkaku/Diaoyu Islands Dispute: Issue Linkage and Coercive Diplomacy', *Asian Security*, 5/2 (June 2009), 170–93. https://doi.org/10.1080/14799850902886617.

Wiegand, Krista E., and Emilia Justynia Powell, 'Unexpected Companions: Bilateral Cooperation Between States Involved in Territorial Disputes', *Conflict Management and Peace Science*, 28/3 (July 2011), 209–29. https://doi.org/10.1177/0738894211404792.

Wiegand, Krista Eileen, *Enduring Territorial Disputes: Strategies of Bargaining, Coercive Diplomacy, and Settlement* (University of Georgia, 2011).

Wilkinson, Rorden, 'Building Asymmetry Concluding the Doha Development Agenda', in Donna Lee and Rorden Wilkinson, eds., *The WTO after Hong Kong Progress in, and Prospects for, the Doha Development Agenda* (Routledge, 2007), 248–61.

Wilkinson, Rorden, 'Power, Performance and the WTO' (International Studies Association Venture Workshop on International Organisation Performance, March 2008).

Williamson, Oliver E., *The Economic Institutions of Capitalism: Firms, Markets, Relational Contracting* (Collier Macmillan, 1987).

Williamson, Oliver E., 'Political Institutions: The Neglected Side of the Story: Comment', *Journal of Law, Economics, & Organization*, 6 (1990), 263–66.

Wirth, Christian, 'Emotions, International Hierarchy, and the Problem of Solipsism in Sino-US South China Sea Politics', *International Relations* 34/1 (September 2019). https://doi.org/10.1177/0047117819875995.

Wirth, Christian, 'Whose "Freedom of Navigation"? Australia, China, the United States and the Making of Order in the "Indo-Pacific"', *The Pacific Review*, 32/4 (July 2019), 475–504. https://doi.org/10.1080/09512748.2018.1515788.

Wolanski, Eric, Severine Choukroun, and Nguyen Huu Nhan, 'Island Building and Overfishing in the Spratly Islands Archipelago Are Predicted to Decrease Larval Flow and Impact the Whole System', *Estuarine, Coastal and Shelf Science*, 233 (February 2020), 106545. https://doi.org/10.1016/j.ecss.2019.106545.

Womack, Brantly, *Asymmetry and International Relationships* (CUP, 2016).

Womack, Brantly, 'The Spratlys: From Dangerous Ground to Apple of Discord', *Contemporary Southeast Asia*, 33/3 (2011), 370–87. https://doi.org/10.1355/cs33-3e.

Wong, Catherine, 'Beijing Hopes for Maritime Code of Conduct in South China Sea in Three Years', *South China Morning Post* (13 November 2018), https://www.scmp.com/news/china/diplomacy/article/2172913/south-china-sea-beijing-hopes-maritime-accord-asean-neighbours (last accessed 22 April 2024).

Wu, Shicun, *Solving Disputes for Regional Cooperation and Development in the South China Sea: A Chinese Perspective* (Elsevier, 2013).

Wu, Shicun, and Keyuan Zou, eds., *Maritime Security in the South China Sea: Regional Implications and International Cooperation* (Routledge, 2016).

Wu, Shicun, and Nong Hong, eds., *Recent Developments in the South China Sea Dispute: The Prospect of a Joint Development Regime* (Routledge, 2014).

Wu, Zhengyu, 'Rimland Powers, Maritime Transformation, and Policy Implications for China', in Peter Dutton and Ryan D Martinson, eds., *Beyond the Wall: Chinese Far Seas Operations* (Naval War College, 2015), 13–22.

Xu, Xiaodong, 'China-Vietnamese Fishery Co-Op Needs New Perspectives', *China Daily* (February 2021), https://www.chinadaily.com.cn/a/202102/01/WS601754e3a31024adobaa655e.html (last accessed 24 April 2024).

Xue, Guifang, 'Bilateral Fisheries Agreements for the Cooperative Management of the Shared Resources of the China Seas: A Note', *Ocean Development & International Law*, 36/4 (2005), 363–74.

Xue, Hanqin, 'Chinese Contemporary Perspectives on International Law', *Recueil Des Cours de l'Académie de Droit International de La Haye = Collected Courses of the Hague Academy of International Law*, 355 (2012), 47–233.

Xue, Song, 'Why Joint Development Agreements Fail', *Contemporary Southeast Asia*, 41/3 (2019), 418–46.

Yahuda, Michael, 'China's New Assertiveness in the South China Sea', *Journal of Contemporary China*, 22/81 (2013), 446–59.

Yamagami, Shingo, 'Reflections on the Issue of the Senkaku Islands -from the Field of Practice on International Law and Politics', *Japan's Territories Series, Japan Digital Library* (March 2016), http://www2.jiia.or.jp/en/digital_library/japan_s_territories.php (last accessed 24 April 2024).

Yarita, Susumu, 'Toward Cooperation in the East China Sea', in Selig Harrison, ed., *Seabed Petroleum in Northeast Asia: Conflict or Cooperation?* (Woodrow Wilson International Center for Scholars, 2005), 23–9.

Yee, Andy, 'Maritime Territorial Disputes in East Asia: A Comparative Analysis of the South China Sea and the East China Sea', *Journal of Current Chinese Affairs*, 40/2 (2011), 165–93.

Yeh, Yun-Hu et al., 'Taiwan and Japan: A Complex Fisheries Relationship', *Marine Policy*, 51 (2015), 293–301.

Yeo, Andrew, *Asia's Regional Architecture: Alliances and Institutions in the Pacific Century*, Studies in Asian Security (Stanford UP, 2019).

Yoshihara, Toshi, 'China's Vision of Its Seascape: The First Island Chain and Chinese Seapower', *Asian Politics & Policy*, 4/3 (2012), 293–314.

Yoshihara, Toshi, and James R Holmes, *Red Star over the Pacific: China's Rise and the Challenge to U.S. Maritime Strategy* (Naval Institute, 2013).

Yung, Christopher D., and Patrick McNulty, 'An Empirical Analysis of Claimant Tactics in the South China Sea', *Strategic Forum*, 289 (National Defense UP, 2015), 1–13. https://www.proquest.com/openview/1254d9b1cc6ac15ce4a2955eb53d83e7/1?pq-origsite=gscholar&cbl=1036427.

Zartman, I. William, 'Conflict Resolution and Negotiation', in Jacob Bercovitch, Viktor Aleksandrovich Kremeniuk, and I. William Zartman, eds., *The SAGE Handbook of Conflict Resolution* (SAGE, 2009), 322–39.

Zartman, I. William, 'Structures of Escalation and Negotiation', in William I. Zartman and Guy Olivier Faure, eds., *Escalation and Negotiation in International Conflict* (CUP, 2005), 165–84.

Zhang, Feng, 'Assessing China's South China Sea Policy, 2009–2015', *East Asian Policy*, 8/03 (2016), 100–9.

Zhang, Haiwen, 'Is It Safeguarding the Freedom of Navigation or Maritime Hegemony of the United States?—Comments on Raul (Pete) Pedrozo's Article on Military Activities in the EEZ', *Chinese Journal of International Law*, 9/1 (March 2010), 31–47. https://doi.org/10.1093/chinesejil/jmq008.

Zhang, Hongzhou, 'China's Evolving Fishing Industry: Implications for Regional and Global Maritime Security', *RSIS Working Paper*, 246/12 (2012), 1–46.

Zhang, Hongzhou, 'Chinese Fishermen in Disputed Waters: Not Quite a "People's War"', *Marine Policy*, 68 (June 2016), 65–73. https://doi.org/10.1016/j.marpol.2016.02.018.

Zhang, Hongzhou, and Sam Bateman, 'Fishing Militia, the Securitization of Fishery and the South China Sea Dispute', *Contemporary Southeast Asia* (2017), 288–314.

Zhang, Ketian, 'Cautious Bully: Reputation, Resolve, and Beijing's Use of Coercion in the South China Sea', *International Security*, 44/1 (July 2019), 117–59. https://doi.org/10.1162/isec_a_00354.

Zhang, Yunbi, 'Japan-Taiwan Fishery Agreement Raises "concern"', *China Daily* (11 April 2013), http://www.chinadaily.com.cn/china/2013-04/11/content_16391602.htm (last accessed 21 April 2024).

Zhang, Yunbi, 'S. China Sea Code of Conduct Text Advances', *China Daily* (1 August 2019), http://www.chinadaily.com.cn/a/201908/01/WS5d42214fa310d83056402178.html (last accessed 24 April 2024).

Zhang, Xinjun, 'Why the 2008 Sino-Japanese Consensus on the East China Sea Has Stalled: Good Faith and Reciprocity Considerations in Interim Measures Pending a Maritime Boundary Delimitation', *Ocean Development & International Law*, 42/1–2 (2011), 53–65. https://doi.org/10.1080/00908320.2011.542105.

Zou, Keyuan, *China's Marine Legal System and the Law of the Sea*, vol. 48 of Publications on Ocean Development (Martinus Nijhoff, 2005).

Zou, Keyuan, 'Innocent Passage for Warships: The Chinese Doctrine and Practice', *Ocean Development & International Law*, 29/3 (1998), 195–223.

Zou, Keyuan, 'Joint Development in the South China Sea: A New Approach', *The International Journal of Marine and Coastal Law*, 21/1 (2006), 83–109. https://doi.org/10.1163/157180806776639510.

Zou, Keyuan, 'Maritime Boundary Delimitation in the Gulf of Tonkin', *Ocean Development & International Law*, 30/3 (1999), 235–54.

Zou, Keyuan, 'Sino-Japanese Joint Fishery Management in the East China Sea', *Marine Policy*, 27/2 (March 2003), 125–42. https://doi.org/10.1016/S0308-597X(02)00086-6.

Zou, Keyuan, 'Sino-Vietnamese Fishery Agreement for the Gulf of Tonkin', *International Journal of Marine and Coastal Law*, 17/1 (2002), 127–48.

Zou, Keyuan, 'South China Sea Studies in China: Achievements, Constraints and Prospects', *Singapore Yearbook of International Law*, 11 (2007), 85.

Zou, Keyuan, 'The Sino-Vietnamese Agreement on Maritime Boundary Delimitation in the Gulf of Tonkin', *Ocean Development & International Law*, 36/1 (2005), 13–24.

Zou, Keyuan, and Yann-Huei Song, 'Maritime Legislation of Mainland China and Taiwan: Developments, Comparison, Implications, and Potential Challenges for the United States', *Ocean Development & International Law*, 31/4 (2000), 303–45.

Zweig, David, and Jianhai Bi, 'China's Global Hunt for Energy', *Foreign Affairs* (2005), 25–38.

List of Interviews

1. Interview with an international lawyer at the National University of Singapore, Singapore, 14 May 2015.
2. Interview with a former section head of China's Ministry of Foreign Affairs, Singapore, 30 May 2015.
3. Interview with a professor of international law at Shanghai Jiao Tong University, London, 18 July 2016.
4. Interview with a professor of international law at the University of the Philippines, Manila, 22 November 2016.
5. Interview with Philippine Supreme Court Justice Antonio Carpio, Manila, 29 November 2016.
6. Interview with a senior official of the Philippine National Security Council, Manila, 01 December 2016.
7. Interview with a ministerial-level official of the administration of President Arroyo, Manila, 02 December 2016.
8. Interview with a ministerial-level official of the administration of President Arroyo, Manila, 06 December 2016.
9. Interview with a senior official of the French Embassy, Manila, 02 December 2016.
10. Interview with a senior official of the Philippine Foreign Service Institute, Manila, 07 December 2016.
11. Interview with a division chief of the Philippine Bureau on Fisheries and Aquatic Resources, Manila, 09 December 2016.
12. Interview with a former senior Taiwanese official, Ministry of Foreign Affairs, Taipei, 05 April 2017.
13. Interview with a senior Taiwanese official, National Security Council, Taipei, 06 April 2017.
14. Interview with a professor of international law at National Chengchi University, Taipei, 07 April 2017.

15. Interview with a senior Malaysian official, Ministry of Foreign Affairs, Ho Chi Minh, 18 November 2016.
16. Interview with a scholar of a leading think tank on international relations affiliated with Vietnam's Ministry of Foreign Affairs, Nha Trang, 14 November 2016.
17. Interview with a security expert of the Vietnamese armed forces, London, 23 September 2016.
18. Interview with a former senior official, Ministry of Foreign Affairs of Taiwan, London, 07 February 2017.
19. Interview with a former minister-level official, Ministry of Foreign Affairs of Taiwan, London, 03 March 2017.
20. Interview with a scholar on maritime security of a leading think tank on maritime affairs affiliated with China's Ministry of Foreign Affairs, China, 11 April 2017.
21. Interview with an international lawyer of a leading think tank on maritime affairs affiliated with China's Ministry of Foreign Affairs, China, 12 April 2017.
22. Interview with an international lawyer of a leading think tank on maritime affairs affiliated with China's Ministry of Foreign Affairs, China, 13 April 2017.
23. Interview with a scholar on maritime security of a leading think tank on maritime affairs affiliated with China's Ministry of Foreign Affairs, China, 18 April 2017.
24. Interview with a scholar on maritime economy of a leading think tank on maritime affairs affiliated with China's Ministry of Foreign Affairs, China, 19 April 2017.
25. Interview with a professor of international law at Tsinghua University, Beijing, 24 April 2017.
26. Interview with a professor of international law at Tsinghua University, Beijing, 25 April 2017.
27. Interview with a professor of international security at Renmin University, Beijing, 26 April 2017.
28. Interview with a professor of international security at Peking University, Beijing, 26 April 2017.
29. Interview with a professor of international security at Renmin University, Beijing, 27 April 2017.
30. Interview with a professor of international law at Waseda University, Tokyo, 12 July 2017.
31. Interview with a Deputy Director-General level official, Ministry of Defense of Japan, Tokyo, 13 July 2017.
32. Interview with a professor of international relations, Tokyo University of Foreign Studies, Tokyo, 13 July 2017.
33. Interview with a scholar of a leading think tank on security affiliated with Japan's Ministry of Foreign Affairs, Tokyo, 14 July 2017.

34. Interview with a professor of international relations of the University of Tokyo, 18 July 2017.
35. Interview with a senior official of Japan's Ministry of Foreign Affairs, Tokyo, 19 July 2017.
36. Interview with a professor of international security of Hosei University, Tokyo, 20 July 2017.
37. Interview with a General-level member of the Japanese Self-Defense Forces, Tokyo, 21 July 2017.
38. Interview with an officer-level member of the US Navy, Yokohama, 25 July 2017.
39. Interview with a former Admiral of the Japanese Maritime Self-Defense Force, 26 July 2017.
40. Interview with a senior official of Japan's Ministry of Foreign Affairs, Tokyo, 27 July 2017.
41. Interview with a professor of international relations at Keio University, 27 July 2017.
42. Interview with a security analyst of Sumitomo Corporation, Tokyo, 28 July 2017.
43. Interview with a security analyst of a leading US security think tank, Washington DC, 16 October 2017.
44. Interview with a former Admiral of the US Navy, telephone, 07 December 2017.
45. Interview with a senior PLA Navy officer, China, 30 October 2019.
46. Interview with a senior official of China's Ministry of Foreign Affairs, 31 October China, 2019.

Index

For Product Safety Concerns and Information please contact our EU
representative GPSR@taylorandfrancis.com
Taylor & Francis Verlag GmbH, Kaufingerstraße 24, 80331 München, Germany

www.ingramcontent.com/pod-product-compliance
Ingram Content Group UK Ltd.
Pitfield, Milton Keynes, MK11 3LW, UK
UKHW020022200926
475702UK00014B/2013
* 9 7 8 1 0 4 1 1 8 3 6 9 3 *